COMPARATIVE POLITICS

General Editors: Max Kaase and Kenneth Newton
Editorial Board: Brian Barry, Franz Lehner,
Arend Lijphart, Seymour Martin Lipset, Mogens Pedersen,
Giovanni Sartori, Rei Shiratori,
Vincent Wright

Coalition Governments in Western Europe

COMPARATIVE POLITICS

Comparative Politics is a series for students and teachers of political science that deals with contemporary issues in comparative government and politics. As Comparative European Politics it has produced a series of high quality books since its foundation in 1990, but now takes on a new form and new title for the new millennium—Comparative Politics. As the process of globalisation proceeds, and as Europe becomes ever more enmeshed in world trends and events, so it is necessary to broaden the scope of the series.

The General Editors are Max Kaase, Professor of Political Science, University of Mannheim and Research Professor Wissenschaftszentrum Berlin, and Kenneth Newton, Professor of Government at Essex University. The series is published in association with the European Consortium for Political Research.

OTHER TITLES IN THIS SERIES

Mixed-Member Electoral Systems: The Best of Both Worlds
Edited by Matthew Shugart and Martin P. Wattenberg

Parties without Partisans: Political Change in Advanced Industrial Democracies
Edited by Russell J. Dalton and Martin P. Wattenberg

Political Institutions: Democracy and Social Change
Josep H. Colomer

Coalition Governments in Western Europe

Edited by
WOLFGANG C. MÜLLER
and
KAARE STRØM

OXFORD
UNIVERSITY PRESS

Great Clarendon Street, Oxford OX2 6DP

Oxford University Press is a department of the University of Oxford.
It furthers the University's objective of excellence in research, scholarship,
and education by publishing worldwide in

Oxford New York

Athens Auckland Bangkok Bogotá Buenos Aires Calcutta
Cape Town Chennai Dar es Salaam Delhi Florence Hong Kong Istanbul
Karachi Kuala Lumpur Madrid Melbourne Mexico City Mumbai
Nairobi Paris São Paulo Singapore Taipei Tokyo Toronto Warsaw
and associated companies in Berlin Ibadan

Oxford is a registered trade mark of Oxford University Press
in the UK and in certain other countries

Published in the United States
by Oxford University Press Inc., New York

© the various contributors 2000

The moral rights of the author have been asserted

Database right Oxford University Press (maker)

First published 2000

All rights reserved. No part of this publication may be reproduced,
stored in a retrieval system, or transmitted, in any form or by any means,
without the prior permission in writing of Oxford University Press,
or as expressly permitted by law, or under terms agreed with the appropriate
reprographics rights organizations. Enquiries concerning reproduction
outside the scope of the above should be sent to the Rights Department,
Oxford University Press, at the address above

You must not circulate this book in any other binding or cover
and you must impose this same condition on any acquirer

British Library Cataloguing in Publication Data

Data available

Library of Congress Cataloging in Publication Data

Coalition governments in western Europe/edited by Wolfgang C. Müller and Kaare Strøm.
p. cm.—(Comparative European politics)
Includes bibliographical references.
1. Coalition governments—Europe, Western. I. Müller, Wolfgang C., 1957–
II. Strom, Kaare. III. Series.
JN94.A58 C63 2000   328.3'69'094—dc21   00–037465
ISBN 0–19–829760–2

1 3 5 7 9 10 8 6 4 2

Typeset by Hope Services (Abingdon) Ltd.
Printed in Great Britain
on acid-free paper by
TJ International Ltd,
Padstow, Cornwall

Acknowledgement

This volume is the fruit of intensive collaboration over a period of several years. It would not have been possible without the support of a number of institutions and individuals. Heinrich Neisser and Fritz Plasser, respectively the chairman and director of the Vienna Centre for Applied Political Research, invited us to prepare a volume on coalition politics in Western Europe under the auspices of, and with the generous support of, their institute. They also published our preliminary results in the institute's research publication series in the German language. The Austrian Ministry of Science, Research, and the Arts graciously provided the funds for a conference which allowed the contributors to gather at an early phase of our research. We are particularly indebted to Günther Burkert-Dottolo and Christina Maria Lutter for successfully shepherding the project through their agency. We also gratefully acknowledge the most helpful support of the University of Vienna, the University of California, San Diego, the Center of German and European Studies at the University of California, and the University of Bergen. All of these institutions have in their respective ways granted guest professorships that have enabled the editors to overcome the obstacles of geographical distance, distraction, and separation. Further, we have greatly benefited from the financial support of the Bank of Sweden Tercentenary Foundation and Torbjörn Bergman, whose project on Constitutional Change and Parliamentary Democracy (1996–0801) supported extensions and revisions of our earlier research.

Last, but certainly not least, we are indebted to Magnus Blomgren, Scott Kastner, and Benjamin Nyblade for their excellent research assistance, their ingenuity, and their patience.

Wolfgang C. Müller and Kaare Strøm

September 1999

Contents

List of Figures	ix
List of Tables	x
List of Contributors	xv

1 Coalition Governance in Western Europe: An Introduction   1
   Wolfgang C. Müller and Kaare Strøm

2 Germany: Stable Parties, Chancellor Democracy, and the Art of   32
   Informal Settlement
   Thomas Saalfeld

3 Austria: Tight Coalitions and Stable Government   86
   Wolfgang C. Müller

4 Ireland: From Single-Party to Coalition Rule   126
   Paul Mitchell

5 Norway: A Fragile Coalitional Order   158
   Hanne Marthe Narud and Kaare Strøm

6 Sweden: When Minority Cabinets Are the Rule and Majority   192
   Coalitions the Exception
   Torbjörn Bergman

7 Denmark: The Life and Death of Government Coalitions   231
   Erik Damgaard

8 Finland: The Consolidation of Parliamentary Governance   264
   Jaakko Nousiainen

9 Belgium: On Government Agreements, Evangelists, Followers,   300
   and Heretics
   Lieven De Winter, Arco Timmermans, and Patrick Dumont

10 The Netherlands: Still the Politics of Accommodation?   356
   Arco Timmermans and Rudy B. Andeweg

11 Luxembourg: Stable Coalitions in a Pivotal Party System 399
   Patrick Dumont and Lieven De Winter

12 Italy: From 'Constrained' Coalitions to Alternating 433
   Governments?
   Luca Verzichelli and Maurizio Cotta

13 France: Forming and Maintaining Government Coalitions in 498
   the Fifth Republic
   Jean-Louis Thiébault

14 Portugal: The Rationale of Democratic Regime Building 529
   José M. Magone

15 Conclusion: Coalition Governance in Western Europe 559
   Wolfgang C. Müller and Kaare Strøm

Index 593

List of Figures

1.1 Coalition and single-party governments in Western Europe, 1945–1999 — 2

5.1 Pro-urban (1) vs. anti-urban (20) interests: Perceived location of parties — 164

List of Tables

1.1	Left–right placement of parties, party strength (in seats), and party composition of governments	10
1.2	Government formation	14
1.3	Cabinets since 1945	17
1.4	Coalition governance	20
1.5	Size and content of coalition agreements	22
1.6	Distribution of cabinet and junior ministerships	23
1.7	Cabinet termination	24–5
1.8	Electoral costs/benefits of government parties	28
2.1	Left–right placement of parties, party strength (in seats), and party composition of governments in Germany, 1949–1999	41–3
2.2	Government formation in Germany, 1949–1999	49
2.3	German cabinets since 1949	52–3
2.4	Coalition governance in Germany	54–5
2.5	Size and content of coalition agreements in Germany, 1949–1999	56
2.6a	Distribution of cabinet and junior ministerships in Germany, 1949–1999	67
2.6b	Distribution of cabinet and junior ministerships in Germany, 1949–1999	68
2.6c	Distribution of cabinet and junior ministerships in Germany, 1949–1999	69–70
2.7	Cabinet termination in Germany, 1949–1999	72–4
2.8	Electoral costs/benefits of government parties in Germany, 1949–1999	79
3.1	Left-right placement of parties, party strength (in seats), and party composition of governments in Austria, 1945–1999	88–9
3.2	Government formation in Austria, 1945–1999	96
3.3	Austrian cabinets since 1945	98
3.4	Coalition governance in Austria	100
3.5	Size and content of coalition agreements in Austria, 1945–1999	102
3.6	Distribution of cabinet and junior ministerships in Austrian coalitions	114–5
3.7	Cabinet termination in Austria, 1945–1999	118–9
3.8	Electoral costs/benefits of government parties in Austria, 1945–1999	121

List of Tables

4.1	Left–right placement of parties, party strength (in seats), and party composition of governments in Ireland, 1944–1999	127–9
4.2	Government formation in Ireland	134
4.3	Cabinets in Ireland since 1944	136
4.4	Coalition governance in Ireland	139
4.5	Size and content of coalition agreements in Ireland, 1973–1999	142
4.6	Distribution of cabinet and junior ministerships in Irish coalitions	146–7
4.7	Cabinet termination in Ireland	152–3
4.8	Electoral costs/benefits of government parties in Ireland, 1944–1999	154
5.1	Left–right placement of parties, party strength (in seats), and party composition of governments in Norway, 1945–1999	162–3
5.2	Government formation in Norway, 1945–1999	168
5.3	Norwegian cabinets since 1945	171
5.4	Coalition governance in Norway	175
5.5	Size and content of coalition agreements in Norway, 1963–1999	176
5.6	Distribution of cabinet and junior ministerships in Norwegian coalitions	182–3
5.7	Cabinet termination in Norway, 1945–1999	184–5
5.8	Electoral costs/benefits of government parties in Norway, 1945–1999	187
6.1a	Left–right placement of parties, party strength (in seats), and government composition in the First Chamber, Sweden 1945–1970	196–7
6.1b	Left–right placement of parties, party strength, and government composition in the First chamber, Sweden 1945–70	200
6.2	Government formation in Sweden, 1945–1999	206
6.3	Swedish cabinets since 1945	208
6.4	Coalition governance in Sweden	210
6.5	Size and content of coalition agreements in Sweden, 1951–1999	213
6.6	Distribution of cabinet and junior ministerships in Swedish coalitions	216
6.7	Cabinet termination in Sweden, 1945–1996	220–1
6.8	Electoral costs/benefits of Swedish cabinet parties, 1945–1999	224
7.1	Left–right placement of parties, party strength (in seats), and party composition of governments in Denmark, 1945–1999	234–5
7.2	Government formation in Denmark, 1945–1999	240
7.3	Danish cabinets since 1945	242
7.4	Coalition governance in Denmark	247
7.5	Size and content of three Danish coalition cabinets' agreements	249

List of Tables

7.6	Party distribution of cabinet ministerships in Danish coalitions, 1945–1999	251–2
7.7	Cabinet termination in Denmark, 1945–1999	254–7
7.8	Electoral costs/benefits of government parties in Denmark, 1945–1999	259
8.1	Left–right placement of parties, party strength (in seats), and party composition of governments in Finland, 1945–1999	266–7
8.2	Government formation in Finland, 1945–1999	274–5
8.3	Finnish cabinets since 1945	276–7
8.4	Coalition governance in Finland	279
8.5	Size and content of coalition agreements in Finland, 1945–1999	280
8.6	Distribution of cabinet and junior ministerships in Finnish coalitions, 1946–1999	284–7
8.7	Cabinet termination in Finland, 1945–1999	290–1
8.8	Electoral costs/benefits of government parties in Finland, 1945–1999	294–5
9.1a	Left–right placement of parties and party strength (in seats) in Belgium: House of Representatives, 1945–1999	302–4
9.1b	Left–right placement of parties and party strength (in seats) in Belgium: Senate, 1945–1999	305–6
9.2	Government formation in Belgium, 1945–1999	314–5
9.3	Belgian cabinets since 1945	320–1
9.4	Party vote on governmental agreement in Belgium, 1961–1999	323
9.5	Coalition governance in Belgium, 1946–1999	330
9.6	Size and content of coalition agreements in Belgium, 1966–1999	331
9.7	Distribution of cabinet and junior ministerships in Belgium, 1945–1999	336–40
9.8	Cabinet termination in Belgium, 1946–1999	346–8
9.9	Electoral costs/benefits of government parties in Belgium, 1945–1999	350
10.1	Left–right placement of parties, party strength (in seats), and party composition of governments in the Netherlands, 1946–1999	359–62
10.2	Government formation in the Netherlands, 1945–1999	369
10.3	Dutch cabinets since 1945	371
10.4	Coalition governance in the Netherlands, 1945–1999	373–4
10.5	Size and content of coalition agreements in the Netherlands, 1963–1999	374
10.6	Distribution of cabinet and junior ministerships in the Netherlands, 1945–1999	378–9
10.7	Cabinet termination in the Netherlands, 1945–1999	388–9

List of Tables

10.8	Electoral costs/benefits of government parties in the Netherlands, 1945–1999	392
11.1	Left–right placement of parties and party strength (in seats) in Luxembourg, 1945–1999	402–3
11.2	Government formation in Luxembourg, 1945–1999	411
11.3	Cabinets in Luxembourg since 1945	413
11.4	Coalition governance in Luxembourg, 1945–1999	414
11.5	Distribution of cabinet and junior ministerships in Luxembourg, 1945–1999	421–3
11.6	Cabinet termination in Luxembourg, 1945–1999	426
11.7	Electoral costs/benefits of government parties in Luxembourg, 1945–1999	429
12.1	Phases of coalition government in Italy	434
12.2a	Left–right placement of parties, party strength (in seats), and party composition of governments in Italy, 1945–1999: Lower Chamber	436–9
12.2b	Left–right placement of parties, party strength (in seats), and party composition of governments in Italy, 1945–1999: Senate	440–1
12.3	Government formation in Italy	450–1
12.4	Italian cabinets since 1945	454–5
12.5	Coalition governance in Italy, 1946–1998	458–9
12.6a	Distribution of cabinet ministerships (with portfolio) in Italian coalitions, 1945–1999	465–8
12.6b	Distribution and number of cabinet ministerships (without portfolio) in Italian coalitions, 1945–1999	469–70
12.6c	Distribution of junior ministerships in Italian coalitions, 1945–1999	471–7
12.7	Cabinet termination in Italy, 1945–1999	479–87
12.8	Electoral costs/benefits of government parties in Italy	491–2
13.1	Left–right placement of parties, party strength (in seats), and party composition of governments in France, 1959–1999	499–500
13.2	Government formation in France, 1959–1999	504
13.3	French cabinets since 1959	507
13.4	Coalition governance in France, 1959–1999	513
13.5	Size and content of coalition agreements in France: 1959–1999	514
13.6	Distribution of cabinet and junior ministerships in French coalitions, 1959–1999	515–20
13.7	Cabinet termination in France, 1959–1999	523–4
13.8	Electoral costs/benefits of government parties in France, 1959–1999	526
14.1	Left–right placement of parties, party strength (in seats), and party composition of governments in Portugal, 1975–1999	531

14.2	Government formation in Portugal, 1976–1999	537
14.3	Portuguese cabinets since 1974	540
14.4	Coalition governance in Portugal	543
14.5	Size and content of coalition agreements in Portugal, 1978–1985	544
14.6	Distribution of cabinet and junior ministerships in Portugese coalitions	550
14.7	Cabinet termination in Portugal, 1976–1999	552
14.8	Electoral costs/benefits of government parties in Portugal, 1976–1999	554
15.1	Parliamentary cabinets	561
15.2	Government participation of parties with median legislator in Western Europe	564
15.3	Party system indicators in Western Europe	565
15.4	Institutional rules and conventions concerning cabinet formation	566–7
15.5	Cabinet representation of the largest parliamentary party	568
15.6	Cabinet formation	570
15.7	Coalition governance	574
15.8	Size and content of coalition agreements	576
15.9	The proportion of procedural rules in coalition agreements	578
15.10	Coalition discipline in legislation	580
15.11	Coalition discipline in other parliamentary behaviour	580
15.12	Policy agreement	582
15.3	Cabinet duration	585
15.14	Mechanisms of cabinet termination	586
15.15	Terminal events	588
15.16	Electoral gains and losses of government parties	589

List of Contributors

Rudy B. Andeweg is professor of political science at the University of Leiden, the Netherlands.
Torbjörn Bergman is lecturer at Umeå University, Sweden.
Maurizio Cotta is professor of political science at the University of Siena, Italy.
Erik Damgaard is professor of political science at the University of Aarhus, Denmark.
Lieven De Winter is professor of political science at the Université Catholique de Louvain, Louvain-la-Neuve, Belgium.
Patrick Dumont is researcher at the Université Catholique de Louvain, Louvain-la-Neuve, Belgium.
José M. Magone is lecturer in political science at the University of Hull, Great Britain.
Paul Mitchell is lecturer in political science at Queen's University Belfast, Northern Ireland, Great Britain.
Wolfgang C. Müller is professor in political science at the University of Vienna, Austria.
Hanne Marthe Narud is researcher at the University of Oslo, Norway.
Jaakko Nousiainen is professor emeritus of political science at the University of Turku, Finland.
Thomas Saalfeld is senior lecturer in political science at the University of Kent at Canterbury, Great Britain.
Kaare Strøm is professor of political science at the University of California, San Diego, USA and adjunct professor at the University of Bergen, Norway.
Jean-Louis Thiébault is professor of political science at the Université Lille II, France.
Arco Timmermans is lecturer in political science at the University of Twente, the Netherlands.
Luca Verzichelli is lecturer in political science at the University of Bologna, Italy.

1

Coalition Governance in Western Europe

An Introduction

Wolfgang C. Müller and Kaare Strøm

PARLIAMENTARY GOVERNMENT AND COALITIONS

Although democracy can take a variety of institutional forms, the most common democratic regime type, parliamentarism, formally privileges the majority of the people's elected representatives. Parliamentary government implies that government policy making is controlled by a legislative majority. When and where this form of government first emerged, in nineteenth-century Britain, its growth coincided with the development of the classic British two-party system. With two and only two cohesive parties, there would always be a legislative majority for one of these groups. Hence, parliamentary government came to mean party government, a system in which two parties competed for the public's favour and thus for monopoly control of the levers of government.

With the spread of parliamentary government, however, and the reform of electoral systems towards proportional representation, parliamentary democracy has become more complex. Multi-party politics has become the twentieth-century norm. And in multi-party systems, where three or more parties gain parliamentary representation, the possibility always exists that no party alone will command a parliamentary majority. Indeed, that possibility has become the rule, rather than the exception, in the majority of the world's parliamentary systems.

Such minority situations (Strøm 1990a), then, require some sort of inter-party coalition building. Where parliament operates by majority decision rules, as is commonly the case, single parties cannot hope to monopolize political control. Coalitions become a necessity. But the shape of such alliances is by no means foreordained. Coalitions in minority situations could be purely legislative alliances, in which a minority government seeks support from day to day and from issue to issue among its companions in parliament. More commonly, however, coalition building involves more committed agreements that include the offices of the executive branch as well, in the sense that the parties that form the parliamentary majority also share control of the cabinet and the executive branch. Such coalition politics has stimulated a stream of important research since the birth of modern political science, and this is the body of knowledge to which we wish to contribute.

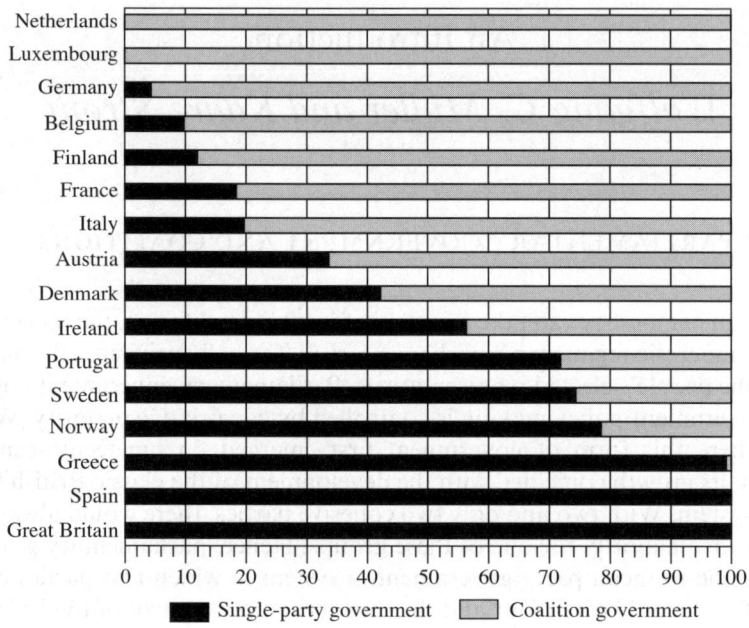

FIGURE 1.1 Coalition and single-party governments in Western Europe, 1945–1999

In order to grasp the real-world importance of coalition politics in parliamentary democracies, it may be useful to take a quick look at its incidence. Figure 1.1 shows the relative frequency of coalition governments in Western Europe. It is based on proportions of time in office rather than on the number of governments of different forms. It is immediately clear that Western European parliamentary democracies vary widely in their experiences with coalition government. Three countries—Britain, Spain, and Greece—stand out because they have had no significant such experience in the post-1945 period. Consequently, they are not covered in this volume, which aims to advance our understanding of parliamentary coalition politics. In the thirteen countries covered in this volume, however, governments have been coalitions either exclusively or frequently. Iceland could be added to this group. Thus, in the great majority of Western European states, coalition politics is at least an occasional occurrence, and often the order of the day. Not all coalitions will interest us equally. This volume will deal with *government* coalitions exclusively. It is nevertheless worth mentioning that most of these countries (but also Britain and Spain) have also made experience with purely *parliamentary* coalitions as a way to build decisive majorities in minority situations. The incidence of minority governments in these various countries will give us a guide to such forms of coalition politics (see Strøm 1990*a*).

Aims of This Volume

The contributors to this volume share an interest in coalition politics in parliamentary democracies (as well as in 'mixed' constitutions such as the French Fifth Republic). Our aim here is to shed some light on the actual coalition politics in the major coalitional systems in Europe.

There are two reasons in particular that this is a timely agenda. One is that the early to mid-1980s witnessed the publication of several most useful volumes detailing coalition politics in European and other parliamentary democracies (Browne and Dreijmanis 1982; Bogdanor 1983; Pridham 1986). For the past decade, however, there has been no similar output (see, however, Laver and Budge 1992, which has a more specific focus), and the standard sources which students of coalition politics have routinely consulted, have therefore become dated. As the interest in coalition politics has grown, the quality of the available surveys has therefore deteriorated.

At the same time, there has been a virtual revolution in our theoretical understanding of coalition bargaining and politics. Advances in spatial and non-cooperative game models of coalition politics, in particular, have brought entirely new or reformulated questions to the forefront of scholarship (see Austen-Smith and Banks 1988, 1990; Baron 1993; Laver and Shepsle 1996; Lupia and Strøm 1995). But the rigorously deductive work in this tradition is not the only source of the gains that have been made in our understanding of coalition politics. At the same time, research frontiers have shifted in response to less formalized work as well (Laver and Budge 1992; Budge and Laver 1993; King et al. 1990; Laver and Schofield 1990; Strøm 1990*a, b*; Warwick 1994, 1999).

This volume seeks to update our empirical knowledge of cabinet coalition politics in parliamentary democracies. In so doing, the contributors seek both to provide a handy set of data on ten or fifteen years of coalition politics that have taken place since the publication of the most prominent previous studies, and to document aspects of cabinet politics that have only recently come to occupy centre stage in the concerns of students of coalition politics. While we shall be happy to serve the first of these functions, to fill the lacuna created by the ceaseless march of time, our major ambition as editors lies in our second objective.

Any successful effort to survey a broad and important set of political phenomena, such as in this case coalition politics, must be based on some theoretical understanding of its subject matter. Consequently, no effort of this sort can hope to succeed without a theoretical underpinning and agenda. In our case, this book is based on four general and fundamental notions about coalition politics:

1. *Coalition politics is strategic.* Taking our inspiration in the rational choice tradition in coalition studies, we conceive of coalition politics as manifested in a set of motivated acts by a set of political actors. Moreover, we are guided by a belief that these behaviours are derived from a persistent pursuit of certain underlying objectives. Finally, we believe that in pursuing their objectives, political actors rationally seek to anticipate the behaviours of those with whom they interact. While these assumptions may sound both general and unspecific, they do lead us to ignore a number of possible foci on coalition politics, such as its symbolic importance, social construction, its personal agonies and ecstasies, as well as its societal functions.

2. *Coalition politics manifests itself as a game between political parties*, but is conditioned by strategic interaction within these parties. As the rest of this chapter will illustrate, we believe that party leaders by and large are the players that matter in coalition politics, and that they define its contents. Consequently, most parts of this survey will focus on the role of parties in this process. But although coalition politics is acted out through parties, it is far from irrelevant what goes on within these organizations. We need to understand the relationships between leaders and followers within political parties and the effects these relationships have on coalition governance. Therefore, several parts of our analytical framework seek to map and illuminate precisely such interactions.

3. *Coalition politics is institutionally conditioned.* We cannot properly understand the formation, performance, or termination of coalition governments without paying attention to their institutional environment, to the rules under which the coalition game is played. These rules vary from country to country, and also often from decade to decade and even from party to party, and they are an indispensable key to the diversity of coalition experiences even in otherwise largely similar advanced democratic societies. Some of the important institutions (e.g. fundamental constitutional provisions) are exogenous to the coalition game in the sense that the actors in this game cannot have any realistic hope of changing them, at least in the short run. Other important institutions are endogenous, which is to say that they are rules that the party actors impose on themselves, often precisely in order to deal with the problems of coalition governance. In coming to terms with the role that institutions play in coalition politics, we have to understand both potential causes and effects of the challenges that political parties face in parliamentary democracies.

4. *Coalition politics is governed by anticipation.* Since we believe that parties and their internal actors are strategic, and since we believe that they are not (always) myopic, it follows that no act of coalition politics can be understood in isolation from others that may occur earlier or later. Too often, students of coalition politics have examined coalition membership in isolation from electoral performance, portfolio allocation in isolation from governance procedures, or termination in isolation from policy programmes. While we cannot in this volume explore all the important interconnections between these manifestations of coalition politics, we wish to lay the basis for their systematic exploration.

These preconceptions have structured the ways in which we try to understand coalition politics in this volume. They have motivated a particular curiosity about certain aspects of coalition politics that have previously more or less escaped scholarly attention. Consequently, our selection of data will in some ways deviate from what has become standard in empirical studies of this sort. Specifically, we shall devote particular attention to two aspects of cabinet coalition politics: (1) the contents and enforcement of coalition agreements, and (2) the causes and conditions of coalition termination or renegotiation. We shall return to these issues below and expand on the reasons for which we are keen to explore these questions in more detail than what they have commonly received.

While this study thus explores in some detail questions which previously have received less attention in the literature, at the same time we wish to minimize any compromises with respect to the information students of coalition politics have come to expect in major empirical surveys. We have therefore sought to extend the records of some of the major data that previous studies have provided, particularly as regards coalition formation and membership. To enhance the usefulness of the volume, the contributors thus provide information on the entire post-World War II period, from the first post-war cabinet until 1 January 1999 (with France, where we cover only the Fifth Republic, and Portugal, where we cover only the period since its transition to democracy, as the only exceptions). We also have sought to cover a broad sweep of the parliamentary democracies in which cabinet coalition bargaining routinely takes place. Although our study is confined to the parliamentary democracies of Western Europe, we have sought to cover all major systems in the region that most typify parliamentary democracy. While the obvious limits of space do apply, we have sought to provide data on all major countries in Western Europe in which coalition politics is a regular occurrence. We have excluded only countries with a very small population and in which the scholarly literature is often spotty and potential contributors scarce (e.g. Iceland) and those in which coalition politics is exceptional rather than normal (e.g. the United Kingdom).

The thirteen country chapters have a common structure. Throughout the book the authors have produced eight standard tables which provide the core information of this volume and which are introduced in the remainder of this introduction. There is a logical sequence to these topics and tables, one that reflects our interest in coalition politics 'from cradle to grave'. Hence, the data are presented in the general sequence in which they would be encountered in coalition politics. The numbering of the tables is largely consistent. Exceptions are only those cases where a specific table was not applicable (because, for instance, in a particular country written coalition agreements are not publicly available), or where country-specific circumstances justify the inclusion of additional tables. In order to illustrate the standard tables and to provide an easy key to the tables contained in this book, we have constructed hypothetical standard tables which are presented below.

BUILDING BLOCKS OF CABINETS: POLITICAL PARTIES

First of all, what are the units (the players) of which coalitions are composed? As Laver and Schofield (1990) point out, this question can in principle be answered in many different ways; yet in practice the literature almost always identifies the answer in terms of parliamentary political parties, which are typically, explicitly or implicitly, assumed to be unitary actors.

This is by no means a foregone conclusion. Rational choice theories are fundamentally committed to the assumption of methodological individualism, to the principle that social events ultimately can only be adequately explained as the results of individual choices and actions, and that every collective phenomenon is reducible to such analysis. By this logic, which underlies the most important research tradition in the field, any ultimately satisfactory account of cabinet membership would have to cast its analysis in terms of the actions and motivations of individuals. Political parties, of course, are not (or extremely rarely) individuals, but rather groups or organizations, aggregates to which we cannot legitimately ascribe motivations or rationality (Arrow 1951). Ideally, then, parties should be analysed as coalitions of individual politicians.

While such analysis may be too patently intractable, there are at least two ways in which parties could be disaggregated short of an individual-level account. One would be a horizontal conception of intra-party politics: a focus on the competing groups of which parties are composed. Some parties, most notoriously perhaps the Japanese Liberal Democrats and the now defunct Italian Christian Democrats, consist of easily identifiable, openly organized, and often powerful factions (Sartori 1976: 71–82; Belloni and Beller 1978). The other possibility is to try to capture the hierarchies of party politics through a vertical conception of the party as an organization in which leaders operate within the constraints imposed by their followers. Agency models of principals (here, perhaps, party members) and agents (their leaders) might provide the tools for rigorous analysis of such hierarchies. Though we believe that such models can make great contributions to the study of parliamentary democracy (see Strøm 2000), they are technically demanding, and their application is by no means straightforward (Müller 2000).

Recognizing, perhaps, the daunting nature of these analytical challenges, coalition theorists brazenly and virtually unanimously continue to stipulate cohesive political parties as their unit of analysis. Their reasons are in part pragmatic: the explicit analysis of all feasible coalitions in a parliament of, say, 300 or 400 members, would be a task of such daunting complexity as to practically preclude any possibility of tractable theoretical analysis (Laver 1989). Besides, empirical knowledge of the real world of cabinet politics firmly suggests that party unity is so much more the rule, rather than the exception. In rational choice terms, it seems reasonable to suggest that the parliamentary representatives, and more generally the leaders, of a political party have a collective interest in cohesive behaviour vis-à-vis other parties. They may have a related collective action problem, but the empirical records amply suggest that they are able to solve this problem most of the time (Laver and Schofield 1990).

In this study, we shall follow the overwhelming majority of cabinet coalition studies and identify cabinet membership by party. This does not mean, however, that we want to ignore completely the internal politics of political parties and its effects on cabinet bargaining and membership. On the contrary, in several parts of the analysis, the contributors have been explicitly asked to assess the impact of intra-party politics on cabinet coalitions. In future studies (Strøm, Müller, and Bergman, n.d.), we plan to explore this theme in greater depth.

THE CONTEXT: PARLIAMENTARY PARTY SYSTEMS

Before we examine the specific coalitions and cabinets in the various countries with which this book is concerned, we shall begin by identifying the parameters imposed by the parliamentary party systems in which these executive coalitions were formed. Parliamentary elections provide the respective parties with bargaining power, which they can in turn convert into the pay-offs they may derive from participation in executive coalitions. The two factors that most decisively determine a party's bargaining power are (1) its share of seats in parliament and (2) its position relative to the other parliamentary parties in policy space.

Formal coalition theories differ in the weight they attribute to these two factors. Classical office-driven (or 'policy-blind') coalition theory assumes that the former parameter completely dominates the latter (for reviews, see Lijphart 1984; Laver and Schofield 1990), whereas the various versions of policy-driven theory attributes at least some weight to policy. In the most radical versions (specifically, in one-dimensional 'pure policy' models), weights (i.e. shares of parliamentary seats) are of no significance at all beyond the minimum threshold of parliamentary representation, as the median party monopolizes coalition bargaining power (Laver and Budge 1992; Laver and Schofield 1990). In short, when all party preferences can be represented by a single policy dimension, no majority can form that prefers any alternative to the ideal point of the median legislator.

Our contributors provide data on the number of parliamentary seats won by each parliamentary party in every election since World War II. Their tables also report the total number of seats in each legislative session. Location in policy space is, of course, less easily captured by any single numerical measure. Our contributors have here applied the best available measures that reflect important concerns in the theoretical literature. Much of that literature, and particularly many influential early works, assume a one-dimensional spatial representation. Later empirical work has shown that it is in most countries possible to identify several significant policy dimensions (Budge, Robertson, and Hearl 1987). While the empirical literature on policy representations suggests significant differences in dimensionality from country to country, it does suggest that the unidimensional left–right scale provides a meaningful representation of the policy spaces of most parliamentary democracies. We have therefore provided such a spatial ordering for each country in this study.

Even among scholars who agree on the utility of the left–right representation, there is disagreement on the most helpful instrument with which such a scale can be generated. Three sources of data are particularly common: (1) general election surveys in which respondents subjectively place the various political parties (e.g. Sani and Sartori 1983), (2) content analysis of the programmatic statements (typically the platforms or 'manifestos') of the political parties themselves (Budge, Robertson and Hearl 1987; Laver and Budge 1992), and (3) so-called 'expert judgements' obtained through small-scale surveys of academic and other experts, in which the respondents are asked to use standard instruments such as a ten-point scale (Castles and Mair 1984; Huber and Inglehart 1995; Laver and Hunt 1992).

Each of these methods has its problems. General election surveys measure the perceptions of the average voter, who is obviously much less well informed about party politics than the party leaders themselves. Also, the issues that most concern the average voter are not necessarily those that are most decisive for cabinet bargaining. Finally, representative samples of voters 'over-represent' the perceptions of the supporters of the larger parties. In party-to-party bargaining, the issue perceptions of smaller parties do not necessarily matter less than those of the larger ones. Content analysis of party programmes get more directly at the issues as they are defined or understood by party leaders. On the other hand, the process of generating spatial representation from such data is much more indirect and consequently controversial (Janda et al. 1995). Finally, expert judgements typically accord a great deal of significance to the perceptions of a small number of authorities, whose own political orientations may often be highly skewed relative to the electorates to which their judgements are related. Moreover, when experts try to use policy positions to explain the membership of cabinets they know, they may consciously or unconsciously let their judgements of the relevant party policy positions be coloured by the very coalitions they are trying to explain. If they know, for example, that two parties ended up forming a coalition, then they may be tempted to infer that the policy distance between these parties was smaller than they would otherwise have believed. But this raises the risk of circular reasoning, and in this way we may easily overestimate the importance of policy distance for coalition formation.

Our own choice, which seeks to make the best of an imperfect world, has been to rely on what we consider the most suitable exemplar of expert judgements, qualified by the best country-specific evidence our contributors might have. In this study, we have therefore drawn on the recent Laver and Hunt (1992) study, since it includes a standard left–right scale and is recent, methodologically rigorous, and geographically comprehensive. The Laver–Hunt placement carries no explicit temporal reference, though the survey was conducted around 1990. We have assumed these placements to be invariant over time in each country, except when our country experts have marshalled strong evidence to the contrary. The first table in each chapter is therefore based on Laver and Hunt's left–right party placements (Table 1.1). From this policy dimension, we have for each parliament identified the party holding the median legislator, i.e. the member with an equal number of other members on his or her left and right. Finally, the initial table identifies the parties participating in each coalition (see above for our definition of this term). In cases where two or more coalitions appeared in the same legislative term (between two consecutive general elections), our contributors have provided separate data on each coalition, which can then be identified in the table by the year in which it was formed.

While the left–right policy dimension with the possible exception of Ireland is the most important one in all Western European countries (Lipset and Rokkan 1967), it is by no means the only relevant one. In some countries, such as Belgium, the assumption of a single policy dimension is clearly unrealistic. The existence of a second or even third relevant policy dimension makes coalition politics much more complex (see Laver and Schofield 1990: 131–42). Where second or third relevant policy dimensions exist, our contributors identify the party which included the median legislator for each election.

TABLE 1.1. *Left–right placement of parties, party strength (in seats), and party composition of governments*

Government	Proximity to election	CP	SD	CE	LP	CO	Median party in second policy dimension	Effective number of legislative parties	Government strength	Total number of seats
1945	FE	18	80	18*	10	74	LP	3.17	102	200
1949	F	38	40	40*	0	82	CO	3.52	122	200
1951	E		**40**			82			122	200
1952	FE	22	74	22*	2	80	LP	3.11	102	200
1955	FE	22	74	22*	2	80	LP	3.11	102	200
1959	FE	18	80	18*	10	74	LP	3.17	102	200
⋮										200
1992	FE	**22**	**80***	22	**2**	74	SD	3.11	104	200

Proximity to election
F   Coalition immediately following an election
E   Coalition ended by an election
FE Coalition immediately following an election and ended by the next election

Parties
CP Communist Party
SD Social Democratic Party
CE Centre Party
LP Liberal Party
CO Conservative Party

Parties which are introduced in **bold** are those which formed the **governments**.
* Party with median legislator.

The parties are placed from left to right according to Laver and Hunt's (1992) 'pro public ownership vs. anti public ownership' or 'increase services vs. cut taxes' policy scales. Parties not covered by the Laver and Hunt survey (e.g. newly created ones) are located on the basis on the available literature and the expertise of the country experts. In the case of government formation between elections (i.e. not immediately following an election) only the number of seats of the governing parties is repeated.

Median party in second policy dimension: Party with the median legislator in the second relevant policy dimension, e.g. the religious dimension.
Effective number of legislative parties: According to Laakso and Taagepera (1979).
Government strength: Total number of seats of government parties.

INSTITUTIONAL BACKGROUND

Coalition theory long treated political parties involved in government formation as if they acted in an institution-free world. Only the votes and preferences of political parties mattered, not the rules under which they made their deals. In practice, however, institutions often constrain coalition bargaining in various ways. A constraint is any restriction on the set of feasible cabinet coalitions that is beyond the short-term control of the players (Strøm, Budge, and Laver 1994: 308). Constraints may take the form of formal rules, such as constitutions or other statutory instruments, or they may flow from less formal, but nonetheless consequential, precommitments made by political parties or other players. Although political institutions can in principle be changed by political actors (Müller 1993), in a given cabinet formation situation they exist and may limit the actors' options. Moreover, political institutions are often protected by special rules of decision making. Institutional change may require qualified majorities, referenda, the consent of subnational units, etc. Political parties, therefore, may be forced to consider political institutions as given, even during the reign of their governments.

The contributions to this volume discuss the relevance of political institutions on government formation, coalition governance, and coalition termination. In particular, they consider whether government formation is affected by specific rules concerning cabinet formation, its size and composition, investiture rules (Bergman 1993), or recognition rules (see Baron 1991). The chapters also discuss the potential impact of cabinet decision making rules and cabinet termination rules, decision rules in the legislature, its dissolution rules, and electoral rules, which may have a direct impact on coalition governance and termination and an indirect influence on coalition formation (see Strøm, Budge, and Laver 1994, for a systematic discussion of these factors).

What is a Cabinet?

Throughout most of this volume, the basic unit of observation is a cabinet. While such executive organs go by a variety of formal designations, they exist in all our relevant countries. A cabinet is the set of politically appointed executive offices involved in top-level national policy making. In the terms of this study, a cabinet consists of a set of individuals (typically, perhaps, 15 to 25) with voting rights in this peak executive organ. We do not count as members of that body individuals (e.g. under-secretaries of state and the like) who may occasionally be invited to attend sessions and give testimony but do not have regular voting rights.

What offices make up a cabinet? When does the life of one cabinet end and that of another begin? In answering these questions, the contributors to this volume have had to steer a joint course between two extreme options, each of which would have jeopardized the institutionally sensitive comparison which is our goal. One possibility is to accept whatever conventions exist in the particular political system with which we are concerned. For example, we could record a new cabinet whenever the official records of state do. Doing so, however, would greatly hinder any cross-national comparison we might wish to undertake. At the other extreme, we could adopt a strict set of cross-national standards a priori, such that each term (cabinet, portfolio, etc.) was strictly defined in a way that left no concessions to local (i.e. national) peculiarities. The problem with this latter approach is that the terms involved, and the actual coalitions we identify, may bear little resemblance to common usage or political realities in any of the countries we examine. Also, we might lose sight of critical institutional factors that shape coalition politics in particular countries.

We try to steer a course between these extremes, to gain comparability without losing all resemblance with local institutions and usage. Our choice has been to define a change of cabinet in rather general terms that are not specific to any particular constitution or political system. On the other hand, we conceive of the make-up of a cabinet in rather more permissive terms that permit national peculiarities (see below). We thus count a change of cabinet with the occurrence of any one of the following conditions:

1. *Any change in the set of parties holding cabinet membership.* Recall that we count as members of the cabinet those and only those parties that have designated representatives with cabinet voting rights. External support parties, i.e. parties that support the cabinet in parliament without holding cabinet portfolios, are not included.
2. *Any change in the identity of the prime minister.* By prime minister, we mean the head of the cabinet, whatever title that office might have (e.g. federal chancellor, president of the council of state, etc.).
3. *Any general election*, whether mandated by the end of the constitutional inter-election period (CIEP) (see King et al. 1990), or precipitated by a premature dissolution of parliament.

Collectively, these three conditions constitute a relatively restrictive definition of a cabinet. That is to say, this usage may in some cases result in a somewhat larger number of cabinets than the national convention. Its advantage lies in the fact that it eliminates potential ambiguities concerning the characteristics of individual cabinets. For that reason, it has become the most common standard in cross-national studies of cabinet coalitions in parliamentary democracies.

It is useful to have a less restrictive term by which we can refer to successive cabinets that share a large number of significant characteristics. By the criteria, these may only be separated by technical counting rules and not by any discretionary or decisional change on the part of any of the parties or parliamentarians involved. Very often in such cases, national convention (though not necessarily official counting rules) would lump these cabinets together under a common designation. In this study, we use the term 'government' to refer to successive cabinets in which there is no change in conditions (1) or (3) above; that is to say, executives with a constant party composition between general elections. Successive cabinets under different prime ministers may thus constitute a single government, as when a prime minister suddenly dies or retires for health reasons.

CABINET FORMATION

Cabinet formation has long been one of the dominant concerns of the coalitions literature. In many ways, the cabinet coalitions literature resembles the romantic Hollywood films of the 1950s. Much is made of the courtship process and 'who gets whom', whereas relatively little light is shed on how such alliances actually work or their prospects for long-term success. Yet, the fine detail of coalition bargaining and formation is notoriously difficult to pin down. It is relatively easy to report the external parameters of the bargaining process (e.g. its duration), as well as its result in partisan composition and portfolio allocation. It is much more difficult to establish the exact route by which the parties arrived at this destination. Yet, the latter question may be just as interesting as the former to the theoretically driven student of cabinet politics.

Two recent trends in coalition studies have led to renewed interest in the process of coalition formation itself. One derives more from theoretical works, the other more from the empirical literature. On the theoretical side, the past five to ten years have witnessed the introduction of non-cooperative game theory to the study of cabinet coalitions (Austen-Smith and Banks 1988; Baron 1991, 1993; Laver and Shepsle 1996; Lupia and Strøm 1995). Contrary to the previously dominant cooperative-theory approaches, such theories try to explicitly model the bargaining process from which cabinet coalitions emerge. And differences in the rules by which this game is played can made a big difference to the outcome. Baron (1991), for example, shows that such consequences can flow from differences in recognition rules, the rules that determine who gets to 'bid' for control of the government, and in what order.

The empirical motivations stems from results that suggest that characteristics of the formation process (such as duration or the number of bargaining rounds) may provide a clue to the subsequent performance of the coalition, specifically its duration (King et al. 1990; Warwick 1992, 1994; Alt and King

1994). The nature and significance of these effects, however, remain controversial. The recent literature includes efforts to understand the coalition bargaining process with the help of formal models of bargaining under asymmetric information (Diermeier and van Roozendaal 1998).

Bargaining Rounds

In response to these concerns in the more recent literature, our contributors provide a survey of the coalition bargaining process in their respective countries. Collectively, these descriptions constitute the most comprehensive account yet of coalition bargaining process across this wide range of parliamentary democracies. Each chapter describes the constitutional process and the general rules that impinge on it in general and qualitative terms. The contributors then go on to describe in more quantitative terms the actual characteristics of the post-1945 formation processes in their respective countries (Table 1.2). In each case, we describe the number of parties in parliament, a useful parameter for our understanding of the complexity of the bargaining situation.

Next, each contributor provides a critical and much less easily accessible characteristic of each coalition bargaining process: the number of formation (bargaining) rounds. The number of bargaining rounds is affected by two

TABLE 1.2. *Government formation*

Government	Number of parties in parliament	Number of previous bargaining rounds	Parties involved in the previous bargaining rounds	Number of days required for government formation
SD–CO–CP–CE–LP 1945	(5)	0	—	5
CO–CE–LP 1945	5	1	SD–CO	15
CO–CE 1949	4	0	—	30
CO–SD 1951	4	0	—	9
CO–CE 1952	5	2	(1) CO–SD (2) SD–CP–CE	93
...	...	...	...	...
SD–CP 1996	5	1	SD–CE	39

Government: A 'government' is defined by the criteria 'same party composition' and 'same electoral period'.

Number of parties in parliament: ( ) No parliament; provisional government before first general election.

Number of previous bargaining rounds: A 'previous bargaining round' is any 'change in the party composition' and 'change in the *formateur* or *informateur*', except when we have reason to believe that the *informateur*'s mission was successful.

Number of days required for government formation: Time between election day and official 'date in' (see Table 1.3).

factors: the sets of parties involved, and, if any, the designated *formateur*, or bargaining coordinator (a *formateur* is a bargaining coordinator who is also the intended prime minister). We count a new bargaining round with every change in the set of parties involved, and with every change in the identity of the *formateur* or coordinator. Such counts are notoriously difficult, of course. In some countries, *formateurs* and coordinators are officially designated and given explicit mandates, which naturally helps in counting. Students of other systems, however, will be less lucky. In any case, there are a multitude of pitfalls in measurement. Some parties may not bargain in good faith and thus render an 'official' attempt a sham. In some cases, parties and observers may distinguish between real negotiations and preliminary, non-committal, talks. Then again, some negotiations may be secret to the public and even to well-informed observers. Our contributors have bravely put their skills and insight to the task of overcoming these difficulties and providing a maximally comparable measure of the number of bargaining attempts. In so doing, they have sought to include every publically known case, regardless of whether it was official or non-official, and conducted in better or worse faith. We have, however, abstained from including cases of secret talks or negotiations which did not lead to the formation of a new government. The authors of the country chapters have also supplied the total number of parties involved in any phase of the bargaining process leading up to the formation of each coalition. Finally, for each bargaining process we provide the duration of the government formation process, measured in the number of days elapsed between the resignation of the previous cabinet (or election date in cases where this was the cause of termination) and the inauguration of the one to which the negotiations gave rise.

CABINET MEMBERSHIP

By far the predominant theme in the literature on cabinet coalitions is coalition membership, or specifically the question of who gets included in the set of parties that sustain the cabinet in parliament. Since Riker's (1962) seminal work, this literature has been heavily influenced by rational choice, and specifically game-theoretic approaches. Riker's influential prediction, the size principle, stipulated that parties seek to build coalitions that are big enough (in terms of parliamentary votes) to win, but no larger. Subsequent scholarship has suggested that under some circumstances, parties may rationally seek supermajorities, either because institutions require it (Strøm, Budge, and Laver 1994), or to avoid some risk of defection (Taylor and Laver 1973). Other scholars have essentially argued that transaction costs would motivate parties to minimize the number of coalition parties, rather than their majorities (Leiserson 1966). The broad school of policy-based coalition theory suggest that policy concerns supplement, or trump, size considerations in coalition membership (e.g. Laver and Schofield 1990). Yet, before we can meaningfully answer any question concerning coalition membership, several operational questions must be addressed.

Cabinet Summary Data

The next table in each chapter provides summary data on each post-1945 cabinet, including both its membership and the dates of its formation and termination (Table 1.3). The contributors supply three dates by which the cabinet's duration can be measured: (1) the date on which the cabinet was installed or inaugurated, (2) the date on which its formal resignation was tendered by the prime minister or equivalent, and (3) the date on which the cabinet actually left office (typically identical with the date on which the next cabinet was installed). In cases where 'formal resignation' refers to changes of prime minister or general elections, the dates refer to the timing of these events.

On the basis of these dates, we have calculated the maximum feasible duration of each cabinet, as well as the time it actually served. Maximum potential duration refers to the amount of time left in the constitutional inter-election period at the time the cabinet was installed. Actual duration, of course, may be a larger or smaller proportion of this hypothetical maximum. Both of these variables have been measured in days. Finally, the parties with full participation in the cabinet (i.e. whose designated representatives hold full voting rights in the cabinet) have been included. In each case, the party of the prime minister or equivalent has been listed first.

COALITION GOVERNANCE

Too often, studies of cabinet coalitions have satisfied themselves with a recording of the formal membership, and perhaps the duration, of these governments. A small body of recent theoretical literature, however, reflects a greatly enhanced interest in the process of governance once a cabinet coalition has been formed. Theoretical forays into the questions of coalition governance have been based on rather divergent assumptions. In their seminal work on *Making and Breaking Governments*, Laver and Shepsle (1996) make the radical assumption of ministerial government (in some early efforts referred to as ministerial policy dictatorship). In this view, coalition policy is ultimately implemented through ministerial departments, for which minister (heads of departments who typically serve in the cabinet) are responsible. This implementation mechanism, these authors argue, leave no room for the

TABLE 1.3. *Cabinets since 1945*

Cabinet number	Prime minister	Date in	Formal resignation	Maximum potential duration (in days)	Duration (in days)	Government composition
1	Green	1 Feb. 1945	15 Dec. 1945	—	318	SD-CO-CE-CP-LP
2	Brown I	15 Dec. 1945	31 Jan. 1949	1,446	1,144	CO-CE-LP
3	Brown II	31 Jan. 1949	30 Nov. 1951	1,431	1,034	CO-CE
4	Brown III	30 Nov. 1951	20 June 1952	397	122	CO-SD
5	Grey	20 June 1952	10 Sept. 1955	1,368	1,246	CO-CE
...	...	...	...	...	...	...
16	White*	10 Sept. 1973	11 Oct. 1973	246	32	CO-CE
...	...	...	...	...	...	...
31	Black IV	12 Mar. 1996		1,392		SD-CP

Maximum potential duration (in days): Remainder of the parliamentary term when the government assumes office: period from 'date in' until the next constitutionally mandated date of parliamentary election, or to the date of presidential elections if it is required or customary for governments to resign at the time of presidential elections. In our example cabinet, Brown I was formed after the general election of 1 Dec. 1945. Cabinet formation required 15 days (see Table 1.2). Therefore the potential duration was 1,446 days (the full parliamentary term of four years [1,461 days] minus the time consumed for cabinet formation). However, the four-year term was not fully exhausted. Elections were held on 1 Jan. 1949. Therefore duration was 1,144 days (see next column).

Duration (in days): Period from 'date in' until 'formal resignation' or date of general election, whichever comes first.

* Cabinet formed to conduct elections only.

effective cabinet oversight of the individual ministers, who consequently are capable of implementing policies corresponding to their own (or their party's) ideal point.

Laver and Shepsle's argument implies that coalition members have no effective mechanism by which they can induce cabinet ministers to implement any policy position other than their ideal point. While the argument in this stark form may strike many empiricists as implausible (see the country chapters in Laver and Shepsle 1994), it certainly does seem to contain a kernel of truth. No doubt cabinet portfolios imply a certain measure of agenda power, which individual ministers can use to shift coalition policy in directions they personally favour. Prime ministers, or coalition negotiators trying to reach a policy agreement, may thus realize that they cannot perfectly implement their most preferred policy package.

Such slippage, or agency loss, however, begs the question of how the coalition parties might try to cooperate to limit the power of individual ministers to impose undesirable policy outcomes on their coalition partners. Though this is a politically important and theoretical intriguing question, we have no systematic empirical understanding of it. Part of the answer may lie in coalition agreements that coalition parties enter before going into executive branch collaboration. Coalition agreements may be formal or informal, and they may be intended for internal use only or designed for public consumption. In this study, we have subjected such agreements to a more intensive scrutiny than in any other empirical study of which we are aware. Throughout this volume coalition agreements are defined as the most binding written statements joined by all parties, i.e. the most authoritative document which constrains party behaviour. While some of these documents regulate coalition life in some detail, working out and signing such a 'contract' is not the only way to agree on the 'rules of the game' within a government coalition. Therefore, in Table 1.4 our contributors have taken into consideration all clearly identifiable informal rules governing the internal life of coalitions. It is important to note, however, that Table 1.4 provides information about rules rather than actual behaviour.

In analysing the coalition agreements, the contributors have coded one agreement per government, rather than per cabinet, in cases where several successive cabinets operated under the same coalition agreement (Table 1.4). We first indicate whether or not a formal agreement existed, then for known agreements whether these terms were designed to be made public during the cabinet's (or coalition's) lifetime.

The contributors further indicate whether the coalition agreements set up a specific conflict management mechanism, such as a coalition committee, inner cabinet, or various other arrangements. In cases where such mechanisms do not exist, disputes and uncertainties would presumably have to be resolved through existing constitutional mechanisms, such as cabinet or sub-cabinet deliberations or negotiations between coalition party leaders. In characterizing the rules of coalition governance, our contributors have identified both the most common conflict management mechanism, and the one used under the most serious circumstances.

Coalition agreements may contain a variety of other regulations of coalition behaviour. Some agreements contain an explicit 'election rule', which commits the parties to submit themselves to a popular election in case the government were to be terminated. Such a rule would prevent existing coalition members from renegotiating at will and thus constrain their bargaining power. Of course, such agreements are only feasible (or at least enforceable) in countries that allow parliamentary dissolution at the discretion of the prime minister or the parliamentary majority.

Coalition agreements, formal or informal, impose various degrees of coalition discipline in parliamentary votes, as well as in other parliamentary activities. Another set of matters that may or may not be regulated through coalition agreements is cabinet and sub-cabinet appointments. Some agreements allow each coalition party full discretion in its choice of cabinet ministers, whereas others subject such appointments to a mutual veto. Similarly, coalition agreements may impose more or less rigorous guidelines on the appointment of junior ministers (ranking political appointees in various ministerial departments but without cabinet rank and voting rights) and other political appointees, for other parliamentary chairmanships, or heads of public enterprises.

The contributors also discuss in which ways coalition agreements are enforceable and to which extent they actually have been observed by the coalition parties. Where written coalition agreements have been available, the contributors have analysed their contents and examined the balance between policy commitments, portfolio and other office agreements, and rules by which coalition disputes would be settled (Table 1.5). There are three general issue areas contained in coalition agreements: (1) policy, (2) office allocation, and (3) procedure. Most coalition agreements contain substantial and explicit policy commitments. Some also include fairly detailed procedural rules, and a few may contain rules about the allocation of public offices. In their contributions, our country experts have calculated the proportion of space devoted to each of these topics in all available agreements.

CABINET AND JUNIOR MINISTERSHIPS

Cabinets are political executive organs made up by a number of individual ministers. In most parliamentary democracies it is customary for each, or at least most, of these ministers to be the head of a ministerial department.

TABLE 1.4. *Coalition governance*

(1) Coalition	(2) Coalition agreement	(3) Agreement public	(4) Election rule	(5) Conflict management mechanisms	(6) Most common management mechanisms	(7) Mechanisms for most serious conflicts	(8) Coalition discipline in legislation	(9) Coalition discipline in other parliamentary behaviour	(10) Freedom of appointment	(11) Policy agreement	(12) Junior ministers	(13) Non-cabinet positions
1945	N	—	N	IC	IC	IC	1	1	Y	0	Y	Y
1949	PRE	N	Y	CaC,IC	CaC	IC	2	2	N	1	N	N
1951	POST	Y	Y	CoC, IC	CaC	IC	3	3	Y	2	Y	Y
1952	IE	Y	Y	Parl, IC	Parl	IC	4	4	N	3	N	N
1955	PRE, POST	Y	N	PCa PS	PCa	PS	1	4	Y	4	Y	Y
1959	POST	Y	Y	CaC, PS	CaC	PS	2	3	Y	2	Y	N
⋮	⋮	⋮	⋮	⋮	⋮	⋮	⋮	⋮	⋮	⋮	⋮	⋮
1996	POST	N	Y	PS, O	O	PS	2	3	N	1	N	N

(2) *Coalition agreement*: Coalition agreements are defined as the most *binding written* statements between the parties, i.e. the most authoritative document which constrains party behaviour. If no such written statements exists, the 'coalition agreement' column indicates 'No'. If one and the same coalition agreement was maintained under different cabinets or even governments, the coding of the coalition agreement does not change.

- N   No written coalition agreement
- PRE   Pre electoral written coalition agreement
- POST Post-electoral written coalition agreement
- IE   Written coalition agreement in the case of coalitions formed during the parliamentary term (not immediately following elections)
- PRE, POST Pre- and post-electoral written coalition agreement

(3) *Agreement public*: The column 'agreement public' refers to the same written statement. Answer to the question: Is the coalition agreement intended to be public during the lifetime of the coalition? If no coalition agreement exists, the column reports 'not applicable'.
- Y Yes
- N No

(4) *Election rule*: Answer to the question: Is the coalition based on an 'election rule', i.e. if the coalition breaks down will this automatically lead to a new election (rather than to the formation of a new government in the existing parliament)?
- Y Yes
- N No

(5) *Conflict management mechanisms*: Answer to the question: Is there a specifically designed conflict management mechanism between the parties?
- IC   Inner cabinet: a subset of cabinet ministers which is not issue-specific and which is stable over time

CaC   Cabinet committee(s): typically issue-specific; they may include cabinet ministers, junior ministers, and/or civil servants
CoC   Coalition committee: typically permanent with relatively stable membership, consisting of party leaders but not limited to cabinet members
Parl Parliamentary leaders (heads of the coalition parties' parliamentary groups)
PCa   Combination of cabinet members and parliamentarians
PS   Party summit: typically ad hoc, consisting of one or several leaders for each coalition party, some but not all of whom may be cabinet members.
O   Other

One or more of these can be entered.

(8) *Coalition discipline in legislation*: Answer to the question: Is the coalition based on the understanding that there will be coalition discipline in parliamentary votes on legislative proposals?
1 Yes always
2 Yes, on all policies except those explicitly exempted
3 No, except those policies explicitly specified
4 No

(9) *Coalition discipline in other parliamentary behaviour*: Answer to the question: Is the coalition based on the understanding that there will be coalition discipline in other parliamentary behaviour (e.g. questioning of ministers, investigative committees, appointments)?
1 Yes always
2 Yes, on all matters except those explicitly exempted
3 No, except those matters explicitly specified
4 No

(10) *Freedom of appointment*: Answer to the question: Do the coalition parties have freedom of appointment for the ministerial posts allocated to them?
Y Yes
N No (= subject to coalition approval/veto)

(11) *Policy agreement*: Answer to the question: Is the coalition based on a substantial and explicit policy agreement?
0 No explicit agreement
1 On few selected policies
2 On a variety of issues, but not comprehensive
3 Comprehensive policy platform

(12) *Junior ministers*: Answer to the question: Do the coalition parties agree on the distribution of junior ministers?
Y Yes
N No

(13) *Non-cabinet positions*: Answer to the question: Do the coalition parties agree on the distribution of non-cabinet positions (e.g. parliamentary chairmanship or offices in the public sector)?
Y Yes
N No

TABLE 1.5. *Size and content of coalition agreements*

Coalition	(1) Size	(2) General procedural rules (in %)	(3) Specific procedural rules (in %)	(4) Distribution of offices (in %)	(5) Distribution of competences (in %)	(6) Policies (in %)
CO–CE 1949	1,500	25	15	10	25	15
CO–CE 1952	2,800	10	21	19	10	40
SD–CP 1996	23,000	*	0	2	2	96

Size: In words.

Specific procedural rules: Procedural rules that apply only to certain policy areas, issues, etc.

Columns (2) through (6) represent percentages of all words in the respective coalition agreements. They are mutually exclusive and sum to 100, except for rounding errors.

* Less than 0.5%.

Nonetheless, in some countries ministers without portfolio are fairly common, and in other cases, two or more ministers may share responsibility for a single department. The early literature tended to see view ministerial portfolios as discrete and interchangeable rewards given to parties or particular politicians. The main scholarly interest lay in trying to understand the forces that governed the distribution of these rewards, such as norms of proportionality or bargaining power (Browne and Franklin 1973; Schofield and Laver 1985).

The more recent theoretical literature has stressed the policy implication of portfolio allocation. Laver and Shepsle (1996), whose work has been discussed above, see portfolio allocation as a distribution of political 'property rights' over their respective jurisdictions. Under ministerial government, whatever party controls a particular portfolio also has strong discretionary control over policy decisions in that particular policy area. Budge and Keman (1990) stress the strong cross-national regularities in the classes of portfolios sought and gained by particular families of parties.

In Table 1.6, the contributors provide detailed information on ministerial portfolio allocation for each coalition cabinet. To facilitate comparison and for ease of use, we have in each case listed what we consider to be the most important portfolios first and in the following order: Prime Minister, Deputy Prime Minister (where applicable), Finance Minister, and Minister of Foreign Affairs. This ranking is in general borne out by the available evidence, including the expert survey in Laver and Hunt (1992). Beyond these standard portfolios, the remaining posts are ranked in declining order, again based on Laver and Hunt and the best evidence available to the country experts.

TABLE 1.6. *Distribution of cabinet and junior ministerships*

Cabinet Number	Cabinet	(1) Prime Minister	(2) Deputy Prime Minister	(3) Finance	(4) Foreign	(5) Interior	(6) Social Affairs	(7) Science	...	(23) Without portfolio
1	Green	SD	CO	CO, sd	LP, co/ce	SD	CP	—	...	—
2	Brown I	CO	CE	CO/LP	LP/CO	CO	CE	—	...	—
3	Brown II	CO	CE	CO	CO/, ce/	CO	CO	—	...	CE
4	Brown III	CO	SD	CO	CO	SD/, co/	SD	—	...	—
5	Grey	CO	CE	LP, CO	I	CE	CE	CO, ce//ce	...	CO/
...										
16	White*	CO	CO	I	CO	CE	CE	CE	...	—
...										
31	Black IV	SD	CP	SD	SD	SD	CP	SD	...	CP, i

Cabinet ministers: Cabinet ministers are entered by the initials of their party, in capital letters (e.g. SD). Columns (1) through (4) are listed in the same order for all countries. Ministers without portfolio are always listed last.

Junior ministers: Junior ministers are only inserted if they come from a party not holding the respective cabinet ministership. They are defined as political appointees who do not have voting rights in the cabinet (in Germany and Austria *Staatssekretär*, in Sweden *statssekreterare*, etc.). If more than one category of junior ministers exists, only the highest is inserted.

Junior ministers are entered by the initials of their party, in small letters (e.g. sd). Thus, a department which is headed by a minister from the CO and also has a junior minister from the SD is coded as CO, sd.

Changes during the reign of a cabinet

LP/CO   A cabinet minister from the Liberals is replaced by a Conservative
LP, CO The ministry was shared by ministers from the Liberals and Conservatives
co/ce   A junior minister from the Conservative Party was replaced by a junior minister from the Centre Party
CO/   The Conservative Party had a cabinet minister when the cabinet assumed office; later this position was abolished
/co   The Conservative Party got a junior minister during the reign of the cabinet; this position was maintained until the end of the cabinet
/col   The Conservative Party got a junior minister during the reign of the cabinet; this position was abolished before the end of the cabinet
ce//ce The Centre Party had a junior minister when the cabinet assumed office; during the reign of the cabinet this position was abolished, but it was reintroduced before the end of the cabinet

I and i   Independent

TABLE 1.7. *Cabinet termination*

Cabinet number	Cabinet	Mechanisms of cabinet termination					
		Technical			Discretionary		
		(1) Regular parliamentary election	(2) Other constitutional reasons	(3) Death of prime minister	(4) Early parliamentary election	(5) Voluntary enlargement of coalition	(6) Cabinet defeated by opposition in parliament
1	Green		x				
2	Brown I				x		
3	Brown II				x		
4	Brown III			x		x	
5	Grey						x
...	...	...	...	...	...	...	...
16	White*				x		
...	...	...	...	...	...	...	...
31	Black III	x					

Note: Technical and discretionary terminations are mutually exhaustive and exclusive. A cabinet may, however, have more than one discretionary termination mechanism. Different terminal event categories are non-exclusive.
(1) Regular parliamentary election at the end of the constitutional inter-election term
(2) Other constitutional reasons, e.g. resignation of cabinet after a new head of state assumes office
(7) The initial(s) indicate the party (parties) in which the conflict(s) occurred
(8) Intra-party conflict in coalition party or parties; the initial(s) indicate the party (parties) in which the conflict(s) occurred

Our account, however, goes beyond the point of detailing such cabinet appointments. Even the allocation of junior ministerships, we believe, can give us important insight about coalition policy making, and specifically about the discretion (autonomy) exercised by each cabinet minister. We believe that ministerial autonomy is more likely in situations where the minister can select junior ministers from his or her own party, compared to situations where cabinet ministers face junior ministers from other coalition parties in their own departments. Such 'divided portfolios', we believe, bespeak some division of power within the jurisdiction of each ministry. At the very least, junior ministers from competing parties should serve to undermine the informational advantages of the party controlling the cabinet min-

	Terminal events						Policy area(s)	Comments
(7) Conflict between coalition parties	(8) Intra-party conflict in coalition party or parties	(9) Elections (non-parliamentary)	(10) Popular opinion shocks	(11) International or national security event	(12) Economic event	(13) Personal event		
Policy conflict / Personnel conflict								
CE, LP	CE;L		x					First regular election School legislation
CO, CE						x		Conflict between party leaders
CO; NL					x		3	Budget rejected
...	...	...	...	...	...	...	...	...
...	...	...	...	...	...	...	...	...

L Conflict in national party leadership (national executive committee, cabinet, parliamentary party leadership)
NL Conflict between united national party leadership and non-leaders (party activists, party congress delegates, backbench MPs, regional leaders, etc.)
LNL Conflict in national party leadership involving non-leaders
The initial(s) indicate in which party (parties) the conflict(s) occurred.
(10) Resignation because government has lost public support or resignation because government wants to hold an early election in order to benefit from good public opinion data
Policy area(s): Ministerial jurisdiction(s) (see Table 1.6) in which policy conflicts occurred

ister. They may represent an important mechanism by which coalition agreements are enforced in individual ministries.

COALITION TERMINATION

Somewhat belatedly, perhaps, coalition studies have over the decade or so come to the realization that coalition terminations may be as interesting and consequential as coalition formations, and that, indeed, one phenomenon cannot be properly understood except in the context of the other (see e.g.

Warwick 1994; Grofman and van Roozendaal 1997). Studies of coalition durability and termination have fallen into a number of camps, according to the causal factors and mechanisms they stress: (1) the structural attributes literature, which emphasizes the effects of cabinet, party system, and regime characteristics on cabinet stability, (2) the critical events approach, which has interpreted coalition terminations as response to exogenous events ('shocks') in the coalition's environment, and (3) the strategic interaction approach, which seeks to provides a behavioural explanation of the processes that lead to cabinet termination in the bargaining incentives that individual parties face (see Lupia and Strøm 1995).

These perspectives are certainly not mutually exclusive, and there can be no question that individual cases of cabinet termination can have several interrelated causes. So far, our factual knowledge of the histories of coalition termination is very sparse. The contributors have made a concerted effort to ameliorate this situation, in the recognition that coalition terminations cannot always be assigned to mutually exclusive and exhaustive causes. The pertinent tables on cabinet termination reflect this fact (Table 1.7).

The first three columns in these tables represent a distinctive set of terminations, which in our terminology are technical. These categories represent cabinets that under our definitions were terminated for reasons beyond the control of the relevant parties, namely constitutionally mandated election, deaths of prime ministers, and other constitutional provisions that require the cabinet's resignation (for example, at the time of the accession of a new head of state). A further set of terminations that fall into this general category are prime ministerial resignations for purely personal and non-political reasons, such as failing health. These causes are presumably mutually exclusive, at least in the sense that any one would be sufficient and that they are unlikely to coincide by chance.

The next five columns represent discretionary mechanisms of termination: cases in which the termination resulted from acts that were both political and discretionary. These are the events to which we expect our strategic understanding of coalition politics to apply. Note that these are mechanisms that need not be mutually exclusive: early parliamentary dissolutions, parliamentary defeats at the hands of the opposition, conflicts between coalition parties over policy or personnel matters, and conflict within any of the coalition parties. In cases where a cabinet met its fate due to inter- or intra-party conflict, we have sought to identify the party or parties involved, as well as whether this conflict involved party leaders, the rank and file, or both.

Finally, the last four columns represent the first systematic attempt, to our knowledge, to actually catalog the critical events that toppled specific cabinets. These may in many cases be viewed as the initial developments that generate the conflicts identified above. We distinguish between four types of events: popular opinion developments, national security events (e.g. threats of war or civil war), economic events (recessions, unfavourable shocks such as the 1973–4 oil embargo), and personal events (scandals, health concerns, appointments to other office). Of course, several different kinds of events can contribute to the resignation of the same cabinet. For each cabinet there is at least one coding of termination mechanisms. There may be no, one, or several codings of terminating events. Finally, the country experts have in relevant cases identified the ministerial jurisdiction(s) involved in policy conflicts leading to cabinet termination. They have also in many cases provided brief explanatory comments.

ELECTORAL PERFORMANCE

Most studies of cabinet termination have focused on its implications concerning cabinet stability. Cabinet terminations have been studied because they help us measure and explain government stability. The theoretical questions driving such exercises have been whether certain types of governments systematically 'outlive' others, or whether particular structural or environmental conditions are particularly inducive or inimical to cabinet stability. In the traditional literature, such questions were in turn typically motivated by a concern for the stability not only of the executive as an institution, but of the political system as a whole (for reviews, see Dodd 1976 and Powell 1982). The Weimar Republic and the French Fourth Republic in particular seem to drive home the point that excessive government turnover was a vice that might ultimately threaten the very survival of democracy.

The more recent literature has increasingly questioned the association between cabinet and system stability (e.g. Lijphart 1984). However, in any case there is an association between the government's behaviour—its performance in terms of public appeal and policy making—and the next elections (Rose and Mackie 1983). Attrition or a winning profile in office can shift voter support between government and opposition and between the individual parties.

Although electoral outcomes are shaped by many factors, government or opposition status without doubt is a crucial one. Accordingly, electoral considerations enter the parties' calculations when considering potential gains and costs of their participation in government before they accept office (Strøm 1990a: 123–9).

Thus far, the literature has considered individual parties' gains and costs from government participation mainly with respect to office pay-offs and policy (see Laver and Schofield 1990: 164–94 for an overview). In any case, there should be a relationship between these two and the respective parties' electoral performance. Parties that have trouble getting their policy proposals accepted, for instance, must be prepared to get punished on election day.

TABLE 1.8. *Electoral costs / benefits of government parties* (in % of votes)

Government	In office at time of election	Election year	CP	SD	CE	LP	CO	Government
Brown I	Y	1949			+9.3	−4.5	+3.1	+7.9
Brown II	N	1952			−7.1		−0.9	−8.0
Brown III	Y	1952	+17.1				−0.9	+16.2
Grey	Y	1955			±0		±0	±0
...	...	...	...	...	...	...	...	...
Black III	Y	1996	+1.6	+2.2				+3.8
MEANS			+2.2	+8.6	−2.4	−3.9	+4.5	+3.8

Parties: Mean figures count each election only once, even when one or more parties participated in more than one government during the electoral term

Government: Net aggregate result for all government parties

In this volume we subject the electoral consequences of government participation to systematic investigation. The ultimate table in each chapter (Table 1.8) shows the performance of each government and each government party in the election that followed its term in office. The table always indicates the election year and whether the government was still in office when the election was contested. In calculating the averages per party in the bottom line of the table, each election has been counted only once even if a party served in two or more governments within the same legislative term.

CONCLUSION

The following thirteen chapters apply the research programme we have outlined in this introducion to the most important coalitional systems of Western Europe. They do so in a way designed to maximize consistency and comparability. Whenever applicable and available, all chapters present the same information in the same order. At the same time, we recognize that each author is a respected expert on the country for which he or she is responsible. We have therefore asked each author to convey the particularities of each system in whatever way is most appropriate. Within the confines that any book such as this implies, there must be some trade-off between these objectives. The same book that provides the most extensive and systematically comparable data cannot unfortunately also be the one that gives the richest configurative interpretation. To the extent that a choice between these desiderata has been necessary, we have come down clearly on the former side. This is a choice that we have made for a number of reasons, but most importantly because we believe in and wish to contribute to systematic and cumulative cross-national research. In the conclusion to this volume we provide a preliminary comparative summary of the most important aspects of coalition politics in Western Europe in the post-war period. In future research (Strøm, Müller, and Bergman, forthcoming), we shall pursue these questions in more systematic and rigorous ways.

REFERENCES

Alt, James, and King, Gary (1994). 'Transfer of Governmental Power'. *Comparative Political Studies*, 27: 190–210.
Arrow, Kenneth J. (1951). *Social Choice and Individual Values*. New York: Wiley.
Austen-Smith, David, and Banks, Jeffrey (1988). 'Elections, Coalitions and Legislative Outcomes'. *American Political Science Review*, 82: 405–22.
——(1990). 'Stable Governments and the Allocation of Policy Portfolios'. *American Political Science Review*, 84: 891–906.
Baron, David P. (1991). 'A Spacial Bargaining Theory of Government Formation in a Parliamentary System'. *American Political Science Review*, 83: 1181–1206.
——(1993). 'Government Formation and Endogenous Parties'. *American Political Science Review*, 88: 33–47.
Belloni, Frank P., and Beller, Dennis C. (1978) (eds.). *Faction Politics: Political Parties and Factionalism in Comparative Perspective*. Santa Barbara, Calif.: Clio Press.
Bergman, Torbjörn (1993). 'Formation Rules and Minority Governments'. *European Journal of Political Research*, 23: 55–66.
Bogdanor, Vernon (1983) (ed.). *Coalition Government in Western Europe*. London: Heinemann.
Browne, Eric C., and Dreijmanis, John (1982) (eds.). *Government Coalitions in Western Democracies*. New York: Longman.
——and Franklin, Mark (1973). 'Aspects of Coalition Payoffs in European Parliamentary Democracies'. *American Political Science Review*, 67: 453–69.
Budge, Ian, and Keman, Hans (1990). *Parties and Democracy: Coalition Formation and Government Functioning in Twenty States*. Oxford: Oxford University Press.
——and Laver, Michael (1993). 'The Policy Basis of Government Coalitions: A Comparative Investigation'. *British Journal of Political Science*, 23: 499–519.
——Robertson, David and Hearl, Derek (1987) (eds.). *Ideology, Strategy and Party Change*. Cambridge: Cambridge University Press.
Castles, Francis G., and Mair, Peter (1984). 'Left–Right Political Scales: Some "Expert" Judgments'. *European Journal of Political Research*, 12: 73–88.
Diermeier, Daniel, and van Roozendaal, Peter (1998). 'The Duration of Government Formation in Western Multi-Party Democracies'. *British Journal of Political Science*, 28: 609–26.

Dodd, Lawrence C. (1976). *Coalitions in Parliamentary Government*. Princeton: Princeton University Press.

Eggertsson, Thráinn (1990). *Economic Behavior and Institutions*. Cambridge: Cambridge University Press.

Grofman, Bernhard, and van Rozendaal, Peter (1997). 'Modelling Cabinet Durability and Termination'. *British Journal of Political Science*, 27: 419–51.

Huber, John, and Inglehart, Ronald (1995). 'Expert Interpretations of Party Space and Party Locations in 42 Societies'. *Party Politics*, 1: 73–111.

Janda, Kenneth, Harmel, Robert, Edens, Christine, and Goff, Patricia (1995). 'Changes in Party Identity'. *Party Politics*, 1: 171–96.

King, Gary, Alt, James, Burns, Nancy, and Laver, Michael (1990). 'A Unified Model of Cabinet Dissolution in Parliamentary Democracies'. *American Journal of Political Science*, 34: 846–71.

Laakso, Markuu, and Taagepera, Rein (1979). '"Effective" Number of Parties: A Measure with Applications to Western Europe'. *Comparative Political Studies*, 12: 3–27.

Laver, Michael (1989). 'Party Competition and Party System Change'. *Journal of Theoretical Politics*, 1: 301–24.

——and Budge, Ian (1992) (eds.). *Party Policy and Coalition Government*. London: Macmillan.

——and Hunt, Ben W. (1992). *Policy and Party Competition*. New York: Routledge.

——and Schofield, Norman (1990). *Multiparty Government*. Oxford: Oxford University Press.

——and Shepsle, Kenneth (1990). 'Coalitions and Cabinet Government'. *American Political Science Review*, 84: 873–90.

————(1994) (eds.). *Cabinet Ministers and Parliamentary Government*. Cambridge: Cambridge University Press.

————(1996). *Making and Breaking Governments: Cabinets and Legislatures in Parliamentary Democracies*. Cambridge: Cambridge University Press.

Leiserson, Michael (1966). 'Factions and Coalitions in One-Party Japan: An Interpretation Based on the Theory of Games'. *American Political Science Review*, 62: 70–87.

Lijphart, Arend (1984). *Democracies*. New Haven: Yale University Press.

Lipset, Seymour Martin, and Rokkan, Stein (1967). 'Cleavage Structures, Party Systems, and Voter Alignments: An Introduction', in Seymour Martin Lipset and Stein Rokkan (eds.), *Party Systems and Voter Alignments*. New York: Free Press.

Lupia, Arthur, and Strøm, Kaare (1995). 'Coalition Termination and the Strategic Timing of Parliamentary Elections'. *American Political Science Review*, 89: 648–65.

Mayhew, David R. (1974). *Congress: The Electoral Connection*. New Haven: Yale University Press.

Müller, Wolfgang C. (1993). 'The Relevance of the State for Party System Change'. *Journal of Theoretical Politics*, 5: 419–54.

Müller, Wolfgang C. (2000). 'Political Parties in Parliamentary Democracies Making Delegation and Accountability Work' *European Journal of Political Research*, 37 (forthcoming).

Powell, G. Bingham (1982). *Contemporary Democracies*. Cambridge, Mass.: Harvard University Press.

Pridham, Geoffrey (1986) (ed.). *Coalition Behaviour in Theory and Practice: An Inductive Model for Western Europe*. Cambridge: Cambridge University Press.

Riker, William T. (1962). *The Theory of Political Coalitions*. New Haven: Yale University Press.

Rose, Richard, and Mackie, Thomas (1983). 'Incumbency in Government: Asset or Liability', in Hans Daalder and Peter Mair (eds.), *West European Party Systems: Continuity and Change*. London: Sage.

Sani, Giacomo, and Sartori, Giovanni (1983). 'Polarization, Fragmentation and Competition in Western Democracies', in Hans Daalder and Peter Mair (eds.), *West European Party Systems: Continuity and Change*. London: Sage.

Sartori, Giovanni (1976). *Parties and Party Systems*. Cambridge: Cambridge University Press.

Schofield, Norman, and Laver, Michael J. (1985). 'Bargaining Theory and Portfolio Payoffs in European Coalition Governments 1945–83'. *British Journal of Political Science* 15: 143–64.

Strøm, Kaare (1990a). *Minority Government and Majority Rule*. Cambridge: Cambridge University Press.

——(1990b). 'A Theory of Competitive Political Parties'. *American Journal of Political Science*, 34: 565–98.

——(2000). 'Delegation and Accountability in Parliamentary Democracies'. *European Journal of Political Research*, 37 (forthcoming).

——Budge, Ian, and Laver, Michael J. (1994). 'Constraints on Cabinet Formation in Parliamentary Democracies'. *American Journal of Political Science*, 38: 303–35.

——Müller, Wolfgang C., and Bergman, Torbjörn (n.d.) (eds.) *Coalition Governance in Parliamentary Democracies*. Oxford: Oxford University Press, forthcoming.

Taylor, Michael, and Laver, Michael (1973). 'Government Coalitions in Western Europe'. *European Journal of Political Research*, 1: 205–48.

Warwick, Paul V. (1992). 'Rising Hazards: An Underlying Dynamic of Parliamentary Government'. *American Journal of Political Science*, 36: 857–76.

——(1994). *Government Survival in Parliamentary Democracies*. Cambridge: Cambridge University Press.

——(1999). 'Ministerial Autonomy or Ministerial Accommodation: Contested Bases of Government Survival in Parliamentary Democracies'. *British Journal of Political Science* 29: 369–94.

2

Germany

Stable Parties, Chancellor Democracy, and the Art of Informal Settlement

Thomas Saalfeld

INTRODUCTION

Coalitions have been 'the typical form of government' (Schmidt 1996: 72) in the Federal Republic of Germany. Compared to the first German Republic, the Weimar Republic (1919–33), coalitions in the second (West) German Republic have been relatively stable since 1949 (for data, see Saalfeld 1999: 147). Even severe exogenous shocks such as the political, economic, and social upheavals of the immediate post-war years, the recessions of 1966/7, 1974/5, and 1981/2, or the political and social frictions induced by German unification have not unsettled the stable patterns of German coalition politics. Although such 'exogenous critical events' (Lupia and Strøm 1995: 651) contributed to several coalition realignments, they have so far not led to frequent coalition crises as experienced in the Weimar Republic.

PARTY SYSTEM FEATURES

In September 1949, when the West German Bundestag met for its first session, the stability of coalition government was not necessarily predictable.

I owe thanks to Mr Joachim Hörster, then chief whip (*Erster Parlamentarischer Geschäftsführer*) of the CDU/CSU Bundestag caucus and Dr Peter Struck, now floor leader (*Fraktionsvorsitzender*) of the SPD Bundestag caucus for granting me access to the texts of various coalition agreements in 1996. Eberhard Flessing, Antje Sommer (Archiv der Sozialen Demokratie der Friedrich-Ebert-Stiftung) and Erich Schwarz (Archiv für Christlich-Demokratische Politik der Konrad-Adenauer-Stiftung) kindly provided me with copies of some coalition agreements and other material from the respective archives. Antje Sommer gave me valuable additional information on coalition agreements between 1966 and 1980. I am particularly grateful to Wolfgang C. Müller, Kaare Strøm, and Cornelia Wilhelm for their helpful comments on earlier drafts of this paper.

The political, economic and social upheavals of World War II did not provide an optimal background for stable coalitions. Moreover, the first Bundestag elections produced a relatively polarized multi-party system, similar to the one characteristic of the early Weimar Republic. Eight parties were represented in the Weimar National Assembly of 1919–20. The 'effective number of parties' (Laakso and Taagepera 1979), which weights these parties according to their share of seats in parliament, was 4.10. The Rae index of fractionalization, expressing the probability that two members drawn at random from the universe belong to different parties, was 0.76. The first elections to the Bundestag produced a strikingly similar result. Like in 1919, eight parliamentary parties were returned in 1949. In addition, six extreme right-wing deputies formed the group[1] of the National Right. With 3.99 the effective number of parties was almost as high as in the National Assembly of 1919–20, and with a Rae index of 0.75 the first Bundestag was almost as fractionalized (Saalfeld 1999: 147). Thus, a 'large number of parties, a high level of fragmentation in the party system, and a complex cleavage structure (class, religion, centre–periphery, anti-communism versus communism, and native population versus refugees and exiles) were characteristic of the party system in the first and second legislative periods (1949–57)' (Schmidt 1996: 69).

Yet, the two party systems differed starkly in their subsequent development. In the first five years of the Weimar Republic, the effective number of parties in parliament grew from 4.10 to 7.10 and was reduced only in 1932 as a result of the rise of extremist anti-system parties on the left and the right (Saalfeld 1999: 147). The Bonn Republic, by contrast, witnessed a rapid process of party-system concentration. Between 1949 and 1961 the Christian Democrats (CDU and CSU) in particular expanded their share of the vote at the expense of the smaller parties to their right. This is reflected in the declining number of parties and groups in the Bundestag from nine in 1949 to three in 1961. It is also indicated by the effective number of parties declining from almost four in the first (1949–53) to approximately 2.5 in the fourth Bundestag (1961–5, see Table 2.1). This concentration process was partly a result of the major parties' (especially the CDU/CSU's) electoral success; in part it was helped by changes in the electoral law. In the Bundestag's first legislative term (1949–53), the 5 per cent threshold was applied at the state (*Land*) rather than at the federal level. Thus, small parties with regional

---

[1] The Bundestag's Rules of Procedure distinguish between parliamentary parties ('*Fraktionen*', which enjoy privileged status) and parliamentary groups ('*Gruppen*'). Currently, a number of deputies will only be recognized as a parliamentary party if it comprises at least 5% of the members of the Bundestag. At the discretion of the Bundestag's majority, a smaller number can be granted a special 'group' status with at least some of the parliamentary parties' rights in the plenum and committees. In the first Bundestag (1949–53), the minimum size requirement for a '*Fraktion*' was 10 members.

strongholds such as the Bavarian Party (BP), the Economic Reconstruction League (WAV), the German Party (DP), and the Centre Party (Zentrum) were able to overcome it at least in one state, which was sufficient to achieve proportional representation in the Bundestag. From 1953 onwards the 5 per cent threshold was applied on the federal level (with the exception of the first all-German election of 1990). This more rigorous entry condition immediately eliminated regional parties except the CSU and the DP. When the CDU decided to discontinue its support for the DP (in the form of electoral pacts) at the end of the 1950s, this small conservative regional party, too, was doomed.

This first phase of concentration (1949–61) was followed by a second phase (1961–83) characterized by a three-party system. In 1961, the conservative parties with a regional and/or denominational character as well as the extreme right-wing parties and the Communists had disappeared from the Bundestag either as a result of electoral and organizational failure or of bans declared by the Federal Constitutional Court on grounds of unconstitutionality. Despite occasional resurgences of small extreme right-wing parties (in particular, the NPD in 1969), the three main parties were able to defend their monopoly of parliamentary representation until 1983. The absolute number of parties remained three. Given the smaller size of the FDP, the effective number of parties varied between 2.24 and 2.52 (see Tables 2.1 and 2.2).

A third phase, characterized by a moderate increase in fractionalization, began in 1983, when the Green Party straddled the 5 per cent threshold for the first time. Between 1980 and 1998 the absolute number of parties and party groups represented in the Bundestag increased from three (1980) to five (1994 and 1998, with a brief peak of seven after the accession of 144 eastern German parliamentarians in October 1990). Since 1987 the effective number of parties in the Bundestag has remained slightly above the values for the 1960s and 1970s and ranged from 2.80 to 2.94 (see Tables 2.1 and 2.2). Initially unification made little difference to the pattern of party representation in the Bundestag. The western German party system was largely reproduced in eastern Germany (mainly through the merger of most eastern German parties with their western counterparts). The only major exception is the Party of Democratic Socialism/ Left List (PDS/LL), the successor of the former ruling communist party of the German Democratic Republic (GDR). The PDS has managed to secure representation in the Bundestag as a result of its regional strength in eastern Germany where it has also established itself as a major party participating in a formal government coalition in the federal state of Mecklenburg-West Pommerania (1998). Yet despite some modest advances in some western German urban areas in the 1998 elections, it has failed to establish itself as an all-German party.

Not only was the number of parties greatly reduced between 1949 and 1961. The main parties' ideological nature and social group affiliations changed. The vast majority of the Weimar parties had been '*Weltanschau-*

ungsparteien' firmly entrenched and 'rigid in their devotion to diverse political ideologies and close in rapport with interest groups' (Norpoth 1982: 7). By contrast, the predominant (West) German parties after 1949 have become far more pragmatic in their ideologies (for useful surveys, see Lösche 1993; Mintzel and Oberreuter 1992; Padgett 1993; Stöss 1986c). Even the Green Party, some of whose early spokespersons considered themselves as fundamentally opposed to representative democracy and presented a radical ecological and pacifist programme, have gradually moderated their stance. As a result, the party has gradually become 'coalitionable'. After a number of coalitions with the Social Democrats (SPD) at the local and regional level and the Christian Democrats in some local authorities, the Greens joined their first coalition at the national level in 1998, when they formed a coalition with the SPD under Chancellor Gerhard Schröder.

INSTITUTIONAL RULES

The development of the Federal Republic's party system—both in terms of the number of parties and the predominant parties' ideological orientation—has been a crucial factor stabilizing coalition politics after 1949. The stability of coalitions has also been underpinned by formal and informal 'rules of the game'. Although the Basic Law (*Grundgesetz*) does not mention coalitions explicitly, some of its provisions have had significant implications for the formation and stability of coalitions: constitutional rules on cabinet decision making, the Chancellor's restricted powers to request a dissolution of parliament, the procedures for initiating a legislative vote of no confidence, the Bundestag's voting procedures and majority requirements as well as the implications of 'co-operative federalism'.

Formal Constraints

The Basic Law limits the powers of the Federal President largely to ceremonial tasks. Unlike the Weimar Reich President, the Federal President has in reality 'next to no discretionary powers in the process of government formation' (von Beyme 1983: 16). Even in a relatively 'open' situation like the aftermath of the 1969 elections, when a CDU/CSU–FDP, a CDU/CSU–SPD, and an SPD–FDP coalition were numerically and politically possible and there was no pre-electoral pact, the Federal President did not, and could not, play an active role in the process of coalition formation (although the incumbent had known preferences for a Social-liberal coalition). Only *after* the leaders of the SPD (Willy Brandt) and FDP (Walter Scheel) had agreed on a coalition, they informed President Gustav Heinemann about their intentions

(Bracher, Jäger, and Link 1986: 18–19). Similarly, the Federal President had no role in the process of coalition formation after the elections of 1998, when the party constellation theoretically allowed three different minimal-winning solutions. The Basic Law does not provide any rules on the process of coalition formation. Unlike some other European countries such as Belgium or the Netherlands an institutionalized system of *formateurs* or *informateurs* has never been used, although the Federal President could assume the role of a facilitator in the case of an impasse in the inter-party negotiations. Coalition formation has been the result of 'freestyle bargaining' between party leaders.

The Federal Chancellor's powers are considerably stronger than the ones enjoyed by the Weimar Reich Chancellors. As head of government, he or she is elected by the Bundestag (Art. 63 of the Basic Law). To be elected, a candidate needs an absolute majority of all members of the Bundestag entitled to vote.[2] The Federal President must appoint the candidate elected with an absolute majority of the chamber. If no candidate reaches an absolute majority in the first ballot, there may be an unspecified number of further ballots within fourteen days. If no candidate reaches an absolute majority within this period of time, the Federal President may appoint the candidate with the relative majority of votes or, alternatively, call an election. As yet, this has never been necessary. Once elected, the Chancellor nominates the members of the cabinet who are then appointed by the Federal President. Individual ministers are responsible to the Chancellor. They may be dismissed by him, but not by the Bundestag. Their tenure in office ends with the Chancellor's.

The Chancellor's dissolution powers are constrained as are the Bundestag's powers to dismiss the Chancellor. He and his cabinet can be dismissed by the Bundestag only collectively and only by a 'constructive vote of no confidence' (Art. 67 of the Basic Law), i.e. an absolute majority of the Bundestag members must not only be willing to depose the Chancellor and his cabinet, they must simultaneously elect an alternative candidate. This is to prevent a repetition of the Weimar experience, where a Reich Chancellor could be dismissed at the request of a 'negative' majority, which subsequently could not agree on a successor, encouraging presidential government by decree. The Bundestag has no powers to dismiss individual ministers for political reasons, a right enjoyed by the Weimar Reichstag (Art. 54 of the Weimar Constitution) to the detriment of coalition stability. The Chancellor of the Federal Republic can request a vote of confidence, mainly in order to consolidate his parliamentary support in critical situations. If the Chancellor loses the confidence of the majority, he may ask the President for a dissolution of the Bundestag (Art. 68 of the Basic Law). There is no obligation to resign in the absence of a supporting parliamentary majority for important government bills or motions. If

---

[2] Between 1949 and 1989, the members for Berlin did not have the right to vote on investiture votes.

the Chancellor fails to achieve a sufficient majority in a vote of confidence, he may ask the Federal President for a dissolution of parliament. Alternatively, he may stay in office or request the President to declare a state of legislative emergency. If he decides to do nothing, he cannot be dismissed by the President, as the latter can only act upon the Chancellor's advice.

Voting procedures have been important institutional constraints on coalition formation. The Basic Law and the Bundestag's Rules of Procedure require qualified majorities for a number of decisions: 'The selection of the Chancellor, votes of confidence and the constructive vote of no confidence require the approval of the majority of the members of the lower House. Legislative changes in the constitution require two-thirds majorities in the Bundestag, the lower House, and in the Bundesrat, the upper House' (Schmidt 1996: 75). This has encouraged surplus-majority coalitions during the first two legislative periods (1949–57) with a large number of constitutional amendments and generally strengthened the 'consensus democracy component' (Schmidt 1996: 75) as well as the incentives to maintain elements of a permanent informal 'Grand Coalition' of the two major parties in what Manfred G. Schmidt (1996) calls a 'Grand Coalition State'.

Apart from the dissolution and voting procedures outlined above, there are two further pillars of Chancellor democracy, strengthening the Chancellor's role and influencing coalition governance: the incumbent's powers to organize the executive branch (*Organisationsgewalt*), that is, to establish and change the number and jurisdiction of the federal departments and to formulate guidelines of government policy (*Richtlinienkompetenz*). Whether the Chancellor is able and willing to use these powers depends on the personal and political circumstances. Potentially, however, they strengthen his position vis-à-vis departmental ministers of his own party as well as other coalition parties.

The 5 per cent threshold of the electoral law (*Bundeswahlgesetz*) and the powers of the Federal Constitutional Court to ban anti-constitutional political parties have contributed to a reduction of the number and ideological range of parties in the Bundestag. The exclusion of relevant anti-system parties has avoided the dangers of 'bilateral oppositions' and 'opposition of principle' (Sartori 1976: 132–4). Especially in its final phase, the Weimar parliament was marred by the presence of ideologically extreme anti-system parties. Their parliamentary strength made coalitions of the remaining major pro-system parties, or minority governments, necessary. Under such circumstances cabinets are more likely to collapse as they may lack a parliamentary majority or include very diverse coalition partners. Often 'these partners know they risk little in abandoning governments as their advantage dictates: their chances of returning to office are excellent' (Warwick 1994: 4). In the Federal Republic, by contrast, coalition choices have been restricted to a small number of democratic parties since 1957, facilitating stable coalition government.

The Bundestag is not the only arena of inter-party cooperation and conflict. Indeed, the nature of the German policy process cannot be understood adequately without referring to the phenomenon of 'cooperative federalism' with its emphasis on bargaining and compromise between the federal government and state governments across the party-political government–opposition divide. This has considerable implications for coalition government at the federal level. More than 50 per cent of all federal (virtually all important domestic bills) are subject to mandatory approval by the Federal Council (Bundesrat), the body representing the federal-state governments. Constitutional amendments need a two-thirds majority in the Bundestag and the Bundesrat. This has several implications for coalition government at the federal level: if there are 'parallel' majorities in Bundestag and Bundesrat, the government parties' state prime ministers have to be consulted on important matters of policy and have therefore usually been important actors in coalition politics. This can lead to tensions between the national coalition parties, especially if decisions are made in extra-parliamentary ad hoc meetings rather than formal cabinet and coalition committees. If the main opposition party in the national capital has a blocking majority in the Bundesrat[3] and, hence, the power to veto or delay federal legislation, intra-coalition bargaining is, in addition, influenced by the need to negotiate compromises with one or more opposition parties.[4] This may both restrict or increase the set of strategies available to coalition partners in their mutual negotiations. For example, the Kohl government's dependence (especially between 1991 and 1998) on the support of at least some SPD-led federal states in the Bundesrat occasionally increased the CDU/CSU's leverage vis-à-vis its liberal coalition partner in questions of social or immigration policy. If majorities in both Houses of the legislature are 'divided', such as under Helmut Kohl's chancellorship between 1991 and 1998, intra-coalition bargaining has been of limited significance. Ultimately the decisive negotiations have to be conducted between the federal government and at least some federal-state governments controlled by the main opposition party (cf. Kaltefleiter 1996: 36). The Conference Committee (*Vermittlungsausschuss*) of Bundestag and Bundesrat, whose members are not bound by any directives, has become a very important body.

[3] This was the case most of the time between 1969 and 1982, from May to October 1990, from early 1991 to September 1998, and since February 1999.

[4] The experience of the Kohl cabinets (1982–98) may serve as an example. Given the fact that the SPD governed in various coalitions with the Greens, the CDU, and the FDP in a number of federal states, it cannot be said the SPD 'controlled' the Bundesrat. Nevertheless, the SPD governed in a sufficiently large number of federal states, giving it influence over the respective state governments' voting behaviour in the Bundesrat (cf. generally Kropp and Sturm 1998: 116–17). Therefore, important federal-state governments with SPD participation had to be persuaded, if the Kohl government wanted its legislation to be passed by the Bundesrat (esp. so-called 'consent laws', that is, laws for which Bundesrat consent is mandatory according to the Basic Law).

Informal Constraints

Since the 1960s the leaders of coalition parties have almost regularly constrained their own scope for post-election bargaining by concluding informal pre-election coalition pacts. In electoral terms such pacts are perfectly rational as they reduce the level of electoral competition between the governing parties. Moreover, risk-averse voters have tended to shy away from penalizing incumbents electorally at the national level privileging incumbent government parties (see Table 2.8). Indeed, as Wolfgang Gibowski (1995: 26) pointed out after Chancellor Kohl's fourth election victory in a row in 1994, 'incumbent federal governments do not normally lose elections'. The frequent use of pre-election coalition pacts is a rational response to this incentive structure and has facilitated long-term cooperation beyond one legislative term.

Self-imposed refusals to enter a coalition or to consider another party as a potential coalition partner have also reduced the range of coalition possibilities. Before the first Bundestag elections of 1949, for example, representatives of the BP announced that the party would play the role of a 'constructive opposition' (Mintzel 1986: 420). Before and after the same elections, the CSU insisted that it would not participate in a coalition with the SPD or the BP. All democratic parties rejected cooperation with the KPD in 1949. In 1953 the CDU/CSU announced it would not enter a Grand Coalition with the Social Democrats (Klingemann und Volkens 1992: 194). In 1990, 1994, and 1998, the PDS was rejected as a coalition partner by all other parties in the Bundestag.

Electoral cooperation between (prospective) coalition partners has been facilitated by the electoral system allowing voters to cast two votes, one directly for a constituency candidate, who is elected on the basis of a plurality system, and one for a party's regional state list (*Landesliste*). The distribution of 'second votes' for the various party lists determines to a large extent the distribution of seats in parliament. Germany's 'additional-member system' gives voters opportunities to 'split' their votes and maximize their impact on the outcome to the advantage of a preferred coalition. Vote splitting is also of importance for the parties' campaign strategies. For example, the 'first' or constituency vote was used to secure the electoral 'survival' of the DP in the 1953 and 1957 elections. The CDU concluded electoral pacts with the DP according to which the Christian Democrats did not nominate candidates in a certain number of DP-held constituencies. This helped the DP to win ten constituency mandates in 1953 and six in 1957 (Schindler 1983: 64, nn. 2 and 3). In return, the DP remained a loyal coalition partner under Adenauer as Chancellor (Jesse 1988: 111–12). Since 1969, the 'second vote' has become increasingly relevant as a factor stabilizing coalitions indirectly. There has been a growing tendency of FDP voters, in particular, to 'split' their votes in order to improve the FDP's survival chances as well as the electoral chances of the FDP's preferred coalition partner (Jesse 1988). With a core support of approximately 3 per cent of the electorate, the FDP has often relied on a substantial share of so-called 'borrowed votes' (*Leihstimmen*) to straddle the 5 per cent threshold and secure its representation in the Bundestag. A substantial proportion of the votes for the FDP's party lists have usually been cast by supporters of one of the major parties (usually the FDP's 'prospective' coalition partner). In the elections of 1994, for example, almost two-thirds of the FDP's total share of the 'second votes' came from voters who considered themselves Christian Democrats (Conradt 1996: 157). Since none of the major parties has been likely to win an overall majority in elections, they have, on occasions, publicly (if grudgingly) supported vote borrowing in order to stabilize a coalition in the long run (Jesse 1988: 116–18). Virtually in exchange, many voters, who cast their 'second' vote for an FDP list, have tended to give their constituency vote to the candidate of the FDP's coalition partner in Bonn.

COALITION FORMATION

Coalitions 1949–1999—an Overview

Table 2.1 provides information on the number of seats held by all parties and party groups represented in the Bundestag since 1949.[5] The parties' names are listed in the top row of the table. They have been ordered according to their ideological location on a single left–right continuum (see below). The ranking of the main parties is based on Michael Laver and W. Ben Hunt's (1992: 196–201) rankings derived from expert ratings in 1989 which have been amended for several reasons explained in n. *a* below Table 2.1. The seats of the parties forming the government are printed in bold letters. The party controlling the median legislator for the most important policy dimension (economic policy) is identified by an asterisk (*). The party controlling the median legislator for the second most important policy dimension (foreign policy) is listed separately. Moreover, Table 2.1 provides information on each govern-

---

[5] Table 2.1 measures the strength of the parties and groups represented in the Bundestag at the beginning of each government's term in office. The table only displays the number of West German Members with full voting rights for the period 1949–90. The members for Berlin were excluded for this time because their voting rights were restricted. Due to Berlin's special status as a city under Allied joint occupation until 1990, its Bundestag deputies were not elected directly. Up until 1987, they were appointed by the Berlin federal-state diet (*Abgeordnetenhaus*) and excluded from voting on most important motions. For example, they had no voting rights in the second and third reading of the legislative process, in votes of no confidence or in the election of the Chancellor. They could, however, vote on internal matters of the Bundestag, the first reading of bills and committee meetings.

TABLE 2.1. *Left–right placement[a] of parties, party strength (in seats), and party composition of governments in Germany, 1949–1999[b]*

Government	Proximity to election[c]	KPD	PDS	GR	B'90	SPD	FDP	CDU/CSU	DSU	Z[d]	GB/BHE	DA/FVP	DP	WAV	BP	NR	Median party in second policy dimension[e]	Effective number of legislative parties[f]	Government strength	Total number of seats[g]
1949	FE	15	—	—	—	131	52	140*	—	10	—	—	17	12	17	6	FDP	3.99	209	402
1953	F	—	—	—	—	151	48	244*	—	—	27	—	15	—	—	—	CDU/CSU	2.77	334	487
1955	—	—	—	—	—	151	49	251*	—	—[d]	18[h]	—	15	—	—	—	CDU/CSU	2.67	315	487
1956	E	—	—	—	—	151	34	251*	—	—[d]	18	14[i]	16	—	—	—	CDU/CSU	2.70	281	487
1957	F	—	—	—	—	169	41	270*	—	—	—	—	17	—	—	—	CDU/CSU	2.39	287	497[j]
1960	—	—	—	—	—	169	42	271*	—	—	—	—	6	—	—	—	CDU/CSU	2.38	271	497
1961	F	—	—	—	—	190	67*	242	—	—	—	—	—	—	—	—	FDP	2.51	309	499
1962	—	—	—	—	—	190	67*	241	—	—	—	—	—	—	—	—	FDP	2.52	241	499
1962	—	—	—	—	—	190	67*	241	—	—	—	—	—	—	—	—	FDP	2.52	308	499
1965	E	—	—	—	—	202	49*	245	—	—	—	—	—	—	—	—	FDP	2.38	294	496
1966	F	—	—	—	—	202	49*	245	—	—	—	—	—	—	—	—	FDP	2.38	245	496
1966	E	—	—	—	—	202	49*	245	—	—	—	—	—	—	—	—	FDP	2.38	447	496
1969	FE	—	—	—	—	224	30	242*	—	—	—	—	—	—	—	—	FDP	2.24	254	496
1972	FE	—	—	—	—	230	41	225*	—	—	—	—	—	—	—	—	FDP	2.34	271	496
1976	FE	—	—	—	—	214	39	243*	—	—	—	—	—	—	—	—	FDP	2.31	253	496
1980	F	—	—	—	—	218	53	226*	—	—	—	—	—	—	—	—	FDP	2.44	271	497
1982	—	—	—	—	—	215	53	226*	—	—	—	—	—	—	—	—	FDP	2.47	215	497
1982	E	—	—	—	—	215	53	226*	—	—	—	—	—	—	—	—	FDP	2.47	279	497
1983	FE	—	—	27	—	193	34	244*	—	—	—	—	—	—	—	—	FDP	2.51	278	498
1987	F	—	—	42	—	186	46	223*	—	—	—	—	—	—	—	—	FDP	2.80	269	497
1990	E	—	24	41	7	226	57	305*	8	—	—	—	—	—	—	—	FDP	2.94	370	663[k]
1991[l]	FE	—	17	—	8	239	79	319*	—	—	—	—	—	—	—	—	FDP	2.65	398	662
1994	FE	—	30	—	49	252	47	294*	—	—	—	—	—	—	—	—	FDP	2.91	341	672
1998	n/a	—	36	—	47	298*	43	245	—	—	—	—	—	—	—	—	SPD	2.90	345	669

cont

TABLE 2.1. cont.

a In order to determine the party controlling the median legislator, Laver and Hunt's (1992: 196–201) rankings have to be amended for several reasons: (*a*) They are not comprehensive as Laver and Hunt include only four out of thirteen parties that are relevant in our context (CDU/CSU, FDP, SPD, and Greens). The fifth party ranked, the NPD, has never been represented in the Bundestag. (*b*) The rankings provide a snapshot of the situation in 1989 but disregard changes across time. It is uncontroversial amongst experts, however, that the FDP's position in the party space has changed several times. (*c*) Laver and Hunt (1992: 56) themselves recognize that the FDP presents a problem because its location varies across different policy dimensions. They consider it 'an outlier' because it is 'at the right-hand end of the scale on economic policy but . . . relatively progressive on social policy' (Laver and Hunt 1992: 56). (*d*) Finally, the most salient dimensions identified by Laver and Hunt (1992: 50) in the German case are (i) environmental and (ii) social policies. The relative importance of the former dimension, in particular, is arguably a result of the particular time of measurement. The changes across time are captured more adequately by content analyses of party manifestos as carried out by Klingemann and Volkens (1992: 198, 219–22). The rankings, on which the identification of the party controlling the median legislator are based, will, therefore, be adjusted for each individual parliamentary session between 1949 and 1994. Klingemann and Volkens's (1992: 203) are, however, also far from satisfactory. Their attempt to locate the parties of the 1949–53 and 1953–7 parliaments on a common left–right dimension has led to some implausible results with respect to some of the minor parties. The right-wing WAV is classified as left of the Communists in the first Bundestag (1949–53) as is the SPD. According to Klingemann and Volkens's data, the Zentrum would have to be classified as a left-wing party. In the second Bundestag (1953–7) the location of the GB/BHE poses similar difficulties. Klingemann and Volkens (1992: 197) have to concede that these placements are artefacts of their coding method: as these parties (quantitatively) made massive social service demands on behalf of their specific clientele, their campaign manifestos contained a large number of socio-economic claims that could only be classified as 'left wing'. Therefore, my ranking of the minor parties of the 1950s was largely based on the qualitative material provided by the historical literature.
b Measurement at the beginning of each government's term; 1949–90: appointed members for Berlin excluded.
c F = coalition immediately following an election; E = Coalition ended by an election; FE = Coalition immediately following an election and ended by the next election.
d In the second Bundestag (1953–7), the Zentrum was no longer recognized as a parliamentary party. It had initially two members, later one member.
e According to Laver and Hunt (1992: 105), the second policy dimension is foreign policy.
f Laakso and Taagepera index.
g Includes 'excess mandates' (*Überhangmandate*).
h The "Gruppe Kraft/Oberländer" who left the GB/BHE existed only for one day (14 July 1955) and joined the CDU/CSU on 15 July1955 (initially as "guests", from 23 Feb. 1956 as full members).
i Government supported by members of the DA/FVP, a group of former FDP members, who join the DP on 14 Mar. 1957.
j Number of seats increased on 04 Jan. 1957 after the accession of ten members from Saarland.
k Number of seats increased on 03 Oct. 1990 after the accession of 144 *Volkskammer* members.
l Elections held in 1990, government formed in 1991.

Parties
KPD   Kommunistische Partei Deutschlands (Communist Party)
PDS   Partei des Demokratischen Sozialismus (Party of Democratic Socialism)
GR   Grüne (Greens)
B'90   Bündnis '90 (Alliance '90)
SPD   Sozialdemokratische Partei Deutschlands (Social Democratic Party)
FDP   Freie Demokratische Partei (Free Democratic Party)
CDU   Christlich Demokratische Union Deutschlands (Christian Democratic Union)
CSU   Christlich-Soziale Union in Bayern (Christian Social Union)
DSU   Deutsche Soziale Union (German Social Union)

Z	Zentrum (Centre)
GB/BHE	Gesamtdeutscher Block/ Bund der Heimatlosen und Entrechteten (All-German Bloc)
DA/FVP	Demokratische Arbeitsgemeinschaft (later renamed Freie Volkspartei) (Democratic Working Group, later renamed Free People's Party)
DP	Deutsche Partei (German Party)
WAV	Wirtschaftliche Aufbau-Vereinigung (Economic Reconstruction League)
BP	Bayernpartei (Bavarian Party)
NR	Nationale Rechte (National Right)

Parties in **bold** formed **governments**.
* Party with median legislator for the first policy dimension (economic policy).

Sources: Schindler (1983: 113, 234–51, 356–64; 1994: 173, 371–5, 438–9; 1995: 554); Presse- und Informationsamt der Bundesregierung (1998c); Klingemann and Volkens (1992: 209–10); Laver and Hunt (1992).

ment formation's proximity to the previous and subsequent elections as well as the 'effective number of legislative parties' (already referred to above).

According to our definition (see the Introduction to this volume), there were twenty-four governments between 1949 and 1 January 1999 of which twenty were coalitions.[6] These governments are listed in Table 2.1 and identified by their year of formation. There were only four brief phases of single-party government: (*a*) Between July 1960 and November 1961 (16 months), there was a CDU/CSU majority government supported by some former members of the DP, after the latter had split up and left the coalition while its ministers kept supporting the government and stayed in office until they joined the CDU/CSU; (*b*) in November–December 1962, there was a CDU/CSU minority government under Adenauer for 24 days, after the FDP had withdrawn from the coalition in order to renegotiate the coalition agreement and force Chancellor Adenauer to promise his resignation; (*c*) in October–November 1966, there was a CDU/CSU minority government lasting 33 days, after the FDP's withdrawal from the CDU/CSU–FDP coalition under Chancellor Ludwig Erhard; (*d*) in September 1982, there was a brief SPD minority government (14 days) after the termination of the SPD–FDP coalition under Chancellor Helmut Schmidt and before the formation of the

---

[6] By and large, the counting rules for governments, coalitions, and cabinets, as outlined in the Introduction, could be applied in a straightforward manner. Only the fourth Adenauer coalition (1956–7) requires a certain element of arbitrary judgement: after a coalition crisis in 1956, 16 FDP parliamentarians, amongst them the party's 4 cabinet ministers, left their party and formed the DA, which supported the government. The 4 ministers kept their portfolios. The FDP withdrew from the coalition on 25 Feb. 1956. The DA formally joined the coalition on 21 Mar. 1956. On 26 June 1956, the party was renamed FVP. Informally, its members had never stopped supporting the government. On 14 Mar. 1957, it merged with the DP. As there was neither a change in the number of parliamentarians supporting the government, nor any changes in portfolio allocation (only the party label of the 16 parliamentarians changed), these changes were not considered coalition terminations.

CDU/CSU–FDP coalition under Helmut Kohl. Given the profound dislike for minority governments amongst the German political elite and academic commentators (they are historically associated with government instability and inefficiency; cf. the debate between Renzsch and Schieren 1997 and Steffani 1997), minority governments have always remained exceptional and marked short transition periods between coalitions rather than the result of strategic choices (for the latter, see Strøm 1990).

Governments have become more stable since 1972. Between 1949 and 1972 only one out of thirteen governments (Adenauer's first (1949–53) cabinet) stretched over the whole length of a parliament (symbolized by 'FE' in Table 2.1). By contrast, five out of ten governments between 1972 and 1998 went over a full parliamentary term. After 1972, this pattern of stable coalition government lasting for a full legislative term was only interrupted in 1982 when the FDP's change of coalition technically produced three governments within one year (the initial SPD–FDP coalition government, an SPD minority government and the eventual CDU/CSU–FDP government). The change of 1990 is partly an artefact of our counting rules. The CDU/CSU–FDP government was voluntarily enlarged as to include the eastern German Social Union (DSU), technically producing two governments none of which stretched over a whole parliamentary term. Since 1972 a high degree of government stability (i.e. coalition governments have had a good chance to survive for the full constitutional inter-election period) has been accompanied by a very low degree of alternation of the parties in office from one government to the next ('turnover'). This is remarkable as Mershon (1999: 229–30) generally finds a positive correlation between stability and alternation for post-war Western Europe.

In the period of 1949–61, the prevailing pattern were coalition governments between the CDU/CSU, as the dominant partner, and one or more smaller parties such as the FDP, the German Party (DP),[7] or the All-German Bloc (GB/BHE) (see Table 2.1).[8] Table 2.1 shows that, between 1953 and 1960, coalitions were generally 'oversized' in William Riker's (1962) terminology. They were neither 'minimal-winning coalitions', which would have been turned into minority governments by the subtraction of any of its members, nor were they 'minimum-winning coalitions', a subset of minimal-winning coalitions comprising those parties with the smallest possible majority in parliament (cf. Laver and Schofield 1990: 91–5). Even when the CDU/CSU won an overall majority of seats in the Bundestag (1957), its leadership did not opt for a single-party government but preferred to continue its coalition with the

---

[7] The DP was represented in the Bundestag between 1949 and 1961. For a recent account, see Schmollinger 1986.

[8] The party's full name is *Gesamtdeutscher Block/Bund der Heimatvertriebenen und Entrechteten* (All-German Bloc/Federation of Expellees and Dispossessed). It was represented in the Bundestag from 1953 to 1957. See Stöss 1986a.

DP.⁹ Chancellor Adenauer's interest in surplus-sized coalitions was of a practical as well as a strategic nature. On a practical level, there was the need to secure a broad majority for the passage of important amendments to the Basic Law in the formative years of the Federal Republic's history. Adenauer needed a 'working majority'. On a strategic level, the CDU was faced with a high degree of electoral uncertainty up until the mid-1950s. The average aggregate volatility (measured by the 'Pedersen Index') was in excess of 14 percentage points for the three elections between 1949 and 1951, before it dropped to an average of 5.8 points for the five elections between 1965 and 1980 (Saalfeld 1999: 147). The CDU/CSU's eventual success was by no means predictable in the early 1950s. The party needed to improve its position in the protestant parts of northern Germany, where an electoral pact with the DP was initially in the CDU's interest. It progressively managed to absorb the voters and part of the leadership of its disintegrating coalition partners (Lösche 1993: 112–15; Schmitt 1986: 573). Finally, the coalition governments allowed the Chancellor to 'discipline' his own parliamentary party. The CDU/CSU was divided in some areas such as social policy, economic policy, the establishment of a welfare state, and other issues in domestic policy. During the first two electoral periods of the Bundestag (1949–57), for example, Adenauer could not take the support of his party's trade-union wing for granted. At several occasions large numbers of its members voted with the Social Democrats against important pieces of government legislation (Saalfeld 1995: 137–40). Thus, the support of his conservative coalition partners was very much a bargaining resource and safety device at the hands of Adenauer vis-à-vis the opposition within his own parliamentary party.

Between 1961 and 1966, Riker's (1962) minimum-winning criterion would have led to predict coalitions between SPD and FDP. In actual fact, however, a series of CDU/CSU–FDP (minimal-winning) coalitions were formed and survived despite several crises. The 'Grand Coalition' of 1966–9 between CDU/CSU and SPD, too, was not minimum-winning (but still minimal-winning). Each of the two major parties could have formed a coalition with the FDP, which would have been more advantageous both in terms of portfolio allocation and policy agreement. The Grand Coalition's desirability was contentious in both major parties. However, relationships between CDU/CSU and FDP were strained beyond repair and the predominant judgement in the SPD leadership was that the potential parliamentary majority of SPD and FDP (the minimum-winning solution) would have been too slim to sustain a government. Herbert Wehner, one of the main supporters of a Grand Coalition in the SPD at the time, clearly wanted to demonstrate his party's 'governability' in a successful partnership with the CDU/CSU. Long-term

⁹ Considering the fact that the Members of the Bundestag for Berlin were not allowed to vote at this time, the CDU/CSU already had an absolute majority of one seat in the 1953–7 Bundestag.

considerations—gaining credibility as a government party—outweighed the short-term benefits of an SPD–FDP coalition in terms of portfolio allocation and policy influence. Finally, the first recession after World War II and the need for important constitutional changes, especially with respect to finance laws and emergency provisions, required a broad parliamentary majority (Hildebrand 1984: 241–58). While there was not a single minimum-winning coalition between 1949 and 1969, five out of 12 coalition cabinets between 1969 and 1999 had minimum-winning status the first Brandt cabinet (1969–72, the second and third Schmidt cabinet (1976–80 and 1980–82) and the fifth and sixth Kohl cabinet (1991–94 and 1994–98). Eleven out of 12 coalition cabinets between 1969 and 1999 had at least minimal-winning status. The only exception was the short-lived post-unification cabinet under Helmut Kohl (1990), which included the eastern German DSU.

Despite the dominance of minimal-winning coalitions since 1969, theories based on office-seeking motivations and the size criterion in Riker's tradition leave several questions unanswered: Why have minimum-winning coalitions been exceptional before 1976? Indeed, why has the less stringent minimal-winning criterion such poor predictive power for the time between 1953 and 1961, but not afterwards? Why have particular minimal-winning coalitions been formed at particular times, although numerical alternatives were possible and (according to Riker) even preferable to parties primarily interested in office? In their account of West German coalition politics, Klingemann and Volkens (1992) emphasize the explanatory importance of the parties' location in the ideological space: they use the median legislator theorem in conjunction with the policy affinities between the party controlling the median legislator, on the one hand, and its potential coalition partners, on the other. According to Laver and Schofield's (1990: 111) summary, the median legislator theorem 'predicts a more or less dictatorial role for the party that controls the median legislator' in the policy space. The median legislator theorem has provided a moderately successful predictor of coalition formation in the sense that the party controlling the median legislator for the most important policy dimension (economic policy) was involved in the formation of sixteen out of twenty-four governments (66.7%) between 1949 and 1998. The party controlling the median legislator for the second most important policy dimension (foreign policy) was included in twenty out of twenty-four governments (83.3%, see Table 2.1). Nevertheless, the theorem as such does not help us to predict which coalition partner(s) the party controlling the median legislator chooses. Apart from office-related considerations, the coalition choices appear to have been influenced by the policy distance between the parties involved (Klingemann and Volkens 1992: 195, 200). Also, the mutual trust between party leaders has influenced coalition formation since the 1960s. 'Parties and governments . . . have a history and tend to anticipate interaction well into the future. Interparty commitments are not made and unmade anew for each electoral period or each instance of government formation' (Strøm 1990:

37). The reputation and credibility of actors, derived from the experience of past interactions, shapes the mutual trust of its partners in the future, may reduce transaction costs, and avoid strategic situations resembling a one-shot prisoners' dilemma (Kropp and Sturm 1998: 97; Mitchell 1999: 270–1; Tsebelis 1990: 74–5).

Bargaining

There are no constitutional rules pertaining to coalition bargaining, although Article 63 of the Basic Law sets out certain majority requirements and deadlines for the election of the Federal Chancellor (see above). The process is largely shaped by informal rules and practices. In general, political parties in Germany have tended to state their preferred coalition partner(s) prior to a general election. In eleven out of the first fourteen Bundestag elections, at least some parties (usually the governing parties) announced in advance which coalitions they did and/or did not wish to form after the election (cf. Klingemann and Volkens 1992: 193–4; Völk 1989: 143). Pre-election coalition pacts (*Koalitionsaussagen*) are an essential feature of the bargaining process. After the elections, government formation typically proceeds in two phases: a first phase of extensive informal negotiations between some leaders of the parties concerned is followed by the formal election of the Federal Chancellor and the swearing in of the Chancellor and his cabinet.

Coalition bargaining takes place during the first stage. According to Dexheimer (1973: 154–5), the first phase can be subdivided into five further stages:

1. After the election result has been declared there may a phase of orientation and intra-party talks about important policy issues and possible coalition partners. This phase can be very short or skipped if there has been a pre-election pact.

2. The prospective candidates for the office of Chancellor, the chairpersons of the prospective coalition parties, and the (prospective) chairpersons of the respective parliamentary parties decide about procedural aspects of the negotiations. In addition, experts in the parliamentary parties and party organizations prepare more detailed policy papers for the ensuing negotiations.

3. The negotiation teams—usually consisting of the leaders and relevant experts of the extra-parliamentary and parliamentary parties as well as influential state politicians such as state Prime Ministers—try to achieve a compromise on the future government's policies.[10]

4. It is usually only after completion of this step, that the coalition parties decide how the portfolios are to be distributed and which politicians are acceptable for cabinet and other top-level positions in the government.

---

[10] The size of the negotiation teams has usually been 15–20 persons under Helmut Kohl's chancellorship. For an example, see Bohnsack (1983*b*: 478 n. 11).

Negotiations over portfolios and ministerial candidates are usually conducted in confidential talks between the party leaders concerned (see 'Offices: Allocation of Cabinet and Junior Ministerships', below).[11]

5. Finally, the results of the negotiations are confirmed by the leaders of the parties' negotiation teams—usually the party chairpersons—and ratified by the parties' national executive bodies (at the federal level usually the *Parteivorstand* or *Parteipräsidium*) and/or the parliamentary party and/or a special party conference.[12]

The formal rules of government investiture are laid down in Articles 63, 64, and 67 of the Basic Law. The Federal President proposes to the Bundestag a candidate for the office of Federal Chancellor. The Federal President has to appoint the candidate who has been elected by more than 50 per cent of the members. In a second step, the Federal President appoints the Federal Ministers upon the Chancellor's advice. These steps are in practice a formality after coalition talks have settled the allocation of portfolios including the office of Federal Chancellor.

Table 2.2 lists, for each government between 1949 and 1 January 1999, the number of parties and 'groups' in the Bundestag, the number of previous bargaining rounds, the parties involved in the previous bargaining rounds and the number of days required for government formation. After elections, coalition negotiations have taken a minimum of 24 (1969, 1983) and a maximum of 73 days (1976).[13] When a new coalition was formed during the life of a parliament (1962, 1966, 1982) negotiations tended to be shorter, varying between 14 and 34 days. The duration of coalition negotiations has often depended on the extent of intra- and inter-party differences over policies. However, one should not overlook that delays are sometimes caused by trivial factors.[14] More importantly, the duration of coalition negotiations cannot be considered a perfect predictor of differences over policy as contentious issues are often not resolved in coalition negotiations. Frequently, the bargaining over controversial issues has been postponed to a later point in time. For example, the 1969 negotiations between SPD and FDP were concluded within only 24 days. The party leaders, Brandt (SPD) and Scheel (FDP) were eager to come to a broad agreement quickly and to settle questions of detail later (cf. Bracher, Jäger, and Link 1986: 19). Similarly, the negotiations between

[11] In the 1998 coalition negotiations between the SPD and Greens, discussions and decisions about portfolio allocation and specific ministers were leaked before the policy agreement had been reached.

[12] In Oct. 1998, for example, the coalition agreement between the SPD and Greens was ratified by special party conferences.

[13] The number of 73 days in 1976 is not indicative of particularly difficult negotiations but of the early election and the relative large amount of time available for bargaining due to the fixed length of the Bundestag's legislative term (until 1980, cf. Schindler 1983: 368 n. 5).

[14] The 1990/1 negotiations, for example, were prolonged by the Christmas break.

Germany

TABLE 2.2. *Government formation in Germany, 1949–1999*

Government	Number of parties (and 'groups') in parliament[a]	Number of previous bargaining rounds	Parties involved in the previous bargaining rounds[a]	Number of days required for government formation[b]
CDU/CSU–FDP–DP 1949	9	0	—	32
CDU/CSU–FDP–DP–GB/BHE 1953	5	0	—	33
CDU/CSU–FDP–DP 1955	5	0	—	0
CDU/CSU–DP-DA/FVP 1956	6	0	—	0
CDU/CSU–DP 1957	4	0	—	37
CDU/CSU 1960	4	0	—	0
CDU/CSU–FDP 1961	3	0	—	51
CDU/CSU 1962	3	0	—	0
CDU/CSU–FDP 1962	3	1[c]	CDU/CSU, SPD	22
CDU/CSU–FDP 1965	3	0	—	31
CDU/CSU 1966	3	0	—	0
CDU/CSU–SPD 1966	3	2	(1) CDU/CSU, FDP (2) SPD, FDP	34
SPD–FDP 1969	3	0	—	23
SPD–FDP 1972	3	0	—	25
SPD–FDP 1976	3	0	—	(<73)[d]
SPD–FDP 1980	3	0	—	31
SPD 1982	3	0	—	0
CDU/CSU–FDP 1982	3	0	—	14
CDU/CSU–FDP 1983	4	0	—	23
CDU/CSU–FDP 1987	4	0	—	45
CDU/CSU–FDP–DSU 1990	7	0	—	0
CDU/CSU–FDP 1991	5	0	—	46
CDU/CSU–FDP 1994	5	0	—	30
SPD–Alliance '90/Greens 1998	5	0	—	30

[a] The CDU/CSU is treated as one party here.
[b] The number of days from the day of the election or cabinet termination until the day when the Chancellor is elected by the Bundestag.
[c] There were also informal talks between FDP and SPD which did not amount to full-scale coalition talks.
[d] Calculation method for 1976 inaccurate because of relatively early election and fixed end of previous legislative term (1972–76).

Sources: Schindler (1983: 233, 356–64, 368; 1994: 370, 438–40; 1995: 564); Presse- und Informationsamt der Bundesregierung (1998*b*).

CDU/CSU and FDP in 1982 were concluded within 14 days without full agreement on every detail of policy.

As the parties had usually committed themselves to a particular coalition prior to a general election or there was little choice, the number of unsuccessful bargaining attempts was '0' in the vast majority of cases. Between 1955 and 1957, some coalitions simply changed because the smaller conservative parties split or withdrew from the oversized coalition. Therefore, no new negotiations were needed as in each case the parties' ministers retained their portfolios and, eventually, joined another coalition party (the CDU/CSU or the DP). Also, no bargaining was required when Kohl's (1987–90) government was voluntarily enlarged after the members of the GDR People's Chamber joined the Bundestag in 1990, and the conservative DSU joined the coalition.

Unsuccessful attempts occurred only twice, 1962 and 1966. After the breakdown of the CDU/CSU–FDP coalition in 1962, the CDU/CSU engaged in parallel negotiations both with SPD and FDP, while SPD and FDP held informal talks (*Informationsgespräche*), which did not amount to full-scale coalition negotiations (Schwarz 1983: 273–88). The CDU/CSU's parallel negotiations of 1962 may have ultimately served the Chancellor's tactical goal to bring the FDP back into line. Adenauer and his negotiators were still in control of the events. In the negotiations prior to the formation of the Grand Coalition of 1966–9, by contrast, both major parties simultaneously negotiated with the FDP as well as with each other. The CDU/CSU was in a less favourable situation than in 1962 and had to make a much 'costlier' coalition offer to the SPD in order to avoid the first SPD–FDP coalition on the federal level (Hildebrand 1984: 243–56). After the elections of 1969, there were, again, preliminary talks between all three parties, yet only those between SPD and FDP developed into full-scale coalition negotiations (Bracher, Jäger, and Link 1986: 18–19).

Unlike in Tables 2.1 and 2.2, the unit of analysis in Table 2.3 is not a government, but a cabinet (for definitions, see Introduction). Table 2.3 lists the name of the Chancellor as well as the cabinets' party compositions, the number of the respective cabinet, the date on which the cabinet assumed office (usually the election of the Chancellor), and the date on which it formally resigned (or on which an election was held, which terminated the cabinet according to the definitions used here). Moreover, it provides information on the maximum potential duration of each cabinet at the stage of its formation and its actual duration in days. The maximum cabinet duration for a full legislative term has been between 1,455 and 1,460 days. When a cabinet was formed later in the legislative term, the maximum potential duration was obviously shorter. Table 2.3 shows that 13 out of 25 cabinets between 1949 and 1998 have been terminated significantly earlier than their maximum potential duration. The causes of these premature terminations will be dealt with in the section on cabinet termination.

COALITION GOVERNANCE

In this section, we will look at some mechanisms of coalition governance in Germany. How are conflicts between coalition parties managed once a coalition is formed? How strong is the individual ministers' discretion to dictate policy without regard to the coalition agreements made during the formation of a coalition? Are there specific devices to limit the powers of individual ministers to impose undesirable policy outcomes on their coalition partners? Are written coalition agreements effective devices to avoid—in the terminology of the principal-agent literature—'agency loss', 'moral hazard', and ministerial 'opportunism'?

Rules of the Game

The rules of coalition governance are largely unwritten ones. Nevertheless, there are some constitutional rules pertaining to the cabinet, which in most coalition governments, is one of the main bodies of coalition governance (cf. Mackie and Hogwood 1985: 12–13). Article 65 of the Basic Law provides the main rules influencing the political cost of cabinet controversies: 'The Chancellor determines and bears responsibility for the general policy of the Government. Within this general framework, each minister conducts the affairs of his department independently under his own responsibility. The Government as a whole decides on differences of opinion between ministers.'[15] Thus, the constitution gives cabinet ministers responsibility for all matters within their department's ambit (*Ressortprinzip*). However, their powers to dictate policy is constrained (*a*) by the Federal Chancellor's power to determine the broad guidelines of government policy (*Richtlinienkompetenz, Kanzlerprinzip*) and (*b*) the need to settle disagreements with other ministers in cabinet (*Kabinettsprinzip, Kollegialprinzip*).

The Federal Chancellor is the only member of the cabinet who is directly elected by the Bundestag. The individual ministers' tenure in office is tied to the Chancellor's. The ministers' policies within their departmental responsibilities must not contradict the Chancellor's broad guidelines of government policy. Formally, the Chancellor could achieve compliance with his general guidelines by requesting the Federal President to dismiss a minister. Nevertheless, the Chancellor cannot give orders to departmental ministers with respect to their departmental duties. The question of whether an issue falls under a departmental minister's competences or the Chancellor's right to determine the government's overall policy is sometimes ambiguous. The resolution of such conflicts often depends on the personal 'chemistry', the

---

[15] I use Müller-Rommel's (1994: 152) translation.

52   Thomas Saalfeld

TABLE 2.3. *German cabinets since 1949*

Cabinet number	Chancellor	Date in[a]	Formal resignation[b]	Maximum potential duration[c] (in days)	Duration[d] (in days)	Government composition
1	Adenauer I	15 Sept. 1949	nfr	1,452	1,452	CDU/CSU–FDP–DP
2	Adenauer II	9 Oct. 1953	nfr	1,457	652	CDU/CSU–FDP–DP–GB/BHE
3	Adenauer III	23 July 1955	nfr	805	217	CDU/CSU–FDP–DP
4	Adenauer IV	25 Feb. 1956	nfr	588	568	CDU/CSU–DP–DA/FVP[e]
5	Adenauer V	22 Oct. 1957	nfr	1,453	984	CDU/CSU–DP
6	Adenauer VI	2 July 1960	nfr	469	442	CDU/CSU
7	Adenauer VII	7 Nov. 1961	nfr	1,439	377	CDU/CSU–FDP
8	Adenauer VIII	19 Nov. 1962	nfr	1,062	24	CDU/CSU
9	Adenauer IX	13 Dec. 1962	15 Oct. 1963	1,038	307	CDU/CSU–FDP
10	Erhard I	16 Oct. 1963	nfr	731	704	CDU/CSU–FDP
11	Erhard II	20 Oct. 1965	nfr	1,459	373	CDU/CSU–FDP
12	Erhard III	28 Oct. 1966	30 Nov. 1966	1,086	34	CDU/CSU
13	Kiesinger	1 Dec. 1966	20 Oct. 1969	1,052	1,032	CDU/CSU–SPD
14	Brandt I	21 Oct. 1969	nfr	1,459	1,125	SPD–FDP
15	Brandt II	14 Dec. 1972	16 May 1974	1,459	518	SPD–FDP
16	Schmidt I	16 May 1974	nfr	941	898	SPD–FDP
17	Schmidt II	15 Dec. 1976	nfr	1,459	1,390	SPD–FDP
18	Schmidt III	05 Nov. 1980	nfr	1,459	681	SPD–FDP
19	Schmidt IV	17 Sept. 1982	1 Oct. 1982	778	14	SPD
20	Kohl I	1 Oct. 1982	nfr	764	156	CDU/CSU–FDP
21	Kohl II	29 Mar. 1983	nfr	1,460	1,398	CDU/CSU–FDP
22	Kohl III	11 Mar. 1987	nfr	1,439	1,329	CDU/CSU–FDP
23	Kohl IV	30 Oct. 1990	nfr	110	33	CDU/CSU–FDP–DSU[f]
24	Kohl V	17 Jan. 1991	nfr	1,432	1,368	CDU/CSU–FDP
25	Kohl VI	15 Nov. 1994	nfr	1,455	1,412	CDU/CSU–FDP
26	Schröder	27 Oct. 1998	n/a	1,459	n/a	SPD–Alliance '90/Greens

cont./

coalition parties' relative weight and their leaders' intra-party authority. It can be extremely difficult for a Chancellor to 'discipline' a minister who is a member of a vital coalition partner and enjoys the full support of his or her own party's leadership. One of the Chancellor's most important organizational resources is the Federal Chancellor's Office (*Bundeskanzleramt*). With a staff of approximately 500 and usually headed by a cabinet minister close to the Chancellor, 'the *Kanzleramt* provides him with the essential reins of government co-ordination' (Smith 1991: 50). The Chancellor's Office has been an important instrument of coalition management (especially communication and monitoring).

Table 2.4 summarizes some important information on coalition governance. The first written coalition agreement, whose existence and exact contents have been verified beyond doubt, was the one between CDU/CSU and FDP in 1961. It was amended in 1962. The previous coalition agreements of 1949, 1953, and 1957 had mainly consisted of verbal arrangements and exchanges of letters between the party leaders involved. Little is known about their contents (see below). It is known that after the elections of 1957, the DP entered the coalition negotiations with a draft treaty whose contents were discovered in the personal papers of Heinrich von Merkatz (reprinted in Küpper 1985: 587–8), one of the leading DP representatives in the 1957 coalition negotiations, who later joined the CDU. It remains uncertain, however, whether or to what extent this agreement was accepted by Chancellor Adenauer (Küpper 1985: 251). The policy contents of the coalition agreements of 1966, 1969, and 1972 were summarized in the Chancellor's inaugural Government Declaration. Between 1966 and 1976, there were no single contract-type documents, which both coalition partners publicly agreed upon.

TABLE 2.3. *cont.*

a Election of the Federal Chancellor.
b If the cabinet was terminated by an election, the election date was taken as cut-off point.
c According to Article 39(1) of the Basic Law, the Bundestag's term ended four years after its constituent meeting until 1976. After an amendment to the Basic Law, the Bundestag's term now (since 1980) ends with the constituent meeting of the subsequent Bundestag. The maximum potential duration is the time between the date when the government assumes office and the latest possible election date according to the Basic Law. The dates were largely taken from Schindler (see above).
d The duration was calculated as the time between a government's first day in office and its last day in office or the date of the election (whichever comes first).
e On 23 Feb. 1956, 17 members of the FDP (19 including Berlin members), the 'Euler group', left the party and kept supporting the government. On 15 Mar. 1956, they founded the DA. On 26 June 1956, the DA was renamed FVP. The 15 remaining FVP members joined the DP on 14 Mar. 1957 and formed the DP/FVP. This merger has not been counted as a new cabinet.
f 144 new members elected by the GDR People's Chamber joined the Bundestag on 03 Oct. 1990. The eastern German DSU was incorporated into the coalition.

nfr = no formal resignation

Sources: Schindler (1983: 21, 356–64; 1994: 31, 437–40); Presse- und Informationsamt der Bundesregierung (1998*a*).

TABLE 2.4. *Coalition governance in Germany*

(1) Coalition	(2) Coalition agreement[a]	(3) Agreement public[b]	(4) Election rule	(5) Resolution mechanisms	(6) Most common management mechanisms	(7) Mechanisms for most serious conflicts	(8) Coalition discipline in legislation	(9) Coalition discipline in other parliamentary behaviour	(10) Freedom of appointment	(11) Policy agreement	(12) Junior ministers	(13) Non-cabinet posts
1949	N	n/a	N	PCa,Parl	PCa,Parl	PCa	1	1	N	1	n/a	Y
1953	N	n/a	N	PCa	PCa	PCa	1	1	N	1	n/a	Y
1955	N	n/a	N	PCa	PCa	PCa	1	1	N	1	n/a	Y
1956	N	n/a	N	PCa	PCa	PCa	1	1	N	1	n/a	Y
1957	N[c]	n/a	N	PCa	PCa	PCa	1	1	N	1	n/a	Y
1961	POST	N[b,d]	N	Parl	Parl	Parl	1	1	N	2	n/a	Y
1962	IE[e]	N[b,d]	N	Parl,PCa	PCa	PCa	1	1	N	1	n/a	Y
1965	N	n/a	N	PCa	PCa	PCa	1	1	N	1	n/a	Y
1966	N	n/a[b]	N	PCa,Parl	Parl	PCa	2[f]	2[f]	N	1	Y	Y
1969	N	n/a[b]	N	—[g]	—[g]	—[g]	1	1	N	2	Y	Y
1972	N	n/a[b]	N	—[g]	—[g]	—[g]	1	1	N	2	Y	Y
1976	N	n/a[b]	N	—[g]	—[g]	—[g]	1	1	N	2	Y	Y
1980	POST	Y	N	Parl,PS,IC,PCa	PS	PS	1	1	N	2	Y	Y
1982	POST	Y	N	Parl,PS,IC,PCa	PS	PS	1	1	N	2	Y	Y
1983	POST	Y	N	Parl,PS,IC,PCa	PS	PS	1	1	N	2	Y	Y
1987	POST	Y	N	Parl,PS,IC,PCa	PS	PS	1	1	N	3	Y	Y
1990	N	n/a	N	Parl,PS,IC,PCa	PS	PS	1	1	N	3	Y	Y
1991	POST	Y	N	CoC,PS,IC,CaC	PS	PS	1	1	N	3	Y	Y
1994	POST	Y	N	Parl,PS,IC,PCa	PS	PS	1	1	N	3	Y	Y
1998	POST	Y	N	CoC,PCa	CoC	PCa	1	1	N	3	Y	Y

cont./

Indeed, in 1972 SPD and FDP, the two coalition partners, explicitly stated that a common paper was unnecessary because its contents would be summarized in Chancellor Brandt's Government Declaration. After 1961, the first coalition treaty in the sense of a common paper that was publicly agreed upon by both coalition partners was the agreement of 1980.

Since 1980, written, post-electoral coalition agreements have become the norm. These agreements are usually well-publicized documents and represent 'the institutionalized mutual distrust of coalition partners' (Kropp and Sturm 1998: 89, my translation). They summarize the results of coalition negotiations and attempt to insure each partner against changing preferences or opportunism of the other. They can also lay down rules for conflict management. Coalition agreements can stabilize the exchange between parties as the give-and-take is usually sequential rather than simultaneous. They stabilize

---

TABLE 2.4. cont.

[a] Only written agreements were considered, which had the character of binding documents for all coalition parties. Mere unilateral statements and press releases were not included.
[b] The results of the coalition negotiations are always summarized in the Chancellor's initial Government Declaration. Thus, the main policy issues agreed upon are publicly known, even if the coalition agreement as such may not be published.
[c] There are various draft agreements. It has, however, never been established, whether an agreement was signed at all (see Küpper 1985: 587–8).
[d] The agreement was not originally intended to be publicized but was subsequently leaked to the press.
[e] The original coalition agreement was amended.
[f] There was a general understanding that the coalition parties would not be able to agree on every policy.
[g] No evidence of particular resolution mechanisms beyond the Cabinet table until 1979. For 1979–80 see entry for 1980.

Note that variables (4)–(11) have not usually been part of formal coalition agreements.

Abbreviations
Y = yes; N = no.
Column 2: N = no written coalition agreement; POST = post-electoral written coalition agreement; IE = written coalition agreement in the case of coalitions formed during the parliamentary term (not immediately following elections).
Column 5: CoC = coalition committee; PS = party summit (including 'Koalitionsgespräche'); IC = inner cabinet (including regular discussions between Chancellor and Deputy Chancellor); PCa = combination of cabinet members and parliamentarians (including attendance of cabinet meetings by leaders of parliamentary parties and 'Koalitionsgespräche' without participation of representatives of the extra-parliamentary parties); Parl = Parliamentary leaders (particularly heads of the coalition parties' parliamentary groups).
Column 9: 1 = The coalition is based on a substantial and explicit policy agreement on few selected policies; 2 = on a variety of issues, but not comprehensive; 3 = on a comprehensive policy platform.

Sources: 1961 and 1962: Schüle (1964: 137). 1969–94: Unpublished materials from the Parliamentary Party of the CDU/CSU, the Archiv der Sozialen Demokratie der Friedrich-Ebert-Stiftung and the Archiv für Christlich-Demokratische Politik der Konrad-Adenauer-Stiftung; 1998: http://www.spd-fraktion-mv.de/koalition/i00000.htm (10 May 1999). Resolution mechanisms: Rudzio (1991), von Beyme (1997).

TABLE 2.5. Size and content of coalition agreements in Germany, 1949–1999

Coalition	Size	General procedural rules (in %)	Specific procedural rules[a] (in %)	Distribution of offices (in %)	Distribution of competences	Policies (in %)
CDU/CSU–FDP–DP 1949	—	—	—	—	—	—
CDU/CSU–FDP–DP–GB/BHE 1953	—	—	—	—	—	—
CDU/CSU–FDP–DP 1955	—	—	—	—	—	—
CDU/CSU–DP 1956	—	—	—	—	—	—
CDU/CSU–DP 1957	—	—	—	—	—	—
CDU/CSU–FDP 1961	1,837	16.4	3.4	0	0	80.2
CDU/CSU–FDP 1962	513	27.9	4.1	0	0	68.0
CDU/CSU–FDP 1965	—	—	—	—	—	—
CDU/CSU–SPD 1966	—	—	—	—	—	—
SPD–FDP 1969	—	—	—	—	—	—
SPD–FDP 1972	—	—	—	—	—	—
SPD–FDP 1976	—	—	—	—	—	—
SPD–FDP 1980	1,199[b]	0	0	0	0	100.0
CDU/CSU–FDP 1982	3,350	0	0	0	0	100.0
CDU/CSU–FDP 1983	2,341	0	0	0	0	100.0
CDU/CSU–FDP 1987[c]	7,153	0	0	0	0	100.0
CDU/CSU–FDP–DSU 1990	—	—	—	—	—	—
CDU/CSU–FDP 1991	15,322	0	0	0	0	100.0
CDU/CSU–FDP 1994	10,580	0	0	0	0	100.0
SPD–Greens/Alliance '90 1998	16,536	1.6	0	1.1	0	97.3

[a] Procedural rules that apply only to certain policy areas, issues, etc.
[b] Word count based on the communiqué of the SPD party executive committee (Parteivorstand) and other executive bodies (Parteirat and Kontrollkommission) of 7 Nov. 1980.
[c] The 1987 agreement consisted of a number of separate policy-specific agreements.

Sources: Schindler (1983: 370–1; 1994: 452); 1961 and 1962: Schüle (1964: 137–45). 1969–94: Unpublished materials from the Parliamentary Party of the CDU/CSU, the Archiv der Sozialen Demokratie der Friedrich-Ebert-Stiftung and the Archiv für Christlich-Demokratische Politik der Konrad-Adenauer-Stiftung; 1998: http://www.spd-frakti.on-mv.de/koalition/i00000.htm (10 May 1999).

exchange over time with 'deferred reciprocal compensation' (Sartori 1987: 229). Frequently, coalition agreements exclude unresolvable conflicts or just flag them up and effectively postpone a settlement to a later stage in the life of a coalition. 'Flagging up' may speed up coalition negotiations. It also allows party leaders to signal to their rank and file that they have stood by the parties' principles in the coalition negotiations. Yet, this strategy is risky and has often led to serious coalition crises at a later stage. An alternative to the 'flagging up' of differences and conflict postponement are vague 'formula compromises' whose interpretation is left to future negotiations. This strategy may also be associated with the risk of mere conflict postponement, although formula compromises do not commit the party leaderships as strongly as in cases where the parties publicly agree to disagree in principle. Coalition agreements can be an initial working programme for a government, although they remain subject to adjustments throughout the parliamentary term. Finally, coalition agreements are an important document for the legitimatization of coalition compromises *within* the coalition parties (Kropp and Sturm 1998: 98–105).

Table 2.5 illustrates that the published agreements between 1980 and 1994 were pure policy documents. Historical evidence on the informal exchanges of letters in 1949 and 1953 suggests that the emphasis on policy was also true for earlier informal agreements (Küpper 1985: 242). Procedural rules of coalition governance, the distribution of portfolios, executive offices and competences were not usually part of the published agreements. The agreements always have to be read in conjunction with the Chancellor's inaugural Government Declaration. The actors usually perceive the latter to mark the end of the coalition negotiations and refer to it throughout the lifetime of a government.

As Tables 2.4 and 2.5 also show, coalition agreements have grown considerably in length and coverage, especially since 1987. During the 1950s and early 1960s, the informal coalition agreements seem to have been relatively general and/or selective in terms of their coverage of policy areas. The four coalition agreements since 1987, by contrast, covered all major policy areas, although provisions were not uniformly precise.

Between 1965 and 1994, questions of coalition governance (Table 2.4) were not covered by the publicly accessible coalition agreements. There has never been an 'election rule' stipulating new elections in the case of a coalition breakdown. Coalition discipline in legislation and other parliamentary behaviour was one of the unwritten rules (see, however, Bohnsack 1983*b*: 481, n. 26), although it has been handled with varying degrees of flexibility depending on the nature of the issue and the government's majority (Arndt 1989: 671). During the Grand Coalition (1966–9) with its large majority, for example, CDU/CSU and SPD allowed each other a certain degree of occasional opposition (*Bereichsopposition*).

Coalition parties are, in constitutional law and political practice, not completely free to appoint their own candidates once portfolios are allocated. Candidates who are unacceptable for one side can be, and have been, vetoed. The fate of Gerhart-Rudolf Baum, an FDP Minister of the Interior under Helmut Schmidt (1978–82) may serve as an example. During the negotiations between CDU/CSU and FDP in 1982, CDU/CSU leaders made it clear that Baum, an open supporter of a continued Social-liberal coalition, was not acceptable and was, hence, rejected, although his party leaders initially suggested him to take over the Ministry of the Interior again. Very much seems to depend on the relative strength and the degree of dependence of each coalition party as well as the support a prospective minister enjoys within his or her own party. In 1982, for example, the FDP was highly dependent on the CDU/CSU (especially on the Christian Democrats concession to postpone an election in the face of devastating FDP results at state elections). In 1962, by contrast, the CDU/CSU could only form a renewed coalition with the FDP after Adenauer, the Chancellor, had promised to step down in 1963. Thus, in this case the smaller coalition partner successfully 'vetoed' a particular Chancellor candidate (indeed, the incumbent). The FDP's 'success' was only possible because Adenauer's grip on his own party was waning (Kaltefleiter 1996: 29). Informal agreements have usually incorporated the allocation of junior ministerial and non-cabinet posts. Conflict management mechanisms will be dealt with specifically below.

Before 1998, only the coalition agreement of 1961 between CDU/CSU and FDP is known to contain a significant amount of 'rules of the game'. The 1961–2 coalition of CDU/CSU and FDP was the first one to have a written coalition 'treaty' officially signed by both parties in the Chancellor's Office. Its contents were not intended to be published, yet the document was leaked to the press. The initiative for the treaty came from the smaller coalition partner, the FDP, who made their participation in government contingent upon certain rules of institutionalized consultation and coalition management. The treaty was very much a result of the FDP's experience as an arithmetically dispensable 'junior partner' in the oversized coalitions of 1953–7. The agreement contained provisions in several policy areas. In procedural terms the FDP promised to support Adenauer's candidature for the Chancellorship in the Bundestag in return for the CDU/CSU's promise that Adenauer's term in office would end after two years. The partners assured each other not to accept a coalition offer from any other party during the parliamentary term. The coalition parties were not allowed to vote with changing majorities (i.e. with the opposition) in the Bundestag. A coalition committee was to be established and its competences were defined. The chairmen of the parliamentary parties were granted the right to attend cabinet meetings (cf. Schüle 1964: 137–8). The coalition agreement of 1961 was very much the result of the FDP's lack of trust in the Chancellor, yet the evidence suggests that the elaborate efforts of the FDP to tie the Government down to particular policies by means of an agreement that the coalition would always vote together in the Bundestag, and by forming a coalition committee to iron out differences were . . . unsuccessful. They offended not only against constitutional provisions concerning the independence of Members and the policy-making prerogatives of the Chancellor, but also against political realities which soon led the Free Democrats themselves to vote against the CDU/CSU on some conspicuous issues (Löwenberg 1967: 255).

The 1962 amendments to this agreement were also leaked to the press. Although its contents as printed in the *Frankfurter Allgemeine Zeitung* (14 Dec. 1962, reprinted in Schüle 1964: 143–5) were never denied by the parties involved, its precise terms and length are not known with absolute certainty. It is a very short document, amending the 1961 agreement in some policy areas and in questions of government organization. It states explicitly that the cooperation between the parliamentary parties of CDU/CSU and FDP as well as between the government and the parliamentary parties needed improvement. The severity of the crisis between the two coalition partners finds expression in the assertion that mutual trust had to be rebuilt. The document refers explicitly to the importance of two Government Declarations, a budgetary speech and a common parliamentary resolution of the two parties as crucial formulations of coalition policy objectives (Schüle 1964: 144). After the termination of the coalition in 1965 (by regular elections), the use of a formal coalition treaty was widely regarded as unsuccessful by leading CDU/CSU and FDP politicians. Therefore, when a new coalition between the two parties was formed in 1965, they reverted to the previous practice of an informal agreement (Schwarz 1983: 283).

The 1998 coalition treaty between SPD and Greens was unusually explicit in spelling out portfolio allocation, basic rules of coalition governance, and the mechanisms of conflict management. Its formulations are largely consistent with a large number of coalition agreements at the federal-state level (see the detailed analysis of Kropp and Sturm 1998: 106–12). The rules of coalition governance in the 1998 agreement can, thus, be taken to be typical of modern formulations of the general rules of the game of coalition governance in Germany. It is therefore worth summarizing some of its main provisions. The parties agree to coordinate their work in parliament and government constantly and to decide procedural issues, policies, and the allocation of public offices by mutual agreement. A coalition committee is to be established to coordinate decision making on issues of fundamental importance. It consists of sixteen members, eight representatives of each party. It meets at the request of one or both of the coalition parties. In the event of conflicts, the coalition committee is to be the main locus of conflict management. Coalition discipline is to be maintained both in legislation and other parliamentary business. The parties agree to vote together in the Bundestag and all constitutional bodies to which the Bundestag or the Cabinet sends several representatives (for example, the Federal Assembly for the election of the Federal President). The obligation to vote together also includes issues not covered by the coalition agreement. The coalition parties will work together in all aspects of parliamentary business. Resolutions, draft bills, and parliamentary questions are to be moved by both parliamentary parties or, failing that, by one party after mutual agreement. In cabinet, no party must be outvoted on issues, which are of fundamental importance to it. The parties explicitly agree to maintain a common position in European Union bodies. Both parties are represented in all cabinet committees and in all bodies in which the cabinet is represented. The power to determine the organization of the Federal Government (*Organisationsgewalt*) remains with the Federal Chancellor (as the Basic Law stipulates), but significant changes in a ministry's jurisdiction require the agreement of both coalition partners. In the section on portfolio allocation, the two parties agree to elect Gerhard Schröder (SPD) as Federal Chancellor. Joschka Fischer (Alliance '90/Greens) is to be Deputy Chancellor. The agreement specifies the eleven portfolios allocated to the SPD and the three portfolios allocated to the Greens.

Coordinating Bodies

Although the cabinet is one important arena of conflict management in a coalition, it is in practice not the most important one. Under Kohl's chancellorship, for example, the Head of the Chancellor's Office repeatedly rejected agenda items for cabinet meetings, if agreement between the ministries involved had not been reached beforehand (Korte 1998: 49).[16] This indicates that conflicts were routinely dealt with in other bodies. Cabinet committees have always played an important role in the interdepartmental coordination of policy, although their meetings are usually attended and dominated by civil servants. In practice, therefore, most cabinet committees belong to the administrative rather than the political 'sphere' and cannot be considered as important mechanisms of political conflict or coalition management. Their number has declined from twelve in the second half of the 1970s to six or seven between 1986 and 1997.[17] Cabinet committees are chaired by the Federal Chancellor or his Deputy. Only in their absence, the departmental minister concerned is in the chair. Their meetings are prepared and managed

---

[16] The declining length of the weekly cabinet meetings seems to corroborate the claim that the cabinet's importance as a body of (coalition) governance declined during Kohl's chancellorship. Between 1982 and 1984, cabinet meetings lasted on average two to three hours. By 1988/9, their average length had dropped to about one hour (Korte 1998: 48–51).

[17] In 1997 there were cabinet committees on National Security, EU Policy, the East German Federal States, Economic Policy, Future Technologies, the Environment and Health, and Space Technology (Busse 1997: 92–3).

by the Chancellor's Office. Most cabinet committees meet only irregularly.[18] A number of them (especially the cabinet committees for Future Technologies, Space Technology, and the Environment and Health) predominantly deal with difficult technical issues that cut across departmental boundaries, but are too complex and detailed to be discussed in cabinet. Some of them (such as the cabinet committee on EU Policy) have never managed to establish a strong coordinating role vis-à-vis the main departments concerned. The most important cabinet committee is the one on National Security which often deals with classified material and the coordination of foreign and defence policy on the one hand and external trade implications on the other (Busse 1997: 92–3; Rudzio 1996: 270–1). On the whole, these committees are not the locus of conflict management in coalitions.

Table 2.4 lists the mechanisms of coalition management used by all coalitions between 1949 and 1 January 1999 using the general coding categories for this volume. The first Adenauer cabinet (1949–53) was a minimal-winning coalition of CDU/CSU, FDP, and DP. Informal communication and decision making structures began to emerge from the end of 1949 onwards, largely on the initiative of the smaller coalition parties FDP and DP. A formal coalition committee did not exist. Leading members of the governing parliamentary parties attended important cabinet meetings. There were regular meetings between members of the government and the parliamentary parties. The Chancellor, for example, held regular meetings with the parliamentary party leaders. Furthermore, leading representatives of the parliamentary parties met regularly without government participation in order to coordinate work in the Bundestag (Küpper 1985: 154–6; Rudzio 1991: 126–7).

The two legislative terms between 1953 and 1961 were characterized by (*a*) surplus-size coalitions dominated by the CDU/CSU and (*b*) the instability and partial disintegration of the smaller coalition parties. Indeed, the CDU/CSU was close to an overall majority in the 1953–7 Bundestag (it controlled an overall majority if members for Berlin are disregarded, whose voting rights were restricted) and commanded an overall majority in the 1957–61 parliament. This situation contributed to less and less consultation of the smaller coalition parties. The management of government and coalition was heavily dominated by the Chancellor and an informal circle of six to seven cabinet ministers and seven to ten leading members of the CDU/CSU parliamentary party (Rudzio 1991: 127–8).

The experience of the 1953–61 period motivated the FDP to demand the first coalition treaty and a formal coalition committee in the 1961–5

---

[18] The Cabinet Committee for All-German Affairs (*Kabinettsausschuß für innerdeutsche Beziehungen*) may be an extreme case. It was established in 1969 and met for the last time on 8 July 1971, although it continued to exist until 1990. In 1990 it was replaced by the Cabinet Committee on German Unity (cf. Korte 1998: 60).

Bundestag. This coalition committee was composed of leading members of the parliamentary parties. Its ability to manage coalition conflicts was severely limited as the federal government was not represented in it.[19] The committee's ineffectiveness led to uncoordinated voting behaviour of CDU/CSU and FDP in parliament and a coalition crisis in 1962. From 1962 onwards, the coalition parties decided to complement the coalition committee with regular meetings of cabinet ministers and leading members of the governing parliamentary parties ('coalition talks'). The coalition committee was to coordinate the government's legislative programme, but more serious issues were to be decided in the coalition talks. This distribution of labour was maintained under Adenauer's successor, Ludwig Erhard (Rudzio 1991: 128–9).

The 1965–6 coalition between CDU/CSU and FDP did not establish a coalition committee, but retained the coalition talks between leading members of the government and the parliamentary parties. The Grand Coalition between CDU/CSU and SPD (1966–9) required new coordination mechanisms as both coalition partners were of similar parliamentary strength and a number of the government's decisions were highly controversial both between and within the coalition parties. Initially, the cabinet was to be the locus of conflict management. Within a short period of time, the cabinet solution proved to be ineffective, however. The *Kreßbronner Kreis* was established as the coalition's legendary coordinating body. It consisted of Chancellor Kiesinger (CDU), Deputy Chancellor Brandt (SPD), the leaders of both parliamentary parties—Rainer Barzel (CDU/CSU) and Helmut Schmidt (SPD), and occasionally some additional members. Increasingly, however, the regular meetings (*'parlamentarische Tischrunde'*) of the parliamentary party leaders Barzel, Schmidt, Richard Stücklen (CSU), and Alex Möller (SPD) gained in importance and were dubbed as the 'counter-government Barzel/Schmidt' (Rudzio 1991: 133).

Initially, the SPD–FDP coalitions between 1969 and 1982 seemed to have relied on the cabinet as its main coordination device. According to Göttrik Wewer (1990: 147), the Social Democratic Chancellors Brandt and Schmidt attempted to resolve conflicts with the FDP without resorting to special coalition bodies. 'Coalition talks' were held irregularly and informally. With growing tensions at the later stages of the Social-liberal coalition, more regular institutional structures were required. From 1979 onwards, leading representatives of the two parliamentary parties met weekly. In addition, there were regular talks between the leaders of the extra-parliamentary parties, Brandt and Genscher. Within the government, there were regular discussions between Chancellor Schmidt and Deputy Chancellor Genscher, which were

---

[19] Therefore, the coalition committee of 1961–5 was not coded as 'CoC' (coalition committee) in Table 2.4, but as 'Parl' (parliamentary leaders).

coded as 'inner cabinet' in Table 2.4. Similar to the first Adenauer cabinet, leading members of the parliamentary parties were occasionally invited to attend cabinet meetings. The most important conflict management mechanism, however, were 'coalition talks' between members of the cabinet, leaders of the parliamentary parties, and leaders of the extra-parliamentary parties. The coalition talks were held regularly. The cabinet was often left with the task of ratifying decisions taken in coalition talks.

The CDU/CSU–FDP coalitions under Chancellor Kohl (1982–98) used a similar mix of coordinating bodies. Under Kohl there were regular meetings between Kohl and his Vice Chancellors, Genscher (1982–92) and Kinkel (1992–8). Moreover, Kohl established regular 'coalition talks' between members of the government and leaders of the parliamentary parties. Until 1988, the delicate relationship between Kohl and the late CSU chairman Franz Josef Strauß, who was at that time Prime Minister of the state of Bavaria but not a member of the cabinet, required regular bilateral consultations between Kohl and Strauß. Strauß also insisted on regular meetings of the party chairmen, i.e. himself, Kohl, Genscher, and the latter's successors (Martin Bangemann and Otto Count Lambsdorff). This body was occasionally enlarged by party experts, or briefed by small working groups of party experts. Specialized working groups of coalition experts were used to reach compromises over detailed policy questions (Schreckenberger 1994: 335). The red–green coalition under Chancellor Schröder (since 1998) established a formal coalition committee, but the handling of the first minor coalition crises in 1998–9 suggests an increasing reliance on the flexible bodies used by Schmidt and Kohl.

The 'Special Relationship' of CDU and CSU

One peculiarity of German coalition politics requires mentioning: the cooperation of the two Christian democratic parties, the Christian Democratic Union (CDU) and its Bavarian sister organization, the Christian Social Union (CSU). Outside the Bundestag, the two parties operate as separate organizations.[20] Inside the Bundestag, however, they have formed a common parliamentary party at the national level since 1949. Indeed, formalized cooperation dates back to the Frankfurt Economic Council (1947–9). This close cooperation of two distinct parties has been formally renewed after every election. Cooperation has not always been free of tensions. Especially from the early 1960s onwards, the two parties' relationship has often been characterized by differences over policy and strategy (Mintzel 1977: 345–7).

The CSU forms its own 'state group' (*Landesgruppe*) within the common parliamentary party, which (unlike other 'state groups' within the CDU or

[20] Electorally, the CSU operates in Bavaria only, the CDU competes in the rest of the Federal Republic excluding Bavaria.

SPD) has consistently pursued the objective of establishing an organizational structure with a degree of autonomy vis-à-vis the common parliamentary party, which has always been dominated by the CDU. Nevertheless, the CSU is treated as part of the CDU/CSU parliamentary party in procedural terms (e.g. in the allocation of time for parliamentary debates). The state group has had its own office since 1949, which has been steadily expanded from 1955 onwards. From 1955 the CSU state group has had its own formal rules of procedure. Since 1969 it has had its own internal working groups and specialized committees. Within the common parliamentary party, the CSU usually operates as a cohesive 'block'. Its Bundestag leadership's participation in internal CDU/CSU decision making has been increasingly formalized. In the first common parliamentary parties, the chairman of the CSU state group was informally the deputy chairman of the parliamentary party. Since 1965 there have been formal rules to the effect that the CSU state group is represented on the common parliamentary party's executive bodies and all specialist internal working groups and committees in proportion to its number of seats. The same is true for the Bundestag committees. The CSU state group has the right to nominate certain Bundestag committee chairpersons from its own ranks. Its participation in common negotiation teams (e.g. for coalition negotiations) is formally laid down in a contract with the CDU. Since 1972, the CSU has formally had the right to veto decisions of the common parliamentary party in case of disagreement between the two parties. That is to say, its members, who are in a minority within the common parliamentary party, cannot be outvoted by the majority of CDU members. The nature of the CSU as a partner with equal rights has been strengthened in the inter-party treaty of 1976. Henceforth, the CDU/CSU leadership has had to negotiate a common position before it entered negotiations with a coalition partner or the opposition (Mintzel 1977: 345–63, 400, 409–12).

Policies

Since 1980, a coalition's policies have largely been laid down in the coalition agreements and the Federal Chancellor's Government Declarations (*Regierungserklärungen*). Prior to 1980, the Chancellors' inaugural Government Declarations have implicitly or explicitly (1966, 1969, 1972) served as substitutes for public written coalition agreements. Since 1980, the volume of coalition agreements has grown considerably, from approximately 1,200 words in 1980 to more than 16,500 words in 1998 (see Table 2.5). The coalition agreements since 1980 have largely been related to the government's policy objectives. The wording of the agreements has tended to be relatively general (excepting budgetary and financial matters, where coalition negotiations have often resulted in relatively precise overall figures (*Eckwerte*)). They form the basis of the Federal Chancellor's first Government Declaration in a parliament. The coalition partners often exchange further documents which remain confidential. However, they are not binding in a legal sense. To what extent have coalition agreements been a binding political constraint on coalition partners? In the scholarly literature, this is a matter of some contention. Müller-Rommel (1994: 165) asserts: 'Although ministers in Germany maintain the autonomy of their departments, they are nevertheless bound to the coalition policy "treaty," which is a very precise agreement over draft bills and leaves hardly any room for deviation or interpretation. Bureaucrats in the ministries as well as in the chancellor's office constantly control and monitor the implementation of this coalition treaty.' Völk (1989: 147–50), the author of the most extensive study on German coalition politics at the national level in recent years, by contrast, contends that the power of coalition agreements as a constraint on the government and the coalition partners should not be overestimated (for similar evaluations, see Bermbach 1978: 322; Bracher, Jäger, and Link 1986: 19; Eschenburg 1956: 680).

In sum, the publicly accessible coalition agreements in Germany fulfil three main functions:

1. They are documentations of the policy results agreed upon during the coalition negotiations. Not only do the agreements serve as a 'reference point' for the coalition parties but also for individual ministers. Violations of the letter and spirit of coalition agreements have, however, not usually been damaging for the violating party, especially when the sanctioning capacity of the other party was low or non-existent.

2. The coalition agreements have an important function for the ratification process within the individual coalition parties. Coalition agreements have to be ratified by party bodies. They serve as proof that the party leaderships have achieved relevant party goals during the negotiations and as a means of internal legitimation.

3. The agreements serve as a government's initial 'working programme' which is subject to adaptations as the legislative term proceeds.

Offices: Allocation of Cabinet and Junior Ministerships

The numerical distribution of portfolios in Germany has usually approximated the proportional-allocation norm, although the FDP and other smaller parties have frequently been slightly over-represented in cabinet (for the 1998 red–green coalition, see Lees 1999). As noted above, portfolios are usually allocated at a relatively late stage of the coalition bargaining process. After the allocation of portfolios to particular parties, an inner circle of party leaders will discuss what politicians are acceptable for cabinet and other top-level positions in the executive branch of government. Over time, some parties have developed preferences for particular portfolios reflecting the relative importance different parties give to different policy areas (cf. Kropp and

Sturm 1998: 34). The CDU and SPD always held the Department of Family Affairs (dealing with family, youth, and health affairs as well as women and senior citizens), Labour and Social Affairs when one of them was in a coalition with the FDP or another small party. Between 1969 and 1998, the FDP usually held the Foreign Ministry and (1972–98) the Ministry of Economic Affairs. CDU or CSU held the Ministry of Food, Agriculture, and Forestry when in government. Usually, the coalition partners' right to nominate suitable candidates will be respected. As was noted above, however, there is no enforceable right to nominate a particular candidate against the wishes of a coalition partner or, indeed, the Federal Chancellor.

Table 2.6 is a synopsis of portfolio allocation in all coalitions since 1949. The ministries in Table 2.6a are listed according to Laver and Hunt's (1992: 196) scores which reflect the 'saliency' of departments in the eyes of nineteen experts in 1989. The ranking is not exhaustive. Nor does it reflect variations in saliency across time and different incumbents. The notes below Table 2.6 list some of the more important changes in the departments' jurisdictions. Such differences may be absolutely crucial for the real political influence of a minister and are often disregarded in studies of portfolio allocation. The function of Deputy Chancellor is not a separate portfolio (as in Belgium) but a position held by a senior cabinet member in addition to his portfolio. It has usually been occupied by a minister from the second largest party in the coalition.

A closer look at the nature of portfolio allocation is more fruitful than establishing its numerical principles. There are some recognizable patterns. Coalition politicians utilize what Keith Krehbiel (1991: 84) terms the 'heterogeneity principle' in the context of Congressional committees: by dividing up responsibilities in a particular policy area between ministers of different parties, or by 'planting' junior ministers of one coalition party in a ministry controlled by another party, the Chancellor and coalition party leaders can create political heterogeneity and improve the monitoring of individual departments' activities. There have been three principal means of creating heterogeneity:

1. Portfolios which have access to information across departmental boundaries are often divided up between the coalition parties. Portfolios with competences cutting across departmental boundaries are the Chancellor's Office, the Ministry of Finance, and the Ministry of Justice. Table 2.6 reveals that the office of Federal Chancellor and, except for the period 1961–2, the Finance Ministry have always been allocated to members of the largest coalition party, i.e. either the CDU/CSU or the SPD. This has strengthened the Chancellor and the largest coalition party. Control of the Ministry of Finance is particularly important because it routinely screens information on all departments' budgets. A similar cross-cutting function is fulfilled by the Ministry of Justice which screens all government legislation prior to its

TABLE 2.6a. *Distribution of cabinet and junior ministerships in Germany, 1949–1999, (1)–(10)*

Cabinet number	Cabinet	(1) Federal Chancellor	(2) [Deputy Chancellor]	(3) Finance[a]	(4) Foreign Affairs	(5) Economic Affairs[b]	(6) Environment	(7) Defence	(8) Transport[c]	(9) Interior	(10) Family Affairs[d]
1	Adenauer I	CD	F	CS	CD	CD	—	—	DP	CD	—
2	Adenauer II	CD	F	CS	CD	CD	—	CD	DP	CD	CD
3	Adenauer III	CD	F	CS	CD	CD	—	CD	DP	CD	CD
4	Adenauer IV	CD	DA/FVP (DP)	CS	CD	CD	—	CD/CS	DP	CD	CD
5	Adenauer V	CD	CD	CD	CD	CD	—	CS	DP (CD)	CD	CD
6	Adenauer VI	CD	CD	CD	CD	CD	—	CS	CD	CD	CD
7	Adenauer VII	CD	CD	F	CD	CD	—	CS	CD	CS	CD
8	Adenauer VIII	CD	CD	[F]	CD	CD	—	CS	CD	CS	CD
9	Adenauer IX	CD	CD	F	CD	CD	—	CS/CD	CD	CS	CD
10	Erhard I	CD	F	F	CD	CD	—	CD	CD	CS	CD
11	Erhard II	CD	F	F	CD	CD	—	CD	CD	CD	CD
12	Erhard III	CD	CD	CD	CD	CD	—	CD	CD	CD	CD
13	Kiesinger	CD,cs	S	CS,cd	S	S	—	CD	S	CD	CD
14	Brandt I	S	F	S	F	S	—	S	S	F,	S
15	Brandt II	S	F	S	F,s	F	—	S	S	F,	S
16	Schmidt I	S	F	S	F,s	F	—	S	S,f	F,s	S
17	Schmidt II	S	F	S	F,s	F	—	S	S	F	S
18	Schmidt III	S	F	S	F,s	F	—	S	S	F	S
19	Schmidt IV	S	S	S	S	S	—	S	S	S	S
20	Kohl I	CD	F	CD	F,cd	F	—	CD,f	CD	CS,cd	CD
21	Kohl II	CD	F	CD,cs	F,cd	F,cd	CD	CD	CS,cd	CS,cd	CD
22	Kohl III	CD	F	CD/CS,cs	F	F,cd/,cs	CD,f,cs	CD	CS,cd	CS/CD,cs,cd	CD
23	Kohl IV	CD	F	CS,cd	F	F,cs	CD,f,cs	CD	CS,cd	CD,cs	CD
24	Kohl V	CD	F	CS,2cd	F	F,cs	CD	CD	CD	CD,cs	CD
25	Kohl VI	CD	F	CS,cd	F,cd	F,cd	CD,f	CD,cs	CD	CD,cs	CD
26	Schröder	S	G	S	G,s	NP	G	S	S	S	S

TABLE 2.6b. *Distribution of cabinet and junior ministerships in Germany, 1949–1999, (11)–(20)*

Cabinet number	Cabinet	(11) Labour and Social Affairs	(12) Food, Agriculture, and Forestry	(13) Justice	(14) Science and Education[e]	(15) Post and Telecommunications[f]	(16) Construction and Housing[g]	(17) Expellees, Refugees, and War Invalids	(18) Intra-German Affairs[h]	(19) Federal Council and Federal States	(20) Economic Cooperation[i]
1	Adenauer I	CD	CS	F	—	CS	F	CD	CD	DP	—
2	Adenauer II	CD	CD	F	CS	CS	F	GB/BHE	CD	DP	F
3	Adenauer III	CD	CD	F	CS	CS	F	CD	CD	DP	F
4	Adenauer IV	CD	CD	DA/FVP (DP)	CS	CS	DA	CD	CD	DP	DA
5	Adenauer V	CD	CD	CS	CS	CS	CD	CD DP, (CD)	CD	DP (CD)	—
6	Adenauer VI	CD	CD	CS	CS	CS	CD	F	CD	CD	F
7	Adenauer VII	CD	CD	F	CS	CS	CD	F	CD	CD	F
8	Adenauer VIII	CD	CD	[F]	CS	CS	CD	[F]	CD	CD	[F]
9	Adenauer IX	CD	CD	F	F	CS	CD	F	CD	CS	F
10	Erhard I	CD	CD	F	F	CS	CD	CD	F	CS	F
11	Erhard II	CD	CS	CD CS	CD	CS	F	CD	F	CS	F
12	Erhard III	CD	CS	CS	CD	CS	CD	CD	CD	CS	CS
13	Kiesinger	CD	CS	s	NP,s	CS	s	CD	s	s	s
14	Brandt I	s	F	s	s	—	s	—	s	—	s
15	Brandt II	s	F	s	s	—	s	—	s	—	s
16	Schmidt I	s	F	s	s	—	s	—	s	—	s
17	Schmidt II	s	F	s	s	—	s	—	s	—	s
18	Schmidt III	s	F	s	s	s	s	—	s	—	s
19	Schmidt IV	CD	F	s	s	s	s	—	s	—	s
20	Kohl I	CD/cs	CS,f,cd	F,cd	CD	CD	CD	—	CD	—	CD
21	Kohl II	CD,cs	CS,f,cd	F,cd	CD	CD	CS,cd	—	CD	—	CS,cd
22	Kohl III	CD,cs	CS,f,cd	F,cd	CD	CD	CS,cd	—	CD	—	CS,cd
23	Kohl IV	CD,cs	CS,f,cd	F,cd	F,cd	CS,cd	CS,cd	—	CD	—	CS,cd
24	Kohl V	CD,cs	CS,f,cd	F,cd	F,cd	CD	F,cd	—	—	—	CS,cd
25	Kohl VI	CD,cs	CD,cs	F	CD	CS	CD,f	—	—	—	CS,cd
26	Schröder	s	s	s	s	—	—	—	—	—	S,g

TABLE 2.6c. *Distribution of cabinet and junior ministerships in Germany, 1949–1999, (21)–(27)*

Cabinet number	Cabinet	(21) Federal Treasurer[j]	(22) Health[k]	(23) Chairman of Federal Defence Council	(24) Research and Technology	(25) Women and Youth	(26) Marshall Plan Affairs	(27) Without Portfolio
1	Adenauer I	—	—	—	—	—	F	—
2	Adenauer II	—	—	—	—	—	—	1 CD, 1 F, 1 GB/BHE, 1 CS
3	Adenauer III	—	—	—	—	—	—	—
4	Adenauer IV	—	—	—	—	—	—	—
5	Adenauer V	—	—	—	—	—	—	—
6	Adenauer VI	F	—	—	—	—	—	—
7	Adenauer VII	[F]	CD	—	—	—	—	1 CD
8	Adenauer VIII	CS	CD	—	—	—	—	1 CD
9	Adenauer IX	CS	CD	—	—	—	—	1 CD
10	Erhard I	CS	CD	CD	—	—	—	2 CD
11	Erhard II	CS	CD	CD	—	—	—	1 CD
12	Erhard III	CS	CD	CD	—	—	—	1 CD
13	Kiesinger	CD	S	—	—	—	—	—
14	Brandt I	—	—	—	S	—	—	1 S
15	Brandt II	—	—	—	S	—	—	1 S, 1 F
16	Schmidt I	—	—	—	S	—	—	—
17	Schmidt II	—	—	—	S	—	—	—
18	Schmidt III	—	—	—	S	—	—	—
19	Schmidt IV	—	—	—	—	—	—	—
20	Kohl I	—	—	—	CD,cs	—	—	—
21	Kohl II	—	—	—	CD,cs	—	—	1 CD
22	Kohl III	—	—	—	CD,cs	—	—	1 CD, 1 CS
23	Kohl IV	—	—	—	CD,cs	—	—	4 CD, 1 CS, 1 DSU, 1 F
24	Kohl V	—	CS,cd	—	CD	CD	—	1 CD
25	Kohl VI	—	CS,cd	—	—	—	—	1 CD
26	Schröder	—	G	—	—	—	—	1 S, 1 s, 1 np (non-cabinet)

cont./

TABLE 2.6c. cont.

a 1971–2: The ministries for Finance and Economic Affairs were temporarily merged; in 1998, important sections of the Ministry of Economic Affairs were incorporated into the Ministry of Finance.
b In 1998 renamed Ministry for Economic Affairs and Technology.
c In 1998 the competences of the Ministry of Transport were significantly enlarged by the incorporation of the Ministry of Construction and Housing.
d 1957–61: Department of Family and Youth Affairs; 1969–72: Department of Youth, Family and Health; 1986–90 Department of Youth, Family, Women, and Health; 1990–94: Department of Family and Senior Citizens; 1994: Department of Family, Senior Citizens, Women, and Youth.
e 1953–7: Department of Nuclear Affairs; 1957–61: Department of Nuclear Energy and Water Management; from 1962: Department of Scientific Research; from 1972: Department of Education and Science; 1994: Department of Education, Science, Research and Technology.
f 1969–72 merged with Department of Transport; 1972–4 merged with Department of Research and Technology; 1974–80: merged with Department of Transport.
g 1949–50: Department of Reconstruction; 1950–61: Department of Housing; 1961–5: Department of Housing, Urban Construction, and Urban Planning.
h 1969 renamed Department of Intra-German Affairs.
i Department of Overseas Development.
j 1963–5: Department of Federal Property.
k From 1972 merged with the Department of Youth and Family.

Note: In some instances there was only a brief coalition crisis. A party withdrew, the minister stayed in office for a short while. These instances have been marked by the party name brackets. CD=CDU, CS=CSU, D=DP, F=FDP, G=Greens, S=SPD, NP=non-party appointment. Cabinet ministers are in capital letters, non-cabinet (junior) ministers (*parlamentarische Staatssekretäre*) in lower-key letters

Sources: Schindler (1983: 304–52, 1994: 414–29), Kürschers Volkshandbuch (1995), Presse- und Informationsamt der Bundesregierung (1998*b*:878–79).

introduction. Under Kohl's chancellorship, the Ministry of Justice was consistently occupied by a member of the FDP as the smaller coalition partner. In the red–green coalition formed in 1998, by contrast, the SPD holds all the important ministries with functions cutting across departmental boundaries.

2. In certain 'neighbouring' or overlapping policy areas, competences are divided up between the coalition partners, i.e. the respective ministries have usually been controlled by ministers from different parties: when the Foreign Office was occupied by an FDP politician, for example, the CDU/CSU or SPD controlled the Ministry of Economic Cooperation (development aid). Similarly, the Ministries of Finance and Economic Affairs as well as the Ministries of the Interior and Justice have usually not been controlled by politicians of the same party. Cooperation and coordination between such 'neighbouring' ministries is usually close and involves early and regular mutual information and consultation. Legislative proposals are frequently sponsored by two or more such departments with one in charge of the overall coordination process. If ministries controlled by both coalition partners are involved in the drafting process, both parties gain early, low-cost information on the 'other side's' compliance with the letter and spirit of the coalition agreement.

3. Since 1967 most ministries have had one or two 'parliamentary secre-

taries of state' (*Parlamentarische Staatssekretäre*), who are essentially junior ministers below cabinet rank.[21] Moreover, the Chancellors' Office was staffed with junior ministers and usually with one or several cabinet ministers without portfolio, who have had an important role in the coordination and management of policy and coalitions, adding to the weight of the Federal Chancellor (for examples, see Korte 1998: 24). During the Grand Coalition and under Brandt's Chancellorship, ministers seem to have been free to select junior ministers from their own party. Interestingly, this pattern changed under Schmidt and Kohl (at least in Kohl's early cabinets). During Schmidt's Chancellorship, the number of junior ministers in some key departments was doubled and several important FDP-led ministries were staffed with an additional junior minister—who was a member of the SPD. This may be seen as an indicator for an attempt of the Chancellor to improve his monitoring capacity through the creation of 'bridge heads' in some key departments such as the Foreign Ministry. The creation of such 'bridge heads' in important FDP-led ministries was also practised in the two first two Kohl cabinets and then gradually reduced as the FDP regained some of the bargaining power it had lost vis-à-vis the CDU/CSU in the events following the break-up of the SPD–FDP coalition in 1982 (Table 2.6, see also Korte 1998: 56). The 1998 coalition agreement between SPD and Greens leaves the nomination of junior ministers largely to the respective cabinet ministers. There are only two exceptions: the SPD nominates one junior minister in the Foreign Ministry (controlled by the Greens), the Greens are compensated for with one junior minister in the Ministry of Economic Cooperation (in charge of development aid and controlled by the SPD).

COALITION AND CABINET TERMINATION

Cabinet Duration

At the time of writing (May 1999), Chancellor Gerhard Schröder is leading the twenty-sixth post-war cabinet. Four out of twenty-five cabinets, that were terminated between 1949 and 1999, were single-party governments. Two cabinets (1963 and 1974) were terminated as a result of changes in the chancellorship without changes in the composition of the coalition (Adenauer––Erhard and Brandt–Schmidt). Although these changes, according to our counting rules, led to new cabinets under new Chancellors, they are not considered as terminations of the existing coalitions and governments. Nineteen out of the twenty-five cabinets terminated between 1949 and 1999

---

[21] 'Parliamentary secretaries of state' are to be distinguished from 'ministers of state' (*Staatsminister*), who constitute another type of junior minister. Both are treated as one category in Table 2.6.

TABLE 2.7. *Cabinet termination in Germany, 1949–1999*

Cabinet number	Cabinet	Mechanisms of cabinet termination							Terminal events			Policy area(s)	Comments
		Technical	Discretionary										
		(1) Reg. parliamentary election	(4) Early parliamentary election	(5) Voluntary enlargement	(6) Cabinet defeated by opposition in parliament	(7) Conflict between coalition parties		(8) Intra-party conflict in coalition party or parties	(12) Economic	(13) Personal		
						Policy	Personnel					
1	Adenauer I	X										
2	Adenauer II					X		G, L			4	GB/BHE split, majority of party withdraw from coalition, minister wing remain in government and later join the CDU/CSU
3	Adenauer III					X		F, LNL		X	4	FDP split, majority of party withdraw from coalition, minister wing remain in government and later merge with the DP
4	Adenauer IV	X										
5	Adenauer V							D, L				DP split, majority of party withdraw from the coalition, minister wing remain in government CDU/CSU government
6	Adenauer VI	X										
7	Adenauer VII					X	X				3	FDP withdraw from the coalition on 19 Nov. 1962

#	Government				Notes
8	Adenauer VIII	X			CDU/CSU minority government; FDP rejoin the coalition on 11 Dec. 1962 after Adenauer has promised his resignation
9	Adenauer IX		X	C, L	Change of Chancellor, no change of coalition
10	Erhard I	X			
11	Erhard II		X	C, L	FDP withdraws from the coalition on 28 Oct. 1966
12	Erhard III	X			CDU/CSU minority government; formation of Grand Coalition
13	Kiesinger	X			General election. The Grand Coalition was perceived by all parties to be a transitory arrangement
14	Brandt I		X	S, F, L	Government lose majority after a series of defectioins and calls an early election after being defeated in a vote of confidence
15	Brandt II			S, L	Change of Chancellor, no changes in coalition
16	Schmidt I	X			
17	Schmidt II	X			
18	Schmidt III		X	S, LNL	FDP withdraws from the coalition on 17 Sept. 1982

TABLE 2.7. cont.

Cabinet number	Cabinet	Mechanisms of cabinet termination								Terminal events		Policy area(s)	Comments
		Technical	Discretionary										
		(1) Reg. parliamentary election	(4) Early parliamentary election	(5) Voluntary enlargement	(6) Cabinet defeated by opposition in parliament	(7) Conflict between coalition parties Policy	(7) Conflict between coalition parties Personnel	(8) Intra-party conflict in coalition party or parties		(12) Economic	(13) Personal		
19	Schmidt IV				X								SPD minority government; Schmidt replaced by Kohl through constructive vote of no confidence
20	Kohl I		X										Early election after FDP's change of coalition during a legislative term
21	Kohl II	X											
22	Kohl III			X									Coalition joined by DSU
23	Kohl IV	X											
24	Kohl V	X											
25	Kohl VI	X											

C = CDU/CSU; S = SPD; F = FDP; G = GB/BHE; D = DP.
L = conflict in national party leadership (national executive committee, cabinet, parliamentary party leadership); LNL = conflict in national party leadership involving non-leaders.

Note: The codes for the policy areas correspond to the column number given to the Federal Departments in Table 2.6.

were coalitions. Ten out of nineteen coalitions between 1949 and 1999 (and 11 out of 25 cabinets) were terminated through regular elections.

Two cabinets were terminated by early elections. Brandt's 1969–72 government had lost its majority in May 1972 as a consequence of several SPD and FDP backbenchers defecting to the opposition. There were severe intra-party conflicts in both government parties over the government's *Ostpolitik*, which was considered by some parliamentarians as a sell-out of national interests. The CDU/CSU's attempted constructive vote of no confidence in 1972 failed, however. Nevertheless, the government was left without a majority and defeated in the Bundestag over the 1973 budget for the Chancellor's Office. Brandt, therefore, asked for a vote of confidence which he was (unsurprisingly) denied as some government supporters abstained. The Federal President then called for early elections (Bracher, Jäger, and Link 1986: 67–76).

Kohl's first (1982–3) cabinet was terminated prematurely by an early election in March 1983, although the government had a sufficient parliamentary majority. The FDP had changed coalitions during a parliamentary term in 1982 after having made an explicit pre-election commitment in 1980 to continue the SPD–FDP coalition for a whole parliamentary term. As this cast doubts on the democratic legitimacy of his government, Kohl and large parts of the CDU/CSU leadership—in line with public opinion—wanted elections early in 1983. In order to dissolve the Bundestag, the Chancellor asked for a vote of confidence which he lost as a result of some parliamentary 'engineering': a high number of government supporters abstained. This manipulation raised serious concern amongst some constitutional lawyers and the Federal President, since it clearly violated the spirit of the Basic Law.

The premature 'termination' of Kohl's third (1987–90) cabinet is a termination only in a technical sense. It can be classified as a 'voluntary enlargement of the coalition' (Table 2.7) resulting from German unification. In October 1990, 144 new members were nominated by the GDR People's Chamber to represent eastern Germany in the Bundestag until all-German elections were held. The cabinet and the coalition were enlarged by representatives of the German Social Union (DSU). Three new CDU cabinet ministers, one new FDP cabinet minister, and one new DSU cabinet minister from eastern Germany were appointed. Since the coalition's party-political composition changed, our counting rules suggest that 3 October 1990 be considered as the end of Kohl's 1987–90 and the beginning of his 1990 government.

In two instances (Adenauer's eighth (1962) and Erhard's third (1966) cabinet), single-party minority governments were replaced by a coalition after a brief coalition crisis. In the absence of an appropriate category, no reason for the cabinets' termination was given in Table 2.7. Schmidt's fourth (1982) minority cabinet was replaced by Kohl's first (1982–3) cabinet through a successful constructive vote of no confidence. This instance was coded as 'cabinet defeated by opposition in parliament'.

Each of the remaining six premature cabinet terminations have been the result of a variety of causes. Certain 'random events' such as an economic recession may have aggravated a chronic coalition crisis. Nevertheless, their impact appears to have been largely catalytic. In all cabinets that were terminated prematurely, the 'stock of commonalities' between two coalition partners (*Vorrat an Gemeinsamkeiten*), as Walter Scheel once remarked with regard to the SPD–FDP coalition of 1969–82, had gradually been used up in a prolonged process of alienation. Policy conflicts between as well as within the coalition parties have invariably played an important role. Nevertheless, policy disagreements, too, have usually been necessary but insufficient conditions of a premature coalition termination. There has invariably been a mix of different variables, which will be characterized in some short descriptions of the events surrounding these terminations.

The premature termination of Adenauer's second (1953–5) government was a result of the GB/BHE's disintegration, which was precipitated by a conflict over foreign policy: the Franco-German agreement on the future of the Saarland in 1954 (cf. Bark and Gress 1993: 333–4). This agreement was bitterly opposed by a majority of GB/BHE Bundestag deputies, while the party's leaders, the cabinet ministers Waldemar Kraft and Theodor Oberländer, accepted Adenauer's policy in principle as a strategy to regain national sovereignty. When it came to the ratification of the Saar Statute in the Bundestag (1954), the majority of the GB/BHE parliamentary party decided to withdraw from the coalition and to vote against it, while the group around Kraft and Oberländer continued to support the Chancellor. The latter kept their ministerial portfolios and joined the CDU in 1955 (Stöss 1986*a*: 1436–7). Adenauer's second (1953–5) cabinet was thus terminated because the official GB/BHE left the coalition whose majority, however, did not depend on the GB/BHE.

The first major coalition crisis between CDU/CSU and FDP, which resulted in the termination of Adenauer's third (1955–6) cabinet, was caused by a combination of at least four separate factors: (*a*) Adenauer's policy of western integration at the expense of swift national reunification, which was opposed by the nationalist wing of the FDP; (*b*) the Chancellor's attempt to discipline the FDP by threatening to reform the electoral system by strengthening the plurality element aggravated the policy-induced crisis considerably; (*c*) a serious rift occurred within the FDP, where a reformist group of 'young turks' in North-Rhine-Westphalia withdrew from the regional CDU–FDP coalition and formed a coalition with the SPD. This strained the relationships between the CDU/CSU and FDP at the national level even further; (*d*) a 'random event', the personality clash between Adenauer and the FDP's parliamentary leader, Thomas Dehler, played a major role. The FDP as a party decided to withdraw from the government. Sixteen out of fifty-four FDP parliamentarians, however, rebelled against this decision and left their party, amongst them the party's four cabinet ministers. They eventually formed a new party, the Free People's Party (FVP), and remained in the government. After a series of electoral defeats at the state level, the FVP merged with the DP (Schwarz 1981: 303–12).

The failure of the CDU/CSU–DP coalition in 1960 followed a similar pattern as the two previous coalition crises. As early as in 1959, the CDU refused to renew the electoral pact which it had concluded with the DP for the 1957 elections and which had secured DP representation in the Bundestag. The CDU increasingly attempted to persuade DP leaders to agree to a fusion of the two parties (Völk 1989: 216–17). In 1960, the DP split up like the GB/BHE in 1955 and the FDP in 1956. Nine members, including the DP cabinet ministers remained in government and eventually joined the CDU. The rest of the party withdrew from the coalition.

Adenauer's seventh (1961–2) cabinet was terminated as a result of three main factors: policy disagreement between the coalition parties over the budget, long-standing controversies between some FDP leaders and the CSU leader and Defence Minister Franz Josef Strauß and a triggering external event (the '*Spiegel* Affair'). A fourth factor may have been the continuing fear of the FDP to be absorbed by the CDU/CSU or destroyed through electoral reform (Schwarz 1983: 261–73).

The fall of Erhard's second (1965–6) cabinet was also caused by a number of factors. External events such as the recession of 1966/7, which began as a slowdown in 1965, and several severe CDU/CSU defeats in state elections played an important role. Erhard was widely considered to be a weak leader. The CDU/CSU was internally divided. The coalition crisis was triggered by severe disagreements between CDU, CSU and FDP over the 1967 federal budget. The negotiations were exceedingly tough. The leaders of the CDU and CSU parliamentary parties in the Bundestag, Rainer Barzel and Franz Josef Strauß were prepared to risk a break-up of the coalition, which would also help them to depose of Erhard as Chancellor. As in the 1950s, the CDU/CSU considered striking a deal with the SPD to introduce a new electoral system to the detriment of the FDP and other small parties (including the extreme right-wing NPD). Finally Barzel and other opponents of Erhard's persuaded the Chancellor to resign (Hildebrand 1984: 218–40).

Like Adenauer's fifth (1957–60) and Erhard's second (1965–6) cabinets, the premature termination of Schmidt's third (1980–2) cabinet was partly caused by inter-party disagreement over budgetary policy. Again, the FDP demanded rigorous expenditure cuts, while Chancellor Schmidt needed to carry his own party, which wanted more moderate spending cuts and some tax increases. Again, an external shock, the recession of 1981 aggravated the tensions. Finally, similar to the previous premature terminations, there were increasing intra-party tensions as for the desirability of a continued coalition. Chancellor Schmidt found it increasingly difficult to maintain the support of his party's left wing over issues such as nuclear energy and the deployment of new US middle-range missiles in Western Europe. Like Adenauer, he had 'used' the FDP to 'discipline' his own party, with negative long-term effects for intra-party cohesion. Some external events, such as a series of negative results in state elections, convinced some FDP leaders around Genscher and Count Lambsdorff that a change of coalitions ('*Wende*') had to be initiated in order to secure the party's survival and necessary changes in fiscal policy. As in previous terminations, the change put an end to the coalition after a prolonged period of alienation (Jäger and Link 1987: 188–251).

The Electoral Costs and Benefits of Government Participation

Unlike the Weimar Republic, voters have generally not penalized the Federal Republic's government parties severely for their participation in government coalitions. Eighteen out of nineteen governments of the Weimar Republic faced severe electoral losses in the following election. There is strong evidence that the electoral 'disincentive' of government participation, which was very strong during the inter-war years, has vanished. Indeed, governments are frequently believed to enjoy an incumbency 'bonus' at elections. Between 1949 and September 1998, no German federal government was completely replaced by the opposition as a direct result of elections. The change of 1998 was a political novelty, therefore. Nevertheless, as noted above, several coalition realignments have been partly responses to electoral decline. Especially a string of losses at state level has frequently contributed to premature coalition terminations, for example in 1966 and 1982.

Eleven out of the twenty-three governments (approximately 48%) terminated between 1949 and 1999 were 'rewarded' in the following election. With average aggregate losses of 0.6 per cent for the twenty-three governments, government participation seems to have had little effect on the relevant parties' electoral fortunes in the next election. Overall figures for the individual parties show government participation was correlated with slight gains for the CDU/CSU and minor losses for the SPD and FDP.

The total averages for each party conceal some differences over time, however. The CDU/CSU–FDP governments of 1991–4 and 1994–8 suffered heavy aggregate losses (6.4% in 1994 and 7.1% in 1998). The losses were particularly severe for the FDP in 1994 and the CDU/CSU in 1998. The CDU/CSU benefited from government participation mainly until 1965 (average gains of 2.9%). Since 1982, its government participation has been correlated with modest average losses (1.7%). The SPD gained most during its first two terms in government (1966–72: +3.3%). After 1972, SPD government participation was correlated with losses (2.5% on average). For the FDP, government

TABLE 2.8. *Electoral costs/benefits of government parties in Germany, 1949–1999* (in % of votes)

Government	In office at time of election	Election year	CDU/CSU	SPD	FDP	GB/BHE	DP	Government
CDU/CSU–FDP–DP 1949–53	Yes	1953	+14.2	—	-2.4	—	-0.7	+11.1
CDU/CSU–FDP–DP–GB/BHE 1953–5	No	1957	+5.0	—	-1.8	-1.3	+0.1	+2.0
CDU/CSU–FDP–DP 1955–6	No	1957	+5.0	—	-1.8	—	+0.1	+3.3
CDU/CSU–FDP–DA/FVP 1956–7	Yes	1957	+5.0	—	—	—	+0.1	[+5.1]ᵃ
CDU/CSU–DP 1957–60	No	1961	-4.9	—	—	—	—	[-4.9]ᵇ
CDU/CSU 1960–1	Yes	1961	-4.9	—	—	—	—	-4.9
CDU/CSU–FDP 1961–2	No	1965	+2.3	—	-3.3	—	—	-1.0
CDU/CSU 1962	No	1965	+2.3	—	—	—	—	+2.3
CDU/CSU–FDP 1962–5	Yes	1965	+2.3	—	-3.3	—	—	-1.0
CDU/CSU–FDP 1965–6	No	1969	-1.5	—	-3.7	—	—	-5.2
CDU/CSU 1966	No	1969	-1.5	—	—	—	—	-1.5
CDU/CSU–SPD 1966–9	Yes	1969	-1.5	+3.4	—	—	—	+1.9
SPD–FDP 1969–72	Yes	1972	—	+3.1	+2.6	—	—	+5.7
SPD–FDP 1972–6	Yes	1976	—	-3.2	-0.5	—	—	-3.7
SPD–FDP 1976–80	Yes	1980	—	+0.3	+2.7	—	—	+3.0
SPD–FDP 1980–2	No	1983	—	-4.7	-3.6	—	—	-8.3
SPD 1982	No	1983	—	-4.7	—	—	—	-4.7
CDU/CSU–FDP 1982–3	Yes	1983	+4.3	—	-3.6	—	—	+0.7
CDU/CSU–FDP 1983–7	Yes	1987	-4.5	—	+2.1	—	—	-2.4
CDU/CSU–FDP 1987–90	No	1990	-0.5	—	+1.9	—	—	+1.4
CDU/CSU–FDP–DSU 1990	Yes	1990	-0.5	—	+1.9	—	—	[+1.4]ᶜ
CDU/CSU–FDP 1991–4	Yes	1994	-2.3	—	-4.1	—	—	-6.4
CDU/CSU–FDP 1994–8	Yes	1998	-6.4	—	-0.7	—	—	-7.1
MEANS			+0.7	-0.2	-0.7	-1.3	-0.3	-0.6

ᵃ The FVP was not listed because it did not compete in two consecutive Bundestag elections. The government's aggregate gains are therefore set in brackets (differences could not be calculated).

ᵇ The DP did not compete in the 1961 Federal elections. The government's aggregate losses are therefore set in brackets (differences could not be calculated).

ᶜ The DSU did not compete in the 1987 Federal elections. The government's aggregate gains are therefore set in brackets (differences could not be cal-

participation was correlated with losses until 1966 (2.7% on average), whereas, since 1969, the picture has been neutral (an average loss of 0.1%).

CONCLUSION

The structure of the party system and the nature of party competition have been the main parameters of coalition government in the German Federal Republic (Kaltefleiter 1996: 34). The main causes of relative coalition stability can be found in the party system. In the first decade after 1949, the party system developed from one that was characterized by 'polarized' pluralism to a moderately pluralist, bipolar party and coalition system. The logic of centrifugal party competition was replaced by a new coalition logic: the two major parties competed to win over a pivot party in the centre: the FDP. The FDP lost this position in the 1998 elections. Nevertheless, the coalition of 1998 stabilizes a two-block system with SPD and Greens, on the one hand, and CDU/CSU and FDP, on the other, and the PDS in an isolated position (at least at the national level). The centripetal form of party competition has been possible because all three main parties have adopted broad, pragmatic programmes enabling them to extend their electoral appeal beyond their predecessors' narrow inter-war clienteles. With considerable tactical skill the CDU/CSU in particular managed to 'embrace', wear down, and absorb all serious competitors to its right. The SPD and FDP also managed to incorporate social groups or political factions that had never been reached by their respective predecessors during the Weimar years. Moreover, the German form of federalism 'introduces powerful Grand Coalition components and consociational elements to the architecture of government in the Federal Republic' (Schmidt 1996: 68) and has favoured a 'coexistence of competition, partisan struggles and majority rule together with consensus formation through compromises or unanimity in decision-making' (Schmidt 1996: 73).

Historical learning from the catastrophe of 1933, resulting in some major constitutional and legal innovations, has also played an important role in stabilizing coalition governments: the restriction of the Federal President's role to ceremonial functions, the Federal Chancellor's strong position *vis-à-vis* the Bundestag (constructive vote of no confidence), the removal of dissolution powers from the head of government and the Chancellor's power to formulate the guidelines of government policy have been important developments as was the 5 per cent threshold of the electoral law. Nevertheless, the main strength of the Chancellor and the main variables influencing coalition stability have been the structure of the party system, the Chancellor's ability to control his own party, and the degree of consensus and support for a coalition within individual coalition parties (cf. Saalfeld 1999).

Coalition governance has largely been achieved by informal means. Coalition 'treaties' have not been of prime importance in this respect. Before 1998, coalition agreements with explicit rules of the game were exceptional. The only verified agreement for Adenauer's seventh (1961–2) cabinet followed complaints from the smaller coalition parties about a decline in consultation by the Chancellor during the two previous parliaments (1953–61). Formal cabinet meetings or cabinet committees have never been the main locus of conflict management between the coalition partners. Informal, but regular 'coalition talks', coalition roundtables with a flexible composition and negotiations between the federal government and state governments have been the crucial devices of coalition governance. Indeed, as some observers (Rudzio 1991; see also Schreckenberger 1994) argue, the various, highly flexible coalition committees are the real locus of political power (and coalition government) in the German Federal Republic.

REFERENCES

Arndt, Claus (1989). 'Fraktion und Abgeordneter', in Hans-Peter Schneider and Wolfgang Zeh (eds.), *Parlamentsrecht und Parlamentspraxis in der Bundesrepublik Deutschland*. Berlin and New York: Walter de Gruyter.
Bark, Dennis L., and Gress, David R. (1993). *A History of West Germany*, i. *From Shadow to Substance*, 2nd edn. Oxford: Blackwell.
Bermbach, Udo (1970). 'Stationen der Regierungsbildung 1969'. *Zeitschrift für Parlamentsfragen*, 1 (1): 5–23.
——(1977). 'Stationen der Regierungsbildung 1976'. *Zeitschrift für Parlamentsfragen*, 8 (2): 159–82.
——(1978). 'Koalitionen', in Kurt Sontheimer and Hans H. Röhring (eds.), *Handbuch des politischen Systems der Bundesrepublik Deutschland*. Munich: Piper.
——(1981). 'Stationen der Regierungsbildung 1980'. *Zeitschrift für Parlamentsfragen*, 12 (1): 58–83.
Beyme, Klaus von (1983). 'Coalition Government in Western Germany', in Vernon Bogdanor (ed.), *Coalition Government in Western Europe*. London: Heinemann.
——(1997). *Der Gesetzgeber: Der Bundestag als Entscheidungszentrum*. Opladen: Westdeutscher Verlag.
Bohnsack, Klaus (1983*a*). 'Die Koalitionskrise 1981/82 und der Regierungswechsel 1982'. *Zeitschrift für Parlamentsfragen*, 14 (1): 5–33.
——(1983*b*). 'Regierungsbildung und Oppositionsformierung 1983'. *Zeitschrift für Parlamentsfragen*, 14 (4): 476–86.
Bracher, Karl Dietrich, Jäger, Wolfgang, and Link, Werner (1986). *Republik im Wandel 1969–1974: Die Ära Brandt (Geschichte der Bundesrepublik Deutschland,* 5/i). Stuttgart: Deutsche Verlags-Anstalt/Mannheim: Brockhaus.

Busse, Volker (1997). *Bundeskanzleramt und Bundesregierung: Aufgaben, Organisation, Arbeitsweise.* Heidelberg: Hüthig.
Conradt, David P. (1996). *The German Polity*, 6th edn. New York and London: Longman.
Dexheimer, Wolfgang F. (1973). *Koalitionsverhandlungen in Bonn, 1961, 1965, 1969: Zur Willensbildung in Parteien und Fraktionen.* Bonn: Eichholz-Verlag.
Eschenburg, Theodor (1956). *Staat und Gesellschaft in Deutschland.* Stuttgart: Curt E. Schwab.
Gibowski, Wolfgang (1995). 'Election Trends in Germany: An Analysis of the Second General Election in Reunited Germany', in Geoffrey K. Roberts (ed.), *Superwahljahr: The German Elections in 1994.* London: Cass.
Heinrich, Gudrun (1995). 'Koalitionsverhandlungen und Regierungsbildung auf Bundesebene 1994 im Spiegel der Presse'. *Zeitschrift für Parlamentsfragen*, 26 (2): 193–203.
Hildebrand, Klaus (1984). *Von Erhard zur Großen Koalition 1963–1969* (*Geschichte der Bundesrepublik Deutschland*, 4). Stuttgart: Deutsche Verlags-Anstalt/ Mannheim: Brockhaus.
Jäger, Wolfgang, and Link, Werner (1987). *Republik im Wandel 1974–1982: Die Ära Schmidt* (*Geschichte der Bundesrepublik Deutschland*, 5/ii). Stuttgart: Deutsche Verlags-Anstalt/Mannheim: Brockhaus.
Jesse, Eckhard (1988). 'Split-Voting in the Federal Republic of Germany: An Analysis of the Federal Elections from 1953 to 1987'. *Electoral Studies*, 7 (2): 109–24.
Kaarbo, Juliet (1996). 'Power and Influence in Foreign Policy Decision Making: The Role of Junior Coalition Partners in German and Israeli Foreign Policy'. *International Studies Quarterly*, 40: 501–30.
Kaltefleiter, Werner (1996). 'Die Kanzlerdemokratie des Helmut Kohl'. *Zeitschrift für Parlamentsfragen*, 27 (1): 27–37.
Klingemann, Hans-Dieter, and Volkens, Andrea (1992). 'Coalition Governments in the Federal Republic of Germany: Does Policy Matter?', in Michael J. Laver and Ian Budge (eds.), *Party Policy and Government Coalitions.* Basingstoke and London: Macmillan.
Korte, Karl-Rudolf (1998). *Deutschlandpolitik in Helmut Kohls Kanzlerschaft: Regierungsstil und Entscheidungen 1982–1989.* Stuttgart: Deutsche Verlags-Anstalt.
Krehbiel, Keith (1991). *Information and Legislative Organization.* Ann Arbor: University of Michigan Press.
Kropp, Sabine, and Sturm, Roland (1998). *Koalitionen und Koalitionsvereinbarungen: Theorie, Analyse und Dokumentation.* Opladen: Leske und Budrich.
Küpper, Jost (1985). *Die Kanzlerdemokratie: Voraussetzungen, Strukturen und Änderungen des Regierungsstiles in der Ära Adenauer.* Frankfurt am Main: Peter Lang.
Kürschners Volkshandbuch (1995). *Deutscher Bundestag: 13. Wahlperiode.* Darmstadt: Neue Darmstädter Verlagsanstalt.
Laakso, Markku, and Taagepera, Rein (1979). '"Effective" Number of Parties: A Measure with Applications to Western Europe', *Comparative Political Studies*, 23: 3–27.
Lange, Rolf, and Richter, Gerhard (1973). 'Die vorzeitige Auflösung des Bundestages. Stationen vom konstruktiven Mißtrauensvotum bis zur Vereidigung der zweiten Regierung Brandt/Scheel'. *Zeitschrift für Parlamentsfragen*, 4 (1): 38–75.

Laver, Michael (1999). 'Divided Parties, Divided Government'. *Legislative Studies Quarterly*, 24 (1): 5–30.
——and Hunt, W. Ben (1992). *Policy and Party Competition*. New York and London: Routledge.
——and Schofield, Norman (1990). *Multiparty Government: The Politics of Coalition in Europe*. Oxford: Oxford University Press.
——and Shepsle, Kenneth A. (1996). *Making and Breaking Governments: Cabinets and Legislatures in Parliamentary Democracies*. Cambridge: Cambridge University Press.
Lees, Charles (1999). 'The Red–Green Coalition', in Stephen Padgett and Thomas Saalfeld (eds.), *Bundestagswahl '98: End of an Era?* London: Cass.
Lösche, Peter (1993). *Kleine Geschichte der deutschen Parteien*. Stuttgart: Kohlhammer.
Löwenberg, Gerhard (1967). *Parliament in the German Political System*. Ithaca, NY: Cornell University Press.
Lupia, Arthur, and Strøm, Kaare (1995). 'Coalition Termination and the Strategic Timing of Parliamentary Elections'. *American Political Science Review*, 89 (3): 648–65.
Mackie, Thomas T., and Hogwood, Brian W. (1985). 'Decision-Making in Cabinet Government', in Thomas T. Mackie and Brian W. Hogwood (eds.), *Unlocking the Cabinet: Cabinet Structures in Comparative Perspective*. London: Sage Publications.
Mershon, Carol (1999). 'The Costs of Coalition: A Five-Nation Comparison', in Shaun Bowler, David M. Farrell, and Richard S. Katz (eds.), *Party Discipline and Parliamentary Government*. Columbus: Ohio State University Press.
Mintzel, Alf (1977). *Geschichte der CSU: Ein Überblick*. Opladen: Westdeutscher Verlag.
——(1986). 'Die Bayernpartei', in Richard Stöss (ed.), *Parteienhandbuch: Die Parteien der Bundesrepublik Deutschland 1945–1980*. Special edition, Volume 1, Opladen: Westdeutscher Verlag.
——and Oberreuter, Heinrich (1992) (eds.). *Parteien in der Bundesrepublik Deutschland*, 2nd edn. Bonn: Bundeszentrale für politische Bildung.
Mitchell, Paul (1999). 'Coalition Discipline, Enforcement Mechanisms and Intraparty Politics', in Shaun Bowler, David M. Farrell, and Richard S. Katz (eds.), *Party Discipline and Parliamentary Government*. Columbus: Ohio State University Press.
Müller-Rommel, Ferdinand (1994). 'The Role of German Ministers in Cabinet Decision Making', in Michael Laver and Kenneth A. Shepsle (eds.), *Cabinet Ministers and Parliamentary Government*, Cambridge: Cambridge University Press.
Norpoth, Helmut (1982). 'The German Federal Republic: Coalition Government at the Brink of Majority Rule', in Eric C. Browne and John Dreijmanis (eds.), *Government Coalitions in Western Democracies*. New York and London: Longman.
Padgett, Stephen (1993) (ed.). *Parties and Party Systems in the New Germany*. Aldershot: Dartmouth.
Presse- und Informationsamt der Bundesregierung. (1998*a*). *Bulletin*, No. 69: 859–68.
——(1998*b*). *Bulletin*, No. 70.
——(1998*c*). *Bulletin*, No. 71.

Renzsch, Wolfgang, and Schieren, Stefan (1997). 'Große Koalition oder Minderheitsregierung: Sachsen-Anhalt als Zukunftsmodell des parlamentarischen Regierungssystems in den neuen Bundesländern?', *Zeitschrift für Parlamentsfragen*, 28 (3): 391–407.

Riker, William H. (1962). *The Theory of Political Coalitions*. New Haven: Yale University Press.

Rudzio, Wolfgang (1991). 'Informelle Entscheidungsmuster in Bonner Koalitionsregierungen', in Hans-Hermann Hartwich and Göttrik Wewer (eds.), *Regieren in der Bundesrepublik II: Formale und informale Komponenten des Regierens in den Bereichen Führung, Entscheidung, Personal und Organisation*. Opladen: Leske und Budrich.

——(1996). *Das politische System der Bundesrepublik Deutschland*, 4th edn. Opladen: Leske und Budrich.

Saalfeld, Thomas (1995). *Parteisoldaten und Rebellen: Eine Untersuchung zur Geschlossenheit der Fraktionen im Deutschen Bundestag (1949–1990)*. Opladen: Leske und Budrich.

——(1999). 'Coalition Politics and Management in the Kohl Era (1982–1998)', in Stephen Padgett and Thomas Saalfeld (eds.), *Bundestagswahl '98: End of an Era?* London: Cass.

Sandschneider, Eberhard (1987). 'Regierungsbildung 1987: Koalitonsverhandlungen und Personalentscheidungen'. *Zeitschrift für Parlamentsfragen*, 18 (2): 203–21.

Sartori, Giovanni (1976). *Parties and Party Systems: A Framework for Analysis*, i. Cambridge: Cambridge University Press.

——(1987). *The Theory of Democracy Revisited. Part One: The Contemporary Debate*. Chatham, NJ: Chatham House.

Schindler, Peter (1983). *Datenhandbuch zur Geschichte des Deutschen Bundestages 1949 bis 1982*, 2nd edn. Bonn: Presse- und Informationszentrum des Deutschen Bundestages.

——(1994). *Datenhandbuch zur Geschichte des Deutschen Bundestages 1983 bis 1991*. Baden-Baden: Nomos.

——(1995). 'Deutscher Bundestag 1976–1994: Parlaments- und Wahlstatistik'. *Zeitschrift für Parlamentsfragen*, 26 (4): 551–66.

Schmidt, Manfred G. (1983). 'Two Logics of Coalition Policy: The West German Case', in Vernon Bogdanor (ed.), *Coalition Government in Western Europe*. London: Heinemann.

——(1996). 'Germany: The Grand Coalition State', in Josep M. Colomer (ed.), *Political Institutions in Europe*. London: Routledge.

Schmitt, Ute (1986). 'Die Christlich Demokratische Union Deutschlands', in Richard Stöss (ed.), *Parteienhandbuch: Die Parteien der Bundesrepublik Deutschland 1945–1980*, Special edition, vol. i. Opladen: Westdeutscher Verlag.

Schmollinger, Horst W. (1986). 'Die Deutsche Partei', in Richard Stöss (ed.), *Parteienhandbuch: Die Parteien der Bundesrepublik Deutschland 1945–1980*, Special edition, vol. ii. Opladen: Westdeutscher Verlag.

Schreckenberger, Waldemar (1994). 'Informelle Verfahren der Entscheidungsvorbereitung zwischen der Bundesregierung und den Mehrheitsfraktionen: Koalitionsgespräche und Koalitionsrunden'. *Zeitschrift für Parlamentsfragen*, 25 (3): 329–346.

Schüle, Adolf (1964). *Koalitionsvereinbarungen im Lichte des Verfassungsrechts: Eine Studie zur deutschen Lehre und Praxis.* Tübingen: Mohr (Siebeck).
Schwarz, Hans-Peter (1981). *Die Ära Adenauer: Gründerjahre der Republik 1949–1957* (*Geschichte der Bundesrepublik Deutschland*, vol. 2). Stuttgart: Deutsche Verlags-Anstalt/Mannheim: Brockhaus.
——(1983). *Die Ära Adenauer: Epochenwechsel 1957–1963* (*Geschichte der Bundesrepublik Deutschland*, vol. 3). Stuttgart: Deutsche Verlags-Anstalt/Mannheim: Brockhaus.
Smith, Gordon (1991). 'The Resources of a German Chancellor', in G.W. Jones (ed.), *West European Prime Ministers.* London: Frank Cass.
Steffani, Winfried (1997). 'Zukunftsmodell Sachsen-Anhalt? Grundsätzliche Bedenken. Bemerkung zum Beitrag von Wolfgang Renzsch und Stefan Schieren in Heft 3/1997'. *Zeitschrift für Parlamentsfragen*, 28 (4): 717–22.
Stöss, Richard. (1986*a*). 'Der Gesamtdeutsche Block/BHE.' In Richard Stöss (ed.), *Parteienhandbuch: Die Parteien der Bundesrepublik Deutschland 1945–1980*, Special edition, vol. 3. Opladen: Westdeutscher Verlag.
——(1986*b*) (ed.). *Parteienhandbuch: Die Parteien der Bundesrepublik Deutschland 1945–1980*, Special edition. Opladen: Westdeutscher Verlag.
Strøm, Kaare (1990). *Minority Government and Majority Rule.* Cambridge: Cambridge University Press.
Tsebelis, George (1990). *Nested Games: Rational Choice in Comparative Politics.* Berkeley: University of California Press.
Völk, Josef Anton (1989). *Regierungskoalitionen auf Bundesebene: Dokumentation und Analyse des Koalitionswesens von 1949 bis 1987.* Regensburg: S. Roderer.
Vorbeck, Antje (1991). 'Regierungsbildung 1990/91: Koalitions- und Personalentscheidungen im Spiegel der Presse'. *Zeitschrift für Parlamentsfragen*, 22 (3): 377–89.
Warwick, Paul V. (1994). *Government Survival in Parliamentary Democracies.* Cambridge: Cambridge University Press.
Wewer, Göttrik (1990). 'Richtlinienkompetenz und Koalitionsregierung: Wo wird die Politik definiert?', in Hans-Hermann Hartwich and Göttrik Wewer (eds.), *Regieren in der Bundesrepublik I: Konzeptionelle Grundlagen und Perspektiven der Forschung.* Opladen: Leske und Budrich.

3

Austria

Tight Coalitions and Stable Government

Wolfgang C. Müller

INTRODUCTION: CENTRAL FEATURES OF THE PARTY SYSTEM

For most of the post-war period the Austrian party system displayed a remarkable degree of stability and concentration. Until 1986 two major political parties, the Social Democratic (Socialist until 1991) Party (SPÖ) and the Christian democratic Austrian People's Party (ÖVP) held 87.3 to 96.4 per cent of the parliamentary seats between themselves. Despite the PR electoral formula five of the twelve elections in the 1945–83 period resulted in absolute majorities for single parties (in 1945 and 1966 for the ÖVP and in 1971, 1975, and 1979 for the SPÖ). Since 1986, however, the party system has been going through a process of deconcentration (Müller 1996*a*). The number of relevant parties increased from three (in 1983) to five (since 1993) through the establishment of the Greens (in 1986) and the Liberal Forum (in 1993). The single most important factor for bringing the SPÖ–ÖVP dominance to an end, however, was the rise of the Freedom Party (FPÖ) which increased its share of the vote dramatically, from 5 per cent (in 1983) to 21.9 per cent (in 1995). This leaves the two traditional major parties with about two-thirds of the parliamentary seats in the mid-1990s.

While only the two major parties existed throughout the whole post-war period several other parties had or still have parliamentary representation and directly or indirectly had an impact on coalition politics. These parties are the League of Independents (VdU) (since 1949) and its successor the FPÖ (since 1956), the Communist Party (KPÖ) in the immediate post-war period, and more recently the Greens and the Liberal Forum (LF).

The traditional major parties, the SPÖ and ÖVP, also have dominated government, either by joining forces in 'grand coalition' governments (1947–66 and since 1987) or by forming single-party governments (1966–83). Government participation of the Communists (1945–7) and the FPÖ

(1983–7) has been no more than episodes. It is this predominance of 'grand coalition' government which makes Austria a particular interesting and unique case in coalition studies.

Party competition has been primarily structured by a socio-economic left–right dimension, with the size and function of the public sector, tax policy, and welfare spending being major and recurrent issues. Table 3.1 places the parties according to this dimension. It draws on the expert survey conducted by Laver and Hunt (1992) which is largely consistent with alternative measures of the left–right placement of Austrian parties.[1] Some observers may find the placement of the LF at the very right of this scale striking. However, it has to be recalled that this scale is based on socio-economic questions exclusively. The LF indeed has a clear market economy programme and it directs its appeal to the upper middle classes. In contrast to the ÖVP, it has not to accommodate a trade union wing and in contrast to the FPÖ, it does not try to appeal to the working class by populist slogans.

The second relevant policy dimension is the religious one. Historically, it divided the Social Democrats and the Christian Socials as much as the socio-economic one. Although the accommodation of Social Democrats and the Catholic Church in the late 1960s and increasing secularization have reduced the relevance of this dimension, it still is important. Since the 1970s moral issues such as abortion, divorce, and more recently the question of homosexual relationships, their public recognition and similar issues rather than state–church relations in the narrow sense constitute the core of this policy dimension. The ÖVP is still closest to the moral teaching of the Catholic Church and constitutes the one end of the scale. Though traditionally an anti-clerical party, the FPÖ comes next because of the social conservatism of the majority of its voters, members, and leaders. The SPÖ covers the middle ground. On the one hand, it has an anti-clerical tradition and some of its activists share libertarian views on social issues. However, on the other hand, most of its voters and members tend to be socially rather conservative. It is the Greens and the LF which constitute the libertarian end of this policy dimension.

---

[1] Party placement in Table 3.1 is consistent with the expert survey of Campbell (1992) who incorporated a time dimension by asking his respondents to locate the parties for three dates in the 1975–91 period. There are some temporary variations of party placements in studies which draw on survey and manifesto data. According to Plasser and Ulram (1995: 478–9) and Plasser, Ulram, and Seeber (1996: 166), the FPÖ was considered to be left of the ÖVP by survey respondents during the 1970s and 1980s. However, at this time the FPÖ was an obviously office-driven party, eager to form a coalition with the SPÖ (Luther 1997). So it seems more likely that the FPÖ's placement in the survey reflects its office rather than policy preferences. This interpretation is shared by the historical accounts of this coalition (see Pelinka 1993; Luther 1995). Manifesto data also display some variation of the parties' left–right placement over time (Horner 1987; Müller, Philipp, and Jenny 1995). These are almost exclusively related to the placement of the FPÖ which traditionally has not provided a fully-fledged manifesto, covering more or less all policy areas. These variations therefore can be considered an artefact of the method employed in these studies.

TABLE 3.1. *Left–right placement of parties,*[a] *party strength (in seats), and party composition of governments in Austria, 1945–1999*

Government	Proximity to election	KPÖ	GA	SPÖ	ÖVP	VdU/FPÖ[b]	LF	Median party in second policy dimension[c]	Effective number of legislative parties	Government strength	Total number of seats
1945	F	**4**	—	76	**85***	—	—	ÖVP	2.20	165	165
1947	E		—	76	**85***	—	—	ÖVP	2.20	161	165
1949	FE	5	—	67	**77***	16	—	VdU	2.87	144	165
1953	FE	4	—	73	**74***	14	—	VdU	2.77	147	165
1956	FE	3	—	74	**82***	6	—	FPÖ	2.46	156	165
1959	FE		—	78	**79***	8	—	FPÖ	2.35	157	165
1963[d]	FE		—	76	**81***	8	—	FPÖ	2.38	157	165
1966	FE		—	74	**85***	6	—	ÖVP	2.34	85	165
1970	FE		—	**81**	78*	6	—	FPÖ	2.28	81	165
1971	FE		—	**93***	80	10	—	FPÖ	2.37	93	183
1975	FE		—	**93***	80	10	—	SPÖ	2.37	93	183
1979	FE		—	**95***	77	11	—	SPÖ	2.40	95	183
1983	FE		—	**90**	81*	**12**	—	SPÖ	2.43	102	183
1987[e]	FE		8	**80**	**77***	18	—	FPÖ	2.98	157	183
1990	FE		10	**80**	**60***	33	—	FPÖ	3.30	140	183
1994	FE		13	65	**52***	42	11	FPÖ	4.14	117	183
1996[f]	F		9	**71**	**53***	40	10	FPÖ	3.92	124	183

There are other policy dimensions of relevance, in particular in recent years. The establishment of the Greens indicated the importance of a policy dimension with the opposite poles of economic growth and ecology. More recently, the issue of immigration figured prominently on the political agenda. Here political parties place themselves in a way similar to that of moral issues, though for different reasons.

INSTITUTIONAL BACKGROUND

According to the constitution the government is appointed by the federal president. It is him who appoints the federal chancellor and at the chancellor's proposal the other cabinet members plus the secretaries of state (junior ministers). The constitution contains no restriction whatever as to whom should be invited to form a government and of which components it should consist. However, *de facto* the federal president has little room for manœuvre. The government needs parliamentary support in order to survive and govern effectively. The president will therefore refrain from appointing a cabinet which is opposed by a parliamentary majority. In theory this may still leave some leeway for the president. In practice, however, the president has confined himself largely to ratify what the parties agree on and in so doing may find himself pre-empted by public declarations of the parties or even pre-electoral commitments. It is the clear convention that the task of forming a gov-

---

TABLE 3.1. *cont.*

a Based on Laver and Hunt's (1992: 142) 'pro public ownership vs. anti public ownership' and 'increase services vs. cut taxes' policy scales which produce the same left–right placement. The LF was founded only in 1993. Its left–right placement refers to the socio-economic policy dimension and is based on an analysis of its electoral manifesto 1995 (Müller, Philipp, and Jenny 1995: 156).
b FPÖ since 1956.
c Religious dimension, based on Laver and Hunt's (1992: 143) 'anti-clerical vs. pro-clerical' and updated by an analysis of electoral manifestos (Müller, Philipp, and Jenny 1995: 156).
d Election was held in 1962, the government was formed in 1963.
e Election was held in 1986, the government was formed in 1987.
f Election was held in 1995, the government was formed in 1996.

Parties
KPÖ   Kommunistische Partei Österreichs (Communist Party of Austria)
GA   Grüne Alternative (Green Alternative)
SPÖ   Sozialdemokratische (Sozialistische) Partei Österreichs (Social Democratic [Socialist until 1991] Party of Austria)
ÖVP   Österreichische Volkspartei (Austrian People's Party)
VdU   Verband der Unabhängigen (League of Independents)
FPÖ   Freiheitliche Partei Österreichs (Freedom Party of Austria)
LF   Liberales Forum (Liberal Forum)

Parties in **bold** formed **governments**.
* Party with median legislator.

ernment is first given to the leader or 'chancellor candidate' of the largest parliamentary party (Welan 1986: 76–7). Up until now the largest party (and with one exception—Leopold Figl in 1953—also the person who was first officially designated chancellor candidate by the president) has always succeeded in forming a viable government.

It would be wrong, however, to consider the president as not constraining government formation at all (Müller 1999a). Potentially presidents gain influence when alternative majority coalitions can be formed and the coalition preferences of the parties are not (yet) fixed. In two cases of government formation the president intervened in the game which was going on between the parties. In 1953, President Theodor Körner publicly rejected an ÖVP proposal of including the VdU in the government (Kollmann 1973: 374).[2] The same happened in 1959 in private consultations between ÖVP leader Raab and President Schärf with regard to the former's proposal of including the FPÖ in what then would have been an all-party government.[3] In both the 1953 and 1959 elections the SPÖ had won more votes than the ÖVP, but due to the electoral system remained one seat behind it. The ÖVP's proposals aimed at strengthening the non-socialist forces in cabinet. Moreover, political observers and actors saw the inclusion of the VdU or FPÖ in the government as preparing the ground for governments which excluded the SPÖ. Though both attempts of enlarging the coalition eventually failed, at least the first one nevertheless constituted a credible threat to the SPÖ and was instrumental for the ÖVP during coalition negotiations.

In 1962/3 President Schärf urged the parties to complete what he considered too long coalition negotiations. Later interventions of the presidents, in particular Kurt Waldheim and Thomas Klestil's expressed preference for 'grand coalition' government in the 1980s and 1990s, were hardly more than 'tailwind' for what was emerging in party negotiations.

Several presidents also tried to help overcome coalition crises. Notable cases are Presidents Körner (in 1952) and Schärf's (in 1960) rejections to cabinet resignations over problems to agree on a budget.

Once formed and sworn in the cabinet must present itself to parliament (the Nationalrat) within one week after assuming office. In so doing it does not go through an investiture vote. However, this occasion can be used to introduce a vote of no confidence. Since the constitutional reform of 1929 Austria falls in the rubric of 'negative' parliamentarism (cf. Bergman 1993), meaning that the burden of proof rests with the opposition. To unseat a government

---

[2] According to the ÖVP proposal, the government would have consisted of ÖVP, SPÖ, and VdU, leaving out only the tiny Communist Party. It remains a question, however, how serious the ÖVP proposal was. Anticipating the president's reaction it may have been no more than an attempt to maintain good relations with the VdU and blaming the president and the SPÖ with its exclusion from government.

[3] Adolf Schärf, 'Bundespräsident', unpublished manuscript, NL Schärf (KK15).

requires a quorum of at least 50 per cent and a majority of those MPs who are present. No government had to face a vote of no confidence when it first presented itself to parliament and only once an individual minister had to do so.[4]

Legislative decision rules constitute some kind of incentive to form broadly based coalitions (Müller 1993). In Austria constitutional amendments require a two-thirds majority in the Nationalrat (with a 50% quorum) and there are many of them. Back in 1993 constitutional lawyers counted no less than 63 constitutional amendments, 225 separate constitutional laws, 427 clauses with constitutional rank in ordinary legislation, and 181 state treaties with constitutionally relevant clauses enacted since 1920 (the vast majority of which date from the post-war period). These figures include the laws concerning economic intervention (*Marktordnungsgesetze*), in particular in the agricultural sector. These laws had a temporary character and thus appeared on the political agenda on a regular basis until their abolishment in 1995, which resulted from Austria's membership in the European Union. Put simply, these laws provided the basis for giving subsidies to farmers and maintaining a uniform price level for agricultural products all over Austria. Since 1962 school legislation requires a two-thirds majority, too. Since legislation in these fields severely affects the clientele of the major parties, in particular the ÖVP, they constitute an incentive to search for large majorities when forming a government. However, the importance of these legislative decision rules should not be overestimated. Interviews with politicians who were involved in government formation suggest that this factor was considered in internal deliberations, but was not decisive. And indeed single-party governments have managed to find two-thirds majorities whenever it was necessary. Likewise, no party was added to the SPÖ–ÖVP government in the 1994–5 period, when the SPÖ and ÖVP had lost the two-thirds majority which they had held between themselves since 1945. The advantage of commanding a two-thirds majority probably would have been more than outweighted by the increased difficulties resulting from the need to coordinate three governmental parties. In the future these legislative decision rules are likely to have even less importance for government formation.

The Austrian electoral system has been a relatively pure PR system which has created only small (until 1970) or even negligible (since 1971) distortions (Müller 1996*b*). It does not create incentives for pre-electoral coalitions. Nevertheless political parties have frequently made clear their coalition preferences before the elections as part of their campaign strategy. They wanted to exploit the popularity or unpopularity of specific potential coalitions in the electorate or their potential constituency. More specifically, during the

---

[4] The case occurred in 1990, when the new Minister of Social Affairs, Josef Hesoun, had to face a no confidence vote (which was rejected). Hesoun had attracted the fire of the opposition, in particular the Greens, in his previous position as a leading trade unionist, taking a 'hardliner' position against the ecological movement.

1945–66 period the ÖVP and SPÖ regularly indicated their willingness to continue cooperation in the 'grand coalition' after the elections. Considering themselves unable to win absolute majorities, they even made this a campaign issue. According to their propaganda 'absolute rule' (*Alleinherrschaft*) of the other party would endanger democracy (Hölzl 1974). In contrast, in the 1970–83 elections, the respective government parties explicitly campaigned for a renewal of their absolute majorities (or, as the SPÖ did in 1971, for making their plurality a majority). Understandably, they did not want to compromise their claim by issuing coalition preferences. The opposition parties did not issue coalition statements either. Since 1986 the situation has changed. The SPÖ in all cases indicated that it would aim at forming a coalition with the ÖVP and explicitly excluded a coalition with the FPÖ from its options. The ÖVP was more reluctant to commit itself. Only before the 1994 elections party chairman Erhard Busek declared that 'grand coalition' government would be continued with 'no ifs and buts'. Since this did not prove a viable electoral strategy, in 1995 the ÖVP did not indicate a coalition preference or exclude any of the options from its agenda. In the 1990s the Greens and the LF have become part of the pre-electoral coalition game. They choose to exclude only any coalition which would include the FPÖ from the range of their options.

COALITION FORMATION

Over the whole post-war period four parties enjoyed being in government. For two of them, however, government participation did not last long. The Communists were represented in government only in the special situation immediately after World War II (1945–7). The FPÖ's participation in government also was short (1983–7). It is the two major parties, the SPÖ and ÖVP, which have mainly provided the country's government. The SPÖ has turned out as the permanent party of government in the post-war period, participating in government for no less than 47 out of 51 post-war years (and still being in office in 1999). After being the leading force in the provisional government of 1945, the SPÖ was the junior partner first in the brief all-party government and then in the old 'grand coalition'. A four-year term in opposition (1966–70) was followed by 13 years of single-party government by the SPÖ (1970–83). The SPÖ–FPÖ coalition of 1983–7 can be considered the aftermath of SPÖ single-party rule. Though reduced in its capacity to determine government policy the SPÖ has managed to hold on power since then, forming a 'grand coalition' government with the ÖVP in 1987. The ÖVP constitutes the mirror picture of the SPÖ's fortunes. It was the leading force in the old 'grand coalition' government until 1966 and then ruled alone until

1970. After 16 years in opposition it returned to government as the junior partner of the SPÖ in the new 'grand coalition' in 1987.

Post-war coalition politics has been enormously stable (cf. Franklin and Mackie 1983). Over the whole post-war period the party composition of coalitions was changed only twice. In 1947 the KPÖ left the government and in 1986 the SPÖ abandoned its coalition with the FPÖ, reacting to a change in the FPÖ leadership which was perceived as fundamental. Otherwise the existing coalitions were returned after the election, except the 'grand coalition' in 1966 when the ÖVP won an absolute majority. However, even then ÖVP and SPÖ conducted serious negotiations to continue 'grand coalition' government despite the ÖVP's absolute majority (Müller 1999b).

All but the first two regular post-war governments formed in 1945 and 1947 (Figl I and II) were minimal-winning coalitions, i.e. a coalition turned into a losing one by the subtraction of any of its members. Not a single minimum-winning coalition (Riker 1962), i.e. a winning coalition comprising the smallest total weight, was formed since 1945. All governments were based on overly large parliamentary majorities. It was the SPÖ–FPÖ coalition formed in 1983 (based on 102 of 183 seats) which came closest to a minimum-winning coalition. This type, however, would have been an ÖVP–FPÖ coalition (93 seats).

According to Table 3.1, in all but one case 'policy-connected' coalitions were formed, i.e. the coalitions were formed by adjacent parties in the major policy dimension. The deviant case is the SPÖ–FPÖ coalition of 1983.[5] Finally, all but one coalition—the SPÖ–FPÖ coalition—were minimal connected winning (Axelrod 1970), i.e. consisted of adjacent parties and the loss of a member would have rendered the coalition either no longer winning or no longer connected.

From this evidence the following questions emerge. First, why the median party, the ÖVP, chose the SPÖ and formed overly large coalitions until 1966? Second, why the median party, the ÖVP, was excluded from government in the 1983–7 period? Third, why the government has again been overly large since 1987, or, in other words, why the median party, again the ÖVP, did not engage in a coalition with the FPÖ?

The institutional features discussed above, in particular the need for two-thirds majorities in many instances, provide some incentive for forming overly large coalitions. Likewise, the convention of giving the task of government formation to the largest party and the general expectation that the strongest parliamentary party will also become the leading party in government have somewhat improved the SPÖ's position in coalition formation situations since 1970. However, these factors do not provide sufficient answers

---

[5] In contrast to the expert placements and manifesto data, survey data about the parties' left–right placements suggest that SPÖ and FPÖ were adjacent parties. See Note 1.

to the above questions. Rather it is necessary to look at constraints which result from the party system and the political agenda. Both are soft rather than hard constraints, i.e. they do not outrule certain alternative outcomes, but they 'load the dice' for the parties' coalition strategies (cf. Strøm, Budge, and Laver 1994: 309).

Party System Constraints

First, in the early years of the Second Republic the legacy of the inter-war period when Christian Socials and Social Democrats had fought each other in a civil war in 1934 constituted a major burden. The elites of their successors, the ÖVP and SPÖ, had learned their lessons from history. In 1945 they deliberately engaged in cooperative politics, later to be labelled consociationalism (Lijphart 1968), one central feature of which was to share government office.

Second, the other parties represented in parliament seemed not to be fit for government. The third traditional 'camp' (*Lager*) in Austrian politics, the German-national one, carried the burden of its entanglement with the Nazi movement. Initially it was even disqualified for participation in elections (until 1949). When the German nationals had re-established themselves as a parliamentary party, the VdU, it was treated as not being acceptable as a government party, as lacking *Koalitionsfähigkeit* (cf. von Beyme 1985). Although occasionally one of the major parties made an attempt to bring the VdU or its successor, the FPÖ, into the coalitional game, none of the parties was really determined to do so before the 1970s.

The Communist Party lacked parliamentary strength and legitimacy. Only once, in 1956, a coalition between the ÖVP and KPÖ would have been feasible in arithmetical terms (85 of 165 seats). This potential coalition, however, was never considered. The KPÖ's inclusion in the provisional and the first regular government had been mainly due to the Communists' good relations with the Soviets who occupied the eastern part of Austria. After 1947, during the Cold War, the KPÖ was considered 'anti-system' and therefore was not a suitable coalition partner for any of the major parties.

During the 1970s and early 1980s all combinations of parliamentary parties were considered suitable coalitions by the relevant actors. Indeed, they were either actually formed (as the 1983 SPÖ–FPÖ coalition) or would have been formed if the elections would not have resulted in absolute majorities for single parties. With hindsight it can be said that in 1971 and 1975 an SPÖ–FPÖ coalition would have been the most likely outcome, provided that the SPÖ would not have won (in 1971) or lost (in 1975) its absolute majority. In contrast, in 1979 an ÖVP–FPÖ coalition would have emerged under this provision.

The radical change of the party system in recent years, however, has introduced new constraints. Thus, the transformation of the FPÖ since 1986 into a populist protest party with alledgedly unclear boundaries to the extreme right has again considerably reduced its coalition potential. The Greens and the LF are small parties and even in combination they had coalition potential in arithmetical terms only in the 1993–4 period during which no government formation situation emerged. Then their votes could have combined to a majority with those of the SPÖ. This, however, may change in the future. Although the Greens started as a fundamental opposition, nowadays both parties are generally considered to be coalitional and indeed appear interested in governmental office.

Political Agenda Constraints

The immediate post-war political agenda contained two major issues: achieving national sovereignty and economic reconstruction. Austria was occupied for ten years by allied forces. Getting the foreign troops out of the country was *the* major national goal and it tied together the major parties. They agreed that this required speaking with one voice and this, in turn, was seen to require sharing government office. The second goal, economic reconstruction, required the cooperation of farmers, capital, and labour. In parliament, these groups were represented by the ÖVP and SPÖ, respectively. It appeared easier to get each group accepting certain sacrifices as long as its leaders were represented in government and thereby could ensure a fair division of the burdens (Müller 1988*b*).

Two other major issues have pushed and pulled the SPÖ and ÖVP towards 'grand coalition' government in recent years. First, there was the need for budgetary restraint, after large-scale deficit-spending policies of the 1970s and early 1980s. Second, there was a consensus between the traditional political elites that Austria should move closer towards the European Community/ Union when the creation of the Single European Market turned out to severely disadvantage non-EC members. While it is true that some political decisions within the scope of budgetary and integration policies require a two-thirds majority, the rationale for the installment and maintainance of 'grand coalition' government in the 1980s and 1990s is not simply a technical matter, i.e. providing the government with a two-thirds majority. Rather the SPÖ and ÖVP agreed that major policy changes and indeed sometimes highly unpopular policies would need broad party and interest group support which could only be provided by both major parties joining forces (Müller 1988*a*). A government lacking this support would fail to introduce the required reforms because of the anticipated electoral punishment. While the 'grand coalition's' policies since 1987 certainly have not exhausted the reform agenda as defined by the government parties themselves, their electoral punishment has been severe, indeed (see Table 3.8).

According to Table 3.2 the government formation process in postwar Austria was rather straightforward. Only during four (of eighteen)

TABLE 3.2. *Government formation in Austria, 1945–1999*

Coalition	Number of parties in parliament	Number of previous bargaining rounds	Parties involved in the previous bargaining rounds	Number of days required for government formation[a]
SPÖ–ÖVP–KPÖ 1945	(3)	0	—	7
ÖVP–SPÖ–KPÖ 1945	3	0	—	25
ÖVP–SPÖ 1947	3	0	—	0
ÖVP–SPÖ 1949	4	0	—	30
ÖVP–SPÖ 1953	4	1	ÖVP–[SPÖ]–VdU[b]	39
ÖVP–SPÖ 1956	4	0	—	47
ÖVP–SPÖ 1959	3	0	—	67
ÖVP–SPÖ 1963	3	0	—	129
ÖVP 1966	3	1	ÖVP–SPÖ	44
SPÖ 1970	3	1	SPÖ–ÖVP	51
SPÖ 1971	3	0	—	25
SPÖ 1975	3	0	—	23
SPÖ 1979	3	0	—	30
SPÖ–FPÖ 1983[c]	3	2 (parallel)	(1) SPÖ–ÖVP (2) ÖVP–FPÖ	30
SPÖ–ÖVP 1987	4	0	—	59
SPÖ–ÖVP 1990	4	0	—	71
SPÖ–ÖVP 1994	5	0	—	51
SPÖ–ÖVP 1996	5	0	—	86

[a] Time between election day and official 'Date in' (see Table 3.3), except for 1945 (number of days between first round of negotiations and official 'Date in').
[b] The ÖVP aimed at an ÖVP–SPÖ–VdU coalition and negotiated with the VdU; the SPÖ rejected this coalition.
[c] The result of the 1983 coalition negotiations to a large extent was a foregone conclusion. The president had entrusted the SPÖ nominee with the official government formation task. The SPÖ aimed at an coalition with the FPÖ but started negotiations with both the ÖVP and the FPÖ. The negotiations between SPÖ and ÖVP mainly served the propaganda purposes. The SPÖ wanted to demonstrate its readiness for broad consensus. The ÖVP, in turn, did not believe in the SPÖ's claim. Seeing no realistic chance for government participation, it did not want to compromise any of its electoral pledges in the coalition negotiations.

government formations alternative party compositions were explored in bargaining attempts between parties. Moreover, it remains questionable how serious these unconclusive bargaining rounds were. The ÖVP's attempt to enlarge the 'grand coalition' in 1953 by bringing in the VdU can be interpreted as a signalling game *vis-à-vis* the SPÖ, designed to reduce the latter's claims after its success in this year's election.[6] The 1966 coalition negotiations between the ÖVP and SPÖ took place on the basis of an absolute parliamen-

[6] The SPÖ had won more votes than the ÖVP, which, however, remained one seat ahead.

tary majority of the ÖVP. Although negotiations were serious, in retrospect there was little chance for their successful completion (Müller 1999*b*). In 1970 negotiations between the SPÖ and ÖVP broke down as a result of mutually exclusive strategies applied by the two parties. On the one hand, SPÖ leader Kreisky was not keen to form a 'grand coalition' with the ÖVP. Rather he was aiming at an SPÖ minority government (which was eventually formed) for which he had alredy ensured himself the FPÖ's parliamentary support (cf. Fischer 1993: 63–6 and 71–6). On the other hand, the ÖVP tried to exploit the fact that a 'grand coalition' of the SPÖ and ÖVP was the only majority-based government which had not been precluded by electoral precommitments and statements made immediately after the publication of the electoral result. The ÖVP's making large claims played into the hands of Kreisky, who found it easier to reject this broad coalition and to form a minority government.

Finally, also the result of the 1983 coalition negotiations to a large extent was a foregone conclusion. The president had entrusted the SPÖ nominee with the official government formation task. The SPÖ aimed at a coalition with the FPÖ but started negotiations with both the ÖVP and the FPÖ. The negotiations between SPÖ and ÖVP mainly served propaganda purposes. The SPÖ aimed at demonstrating its readiness for broad consensus. The ÖVP, in turn, did not believe this claim of the SPÖ. Seeing no realistic chance for government participation, it did not want to compromise any of its electoral pledges in the coalition negotiations. Both the ÖVP and the FPÖ tried to improve their position vis-à-vis the SPÖ through parallel talks with each other. These were cancelled by the FPÖ, however, once it realized that the SPÖ was serious about forming a government with the FPÖ.

Formation Duration

Leaving aside the exceptional cases of the provisional government in 1945 and the Figl II government in 1947, government formation in Austria required between 23 and 129 days, with an average of 50.4 days (see Table 3.2). With an average of 57.6 days the formation of coalition governments was significantly more time-consuming than that of single-party governments (34.6 days). As one might have expected, the formation of majority-based single-party governments was the easiest task (30.5 days).

The length of coalition negotiations gives some indication about the size of the gap between the parties which needed to be bridged. The quality of this gap, however, differed. In the longest coalition negotiations, those of 1962/3 (more than one-third of a year), the SPÖ and ÖVP disagreed first and foremost about portfolio allocation. In contrast, the longish coalition negotiations of the 1990s centred on policies. Tactical considerations also influenced the duration of coalition negotiations. In 1959 and 1962/3 the parties which had lost seats in the elections were deliberately slow moving in the coalition

TABLE 3.3. *Austrian cabinets since 1945*

Cabinet number	Chancellor	Date in	Formal resignation	Maximum potential duration (in days)[a]	Duration (in days)[b]	Government composition
1	Renner	27 Apr. 1945	20 Dec. 1945	—	237	SPÖ–ÖVP–KPÖ
2	Figl I	20 Dec. 1945	nfr	1,461	700	ÖVP–SPÖ–KPÖ
3	Figl II[c]	20 Nov. 1947	11 Oct. 1949	761	689	ÖVP–SPÖ
4	Figl III	08 Nov. 1949	25 Feb. 1953	1,462	1,202	ÖVP–SPÖ
5	Raab I	02 Apr. 1953	14 May 1956	1,447	1,137	ÖVP–SPÖ
6	Raab II	29 June 1956	12 May 1959	1,441	1,045	ÖVP–SPÖ
7	Raab III[d]	16 July 1959	11 Apr. 1961	1,425	635	ÖVP–SPÖ
8	Gorbach I	11 Apr. 1961	20 Nov. 1962	790	586	ÖVP–SPÖ
9	Gorbach II	27 Mar. 1963	02 Apr. 1964	1,359	335	ÖVP–SPÖ
10	Klaus I	02 Apr. 1964	25 Oct. 1965	987	571	ÖVP–SPÖ
11	Klaus II	19 Apr. 1966	03 Mar. 1970	1,442	1,412	ÖVP
12	Kreisky I	21 Apr. 1970	19 Oct. 1971	1,441	537	SPÖ
13	Kreisky II	04 Nov. 1971	08 Oct. 1975	1,462	1,431	SPÖ
14	Kreisky III	28 Oct. 1975	09 May 1979	1,469	1,286	SPÖ
15	Kreisky IV	05 June 1979	26 Apr. 1983	1,462	1,419	SPÖ
16	Sinowatz	24 May 1983	16 June 1986	1,457	1,119	SPÖ–FPÖ
17	Vranitzky I	16 June 1986	25 Nov. 1986	338	160	SPÖ–FPÖ
18	Vranitzky II	21 Jan. 1987	09 Oct. 1990	1,427	1,355	SPÖ–ÖVP
19	Vranitzky III	17 Dec. 1990	11 Oct. 1994	1,420	1,392	SPÖ–ÖVP
20	Vranitzky IV	29 Nov. 1994	19 Dec. 1995	1,440	383	SPÖ–ÖVP
21	Vranitzky V	12 Mar. 1996	15 Jan. 1997	1,404	309	SPÖ–ÖVP
22	Klima	15 Jan. 1997		1,095		SPÖ–ÖVP

[a] Remainder of the parliamentary term when the government assumes office (i.e. remainder of four years, beginning with the first meeting of a newly elected parliament).
[b] Period from 'date in' until 'formal resignation' or date of general election, whichever comes first.
[c] According to conventional numbering cabinet Figl II does not exist and what is Figl III in Table 3.3 is split into two cabinets (officially Figl II (resignation date 28 Oct. 1952) and III (date in 28 Oct. 1952)).
[d] According to conventional numbering cabinet Raab III resigned 3 Nov. 1960 and was followed by cabinet Raab IV which assumed office at the same day.

negotiations. Eventually the electoral success of their negotiation partners 'faded away' and government formation required less concessions on their part than would have been the norm on the basis of the 1949–56 record.

Coalition Membership

From a coalitional perspective, Austria's post-war history falls into three main parts. During the first two post-war decades all-party or 'grand coalition' governments were in office. The second period, beginning in 1966, was characterized by single-party governments, first of the ÖVP and then the SPÖ. Since 1983 coalition governments have been in office again. Except for the all-party coalition of the immediate post-war period and a short-lived coalition between the SPÖ and FPÖ in the 1980s all governments were either single-party or 'grand coalitions' of the SPÖ and ÖVP.

Table 3.3 gives an overview of all post-1945 Austrian cabinets. Until 1 January 1999, the end date of this project, there have been twenty-two cabinets. They break down in five single-party and seventeen coalition cabinets. All but one (Kreisky I, 1970–1) have controlled a parliamentary majority.

COALITION GOVERNANCE

How to organize coalition governance has been given considerable attention by the Austrian parties. This topic was an important, sometimes the most important issue in coalition negotiations. These have led to sophisticated decision making rules, a wide range of coalitional institutions, and quite elaborated coalition agreements. Table 3.4 provides an overview of the specific rules and mechanisms employed by Austrian coalition governments. It is based on the coalition agreements, archival research, interviews with more than eighty former cabinet ministers and other politicians involved in coalition politics (e.g. parliamentary party group leaders) and the relevant literature.[7]

Coalition Agreements

In the post-war era (1945–99) Austria has experienced eleven coalition governments (until 1 January 1999). With the exception of the provisional government of 1945 and the first regular government assuming office in

---

[7] Secher 1958; Naßmacher 1968; Rudzio 1971; Rauchensteiner 1987; Pelinka 1993; Müller 1988a, 1997.

TABLE 3.4. *Coalition governance in Austria*

(1) Coalition	(2) Coalition agreement	(3) Agreement public	(4) Election rule	(5) Conflict management mechanism	(6) Most common management mechanisms	(7) Management mechanisms for the most serious conflicts	(8) Coalition discipline in legislation	(9) Coalition discipline in other parliamentary behaviour[a]	(10) Freedom of appointment	(11) Policy agreement	(12) Junior ministers	(13) Non-cabinet positions
1945	N	—	N	CoC,CaC	CaC	CoC	1	1/2	Y	0/1	Y	N
1947	N	—	N	CoC,CaC	CaC	CoC	1	1/2	Y	0/1	Y	N
1949	POST	N	Y	CoC,CaC	CaC	CoC	1	1	Y	0/1	Y	Y
1953	POST	N	Y	CoC,CaC	CaC	CoC	1	1	Y	0/1	Y	Y
1956	POST	Y	Y	CoC,CaC	CaC	CoC	1	1	Y	0/1	Y	Y
1959	POST	Y	Y	CoC,CaC	CaC	CoC	1	1	Y	0/1	Y	Y
1963	POST	Y	Y	CoC,IC,CaC	CaC	IC	1	1	Y	0/1	Y	Y
1983	POST	Y	Y	CoC,IC,CaC	CaC	IC	1	1	Y	2	Y	N
1987	POST	Y	Y	CoC,IC,CaC	CaC	IC	1	1	Y	3	Y	N
1990	POST	Y	Y	CoC,IC,CaC	CaC	IC	1	1	Y	3	Y	N
1994	POST	Y	Y	CoC,IC,CaC	CaC	IC	1	1	Y	3	Y	N
1996	POST	Y	Y	CoC,IC,CaC	CaC	IC	2	1	Y	3	Y	N

[a] The coalition agreements do not contain explicit references to other parliamentary behaviour. In coalition practice, however, coalition discipline was a behavioural norm. The column codifies this norm.

November 1945,[8] all coalition governments were based on coalition agreements. Since such documents are worked out only after elections but not after a change in the position of Chancellor, altogether ten coalition agreements were produced. Initially, they were not meant for publication and the coalition agreements of 1949 and 1953 were not published at that time (Schneider 1961). The 1953 agreement, however, was leaked to the press while the respective coalition was in office. Recognizing that it would be impossible to maintain the secrecy of the coalition agreements, political parties have published them since 1956.

While coalition agreements are the most important and general documents of inter-party cooperation, they are not the only ones. Important policy issues and questions of long-term distribution of spoils which had appeared on the political agenda outside the context of post-electoral coalition negotations traditionally have been made the subject of formal party agreements, which also take a written form. Such documents fixed, for instance, the parties' nomination rights for constitutional court judges (Welan 1974), Austria's policy of integration in the EU (in 1989), and a major change in the policy of privatization of the SPÖ–ÖVP coalition (in 1993) (Meth-Cohn and Müller 1994).

Policy Agreement

According to Table 3.5 there are substantial differences between the coalitions regarding the weight given to hammering out a policy programme during the coalition negotiations (Müller 1994a). In particular, there is a striking contrast between the old and new 'grand coalitions', with the SPÖ–FPÖ coalition covering the middle ground. The coalition agreements of the ÖVP–SPÖ 'grand coalitions' (until 1966) hardly dealt with policy questions in a substantive way. Rather specific mechanisms were set up to decide on specific policy questions. Only a few policy decisions were explicitly made during the coalition negotiations, mostly concerning those issues which had caused particular tension in the previous government and may have caused its early termination.

The coalition agreement between the SPÖ and FPÖ in no respect was very detailed and in policy terms by and large contained rather general and noncommital statements. The most important exception from this rule was the

---

[8] In building cabinet Fig. I, the party leaders of the ÖVP and SPÖ had met and agreed on principles of cooperation and a few very general policy guidelines. These, however, were not put in the form of a coalition agreement, probably because the ÖVP, which had won an absolute majority of seats in the preceeding election, did not want to commit itself more than necessary. SPÖ chairman Schärf summarized the results of these negotiations. He then sent his summary to the ÖVP which did not reject it (but cautiously refrained from formally confirming it).

TABLE 3.5. *Size and content of coalition agreements in Austria, 1949–1999*

Coalition	Size[a]	General procedural rules (in %)	Specific procedural rules (in %)	Distribution of offices (in %)	Distribution of competences (in %)	Policies (in %)
ÖVP–SPÖ 1949	1,600	11	44	16	25	5
ÖVP–SPÖ 1953[b]	700	28	33	30	4	4
ÖVP–SPÖ 1956	1,700	41	30	4	24	0
ÖVP–SPÖ 1959[c]	1,200	50	13	26	6	6
ÖVP–SPÖ 1963	4,400	21	27	19	24	9
SPÖ–FPÖ 1983	2,900	7	0	3	0	90
SPÖ–ÖVP 1987	13,900	2	1	1	*	96
SPÖ–ÖVP 1990	23,300	1	0	1	0	98
SPÖ–ÖVP 1994	11,700	6	4	1	0	88
SPÖ–ÖVP 1996	11,200	8	3	1	0	87

[a] Word count 'Word 6.0.1' Macintosh, rounded to full hundreds.
[b] The official document has been supplemented by the list of the government posts. The parties had dealt with this question in the same way as in all other coalition negotiations but did not include the resulting list in their written agreement.
[c] The official document has been supplemented by the 1956 appendix on state secretaries to which shorthand reference is made.

introduction of a new tax on interest income from bank savings. This tax had been a critical issue in the 1983 election campaign, dividing SPÖ and FPÖ. A compromise was hammered out in the coalition negotiations and consequently made part of the coalition agreement.

In contrast, the coalition agreements of the SPÖ and ÖVP since 1987 contain detailed and rather precise policy proposals for many of the policy areas. To provide one example, the SPÖ–FPÖ coalition agreement claimed that the government would apply the 'strictest measures of budgetary restraint', without providing further details (except about the new tax mentioned above). The 1987 SPÖ–ÖVP coalition agreement, in contrast, contained a substantial section on this issue, providing figures for both the goals and means of budgetary policy. How can this difference between the old and new 'grand coalitions' be explained? First, the coalition agreements of the new 'grand coalition' reflect the focus of coalition negotiations which was on policy. Having a detailed government programme was considered useful by both SPÖ and ÖVP which had faced each other for more than twenty years as government and opposition. This was the case in particular, because the return to 'grand coalition' government was intended to imply major policy changes. Second, the negotiators eagerly wanted to avoid the appearance of 'old style party politics', which had been a famous-infamous trade mark of the old 'grand coalition'. In 1986/7 the emerging new 'grand coalition' met a lot of criticism from the media which was based on the expectation that the new 'grand coalition' would match the old one in this respect. A 'rational', policy-based coalition agreement was meant to signal that these gloomy perspectives were wrong. However, the coalition negotiators have been aware that what is hammered out by a few top leaders within a few weeks or months cannot contain unambiguous solutions for all issues which emerge during the reign of a government. Therefore, the recent coalition agreements also contain a substantial procedural part. Indeed, the negotiators were no less careful in framing the procedural rules than in the 1950s and 1960s.

Election Rule

The Austrian parliament (Nationalrat) has a four-year term, which, however, can be cut short. According to the constitution the parliament can dissolve itself or it can be dissolved by the president.[9] Constitutionally, the president is restricted only inasmuch as he can dissolve parliament only once for any one particular reason (Art. 29).[10] However, the president's dissolution right has not been used since 1930.[11] It would constitute a sharp break with established conventions if the president would intervene in such a way.

The norm is rather that parliament dissolves itself and that it does so on the basis of a private member's bill, even if de facto it had been decided within government to go for early elections. Therefore, the regulation of when and under which conditions early elections should be held is a potentially important task for coalition agreements. From 1949 onwards, all coalitions were based on an 'election rule'. The coalition agreements stated that a breakdown of the coalition would automatically lead to a new election (rather than to the formation of a new government in the sitting parliament). Moreover, the parties took care to include a clause in the coalition agreements stating that the next election (regular or early) would be organized and carried out by the government which was established by the present agreement (rather than by an interim government). Indeed eight of the fifteen parliamentary terms in the 1945–95 period were brought to an end before their full length of four years had expired. In all but two cases the parliamentary term was reduced by half a year or a year. Only in 1971 and in 1995 governments went to elections without having reached half-term.

[9] The term of parliament may also be cut short by a failed attempt to dismiss the president by referendum. According to the constitution this automatically leads to the dissolution of the Nationalrat. This, however, has never happened.

[10] The case is complicated, however, by the fact that the constitution does not oblige the president to state his reason when dissolving parliament.

[11] In 1930 the president appointed a government which lacked a parliamentary majority. The chancellor then convinced the president to dissolve parliament before having to face it (Müller, Philipp, and Steininger 1995: 76). This episode resulted in an electoral disaster for the government party. This is probably one of the reasons why presidential dissolution power has not been used again.

Cabinet Decision Rules

According to constitutional practice cabinet decisions are made by the unanimity rule.[12] The unanimity requirement for cabinet decisions, which gives each minister (and hence government party) an absolute veto power, is the ruling interpretation of the constitution, though an alternative interpretation would probably not be unconstitutional (see Pfeifer 1964). To avoid potential problems from conflicting interpretations of cabinet decision making rules, several of the coalition agreements explicitly referred to the unanimity rule. Thus, the cabinet decision making rule is a strong constraint for coalition governance. However, the unanimity rule in cabinet could easily be circumvented by introducing those bills which do not get the cabinet's approval as private member bills in parliament.

Implementation of laws normally does not rest with the cabinet but with individual ministers. Coordination of parties or individual ministers can nevertheless be enforced by introducing an 'accord' clause *(Einvernehmens-Klausel)* in the respective law. This clause then states that the ministers mentioned must agree on the administrative decisions to be taken in the law's implementation (Barfuß 1968). To the chagrin of administrative reformers, coalition governments indeed make frequent use of 'accord' clauses in their legislation in order to guarantee inter-party consensus in the implementation of relevant laws.

Conflict Management Mechanisms

All coalition agreements established a mechanism of coordination and conflict management between the coalition parties. According to the 1949 agreement, three committees were established, the task of which was to coordinate the parties, the party teams in government, and the parliamentary party groups, respectively. Additional mechanisms were introduced to ensure consensus between the Minister of Interior (SPÖ) and his Secretary of State (ÖVP) and to give each coalition party a share in making decisions about the public sector of the economy. In 1953 the number of coalition committees was reduced to one which continued to exist until the end of the old 'grand coalition' in 1966. Although its official name, size, composition, and relevance varied over this period, it is save to say that it was the most important conflict management mechanism, at least until 1964. Among its constant features was the membership of the coalition parties' chairmen which, leaving aside short periods of transition, also occupied the positions of Chancellor and Vice-Chancellor, respectively. Other constant participants were the leaders of the parliamentary groups and the central party secretaries.

---

[12] See Welan and Neisser 1971; Gerlich and Müller 1996; Müller 1997.

The return to coalition government in 1983 after seventeen years of single-party governments also saw the reintroduction of coalition committees. Both the SPÖ–FPÖ and the SPÖ–ÖVP governments established coalition committees. While these committees have been very important conflict management mechanisms, they clearly have not had the relevance of their predecessor in the old 'grand coalition'. In contrast to the coalition committee until 1966, for most of the post-1987 period it has not included the most important politicians, i.e. the party chairmen who also occupy the highest governmental offices (Chancellor and Vice-Chancellor). The 'classic' coalition committee used to make subject matter decisions which then were enforced on the relevant cabinet members. In contrast, coalition committees since 1983 have identified problems and have been making procedural decisons about the further handling of these matters.

Critical decisions have been referred to the weekly meeting of the coalition parties' chairmen since 1983. This is meant by reference to an inner cabinet (IC) in Table 3.5. While it is true that the party chairmen also met privately during the old 'grand coalition' and many decisions were indeed prepared in this way, the decision making process was nevertheless much more collective then. In the old days the party chairmen would report back to their party executives or their respective party's team in the coalition committee before a final decision was taken, which typically would happen in the coalition committee rather than between the party leaders.

All governments have made use of cabinet committees as conflict management mechanisms, i.e. two or more cabinet members were given the task to work out solutions for specific problems. In the post-1987 period this has been quantitatively by far the most important mechanism to find inter-party consensus in substantive matters, in particular if combinations of ministers and parliamentary spokespersons are also counted as 'cabinet' committees.

Legislative Coalition Discipline

Due to Austria's legalistic culture, expressed for instance in Article 18 of the Constitution,[13] policy making to a large extent is law-making. Legislative behaviour is probably even more important for coalition politics in Austria than elsewhere. All coalitions were indeed based on the understanding that there will be coalition discipline in parliamentary votes on legislative proposals. The coalition agreements in various formulations were more or less explicit about this. The variations were partly due to the intention of publishing the agreements. The 1953 agreement, for instance, which was not intended for publication, boldly said: 'The legislative proposals which had been accepted by the government are obligatory for the parliamentary

---

[13] Art. 18 reads: 'The entire public administration shall be based on law.'

parties. Amendments can only be introduced in consultation with and the consent of the relevant cabinet minister.' This and similar formulations in the 1956 and 1959 coalition agreements, of course, did not respect the constitutionally guaranteed free mandate of MPs. Consequently they were criticized as violating the spirit of the constitution and the MPs increasingly perceived such formulations as violating their dignity. The 1963 coalition agreement eventually took this criticism into consideration. Accordingly, the coalition parties 'oblige(d) themselves to recommend their MPs to support these (i.e. government) proposals'. The coalition agreements since 1983 were also worded in a way which avoids the alienation of MPs but leaves no doubt that the parties commit themselves to coalition discipline in parliamentary votes on legislative proposals. In practice, coalition discipline indeed was maintained.

Whether coalition discipline in legislation should apply to all cases was a recurring issue in coalition negotiations between the SPÖ and ÖVP. The ÖVP (which is more likely to find an alternative majority) has been in favour of a loose coalition while the SPÖ has wanted a tight coalition, committing its members to full coalition discipline. In response to the ÖVP's demand the coalition agreements of 1953, 1956 and 1959 mentioned a 'coalition free area', i.e. the possibility of legislation which was not supported by both government parties. The required details were, however, not worked out before 1963. The complicated procedure for law-making in the 'coalition free area' as introduced 1963, however, was never used until the end of 'grand coaltion' government in 1966.[14]

With the return to 'grand coalition' government in 1987, the 'coalition free area' emerged again on the agenda of the coalition negotiators. Although the coalition agreement emphasized that legislative proposals should be worked out jointly by the coalition parties, either in cabinet or in parliament, legislative proposals of individual parties were anticipated. In these cases the coalition agreement obliged the leaders of the parliamentary parties to search for

---

[14] According to the 1963 coalition agreement the parties should as a rule search for consensus for their legislative proposals in cabinet. If these attempts came to nothing, the issue would be referred to the coalition committee. If three months expired without reaching a consensus in the coalition committee, the parties would be free to introduce their proposals in parliament. These proposals would constitute the basis for an attempt to reach consensus between the parliamentary groups of the government parties. If five months expired without reaching a consensus between them, the legislative proposals would be free for parliamentary treatment in committees and eventually floor voting. However, the coalition agreement granted the losing party the right to ask for a referendum on the respective issue. If the proposal for a referendum was not accepted by the winning party, the losing one was granted the right to demand an early election. Moreover the coalition agreement defined a number of policies which were exempted from this procedure and in any case required the consensus of the government parties (conscience issues, the introduction of financial burdens for citizens, additional expenditures, changes in the present fiscal year's budget, the selling-off of state property).

consensus. Both leaders were granted veto right. In the case of a veto or if the proposal would trigger substantial financial costs, the governing parties would not outvote each other. In practice, the formal veto was rarely employed. The coalition parties made clear at an early stage that they would veto a specific proposal and the respective other party then normally refrained from introducing a bill to parliament. When they occasionally did, it was to demonstrate their respective policy preferences; however, these bills were never subject to a parliamentary reading.

In 1994 the mutual veto power of the coalition parties was abolished. The coalition agreement rather outlined an obligatory procedure of mutual consultation and mechanisms of consensus building in the case of single-party proposals. Accordingly the coalition parties will inform each other before introducing bills to parliament. An attempt to arrive at a joint proposal of both parties will precede the formal introduction of any legislative proposal. If no consensus can be reached before the formal introduction of a proposal, a two-party committee is established immediately after first reading in parliament, in order to achieve consensus. Some politicians deeply involved in coalition politics say that only the wording of the coalition agreement (but not its content) had been changed. Others claim that it makes a difference for issues which are not very politicized. Accordingly, the first reading exposes the party positions to a greater extent to public scrutiny than the previous procedure. This, in turn, makes parties more willing to compromise if they find their issue position electorally disadvantageous.

Furthermore the 'coalition free area', one of the ÖVP's prestige projects in the 1995/6 coalition negotiations, was enlarged, explicitly exempting a number of issues from coalition discipline. A closer look at these issues reveals, however, that they either lack a majority to change the status quo or require a two-thirds majority (which is impossible without the SPÖ and extremely unlikely without both government parties supporting it). Thus the enlargement of the 'coalition free area' in 1996 has largely been a symbolic response to the needs of the ÖVP.

Coalition Discipline in Non-Legislative Parliamentary Behaviour

The coalition agreements have been silent concerning other parliamentary behaviour than voting on legislative proposals. The practice under the various 'grand coalition' governments was one of *Bereichsopposition*, i.e. the SPÖ assumed a kind of opposition position vis-à-vis the ministers of the ÖVP and vice versa.[15] Ministers of the coalition partner were asked critical questions (while party comrades in the government were asked questions that allowed them to announce good news). In the 1950s and 1980s a few investigation

---

[15] See Engelmann 1966; Leclaire 1966; Gerlich 1973; Müller 1993.

committees were established by one of the government parties joining forces with the opposition to examine scandals which emerged in one-party dominions of either of the coalition parties (Müller 1993). However, *Bereichsopposition* has been a contained form of opposition. Not only would it have been inconceivable to practice sanctioned control, i.e. to remove a minister by a vote of no confidence in one of the government parties joining forces with the opposition. The government parties have also cooperated closely in determining the parliamentary agenda and the use of the more powerful parliamentary instruments such as investigation committees. Exceptions to this rule, as mentioned above, constituted coalitional crises. In the old 'grand coalition' (1945–66) each of the governing parties even practised some form of control over parliamentary questions in order to avoid problems with the coalition partner because of too critical questioning of its cabinet members. Since 1987 the government parties' MPs are no longer subject to systematic control of their parliamentary questions, however, the parliamentary party group leaders keep them at bay so that they cannot rock the coalition boat.

In contrast to 'grand coalition' governments, the SPÖ–FPÖ government faced a strong opposition. It therefore tried to maintain a uniform front *vis-à-vis* parliament and by and large has practised a rather contained form of *Bereichsopposition*.

Freedom of Appointments

All coalitions were based on the principle that the coalition parties have freedom of appointment for the ministerial and junior ministerial posts allocated to them. Vice-Chancellor Pittermann once referred to this principle as the 'chimpanzee principle', meaning that if one party choses a chimpanzee as minister this must be accepted by its coalition partner. This principle was violated only once. In the 1990 coalition negotiations the SPÖ responded to the ÖVP's rejection of a candidate for the minister of justice (who already had been accepted as an independent candidate in the negotiations) by rejecting its former general secretary as a secretary of state. During the 1995 electoral campaign individual ÖVP politicians claimed that the SPÖ would need to replace several of its ministers as a precondition for a new coalition with the ÖVP, but later the ÖVP made clear that the principle of mutual non-interference was still upheld.

Junior Ministers

Junior ministers (*Staatssekretäre*) have been an important feature of Austrian coalitions. In the provisional government of 1945 they were used to grant all parties representation in each government department (except the Ministry of Finance). In the old 'grand coalition' this principle was applied to several of the key departments (Foreign, Interior, Defence, Trade). The recent 'grand coalition' until 1995 also subscribed to this policy, though (given its unpopularity) in a more restricted way. The general idea behind agreeing on those junior ministerships in the coalition negotiations is to establish a permanent link between the respective government department and the party who is not in charge of it. This should guarantee mutual information in good time and thereby smooth the work of the coalition. In practice, some secretaries of state have confined themselves to a monitoring function on behalf of their party while others have tended to become the ambassadors of their department. It was the ÖVP secretary of state in the finance department in the 1987–95 period, who had the greatest policy impact.

Enforcement Mechanisms

All coalition agreements were set up as contracts between the political parties which formed the coalitions. They were signed on behalf of their parties by the party chairmen and the other high-ranking party leaders who had participated in the coalition negotiations. These leaders, in turn, had been officially nominated coalition negotiators by their respective party executives. Moreover, the leading party bodies had received reports during the negotiations and had formally accepted the coalition agreement. The SPÖ had even summoned twice a party congress to ratify the coalition the party leaders wanted to go into.[16] So it was indeed agreements between the parties. Changes in the party leadership normally did not affect the parties' recognition of the validity of the coalition agreement. The exception to this rule was the SPÖ's termination of the coalition with the FPÖ in 1986 as a response to the election of Jörg Haider to party leadership. The SPÖ claimed that this was not a normal change in personnel but one which changed the FPÖ so fundamentally that it no longer could be considered the same party. The thorough transformation of the FPÖ since then (Luther 1997) supports this claim.[17]

---

[16] These cases were the party's participation in the first regular government in 1945 and the forming of the coalition with the FPÖ in 1983.

[17] It was only once that the validity of the coalition agreement was challenged after a 'normal' leadership change in one of the coalition parties. This was when Alfons Gorbach was replaced as Federal Chancellor by Josef Klaus in 1964. Both the new ÖVP Party chairman Josef Klaus and the general secretary Hermann Withalm deliberately had not signed the 1963 coalition agreement (*ÖVP-Pressedienst*, 29 Mar. 1963). They had disagreed with Gorbach over the content of the coalition agreement, considering him too compliant vis-à-vis the Social Democrats. So the SPÖ raised this issue when Klaus assumed the office of Federal Chancellor. Eventually, Klaus and Withalm gave in and signed the existing coalition agreement. (See SPÖ, *Parteivertretung*, 5 Sept. 1963; 25 Feb. 1964; 3 Mar. 1964; SPÖ, *Parteitagsbericht* 1965, p. 12. The historic account of Rauchensteiner (1987: 452) who without citing specific sources claims that Klaus had signed the coalition agreement already in 1963 in behalf of Withalm is obviously wrong.)

In practice the coalition agreements are interpreted first and foremost by those individual politicians who serve in governmental, parliamentary, or party office. If conflicting interpretations arise between the coalition parties, this interpretation is made by the coalition committee or the two party chairmen. In addition to this, in the 1987–95 period the minister of finance (SPÖ) and his secretary of state (ÖVP) were of central importance for all questions with financial implications. If the government parties do not agree on the interpretation of the coalition agreement, however, the question is which means they have available to enforce their respective interpretation on their coalition partner. In the 1960s academics had raised the question of whether coalition agreements can be legally enforced by an appeal to the judicial system. However, political parties had agreed then and still do so that coalition contracts are gentlemen's agreements and the only way to enforce them is a political one (Marcic 1966).

In the old days of exclusively procedure-based coalition agreements, the only possible violation was one of the rules of the game. The coalition agreements were unambiguous and their interpretation could be straightforward. The largely policy-based coalition agreements of the 1980s and 1990s naturally leave more room for interpretation and hence for potential disagreement. It is simply not possible (nor wise) to map out government policies in such detail that this cannot happen. Moreover, the coalition agreements' prescribed policies and rules of the game may constitute conflicting reference points in specific situations. While one party may demand specific legislation on the basis of the coalition agreement's policy content, the other party may try to block this by not agreeing on a joint legislative proposal but insisting on (and exploiting) the rule of coalition discipline in the legislative arena.

If a decision rests within ministerial discretion (uncontained by specific accord clauses) the party which occupies this department may decide to implement its interpretation of the coalition agreement (cf. Laver and Shepsle 1996). If the decision to be taken rests with the cabinet, however, there is an in-built advantage for the status quo because of the unanimity requirement. Of course, the party losing in cabinet can still try to bypass the cabinet and to find a parliamentary majority for its proposal, reneging parliamentary coalition discipline. The other party, in turn, may threaten to respond, either by behaving in the same way when it comes to other issues or by terminating the coalition or at least the cabinet. In the end it boils down to the question of whether a party is willing to risk early elections or even the termination of the coalition. Within the individual parties, major decisions such as going for early elections or to compromise a major electoral pledge require the consent of party executive bodies.

In practice, Austrian government coalitions have obeyed the coalition agreements very closely. Manifest violations can hardly be identifed. An example in the old 'grand coalition' concerned the role of the secretaries of state. The coalition agreements had extended their role considerably beyond that of being a servant of the minister, as prescribed by the constitution. While this was respected by the majority of ministers, a few of them did not.[18] A more spectacular conflict in the old 'grand coalition' was the 'Habsburg crisis' in 1963, when the SPÖ joined forces with the FPÖ. They outvoted the ÖVP in two parliamentary resolutions in order to prevent the return of the last emperor's son, Otto Habsburg, to Austria. However, while the SPÖ's behaviour certainly violated the spirit of the coalition agreement (and indeed was seen so by the relevant SPÖ politicians), it did not violate its actual content (which did not say a word on non-legislative parliamentary behaviour). The same can be said for a few cases in the new 'grand coalition', including the lifting of the parliamentary immunity of the SPÖ's former chairman Sinowatz (which actually was pre-empted by his resignation from parliament), the establishment of two investigation committees in the 1986–90 parliament, and the election of the audit office's president in 1992 by an ÖVP–FPÖ voting coalition in parliament. In these cases one of the coalition parties was outvoted by the other one joining forces with the opposition.

More important, however, are anticipated violations of the coalition discipline. In these cases the party in the losing position anticipates the break of 'coalition discipline' by its coalition partner and gives in. Rather than being defeated in a parliamentary showdown it votes together with its coalition partner for a proposal which it would never have accepted if the coalition partner would have been willing to strictly observe the coalition agreement. The termination of the SPÖ–FPÖ coalition in 1986 (by the SPÖ), the termination of the Vranitzky IV cabinet in 1995 (by the ÖVP), and the lifting of coalition discipline for legislative voting in an extra meeting of parliament after the 1995 cabinet termination (on the ÖVP's pressure) are the most prominent examples. Though these are important cases and there are more of them, they are clearly exceptions. The general pattern is that parties obey the coalition agreement.

Finally, it is worth asking the question why political parties generally obey the coalition agreements (see Shepsle 1996: 229–31). There is no external enforcement mechanism and normally a decision on any specific issue is also not a pure coordination game which gives both parties the same incentive to obey the coalition agreement. Perhaps the answer is that the parties know that politics is not a one-shot game and that they are concerned about their reputation. It is as important *vis-à-vis* the actual coalition partner as well as *vis-à-vis* potential coalition partners to maintain credibility. If the coalition

---

[18] The behaviour of the Minister of Interior, Franz Olah, the SPÖ's *enfant terrible*, was notorious (also) in this respect. It was matched by the behaviour of the ÖVP's Minister of Defence, Georg Prader. Both did their best to prevent the secretaries of state from seeing important departmental papers. They even issued orders to their secretaries of state that they were not allowed to visit military and police units, respectively.

agreement is not observed, this also may have negative spillover effects in other arenas, in particular the corporatist one. More research is needed to provide a full explanation of this aspect of Austrian coalition politics.

PORTFOLIO ALLOCATION

The mass for manoeuvre in coalition negotiations consists of ministerial posts, secretary of state posts and competences, which, in turn, may include considerable appointment power for jobs in the civil service or public sector. In the coalition negotiations a few conventions and patterns got established which are by and large unchallenged. First, the position of Chancellor goes to the government party with the larger number of parliamentary seats. Second, the second government party nominates the Vice-Chancellor. Third, the positions of the Minister of Finance, *the* major ministerial post, is tied to the Chancellorship, i.e. it goes to the strongest party in government. This convention was not even challenged when the margin between the government parties was very small.[19] Fourth, the distribution of ministerial posts is roughly proportional to the parliamentary strengths of the coalition parties. To some extent secretary of state posts and competences are used to balance the division of ministerial office spoils. If a coalition is maintained after an election, changes in the parliamentary strength of parties are taken into account. Fifth, each party gets those departments which correspond most closely to its constituency (cf. Budge and Keman 1991). Thus, whenever the respective parties are represented in government, the Social Democrats get Social Affairs and Transportation (including the railways and postal services) and the ÖVP gets Agriculture and Trade. Sixth, there is a tradition to avoid one-party monopolies in broad branches of government. Thus, because of historical reasons (the civil war in 1934), the old 'grand coalition' divided the responsibility for the armed forces between SPÖ (Interior) and ÖVP (Defence). The new 'grand coalition' maintained this pattern and applied it also to the two educational departments.

Portfolio allocation always has been an important and occasionally even the most conflictual issue in coalition negotiations. The longest ever coalition negotiations for instance, those of 1962/3, took more than four months mainly because of the ÖVP and SPÖ's battle over the Foreign Ministry. In contrast, in recent years negotiations over portfolio allocation has been decided in a few meetings of the negotiation teams. However, several of them lasted for hours and hours and were not completed before the early hours of

[19] When ÖVP chairman Julius Raab, sick of the financial demands of SPÖ ministers, offered the Finance Ministry to the SPÖ in the 1959 coalition negotiations, this caused an outcry in his own party. Raab was forced to withdraw his offer.

the morning. All this can be read as indirect support for the portfolio allocation approach of Laver and Shepsle (1996) and indeed it contains a kernel of truth (Müller 1994*b*). While it is true that the formal cabinet decision rules and the coalition governance mechanisms as described above, substantially constrain ministerial discretion, holding a portfolio is still is a major advantage in policy making. This is particularly true in terms of agenda control: it is very difficult to bypass a minister with an initiative which falls in his or her domain. And despite all instruments of mutual control a minister is in a privileged position to influence policies for which he or she is formally responsible. Thus, the struggle over portfolio allocation is clearly related to the coalition parties' policy making capacity. Of course, parties also try hard to win minister posts because they value office as such. Several of the party representatives in the negotiators will be appointed to cabinet after their successful completion and they want a suitable portfolio. Finally, the leaders of the parties have a strong additional incentive to work towards a maximization of portfolios: their desire to remain party leaders (cf. Luebbert 1986). Their popularity within their own party also depends on their ability to deliver offices.

Table 3.6 contains all cabinet ministers and those junior ministers (*Staatssekretäre*) who came from a different party than the minister. Major changes in the departmental structure have been indicated in Table 3.6. Generally the new departments which were created during the period under investigation have been located next to the ones which provided the bulk of competences and civil servants for the new ones. Most of the new departments are not considered to be as important as the traditional ones. Table 3.6 also shows that junior ministers have been used as instruments of mutual control and coordination, in particular during the second half of the old grand coalition.

Non-cabinet Positions

In the first period of coalition governments (until 1966) the parties agreed on and were explicit about the distribution of non-cabinet positions in their written agreements. In 1945 and 1949 the ÖVP and SPÖ included even subnational government positions (in the *Länder* and in local communities with more than 10,000 inhabitants) in their coalition agreement at the national level.

In the Austrian governmental system the 'spoils system' is restricted to genuinely political positions, i.e. those of ministers and secretaries of state. Civil servants remain in their posts, regardless of whatever cabinet is in office. However, party affiliation has been a major criterion in recruiting and promoting civil servants. Since several departments remained under the control of the same party for decades, the accumulated appointments have led to the

TABLE 3.6. Distribution of cabinet and junior ministerships in Austrian coalitions

Cabinet number	Cabinet	(1) Chancellor	(2) Vice-Chancellor[a]	(3) Finance	(4) Foreign	(5) Interior	(6) Defence	(7) Justice	(8) Social Affairs[b]	(9) Health Environment	(10) Health and Consumer Protection	(11) Environment (Youth, Family)[c]	(12) Family and Consumer Protection
1	Renner	S,v/v,v	S,V,K	I(V)	—	K,s,v,/v	—	I,s,v,k	S,v,k	—	—	—	—
2	Figl I	V	S	I(V)	V	S,v	—	I(S)	S	—	—	—	—
3	Figl II	V	S	I(V)	V	S,v	—	I(S)	S	—	—	—	—
4	Figl III	V	S	I(V)/V	V	S,v	—	S/I(S)	S	—	—	—	—
5	Raab I	V	S	V	V,s	S,v	V,s	I(S)	S	—	—	—	—
6	Raab II	V	S	V	V,s	S,v	V,s	S	S	—	—	—	—
7	Raab III	V	S	V	S,v	S,v	V,s	S	S	—	—	—	—
8	Gorbach I	V	S	V	S,v	S,v	V,s	S,v	S	—	—	—	—
9	Gorbach II	V	S	V	S,v	S,v	V,s	S,v	S	—	—	—	—
10	Klaus I	V	S	V	S,v	S,v	V,s	S,v	S	—	—	—	—
16	Sinowatz	S	F*	S,f	S	S	F	F	S	s	—	—	—
17	Vranitzky I	S	F*	S,f	S	S	F	F	S	s	s	—	s
18	Vranitzky II	S	V*	S,v	V,*/	S	V	I	S	—	—	V	s
19	Vranitzky III	S	V*	S,v	S	S	V	I	S	—	s	V	—
20	Vranitzky IV	S,v	V*	S,v/	V,/*	S	V	I	S	—	s	V	—
21	Vranitzky V	S	V*	S	V*	S	V	I	S	—	—	V	—
22	Klima	S	V*	S	V*	S	V	I	S	—	—	V	—

Austria

Cabinet number	Cabinet	(13) Trade and Commerce	(14) Construction	(15) Economic Planning	(16) Transport[d]	(17) Education[e]	(18) Science, Research[f]	(19) Agriculture	(20) Food	(21) Electrification[g]	(22) Women (and Consumer Protection)[h]	(23) Without portfolio[i]
1	Renner	V,s,k	V,s,k	IV,/s,/k	—	K,v,s	—	V,s,k	S,k,v	—	—	—
2	Figl I	V	—	V,s	S	V	—	V	S	K	—	V
3	Figl II	V	—	V,s	S	V	—	V	S	S	—	V
4	Figl III	V	—	—	S	V	—	V	—	—	—	—
5	Raab I	V,s	—	—	S	V	—	V	—	—	—	—
6	Raab II	V,s	—	—	S	V	—	V	—	—	—	—
7	Raab III	V,s	—	—	S	V	—	V	—	—	—	—
8	Gorbach I	V,s	—	—	S	V	—	V	—	—	—	—
9	Gorbach II	V,s	—	—	S	V	—	V	—	—	—	—
10	Klaus I	V,s	—	—	S	V	—	V	—	—	—	—
16	Sinowatz	F*,s	S	—	S	S	S	S,f	—	—	—	/S
17	Vranitzky I	F*,s	S	—	S	S	S	S,f	—	—	—	—
18	Vranitzky II	V	—	—	S	S	V	V	—	—	—	—
19	Vranitzky III	V	—	—	S	S	V,/*	V	—	—	S	S,V,/*
20	Vranitzky IV	V,/*	—	—	S,v	V,/*	S	V	—	—	S	V,*/
21	Vranitzky V	V	—	—	—	V	S	V	—	—	S	—
22	Klima	V	—	—	—	V	S	V	—	—	S	—

* Vice-Chancellor who also was a cabinet minister. The second * indicate the specific department held by the Vice-Chancellor.
I = Independent
I(S) = Independent, nominated by the SPÖ

[a] Vice-Chancellor Pittermann (S) had departmental responsibility for the nationalized industries in the 1959–66 period. Nationalized industries belonged to the domain of the Federal Chancellory. Vice-Chancellor Riegler (V) in the 1989–91 period also had departmental responsibility for administrative reform and federalism within the Federal Chancellory.
[b] Including Health until 1970 (cabinet 12, Kreisky I) and since 1997 (cabinet 22, Klima).
[c] In cabinet no. 20 Environment only.
[d] Including Nationalized Industries in cabinets nos. 4 and 5. The department was merged with the Science Department (dept. 18) in 1996.
[e] Including Science and Research (dept. 18) until 1970 (cabinets 1–11), Sports until 1991 (cabinets 1–18) and Arts until 1994 (cabinets 1–19).
[f] Including Arts since 1991 (cabinets 19ff.) and Transport (dept. 16) since 1996 (cabinet 21).
[g] The department was created in order to give the sole Communist minister a not too important task.
[h] Technically Women's Affairs is not a department but a relatively small office within the Federal Chancellory and in this respect not different to the ministers listed under 23. In 1997 (cabinet 22, Klima) Consumer Protection was given to the Women's minister as a 'real' competence (including the division of a ministry).
[i] Ministers in the Federal Chancellory whose main task was the coordination between the coalition partners.

creation of one-party dominions, e.g. in the Departments of Social Affairs (SPÖ) and Agriculture (ÖVP) (Secher 1958: 796–808; Steiner 1972: 383–97; Dreijmanis 1982: 252–3; Müller 1989). Ministers are free, however, to appoint a few personal secretaries to the departments which they control. This practice has become more important since 1966. Very often the ministers' secretaries are recruited from the respective department's permanent staff and assume leading civil service positions once they leave the ministerial cabinets. This policy has long-term effects on the political affiliation of the higher echelons of the civil service (Müller, Philipp, and Steininger 1996). Ministerial appointment power is limited, however. Top civil servant appointments require a unanimous cabinet decision and the formal appointment through the president. In practice, the parties have largely followed a policy of mutual non-interference in departmental appointments, but have been careful to maintain some balance in key positions, such as important ambassador posts.

In all coalition agreements of the 1949–66 period the management positions in the nationalized sector figured prominently. The established pattern was to divide the positions evenly and to grant one party the head of the *Aufsichtsrat* and the other party the head of the *Vorstand* in any particular firm.[20] This *Proporz* was even largely maintained during the period of single-party governments (Dobler 1983) and got officially abolished only after the financial breakdown of most of the nationalized industries in the mid-1980s (Meth-Cohn and Müller 1994). The coalition agreements since the 1980s have not contained any reference to the division of spoils at the non-cabinet level. However, the parties have maintained a strong influence to fill important public sector positions with their adherents and occasionally have engaged in public fights over positions such as the president of the largest commercial bank or the president of the central bank (Müller, Philipp, and Steininger 1996). In most cases, however, the government parties were able to agree about important appointments in private negotiations. Some of these resulted in unpublished side letters to the post-1987 coalition agreements.

COALITION TERMINATION

Leaving out the provisional government of 1945, the average cabinet duration has been 2.4 years (885 days) (Figl I to Vranizky V). Single-party cabinets on average have lasted much longer (1217 days) than coalition cabinets (774 days). Single-party cabinets have exhausted 84 per cent of their potential duration while coalition cabinets have exhausted a mere 63 per cent

---

[20] The *Aufsichtsrat* represents the firm owners and supervises the *Vorstand* which is in charge of the operative management decisions.

(unweighted averages). These differences are substantially reduced, however, if governments rather than cabinets are made the unit of investigation (again 1,217 days and 84% for single-party governments, but 1,028 days and 76% for coalition governments). The most durable type of government, however, was single-party majority governments/cabinets, which have an average duration of 1,387 days and have exhausted 95 per cent of their potential duration (see Table 3.3). Compared to coalition cabinets and governments in most other West European countries, however, the Austrian ones have been among the most stable.

Table 3.7 provides an overview of the causes of cabinet termination. The vast majority of cabinets have been terminated by parliamentary elections, seven regular and nine early ones. Leaving aside the first two elections (1945 and 1949) and the Kreisky II cabinet, the termination of a cabinet by regular elections tends to indicate its relative unpopularity: nothing was to be gained from early elections (cabinets 11, 15, 18, 19). In contrast, early elections under single-party governments (Kreisky I and III) were strategically timed and indeed resulted in a strengthening of the government. Under coalition governments early elections normally were a means to overcome a deadlock over policy issues (cabinets 4, 5, 6, 10, 20). Of course, the individual coalition parties considered their electoral prospects before they decided to go for early elections. Conflicts between coalition parties typically have been policy conflicts. The only exception is the termination of the SPÖ–FPÖ coalition. In this case no specific policy issues were at stake. Rather cabinet termination was the SPÖ's and in particular Chancellor Vranitzky's response to a leadership change in the FPÖ (which is coded in column 7). When the FPÖ replaced Vice-Chancellor Norbert Steger as party chairman by Jörg Haider, the SPÖ interpreted this not as a normal change in party leadership (which is an internal matter of each of the coalition parties and has no direct impact on coalition politics). In addition to this case, intra-party events were relevant in three further cabinet terminations (cabinets 4, 7, 9) and they were the only reason for two of them (cabinets 7, 9). In all these cases the Chancellor was sacked by his own party, the ÖVP, or resigned to pre-empt such a move of his party (Raab). Major external events account for only two cases of cabinet termination. The withdrawal (or exclusion) of the Communists from government, which brought to an end the cabinet Figl I, resulted from the beginning of the Cold War and related domestic policy decisions (participation in the Marshall Plan, currency reform). The Sinowatz cabinet was terminated by the voluntary resignation of the Chancellor, following his party's electoral disaster in the 1996 presidential election. This election had clearly indicated that the SPÖ had lost its plurality in the electorate. Sinowatz's resignation was well-timed and gave way to the inauguration of a much more popular Chancellor, Franz Vranitzky, who indeed helped the SPÖ to regain its plurality in the electorate until the upcoming parliamentary election. The policy

TABLE 3.7. *Cabinet termination in Austria, 1945–1999*

Cabinet number	Cabinet	Mechanisms of cabinet termination			
		Technical		Discretionary	
		(1) Regular parliamentary election	(2) Other constitutional reason	(4) Early parliamentary election	(7) Conflict between coalition parties
					Policy conflict / Personnel conflict
1	Renner	(X)			
2	Figl I				X
3	Figl II	X			
4	Figl III			X	X
5	Raab I			X	X
6	Raab II			X	X
7	Raab III				
8	Gorbach I			X	
9	Gorbach II				
10	Klaus I			X	X
11	Klaus II	X			
12	Kreisky I			X	
13	Kreisky II	X			
14	Kreisky III			X	
15	Kreisky IV	X			
16	Sinowatz		X		
17	Vranitzky I			X	X
18	Vranitzky II	X			
19	Vranitzky III	X			
20	Vranitzky IV			X	X
21	Vranitzy V		X		

	Terminal events				Policy area(s)	Comments
(8) Intra-party conflict in coalition party or parties	(9) Elections (non-parliamentary)	(10) Popular opinion shocks	(11) International or national security event	(12) Economic event		
						First regular election
		X	X		3,4	Communists leave government over currency reform and Marshall Plan – beginning of Cold War.
						Regular election
					3	Budget
						Nationalization
						Several issues, including privatization, social insurance, housing
V,L						Half-enforced resignation of Raab because of party strategy *vis-à-vis* coalition partner
						Consensual early elections
V,L						Gorbach lost confidence vote in party execututve
					3	Budget
						Regular election
						SPÖ attempt at winning absolute majority
						Strategic timing of election
						Strategic timing of election
						Regular election
	X		X			Voluntary resignation of the Chancellor after defeat of SPÖ in presidential election
F,LNL						Change in FPÖ leadership
						Regular election
						Regular election
					3	Budget
						Voluntary retirement of the Chancellor

areas which caused coalition conflict and subsequent cabinet termination all belong to the socio-economic domain, which has been identified as the major policy dimension above.

GOVERNMENT PARTICIPATION AND ELECTORAL PERFORMANCE

Looking at the whole post-war period, government participation in electoral terms was more a liability than an asset. According to Table 3.8, government parties collectively lost 1.7 per cent of their votes in each election. There are relevant differences between the individiual parties. The ÖVP lost considerably more than the SPÖ, the KPÖ almost maintained its strength, and the FPÖ even substantially increased its vote after having held governmental office. This requires qualification, however. The KPÖ did not face the electorate as a government party, having retreated from office two years before the 1949 election. Similarly, the FPÖ was no longer considered a government party when the 1986 elections were held. The SPÖ had cancelled the coalition with the FPÖ over a change in the FPÖ's leadership and had initiated early elections. When these elections were held, the FPÖ was still represented in the government by a team headed by its previous chairman. At the same time, however, the party under its new leader, Jörg Haider, had assumed the role of a populist opposition party. It was judged by the voters not on the basis of its government record but on the grounds of its new role in Austrian politics (Plasser and Ulram 1995).

The finding that government office is an electoral liability also needs qualification in terms of its time dimension. Leaving out the 1949 election, which was hardly more than the return to 'normality' after the lifting of the post-war voting right limitations,[21] it turns out that government parties increased their share of votes at an average of 1.7 per cent in each election in the 1953–66 period. In sharp contrast to the electoral performance of the old 'grand coalition', the new 'grand coalition' has suffered an average loss of 4.7 per cent in each election (1990–5). The single-party governments which were in office between the two periods of 'grand coalition' government cover the middle ground with an average loss of 0.9 per cent. Clearly, governmental office has become an electoral liability over time, in particular with the drastic decline of party loyalties since the 1970s (Plasser, Ulram, and Grausgruber 1992).

---

[21] In 1945 competition was limited to three parties by the Allied occupation. The 'third camp', which in the 1930s largely was absorbed by the Nazi Party, was not allowed to run and more than 500,000 former Nazis were not allowed to vote (disfranchised). In 1949 the 'third camp' contested the election successfully.

TABLE 3.8. *Electoral costs/benefits of government parties in Austria, 1945–1999*
(in % of votes)

Government	In office at time of election	Election year	SPÖ	ÖVP	KPÖ	FPÖ	Government
ÖVP–SPÖ–KPÖ 1945–7	No	1949	−5.9	−5.8	−0.3	—	−12.0
ÖVP–SPÖ 1947–9	Yes	1949	−5.9	−5.8	—	—	−11.7
ÖVP–SPÖ 1949–53	Yes	1953	+3.8	−2.7	—	—	+1.1
ÖVP–SPÖ 1953–6	Yes	1956	+1.0	+4.7	—	—	+5.7
ÖVP–SPÖ 1956–9	Yes	1959	+1.8	−1.8	—	—	±0
ÖVP–SPÖ 1959–63	Yes	1962	−0.8	+1.2	—	—	+0.4
ÖVP–SPÖ 1963–6	Yes	1966	−1.4	+2.9	—	—	+1.5
ÖVP 1966–70	Yes	1970	—	−3.6	—	—	−3.6
SPÖ 1970–1	Yes	1971	+1.6		—	—	+1.6
SPÖ 1971–5	Yes	1975	+0.4		—	—	+0.4
SPÖ 1975–9	Yes	1979	+0.6		—	—	+0.6
SPÖ 1979–83	Yes	1983	−3.3		—	—	−3.3
SPÖ–FPÖ 1983–6	Yes	1986	−4.6		—	+4.8	+0.2
SPÖ–ÖVP 1987–90	Yes	1990	−0.3	−9.2	—	—	−10.1
SPÖ–ÖVP 1990–4	Yes	1994	−7.9	−4.4	—	—	−12.3
SPÖ–ÖVP 1994–5	Yes	1995	+3.2	+0.6	—	—	+3.8
MEANS			−0.8	−1.8	−0.3	+4.8	−1.7

Coalition governments with their inherent internal conflicts and compromises appear particularly vulnerable.

CONCLUSION

Stability has been the hallmark of government politics in post-war Austria. Except for the all-party coalition of the immediate post-war period and a short-lived (by Austrian standards) coalition between the SPÖ and FPÖ in the 1980s, all governments were either single-party or 'grand coalitions' of the SPÖ and ÖVP. Moreover the government formation process was also straightforward, with alternative party compositions being hardly explored in bargaining attempts in government formation situations. Institutional constraints, party system constraints, and constraints resulting from the political agenda account for this stability and the predominance of 'grand coalition' governments in particular.

It would be wrong, however, to underrate the dynamics of party competition. Precisely to tame these dynamics tight coalitions have been designed. Tight coalitions mean sophisticated decision making rules, a wide range of coalitional institutions, quite elaborated coalition agreements, and an encompassing understanding of the division of spoils far beyond the allocation of government portfolios. However, over time tight coalitions have become more and more unpopular among the parties' rank and file, MPs, and in the media and, since the 1980s, also in the electorate. In 1966 single-party governments had emerged as a solution (lasting until 1983). The new 'grand coalition', inaugurated in 1987, faces the same problem as its historic predecessor. However, this time there is no chance for replacing it by single-party government. Rather new forms of coalitions constitute the alternative, in particular coalitions between the ÖVP and FPÖ, on the one hand, and the SPÖ, LF, and Greens, on the other. If these alternatives indeed will be formed, coalitions are likely to turn out both less tight and less stable than the classic 'grand coalition' type.

REFERENCES

Axelrod, Robert (1970). *Conflict of Interest*. Chicago: Markham.
Barfuß, Walter (1968). *Ressortzuständigkeit und Vollzugsklausel*.Vienna: Springer.
Bergman, Torbjörn (1993). 'Formation Rules and Minority Governments'. *European Journal of Political Research*, 23: 55–66.
Budge, Ian and Keman, Hans (1991). *Parties and Democracy*. Oxford: Oxford University Press.
Campbell, David (1992). 'Die Dynamik der politischen Links-rechts-Schwingungen in Österreich'. *Österreichische Zeitschrift für Politikwissenschaft*, 21: 165–79.
Dobler, Helmut (1983). 'Der persistente Proporz: Parteien und verstaatlichte Industrie', in Peter Gerlich and Wolfgang C. Müller (eds.), *Zwischen Koalition und Konkurrenz. Österreichs Parteien seit 1945*. Vienna: Braumüller.
Dreijmanis, John (1982). 'Austria: The "Black"–"Red" Coalitions', in Eric C. Browne and John Dreijmanis (eds.), *Government Coalitions in Western Democracies*. New York: Longman.
Engelmann, Frederick E. (1962). 'Haggling for the Equilibrium: The Renegotiation of the Austrian Coalition, 1959'. *American Political Science Review*, 56: 651–62.
——(1966). 'Austria: The Pooling of Opposition', in Robert A. Dahl (ed.), *Political Oppositions in Western Democracies*. Yale: Yale University Press.
Fischer, Heinz (1993). *Die Kreisky-Jahre 1967–1983*. Vienna: Löcker.
Franklin, Mark, and Mackie, Thomas T. (1983). 'Familiarity and Inertia in the Formation of Governing Coalitions in Parliamentary Democracies'. *British Journal of Political Science*, 13: 275–98.
Gerlich, Peter (1973). *Parlamentarische Kontrolle im politischen System*. Vienna: Springer.
——and Müller, Wolfgang C. (1996). 'Austria: Routine and Ritual', in Jean Blondel and Ferdinand Müller-Rommel (eds.), *Cabinets in Western Europe*. London: Macmillan.

——Philipp, Wilfried (1988). 'Potentials and Limitations of Executive Leadership: The Austrian Cabinet since 1945'. *European Journal of Political Research,* 16: 191–205.

Hölzl, Norbert (1974). *Propagandaschlachten. Die österreichischen Wahlkämpfe 1945–1971.* Vienna: Verlag für Geschichte und Politik.

Horner, Franz (1997). 'Austria 1949–1979', in Ian Budge, David Robertson, and Derek Hearl (eds.), *Ideology, Strategy and Party Change: Spacial Analyses of Post-War Election Programmes in 19 Democracies.* Cambridge: Cambridge University Press.

Kollmann, Eric C. (1973). *Theodor Körner. Militär und Politik.* Vienna: Verlag für Geschichte und Politik.

Laver, Michael, and Hunt, Ben W. (1992). *Policy and Party Competition.* New York: Routledge.

——and Shepsle, Kenneth (1996). *Making and Breaking Governments.* Cambridge: Cambridge University Press.

Leclaire, Alfred (1966). *Große Koalition als permanente Krisenregierung.* Ph.D. University of Heidelberg.

Lijphart, Arend (1968). 'Consociational Democracy'. *World Politics,* 21: 207–25.

Luebbert, Gregory M. (1986). *Comparative Democracy.* New York: Columbia University Press.

Luther, Kurt Richard (1995). 'Friedrich Peter' and 'Norbert Steger', in Herbert Dachs, Peter Gerlich, and Wolfgang C. Müller (eds.), *Die Politiker.* Vienna: Manz.

——(1997). 'Die Freiheitlichen', in Herbert Dachs, Peter Gerlich, Herbert Gottweis, Franz Horner, Helmut Kramer, Volkmar Lauber, Wolfgang C. Müller, and Emmerich Tálos (eds.), *Handbuch des politischen Systems Österreichs.* Vienna: Manz.

Marcic, René (1966). *Die Zukunft der Koalition.* Vienna: Europa Verlag.

Meth-Cohn, Delia, and Müller, Wolfgang C. (1994). 'Looking Reality in the Eye: The Politics of Privatisation in Austria', in Vincent Wright (ed.), *Privatisation in Western Europe. Pressures, Problems and Paradoxes.* London: Francis Pinter.

Müller, Wolfgang C. (1988*a*). 'Die neue große Koalition in Österreich'. *Österreichische Zeitschrift für Politikwissenschaft,* 17: 321–47.

——(1988*b*). 'SPÖ und große Koalition', in Peter Pelinka and Gerhard Steger (eds.), *Auf dem Weg zur Staatspartei.* Vienna: Verlag für Gesellschaftskritik.

——(1989). 'Party Patronage in Austria', in Anton Pelinka and Fritz Plasser (eds.), *The Austrian Party System.* Boulder, Colo.: Westview.

——(1992). 'Austrian Governmental Institutions: Do They Matter?' *West European Politics,* 15 (1): 99–131.

——(1993). 'Executive–Legislative Relations in Austria: 1945–1992'. *Legislative Studies Quarterly,* 18: 467–94.

——(1994*a*). 'Koalitionsabkommen in der österreichischen Politik'. *Zeitschrift für Parlamentsfragen,* 25: 346–53.

——(1994*b*). 'Models of Government and the Austrian Cabinet', in Michael Laver and Kenneth A. Shepsle (eds.), *Cabinet Ministers and Parliamentary Government.* Cambridge: Cambridge University Press.

——(1996*a*). 'Political Parties', in Volkmar Lauber (ed.), *Contemporary Austrian Politics.* Boulder, Colo.: Westview.

Müller, Wolfgang C. (1996*b*). 'Wahlsysteme und Parteiensystem in Österreich 1945–1995', in Fritz Plasser, Peter A. Ulram and Günther Ogris (eds.), *Wahlkampf und Wählerentscheidung*. Vienna: Signum.

——(1997). 'Regierung und Kabinettsystem', in Herbert Dachs, Peter Gerlich, Herbert Gottweis, Franz Horner, Helmut Kramer, Volkmar Lauber, Wolfgang C. Müller and Emmerich Tálos (eds.), *Handbuch des politischen Systems Österreichs*. Vienna: Manz.

——(1999*a*). 'Austria', in Robert Elgie (ed.), *Semi-Presidentialism in Europe*. Oxford: Oxford University Press.

——(1999*b*). 'Decision for Opposition: The Austrian Socialist Party's Abandonment of Government Participation in 1966', in Wolfgang C. Müller and Kaare Strøm (eds.), *Votes, Office, or Policy? How Political Parties in Western Europe Make Hard Decisions*. Cambridge: Cambridge University Press.

——Philipp, Wilfried, and Jenny, Marcelo (1995). 'Ideologie und Strategie österreichischer Parteien: Eine Analyse der Wahlprogramme 1949–1994', in Wolfgang C. Müller, Fritz Plasser, and Peter A. Ulram (eds.), *Wählerverhalten und Parteienwettbewerb*. Vienna: Signum.

——Steininger, Barbara (1995). 'Die Regierung', in Emmerich Tálos, Herbert Dachs, Ernst Hanisch, and Anton Staudinger (eds.), *Handbuch des politischen Systems Österreichs. Erste Republik 1918–1933*. Vienna: Manz.

——(1996). 'Austria: Party Government within Limits', in Jean Blondel and Maurizio Cotta (eds.), *Party and Government*. London: Macmillan.

Naßmacher, Karl-Heinz (1968). *Das österreichische Regierungssystem*. Cologne: Westdeutscher Verlag.

Pelinka, Anton (1993). *Die kleine Koalition SPÖ–FPÖ 1983–1986*. Vienna: Böhlau.

Pfeifer, Helmut (1964). 'Über die Beschlußfassung der Regierung und die Verantwortlichkeit ihrer Mitglieder'. *Juristische Blätter* 86: 485–500 and 541–52.

Plasser, Fritz, and Ulram, Peter A. (1995). 'Wandel der politischen Konfliktdynamik: Radikaler Rechtspopulismus in Österreich', in Wolfgang C. Müller, Fritz Plasser, and Peter A. Ulram (eds.), *Wählerverhalten und Parteienwettbewerb*. Vienna: Signum.

——Grausgruber, Alfred (1992). 'The Decline of "Lager Mentality" and the New Model of Electoral Competition in Austria', in Kurt Richard Luther and Wolfgang C. Müller (eds.), *Politics in Austria: Still a Case of Consociationalism?* London: Frank Cass.

——Seeber, Gilg (1996). '(Dis-)Kontinuitäten und neue Spannungslinien im Wählerverhalten: Trendanalysen 1986–1995', in Fritz Plasser, Peter A. Ulram, and Günther Ogris (eds.), *Wahlkampf und Wählerentscheidung*. Vienna: Signum.

Rauchensteiner, Manfred (1987). *Die Zwei. Die Große Koalition in Österreich 1945–1966*. Vienna: Österreichischer Bundesverlag.

Riker, William H. (1962). *The Theory of Political Coalitions*. New Haven: Yale University Press.

Rudzio, Wolfgang (1971). 'Entscheidungszentrum Koalitionsausschuß—Zur Realverfassung Österreichs unter der großen Koalition'. *Politische Vierteljahresschrift*, 12: 87–118.

Schneider, Kurt (1961). *Die österreichische Parteiendemokratie in Recht und Wirklichkeit*. Ph.D. University of Vienna.

Secher, Herbert P. (1958). 'Coalition Government: The Case of the Second Republic'. *American Political Science Review*, 52: 791–809.

Shepsle, Kenneth A. (1996). 'Political Deals in Institutional Settings', in Robert E. Goodin (ed.), *The Theory of Institutional Design*. Cambridge: Cambridge University Press.

Steiner, Kurt (1972). *Politics in Austria*. Boston: Little, Brown.

Strøm, Kaare, Budge, Ian, and Laver, Michael (1994). 'Constraints on Cabinet Formation in Parliamentary Democracies'. *American Journal of Political Science*, 28: 303–35.

von Beyme, Klaus (1985). *Political Parties in Western Democracies*. Aldershot: Gower.

Welan, Manfried (1974). 'Der Verfassungsgerichtshof—eine Nebenregierung?', in Heinz Fischer (ed.), *Das politische System Österreichs*. Vienna: Europaverlag.

——(1986). *Das österreichische Staatsoberhaupt*. Vienna: Verlag für Geschichte und Politik.

——and Neisser, Heinrich (1971). *Der Bundeskanzler im österreichischen Verfassungsgefüge*. Vienna: Hollinek.

4

Ireland

From Single-Party to Coalition Rule

Paul Mitchell

INTRODUCTION

Until recently there was no real consensus that Ireland should even be included in the group of European countries labelled 'coalition systems'. As late as 1983 Farrell noted that 'despite the operation of STV, the typical outcome has been single-party government' (Farrell 1983: 249), while a few years later Laver and Higgins concluded that 'until Fianna Fáil shows a willingness to share power with others, or until it loses support to smaller parties, Ireland is not really a coalition system at all' (1986: 196). Fianna Fáil, for long the predominant party in the system, has now done both, gradually losing votes until finally they agreed to take part in coalition governments. Previously after every election there was a relatively straightforward and stark choice: either Fianna Fáil would form a single-party government if it won a majority (or could attract the support of independents to sustain minority administrations) or a coalition of almost the entire opposition would have to sink their policy differences and combine as the only method of displacing the dominant party. Fianna Fáil's participation in coalition (since 1989) removes the single biggest constraint on the bargaining environment and facilitates the recent emergence of a fully-fledged coalition politics of rival alliances competing for the keys to the cabinet door.

This recent expansion of governing alternatives should not, however, obscure the fact that experience of executive coalitions dates back over fifty years, even if in earlier decades the role of coalitions was to punctuate long periods of single-party rule (and hence provide *some* alternative) whereas more recently coalitions have become the 'normal' outcome of a formation period.[1]

[1] In the period 1944–73 single-party administrations accounted for 78.7% of government duration and coalitions 21.3%. In more recent decades (1973–99) the pattern is almost a mirror image of the earlier period, with coalitions accounting for 72.5% of duration and single-party (Fianna Fáil) governments 27.5% (figure calculated until 1 Jan. 1999).

TABLE 4.1. *Left–right placement of parties[a], party strength (in seats) and party composition of governments in Ireland, 1944–1999*

Governments	Proximity to election	WP/DL	Lab	CnP	CnT	FF	FG	PD	Others	Median party in second policy dimension[b]	Effective number of legislative parties[c]	Government strength	Total number of seats
1944	FE		12[d]		11	76*	30		9	FF	2.77	76	138
1948	FE		19[d]	10	7	68*	31		12	FF	3.62	67	147
1951	FE		16	2	6	69*	40		14	CnT	3.26	69	147
1954	FE		19	3	5	65*	50		5	CnT	3.05	74	147
1957	FE		12	1	3	78*	40		13[e]	FF	2.76	78	147
1961	FE		16	1	2	70*	47		8[f]	FF	2.16	70	144
1965	FE		22	1		72*	47		2	FF	2.63	72	144
1969	FE		18			75*	50		1	FF	2.46	75	144
1973	FE		19			69*	54		2	Lab	2.59	73	144
1977	FE		17			84*	43		4	FF	2.38	84	148
1981	FE	1	15			78*	65		7[g]	Lab	2.62	80	166
1982–1	FE	3	15			81*	63		4	Lab	2.56	81	166
1982–2	FE	2	16			75*	70		3	Lab	2.56	86	166
1987	FE	4	12			81*	51	14	4	Lab	2.90	81	166
1989	F	7	15			77*	55	6	6[h]	Lab	2.98	83	166
1992[i]	n.e. E	7[j]	15			77*	55	6	6	Lab	2.98	83	166
1993[k]	F	4	33			68*	45	10	6[h]	Lab	3.51	101	166
1994	n.e.	6	32			66*	46	8	7[h]	Lab	3.63	84	166
1997	F	4	17			77*	54	4	10[l]	Lab	3.00	81[m]	166

cont./

TABLE 4.1. *cont.*

ᵃ Based on Laver's (1994: 160) expert survey of the Irish party system (an update of Laver and Hunt 1992). The left–right placement is based on the 'increase public services vs. cut taxes' policy scale. There is some doubt that the Laver and Hunt and Laver data (expert judgements that are by definition 'snaphots' of estimated party placements in 1989 and 1992 respectively) accurately reflect the correct order of party placement (left–right scale) for the entire post-war period. For example, using manifesto data Mair argues that Fine Gael can be placed to the left of Fianna Fail for the period 1965–77 (Mair 1986: 463–5).

ᵇ The Northern Ireland dimension based on Laver's (1994, 1998) 'Oppose permanent British presence in Northern Ireland versus defend permanent British presence in Northern Ireland'. Note that in the 1997 survey Northern Ireland was judged to be the most salient dimension. However, some caution should be exercised in interpreting the identity of the median party on the second dimension. First, as in all other countries we can be more confident in judging ordinal party placement in more recent parliaments that are close in time to the surveys. Using surveys conducted in the 1990s to read backwards several decades is obviously problematic. Second, the existence in Ireland of multiple independent deputies complicates the task of identifying the median legislator on the second dimension (though note that FF always controls the median deputy on the first dimension regardless of assumptions made about independents). For example, while Labour clearly controls the median legislator on the Northern Ireland dimension after the 1992 election (i.e. regardless of independents), it only continues to do so after the 1997 election based on one's assumptions concerning the policy preferences of independents. Alternatively, if all independents in 1997 are excluded then Labour clearly controls the median legislator.

The first two decades after 1945 contain two parties, Clann na Poblachta and Clann na Talmhan, that ceased to win any seats after 1965 and thus are not included in any of the surveys. The assumption made here (based partly on profiles of these parties in Gallagher 1985), is that with respect to the Northern Ireland dimension the ordinal party placement (from most republican) was CnP–FF–CnT–Lab–FG. Also, the large number of independents and others in these decades make the identification of the median party very tentative.

During 1998 Democratic Left merged with the Labour Party. The new party is known as the Labour Party.

ᶜ The Laakso and Taagepera index by seat shares (excluding 'Others').

ᵈ The figures for the Labour Party in 1944 and 1948 are the combined totals of Labour and National Labour, the latter a temporary split from the Labour Party.

ᵉ The total of 13 others includes 4 Sinn Fein deputies who declined to take their seats.

ᶠ The total of 8 others elected in 1961 includes 2 National Progressive Democrats (former independents who later joined the Labour Party in Nov. 1963).

ᵍ The total of 7 others includes 2 National H-Block Committee republican prisoners who did not take their seats.

ʰ At the 1989 and 1992 elections the total number of 'others' includes one deputy elected on each occasion for the Green Party.

ⁱ Using counting rules 1 and 3 the 1992 Reynolds 1 government would not be listed because there was a change of PM but no election or change in partisanship. However, this case clearly warrants classification as an episode of coalition bargaining rather than a 'technical' termination (by death or voluntary early retirement of PM). The smaller coalition party, the Progressive Democrats, issued an ultimatum to Fianna Fáil: unless Fianna Fáil replaced Haughey as leader they would break the coalition. Since an immediate general election was projected to be disastrous for FF, Haughey resigned enabling the coalition to continue under a new PM.

ʲ The Workers' Party split during 1992 with the majority faction renaming itself Democratic Left and won four seats at the 1992 election. The rump party continued as the Workers' Party but won no seats.

ᵏ Election was held in 1992, the government was formed in 1993.

ˡ The total of 10 others elected in 1997 includes 2 from the Green Party and 1 Sinn Fein.

ᵐ Although the government that formed in 1997 is a minority coalition administration it secured the external support during formation negotiations of three independent deputies and hence had a legislative majority.

Parties
WP Workers' Party
DL Democratic Left
Lab Labour Party
CnP Clann na Poblachta (Party of the Republic)
CnT Clann na Talmhan (Party of the Land)
FF Fianna Fáil (Soldiers of Ireland)
FG Fine Gael (Irish Race)
PD Progressive Democrats

n.e. = no general election
Parties in **bold** formed **governments**.
* Party with median legislator.

Median legislator: Given the order of party placement in Table 4.1 Fianna Fáil always controls the median legislator, irrespective of any assumptions that are made about the placement of the 'others'.

The history of formal coalition politics can be quite conveniently divided into three periods: before 1973, 1973–89, and after 1989. First, before 1973 Ireland had a multi-party system in which the typical outcome of an election was single-party (though quite often minority) government. Fianna Fáil dominated these decades governing for most of this time including two separate periods of continuous sixteen-year rule (1932–48, 1957–73). Indeed, after Fianna Fáil first came to power in 1932 it was displaced on only two occasions during the entire period (until 1973) and it required coalitions of almost the entire opposition to do so. The first 'inter-party' government (Fianna Fáil so dominated the rules of competition that the other parties eschewed the word 'coalition' believing it to be pejorative) served between 1948–51, a diverse coalition spanning the spectrum in which five parties and an independent held cabinet seats. This alternation in government was facilitated by a (then) unprecedented slump in Fianna Fáil's vote and a corresponding surge by two small parties, Clann na Talmhan (a centre-left farmers party) and particularly by Clann na Poblachta (a socially radical republican party) that took 13.2 per cent of the vote in 1948, its first election. The coalition was completed by the two other traditional parties in the system: Fine Gael (the second largest political party and the 'pro-treaty' side of the civil war political cleavage that structured politics in the new state) and the long-suffering Labour Party, the third largest party in Ireland but traditionally the weakest social democratic party in Western Europe.

By the time of the second 'inter-party' government of 1954–7, a three-party coalition of Fine Gael, Labour and Clann na Talmhan (with a pledge of external support from Clann na Poblachta), the fortunes of the latter two parties were in terminal decline and both ceased to exist in 1965 (Gallagher 1985; Mair 1987). The second coalition was a fairly unhappy experience for its participants and resulted in severe electoral setbacks for all parties involved (see Table 4.8). Fine Gael and Labour then pursued mutually exclusive strategies 'with each hoping, if only fancifully, that it might one day acquire sufficient support to challenge for government on its own' (Mair 1993b: 97). The reality, however, was that Fine Gael and Labour's efforts to forge separate destinies ushered in the second period of sixteen-year continuous Fianna Fáil rule (1957–73). Fianna Fáil's pivotal position was such that, if the opposition parties refused to combine against it, then no governing alternative existed. Fianna Fáil rule was the party system's default option.

The second period of coalition government began in 1973 and ended in 1989. The logic of competition—Fianna Fáil versus 'the rest'—remained the same as before but 'the rest' had now been streamlined to just two parties (Fine Gael and Labour) rather than the five that had been necessary to remove Fianna Fáil from office in 1948. This simplification of coalition bargaining to just two parties combined with greater policy affinity between Fine Gael and Labour in the 1970s and early 1980s meant that a non-Fianna Fáil coalition alternative was viable.[2] Thus, during the sixteen-year period 1973–89 and in a major departure from earlier decades, no Irish government served two consecutive terms.[3] Fianna Fáil single-party governments alternated with 'the coalition' after each government resignation.

However, while Fine Gael and Labour enjoyed a more regular taste of power both parties were still heavily constrained by Fianna Fáil's refusal to play the coalition game. Basically, if they wanted to be relevant in the government formation stage, then they were stuck with each other, for better or worse. And as the 1980s progressed there was a lot of 'worse' as the earlier policy affinity between the parties evaporated with the economic recession. As Fine Gael increasingly stressed fiscal rectitude (a tendency strengthened by the need to defend its flank from the competition of a new right-wing party, the Progressive Democrats), the Labour Party's divisions over 'the coalition question' intensified. As Mair has argued: 'Labour, in particular, was wholly hemmed in' (1993a: 170). To maintain an independent policy stance by refusing to participate with Fine Gael made it irrelevant to the process of government formation and thus limited its possible electoral growth. To participate in government, on the other hand, meant accepting the only coalition that was available. To compound matters Labour's bargaining power within a government dominated by its larger conservative partner would be restricted, since threats to bring down the government depend substantially on the exis-

---

[2] Other factors also loosened Fianna Fáil's grip on power. Although the party continued to attract around 45% of votes the increasingly proportional seat distribution (partially due to an independent boundary commission) denied them the same scale of 'seat bonuses' that had traditionally accrued to Fianna Fáil. Also, and quite importantly, there were now far fewer independent deputies (see Table 4.1) with whom Fianna Fáil could build legislative majorities (Mair 1993a). However, 10 independents were elected in 1997.

[3] Incidentally, this pattern of alternating governments continued after 1989.

tence of alternative coalitions. Thus, in or out of coalition, the Fianna Fáil imposed constraint, placed Labour in a strategically weak position.

The bargaining environment was transformed in 1989 by Fianna Fáil's decision to enter its first executive coalition, ceding two cabinet seats to the Progressive Democrats. Since 1989 five successive coalition governments have formed thus breaking the earlier pattern of alternating single-party and coalition governments. Why Fianna Fáil abandoned its objection 'in principle' to coalitions, thus undermining the traditional structure of party competition, is a complex and fascinating issue (Gallagher and Sinnott 1990; Marsh and Mitchell 1999*b*). Laver and Arkins (1990) argue that negotiating a coalition that would allow Fianna Fáil to remain in office was probably the only way that the Fianna Fáil leader could protect his position: another election was expected to leave Fianna Fáil in an even weaker position, while a return to opposition would have resulted in a leadership challenge. Thus, Laver and Arkins suggest that there may well have been a sharp 'conflict of interest between the Fianna Fáil party and its leader' (1990: 205).

The important point here, however, was that Fianna Fáil was now just an 'ordinary' (but still the biggest) political party. While Fianna Fáil may at some point in the future be in a position to form a single-party government, coalitions are now fully legitimate. The five-party system of the 1990s[4] combined with Fianna Fáil's new availability as a partner in government means that the other parties for the first time have a choice of coalition partners. And in coalition politics choice is power.

INSTITUTIONAL CONSTRAINTS

Although the process of government formation has been heavily influenced by self-imposed behavioural constraints (most notably the changing attitudes of Fianna Fáil and Labour towards coalitions), institutional constraints have played a fairly small role in shaping coalition politics in Ireland, at least relative to some other European countries. Patterns of government formation have closely corresponded to what Laver and Schofield have described as 'freestyle bargaining between elites' (1990). There are no size or composition requirements and no recognition rules, *formateurs* or *informateurs* (see Strøm, Budge, and Laver 1994 for a review of constraints). There is an investiture requirement so that a proposed Taoiseach (prime minister) must win a plurality vote in the legislature (Art. 13.1.1–2). This has not, however, prevented

---

[4] A 'six-party' system if the Green Party is counted (one deputy elected in 1989 and 1992 and two deputies at the 1997 elections. However, as previously noted DL has subsequently merged with Labour). Table 4.1 shows that the 'effective number of parties' has significantly increased, at least until the 1997 election.

the quite frequent incidence of minority governments (by means of the support of independents or the abstention of other parties).

More surprisingly, although there is a directly elected president, he or she plays no role in forming the government. There is, however, a constitutional clause relating to the powers of legislative dissolution which could influence government composition if invoked by the president.[5] In normal circumstances, when a Taoiseach requests the president to dissolve the Dáil, in order to hold an election, the president is required to do so (Art. 13.2.1). However, according to Article 13.2.2, the president 'may in his absolute discretion refuse to dissolve Dáil Éireann on the advice of a Taoiseach who has ceased to retain the support of a majority in Dáil Éireann' (see Gallagher 1988). By using this power, a president could encourage coalition renegotiation during an inter-electoral period as an alternative to the traditional resort to an election as soon as a government resigns. While no president has yet exercised this power, it could become a source of controversy, in an era of fully-fledged coalition politics. In 1994 the issue was almost put to a test but in the event the Taoiseach resigned in advance of his almost certain defeat on a tabled confidence motion. The President very publicly consulted the Chairman of the Bar Council on her constitutional powers, a move widely interpreted as a signal that she may indeed refuse to dissolve the Dáil if called upon to do so.[6] In the event, Fianna Fáil elected a new leader and was forced into opposition. For the first time ever one coalition replaced another during an inter-electoral period.

Another institutional rule that significantly structures coalition politics is the nature of the electoral system. The Single Transferable Vote (STV) electoral system by encouraging voters to rank-order candidates (and thus, parties) rewards cooperative electoral strategies. This means that there is a significant coalition formation phase *before* elections because leaders are induced to encourage party supporters to transfer their lower preference votes (once the transfer becomes 'terminal') to the most likely prospective coalition partners. High transfer rates between parties can make all the difference to the distribution of a fairly small number of seats. However, given that the Dáil is often delicately balanced[7] and governments rarely enjoy size-

---

[5] Note that the legislature and non-PM parties do not have the power to impose a dissolution on the PM. To force a dissolution, the non-PM parties must defeat the government, elect a rival PM, and then dissolve parliament. Thus, Ireland is a good example of a system in which there is an important 'strategic asymmetry' between the PM's party and all others with regard to legislative dissolution powers (Laver and Shepsle 1996).

[6] Since the then President (Mary Robinson) is a prominent constitutional lawyer, she could quite easily have requested legal advice more privately if there had been no intention to send a signal. Thanks to Michael Gallagher for this point.

[7] Indeed, a problem for the application of conventional coalition theories in Ireland is that the 'key "pivotal" group was, as often as not, the "others"' (Laver and Higgins 1986: 179). However, these were not of course a 'unified bargaining actor' so that the effective 'winning' threshold of legislative votes for any prospective government was often less than half the seats (ibid).

able majorities (if they have one at all) transfers can make or break a prospective coalition. Occasionally, as in 1973 and 1977 an explicit pre-ballot transfer pact existed between Fine Gael and the Labour Party, but more typically pre-electoral coalitions are implicit.[8] Moreover, the electorate appear to be highly responsive to these explicit or implicit signals regarding electoral coalitions. For example, during the 1973–87 period (containing three Fine Gael–Labour coalition governments), these parties consistently transferred to each other at rates of 60–70 per cent. However, 'in 1987, following the break-up of the Fine Gael–Labour coalition, the voters for the two parties followed their leaders and went their separate ways . . . transfers plummeted to . . . just over 30 per cent each way' (Sinnott 1995: 215).

There is therefore a distinction between pre-ballot electoral coalitions designed to maximize the parliamentary bargaining power of a particular set of cooperative parties and the negotiation of formal executive coalitions. These are analytically separate bargaining environments and parties may cooperate with *different* parties in each stage (although they *may* risk incurring credibility costs if they do so). For example, at the 1992 election, Fine Gael in an attempt to maximize the non-Fianna Fáil vote, floated the possibility of a 'rainbow coalition' of itself, Labour, and the Progressive Democrats. However, while the Fine Gael leader recommended that his supporters transfer their lower preferences to these two parties, the Labour Party enjoying an unprecedented surge in the opinion polls, refused to reciprocate, judging that it could maximize its vote by not indicating any coalition preferences (and hence not alienating Fianna Fáil voters). The destination of Labour terminal transfers suggest that its supporters were not enthusiastic about a coalition with Fianna Fáil. In situations (24 cases) where both Fine Gael and Fianna Fáil candidates were available to receive Labour terminal transfers, Fine Gael received over twice as many as Fianna Fáil (Gallagher 1993*b*: 68–9). Nevertheless, having increased its bargaining power in its best ever electoral performance, Labour negotiated an executive coalition with Fianna Fáil in the quite different strategic context of government formation.

COALITION FORMATION

Compared with some other countries coalition building in Ireland is a fairly unstructured process in which party leaders engage in (relatively) freestyle bargaining. There are no recognition rules and no one is officially designated to lead or chair the negotiations. Until recently there has never been a choice

[8] In 1997, for the first time, two alternative coalitions offered themselves in the election: the incumbents (FG, Labour, and DL) and the challengers FF and the PDs. See Marsh and Mitchell 1999*a*.

of more than two alternative governments. If, following an election, Fianna Fáil had the numbers they would form a single-party administration. If they did not, then the outcome would depend on the current attitude of Fine Gael and Labour to a coalition with each other. If they did not agree to sink their policy differences and coalesce, then there would be a Fianna Fáil government by default. This facilitated speedy government formation so that all governments (before 1993) were put together within the 'official gap' between the dissolution of parliament for the purposes of elections and the first scheduled meeting of the new Dáil. Table 4.2 indicates that all governments before 1989 were put together in between one to three weeks.

TABLE 4.2. *Government formation in Ireland*

Coalition	Number of parties in parliament	Number of previous bargaining rounds	Parties involved in the previous bargaining rounds	Number of days required for government formation
FF 1944	5	0		10
FG–LAB–NL–CnT–CnP 1948	6	1	FG, Lab, CnP, CnT, NL	14
FF 1951	5	0		14
FG–LAB–CnT 1954	5	0		14
FF 1957	5[a]	0		15
FF 1961	6	0		7
FF 1965	4	0		14
FF 1969	3	0		14
FG–LAB 1973	3	0		14
FF 1977	3	0		19
FG–LAB 1981	4[b]	0		19
FF 1982–1	4	0		19
FG–LAB 1982–2	4	0		20
FF 1987	5	0		21
FF–PD 1989	6	0		27
FF–PD 1992	6	0		7
FF–LAB 1993	6	1	FG, Lab, DL, PD, FF	48
FG–LAB–DL 1994	6	1	FF, Lab, FG, DL	29
FF–PD 1997	7[c]	0		20

[a] A sixth party, Sinn Fein, won 4 seats at the 1957 election but did not take up their seats.
[b] A fifth party, Sinn Fein, won 2 seats at the 1981 election but did not take up their seats.
[c] Sinn Fein won one seat, its first since abandoning its abstentionist policy.

The expansion in the number of governing alternatives since 1989 has complicated and tended to lengthen the process, so that during the two formation periods (1992–3 and 1994) the government could not be put together before the first scheduled meeting of the Dáil. Since no one could be elected Taoiseach at these first meetings, the Dáil had to be adjourned for a period of time to allow coalition negotiations to progress. Government formation after the 1992 election was unprecedented in taking just over seven weeks, even although this is still a relatively modest period compared to some of the longest formation episodes in countries like the Netherlands.

All post-1945 cabinets are listed in Table 4.3. Of the twenty-two administrations, twelve have been single-party governments (8 with majorities and 4 minority governments) and there have been ten coalitions (7 majority and 3 minority). The trend since 1973 has been towards more coalition governments, a pattern that tends to increase the proportion of majoritarian administrations, since most coalitions build up to or past a bare majority.

A closer look at the 1992–3 coalition negotiations provides a clearer impression of the pattern of government formation in Ireland's multi-party coalition system. It is noticeable that the closest approximation to a *formateur* in this period was Dick Spring (Labour Party) the leader of only the third largest party.[9] This suggests that this role can be captured by a leader with a sense of 'momentum' (Labour had been the clear 'winners' of the election, doubling in size while the two larger parties declined significantly) or by a party that is pivotal in some spatial sense (Mitchell 1993; Laver and Shepsle 1996). Fianna Fáil, following the electoral setback seemed resigned to opposition, while Fine Gael as the second largest party assumed that it would almost certainly form a government with Labour and the Progressive Democrats. The reality, however, was that assuming that Fianna Fáil and Fine Gael would refuse to contemplate a grand coalition in the centre (this remains a major behavioural constraint), the Labour Party was indispensable to any majority coalition with a realistic chance of forming.[10] In terms of a two-dimensional plot of the most salient cleavages, Fianna Fáil controlled the median legislator on the public ownership dimension while the median legislator on the Northern Ireland dimension was controlled by Labour (Laver 1994: 159). In Laver and Shepsle's terms a Fianna Fáil–Labour coalition constituted the dimension by dimension median cabinet (1996: 142–3).

Since Labour were indispensable they could afford to shop around for the best deal. Labour determined not only much of the content but also the format of negotiations. For example, while Fine Gael impatient to build a government tried to insist on trilateral talks between themselves, Labour, and the Progressive Democrats, Labour refused to attend, preferring bilaterals with each party. Labour also infuriated Fine Gael by first holding side-talks with Democratic Left (a party Fine Gael had ruled out as partners) to agree

---

[9] It is probably more accurate to say that Spring was in a strong bargaining position which he used to attempt to direct coalition negotiations. Spring was not the *formateur* in the sense of being the Prime Minister designate.

[10] Theoretically Fianna Fáil could have formed a majority coalition without Fine Gael or Labour. To do so Fianna Fáil would need to have been able to build an ideologically diverse coalition of itself, the Progressive Democrats, Democratic Left, the Green Party, and at least one independent deputy. Excepting this eventuality (which was not even considered) and the even more unlikely grand coalition (of Fianna Fáil and Fine Gael), Labour could not be excluded from any majority coalition.

TABLE 4.3. *Cabinets in Ireland since 1944*

Cabinet number	Taoiseach	Date in	Formal resignation	Maximum potential duration (in days)	Duration (in days)	Government composition
1	de Valera VI	9 June 1944	4 Feb. 1948	1,790	1,315	FF
2	Costello I	18 Feb. 1948	30 May 1951	1,786	1,182	FG–LAB–NL–CnT–CnP
3	de Valera VII	13 June 1951	18 May 1954	1,786	1,055	FF
4	Costello II	2 June 1954	5 Mar. 1957	1,786	993	FG–LAB–CnT
5	de Valera VIII	20 Mar. 1957	23 June 1959	1,785	783	FF
6	Lemass I	23 June 1959	4 Oct. 1961	1,002	821	FF
7	Lemass II	11 Oct. 1961	7 Apr. 1965	1,793	1,256	FF
8	Lemass III	21 Apr. 1965	10 Nov. 1966	1,786	559	FF
9	Lynch I	10 Nov. 1966	18 June 1969	1,227	938	FF
10	Lynch II	2 July 1969	28 Feb. 1973	1,786	1,316	FF
11	Cosgrave I	14 Mar. 1973	16 June 1977	1,786	1,532	FG–LAB
12	Lynch III	5 July 1977	12 Dec. 1979	1,781	877	FF
13	Haughey I	12 Dec. 1979	11 June 1981	904	545	FF
14	FitzGerald I	30 June 1981	18 Feb. 1982	1,787	228	FG–LAB
15	Haughey II	9 Mar. 1982	24 Nov. 1982	1,781	255	FF
16	FitzGerald II	14 Dec. 1982	17 Feb. 1987	1,780	1,503	FG–LAB
17	Haughey III	10 Mar. 1987	15 June 1989	1,779	815	FF
18	Haughey IV	12 July 1989	11 Feb. 1992	1,773	899	FF–PD
19	Reynolds 1	11 Feb. 1992	25 Nov. 1992	874	284	FF–PD
20	Reynolds 2	12 Jan. 1993	17 Nov. 1994	1,752	665	FF–LAB
21	Bruton 1	15 Dec. 1994	6 June 1997	1,087	892	FG–LAB–DL
22	Ahern 1	26 June 1997		1,780		FF–PD

a 'left-wing' policy agenda and presumably cover Labour's flank if it subsequently went into government without Democratic Left. The negotiations with Fine Gael eventually broke down and Labour immediately opened 'official' negotiations with Fianna Fáil (there had already been private meetings between these parties while Labour was still negotiating with Fine Gael) which concluded successfully (Farrell 1993*a*). One key difference was that while Fine Gael continued to treat Labour as though it were a junior coalition partner (on the model of the coalitions of the 1970s and 1980s) Fianna Fáil nimbly adjusted to Labour's new bargaining strength, offering 'partnership government' (more below). Fianna Fáil was also prepared to include most of Labour's policy demands in the coalition policy document and to restructure the departmental and decision making process in line with Labour's insistence that it would be a full governing partner. Therefore, in this example of 'freestyle bargaining' the parties that adjusted most rapidly to the new environment and played to their strengths, claimed the prize.

Another aspect of government formation, more fully revealed by the 1994 negotiations, may be a tendency to proceed by means of proto-coalition formation rather than the inclusive trilateral talks that Fine Gael had tried to insist on in 1992. Briefly, in 1994 following the collapse of the Fianna Fáil–Labour government in acrimonious circumstances, Fianna Fáil were temporarily ruled out as coalition partners by a series of scandals. This meant that an alternative three- or four-party coalition might be formed by Fine Gael and Labour with one or both of the two smaller parties. Fine Gael favoured a four-party government, hoping that the Progressive Democrats and Democratic Left would balance each other ideologically, while Labour preferred a three-party coalition that would exclude the Progressive Democrats (on policy grounds). Interestingly, both the Progressive Democrats and Democratic Left also preferred a three-party minimum-winning coalition— not because they would get a bigger share of the prize as traditional coalition theory suggests—but because whichever of the small parties was included would then have the ability to bring down the government. The process followed was that Fine Gael and Labour held a series of bilateral negotiations to agree a policy document. Only then did they decide to invite Democratic Left to join them. Thus, in both the 1992–3 and 1994 formation periods, coalition negotiations proceeded by proto-coalition formation and there were two bargaining attempts on each occasion.[11]

The continuing mutual avoidance of Fianna Fáil and Fine Gael is the last major behavioural constraint and places some practical limits on the extent of coalition reshuffles. Of the parties still in existence in 1999 only four have been

---

[11] A slightly different but logically similar process ensued in 1997. The FF–PD pre-electoral coalition, following the result of the general election, first negotiated a two-party executive coalition and then opened talks with independent deputies to secure a viable legislative coalition (Mitchell 1999*b*).

in government (Fianna Fáil, Fine Gael, Labour, and Progressive Democrats), and given the embargo on the grand coalition of the first two parties and the improbability of a Fianna Fáil majority government, the feasible alternatives involve one or other of the biggest parties in coalition with Labour, the PDs, or both.[12]

COALITION GOVERNANCE

Rules and Procedures

Apart from the constitutional doctrine of collective cabinet responsibility, which increases the political cost of lost cabinet battles, there are no real 'official rules' of coalition politics. The practice of coalition governance—see Table 4.4—has evolved from the early coalitions that made essentially *ad hoc* minor adaptations to the policy and decision making procedures that prevailed during single-party governments,[13] to the more recent practice of the coalition parties adjusting the policy process and informal norms of behaviour, in order to better facilitate coalition governance.

The style of cabinet decision making is structured by Art. 28.4.2 of the Constitution: 'The Government shall meet and act as a collective authority, and shall be collectively responsible for the Departments of State administered by the members of the Government.' The cabinet acts as a clearing house for most major decisions and the doctrine of collective cabinet responsibility 'normally denies ministers the right to record private dissent, let alone public opposition, to cabinet decisions' (Farrell 1993*b*: 174). This doctrine poses a particular problem for coalition governments, in that a party having lost a major policy debate in cabinet will be obliged to defend the policy in public. As Laver and Higgins note, 'this can on occasion place them in an

---

[12] This produces a set of six possible coalitions, though some are more probable than others (e.g. an FG–PD combination is unlikely to have the numbers). A seventh logical possibility, a Labour–PD coalition depends upon even more wildly optimistic forecasts of the future electoral growth of these parties. In 1997 the Green Party for the first time grew to two seats so that further progress could make it a relevant coalition actor. Finally, the presence of independent deputies (in 1997, 10) can make it much easier for 'nearly winning' minority governments to be viable. See Laver 1999 for a fuller discussion of future options.

[13] To take a small example, during the Fine Gael–Labour Party coalition of 1973–7 (the first in the 'modern' era) the ministers did not act as party blocs within the cabinet. Indeed, the ministers of each party did not even sit together in party teams: 'the decision not to do so was taken at the start, as a token of the two parties' willingness to operate amicably' (Gallagher 1982: 219). Given the normative prejudice (encouraged by Fianna Fáil) that 'coalition politics' equals 'weak government', they tried as far as possible, to behave 'as if' they were a united single-party government. And indeed there was relatively little coalition conflict during this administration which lasted more than four years (though of course this should not necessarily be attributed to seating arrangements!).

TABLE 4.4. *Coalition governance in Ireland*

(1) Coalition	(2) Coalition agreement	(3) Agreement public	(4) Election rule	(5) Conflict management mechanism	(6) Most common management mechanism	(7) Mechanism for most serious conflicts	(8) Coalition discipline in legislation	(9) Coalition discipline in other parliamentary behaviour	(10) Freedom of appointment	(11) Policy agreement	(12) Junior ministers	(13) Non-cabinet positions
1948	N	NA	N	Parl; PS	PS	Parl	1	1	Y	0	Y	Y
1954	N	NA	N	Parl; PS	PS	Parl	1	1	Y	0	Y	Y
1973	PRE	Y	N	Parl; PS	PS	Parl	2	1	Y	1	Y	Y
1981	POST	Y	N	Parl; PS	PS	Parl	1	1	Y	2	Y	Y
1982–2	POST	Y	N	Parl; PS	PS	Parl	2	1	Y	2	Y	Y
1989	POST	Y	N	Parl; PS	PS	Parl	1	1	Y	2	Y	Y
1992	POST	Y	N	Parl; PS[a]	PS	Parl	1	1	Y	2	Y	Y
1993	POST	Y	N	Parl; PS	CaC; O[b]	Parl	1	1	Y	2	Y	Y
1994	IE	Y	N	Parl; PS	CaC; O[b]	Parl	1	1	Y	2	Y	Y
1997	POST	Y	N	Parl; PS	PS	Parl	1	1	Y	2	Y	Y

[a] There was very little conflict resolution of any kind during this short-lived cabinet. The parties and party leaders of the governing coalition were hostile to each other and clearly positioning themselves for the next election.

[b] During the 1993–7 period (covering two coalitions) each minister had a 'programme manager' and a ministerial cabinet. Regular meetings of the programme managers and ministerial advisers prior to the actual cabinet meetings were used to resolve problems, and coordinate and track policy development and implementation (with clear brief to troubleshoot emerging problems and especially to ensure that the programme for government—the coalition document—is being implemented in a timely fashion. Each party would be represented by party advisers and usually a junior minister reporting directly to the party leader. For example for the largest party this would typically be the government chief whip (a junior minister) while for the Labour Party it would be a junior minister in the office of the Tanaiste (the office of deputy PM held by the Labour leader). Hence the committee was composed of (1) the most important junior minister from each governing party, and (2) party advisers and programme managers, non-elected but high-powered administrative and party political spin doctors who leave office with the government. Most conflicts during these cabinets were dealt with/resolved here. If not resolved here—a serious conflict—then the party leaders would have to sort it out informally and in person.

almost untenable position as far as their personal credibility is concerned and has the effect of forcing parties that lose policy debates in cabinet to pay a high public price' (1986: 176). The net effect is to raise the salience of any serious policy conflict between the parties. The parties have responded to these dangers with a variety of enforcement mechanisms ranging from the evolution of comprehensive coalition policy documents, to teams of programme managers and ministerial cabinets, to monitor and improve the party's 'performance' in government (more below).

There are no official channels of conflict management similar to the coalition committees that exist in some other coalition systems. Essentially, battles are fought out in cabinet or decided in private meetings of the party leaders and their key advisers. On several occasions during the 1982–7 coalition, for example, head-to-head policy conflicts could only be resolved by a temporary adjournment of the cabinet so that the two leaders (of Fine Gael and Labour) could meet privately to reach a compromise. On crunch issues the 'context' of these meetings might be that Labour would threaten to pull out of government if there was no satisfactory resolution. Therefore, the normal practice is that key party issues that have resulted in stalemate in cabinet will have to be resolved by *ad hoc* private meetings of the party leaders and/or their advisers. Occasionally, a junior coalition partner might underline the seriousness of its objections by boycotting cabinet meetings until the dispute is satisfactorily resolved.

Coalition discipline is typically very strong in Ireland with parties behaving 'as if' they were unitary actors, at least for the purposes of legislative votes. The fact that most Irish governments have had a slim parliamentary majority, combined with the British parliamentary legacy of 'whipping' deputies into line, means that backbenchers know that they face immediate expulsion from the parliamentary party if they vote against the government (without permission). Threatened revolts by individual deputies are often faced down by the government. One of the more dramatic examples was the rebellion in November 1986 by Michael O'Leary, a Fine Gael deputy. By this time the coalition was a minority government that needed O'Leary's vote to survive. Even although he had been clearly stating all day (on national radio and television) that he would vote against the government, O'Leary ultimately acceded to the pressure to remain loyal. One of his colleagues (a cabinet minister) 'told O'Leary in no uncertain terms that he was dead, gone as far as Fine Gael was concerned if he didn't support the government' (Kenny and Keane 1987: 19). Control of candidate selection meant that Fine Gael could credibly threaten to end his political career.

The discipline that is expected of government backbenchers is required of government ministers. An individual minister who disagrees with government policy is expected to remain loyal or exit the government. In 1983, Frank Cluskey, became one of the very few cabinet ministers to resign for what were ostensibly 'policy' reasons. Voting against government policy is simply not an option for a cabinet minister. Undoubtedly, the most dramatic exception to this rule occurred on 16 July 1974 when the Taoiseach and another cabinet minister voted against their government's own Bill to liberalize contraception laws. This was unprecedented and rather bizarre in that the Taoiseach 'had given no prior indication [even in cabinet] that he opposed the Bill' (Gallagher 1982: 203). However, this example is of more than anecdotal interest: it illustrates that it is possible (though not encouraged) for a minister to vote against government policy if the government has conceded a free vote (as it had in this case) or if the issue has been explicitly exempted from the normal requirements of coalition discipline by a provision inserted in the coalition policy document. Such clauses and free votes are quite rare and almost exclusively apply to areas that are accepted as relating to controversial issues that concern 'individual moral conscience' rather than party politics.[14]

While strong party discipline in legislative votes is a prerequisite of government survival, parties need not act in such a unitary fashion in other arenas. If we were primarily interested in public policy outcomes, for example, then it is clear that intra-party politics acts as a significant constraint on policy bargaining between the parties' ministerial teams in cabinet (Mitchell 1996, 1999a). In particular, sections of the parliamentary parties may have specific incentives to police the coalition policy document, by attempting to prevent 'policy drift' through compromise in cabinet. It seems clear that a delicate trade-off has to be struck between negotiations within and between parties.

Coalition agreements do not exist before 1973 and only really evolved in the 1980s and 1990s into substantial documents. These written and published documents are not coalition 'agreements' in the wider sense, rather they are coalition policy documents. These policy documents are getting longer and more detailed (see Table 4.5). The first agreement in 1973 was a pre-electoral manifesto presented as a simple 14-point plan that amounted to only about 1,200 words. By contrast, the 1993 coalition presented a post-electoral document of approximately 23,500 words for ratification by their parliamentary parties.[15]

[14] In particular, capital punishment, church/state issues, reproduction, and sexual morality. For example, during the campaign leading to the Nov. 1982 general election, Fine Gael promised to introduce and support a 'pro-life' amendment to the constitution, making abortion unconstitutional (it was already illegal). In the subsequent coalition policy document negotiated with the Labour Party, the commitment to introduce such an amendment appears, but with an important opt-out clause for Labour: 'The Parliamentary Labour Party reserves the right to a free vote on this issue' (*Joint Programme for Government*, quoted in Mitchell 1996: 145).

[15] While the coalition programmes are now substantial and lengthy documents, there does not appear to be any unilinear trend towards ever longer documents. For example, the 1993 programme is more than three times longer than the 1997 document.

TABLE 4.5. *Size and content of coalition agreements in Ireland, 1973–1999*

Coalition	Size	General procedural rules (in %)	Specific procedural rules (in %)	Distribution of offices (in %)	Distribution of competences (in %)	Policies (in %)
1973	1,248	0	0	0	0	100
1981	9,717	0	0	0	0	100
1982–2	5,877	0	0	0	0	100
1989	n.a.	n.a.	n.a.	n.a.	n.a.	n.a.
1993	23,500	0	0	0	0	100
1994	13,270	0	0	0	0	100
1997	7,351	0	0	0	0	100

n.a. = Coalition agreement is not available.

Parties do take these policy negotiations seriously for a variety of reasons. First, in the case of the Labour Party, the coalition policy document and the decision to enter a coalition government has to be approved by a vote at a specially convened delegate conference. The decision to join a coalition has usually been a highly controversial one for the Labour Party (the period since the 1992 election was exceptional in that regard) with many in the party believing that participation in governments dominated by Fine Gael severely compromised Labour's reputation as a left-wing party and contributed to electoral stagnation (see Gallagher 1982; Mair 1987; Marsh and Mitchell, 1999*b*). Throughout the 1980s when Labour was quite evenly divided on the coalition question, this meant that the Labour leaders (interested in getting into the cabinet) had strong incentives to negotiate a policy package that their party conference would accept.

Second and more generally, although we have very little direct evidence of the precise relationship between the policy 'performance' of a coalition and its subsequent electoral fate, the parties involved certainly behave as though there is a strong tangible connection. Parties in government vigorously attempt to implement their key policies. And because they are aware of the multiple dangers to their policy agendas, such as policy drift and partners reneging on commitments, they attempt to include their key policies in the coalition policy document as insurance. This is of considerable practical importance in the subsequent life of the government (more below). Certainly, detailed analysis of the coalition governments in the 1980s suggests that it will be almost impossible for a party to secure acceptance of a policy during the life of the government if it failed to do so during coalition formation (Mitchell 1996).

Of course this does not mean that coalition negotiations during a government formation period are exclusively concerned with the policy programme.

There is often hard bargaining concerning the distribution of offices and sometimes the rules of the game, but these have to be inferred from other sources, such as leaks to journalists. There are three principal 'stages' to coalition negotiations: the selection of partners, the negotiation of the coalition policy document, and the distribution of portfolios. These are analytically discrete processes even if they occur contemporaneously. In other words, parties typically do not trade a cabinet portfolio for a greater input of its policies into the coalition policy document. Parties fight to maximize their share of both (subject to some 'fairness' conventions).

Offices

The distribution of cabinet portfolios in Ireland has broadly approximated the proportional allocation norm, although smaller parties can usually expect to get slightly more than their proportional share (the 'relative weakness effect', Browne 1973). Thus, the Labour Party in 1993 received 40 per cent of cabinet portfolios (6 ministers), although their contribution to government votes was only 32.7 per cent.[16]

The numerical and qualitative distribution of offices can be a source of significant stumbling blocks in negotiations. For example, a crisis occurred during the 1994 formation negotiations when Labour insisted on retaining six cabinet posts, Fine Gael demanded a minimum of eight, and Democratic Left wanted two (the same that the Progressive Democrats received in the 1989 coalition, when they like Democratic Left had 6 deputies). Since there is a constitutional maximum of fifteen cabinet portfolios somebody had to give way and Democratic Left blinked first. A fudge was agreed so that Democratic Left would get one cabinet minister and one 'super' junior minister who would be allowed to attend cabinet meetings, although not officially a full cabinet minister.

Moreover, this hard bargaining also extends to the allocation of junior ministers. While there is an element of 'signalling the score' this also suggests that junior ministers are regarded as a significant resource. Müller and Strøm's remarks (Introduction) concerning the possible limitations to ministerial autonomy posed by 'divided portfolios' certainly seem theoretically and intuitively plausible. The short, if unhelpful, empirical answer is that this requires further work, at least for the Irish case. To my knowledge no one has published a study analysing the role of junior ministers. While this practice seems likely to have been less significant in the past when there were very few

---

[16] The outcome in 1994 marked a slight departure from the 'relative weakness effect' in that the smallest party, Democratic Left, only managed to secure one cabinet portfolio (slightly less than its proportional share, and not counting the 'super junior' minister). The PDs' one full cabinet member in 1997 is more than their strictly proportional share, though obviously one cannot allocate a fraction of a minister!

junior ministers, there has been a considerable expansion in the number and roles of junior ministers. For example, former Taoiseach Garret FitzGerald notes: 'I was concerned that all Ministers of State [junior ministers] should have specific tasks formally delegated to them by their ministers, something that in the past had often not been the case. Accordingly, I decided in each instance the duties of the junior Minister, and asked that the formal assignment of these functions be made by the member of the Government concerned' (FitzGerald 1991: 433). It seems likely that the junior minister might be most effective when he or she is delegated a significant area within one ministry's competence. Occasionally, a junior minister is given a more general role. For example, Nuala Fennell was asked to co-ordinate women's affairs across a number of departments dealing with women's rights during the 1982–7 coalition. This did not work particularly well in that the minister's and civil servants from these departments were not very cooperative: 'in some cases this reflected a measure of male chauvinism, but for the most part it was simply the instinctive response of Ministers and civil servants to any attempt at co-ordination that impinged upon their responsibilities' (FitzGerald 1991: 434).

Certainly, even a quick glance at the most recent coalitions in Table 4.6, reveals that most ministries and certainly those in the key policy areas now have cabinet ministers and junior ministers from different parties.[17] This must at minimum undermine the informational advantages to the party holding the cabinet jurisdiction, but the extent to which junior ministers can be used to uphold party policy in areas where the party does not control the cabinet minister, must remain an open question pending study of decision making processes within ministries.

Patronage appointments (of which the government has many) can also be a source of 'office' competition between the parties. In general, these must be agreed between the parties in the coalition if the competition is to be contained to manageable levels. As part of the 1992–3 formation negotiations, for example, Fianna Fáil and Labour agreed Ireland's next nominee for the European Commission. During the 1982–7 coalition, however, the nomination to the same job caused a major government crisis. In the end, the Fine Gael candidate for the European post (the then Attorney General) was only accepted by Labour on the condition that they could nominate his successor as Attorney General. Therefore, the general rule is that all major appointments (those that transcend the responsibilities of individual departments) have to be agreed between the parties. Indeed, dramatic events in 1994 underlined the dangers of departing from this convention: the Fianna Fáil Taoiseach appointed his nominee as President of the High Court against the

[17] This is best seen by examining Reynolds II and Bruton I (1992–7). During Ahern I (1997–) the extremely small size of the junior coalition partner, the PDs, imposed practical limits on the extent of this form of ministerial cross-checking.

express wishes of the Labour Party. Labour immediately withdrew from the cabinet.

Similar norms of consultation and agreement between party leaders applies to any cabinet reshuffle of portfolios. While reshuffles are not as common in coalition governments they have occasionally occurred. Just as each party normally has full discretion as to its original choice of ministers, the Taoiseach cannot realistically fire or even move a minister of another party without that party's consent. This was dramatically highlighted in 1986 when the Fine Gael Taoiseach as part of an extensive reshuffle wanted to move the Minister for Health, Barry Desmond, who was also deputy leader of the Labour Party. Desmond refused point blank to be moved to any other portfolio, saying that the Taoiseach would have to sack him to get him out of the Department of Health. Although the Taoiseach under Article 28.9.4 of the Constitution, can 'for reasons which seem to him sufficient', fire any member of the government, this power is in effect amended during coalition governments. The leader of the Labour Party could hardly allow his deputy to be fired by Fine Gael and informed the Taoiseach that Labour would resign from government if Desmond was fired. Facing an electoral disaster, in the event of a coalition break-up triggering a certain general election, the Taoiseach left Desmond at the Department of Health.

Policy

In Ireland parties do bargain vigorously over policy and many of the key events that destabilize coalition governments are policy conflicts. Whatever the precise relationship, parties believe that their electoral futures significantly depend upon the perception of their policy performance in government and expend enormous effort and resources to this end. Given the existence of multiple dangers which might sidetrack the implementation of a party's policies, such as the obstruction and opposition of the other parties in the coalition, policy erosion by detail, or simply being derailed by a fast-moving and busy government agenda, parties in coalitions increasingly resort to detailed policy documents at formation. Each party bargains to imprint a selection of its key policies in the coalition policy document as partial insurance that the measure has minimal agreement.

Although the coalition policy document is a highly strategic device that includes much window-dressing and empty aspirations, it increasingly incorporates fairly detailed commitments in a wide range of policy areas. While the level of specificity does not of course rival the eventual draft legislation (and there is therefore much still to play for) it does include definite commitments, some of which are costed. For example, the *Fianna Fáil and Labour Programme for a Partnership Government 1993–1997* (reproduced in Gallagher and Laver 1993), includes specific commitments to institutional

TABLE 4.6. *Distribution of cabinet and junior ministerships in Irish coalitions*

		(1) Taoiseach	(2) Finance	(3) Industry/ Enterprise	(4) Foreign	(5) Agriculture	(6) Justice	(7) Health/ Social Welfare	(8) Environment
2	Costello I	FG	FGcnt		CnP	Ind[a]	FG	CnP	L
4	Costello II	FG	FG	L*	FG	FG	L	FG	FG
11	Cosgrave I	FG	FG	L	FG	FG	FG	L*fg	Lfg
14	FitzGerald I	FG	FGl	L*fg	FG	FG	FGl	Lfg	FG
16	FitzGerald II	FG	FGl	FG	FG	FG	FG	Lfg	L*
18	Haughey IV	FF	FF	PDff	FF	FF	FF	FF	FFpd
19	Reynolds I	FF	FF	PDff	FF	FF	FF	FF	FFpd
20	Reynolds II	FF	FFl	Lff	L*ff	FFl	FF	Lff, FFl[8]	FFl
21	Bruton I	FG	Lfg	FGdl	L*fg	FG	FG	FG, DLfg[12]	Ldl
22	Ahern I	FF	FF	PDff	FFpd	FF	FF	FF; FF[14]	FFpd

* Indicates party holding the office of Tanaiste (Deputy Prime Minister).
[a] During the 1948–51 coalition the Ministry of Agriculture was held by James Dillon an independent (the only independent minister that Ireland has had). At this time he was in exile from Fine Gael and later became leader of that party.
[b] The Deputy Prime Minister held the Ministry of Social Welfare. During many cabinets the separate ministries of Health and Social Welfare are represented by the same cabinet minister.
[c] Social Welfare.
[d] During the 1973–7 coalition the Department of Transport was held by Fine Gael and the Department of Posts and Telegraphs (Communications) by the Labour Party.
[e] The Department of Fisheries and Forestry.
[f] The Department of Public Service.

and taxation reform, promises to raise child benefit by a stated amount, promises to recruit 500 new remedial teachers, and even mentions a new hospital in Tallaght (to begin construction Spring 1993) which is to have exactly 467 beds!

The policy document does provide some structure to policy competition during the life of the coalition. Certainly, as already mentioned, if a party failed to have one of its key policies inserted in this document at formation, then it will have very little chance subsequently of forcing the issue onto the government's agenda and securing its adoption. It seems that to do so requires exercises in brinkmanship, explicit threats to break the government. The policy document is particularly important for smaller parties in coalition, as they have reason to be fearful of the progressive erosion of their policy commitments (and political identity) through the accumulation of lost cabinet battles and because they control fewer ministries. The coalition policy document provides a legitimating reference point, outside of the logic of cabinet arithmetic and portfolio distribution, that can be periodically invoked to protect the smaller parties' vital policy interests.

(9) Labour/ Employment	(10) Education	(11) Transport/ Communications	(12) Defence	(13) Trade/ Tourism	(14) Gaeltacht	(15) Lands	(16) Other
	FG	NL	FGl			CnT	L*b
	FG	L	FG			CnT	Lc
L	FGl	FG, Ld	FG		FG	FG	
L	FG	FG	L	FG	FG		FGe
L	FG	FG	FG	Lfg	FG		FGf
FF	FF	FF	FF*	FF	PD		PD, FFh
FF	FF	FF	FF*	FF			PD, FFh
	Lff	FF	FF	FF	Li		Lffj
	Lfg	FGl	FGl	FG	Li		Lj
	FF	FF	FF	FF	FFi		FFm

h During the Haughey IV and Reynolds I governments, the Department of Energy was held by the Progressive Democrats and the Department of the Marine by Fianna Fáil.
i During the 1993–95 coalition the Department of Health was assigned to a Labour minister and the Department of Social Welfare to Fianna Fail.
j The department of Arts, Culture and the Gaeltacht.
k A new ministry the Department of Equality and Law Reform.
l In the coalition formed in Dec. 1994, the Departments of Health and Social Welfare were again held by different cabinet ministeres, Health by Fine Gael and Social Welfare by Democratic Left.
m In 1997 the Departments of Health and Social Welfare were again assigned to different cabinet ministers.
n In 1997 a Ministry of Natural Resources was created.

The document is quickly 'politicized' and often becomes a battleground as the media and the parties identify which parts of the supposedly 'joint' programme belong to each party. Party effectiveness can then be judged in terms of their success in implementing 'their parts' of the programme. None of this is meant to suggest that the coalition policy document is simply 'implemented' in some unproblematic fashion. Rather, many of the key items in the document will be the source of much subsequent conflict as the parties battle to interpret the true 'meaning' of a commitment or fight over the details.

Also, since parties will have suffered policy costs by making concessions at coalition formation as part of their eagerness to get into office, they will often try to renege on these commitments once installed in government. Such defections will be resisted. If a precise commitment was secured at formation and included in the coalition's policy document, attempted defections from this policy by a party's coalition partners will be highly destabilizing, since they will be regarded not simply as 'ordinary' policy debate, but as a 'breach of faith' and an assault on formation conditions. However, there are multiple strategies by which a party can attempt to disguise a defection, presenting it as 'policy development', or by rationalizing 'changed circumstances' and 'economic realities'. Of course, a party will be greatly aided in this task if it controls the relevant portfolio.

Close examination of the coalition governments in the 1980s suggests that a key enforcement mechanism for the coalition policy document was provided by intra-party opposition to the concessions made by each parties' ministers in cabinet (Mitchell 1996, 1999a). While parliamentary discipline is generally high, clear departures from the party policies that were negotiated into the coalition policy document, proved to be dangerous for ministers. Ministers, who after all occupy the top jobs, have greater incentives to see the virtues or at least the necessity of inter-party concessions in cabinet. The parliamentary party, on the other hand, typically sees less advantage (and potentially a lot of electoral danger) in compromising key party policies. Coalition policy compromises were repeatedly destabilized by revolts in the government's constituent parties. These do not usually show up in a legislative roll call analysis because deputies rarely actually vote against the government. Rather, the interaction of inter-party and intra-party bargaining is such that negotiations in cabinet occurred in the context of an anticipated need to 'carry' the coalition's parliamentary parties. However, on many occasions the ministers miscalculated how much departure from party policy their backbenchers would tolerate, so that a revolt would develop in the parliamentary party and party organization. While ministers would sometimes attempt to face down such rebellions, the more typical response was to take the threat seriously and renegotiate the policy between the parties at cabinet level. Thus, most intra-party rebellions become a part of a government's policy development phase and do not show up as legislative defections. It seems then, that sections of parliamentary parties distinct from a party's ministerial team, in becoming advocates for party policy, form part of an enforcement mechanism for the coalition policy document.

Notwithstanding the above points, a party's ministerial team also has electoral and office-seeking incentives to try to implement party policies. During the 1992–3 formation negotiations the Labour Party insisted on a series of institutional and structural changes to government departments—essentially enforcement mechanisms—that were designed to ensure that Labour would have a major impact across a wide range of policy areas (for example, policy areas where they did not control the portfolio). Labour had been disappointed by its performance in previous coalitions led by a larger party in which it had been perceived to play a junior role. Labour, in a position of unprecedented strength after the 1992 election, wanted to change the rules of coalition governance, in order to break out of the pattern of participation in a coalition dominated by its larger rivals leading to electoral decline. Thus, the impetus for institutional change was primarily electoral: if electorates do engage in retrospective voting, then Labour might expect popularity gains at the next election, if only it could win the battle of perception that it was effective whilst in government.[18]

Three principal changes were made. First, Labour wanted the role of their party leader in the coalition government to be institutionally strengthened. Dick Spring (the Labour leader) was appointed foreign minister and Tánaiste (deputy prime minister). While the leader of the second largest party in a coalition had always been appointed Tánaiste, in the past this had been largely symbolic (a constitutional position, deputizing for the Taoiseach in the event of his absence, incapacity or death). Spring wanted an office of Tánaiste created with a staff to allow him to monitor the broad progress of the government (from Labour's perspective) and to facilitate the implementation of the coalition's policy programme. Such an office was created with a leading junior minister appointed as well as civil servants. It is clear from the official duties allocated to the junior minister (a Labour Party member) at the office of the Tánaiste that her primary function was to ensure that a reasonable amount of Labour policies specifically and the coalition programme in general are implemented. She represented the Labour leader on all the key policy coordinating committees, while the Taoiseach (Fianna Fáil) was represented on these same committees by a Fianna Fáil junior minister who was also the government's Chief Whip.

Second, ministerial cabinets were introduced in which political appointees personally loyal to the minister advised on a wide range of matters relating to both departmental business and other policy areas on the cabinet agenda. One former civil servant nicely summarized the role of these advisers: 'in general, an advisor acts as a replication of the minister in many respects, as an extension of his political personality, as an extra pair of eyes and ears, doing for him what the Minister would do for himself if he had time' (Sean Dooney, quoted in Farrell 1993a: 159).

While political advisers had previously existed on a more informal basis, the third change was more innovative, controversial, and upset many civil servants. This was the appointment by each cabinet minister of a 'partnership programme manager', a senior appointment designed to enhance the minister's ability to monitor and check that the departmental policies are actually being implemented properly. One informed observer noted that 'Labour intended to do more than insist on a comprehensive programme for government. It also wanted an agreed means of ensuring that all policy proposals outlined in any prenuptial agreement with Fianna Fáil would be subject to informed and detailed tracking, fine-tuning and review by trusted officials,

---

[18] Ironically, despite implementing most of its agenda and being a prominent member of a popular government, Labour received a crushing blow at the 1997 general election and was cut in half (see Marsh and Sinnott 1999). One intriguing explanation might be as follows: if a government has implemented almost its entire manifesto, why re-elect it? Thanks to Rudy Andeweg for this latter point.

the partnership programme managers, whose responsibility would be to each minister personally rather than to his or her department' (O'Halpin 1996: 5). One reason why these structural changes are likely to be of lasting significance is that a whole series of new 'political' jobs have been created that can be used to put party staffers on the public payroll (O'Halpin 1996: 10).[19]

It seems clear then that parties in Irish coalition governments do take the need to be seen to be implementing policies quite seriously and they are no longer satisfied with the empty homilies and unrealistic aspirations of previous coalition policy documents. While these documents continue to contain both of these 'feel good' clauses, they increasingly include more specific policies that they intend to implement. Furthermore, parties are increasingly concerned with enforcement mechanisms designed to ensure that they deliver (or are perceived to deliver) the promises they make.

COALITION TERMINATION

In marked contrast to Browne et al.'s (1986: 100) finding that 'regularly scheduled elections are the most common single cause of dissolutions' in Scandinavia (especially, Iceland, Norway, and Sweden), no Irish governments have ever been terminated by a 'regular' parliamentary election at least in the strict sense of an administration serving its full five-year term. The longest lasting government listed in Table 4.3 was the Cosgrave (1973–7) coalition which terminated after serving four years and three months. The average duration of the twenty-one completed governments in Table 4.3 is 891 days[20] (about two years and five months).[21] Of course in a system in which the prime minister has dissolution powers, it is highly improbable that a government will be terminated by reaching its maximum term. The strategic timing of elections is an important resource for the PM's party and few PM's would want to risk being 'boxed-in' (diminishing the other parties' uncer-

---

[19] While these innovations were extensively used during the 1993–4 and 1994–7 governments, they were scaled back by the coalition that came to power in 1997. This was largely because the Progressive Democrats (as a liberal tax and deficit cutting party) had argued in opposition that the creation of an office of Tánaiste and extensive use of programme managers was a wasteful use of public funds. The other parties have less reticence about such 'hired help', so it seems likely that future coalitions will find it prudent to adopt some variation on these reforms.

[20] The standard deviation is 373 days.

[21] Of course all duration estimates are an artefact of counting rules. There are three instances in Table 4.3 of a new cabinet being created by the voluntary retirement of the Taoiseach (de Valera, Lemass, and Lynch). Thus, if such voluntary resignations are not counted as establishing a new cabinet, then the average duration of Irish governments rises to 1,040 days (about two years and ten months). The resignation of Haughey in favour of Reynolds is not included, since it was clearly forced to save the coalition.

tainty) by governing into the last few months of the maximum term. Thus, in one sense, to say that the Cosgrave government ended 'early' (after four years and three months) is somewhat misleading. Certainly, it does not suggest that the government was in any sense terminated by instability or conflict, simply because technically the coalition could have chosen to govern for another few months. In a substantive sense, any government that has lasted perhaps three and a half to four years is conventionally thought of as having lasted a 'full' term.

Thus, Irish governments are rarely ended for purely technical reasons as defined by Table 4.7. Government's do not serve the maximum constitutionally possible period and no Taoiseach has ever died in office. On four occasions, however, the government has been terminated because of the 'mid-term' resignation of the Taoiseach, requiring the succession of a party colleague. On three of the four occasions, the resignation can be said to be primarily a voluntary retirement, while on the fourth (Haughey IV) the Taoiseach was forced to resign by an ultimatum from his coalition partners.

Coalition terminations are typically accompanied by early elections because a government resignation traditionally triggered an election. Indeed, the change of coalition government in 1994 was the first to occur within an inter-electoral period, an occurrence that may—or may not—serve to legitimize this process.

Governments in Ireland have been terminated by combinations of the full range of discretionary mechanisms listed in Table 4.7 (except voluntary enlargement of the coalition). Early elections and conflict within and between the coalition parties are clearly the most frequent events that contribute to coalition break-up. The strategic timing of elections is clearly of considerable importance, although since almost all coalition governments have suffered badly at the subsequent election (Table 4.8) this is more about damage limitation than a 'cut and run' to an early election in order to cash-in on windfall popularity gains. As can be seen from Table 4.7, conflict within and between the coalition partners are probably the largest causes of early resignation, and it seems likely that the opportunity costs of collapse do decrease as it reaches the end of its maximum term (Lupia and Strøm 1995: 656). Nevertheless, some recent coalitions (Reynolds 1, Reynolds 2) fell apart early in their terms due to irreconcilable policy and patronage disputes between the parties. Indeed, the Fianna Fáil–Labour coalition that formed in 1993, despite being a government with by far the largest parliamentary majority in Irish history (and incidentally the government which most leading coalition theories predicted would be a 'stable equilibrium') collapsed in acrimony in less than two years.

TABLE 4.7. *Cabinet termination in Ireland*

Cabinet number	Cabinet	Mechanisms of cabinet termination					
		Technical	Discretionary				
		(2) Other constitutional reason	(4) Early parliamentary election	(6) Cabinet defeated by opposition in parliament	(7) Conflict between coalition parties		(8) Intra-party conflict in coalition party or parties
					Policy	Personnel	
1	de Valera VI		X				
2	Costello I		X				CnP,L
3	de Valera VII		X				
4	Costello II		X		X		CnP, L, FG
5	de Valera VIII	X					
6	Lemass I		X				
7	Lemass II		X				
8	Lemass III	X					
9	Lynch I		X				
10	Lynch II		X				FF,L
11	Cosgrave I		X				
12	Lynch III						FF,NL
13	Haughey I		X				FF,L
14	FitzGerald I		X	X			
15	Haughey II		X	X			FF,L
16	FitzGerald II		X		X		FG,NL Lab, NL
17	Haughey III		X				
18	Haughey IV				X	X	FF,L
19	Reynolds I		X	X		X	
20	Reynolds II					X	
21	Bruton I		X				

(10) Popular opinion shocks	(11) International or national security event	(12) Economic event	(13) Personal event	Policy area(s)	Comments
					Threat of new party, CnP
				5; 7	Lost vote on milk prices when 3 TDs defect
X				2	Minority government lost 2 by-elections and Ind's defect
		X			CnP leaves government. Calls election to avoid confidence vote
			X		PM resigns (retires) to allow succession
X					Early election to cash-in on popularity
X					Lemass (PM), confident of victory after by-election successes during 1964, calls early election (wins narrow overall majority)
			X		PM resigns (retires) to allow succession (also had heart disease)
					Election to consolidate PM's position within party
	X			4	Had become a minority government; election called to restore position (intense factionalism in FF over NI policy; ministers sacked)
					Government calls election, then commissions an opinion poll, finding it is way behind FF!
X			X		PM resigns (retires) to allow succession (also backbench dissent at loss of European and by-elections)
					Haughey seeks personal mandate (sharp factionalism among FF leadership)
				2; 7	Defeated on its Budget (first division on raising beer prices!)
		X			Undermined by fationalism and scandals, government loses confidence motion
X				2; 7	Labour withdraws from coalition
X					High in the polls, FF gambles on an early opportunistic election
			X		Intense factionalism within FF; PM forced to resign by an ultimatum from coalition partner
					PD's withdraw from government after sharp personal conflict with PM
				6	Conflict between PM and Lab. leader. PM resigns but Lab. still leave the government
					No conflict: a popular three-party government holds election to renew its mandate—and loses

TABLE 4.8. *Electoral costs/benefits of government parties in Ireland, 1944–1999 (in % of votes)*

Government	In office at time of election	Election year	WP/DL[a]	LAB	CnP	FF	CnT	FG	PD	Government
FF 1944–8	Yes	1948	—	—	—	−7.0	—	—	—	−7.0
FG–Lab–NL–CnT–CnP 1948–51	Yes	1951	—	+0.1[b]	−9.1	—	−2.7	+6.0	—	−5.7
FF 1951–4	Yes	1954	—	—	—	−2.9	—	—	—	−2.9
FG–Lab–CnT 1954–7	Yes	1957	—	−3.0	—	—	−0.7	−5.4	—	−9.1
FF 1957–61	Yes	1961	—	—	—	−4.5	—	—	—	−4.5
FF 1961–5	Yes	1965	—	—	—	+3.9	—	—	—	+3.9
FF 1965–9	Yes	1969	—	—	—	−2.0	—	—	—	−2.0
FF 1969–73	Yes	1973	—	—	—	+0.5	—	—	—	+0.5
FG–Lab 1973–7	Yes	1977	—	−2.1	—	—	—	−4.6	—	−6.7
FF 1977–81	Yes	1981	—	—	—	−5.3	—	—	—	−5.3
FG–Lab 1981–2	Yes	1982–1	—	−0.8	—	—	—	+0.8	—	±0
FF 1982	Yes	1982–2	—	—	—	−2.1	—	—	—	−2.1
FG–Lab 1982–7	Yes	1987	—	−3.0	—	—	—	−12.1	—	−15.1
FF 1987–9	Yes	1989	—	—	—	0.0	—	—	—	±0
FF–PD 1989–92	Yes	1992	—	—	—	−5.0	—	—	−0.8	−5.8
FF–Lab 1993–4	No	1997	—	−8.9	—	+0.2	—	—	—	−8.7
FG–Lab–DL 1994–7	Yes	1997	−0.3	−8.9	—	—	—	+3.5	—	−5.7
FF–PD 1997–										
MEANS			−0.3[c]	−2.95[d]	−9.1[e]	−2.2	−1.7	−1.97	−0.8	−4.48

[a] The figures for 1992 onwards refers to Democratic Left. Following Gallagher (1993b: 60) Democratic Left 'founded in 1992 by six of the seven Workers' Party TDs, is treated as the continuation of the pre-1992 Workers' Party and the 1992 Workers' Party is treated as a new party'.
[b] Refers to the combined total for the Labour Party and National Labour, a temporary split from Labour. The parties 'merged amicably' in June 1950 before the next election (Gallagher 1985: 110).
[c] DL were only in government on one occasion (n = 1), before they merged during 1998 with the Labour Party.
[d] For the purposes of calculation the mean Labour loss the cell entries for 1994 and 1997 (−8.9) are treated as one case.
[e] Note that in the case of Clann na Poblachta the apparently high 'mean' cost of incumbency refers to only one case (n = 1).

CONCLUSION

Government formation and maintenance has entered a more exciting phase of fully-fledged coalition politics in which there now are a variety of possible outcomes from the bargaining process that previously had been highly restricted by self-imposed behavioural constraints. Most Irish politicians are by now quite adept at coalition politics and have even adapted the rules of the game, departments, and the administrative structure, to facilitate individual parties in their efforts to improve their 'performance' (not least electoral) while in government.

As well as an increasingly available electorate the previously dominant party, Fianna Fáil, is now available for coalition and thus has become an 'ordinary' political party like all the rest. Whether this is in Fianna Fáil's long-term interest is unclear at this point. It is of course still by far the largest party and its central location indicates that it will be a powerful player in coalition bargaining. But it no longer defines the entire structure of party competition as a simple choice between itself or 'the rest', a development that may weaken the party in the long run. What is clear beyond doubt is that the other parties (at least the smaller parties) have been freed from their shackles and are enjoying a wider range of potential governing combinations. They now have options, and as was mentioned earlier, choice is the largest part of power in coalition politics.

REFERENCES

Browne, Eric (1973). *Coalition Theories: A Logical and Empirical Critique.* Beverly Hills, Calif.: Sage.

——Frendreis, J. and Gleiber, D. (1986). 'Dissolution of Governments in Scandinavia: A Critical Events Perspective'. *Scandinavian Political Studies*, 9: 93–109.

Farrell, Brian (1983). 'Coalitions and Political Institutions: The Irish Experience', in Vernon Bogdanor (ed.), *Coalition Government in Western Europe*. London: Heinemann.

——(1993a). 'The Formation of the Partnership Government', in Michael Gallagher and Michael Laver (eds.), *How Ireland Voted 1992*. Dublin: PSAI Press and Folens.

——(1993b). 'The Government', in John Coakley and Michael Gallagher (eds.), *Politics in the Republic of Ireland*, 2nd edn. Limerick: PSAI Press and Folens.

FitzGerald, Garret (1991). *All in a Life: Garret FitzGerald: An Autobiography.* London: Macmillan.

Gallagher, Michael (1982). *The Irish Labour Party in Transition, 1957–82.* Manchester: Manchester University Press.

Gallagher, Michael (1985). *Political Parties in the Republic of Ireland*. Manchester: Manchester University Press.
——(1988). 'The People, the President and the Constitution', in Brian Farrell (ed.), *De Valera's Constitution and Ours*. Dublin: Gill and Macmillan.
——(1993a). 'The Constitution', in John Coakley and Michael Gallagher (eds.), *Politics in the Republic of Ireland*, 2nd edn. Limerick: PSAI Press and Folens.
——(1993b). 'The Election of the 27th Dáil', in Michael Gallagher and Michael Laver (eds.), *How Ireland Voted 1992*. Dublin: PSAI Press and Folens.
——and Laver, Michael (1993) (eds.). *How Ireland Voted 1992*. Dublin: Folens and PSAI Press.
——and Sinnott, Richard (1990) (eds.). *How Ireland Voted 1989*. Galway: Centre for the Study of Irish Elections and PSAI Press.
Kenny, Shane, and Keane, Fergal (1987). *Irish Politics Now: 'This Week' Guide to the 25th Dáil*. Dublin: Brandon and RTE.
Laver, Michael (1994). 'Party Policy and Cabinet Portfolios in Ireland 1992: Results from an Expert Survey'. *Irish Political Studies*, 9: 157–64.
——(1998). 'Party Policy in Ireland in 1997: Results from an Expert Survey', *Irish Political Studies*, 13: 159–71.
——(1999). 'The Irish Party System Approaching the Millennium', in Michael Marsh and Paul Mitchell (eds.), *How Ireland Voted 1997*. Boulder, Colo.: Westview Press.
——and Arkins, Audrey (1990). 'Coalition and Fianna Fáil', in Michael Gallagher and Richard Sinnott (eds.), *How Ireland Voted 1989*. Galway: Centre for the Study of Irish Elections and PSAI Press.
——and Higgins, Michael D. (1986). 'Coalition or Fianna Fáil? The Politics of Inter-Party Government in Ireland', in Geoffrey Pridham (ed.), *Coalition Behaviour in Theory and Practice*. Cambridge: Cambridge University Press.
——and Schofield, Norman (1990). *Multiparty Government: The Politics of Coalition in Europe*. Oxford: Oxford University Press.
——and Shepsle, Kenneth (1996). *Making and Breaking Governments: Cabinets and Legislatures in Parliamentary Democracies*. Cambridge: Cambridge University Press.
Lupia, Arthur, and Strøm, Kaare (1995). 'Coalition Termination and the Strategic Timing of Parliamentary Elections'. *American Political Science Review*, 89: 648–65.
Mair, Peter (1986). 'Locating Irish Parties on a Left–Right Dimension: An Empirical Enquiry'. *Political Studies*, 34: 456–65.
——(1987). *The Changing Irish Party System: Organisation, Ideology and Electoral Competition*. London: Frances Pinter.
——(1993a). 'Fianna Fáil, Labour and the Irish Party System', in Michael Gallagher and Michael Laver (eds.), *How Ireland Voted 1992*. Dublin: PSAI Press and Folens.
——(1993b). 'The Party System and Party Competition', in John Coakley and Michael Gallagher (eds.), *Politics in the Republic of Ireland*, 2nd edn. Limerick: PSAI Press and Folens.
Marsh, Michael, and Mitchell, Paul (1999a) (eds.). *How Ireland Voted 1997*. Boulder, Colo.: Westview Press.
————(1999b). 'Office, Votes and then Policy: Hard Choices for Political Parties in the Republic of Ireland', in Wolfgang C. Müller and Kaare Strøm (eds.), *Policy, Office, or Votes?* Cambridge: Cambridge University Press.

——and Sinnott, Richard (1999). 'The Behaviour of the Irish Voter', in Michael Marsh and Paul Mitchell (eds.), *How Ireland Voted 1997*. Boulder, Colo.: Westview Press.
Mitchell, Paul (1993). 'The 1992 General Election in the Republic of Ireland'. *Irish Political Studies* 8: 111–17.
——(1996). *The Life and Times of Coalition Governments: Coalition Maintenance by Event Management*. Ph.D. EUI, Florence.
——(1999a). 'Coalition Discipline, Enforcement Mechanisms and Intra-Party Politics', in Shaun Bowler, David Farrell, and Richard Katz (eds.), *Party Discipline and Parliamentary Government*. Columbus: Ohio State University Press.
——(1999b). 'Government Formation: A Tale of Two Coalitions', in Michael Marsh and Paul Mitchell (eds.), *How Ireland Voted 1997*. Boulder, Colo.: Westview Press.
O'Halpin, Eunan (1996). 'Partnership Programme Managers in the Reynolds/Spring Coalition 1993–94: An Assessment'. Dublin City University Business School, Research Paper no. 6.
Sinnott, Richard (1995). *Irish Voters Decide: Voting Behaviour in Elections and Referendums since 1918*. Manchester: Manchester University Press.
Strøm, Kaare, Budge, Ian, and Laver, Michael (1994). 'Constraints on Cabinet Formation in Parliamentary Democracies'. *American Journal of Political Science*, 38: 303–35.

5

Norway

A Fragile Coalitional Order

Hanne Marthe Narud and Kaare Strøm

INTRODUCTION

In Norway, coalition government has rarely been more than a transitory phenomenon. Since the post-war resumption of partisan politics in 1945, there have been only eight cabinets representing more than one political party, and half of these have lasted no more than about a year.[1] Moreover, all but the most recent of Norwegian coalitions have occurred in two clearly delimited eras: one lasting from the early 1960s to the early 1970s, and a second covering the period from 1983 to 1990. Both of these periods of coalescence were cut short by the intrusion of the issue of European Community/Union (EC/EU) membership. Outside of these historical parameters, Norway has been governed by single-party, often minority, governments. Before World War II, true coalitions were indeed even more rare, and the only such alliance that emerged with any regularity was the one between the Conservatives and the Moderate Liberals (Frisinnede Venstre), two parties which eventually merged.

During some periods, Norway, like Ireland, has alternated between coalitional and non-coalitional politics. Non-socialist coalitions have replaced

---

We would like to thank Lars Korvald, Gunnar Magnus, Erik Nessheim, Jon O. Norbom, Jarle Skjørestad, Paul Thyness, Henry Valen, and Erik Wickstrøm for valuable comments and information.

[1] Our account of Norwegian post-war governments begins with the cabinet formed by Einar Gerhardsen in Nov. 1945. This was the first cabinet following the Oct. 1945 parliamentary election and the resumption of partisan politics. In accordance with Norwegian convention, however, we refer to this cabinet as Gerhardsen II, since Gerhardsen also headed a short-lived provisional all-party coalition from 25 June until a government based on the results of the 8 Oct. elections could be formed. We exclude Gerhardsen I from any further analysis because it was so clearly a provisional caretaker based on the suspension of ordinary party politics. In so doing, we are in accordance with the most authoritative account of post-war Norwegian parliamentary government (Nordby 1985).

single-party Labour governments, and vice versa. This form of alternation was particularly prominent in the decades from 1960 to 1990, as noted above. But, again somewhat akin to Ireland, established patterns of coalition formation have broken down in the most recent years. Contrary to the Irish case, however, these trends seem to have made cabinet coalitions less, rather than more, likely. As in Denmark and Sweden, it is specifically broad non-socialist coalescence that has recently become less common and credible. To understand the background of these trends in Norwegian coalition bargaining, let us first consider the Norwegian party system.

THE POST-WAR NORWEGIAN PARTY SYSTEM

Until the early 1970s Norway had one of the most stable party systems in Western Europe. Similar in format to those of Sweden and Denmark, the Norwegian party system originated in the late 1880s, and emerged around 1920 into what has been labelled 'the Scandinavian five-party model' (Berglund and Lindström 1978). The party system has been politically defined around six dimensions of political cleavage, determined by economic, geographical, and cultural circumstances (see Rokkan 1967, 1970; Valen and Rokkan 1974). The class cleavage and the sectoral urban-rural cleavage were determined by economic conflicts in the labour market and the commodity market, respectively. A territorial cleavage between centre and periphery partly overlapped with three cultural cleavages: a socio-cultural conflict between two different versions of the Norwegian language; a moral conflict, focused in large part on the abuse of alcohol and articulated by the teetotalist movement; and a religious conflict over the doctrines and organization of the Lutheran state church and its role in social life. A number of cleavages have thus influenced Norwegian politics and the development of its party system. The major division, however, not only in shaping electoral preferences, but also in terms of government alternatives, has been along the left–right axis, between socialists and non-socialists.

Some salient features of the Norwegian party system were established by the 1920s and endured for almost 50 years. A stable Norwegian five-party system pitted a dominant Labour Party (Arbeiderpartiet (A or DNA)) and a much smaller Communist Party (Norges Kommunistiske Parti (NKP)) against three non-socialist parties: the Conservatives (Høyre (H)), the Liberals (Venstre (V)), the agrarian Centre Party (Senterpartiet (SP)).[2] The first deviation from this model occurred in 1933, when a fundamentalist religious faction broke away from the Liberals and founded the Christian

---

[2] The Centre Party was until 1959 known as the Farmers' Party (Bondepartiet).

People's Party (Kristelig Folkeparti (KRF)). The critical issue that provoked this fission was abolition. After the onset of the Cold War, the Communist Party gradually faded into oblivion and lost its parliamentary representation in 1961. At the same time, however, a left-wing Labour faction broke out and formed the Socialist People's Party (Sosialistisk Folkeparti) because of dissent over foreign policy issues and specifically NATO membership. 1973 witnessed additional changes in the party system. The question of Norwegian membership in the European Community (EC) sparked intense conflict within as well as between political parties (see e.g. Valen 1973; Gleditsch and Hellevik 1977; Bjørklund 1982). As a result, the Liberal Party that had dominated Norwegian politics from the 1880s to the 1930s was split in two.[3] The two parties merged again in 1988, but the 'new' Liberal Party has never regained its traditional strength. In addition, two new parties evolved. On the left wing a new socialist party, today called the Socialist Left Party (Sosialistisk Venstreparti), emerged as a result of a union between the Socialist People's Party, the Communist Party, and an anti-EC faction of the Labour Party (AIK). Another new party formed on the right: Anders Lange's Party, named after its founder, a flamboyant and eccentric anti-statist populist. This new party, which called for sharp reductions in taxes and public expenditure, later changed its name to the Progress Party (Fremskrittspartiet). Since the mid-1980s, the Progress Party has campaigned to restrict immigration and curtail the size of the public sector.

Effectively, then, the post-war Norwegian party system has, in Laver and Schofield's (1990) terms, changed from a unipolar, through a bipolar, to a multipolar format. The history of this development can be summarized as follows:

1. *Social Democratic Predominance: 1945–1961.* From World War II until 1961, the Labour Party enjoyed a predominant position (Sartori 1976). Four consecutive elections yielded outright parliamentary majorities and single-party Labour governments. Effectively, the party system was at this time unipolar. The socialist parties jointly obtained about 51 per cent of the popular vote in all elections from 1945 to 1969. The parties of the centre—the Liberals, the (agrarian) Centre Party, and the Christian People's Party—obtained about 29 per cent, and the Conservatives about 20 per cent. Thus, during this early post-war period only marginal electoral shifts occurred from one election to the next.

---

[3] The majority of the members of the Liberal parliamentary party left to form the pro-EC Liberal People's Party (Det Liberale Folkeparti (DLF)). The anti-EC rump retained the name and the party organization. The ill-fated DLF actually went through two name changes. It was first known as the Popular New Liberals and subsequently as the New People's Party, before taking the name used in this analysis. The Liberals and the Liberal People's Party reunited in 1988, sixteen years after their 'divorce'.

2. *Bipolar Stability: 1961–1972*. The 1961 emergence of the Socialist People's Party caused some erosion of Labour's support, while the non-socialist parties gained in strength and cohesion. The effective number of legislative parties increased slightly (see Table 5.1). However, until the early 1970s electoral volatility remained low, and the party system deviated only slightly from its previous five-party format. The socialist and non-socialist blocs were extremely evenly balanced, and minority Labour governments alternated with bourgeois coalitions (see Groennings 1961; Rommetvedt 1984).

3. *Bipolar Fragmentation: 1972–1990*. Following the first European Community referendum in 1972, Norway began to experience more party system change than at any time since the 1920s. This is clearly reflected in Table 5.1, which shows that the effective number of parties increased from 3.2 in 1969 to 4.1 in 1973. From the mid-1970s on, a massive shift could be observed in favour of the parties of the right: the Conservatives and the Progress Party, popularly referred to as 'the swing to the right' (Bjørklund and Hagtvet 1981; Valen 1981, 1992). There was a corresponding decline in support for Labour and the parties of the centre (Sainsbury 1985). The Conservatives reached a peak of support in the early 1980s, from which they have subsequently gradually receded (Kuhnle, Strøm, and Svåsand 1986). The Progress Party, on the other hand, has experienced even greater and less predictable volatility, but have gone on to particular successes in the elections of 1989 and 1997.

4. *Multipolar Fragmentation: 1990–* . The legacy of the political upheaval that began in the 1970s has been a substantially weakened Labour Party, significant new parties on the extreme left and right, a resurgence of the right (though with ebbs and flows), and a simultaneous atrophy of the non-socialist centre. The longer-term party system trend has thus been towards fragmentation, volatility, and some polarization (Heidar 1989). Yet the two major parties (Labour and the Conservatives) weathered the crises reasonably well until 1989, when their combined vote share fell from 71.2 to 56.5 per cent. After returning to 1960s levels in the 1980s, the effective number of parties jumped once again to 4.2 in 1989. The next year, Conservative Jan P. Syse's non-socialist coalition (Syse) fell apart over European Union membership, ending the era of two-bloc politics, at least through the end of the twentieth century.

Just as in the early 1970s, the issue of European integration stirred up almost every cleavage in the system and provoked conflict between the old allies in the non-socialist camp (Aardal and Valen 1995). The 1993 election dramatically changed the distribution of seats within the non-socialist bloc. The Centre Party, which almost tripled its support since 1989, ended up as the second biggest party in the national legislature, the Storting (see Table 5.1). The Conservatives correspondingly lost their status as Norway's second

TABLE 5.1. Left–right placement of parties, party strength (in seats), and party composition of governments in Norway, 1945–1999

Government	Proximity to election	NKP/RV[a]	SF/SV[b]	A	V	KRF	SP	H	FRP	Others[c]	Median party in second policy dimension	Effective number of legislative parties	Government strength	Total number of seats
1945	FE	11	—	76*	20	8	10	25	—	—	A	3.2	76	150
1949	FE	—	—	85*	21	9	12	23	—	—	A	2.7	85	150
1953	FE	3	—	77*	15	14	14	27	—	—	A	3.1	77	150
1957	FE	1	—	78*	15	12	15	29	—	—	A	3.0	78	150
1961	F	—	2	74*	14	15	16	29	—	—	A	3.2	74	150
1963	—	—	2	74*	14	15	16	**29**	—	—	A	3.2	74	150
1963	E	—	2	74*	**14**	**15**	**16**	29	—	—	A	3.2	74	150
1965	FE	—	2	68	18*	**13**	**18**	**31**	—	—	A	3.5	80	150
1969	F	—	—	74	13*	**14**	**20**	**29**	—	—	A	3.2	76	150
1971	—	—	—	**74**	13*	14	20	29	—	—	A	3.2	74	150
1972	E	—	—	74	13*	**14**	**20**	29	—	1	A	3.2	47	150
1973	FE	—	16	62*	2	20	21	29	4	—	A	4.1	62	155
1977	FE	—	2	76*	2	22	12	41	—	—	A	3.0	76	155
1981	F	—	4	66	2	15*	**11**	**53**	4	—	A	3.2	53	155
1983	E	—	4	66	2	**15***	**11**	**53**	4	—	A	3.2	79	155
1985	F	—	6	71	—	**16***	**12**	**50**	2	—	A	3.1	78	157
1986	E	—	6	**71**	—	16*	12	50	2	—	A	3.1	71	157
1989	F	—	17	63	—	**14***	**11**	**37**	22	1	A	4.2	62	165
1990	E	—	17	**63**	—	14*	11	37	22	1	A	4.2	63	165
1993	FE	1	13	**67**	1	13*	32	28	10	—	A	4.0	67	165
1997	F	—	9	65	**6**	**25***	**11**	23	25	1	A	4.4	42	165

cont./

cont.
a The figures from 1945–61 relates to the electoral result of the Communist Party (NKP), whereas the 1993 result applies for the Red Election Alliance (RV).
b SV since 1973.
c This category consists of the following parties: 1973–7: DLF = Det Liberale Folkeparti (Liberal People's Party), 1989–93: FFF = Folkeaksjonen Fremtid for Finmark (Popular Movement for the Future of Finnmark), 1997– : TF = Tverrpolitisk Folkevalgte, also called Kystpartiet (Coastal Party).

Parties
NKP   *Norges Kommunistiske Parti* (Communist Party)
RV   *Rød Valgallianse* (Red Election Alliance)
SF   *Sosialistisk Folkeparti* (Socialist People's Party)
SV   *Sosialistisk Venstreparti* (Socialist Left Party)
A   *Arbeiderpartiet* (Labour Party)
V   *Venstre* (Liberal Party)
KRF   *Kristelig Folkeparti* (Christian People's Party)
SP   *Senterpartiet* (Centre Party)
H   *Høyre* (Conservative Party)
FRP   *Fremskrittspartiet* (Progress Party)

largest parliamentary party for the first time since 1930. As late as 1981, the party had won 53 seats to the Centre Party's 11. The 1997 election brought a rude return to normalcy for the Centre Party, which lost more than half of its votes and close to two-thirds of its parliamentary representation. There was no consolation, however, for the Conservatives, who suffered the ignomy of being reduced to the fourth party in parliament. The victors were the Christian People's Party and the Progress Party, which ended up tied for second in parliamentary seats. The formation of a three-party centrist coalition government represented an important step away from the two-bloc format of the past.

At the electoral level, increased competition between the parties is clearly reflected in the increased number of floating voters. After the early 1970s about one out of three electors shifted position from one election to the next, as compared to the 1960s when the corresponding figure was about one out of four (Valen and Urwin 1985). In the Storting elections of the 1990s, gross individual volatility has reached almost 45 per cent.

Policy Dimensions

The policy dimensions of Norwegian politics have traditionally been shaped in large part by the dominant social cleavages. The socio-economic class cleavage is expressed through the ideological left–right dimension, whereas the territorial and sectoral cleavages are reflected through the centre–periphery and the urban–rural dimension, respectively. Finally, the cultural cleavages have given rise to a moral-religious dimension.[4] These policy

[4] The moral-religious dimension does not include the socio-cultural language question, which in recent times has been more or less absent from the political debate.

dimensions of Norwegian politics have been subject to much scholarly scrutiny. The literature has relied for evidence on voter and/or elite surveys (Narud 1996b; Valen 1981, 1990, 1994), content analysis of party programmes (Bilstad 1986; Grønmo 1975a, 1975b; Strøm and Leipart 1989, 1992, 1993), and records of parliamentary behaviour (Rommetvedt 1984, 1991; Shaffer 1991, 1996). While these studies yield somewhat different spatial representations, they leave no doubt that the dominant dimension of political contention over the past half-century has been the left–right axis. Only in the 1990s has the predominance of this dimension somewhat lessened (Aardal and Valen 1995; Narud 1996b; Shaffer 1996; Jenssen and Valen 1995).

Table 5.1 shows that Labour, as the majority party, controlled the median position on Laver and Hunt's (1992) left–right dimension between 1945 and 1961. After the party lost its majority position in 1961, it continued to hold the median legislator until 1965. The Liberal Party occupied the median position from 1965 until 1973, when Labour again regained this position. Since 1981 the Christian People's Party has controlled the median position on the left–right axis.

Observe, however, that Laver and Hunt's (1992) placement on this left–right scale probably does not do justice to the policy position of the Centre Party in the 1980s and 1990s. Laver and Hunt place this party to the right of the Christian People's Party. This is conventionally considered to be correct for large parts of the early post-war period. Recent studies, however, indicate that these two parties have swapped places on the left–right axis (Narud 1996b; Aardal and Valen 1995). This reflects a leftward drift in the position of the Centre Party since the 1970s, as the party's opposition to European integration has gradually generalized into a greater scepticism towards market economics.

Two other important dimensions in Norwegian politics are strongly inter-correlated: the urban–rural dimension and the centre–periphery axis. The policy positions of the various parties tend to be highly consistent across these two dimensions, as the parties that most favour rural interests are also the strongest defenders of the peripheries, and so forth. And on both these dimensions, the policy positions of the parties differ considerably from those of the left–right dimension.[5] Since Laver and Hunt report only the urban-rural

	FRP	H	A	DLF	SV	V	KRF	SP	
1									20
	4.3	5.4	7.7	10.2	11.1	12.7	14.7	18.6	

FIGURE 5.1. Pro-urban (1) vs. anti-urban (20) interests: Perceived location of parties. (Mean score, party elites, as reported by Laver and Hunt 1992)

---

[5] The urban–rural (cum centre–periphery) dimension has on several occasions influenced coalition politics as well as party competition. For this reason, we have defined it as the second most important dimension. The third most important dimension may be the

dimension, and since this dimension is also most generalizable cross-nationally, we report only those placements here. Figure 5.1 shows the location of the parties on this particular dimension as reported by Laver and Hunt (1992).

As indicated by Figure 5.1, the Progress Party (FRP) is the most pro-urban party, and the Centre Party (SP) the most anti-urban (or pro-rural). The Conservatives (H) are fairly close to the Progress Party, whereas the Christian People's Party (KRF) is adjacent to the Centre Party on the anti-urban side.[6] All other parties hold more centrist positions on this dimension. As we can see, the old allies in the bourgeois camp, which are fairly close neighbours on the left–right axis, are highly polarized along the urban–rural dimension. In addition, Table 5.1 tells us that Labour has controlled the median legislator on the urban–rural dimension for the whole post-war period. This dimension is therefore particularly inimical to non-socialist cooperation.

This secondary dimension has been mobilized in dramatic ways at particular times in the post-war period. Of particular importance to coalition politics are the saliency and the mobilizing effect of the EC/EU issue in the early 1970s and again in the 1990s. On these occasions, the ideological left–right dimension has dramatically declined in significance. No doubt this development has been helped by the fact that the normally dominant dimension has been cross-cut by not just one, but several alternative dimensions, which themselves are highly intercorrelated. The established patterns of left–right opposition have been undermined by the fact that several salient policy dimensions, of which the urban–rural axis is the most consequential, have militated against them.

Of most relevance to non-socialist coalescence is the fact that the Centre Party represents rural economic interests and the peripheral parts of the country, while the Conservatives advocate the interests of urban areas and draw particular support in the region around Oslo. It is anathema to the Centre Party to be part of a coalition that favours EU membership, simply because membership threatens the very existence of the heavily protected and subsidized farming interests that are the backbone of the party. Norwegian EU membership would mean a build-down of the protections that agriculture currently enjoys vis-à-vis the more profitable farming communities in continental Europe. Furthermore, Norwegian fishermen, who are similarly important to the economic life of the country's peripheries, fear that their fisheries

moral-religious axis, on which the Christian People's Party is at one pole and the parties of the left–right extremes (the Socialist Left and the Progress Party) at the other.

[6] Laver and Hunt (1992) provide no information on the placement of the Communist Party (NKP). For this reason, and because a major faction of the party merged with the Socialist People's Party in 1973, we have in identifying the median party given the Communists the same ordinal rank on the urban–rural dimension as the latter. Note that the position of the Communist Party is only relevant for the years the party was represented in the Storting (i.e. between 1945 and 1961) and that it never affects the identity of the median party.

resources would be severely endangered by EU membership. Thus, the Centre Party fiercely opposes accession to the EU. The Christian People's Party opposes European Union membership on less material grounds, most notably the fact that membership would involve more liberal alcohol policies, an issue of remarkable historical significance in Norwegian politics and particularly to the KRF's moral-religious concerns. This gives rise to an anti-European alliance between these two parties. By contrast, the Conservative Party, historically urban, urbane, and socially liberal, has always been the most vocal champion of EU membership.

Thus, the increased saliency of the urban–rural dimension inhibits the traditional bourgeois coalition alternative. Indeed, it has led to the termination of two coalitions (Narud 1995; Rommetvedt 1991), as we shall see below. The nearly identical results of the EC/EU struggles of the 1970s and the 1990s indicate that these conflicts are neither coincidental nor likely to change quickly. Instead, they reflect the importance of traditional conflict dimensions that are likely to constrain even future coalition bargaining in predictable ways.

INSTITUTIONAL BACKGROUND

The Norwegian Constitution of 1814 is the oldest living constitution in Scandinavia. Indeed, among the codified constitutions of the democratic world, it ranks second only to that of the United States. Contrary to Denmark and Sweden, Norway has not fundamentally overhauled and updated its constitution in the period since World War II. Consequently, the Norwegian constitution is silent on many aspects of modern governance, such as the role of political parties. On other issues there are major discrepancies between formal constitutional provisions and contemporary practice. For example, though Norway has in practice been a parliamentary democracy since 1884, the written constitution gives no recognition to this practice. It is important to note, however, that the long-standing practice has given parliamentary government the status of a constitutional convention (*sedvanerett*) (Andenæs 1981).

The fluid and informal Constitution has a permissive impact on Norwegian coalition bargaining. Specifically, it seems to have favoured the formation of numerically weak governments. Norway is one of the world's leaders in the frequency of minority governments (Strøm 1990). No doubt that this record has multiple causes. Partly, however, the explanation is surely institutional, in that several of the rules that govern Norwegian government decision making facilitate minority government formation and maintenance. The same rules may facilitate cabinet stability in more general ways, as we shall see in a later section.

The most obviously important procedural rule in the Norwegian version of parliamentary democracy is what Bergman (1993) calls 'negative parliamentarism', i.e. the rule that governments can be invested and sustained as long as there is no explicit majority vote of opposition in parliament. Norwegian parliamentary procedure contains four more or less formal rules that contribute to this practice:

1. Because parliamentary government has never become codified, there is no formal vote of investiture, and governments are assumed to have the confidence of the Storting until the opposite has been demonstrated.

2. The prime minister is neither formally nor by convention expected to hand in his (or her) resignation at the end of a parliamentary term or on any other formal occasion (e.g. when a new King accedes to the throne).

3. The government is not expected to resign in the event of a parliamentary defeat, unless the bill explicitly has been made the subject of a motion of confidence or no confidence. Even defeats on major legislative initiatives (e.g. parts of the budget) need not lead to the cabinet's resignation, and over time Norwegian governments (especially minority cabinets) have become more and more tolerant of parliamentary defeats. Interestingly, the Brundtland cabinets of the 1990s suffered parliamentary defeats with increasing regularity, while at the same time, they steadily became more, rather than less, entrenched (Rommetvedt 1996).

4. While a Norwegian government must by convention resign if a parliamentary majority adopts an unambiguous motion of no confidence, it may choose to stay in office in case of a so-called 'negative majority'. That is to say, if two or more different motions of no confidence collectively attract the votes of a parliamentary majority, but no single motion has majority support, the government may choose to resign but is under no obligation to do so. Though the negative majority rule, like many other aspects of Norwegian parliamentary procedure, is poorly articulated and historically controversial (see Stavang 1971; also Rasch 1987), the government's discretion has in practice been well established. In 1987, for example, Gro Harlem Brundtland chose to remain in office after an absolute majority of the members of the Storting had voted for at least one of two alternative motions of no confidence (Strøm 1994b).

CABINET MEMBERSHIP

Post-war Norwegian coalition formation, as shown in Table 5.2, falls into two separate and disparate periods. Prior to 1961, Norway experienced stable, single-party, majority governments. The 1961 election, however, deprived the Labour Party of a parliamentary majority, and after that

TABLE 5.2. *Government formation in Norway 1945–1999*

Government	Number of parties in parliament	Number of previous bargaining rounds	Parties involved in previous bargaining rounds	Number of days required for government formation
A 1945	6	0		3
A 1949	5	0		0
A 1953	6	0		0
A 1957	6	0		0
A 1961	6	0		0
H–SP–V–KRF 1963A	6	0		1
A 1963B	6	0		4
SP–H–V–KRF 1965	6	0		16
SP–H–V–KRF 1969	5	0		0
A 1971	6	1	H–SP–V–KRF	11
KRF–SP–V 1972	6	0		11
A 1973	8	0		4
A 1977	6	0		0
H 1981	7	1	H–KRF–SP	5
H–KRF–SP 1983	7	0		7
H–KRF–SP 1985	6	0		0
A 1986	6	0		7
H–KRF–SP 1989	7	0		3
A 1990	7	1	H–KRF–SP	5
A 1993	8	0		0
KRF–SP–V 1997	8	0		4

watershed, Norwegian cabinets have more often than not been 'undersized', and only occasionally coalitions. Labour has never again captured a legislative majority. Its cabinets consequently have relied on legislative coalitions for their survival. In large part, majority building since 1961 has been informal and *ad hoc*.

For the first four years after it lost its parliamentary majority, Labour ran a minority government, interrupted by a four-week episode of bourgeois minority government. The more important development of this period was that the non-socialist parties managed to present a coalition alternative for the first time since the 1930s. Indeed, this was the first coalition of Liberals and Conservatives in stable peacetime circumstances. The bourgeois bloc won the election of 1965, and for the next quarter-century the voters were basically faced with two competing government alternatives: either a bourgeois coalition, or a minority government of Labour based upon a socialist majority. Only in the 1990s has this situation fundamentally changed, so that there are now more than two feasible government alternatives.

While the composition and size of Norwegian governments have changed substantially over the post-war period, other patterns of cabinet formation have remained stable. Among the recurrent properties of Norwegian governments are the following:

1. All Norwegian cabinets have been either socialist or non-socialist. There have been no peacetime coalitions between socialist and non-socialist parties. In fact, the Norwegian Labour Party is the only major social democratic party in Western Europe never to have entered a cabinet coalition with any bourgeois party.

2. Labour has eschewed coalitions not only with non-socialist parties, but also with any of the smaller parties to its left. In several campaigns, the Labour Party has indeed made a campaign issue out of its resistance to coalition politics (again reminiscent of the previous 'anti-coalition' stance of the Irish Fianna Fáil). Thus, a socialist government has meant a cabinet of Labour alone and since 1961 therefore also a minority cabinet.

3. Non-socialist cabinets, on the other hand, have tended to be coalitions (Rommetvedt 1984), and all but one have included at least three parties. The exception is the first Willoch cabinet (1981–3), a purely Conservative administration.[7] Yet many coalitions, including the three most recent ones (Willoch III, Syse, and Bondevik), have been minority cabinets. There have been two types of non-socialist coalitions: centre-right governments including the Conservatives and centrist coalitions consisting only of the Christian People's Party, the Centre Party, and the Liberals. All told, there have been six centre-right coalitions and only two centrist coalitions (Korvald and Bondevik). Both of the latter have formed under circumstances in which dissent over European integration has precluded coalescence between Conservatives and the other non-socialist parties, and specifically the Centre Party. Both have also been led by prime ministers from the Christian People's Party.

The most recent of the broader centre-right coalitions was Syse (1989–90). The cabinet formed after the 1989 election had produced a non-socialist majority in the Storting. This majority, however, rested on the Progress Party, which was not deemed an acceptable coalition partner. Even the cooperation between the three governing parties (Conservatives, Christians, and Centre) looked shaky from the start, and within a year the coalition foundered on policies towards the EU. Since that time, there has been no serious attempt to resuscitate the broad non-socialist coalition. The centrist coalitions of 1972 and 1997 have both been somewhat accidental, though the latter less so than the former. Both were precipitated by the abrupt resignation of a previous Labour cabinet. In Korvald's case (1972), this was due to the result of the first EC referendum and the fact that Prime Minister Bratteli

---

[7] Willoch I (1981–3) nevertheless enjoyed consistent parliamentary support from the Christian People's Party and the Centre Party.

had explicitly tied his fate to the outcome of this vote. In 1997 Thorbjørn Jagland had similarly committed himself to resigning in the event that his party (Labour) failed to gain the level of support it had enjoyed in the previous election (36.9%). In the event, Labour slipped to 35.0%, and Jagland duly resigned, paving the way for Kjell Magne Bondevik's minority coalition. Incidentally, Bondevik's biography provides a bridge between these two coalitions that were twenty-five years apart in time. His uncle was a leading member of the KRF in the 1960s and 1970s (see below), and the younger Bondevik himself served as a junior minister in Korvald's administration.

Table 5.3 presents a survey of all post-1945 Norwegian cabinets. As we see, there have been twenty-six cabinets over these fifty-four years. These break down into eighteen single-party administrations and eight coalitions. Nine cabinets have included representatives of parties that collectively controlled a majority of the seats in the Storting, whereas seventeen have been minority cabinets of one type or another. Most minority governments have relied on ad hoc parliamentary support; only one (Willoch I, 1981–3) could be characterized as having stable and pre-negotiated support from two parties outside the cabinet, namely the Christian People's Party and the Centre Party. Collectively, these three parties controlled a slim parliamentary majority, and in 1983 they formalized their cooperation by forming a three-party majority cabinet, still under Willoch's premiership. The latter cabinet, Willoch II (1983–5), is the only majority administration that has formed since 1969.

The Norwegian record of cabinet formation is thus distinctive in more ways than one. The paucity of coalitions and the extended bifurcation of the party system into socialist and non-socialist blocs are salient features. Also noteworthy is the pattern of coalition avoidance. Yet, minority government has not always been a feature of Norwegian politics. Between 1940 and 1961 there were in fact none, for the simple reason mentioned above: Social Democratic predominance. Since 1961, however, Norway has experienced seventeen minority and only three majority cabinets. Since 1971, minority cabinets outnumber majoritarian ones fourteen to one. Thus, coalitions have failed to form in the majority of situations where they conventionally would be predicted. Moreover, in five of the eight cases in which (non-socialist) coalitions have formed, the coalition building process has stopped short of a majority. Even in these cases, then, some coalition 'avoidance' has taken place. Hence, the failure to coalesce is a general and striking feature of Norwegian party politics.

CABINET FORMATION

Formally, the Constitution gives the King wide discretion to appoint the members of the cabinet, which is still formally known as the King's council.

TABLE 5.3. *Norwegian cabinets since 1945*

Cabinet number	Prime Minister	Date in	Formal resignation	Maximum potential duration (in days)	Duration (in days)	Party composition
1	Gerhardsen II	05 Nov. 1945	10 Oct. 1949	1,435	1,435	A
2	Gerhardsen III	10 Oct. 1949	13 Nov. 1951	1,463	764	A
3	Torp I	19 Nov. 1951	12 Oct. 1953	693	693	A
4	Torp II	12 Oct. 1953	14 Jan. 1955	1,456	459	A
5	Gerhardsen IV	22 Jan. 1955	07 Oct. 1957	989	989	A
6	Gerhardsen V	07 Oct. 1957	11 Sept. 1961	1,435	1,435	A
7	Gerhardsen VI	11 Sept. 1961	27 Aug. 1963	1,491	715	A
8	Lyng	28 Aug. 1963	21 Sept. 1963	775	24	H–SP–V–KRF
9	Gerhardsen VII	25 Sept. 1963	11 Oct. 1965	747	747	A
10	Borten I	12 Oct. 1965	07 Sept. 1969	1,426	1,426	SP–H–V–KRF
11	Borten II	07 Sept. 1969	02 Mar. 1971	1,491	541	SP–H–V–KRF
12	Bratteli I	13 Mar. 1971	07 Oct. 1972	944	574	A
13	Korvald	18 Oct. 1972	12 Oct. 1973	359	359	KRF–SP–V
14	Bratteli II	16 Oct. 1973	09 Jan. 1976	1,461	815	A
15	Nordli I	15 Jan. 1976	11 Sept. 1977	605	605	A
16	Nordli II	11 Sept. 1977	30 Jan. 1981	1,492	1,237	A
17	Brundtland I	04 Feb. 1981	12 Oct. 1981	250	250	A
18	Willoch I	14 Oct. 1981	01 June 1983	1,461	595	H
19	Willoch II	08 June 1983	08 Sept. 1985	823	823	H–KRF–SP
20	Willoch III	08 Sept. 1985	02 May 1986	1,493	236	H–KRF–SP
21	Brundtland II	09 May 1986	13 Oct. 1989	1,250	1,250	A
22	Syse	16 Oct. 1989	29 Oct. 1990	1,461	378	H–KRF–SP
23	Brundtland III	03 Nov. 1990	13 Sept. 1993	1,045	1,045	A
24	Brundtland IV	13 Sept. 1993	23 Oct. 1996	1,490	1,163	A
25	Jagland	25 Oct. 1996	14 Oct. 1997	325	325	A
26	Bondevik	17 Oct. 1997		1,424		KRF–SP–V

In practice, however, the King has exerted no influence on the composition of any cabinet since 1928.[8] The King always follows the advice of the leaders of the parliamentary parties when he formally calls upon someone to form a new government. In practice, there have been few cases in which the choice of the prime minister-designate has been difficult. Because of the absence of formal rules and mechanisms, Norwegian government formation is best described as 'freestyle bargaining'. The use of *informateurs* has no codified place in the Norwegian constitution, and the practice has been rare indeed. In the postwar period, there is only one notable case. In the difficult cabinet crisis of 1971, when a bourgeois majority coalition had just broken down over the EC issue, the King formally gave the President of the Storting, Conservative Bernt Ingvaldsen, the mandate of investigating the feasibility of another non-socialist coalition. It is was obvious that Ingvaldsen, a senior, right-wing, and somewhat formal representative of his party, was never intended to head such an administration. His role was purely that of an *informateur*. At any rate, Ingvaldsen's efforts failed for no fault of his own, and the *informateur* institution has never again been used in the nearly three decades that have passed. If the recent trend towards party system fragmentation and coalition fluidity continues, however, it is not inconceivable that a stronger tradition of *informateurship* may develop.

Cabinet formation in Norway has rarely taken much time or involved repeated rounds. As Table 5.2 shows, the initial attempt at cabinet formation has been inconclusive on only three occasions. In each case, this has been due to a serious policy conflict between the non-socialist parties. In 1971, the four non-socialist parties that had made up the Borten coalitions failed to agree to patch up their differences under the proposed leadership of Kjell Bondevik of the Christian People's Party. Effectively, the Centre Party's opposition to Norwegian EC membership rendered a non-socialist coalition unfeasible. Consequently, Bondevik had to face the media and throw in the towel with the expression, 'I am deeply wounded and disappointed,' words that subsequently became a stock phrase in Norwegian. Ten years later, Willoch's initial attempt to bring the Christian People's Party and the Centre Party into his government also failed, though under much less acrimonious circumstances. This time, the abortion issue was to blame, with the Christian People's Party taking a pro-life position and most of the Conservatives opposed. Finally, the same three parties failed to resuscitate their coalition in 1990, at the time of Syse's resignation, for much the same reason that Bondevik's efforts failed almost twenty years earlier: foreign policy differ-

---

[8] In 1928, King Haakon VII, against the advice of the outgoing prime minister, called upon the leader of the Labour Party to form a new government. This led to the formation of the first socialist government in Norwegian history (see Björnberg 1939). The government proved short-lived but the King's behaviour did much to solidify his support among Norwegian Social Democrats.

ences, specifically over EU membership. All other cabinets, however, have formed 'without a hitch'.

Nor has coalition bargaining typically taken much time. As Table 5.2 shows, there have been only three cases in which coalition bargaining has taken more than one week, namely 1965 (Borten I), 1971 (the case mentioned above, which ultimately led to the formation of a Labour minority government under Bratteli), and 1972, when a three-party minority government (Korvald) was formed by the parties that represented the victorious side in the 1972 EC referendum. The first of these cases was the negotiations that led to the formation of the first durable non-socialist coalition in Norwegian history since independence in 1905. Given the significance and novelty of the task, it is not surprising that it should have taken a little more time than normal. Accounts of this case suggest that bargaining was vigorous and detailed but not acrimonious, and that the attainment of a satisfactory outcome was never seriously in doubt (e.g. Lyng 1976).

In 1971, the outcome was given once Bondevik's attempt had failed: a minority Social Democratic government under Trygve Bratteli, the Labour leader since 1965. In 1972, coalition bargaining was constrained by the fact that Bratteli had just resigned over his government's defeat in the EC referendum. The outcome of this vote meant that the agenda of the new government would be dominated by the need to conclude a satisfactory trade agreement with the EC. Given Bratteli's personal commitments and the Labour Party leadership's rejection of this alternative during the campaign, the party was effectively out of contention for cabinet participation. The Conservative Party was similarly unavailable. Hence, it was clear that the new government would have to consist of parties that had been on the winning side of the EC referendum, although these parties controlled only about a quarter of the seats in Parliament. Despite the fact that the Centre Party was the largest of these parties, the prime ministership went to the Christian People's Party, which had never before enjoyed this favour, and which had taken a less uncompromising attitude towards the European Community.

Note, however, that our measure of crisis duration effectively underreports the period during which bargaining may take place immediately following a parliamentary election. Such elections always take place in mid-September, whereas the official opening of the Storting does not occur until early October. By convention, the outgoing administration does not tender its resignation until the new parliament has been convened. However, when it is clear that the government intends to resign, the parliamentary calendar leaves an interim of several weeks during which unofficial negotiations may take place. This is indeed what happened in 1997, when Jagland announced on election night, 15 September, that he would tender his resignation as soon as the new Storting convened. This commitment allowed the three centrist parties a window during which they could informally negotiate a potential agreement, which in fact resulted in Bondevik's inauguration on 17 October. Similar circumstances occurred in 1965, 1981, and 1989.

COALITION GOVERNANCE

How has Norway been governed under the twenty-six post-war governments? Since eighteen of these have been single-party governments, the rules that have governed policy making in these cases should be sought within these parties rather than in inter-party agreements. Of course, two-thirds of these cabinets (12 out of 18) have been minority cabinets, which means that some agreements necessarily had to be made between the governing party (typically Labour) and parts of the opposition. However, such agreements have rarely been formalized or binding. Policy compromises have largely been reached *ad hoc* and in a decentralized manner, where the parliamentary committees and the respective parties' parliamentary leaders have played key roles. Only Willoch's first (1981) government had anything like a formalized agreement with support parties. Most of the eight coalition cabinets have been formed as a 'bloc' against the dominant Labour Party, whereas the latter, as mentioned above, has never formed a peacetime coalition government with any other party. The two centrist coalitions (Korvald and Bondevik) have tried to pursue a course independent of the rightist parties as well as of Labour. Yet, Bondevik (1997–) faced such hostility and intransigence from the Labour Party that on most issues he was forced to negotiate his support from the Conservatives and the Progress Party.

Coalition Agreements

All Norwegian coalition governments have been based on some formal agreement. The first such post-war coalition agreement was negotiated before the general election of 1965. Since then, centre-right coalition cabinets have normally based their policy platform on the joint non-socialist written opinion submitted with the finance committee's report on the government's programme for the coming four-year period. This is a major policy statement to which the parties normally devote substantial attention, but it does not detail government decision making procedures. Typically, these pre-electoral statements have been supplemented by additional agreements made after the election. Most commonly, however, the pre-electoral platforms have been the most detailed and authoritative agreements between the governing parties. Since all but two coalition agreements have been presented to the voters before elections, they have by definition been public. However, on some core

TABLE 5.4. *Coalition governance in Norway*

(1) Government	(2) Coalition agreement	(3) Agreement public	(5) Conflict management mechanisms	(6) Most common management mechanisms	(7) Management mechanisms for most serious conflicts	(8) Coalition discipline in legislation	(9) Coalition discipline in other parliamentary behaviour	(10) Freedom of appointment	(11) Policy agreement	(12) Junior ministers	(13) Non-cabinet positions[a]
H–SP–V–KRF 1963	POST	Y	NA	NA	NA	—	—	Y	1	Y	N
SP–H–V–KRF 1965	PRE,POST	Y	IC/CAC	CAC	IC	1	2	Y	3	Y	Y
SP–H–V–KRF 1969	PRE,POST	Y	IC/CAC	CAC	IC	1	2	Y	3	Y	Y
KRF–SP–V 1972	POST	Y	PCA/CAC	CAC	PCA	1	2	Y	—	Y	N
H–KRF–SP 1983	PRE,POST	Y	IC	IC	IC	1	2	N	3	N	Y
H–KRF–SP 1985	PRE,POST	Y	IC	IC	IC	1	2	N	3	N	Y
H–KRF–SP 1989	PRE,POST	Y	IC	IC	IC	1	2	Y	2	Y	Y
KRF–SP–V 1997	PRE,POST	Y	IC	IC	IC	1[b]	2	N	3	N	Y

[a] Board of Presidents of Parliament.
[b] In November 1998 four of the cabinet ministers from the Centre Party dissented from the rest of the government on the Veterinary Agreement proposed by the EU. In the votations, the parliamentary group of the Centre Party voted against the proposal.

TABLE 5.5. *Size and content of coalition agreements in Norway, 1963–1999*

Government	Size[a]	General procedural rules (in %)	Specific procedural rules (in %)	Distribution of offices (in %)	Distribution of competences (in %)	Policies (in %)
H–SP–V–KRF 1963	2,941	0	0	0	0	100
SP–H–V–KRF 1965	4,456	0	0	0	0	100
SP–H–V–KRF 1969	5,996	0	0	0	0	100
KRF–SP–V 1972	2,919	0	0	0	0	100
H–KRF–SP 1983	25,137	0	3.5[b]	0	0	96.5
H–KRF–SP 1985	31,138	0	0	0	0	100
H–KRF–SP 1989	6,650	0	0.2[c]	0	0	99.8
KRF–SP–V 1997	20,240	0	0	0	0	100

[a] Number of words based on WP5.1 word count (after having scanned the policy documents). Observe, that for two of the coalition cases—1963 and 1972—no pre-negotiated policy agreement existed. For these two cases we have defined the prime minister's policy declaration as the government's policy contract. In addition, contrary to normal coalition procedure, the 1989 coalition presented the most binding agreement *after* the election, hence, the word count has been based on the length of this particular document. All other counts have been based on the written opinion submitted with the finance committee's report on the government's programme for the coming four-year period (i.e. the pre-negotiated coalition contract).

[b] Contrary to all other policy areas, the coalition agreement expressed each party's own view on the abortion issue.

[c] The coalition agreement contained one sentence about how the EU issue should be handled by the parties.

issues of special salience to the parties, coalition members normally 'agree to disagree'. This part of the agreement is not made public.

The analysis in Table 5.5 is therefore in most cases based on the joint non-socialist opinion submitted with the finance committee's report on the government's programme for the coming four-year period. For two cabinets, Lyng (1963) and Korvald (1972–3), no pre-negotiated policy agreement existed, since these cabinets formed in mid-term, after a Labour government had chosen to resign (Korvald) or been forced to do so (Lyng). For these two cases, we have considered the prime minister's government declaration as the coalition document. Finally, contrary to previous practice, the Syse government (1989–90) presented its most authoritative coalition agreement *after* the election that led to its formation.

The Norwegian coalition agreements have been documents of their times. The first coalition (Lyng, 1963) lasted only four weeks, but nevertheless marked a turning point in Norwegian parliamentary history. Labour had been in power continuously since 1935, though it had lost its majority in 1961. Hence, even though the non-socialist parties had not been able to present a pre-electoral alliance to the voters in 1961, the new coalition was able to present itself and its policies in a detailed document upon taking office in 1963. The document covered all major policy areas. In addition, Lyng presented a budget proposal, which—because of the government's grave doubts about its own survival—was done in two alternative versions: one to be used in the event that the government would be transitory, and one for the unlikely event that Lyng would be able to implement a budget.

From 1965 on, coalition agreements have been 'declarations of intent' by the parties concerned, presented before the election as a joint policy platform. After the election, if a coalition is formed, the parties' joint declaration (their common proposal on the former government's programme) makes up the coalition agreement. The coalition's programme is presented to the Storting by the prime minister in his (or her) first meeting with the Parliament.

Coalition agreements vary in the extent to which post-electoral changes are made during coalition bargaining, for example whether points or details are added to the original (pre-electoral) policy document. In 1983, for example, the coalition agreement was based on the 1981 joint proposal of the non-socialist parties. In that earlier year, the Christian People's Party had refused to enter the coalition due to disagreements with the Conservatives over abortion. In 1983, however, this issue had subsided, and the Christians—together with the Centre Party—joined the Conservatives in the second Willoch cabinet. Despite the fact that two years had passed, Prime Minister Willoch's 1983 policy statement referred to the 1981 policy document, to which only a few changes were made. In 1989, on the other hand, Syse presented to the electorate a new 22-point declaration, instead of referring to the joint programme proposal from the finance committee. The rationale had to do with the government's policy agenda. Because of the divisive upcoming issue of Norwegian EU membership, the coalition parties felt a need for a fairly detailed post-electoral document clarifying their policy platform. Interestingly, the last lines of this particular agreement contained a specific formulation concerning the EU membership issue, which preserved each coalition party's freedom with respect to the future relationship with the EU. This particular provision was labelled the 'suicide paragraph' of the Syse coalition. Hence, unlike the other coalition agreements, the 1989 accord was for the most part hammered out after the election.

Table 5.5 shows that coalition agreements deal almost exclusively with policy matters. They do not contain any general 'rules of the game' concerning decision making procedures in the coalition, nor do they specify the distribution of cabinet portfolios, other offices, or competences. Quite clearly, the procedural rules of coalition politics are not spelled out with as much detail in Norway as in some countries where coalitions are more common (e.g. Austria, Belgium, or the Netherlands). Specific conflict management mechanisms or provisions on coalition discipline cannot be found in any formal inter-party agreements. Since Norwegian parliamentary elections are held every fourth year without any recourse to early parliamentary dissolution, there can be no 'election rule', whereby the parties commit themselves to calling elections in the event that their coalition would break down. Of course, the same constitutional provision precludes coalition parties from manufacturing a cabinet crisis in order to trigger early elections from which they could expect to benefit. Only two coalition agreements have laid out procedural rules for more specific policy areas. In both cases, these agreements amounted to decisions to 'agree to disagree' on important issue areas that had complicated coalition negotiations. In 1983 (Willoch II), the issue was abortion; in 1989 (Syse) it was membership in the European Community.

Governance Mechanisms

Once a coalition government has been formed, the cabinet meets regularly, normally several times per week. There are two forms of cabinet meetings: Councils of State (*statsråd*), in which the King presides, and cabinet conferences. Only Council of State decisions are official. The cabinet conferences are considered to be informal gatherings, and no constitutional rule exists for decision making or for setting the agenda. However, even cabinet conferences may reach decisions that are considered to bind individual ministers (Berggrav 1994). Occasionally the parliamentary leaders of the coalition parties are invited to take part in cabinet conferences, which can thus serve as vehicles for conflict management. Conflicts within the coalition government are discussed at the cabinet conferences, and in situations where no agreement can be reached, individual ministers have the opportunity to dissent.

Normally, the other cabinet members will be informed about the dissent at the preceding cabinet conference. The reports from the cabinet conferences are to be found in the central government's archives, and they are normally not made public before forty years elapse unless all parties of the former coalition government consent to do so (Berggrav 1994).

Cabinet conferences are not, however, suitable venues for all forms of conflict management. If more serious policy disagreements occur within the coalition, the matter will be discussed on party summits consisting of members of the cabinet and the party leadership. Norwegian coalition cabinets have used several competing vehicles as well. The Borten cabinets developed a repertoire of instruments, including an inner cabinet consisting of a few of the leading cabinet members and representing all the coalition parties. Moreover, the coalition parties often subjected controversial proposals to cabinet committees consisting of junior ministers and civil servants. Whereas the inner cabinet (also irreverently known as the 'high council') tended to be involved in managing the most difficult controversies, the cabinet committees probably handled a larger number of issues.

Korvald differed from the Borten cabinets in not having an institutionalized inner cabinet. Instead, this cabinet subjected difficult issues to cabinet committees or to consultations among senior parliamentarians as well as cabinet members. This difference may at least in part reflect the fact that the Korvald coalition was less conflicted than Borten, partly due to its greater policy cohesion, particularly in foreign policy, and partly to its more limited tenure and agenda. When Kaare Willoch formed the next Norwegian coalition government in 1983, he also diverged from the practices of the Borten cabinets (in which he had served as Minister of Trade), but in a different direction. Anticipating the need for conflict management, Willoch relied heavily on an inner cabinet of four cabinet members, including himself, Conservative Finance Minister Rolf Presthus, and the leaders of the two other coalition parties. Willoch ran his cabinets in a much more centralized manner than his predecessors and was less inclined to delegate conflictual matters to junior ministers or civil servants. Willoch's reliance on his inner cabinet has been continued under the two subsequent coalitions, although particularly Syse in practice played a much less authoritative role within the cabinet he led.

Coalition Discipline

Norwegian coalition governments have had no formal or explicit rules concerning parliamentary votes on legislative proposals or other parliamentary behaviour. This should not be read as acquiescence in legislative indiscipline, however. Generally, party cohesion is very strong in the Norwegian parliament (Svåsand, Strøm, and Rasch 1997), and coalition governments have been founded on the expectation of such cohesion. However, it is up to each of the coalition parties to control its own parliamentary group. Interviews with some of the central party actors involved in coalition politics suggest that enforcement mechanisms have not been highly institutionalized. Coalition enforcement procedures must therefore to a large extent be sought in internal party mechanisms. Strict party control over ballot access and political finance are surely among the factors that facilitate party discipline, although some control over these resources is decentralized to the province level.

When in office as a coalition, the bourgeois parties have sought to vote together as a bloc on important issues. Compared to times when cabinet coalitions are not feasible, inter-party agreement in committee reports and on roll call votes has been much higher when the non-socialists have either been in office together or anticipated such coalitions (Rommetvedt 1991; Shaffer 1996). Nevertheless, open disagreement may occur between the coalition and the various parliamentary parties. Interestingly, many such conflicts concern local or regional issues, such as the development of airports, roads, oil installations, or other infrastructure. In some such cases, party representatives may vote against the government's proposal. Other matters of strong personal commitment may also be exempted from coalition discipline. The Bondevik cabinet has experienced two prominent cases in which its representatives have broken rank. One was on the appointment of the bishop of Oslo (traditionally the head of the Norwegian Lutheran church), when the cabinet members of the two smaller coalition parties joined together and defeated Odd Bondevik, the prime minister's cousin, in favour of a more liberal candidate. Not too long thereafter, four Centre Party cabinet members and the party's entire parliamentary delegation voted against the government's proposal to ratify the EEA veterinary agreement.

Bourgeois coalitions have made use of a number of different coordination mechanisms to avoid such overt conflict. Much intra-coalition policy coordination takes place in parliamentary committees. The fact that Norwegian parliamentary committees are relatively small, that each representative is a member of one and only one parliamentary committee, and that committees conduct their business behind closed doors, makes parliamentary committees a conducive arena for legislative compromise (see Mattson and Strøm 1995). Parliamentary committee members are in close communication with their respective parliamentary leaderships, whose coordination and supervision are critical to coalition decision making.

PORTFOLIO ALLOCATION

Portfolio allocation in the seven coalition cabinets has exhibited a number of identifiable patterns. In most cases, the numerical allocation has come very close to the proportionality, or parity, norm that each party's share of the cabinet portfolios has been in proportion to the parliamentary votes it contributes to the coalition. Insider accounts suggest that negotiators have in fact based their decisions on such calculations (Lyng 1976). In recent years, however, the smaller coalition parties have been significantly over-represented relative to the largest party. Under Willoch III and Syse, this meant that the Christian People's Party and the Centre Party were advantaged compared to the Conservatives. Under Bondevik, this practice has continued, but now at the expense of the Christian People's Party, which holds only nine out of nineteen portfolios, despite contributing twenty-five out of the coalition's forty-two votes in Parliament. It is true that in five out of eight coalitions, the prime ministership has gone to the largest coalition party. Nonetheless, the fact that this has *not* happened in almost half of all Norwegian coalitions may be noteworthy by international standards.

A closer look at portfolio allocation reveals a striking association between the traditional policy concerns of the various parties and the cabinet portfolios they have controlled. The Conservatives have held the Ministries of Defence and Industry in all six coalitions in which they have participated. In most cases, they have also captured Justice and Foreign Affairs. The much smaller Christian People's Party has won the large portfolio of Social Affairs in five of its eight coalitions, and that of Church and Education (or its successors) no fewer than six times. The Centre Party, with its rural profile, has won Agriculture and Fisheries each in five of eight coalitions and Transportation four times. Shifts in portfolio allocation between parties have rarely happened during the 'lifetime' of coalition governments.

Although portfolios have generally been allocated to the parties with the most intense preferences, however, this has not been a foregone conclusion. In fact, when the first durable non-socialist coalition was put together in 1965, there was a conscious effort to avoid this outcome, specifically as regarded the Ministry of Church and Education. The Liberals, as well as many members of other coalition parties, were not especially keen to yield this portfolio to Kjell Bondevik of the Christian People's Party (Lyng 1976: 16–41).

In the early coalition cabinets, the selection of individual ministers proceeded in a fairly decentralized manner, though specific practices concerning freedom of appointment have varied. In 1965 as well as 1969, even though all names had been discussed (and approved) by the large negotiating group in advance, in reality each party appointed its own ministers. The prime minister and the other coalition members had little influence (Sejersted 1984: 229). In the coalitions of 1983 and 1985, on the other hand, Prime Minister Willoch insisted that the appointment of ministers and junior ministers (*statssekretærer*) be subject to his approval. Of the two most recent coalitions, Syse seemed closer to the decentralized Borten model, whereas Bondevik has claimed stronger prime ministerial control over cabinet and sub-cabinet appointments.

TABLE 5.6. Distribution of cabinet and junior ministerships in Norwegian coalitions

Cabinet number	Cabinet	(1) Prime Minister	(2) Finance	(3) Foreign	(4) Industry	(5) Environment[a]	(6) Defence	(7) Trade	(8) Oil/Energy[b]	(9) Communications (Transportation)	(10) Health/Social Affairs
8	Lyng	H	SP	KRF	H	—	H	H	—	SP	KRF
10	Borten I	SP	V	H	H	—	H	H	—	H	KRF
11	Borten II	SP	V	H	H	—	H	H	—	H	KRF
13	Korvald	KRF	V	SP	V	SP	V	V	—	SP	KRF
19	Willoch II	H	H,/sp*	H	H	SP	H	KRF	KRF	SP	H
20	Willoch III	H	H,krf	H	H	SP	H	KRF	KRF	SP	H,krf
22	Syse	H	H,krf	KRF	H[g]	SP	H	H[h]	SP	KRF	H
26	Bondevik	KRF,sp,v	SP,krf,v	KRF,sp	V	V	KRF	V[i]	SP	V	KRF,SP[j]

TABLE 5.6 CONTINUED

Cabinet number	Cabinet	(11) Agriculture	(12) Justice	(13) Church/Education	(14) Local Government/Labour	(15) Consumer Affairs/Government Administration	(16) Culture[c]	(17) Family	(18) Fisheries	(19) Foreign Aid[d]	(20) Wages/prices[e] Labour/administration[f]
8	Lyng	SP	KRF	V	V	SP[k]	—	SP[k]	H	—	V
10	Borten I	V	H	KRF	V	KRF[k]	—	KRF[k]	SP	—	SP
11	Borten II	V	H	KRF	V	KRF[k]	—	KRF[k]	SP	—	SP
13	Korvald	SP	KRF	SP	KRF	V	—	—[j]	SP	KRF	—
19	Willoch II	SP	H	KRF	H	H	H	KRF[l]	H	KRF	—
20	Willoch III	SP	H	KRF	H	H	H	KRF	SP	KRF	H[f]
22	Syse	SP	H	KRF	SP	KRF,h	KRF	KRF	H	SP	V
26	Bondevik	KRF	KRF	KRF	SP	V[m]	SP	KRF	SP	KRF	

cont./

Norwegian cabinets have included a fairly limited number of sub-cabinet political appointments. The typical practice has been for each department to have one junior minister, in addition to one personal secretary to the minister (*personlig sekretær*). In the large majority of cases, all appointees within a single department have been drawn from the same party. However, exceptions began to be made in Willoch's third cabinet, in which the smaller coalition parties were given sub-cabinet appointments in key departments controlled by the Conservatives. Syse continued this practice, and under Bondevik it has been expanded. In the three most prestigious ministries (the Office of the Prime Minister, Finance, and Foreign Affairs), junior ministerships are now shared between two or even all three coalition parties. Needless to say, this form of power-sharing has been made possible by an expansion of the number of sub-cabinet appointments. Thus, there are currently five secretaries of state assigned to the Office of the Prime Minister.

COALITION TERMINATION

Table 5.7 provides an overview of coalition terminations in the Norwegian system. Technical reasons is by far the most common cause of cabinet resignation in the post-war period. Out of twenty-five terminated cases, about half

---

TABLE 5.6. *cont.*

* Conservative (H) Junior minister appointed 6 June 1983 was replaced by Centre Party junior minister 17 June 1983.

a Established 1972.
b Established 1978.
c Established 1982 as the Ministry of Culture and Science. In 1990 named Church and Culture, and since 1991 named Ministry of Cultural Affairs.
d Established 1984. From 1990 a sub-ministry under the Ministry of Foreign Affairs, and since 1997 named the Ministry of International Development and Human Rights.
e Abolished 1972.
f The Ministry of Labour and Administration was established 1 Jan. 1990. It was abolished in Dec. 1992, and re-established in Jan. 1998.
g Abolished 1988. Issues transferred to the Ministry of Industry and Energy. Since 1 Jan. 1997, a part of the Ministry of Trade and Industry.
h From 1989 sub-ministry under Ministry of Foreign Affairs.
i Since 1997 the Ministry of Trade and Industry.
j Since 8 Nov. 1993 the Ministry of Health and Social Affairs consists of two sub-ministries: the Ministry of Health and the Ministry of Social Affairs. In the Bondevik government, the first is headed by the KRF, whereas the ministry of Social Affairs is headed by the SP.
k The Ministries of Family and Consumer's Affairs were merged at the time.
l Abolished 1972 and re-established 1990 as the Ministry of Family and Consumer's Affairs. Since 1991 named the Ministry of Children and Family Affairs.
m Since 1998 the Ministry of Labour and Government Administration.

Sources: Nordby 1985, Torp 1994, Strøm 1994b; *Stortinget i navn og tall, 1997–2001*.

TABLE 5.7. Cabinet termination in Norway, 1945–1999

Cabinet number	Cabinet	Mechanisms of cabinet termination					
		Technical		Discretionary			
		(1) Regular parliamentary election	(2) Other constitutional reasons	(5) Voluntary enlargement of government	(6) Cabinet defeated by opposition	(7) Conflict between coalition parties: policy	(8) Intra-party conflict in coalition party
1	Gerhardsen II	X					
2	Gerhardsen III		X				
3	Torp I	X					
4	Torp II						L
5	Gerhardsen IV	X					
6	Gerhardsen V	X					
7	Gerhardsen VI				X		
8	Lyng				X		
9	Gerhardsen VII	X					
10	Borten I	X					
11	Borten II					H,SP, KRF,V	
12	Bratteli I		X				
13	Korvald	X	X				
14	Bratteli II						L
15	Nordli I	X					
16	Nordli II		X				
17	Brundtland I	X					
18	Willoch I			X			
19	Willoch II	X					
20	Willoch III				X		
21	Brundtland II	X					
22	Syse					H,SP	
23	Brundtland III	X					
24	Brundtland IV		X				
25	Jagland	X					

a The Labour government was forced out of office as a result of an accident in the government operated coal mine 'Kings Bay' in Spitsbergen. A publicly appointed investigating committee concluded that the government had not done enough to secure the mine. In addition, the government was accused of withholding information from the Storting about safety precautions in the mines.

(13) have run their maximum constitutional term, which is to say that they have been terminated by a constitutionally mandated regular election (the Norwegian constitution does not permit early dissolutions). Twelve cabinets have been terminated before reaching their maximum constitutional duration.

Terminal events				Policy area(s)	Comments
(9) Election (non-parliamentary)	(11) International or national security	(12) Economic	(13) Personal		
			X		Voluntary 'retirement'
		X	X	2	Gerhardsen returns in 'palace coup'.
		X	X	4	Government cover-up of 'Kings Bay' accident
		X		2	Defeated on government declaration Lost election
	X	X	X	3,1	'Leakage' of EC documents
X	X			3	EC Referendum
	X			3	EC trade agreement concluded
			X		Forced retirement
			X		Personal retirement due to poor health in the face of intensifying leadership conflict in the Labor Party Lost election
				10,13	Lost majority
		X		2	Parliamentary defeat on austerity bill Lost election
	X			3	EC membership
					Voluntary retirement Lost election

Policy controversies between the coalition partners have twice led to a change of governments, mostly due to foreign policy issues. The question of Norwegian membership in the European Community triggered the death of both the Borten II coalition in 1971 and the Syse coalition twenty years later (see e.g. Sejersted 1984; Narud 1995). In addition, the Borten II coalition had the appearance of a scandal, because of the prime minister's indiscretion in regard to a confidential state paper concerning the projected EU membership. Three cabinets have been defeated by the opposition in Parliament, Gerhardsen VI and Lyng in 1963, and Willoch III in 1986. The latter was formed as a minority coalition in 1985 dependent on the parliamentary support of the tiny right-wing Progress Party, which by its two seats was pivotal between socialists and non-socialists in the Storting. After the election the coalition was forced to enter into negotiations with the Progress Party on its budget proposals in parliament, but failed to reach a compromise during the spring session of 1986, and was outvoted on its new budget proposal when the Progress Party joined the socialist opposition and rejected increased taxes on petrol. Willoch I is the only cabinet terminated because of a voluntary enlargement, when the Christian People's Party and the Centre Party joined the Conservatives in 1983.

A majority of the terminal events associated with discretionary terminations have fallen into the category of personal events. Most commonly, this refers to the voluntary or involuntary retirement of the prime minister. In one of these cases, Torp II (1953–5), the poor health of the prime minister coincided with economic budgetary difficulties and factional conflict within the Labour Party. Similarly, in 1976 Bratteli was rather ignominiously forced into giving up the prime ministership. Nordli's 1981 retirement also coincided with intra-party stress, but in this case personal health was also a genuine concern, and it seems reasonable to infer that Nordli jumped more than he was pushed. In total, intra-party leadership conflicts have contributed to three cabinet terminations, whereas interestingly coalition governments have never fallen over personnel conflicts. Similarly, no prime minister has fallen because he has fallen out of grace with the rank-and-file of his party. Overall, Table 5.7 indicates that most cabinets were terminated for reasons beyond the control of the relevant parties. This applies with particular force to single-party cabinets, whether majority or minority.

ELECTORAL PERFORMANCE

Since the 1970s, it has become common in Norwegian journalism and political parlance generally to refer to governments suffering 'wear and tear' (*slitasje*). While this term is hardly defined in any precise way, there is no doubt that losses of popular support, and more specifically anticipated electoral losses, are a major part of the referent of such discussions. The general recognition of this phenomenon has developed along with, and no doubt partly as a result of, a growing tendency for incumbent parties to suffer at the polls. Table 5.8 shows the gains and losses (in votes) of incumbent parties between 1949 and 1997.

TABLE 5.8. *Electoral costs / benefits of government parties in Norway, 1945–1999 (in % of votes)*

Government	In office at time of election	Election year	A	H	SP	KRF	V	Government
A 1945–9	Yes	1949	+4.7	—	—	—	—	+4.7
A 1949–53	Yes	1953	+1.0	—	—	—	—	+1.0
A 1953–7	Yes	1957	+1.6	—	—	—	—	+1.6
A 1957–61	Yes	1961	−1.5	—	—	—	—	−1.5
A 1961–3	No	1965	−3.6	—	—	—	—	−3.6
H–V–SP–KRF 1963	No	1965	—	+1.1	+0.6	−1.5	+1.5	+1.7
A 1963–5	Yes	1965	−3.6	—	—	—	—	−3.6
SP–H–V–KRF 1965–9	Yes	1969	—	−1.5	+0.6	+1.3	−1.0	−0.6
SP–H–V–KRF 1969–71	No	1973	—	−2.2	+0.5	+2.8	−5.9	−4.8
A 1971–2	No	1973	−11.2	—	—	—	—	−11.2
SP–V–KRF 1972–3	Yes	1973	—	—	+0.5	+2.8	−5.9	−2.6
A 1973–7	Yes	1977	+7.0	—	—	—	—	+7.0
A 1977–81	Yes	1981	−5.1	—	—	—	—	−5.1
H 1981–3	No	1985	—	−1.3	—	—	—	−1.3
H–KRF–SP 1983–5	Yes	1985	—	−1.3	−0.1	−0.6	—	−2.0
H–KRF–SP 1985–6	No	1989	—	−8.2	−0.1	+0.2	—	−8.1
A 1986–9	Yes	1989	−6.5	—	—	—	—	−6.5
H–KRF–SP 1989–90	No	1993	—	−5.2	+10.3	−0.6	—	+4.5
A 1990–3	Yes	1993	+2.6	—	—	—	—	+2.6
A 1993–7	Yes	1997	−1.9	—	—	—	—	−1.9
MEANS			−1.2	−2.9	2.4	0.4	−1.8	−1.4

Overall, there is a moderate tendency towards an adverse incumbency effect. That is to say that, in the aggregate, there is a slight tendency for incumbent parties to lose votes when they have to face the voters. The mean net loss amounts to 1.4 per cent of the total national poll. Yet, there are notable exceptions. Labour gained votes in its first three post-war elections, but has since lost ground in five of the seven cases in which it has been in office at election time. Two of the centrist parties, the Christian People's Party and the Centre Party, have actually most often benefited electorally from taking government responsibility. On the other hand, the Conservatives and to some extent the Liberals show a fairly consistent pattern of losing votes as incumbents.

In coalition cabinets, it is rare for all parties to suffer the same fate. This has happened only in 1985, when all three non-socialist governing parties suffered minor setbacks. Yet, all three coalitions that have faced elections have experienced net losses. Public opinion polling data confirm that the Conservative Party tends to be more popular with the voters when they are out of government than when they are in, whereas the other coalition parties are less affected by incumbency (Narud 1993). The above results indicate that, in the Norwegian system, the two traditionally large parties with clearly defined left–right placements seem to derive electoral liabilities from holding office, whereas the two smaller parties with programmatic commitments most clearly related to alternative policy dimensions seem to face less of a dilemma.

It is not clearly whether these differences in electoral fortunes are due to policy profiles, size, or historical accident. Yet, consistent with the results reported from other countries (e.g. Powell and Whitten 1993), the evidence from Norway may suggest that the effect of economic performance varies for cabinets of different ideological leanings. Voters most commonly evaluate Labour more favourably on unemployment and social policies, whereas the non-socialist coalitions do better concerning inflation (Aardal and Listhaug 1986, 1989). How these assessments figure into the voters' retrospective judgements seems to be related to the ideological distinctiveness of the parties (Narud 1996*a*).

CONCLUSION

Norway's history of coalition bargaining reflects a political system in which the political parties have remained key, unified players in the process of governance, and in which party, rather than coalition, governance has in many ways stayed the norm. Coalition politics has been limited to a set of non-socialist parties, in either a centre-right or a centrist format. This is to say that about half of the currently relevant parties (representing a solid majority of the current membership of Parliament) have never participated in any organic cabinet coalition. Coalition bargaining has in most cases involved a fairly small set of top party leaders, and their negotiations have been fairly brief, private, and informal. The prevailing practices can aptly be characterized as freestyle bargaining, and an *informateur* has been appointed on only one occasion. Although all Norwegian coalition cabinets have been based on a formal policy agreement, they have generally not had very elaborate mechanisms of conflict management. Despite this limited experience with coalitions, Norwegian cabinets, including multi-party ones, have generally been durable, and there have been few cases that have terminated existing cabinets or prevented the formation of others. As in most other countries, governing parties have tended to suffer at the polls, but the adverse electoral incumbency effect has in most cases been moderate. All in all, the Norwegian inclination towards minority cabinets and ad hoc legislative coalescence seems to reflect the ease of informal majority building rather than the frustrations of full-blown coalescence.

REFERENCES

Aardal, Bernt, and Listhaug, Ola (1986). 'Economic Factors and Voting Behavior in Norway 1965–1985'. Working paper no. 4. Oslo: Institute for Social Research.
——(1989). 'Økonomi og Stemmegivning', in Bernt Aardal and Henry Valen (eds.), *Velgere, Partier og Politisk Avstand*. Oslo: Statistisk Sentralbyrå.
——and Valen, Henry (1995). *Konflikt og Opinion*. Oslo: NKS-Forlaget.
Andenæs, Johs (1981). *Statsforfatningen i Norge*. Oslo: Tanum-Nordli.
Berggrav, Dag (1994). *Slik Styres Norge*. Oslo: Schibsted.
Berglund, Sten, and Lindström, Ulf (1978). *The Scandinavian Party System(s)*. Lund: Studentliteratur.
Bergman, Torbjörn (1993). 'Formation Rules and Minority Governments'. *European Journal of Political Research*, 23: 55–66.
Bilstad, Karl-Anders (1986). 'Konfliktstruktur og Partiavstand'. Graduate thesis. University of Bergen.
Bjørklund, Tor (1982). *Mot Strømmen: Kampen mot EF 1961–1972*. Oslo: Universitetsforlaget.
——and Hagtvet, Bernt (1981) (eds.). *Høyrebølgen—Epokeskifte i norsk politikk?* Oslo: Aschehoug.
Björnberg, Arne (1939). *Parlamentarismens Utveckling i Norge Efter 1905*. Stockholm: Almqvist & Wiksell.
Gleditsch, Nils Petter, and Hellevik, Ottar (1977). *Kampen om EF*. Oslo: Pax Forlag.
Groennings, Sven (1961). 'Cooperation among Norway's Non-Socialist Political Parties'. Ph.D. thesis. Stanford University.
Grønmo, Sigmund (1975*a*). 'Politiske skillelinjer i norske partiprogrammer: En

analyse av utviklingen fra 1936 til 1973'. Paper prepared for presentation at the meeting of the Nordic Political Science Association Conference, Århus, Denmark.

——(1975b). 'Skillelinjer i partipolitikken 1969–1973: Noen virkninger av EF-striden'. *Tidsskrift for Samfunnsforskning*, 16: 119–53.

Heidar, Knut (1989). 'Norway: Levels of Party Competition and System Change'. *West European Politics*, 12: 143–56.

Jenssen, Anders Todal, and Valen, Henry (1995) (eds.). *Brussel midt imot*. Oslo: Tano Forlag.

Kuhnle, Stein, Strøm, Kaare, and Svåsand, Lars G. (1986). 'The Norwegian Conservative Party: Setback in an Era of Strength'. *West European Politics*, 9: 448–71.

Laver, Michael J., and Hunt, W. Ben (1992). *Policy and Party Competition*. London and New York: Routledge.

——and Schofield, Norman (1990). *Multiparty Government: The Politics of Coalition in Europe*. Oxford: Oxford University Press.

Lyng, John (1976). *Mellom øst og vest: Erindringer 1965–1968*. Oslo: Cappelen.

Mattson, Ingvar, and Strøm, Kaare (1995). 'Parliamentary Committees', in Herbert Döring (ed.), *Parliaments and Majority Rule in Western Europe*. New York: St Martin's Press.

Narud, Hanne Marthe (1993). 'Coalitions and Electoral Trade-offs in Norway: The Dilemma of the Conservative Party'. Paper prepared for the Nordic Political Science Conference, Oslo, 19–21 Aug. 1993.

——(1995). 'Coalition Termination in Norway: Models and Cases'. *Scandinavian Political Studies*, 18: 1–24.

——(1996a). 'Party Policies and Government Accountability: A Comparison between the Netherlands and Norway'. *Party Politics*, 2: 479–507.

——(1996b). *Voters, Parties, and Governments*. Report no. 96: 7. Oslo: Institute for Social Research.

Nordby, Trond (1985) (ed.). *Storting og Regjering 1945–1985*. Oslo: Kunnskapsforlaget.

Powell, G. Bingham, and Whitten, Guy D. (1993). 'A Cross National Analysis of Economic Voting: Taking Account of the Political Context'. *American Journal of Political Science*, 37: 391–414.

Rasch, Bjørn Erik (1987). 'Manipulation and Strategic Voting in the Norwegian Parliament'. *Public Choice*, 52: 57–73.

Rokkan, Stein (1967). 'Geography, Religion and Social Class: Crosscutting Cleavages in Norwegian Politics', in Seymour Martin Lipset and Stein Rokkan (eds.), *Party Systems and Voter Alignments*. New York: Free Press.

——(1970). *Citizens, Elections, Parties*. New York: David McKay.

Rommetvedt, Hilmar (1984). *Borgerlig samarbeid: Sprikende staur eller laftet tømmer?* Stavanger: Universitetsforlaget.

——(1991). 'Partiavstand og partikoalisjoner'. Ph.D. thesis, University of Bergen.

——(1996). 'Norwegian Storting'. Paper prepared for delivery at the Conference on Parliamentary Committees, Budapest, 20–22 June.

Sainsbury, Dianne (1985). 'The Electoral Difficulties of the Scandinavian Social Democrats in the 1970s: The Social Bases of the Parties and Structural Explanations of Party Decline'. *Comparative Politics*, 18: 1–19.

Sartori, Giovanni (1976). *Parties and Party Systems: A Framework for Analysis*. Cambridge: Cambridge University Press.
Sejersted, Francis (1984). *Opposisjon og posisjon*. Oslo: Cappelen.
Shaffer, William R. (1991). 'Interparty Spatial Relationships in Norwegian Storting Roll Call Voting'. *Scandinavian Political Studies*, 14: 59–83.
Stavang, Per (1971). 'Negativt Fleirtal i Norsk Parlamentarisme'. *Lov og rett*, 145–66.
Strøm, Kaare (1990). *Minority Government and Majority Rule*. New York: Cambridge University Press.
——(1994*a*). 'The Political Role of Norwegian Cabinet Ministers', in Michael Laver and Kenneth A. Shepsle (eds.), *Cabinet Ministers and Parliamentary Government*. Cambridge: Cambridge University Press.
——(1994*b*). 'The Presthus Debacle: Intraparty Politics and Bargaining Failure in Norway', *American Political Science Review*, 88: 112–27.
——and Leipart, Jørn Y. (1989). 'Ideology, Strategy and Party Competition in Postwar Norway'. *European Journal of Political Research*, 17: 263–88.
—— ——(1992). 'Norway: Policy Pursuit and Coalition Avoidance', in Michael J. Laver and Ian Budge (eds.), *Party Policy and Government Coalitions*. London: Macmillan.
—— ——(1993). 'Policy, Institutions, and Coalition Avoidance: Norwegian Governments, 1945–1990'. *American Political Science Review*, 87: 870–87.
Svåsand, Lars, Strøm, Kaare, and Rasch, Bjørn E. (1997). 'Party Organization', in Kaare Strøm and Lars Svåsand (eds.), *Challenges to Political Parties: The Case of Norway*. Ann Arbor: University of Michigan Press.
Torp, Olaf C. (1994). *Stortinget i navn og tall: Høsten 1993—Våren 1997*. Oslo: Universitetsforlaget.
Valen, Henry (1973). 'No to EC'. *Scandinavian Political Studies*, 8: 214–26.
——(1981). *Valg og Politikk: Et Samfunn i Endring*. Oslo: NKS-Forlaget.
——(1990). 'Velgere, Politisk Avstand og Koalisjoner'. *Norsk Statsvitenskapelig Tidsskrift*, 6: 17–32.
——(1992). 'Norway', in Mark Franklin, Thomas T. Mackie, and Henry Valen (eds.), *Electoral Change*. Cambridge: Cambridge University Press.
——(1994). 'List Alliances: An Experiment in Political Representation', in M. Kent Jenings and Thomas T. Mann (eds.), *Elections at Home and Abroad*. Ann Arbor: University of Michigan Press.
——and Rokkan, Stein (1974). 'Norway: Conflict Structure and Mass Politics in a European Periphery', in Richard Rose (ed.), *Electoral Behavior: A Comparative Handbook*. New York: Free Press.
——and Urwin, Derek W. (1985). 'De Politiske Partiene', in Trond Nordby (ed.), *Storting og Regjering 1945–1985*, ii. Oslo: Kunnskapsforlaget.

6

Sweden

When Minority Cabinets are the Rule and Majority Coalitions the Exception

Torbjörn Bergman

THE PARLIAMENTARY PARTY SYSTEM

Most Swedish governments have been minority governments. Usually these have been formed by the Social Democratic Party alone. With the exception of the period 1951–7, a third salient feature is that these governments have been either 'socialist' or 'non-socialist' (or bourgeois).[1] This reflects a split of the five traditional parties into two blocs. The Communist Party (today the Left Party) and the Social Democrats constitute the socialist bloc and the Centre (former Agrarian), the Liberal, and the Conservative Parties the other one.[2] The split has been salient in terms of government formation and in elections. In terms of policy making, however, the governments tend to represent the middle ground rather than the politics of one of the blocs (Bergman 1995; Mattson 1996; Klingemann et al. 1994).

---

[1] Ruin (1968, 1985) talks about this distinctive split into a socialist and a bourgeois bloc in terms of a modified two-party system. In this system, competition dominates during electoral campaigns and in government formation while consensus and cooperation characterize much of the everyday proceedings in the Riksdag. Note that the use of the term 'bourgeois' (*borgerlig*) does not imply a class-theoretical perspective. It is simply a label often used by the non-socialist parties themselves.

[2] With regard to the question of English names of Swedish political parties, I follow Westholm (1991: 31), who emphasizes that party names should be readily accessible to an English-speaking audience. I do not translate the names literally, nor do I report more than a few of the name changes that have occurred over time. For practical purposes, I also refrain from discussing a locally constituted party-association (Medborgerlig Samling) which in the mid-1960s argued for more extensive non-socialist cooperation and gained a few seats in the Riksdag. This group was soon subsumed by the traditional parties. I also do not count the 1985 election of the Christian Democratic Party leader to the Riksdag as a instance of a party gaining representation. His seat was a result of an electoral alliance with the Centre Party (Hadenius, Molin, and Wieslander 1993).

Electoral support for the two parties in the socialist bloc has been relatively stable. In its worst electoral performance, in 1998, the Social Democratic Party got 36.4 per cent of the total vote. On average, however, the party has won about 45 per cent of the popular vote.[3] The Communist Party usually gets about 5 per cent of the vote. The party has never held any government portfolio, nor has it seriously demanded such a position. In the first decades after World War II, the Communist policy position was that they would never prevent a working-class government, i.e. a Social Democratic one, from coming to power, nor help unseat such a government. Since the early 1980s, however, Communist support for Social Democratic governments has been less self-evident (Feldt 1991; Sjölin 1993).

Among the non-socialist parties, there has been greater volatility. This is especially true for the Liberal Party. From a post-war peak of 24.4 per cent in 1952, the Liberals share of the popular vote declined to a meager 5.9 per cent in 1982 and then rebounded dramatically to 14.2 per cent in 1985. In 1998 the party was down to 4.7 per cent. The two other non-socialist parties have also experienced surges and declines, with the Centre Party reaching its peak in the 1970s, and the Conservative Party in the 1980s and 1990s. Thus, each one of the three non-socialist parties has at times been the leading party within the bloc. The Liberal Party was in this position in the early 1950s, while in the 1970s it was held by the Centre Party. Today the Conservative Party is the largest of the three.

In a comparative perspective, two features of the Swedish party system are particularly noteworthy (Laver and Schofield 1990: 241). One is the unitary behaviour of the Swedish parties which, with the exception of the Communist Party, have managed to avoid party-splintering. In the Riksdag, with few exceptions, the parties behave as cohesive groups. The second feature is that some of the Swedish parties have close ties to organized interest groups. In general, the Conservative Party has been close to organized business and the Centre Party is strong among organized farmers. The Liberal Party is known for its support among daily newspaper editors (Birgersson and Westerståhl 1992). Since the 1960s, however, this support has been above and beyond the party's support as measured by electoral strength. In terms of membership and organization, the closest link has been the one between the Social Democratic Party and organized labour, in particular the national federation for blue-collar workers (the LO).

The combination of these two features, unitary parties with strong ties to organized interests, sometimes produces intense conflict within parties

---

[3] In fact, in the period 1945–87, in terms of its electoral support, the Swedish Social Democratic Party was Western Europe's most popular party, narrowly beating the Irish Fianna Fáil to take the first place position (Coakley 1987: 159). For the 1948–98 period, the average is 44.5%. For specifics on the parties' electoral support, see Bergman (1995: 67–9) and *Från Riksdag & Departement* (1998: 13).

between those who are close to the relevant interest groups and those who are not. Again, the Social Democratic intra-party struggles, the so-called 'War of Roses' (after the flower which is the party symbol), have gotten the most attention. However, these conflicts lack the permanent leadership and semi-organized characteristic of outright intra-party factions.

The stability of the five-party system was once a third noteworthy feature. Since the 1988 election this is no longer the case. In 1988, the five established parties were joined in the Riksdag by the Green Party. Two other parties that have been elected to parliament are the Christian Democratic Party (1991) and the New Democracy Party (1991).

Table 6.1a shows the alignment of the leadership of each party on the comparative 'Pro-public ownership vs. anti-public ownership' scale used by Laver and Hunt (1992: 305).[4] The New Democracy Party placement is based on its placement in the 1991 electoral survey. This placement was the one about which voters disagreed most (Gilljam and Holmberg 1993: 40–1). The party was also a source of irritation among the four parties in the coalition cabinet. On some occasions, its often radical right-wing views did not prevent New Democracy from siding with the Social Democrats in crucial votes in the Riksdag.

Table 6.1a shows the increase in the number of parliamentary parties that occurred in 1988 and 1991. One way to measure bargaining complexity is in terms of the common Laakso–Taagepera index of the effective number of parties. The higher the score on the index, the more complex is the party system. Table 6.1a shows that the parliamentary party system was the least complex after the 1968 election and the most complex after the 1998 election.

Table 6.1a also makes clear the predominance of single-party Social Democratic minority governments.[5] Both majority and multi-party governments have been the exception rather than the rule. The table demonstrates the crucial importance of the median legislator. With four exceptions, the median legislator party has been part of the government. One exception occurred in 1957 when the median party in the Second Chamber, the Centre

---

[4] On this scale, the placement of the parties' voters is consistent with the placement of the leaders. On an alternative left–right scale, 'increase services vs. cut taxes', the experts surveyed by Laver and Hunt (1992: 304) placed the party leadership (but not the voters) of the Green Party to the left of the Social Democrats. As a time-specific placement, this might be true. However, the scale used for Table 6.1a is better supported by electoral surveys (Gilljam and Holmberg 1995).

[5] Note that until 1961 Speakers did not have the right to vote, nor was a substitute member allowed to replace him. The Social Democrats held this position in the Second Chamber. Thus, in practice, the party had one vote less than mandated by the actual electoral performance (Andrén 1968a: 79). For an example of the practical importance of this, see the Second Chamber vote on mandatory and public pension funds (ATP) in 1959 (Lewin 1992: 293–4). Under the 1975 constitution, a substitute member replaces the MP elected as Speaker. The Speaker does not vote.

Party, left the coalition with the Social Democrats. This situation is discussed in more detail below.

Another exception is the Centre Party in 1973. At that time, the even-numbered Riksdag was split into two blocs of the same size, 175 votes each. Technically speaking, in this case there were two median legislators. One legislator within the Social Democratic Party and the other in the Centre Party. The non-socialist parties were one vote short of being able to unseat the Social Democratic government. Until the subsequent election in 1976, issues were decided by ad hoc policy coalitions or, when a proposal was deadlocked with 175 for and 175 against, by lottery. The third exception, the non-median Liberal Party government in 1978, is probably a technical artefact. Because of the 'frozen' placement of the parties over time, Table 6.1a does not show that the Liberal Party actually was to the left of the Centre Party. Voters placed it slightly to the left of the Centre Party in all four elections from 1973 through 1982.[6] From 1985 through 1991, the voters again put the Centre Party to the left of the Liberals. One should note that the left–right difference between the two parties has been rather marginal (Gilljam and Holmberg 1995: 60; Petersson 1977: 138–48). In Swedish politics, these two parties are sometimes referred to as 'the parties of the middle'. Rather than the left–right alignment, it is the rural, pragmatic, and environmental profile of the Centre Party which stands in contrast to the more urban and white-collar (academic) profile of the Liberal Party. The fourth exception is that the Green Party held the median legislator position after the 1998 election.

In the first two elections in which it gained representation, 1988 and 1994, election surveys placed the Green Party between the Social Democrats and the Centre Party. In 1991, the Christian Democratic Party was by voters placed between the Centre and Liberal Parties. Both of these positions are consistent with the Laver and Hunt (1992) study. The New Democracy Party was not included in that study. It formed only about six months prior to Election Day. In the 1991 election, the New Democracy Party was by voters placed to the right of the Liberal Party and to the left of the Conservatives. This position is consistent with the Swedish manifesto data (Bergman 1995).[7] New Democracy was not returned to parliament by the voters. The other two newcomer parties were re-elected in 1994, and while the Green Party in 1998 got the median legislator position, the Christian Democratic Party gained

---

[6] This is supported by the expert judgements reported by Castles and Mair (1984: 82). According to the experts surveyed, the Liberal Party was to the left of the Centre Party in the early 1980s.

[7] In the 1994 election survey, the left–right alignment of the Liberal, Centre, and Christian Democrats shifted once again. This time, the voters placed the Liberal and Centre Parties in the same (average) position. The Christian Democratic Party was placed to the right of these two parties, in between the parties of the middle and the Conservatives (Gilljam and Holmberg 1995: 60).

TABLE 6.1a. *Left–right placement of parties, party strength (in seats), and government composition in Sweden, 1945–1999*

Government	Proximity to election	Com	SD	Green	Ce	CD	Li	New Dem	Co	Median party in second policy dimension	Effective number of parliamentary parties	Government strength	Total number of seats
1945	E	15	**115***	—	35	—	26	—	39	SD	3.14	115	230
1948	F	8	**112***	—	30	—	57	—	23	SD	3.06	112	230
1951	E	—	**112***	—	**30**	—	—	—	31	—	—	142	—
1952	FE	5	**110***	—	**26***	—	58	—	31	SD	3.09	136	230
1956	F	6	**106**	—	**19***	—	58	—	42	SD	3.18	125	231
1957	E	—	**106**	—	—	—	—	—	—	—	—	106	—
1958	FE	5	**111***	—	32	—	38	—	45	SD	3.17	111	231
1960	FE	5	**114***	—	34	—	40	—	39	SD	3.11	114	232
1964	FE	8	**113***	—	36	—	43	—	33	SD	3.18	113	233
1968	FE	3	**125***	—	39	—	34	—	32	SD	2.81	125	233
1970	FE	17	**163***	—	71	—	58	—	41	SD	3.31	163	350
1973	FE	19	**156***	—	90*	—	34	—	51	SD	3.35	156	350
1976	F	17	152	—	**86***	—	**39**	—	**55**	SD	3.45	180	349
1978	E	—	—	—	—	—	**39**	—	—	—	—	39	—
1979	F	20	154	—	**64***	—	**38**	—	**73**	SD	3.48	175	349
1981	E	—	—	—	**64***	—	**38**	—	—	—	—	102	—
1982	FE	20	**166***	—	56	—	21	—	86	SD	3.09	166	349
1985	FE	19	**159***	—	44	—	51	—	76	SD	3.38	159	349
1988 x	FE	21	**156***	20	42	—	44	—	66	SD	3.66	156	349
1991	FE	16	138	—	**31***	**26**	**33**	25	**80**	SD	4.19	170	349
1994	FE	22	**161***	18	27	15	26	—	80	SD	3.50	161	349
1998	n.a.	43	**131**	16*	18	42	17	—	82	SD	4.29	131	349

cont./

more votes and became the fourth largest party in the Riksdag—after the Social Democrats, the Conservatives, and the (former) Communist Party.

Some aspects of the dominance of the left–right dimension have become weaker in recent years. As mentioned, the Communist Party has become more reluctant to provide unconditional support for the Social Democrats. Another important change with implications for coalition formation is that new parties have gained representation in the Riksdag. A third is that in recent years the voters have become more volatile and make up their minds about how to vote later in the election campaigns (Gilljam and Holmberg 1995). Another important change is that in the 1994 election, the Social Democratic Party was second only to the Conservative Party in its willingness to present the voters with an austerity budget programme (Bergman 1995).

Cross-cutting cleavages based on language, religion, or region are less significant in Sweden than in most other West European countries. To the extent that there exists a main alternative dimension to the left–right one, its opposite poles can be labelled economic growth versus ecology. Its roots go back to an urban–agrarian dimension in the 1950s, when agrarian interests were represented by the Centre Party. In the 1960s and 1970s, this dimension broadened to become a more general centre–periphery dimension and to include issues such as decentralization of society and in the public sector in particular (Back and Berglund 1978). The alternative dimension also came to incorporate a growing concern for green or environmental values. The most salient issue has been the Swedish nuclear power programme. Typically, both the Communists and the Centre Party are characterized as representatives of

TABLE 6.1a. *cont.*

Notes
Parties in **bold** formed **governments**. The number of seats refers to the Second Chamber until 1969 and thereafter to the one–chamber Riksdag.
* Party with median legislator (under the assumed left–right party alignment).
The other legend (x) refers to the fact that the Carlsson (1988–91) cabinet formally resigned in Feb. 1990 and returned to power shortly thereafter. This event does not meet this book's restrictive comparative criteria for when to count a new cabinet or government.

Parties
Com	Left Party–Communist (Vänsterpartiet)
SD	Social Democrats (Arbetarepartiet–Socialdemokraterna)
Green	Environmental Party (Miljöpartiet de gröna)
Ce	Center Party (Centern)
CD	Christian Democratic Party (Kristdemokraterna)
Li	Liberal Party (Folkpartiet liberalerna)
New Dem	New Democracy Party (Ny Demokrati)
Co	Conservative Party (Moderata samlingspartiet)

Sources: *Allmänna valen 1994*: 27; *Statistisk Årsbok för Sverige 1970*: 395 and *1999*: 424.

the ecology position in Swedish politics (Bäck and Möller 1992: 35–6; Vedung 1979: 170).[8]

The alternative dimension was manifest in the election of the Green Party to the Riksdag in 1988 (Bennulf 1994). However, Green value positions are not independent of the left–right dimension (Bennulf 1992, 1994). An affinity between left position and Green values has been observed (Gilljam and Holmberg 1993: 235, 1995). This general pattern also holds for other alternative dimensions such as gender and morality (Bäck and Möller 1995: 39–41; Gilljam and Holmberg 1993: 234–42).

In Table 6.1a there is a column which identifies the median party on the second dimension. Placing parties on an alternative dimension, using an 'Environment vs. growth' scale from the Laver and Hunt (1992: 307) study, reveals that the Social Democrats have always controlled the median legislator. This is because both the Social Democrats and the Conservative Party are seen as being pro-growth, with the Conservatives being the strongest proponent for growth policies. Thus, somewhat ironically, the size and position of the Conservative Party has helped ensure that the Social Democratic Party has had an even better bargaining position on the second, alternative, dimension than on the dominant left–right dimension!

INSTITUTIONAL BACKGROUND

In this section I discuss the institutional context of Swedish governments. In the discussion above, I noted that an informal constraint early in the post-war period was that the Communist Party was not accepted as a viable coalition partner. Its bargaining position might still be weak, but since the party has gained substantially in voter support, it is no longer self-evident that the Social Democrats will be able to exclude it from a future 'socialist' government.[9] The discussion below focuses primarily on the 'hard' and formal con-

---

[8] Centre and Communist Party positions are quite different on other issues. In a factor-analysis of election manifestos, Holmstedt and Schou (1987: 196–7) detected a center-left dimension in which issues such as international peace, democracy, regulation of capitalism, and controlled economy clustered at one pole, while issues of decentralization, incentives, education, traditional morality, and agriculture clustered at the other. The authors conclude that this dimension distinctively separates the Communist Party from the Centre Party. On this dimension, other parties have positions more in the middle.

[9] Further indication of the transformation of the Communist Party is that in 1990 it changed its name to the Left Party (Vänsterpartiet). In the long run, the new role of the party might lead to demands for cabinet portfolios and other concessions from the Social Democrats (on this point, see also Bäck and Möller 1995: 78–82). Of course, another possibility is that electoral success might lead to the opposite development because it provides an incentive for a renewed call for ideological purity from party activists.

straints that constitutional arrangements create for government 'life cycles'. Important elements are electoral laws and parliamentary procedures.

Electoral Laws

The impact of electoral laws on government life cycles can be substantial, albeit indirect. In Sweden, one impact stems from the strictly proportional electoral system which helps to provide a multi-party system in the Riksdag. Another stems from the exclusion of parties that fail to get either 4 per cent of the vote nationally or 12 per cent in one constituency. In some elections this threshold has endangered the parliamentary representation of the Communist Party. If the Communist Party were to fall below the threshold, it would challenge the predominance of the Social Democratic Party.

Electoral laws shape government life cycles in at least one additional way. Elections have to be held at predetermined intervals, regardless of whether an extra election has been held during the legislative term.[10] This constitutional provision has effectively decreased the likelihood of premature (or extra) elections. In 1978 and 1981 such elections were discussed as possible solutions to government crises, but in the end this option was ruled out. In both cases, one of the main reasons was that a mandatory election would have to take place soon after the extra election (Hadenius, Molin, and Wieslander 1993: 263–281; Särlvik 1983: 130–2). At least in 1978, this informal restriction on the cabinet's options helped facilitate a government solution that otherwise might have been avoided.

Parliamentary Procedures

One important reason for the Social Democrats' dominance up to 1970 was in the structure of the two-chamber Riksdag, and the First Chamber in particular. The members of the First Chamber were elected indirectly on the basis of results in local and regional elections. Since only a portion (about one-eighth) of the legislators were elected every year, there was a time lag between changes in electoral support and the distribution of seats in the First Chamber.

The Social Democratic Party held a majority of the seats in the First Chamber until it was abolished with the election of 1970. Even though the directly elected Second Chamber was considered to be the parliamentary basis for governments, a government without support in the First Chamber

---

[10] Until 1970, direct elections to the Second Chamber were held every fourth year. From 1970 through 1994 elections were held every third year. Following the 1994 election, the period between elections has been changed back to four years (Instrument of Government, Chapter 3, Art. 3.)

TABLE 6.1b. *Left–right placement of parties, party strength, and government composition in the First Chamber, Sweden 1945–1970*

Year of government formation	Proximity to elections	Com	SD	Ce	Li	Co	Median party in second policy dimension	Effective number of parliamentary parties	Government strength	Total number of seats
1945	E	2	83*	21	14	30	SD	2.67	83	150
1948	F	3	84*	21	18	24	SD	2.68	84	150
1951	E	—	84*	21	—	—	SD	—	105	150
1952	FE	4	79*	25	22	20	SD	2.67	104	150
1956	F	3	79*	25	30	13	SD	2.83	104	150
1957	E	—	79*	—	—	—	SD	—	79	150
1958	FE	2	79*	22	32	16	SD	2.85	79	151
1960	FE	2	77*	20	33	19	SD	2.93	77	151
1964	FE	2	78*	19	26	26	SD	2.92	78	151
1968	FE	1	79*	20	26	25	SD	2.87	79	151

Notes
The First Chamber was elected indirectly by the elected regional assemblies. Every year a small portion of the legislature was up for re-election (about one–eighth). The exact number varied depending on the number of seats allocated to the specific constituencies whose turn it was to vote. Thus, the distribution of seats changed every year. For practical purposes, the table only shows the distribution for the year following a general direct election to the Second Chamber.
* Party with median legislator (under the assumed left–right party alignment).

Parties:
See Table 6.1a.

would have found it difficult to survive. Table 6.1b shows the Social Democrats' hold on the median legislator in the First Chamber.

While a majority in joint votes (i.e. the sum of the votes in both chambers) was sufficient for budget resolutions, governments needed a majority in each chamber to enact legislation (Andrén 1968a: 101–2; Halvarson 1980: 6–8). As illustrated by Table 6.1b, until the one-chamber Riksdag was established in 1971, a non-socialist coalition could be defeated by the Social Democratic Party in all votes in the First Chamber. As for joint votes, with the support of the Communist Party, the Social Democrats could win all joint votes during the entire 1945–70 period. Thus, even in the period 1952–8, when the Centre Party held the median legislator in the Second Chamber, a non-socialist coalition could not win a joint vote or enact legislation against the will of the two parties in the socialist bloc.

After the abolition of the bicameral parliament, other features of the functioning of the Riksdag have an impact on the role and function of governments. First of all, note that the Riksdag alone can decide on legislation and on the state budget. The constitutional role of the government is primarily to prepare and implement Riksdag decisions. In this role, the government enjoys considerable discretion. Furthermore, Sweden's becoming a member of the European Union on 1 January 1995 led to a transfer of legislative power from the Riksdag to union institutions in many policy areas. This has implications for the government–parliament relationship. However, for the period as a whole, the Riksdag has been the Swedish arena in which all major policies have been formally decided.

The internal organization of the parliament matters for parliament–government relations. To varying degrees, depending mostly on whether the government controls an absolute majority or not, opposition parties in Sweden are able to influence policy decisions via the committee system. The Riksdag has sixteen standing committees, all authorized to take legislative initiatives of their own and with full-time staffs to provide administrative assistance (Arter 1985). The standing committees are specialized in areas that roughly correspond to the jurisdictions of the government ministries, and committee chairs are distributed roughly proportionally among the parties in the legislature. Internal parliamentary structures thus provide opportunities for the opposition to exercise policy influence, thereby reducing the incentives to participate in cabinet. Parties represented in the Riksdag but not in the government are not necessarily without influence over national policy making. This has contributed to the high frequency of minority cabinets (Strøm 1986, 1990: 70–3).[11]

---

[11] In fact, with Belgium, France (Fourth Republic), Iceland, Italy, and Portugal, Sweden ranks in the group of countries which scores the second highest on the index of oppositional influence in Strøm's (1990) sample of 15 parliamentary democracies. Only Norway scores higher. This is because Norway, in contrast to Sweden, has a restriction on the number of

A constitutional reform introduced with the 1970 election was a new procedure for an explicit vote on a declaration of no confidence against the government. In such a vote, an absolute parliamentary majority (i.e. more than half of all members) is needed to bring down the government or an individual minister. This procedure was tried twice in the 1980s, in 1980 and 1985. Both attempts failed (Holmberg and Stjernquist 1995: 196). It was tried again in 1996 and 1998, but the motions failed this time too. The consequence of the design of this voting rule is to promote government stability. Even relatively small minority governments can be stable because abstentions are counted as support for the incumbents.[12]

One of the most important institutional features of Swedish parliamentary democracy is what is known as 'negative' parliamentarism (Bergman 1995).[13] When formation rules require that a new government must have an explicit level of vote support in the parliament, they can be seen as an expression of 'positive' parliamentarism. In negative parliamentarism, the coming to power of a new government is ultimately based on the tolerance of a parliamentary majority, though not necessarily on the active support of such a majority.[14]

Within the category of negative parliamentarism, the Swedish formation rules are in two ways unusual. First, since 1 January 1975 the Head of State (the monarch) is excluded from the cabinet formation process. More important for coalition formation is the nature of the unusual voting rule that came into effect on the same day. A candidate for prime minister (PM) is suggested by the Speaker of the Riksdag. Before a new cabinet can assume power, it must be proven that an absolute majority tolerates the Speaker's candidate. The candidate can form a cabinet if not more than half of the members of the Riksdag vote against him or her.

committees on which a member of parliament can serve. This encourages specialization which in turn facilitates influence. Overall, Ireland and the UK have the lowest scores on the index.

[12] Here government stability should be understood only in a formal sense, i.e. the voting rule makes it difficult to unseat a cabinet already in power. This does not have to mean that any particular government is free from internal conflict or that it necessarily has a stable parliamentary base in the Riksdag.

[13] Negative parliamentarism is found in constitutional monarchies in Northern Europe: Denmark, Norway, Sweden, and the UK. It is also the system in Canada and in some countries with an elected Head of State, specifically Iceland, Finland, and Portugal (Bergman 1995: 42). In the Netherlands, the constitution does not require that there must be a positive vote of investiture before a cabinet assumes power. On the other hand, there is consensus that the outcome of government formation must be a majority government (Timmermans 1996: 117). The norm that the government should have majority support in the parliament, and not just be tolerated by the parliament, is widely accepted. For this reason, I place the Netherlands with the countries with positive parliamentarism.

[14] The weak bargaining position of support parties in negative parliamentarism helps explain the frequent occurrence of minority governments in these countries (Bergman 1995). This is the other side of 'coalition avoidance', i.e. a general unwillingness of support parties to join a government. On coalition avoidance, see Strøm (1990).

Compared with the formation process before 1975, the addition of the new voting rule has had two important consequences. One is that the parties are now forced to show openly whether or not they tolerate a new government before it forms. Because of the voting rule, doing nothing (i.e. abstaining the vote) can more readily be interpreted as tacit support for a new government. Another difference is that the members of the Riksdag have become more involved in the formation process. Before the voting rule, the bargaining process was more easily kept within a small circle of leaders.

With the new voting rule, the party leaders have to consult more widely to ensure that the members of their own party are willing to vote for or against a particular candidate. While the consultations are largely limited to the parliamentary party groups, the trend has been in favour of broader consultations. The Liberal Party has held explicit pre-election discussions of potential coalitions at party conferences and the Centre Party is known to have a time-consuming internal decision making process. Overall, however, government formations and dissolutions have been decided largely by the party leaderships and not by party organizations, party conferences, or by membership votes.

Largely overlooked in the literature on Swedish politics is the distinction between an *informateur* and a *formateur* which is important in the context of government formation in, for example, Belgium and the Netherlands. Before 1975, the King himself acted as something of an *informateur* when he listened to the advise of the party leaders. Since 1975, when the new constitution went into effect, the Riksdag Speaker consults with all party leaders. This is the first step in the formal process of government formation. In this step of the process, the Speaker can be said to have a role which corresponds to that of the head of state in other Western European countries. However, it should be noted that Swedish coalition formation largely is a process of freestyle bargaining among the party leaders. The Speaker can ask one of the party leaders either (1) to find out if a particular government might be formed (i.e. assume the role of an *informateur*) or (2) to attempt to form a government (i.e. assume the role of a *formeateur*), but the party leaders bargaining among themselves without the participation of the Speaker. In Sweden, there is no clear-cut distinction between the two separate roles. Usually, it is assumed that the *informateur* and the *formateur* is one and the same person. Only on one occasion since 1975 has a party leader been an *informateur* but not a *formateur*. This was in 1990 when the Carlsson government (1988–91) formally resigned. The acting Speaker asked the Conservative Party leader to consider the possibility of an alternative coalition. The party leader did not find this to be a viable option and the Carlsson government returned to power shortly thereafter. (This does not meet our strict comparative criteria for counting a new government. The Carlsson 1988–91 government is therefore counted as one cabinet only.)

A final parliamentary procedure concerns the cabinet's authority to dissolve the parliament. In contrast to neighbouring Norway, this is permitted under the constitution. There are few limitations on this right. One has to do with the timing of an extra election, which cannot be held within three months of a preceding one. Another is that a 'caretaker' cabinet cannot dissolve the Riksdag. As discussed above, the use of the extra election rule has in practice been limited as a result of the requirement that mandatory elections be held at set intervals. Only once in the post-war period has the Riksdag been dissolved and an early election held. This was in 1958 following the 1957 breakup of the Social Democratic-Centre Party coalition.

COALITION FORMATION

The Swedish government formation process is short. During a period of a few weeks, the basis for coalitional governance is worked out. In general, the process involves several steps. First a general policy programme is agreed upon. After that, portfolios are distributed. Thereafter the parties appoint junior ministers and other political appointees in the ministries.[15] Simultaneous with the process of government formation, the positions of Speaker and Deputy Speakers and, on occasion, assignments to standing Riksdag committees are decided in parallel negotiations. In practice, however, the process is seldom this linear. For example, in 1951 the Centre Party and the Social Democrats discussed policies, then portfolios, then policies and finally portfolios again (Erlander 1974: 267–85). After the election in 1976, a week of discussions about the overall distribution of portfolios preceded in-depth negotiations on policy (Bohman 1984: 144–51; Hammerich 1977: 113–14). Thus, discussions about portfolios are not always kept neatly separate from discussions of policy. Instead it is mostly a matter of emphasis, with policy usually negotiated before the details of the distribution of portfolios.

Underlying the historical record of government formation is fierce competition for electoral votes, not only between the two blocs but also within the non-socialist bloc (Möller 1986). It is believed that when the non-socialist parties have appeared far apart in their policy positions, this has helped the Social Democrats electorally (Gilljam and Holmberg 1993: 227, 241).

---

[15] There has been an increase in the number of appointments in the post-war period as a whole. However, the number of political appointees in ministries is still relatively small (*Konstitutionsutskottets betänkande 1995/96: KU30*, 11). On 1 Jan. 1996, a total of 127, out of a staff of 3398, were explicitly political appointees (3.7%). At that time, there were 23 junior ministers.

Since the late 1950s the three non-socialist parties, and lately the newcomer Christian Democratic Party, have expressed a preference for a non-socialist government but this has not always meant a commitment to a specific government composition. One or more of the non-socialist parties have at times been open to the formation of non-socialist governments that do not include all the non-socialist parties. This was particularly true in the period before 1976 and since 1976 during inter-election periods (Bergman 1995, Hadenius, Molin, and Wieslander 1993; Pesonen and Thomas 1983). In addition, the Liberals and the Centre Party have now and then found themselves forced to choose between cooperation with the Social Democrats or the Conservative Party. In the late 1970s and early 1980s, in the late 1980s and again in the most recent period, one or both of these two parties have chosen to seek broad long-term policy agreements with the Social Democrats. This has given the Conservative Party the opportunity to profile itself as the only opposition party significantly different from the Social Democrats. At the same time, the non-socialist bloc's credibility as a coherent alternative has weakened.

Table 6.2 shows the historical record of successful and unsuccessful government formations in Sweden since 1945.

From 1945 until the new voting rule came into use in 1975, it was common that the Social Democrats alone or with the Centre Party simply remained in power after a mandatory election. After the election, no bargaining process was initiated, no votes were held. The end result normally was a foregone conclusion—the Social Democratic Party leader held on to the post as prime minister. The process was made even easier by the fact that during the entire period from 1946–69, this was the same person, Tage Erlander. There was but one exception to the absence of a formal bargaining process.

In 1957, when the coalition resigned, the King invited the parties to consultations. At first he wanted to know the possibility of creating a coalition including the Social Democrats and all three non-socialist parties. Erlander, who was very reluctant to the idea of a four-party government, was appointed *informateur/formateur*. When this initiative failed, the King gave the Liberal and Conservative leaders the task of exploring the possibility of a non-socialist government. They assumed the role of *formateurs*. However, the Centre Party declared itself unwilling to join the other two in a cabinet coalition.[16] The attempt to build a non-socialist coalition therefore failed and the

---

[16] Ruin (1968: 262–3) argues that the Centre Party had three major motives in its refusal to join the coalition. First, there was only a weak parliamentary basis for such a government because the socialist parties controlled the First Chamber in the Riksdag. Second, the Centre Party perceived a lack of a common policy platform, esp. in relation to the Conservative Party. Third, the 'lack of decency' that the leadership associated with a sudden shift from one coalition to another. The anticipation that such a behaviour would lead to an electoral backlash seems to have prevented the Centre Party from pursuing cabinet portfolios on this occasion. This thesis gains support from a statement by the chairman of the Centre Party (Hedlund) that the possibility of a non-socialist coalition would increase

TABLE 6.2. *Government formation in Sweden, 1945–1999*

Government	Number of parties in parliament	Number of previous bargaining rounds	Parties involved in previous bargaining rounds	Number of days required in government formation
SD 1945	5	0		0
SD 1948	5	1	SD–Ce	0
SD–Ce 1951	5	0		0
SD–Ce 1952	5	0		0
SD–Ce 1956	5	0		0
SD 1957	5	2	(1) SD–Li–Co–Ce	
			(2) Li–Co–Ce	5
SD 1958	5	0		0
SD 1960	5	0		0
SD 1964	5	0		0
SD 1968	5	0		0
SD 1970	5	0		0
SD 1973	5	0		0
Ce–Li–Co 1976[a]	5	0		18
Li 1978	5	1	Co–Li	8
Ce–Li–Co 1979	5	0		25
Ce–Li 1981	5	0		11
SD 1982	5	0		18
SD 1985	5	0		0
SD 1988	6	0		0
Co–Ce–CD–Li 1991	7	0		18
SD 1994	7	1	Li–SD	18
SD 1998	7	0		0

[a] The first cabinet formation under the constitution which went into effect 1 Jan. 1975. As explained in the text, the new constitution requires a vote to be held before a new cabinet can assume power. However, after a general election, if a cabinet does not resign, or is not forced to resign, it simply continues in power. No vote is held in the Riksdag.

Sources: See Table 6.1a.

Social Democratic party leader subsequently accepted the roles of *formateur* and prime minister (Jonasson 1981; Ruin 1968; von Sydow 1978).

There have been a few other failed efforts to form governments. One example occurred in 1948, when the Social Democrats invited the Centre Party to join the government (Jonasson 1972; Ruin 1968). After the 1948 elections, the Social Democrats were safe in office, but they wanted to secure a long-term majority by cooperating with the Centre Party. The offer was declined and since the talks where publicly known but only informal, they did not have any

after awhile. However, the above discussion about the role of First Chamber indicates that it was the weak parliamentary position that in particular led the Centre Party leadership to decide to avoid a non-socialist coalition (on this point, see also Andrén 1968*b*: 302).

impact on the length of time it took to form a cabinet that year. A similar event occurred in 1994, when the Liberal Party wanted to be invited into the government, but were rejected by the Social Democrats. In this case, it took more than two weeks to form a government (see e.g. Isaksson 1995: 201–20). However, this was for technical reasons. The new voting rule of 1975 artificially increased the length of the government formation process, and not because the bargaining process took a long time.[17] After an election and a resignation of the prime minister, the Riksdag must assemble, a Speaker has to be elected, and a vote must be held. This automatically produces a process lasting over two weeks. In contrast, when the Centre Party–Social Democratic coalition in 1951 had negotiated their policy programme and distributed portfolios, they went to the King and he simply appointed four Centre Party ministers.[18]

The first government formed under the new voting rule was the non-socialist three-party majority coalition in 1976. When it resigned two years later, because of internal conflict over the Swedish nuclear power programme, there was no extra election and the Riksdag remained in session. The Liberal Party avoided a coalition with the Conservatives until abstentions by the Social Democrats and the Centre Party allowed them their own government (Petersson 1979). The whole process, from the formal resignation, took just over a week.

Table 6.3 shows the maximum possible duration of each cabinet as well as the actual duration. In contrast to the preceding tables on governments, this table includes a new unit of analysis (cabinet), also when there is a new prime minister (PM). In Sweden, it is up to the prime minister to select the other members of the cabinet. Before 1975, this was done informally through the formal act of the King. Since 1975, it is the PM who directly appoints the other ministers. In the post-war period, there has to date been twenty-six cabinets. Of these, only five have not included the Social Democrats. There has been a total of seven coalitions. The only single-party cabinet that has not included the Social Democrats was a short-lived cabinet formed by the Liberal Party in 1978–9.

---

[17] In fact, since the Social Democrats declined even to negotiate, the 'bargaining status' of this unsuccessful attempt is ambiguous. It has been included because the talks were known to the general public and because the Liberal Party leaderships' willingness to join a coalition was obvious.

[18] Informal talks had been going on between the two parties, since before the 1948 election. After the 1948 election, there were negotiations about the possibility of forming a coalition. In 1951, when the coalition formed, it was preceded by six months of talks between the party leaders. The actual bargaining process took 9 days (Erlander 1974: 267–84). However, since the Social Democratic cabinet never resigned, the formal formation process did not take any time at all, see Tables 6.2 and 6.3.

TABLE 6.3. *Swedish cabinets since 1945*

Cabinet number	Cabinet	Date in	Date out	Maximum possible duration (days)	Duration (in days)	Cabinet composition
1	Hansson	31 July 1945	06 Oct. 1946	1,146	432	SD
2	Erlander I	11 Oct. 1946	19 Sept. 1948	709	709	SD
3	Erlander II	19 Sept. 1948	01 Oct. 1951	1,463	1,107	SD
4	Erlander III	01 Oct. 1951	21 Sept. 1952	356	356	SD–Ce
5	Erlander IV	21 Sept. 1952	26 Sept. 1956	1,466	1,466	SD–Ce
6	Erlander V	26 Sept. 1956	26 Oct. 1957	1,453	395	SD–Ce
7	Erlander VI	31 Oct. 1957	01 June 1958	1,053	213	SD
8	Erlander VII	01 June 1958	18 Sept. 1960	840	840	SD
9	Erlander VIII	18 Sept. 1960	20 Sept. 1964	1,468	1,468	SD
10	Erlander IX	20 Sept. 1964	15 Sept. 1968	1,456	1,456	SD
11	Erlander X	15 Sept. 1968	14 Oct. 1969	735	394	SD
12	Palme I	14 Oct. 1969	20 Sept. 1970	341	341	SD
13	Palme II	20 Sept. 1970	16 Sept. 1973	1,092	1,092	SD
14	Palme III	16 Sept. 1973	19 Sept. 1976	1,099	1,099	SD
15	Fälldin I	07 Oct. 1976	05 Oct. 1978	1,074	728	Ce–Li–Co
16	Ullsten	13 Oct. 1978	16 Sept. 1979	338	338	Li
17	Fälldin II	11 Oct. 1979	08 May 1981	1,074	575	Ce–Li–Co
18	Fälldin III	19 May 1981	19 Sept. 1982	488	488	Ce–Li
19	Palme IV	07 Oct. 1982	15 Sept. 1985	1,074	1,074	SD
20	Palme V	15 Sept. 1985	01 Mar. 1986	1,099	167	SD
21	Carlsson I	12 Mar. 1986	18 Sept. 1988	921	921	SD
22	Carlsson II	18 Sept. 1988	15 Sept. 1991	1,092	1,092	SD
23	Bildt	03 Oct. 1991	18 Sept. 1994	1,081	1,081	Co–Ce–CD–Li
24	Carlsson III	06 Oct. 1994	18 Mar. 1996	1,445	529	SD
25	Persson I	21 Mar. 1996	20 Sept. 1998	913	913	SD
26	Persson II	20 Sept. 1998	—	1,463	—	SD

Note Before 1975, the column 'date in' refers to the date that the cabinet was appointed by the King. From 1975 the column refers to the date that the vote was taken in the Riksdag. This ends the bargaining process. However, the formal transfer of power takes place a few days later at a session chaired by the Monarch. The column 'date out' refers to the date of the formal resignation or a mandatory election, whichever came first.

Sources: Bergman 1995; Hadenius et al. 1993; *Riksdagens protokoll*, various issues.

COALITION GOVERNANCE

An examination of coalition agreements and cabinet procedures shows that the 1951–8 coalitions between the Social Democrats and the Centre Party had the least formalized policy programmes and conflict resolution mechanisms. Table 6.4 presents a summary of main features of coalition governance in Sweden.

The history behind the first column in Table 6.4 is the following. The first coalition formed three years into an inter-election period. The two party leaders, together with a few senior ministers and party representatives, worked out a policy programme. The content was joint standpoints on some of the policy issues facing the coalition, but far from all of them. This coalition agreement remained in force after the 1952 election. Only after the election in 1956 did the two parties begin to negotiate a revised coalition agreement (Erlander 1974; Jonnergård 1985: 90; Ruin 1968). The Social Democratic–Centre Party coalition marked a period of stability in Swedish politics. The coalition is seen by most observers as one that worked well and without any major coalition disturbances until the two parties took two different paths on the issue of mandatory and public pension funds (ATP) in the mid-1950s.

Broad patterns of coalition governance have remained the same in subsequent coalitions. The parties usually negotiate a coalition programme only after an election (Bergström 1987). In 1990–1, well before the upcoming election, the Liberal and Conservative Party leaders presented the outlines of a joint economic and budgetary policy programme. However, even this policy area was negotiated by all four coalition parties after the election. A second feature is that coalition discipline is high, except on certain issues. That the parties are largely free to appoint their own representatives to cabinet positions is a third. A fourth pattern is that non-cabinet positions (except for junior ministers) are dealt with in parallel but largely separate negotiations.

Finally, coalitions do not prepare for their own demise by, for example, including a rule requiring extra elections if the government resigns. Rather, such issues are explicitly dealt with only when a government crisis occurs. This order of things is probably facilitated by the predetermined date of the next mandatory election. As for the extent of party discipline, certain issues of morals and ethics, such as religious issues, abortion, alcohol, and, more recently, smoking restrictions, are generally left outside of party discipline. This is the case both with regard to party discipline in the Riksdag and within coalitions and has been a constant in Swedish politics throughout the postwar period.

TABLE 6.4. *Coalition governance in Sweden*

(1) Coalition	(2) Coalition agreement	(3) Agreement public	(4) Election rule	(5) Management mechanisms[a]	(8) Coalition discipline in legislation	(9) Coalition discipline in other parliamentary behaviour	(10) Freedom of appointment[b]	(11) Policy agreement	(12) Junior ministers	(13) Non-cabinet positions
Erlander III 1951	IE	Yes	No	IC	2	2	Yes	2	Yes	Yes
Erlander IV 1952c	PRE	Yes	No	IC	2	2	Yes	2	Yes	Yes
Erlander V 1956	POST	Yes	No	IC	2	2	Yes	2	Yes	Yes
Fälldin I 1976	POST	Yes	No	IC, CaC	2	2	Yes	3	Yes	Yes
Fälldin II 1979	POST	Yes	No	IC, CaC	2	2	Yes	3	Yes	Yes
Fälldin III 1981	IE	Yes	No	IC, CaC	2	2	Yes	3	Yes	Yes
Bildt 1991	POST	Yes[d]	No	IC, CaC	2	2	Yes	3	Yes	Yes

[a] For all coalitions, an inner cabinet consisting of party leaders, and occasionally other important ministers, was the conflict management mechanism for the most important conflicts. From 1976 the governments also had cabinet committees as conflict management mechanisms. This was the mechanism used most frequently. When this mechanism failed, issues were handed over to the inner cabinet.

[b] This is the general principle. As explained in the text, occasionally there are exceptions to this principle.

[c] In 1952, the 1951 coalition did not renegotiate the coalition programme or the forms for coalition governance, it simply continued on in power. Thus, the information provided for the 1952 row is identical with the information provided in the 1951 row.

[d] This refers to the 1991 comprehensive coalition agreement which was combined with comprehensive and detailed sub-protocols. The sub-protocols are not public.

Cabinet Portfolios and Procedures

Rules for decision making within the cabinet can be important for cabinet life cycles. The Swedish constitution formally rejects the idea of direct ministerial control of state agencies when these implement law or exercise state authority over individuals. Moreover, administrative state agencies fall under the authority of the cabinet as a collective and not under individual ministers. With minor exceptions, such as internal departmental matters, executive decision making is supposed to express the views of the cabinet as a whole (Holmberg and Stjernquist 1995).

This does not imply that department ministers are without means to enforce their will; they have substantial control over routine matters as well as over the budgetary process. Besides this, they have important agenda-setting powers when preparing collective decisions for the cabinet. Nonetheless, the specific utility of a ministerial portfolio might be more restricted in Sweden than in systems where each minister exercises a more formal and direct control over the implementing agencies. As discussed by Laver (1992: 47–8) in the case of Ireland, the existence of collective cabinet responsibility may force coalition partners and individual ministers to defend coalition policies with which they disagree. This might be a reason not to join a coalition unless there is assurance that its policies will be acceptable.

The general practice concerning ministerial appointment is that parties may choose their own representative for their given portfolios and other positions. There have been notable exceptions, however. In 1951, the deputy party leader of the Centre Party, von Heland, expected to be invited to sit in the coalition cabinet. His party leader brought up his name, but refrained from pushing his candidacy. He probably knew that the Social Democrats would strongly oppose his candidacy. Not only among Social Democrats, but even within his his own party, Heland was known for his aggressive style (Erlander 1974: 282–3; von Heland 1969: 202–28). In a famous incident in 1976, the Conservative Party's Astrid Kristensson was prevented from becoming the Minister of Justice, largely because of opposition from the Liberal Party (Bergström 1987: 223; Bohman 1984: 159–60; Hammerich 1977). However, there are two sides to this coin of excluding particular candidates. The party leaders did not protest very sharply. Parties avoid presenting candidates who know they will be difficult for their coalition partners to tolerate.

In Sweden, the position of junior minister is an administrative one (second in command in the ministry). The tradition has been to appoint an accomplished administrator, often one with party political ties to the minister in question, though not necessarily so (Christoffersson 1983). The positions are usually not filled until after policies have been agreed upon and cabinet portfolios have been distributed. Each minister has the right to suggest his or her own candidate, but the above-mentioned principle of exclusion on the grounds of non-tolerance applies. The candidates are appointed unless one of the coalition partners is strongly opposed (Bergström 1987). There are, however, exceptions to the general principle that ministers are free to choose their junior ministers. One example is that in 1951 Prime Minister Erlander placed a Social Democratic junior minister in the Ministry of Education to oversee future reforms in that policy area (Erlander 1974: 280). The Minister of Education was from the Centre Party. Another example is that in 1976, Prime Minister Fälldin blocked Carl Bildt's appointment as a junior minister (*statssekreterare*) because he held Bildt (the PM in 1991) to be too young and lacking in administrative experience (Bergström 1987: 248, 496).

The features discussed here have largely been constants in cabinet governance. Some change is nonetheless discernable. For instance, freedom of appointment has developed into a higher level of tolerance for a party's preferred candidate, both as regards ministers and junior ministers. Also, in the 1950s there were altogether fewer considerations, fewer junior ministers and fewer non-cabinet positions to put together in the the giant 'jigsaw puzzle' of coalition formation and governance than was the case in the 1991 coalition.

There has been even more obvious change with regard to other aspects of coalition governance. One is that the organization of cabinet procedures has become more elabourate over time. In the 1950s, conflicts within the cabinet were dealt with by the party leaders and sometimes the heads of the most important ministries, who together formed something of an informal inner cabinet. The practice of having an informal inner cabinet of ministers still exists (see e.g. Feldt 1993).

In addition to the informal inner cabinet, from 1976 coalitions have had a system of problem-solving and coordination. The 1976–82 and the 1991 coalitions had cabinet committees (CaC). However, there were significant differences between the 1991 system and the 1976–82 system. In the 1976–82 period, the three parties tried a model of coordination in which each party leader was given a staff of political appointees responsible for cabinet coordination. These staffs were to provide a low-level (or first) arena for resolving policy differences within the coalition. By allowing the party leaders to focus on larger disputes and more important issues, it was hoped to reduce the pressure on the top-level decision makers within each party. The system is reported to have worked reasonably well for most issues, but at times it had the opposite effect of what was intended. By splitting up the staff responsible for trouble-shouting into three distinct party groups, policy disputes sometimes became entrenched rather than resolved (Egardt, interview, 1996; Larsson 1986: 188–93; Pettersson, interview, 1996).

The 1991 coalition deliberately organized the formal structure of coordination quite differently. Instead of having staffs for coordination for every party leader, the coalition arranged for one centrally located staff for this purpose. The status of the staff was raised, by elevating the positions from political appointees in general to the level of junior minister. The junior ministers responsible for policy coordination were all placed in the prime minister's office. This enabled them to become something of an intermediary station between the efforts to coordinate at the ministry-level and efforts in the inner cabinet—i.e. essentially the leader of each party. This system is reported to have worked well, not least in comparison with the 1976–82 system (Egardt, interview, 1996; Pettersson, interview, 1996).

Two other efforts to increase communication and coordination between the parties were made by the 1991 coalition. One was that the leaders of each party's parliamentary group, which is a position separate from party leader, attended the informal weekly meetings at which broad outlines of cabinet policy are discussed. The other invention was that the parliamentary groups of each party occasionally met with each other and with the cabinet ministers to exchange information and engage in policy discussions. Both procedures are reported to have worked well and to have contributed to the four-party coalition's ability to stay in power until the next mandatory election (Egardt, interview, 1996; Pettersson, interview, 1996).

Of course, the increased efforts at coordination and organization of party relations within the cabinet could be an artefact of the higher number of parties (four) in the more recent cabinet coalitions. But the observation that there has been a general trend in favour of more formalized and elaborate arrangements is further supported by the information provided in Table 6.5.

TABLE 6.5. *Size and content of coalition agreements in Sweden, 1951–1999*

Coalition	Size[a]	General procedural rules (in %)	Policy specific procedural rules (in %)[b]	Distribution of offices (in %)	Distribution of competences (in %)	Policies (in %)
SD–Ce 1951	1,100	0	—	0	0	100
SD–Ce 1952	see above	0	—	0	0	—
SD–Ce 1956	1,900	0	2	0	0	98
Ce–Li–Co 1976	2,900	0	8	0	0	92
Ce–Li–Co 1979	3,500	0	4	0	0	96
Ce–Li–1981	1,400	0	—	0	0	100
Co–Ce–CD–Li 1991[c]	5,200 (>50,000)	0	4	0	0	96

[a] The size of the agreement is a rounded approximation (average number of words per sentence X rows per page X number of pages).
[b] The proportion of specific policy rules is a rough estimate based on a difficult distinction between procedural rules meant to constrain or guide the coalition partners and those policy statements that contain a policy trajectory agreed upon by the parties in the coalition.
[c] Non–public sub–protocols were agreed upon by the four parties before they formed the cabinet. Presumably, the proportion of policy–specific procedural rules is about the same as in the public coalition agreements in the public coalition agreement, or perhaps slightly higher (Egardt, interview, 1996; Pettersson, interview, 1996).

In Sweden, it used to be the case that a cabinet's general policy statement to the parliament was presented as the Crown Speech (*trontal*). Until 1975, the coalitions also negotiated separate agreements. Today, the most central and binding document is the cabinet's declaration (*regeringsförklaring*) to the Riksdag. Under the new constitution, the cabinet presents a policy programme when the Riksdag opens each year and when a new cabinet is formed. These statements are part of the publicly available Riksdag Minutes (*Riksdagens protokoll*). For coalition cabinets, this declaration is regarded as being the most central and binding of all documents. It is negotiated in detail and the parties put a lot of time and effort into the wording of each sentence. The declaration is important for single-party cabinets too, but more as a general statement of policy intent. In coalitions, parties regard it as a binding document throughout the duration of the cabinet (Egardt, interview, 1996; Pettersson, interview, 1996; see also Bergström 1987). In 1951 and 1956, coalition policy programmes were published in the newspapers. In 1952, however, there appears not to have been any renegotiation of the 1951 policy programme, which remained in force after the 1952 election (Erlander 1974; Jonnergård 1985: 90; see also Ruin 1968).

Two noticeable patterns are that the written coalition agreements have become longer over time and that they now provide some specific rules or methods for dealing with controversial issues. The 1951 agreement contained approximately 1,100 words and dealt exclusively with the policy content upon which the coalition was based. When the document was renegotiated in 1956, it was expanded to 1,900 words. This time it also contained references to points of disagreement. One such reference was the need for further negotiations on economic policies. The other was a reference to the issue of mandatory and public pension funds (ATP) about which the Centre Party reserved the right to further discussions.

The 1976 agreement was longer still. On the issue of the nuclear power programme, it contained specific references to the steps and procedures according to which the issue was to be handled. The 1979 agreement also contained such references. The coalition formed in 1981 is the exception to the trend. After the Conservative Party resigned from the coalition in dispute over the tax system, the two parties of the middle remained in power. They did so with reference to the programme of the old coalition. By this time the issue of nuclear power had already been decided in a referendum so the parties did not include specific references to particular procedures for resolving it.

The 1991 coalition continued the trend of making coalition agreements larger as measured by number of words. The public document is about five times longer than the one agreed upon by the 1951 coalition. The policy agreements are also very comprehensive, much more so than was the case in 1951. The 1991 programme includes references to specific procedures for resolving issues such as whether the state should make it easier for parents to stay home with their children through an income supplement for those who choose to do so and the issue of whether to build a bridge between Sweden and Denmark. Given the earlier tradition of short coalition agreements, what is remarkable about the 1991 coalition agreement is that it was explicitly supplemented with non-public and comprehensive sub-protocols. The party leaders and their assistants in the negotiations managed to produce approximately 200 pages of sub-protocols governing issues, and follow-up issues, for basically any potential policy dispute they could think of. Of the more than 50,000 words contained in these pages (a very rough estimate), almost all are agreements on issues of policy content. However, as is the case with the government declarations, a small but significant portion of the sub-protocols deal with steps, methods, and procedures to be followed when deciding on the content of specific policy issues (Egardt, interview, 1996; Pettersson, interview, 1996).

In the 1991 cabinet formation, the four coalition partners bargained through a system of working committees, subordinate to the party leaders. These committees worked out much of what is found in the agreements. The most difficult issues were solved by the party leaders. Once the committees and the party leaders had reached broad agreement the government declaration was drafted. The declaration itself was discussed, negotiated, and finalized in a separate round of negotiations. Both the sub-protocols and the government declaration were considered to be binding. However, the fact that the coalition agreement reported to the Riksdag is public enhanced its status as the most important of all coalition documents.

Another basic element of coalition governance is the distribution of portfolios. As explained above, the distribution might be less important in Sweden than it is in countries where individual ministers control state agencies more directly. However, as was also pointed out, individual ministers still have agenda-setting power through the privilege of policy formulation. Table 6.6 shows the distribution of portfolios in the seven cabinet coalitions. The only junior minister that has been identified is the 1951–7 junior minister in the Ministry of Education. Otherwise, junior ministers (*statssekreterare*) belong to the same party as the minister or they are perceived as non-partisan.

Over time, the parties have traded portfolios. Nonetheless, there are some obvious continuities. The Centre Party has held the position of Minister of Agriculture in all Swedish coalitions. This position fits well with its historical roots as a party for small and middle-sized farmers. Another continuity is that, except for the Conservative Party in 1979, the largest party in the coalition has always claimed the office of the prime minister. The possibility of having a deputy prime minister was introduced with the new constitution and the leaders of the Liberal Party have managed to get the title in all coalitions since 1976. The Liberal Party has also appointed the Minister of Finance and

216   *Torbjörn Bergman*

TABLE 6.6. *Distribution of cabinet and junior ministerships in Swedish coalitions*

Cabinet and year formed	(1) Prime Minister	(2) Deputy PM = Honorary title	(3a) Finance	(4) Foreign Affairs	(5) Health and Social Affairs	(6) Labour and Equality Affairs	(7) Environment and Energy	(8) Education and Cultural Affairs	(9) Industry	(10) Defence	(11) Justice	(12) Housing
Erlander III 1951	SD	—	SD	SD	SD	—	—	Ce, sd	—	SD	SD	—
Erlander IV 1952	SD	—	SD	SD	SD	—	—	Ce, sd	—	SD	SD	—
Erlander V 1956	SD	—	SD	SD	SD	—	—	Ce, sd	—	SD	SD	Ce
Fälldin I 1976	Ce	Li	Li	Ce	Ce	Li	—	Li	Ce	Co	non–party	Li
Fälldin II 1979	Ce	Li	Li	Li	Ce	Li	—	Li	Ce	Ce	Co	Li
Fälldin III 1981	Ce	Li	Li	Li	Ce	Li	—	Li	Ce	Ce	non–party	Li
Bildt 1991	Co	Li	Li	Co	Li	Ce	Ce	Co	Co	Co	Co	—

TABLE 6.6. Cont.

Cabinet and year formed	(13) Transport and Communications	(14) Agriculture	(3b) Economy	Interior	Foreign Trade	Civil Affairs/ Local government	Environment and Energy	Education and Cultural Affairs	Industry	Defence	Justice	Housing
Erlander III 1951	SD	Ce	—	Ce	SD	SD	SD	SD	Ca* (13)	—	—	No Portfolio
Erlander IV 1952	SD	Ce	—	Ce	SD	SD	SD	SD	Ce* (13)	—	—	No Portfolio
Erlander V 1956	SD	Ce	—	Ce	SD	SD	SD	SD	Ce* (13)	—	—	No Portfolio
Fälldin I 1976	Co	Ce	Co	—	Co	Ce	Co* (8)	Co* (5)	Li * (12)	Ce	—	No Portfolio
Fälldin II 1979	Ce	Ce	Co	—	Co	Ce	Co* (8)	Co* (5)	Ce * (3a)	Ce* (6)	non–party	No Portfolio
Fälldin III 1981	Ce	Ce	—	—	Li	Ce	Ce* (8)	Li* (5)	Ce* (3a)	—	—	No Portfolio
Bildt 1991 non–party	CD	Ce	—	—	Co	CD	Co	Co	Li	Ce	CD* (4)	No Portfolio

* Instances in which a minister without portfolio has been responsible for preparing certain issues within a ministry led by a minister from another party. The number within the parenthesis identifies the ministry at which the minister without portfolio had such a role.

Note: Ministries in order of importance (Laver and Hunt 1992: 303). Unnumbered ministries were not included in Laver and Hunt (1992)

Sources: Hadenius et al. 1993: 373–380, Erlander 1974: 280–284.

Budget (3a) from among its ranks, though not without consultations with other parties. Twice, in 1976 and 1979, they had to share part of the ministry—macroeconomic analysis—with the Conservative Party leader (Bohman) around whom a separate ministry was created (3b). The Liberals used to have a hold on the Ministry of Education, but in the 1991 coalition two cabinet members from the Conservative Party were appointed to this ministry. These were the Minister of Education and a minister without portfolio. The latter minister was, in practice, Minister for Education up to the level of colleges and universities.

Ministers without portfolios used to be advisers or consultants, especially on legal and administrative matters. Over time they have gradually become ministers responsible for the preparation of policy in a particular area (Larsson 1990). This trend existed already in the 1950s. In 1951, the Centre Party had a minister without portfolio who was responsible for preparing policy concerning roads within the Ministry of Transport and Communications. The ministry was led by a Social Democrat (Erlander 1974: 283–4). The trend that ministers without portfolio were assigned to a particular policy area grew stronger in the 1960s (Andrén 1968b: 300). Today all ministers without portfolio are responsible for a policy area, though they (per definition) do not formally head any particular ministry.

As mentioned above, in 1951 a Social Democratic junior minister was placed in the Department of Education (ministry number 8 in Table 6.6), which at the time was headed by a minister from the Centre Party. This is an unusual practice. Instead the Swedish practice is to appoint a minister and minister without portfolio from different parties. For example, in the 1991 coalition, the Liberal Minister of Finance shared the ministry with a minister without portfolio from the Conservative Party. In practice, the Conservative minister was placed at the ministry to prepare issues concerning taxation. In 1991, the only other multi-party ministry was the Ministry for Foreign Affairs, which contained three ministers, two Conservative ministers (one without portfolio) and the Christian Democratic Party leader who served as a minister without portfolio. However, compared to the period 1976–82, the 1991 coalition actually had fewer multi-party ministries. Ministers sharing ministries are not an exclusive feature of coalition governments, however. Social Democratic cabinets often have more than one minister within the same ministry.

In the 1976–9 coalitions, this practice of multi-party ministries was widespread. A total of eighteen multi-party ministries are identified in Table 6.6. Of these, thirteen occurred during this period. The Centre Party and the Conservative Party have placed the most ministers without portfolio in ministries headed by someone from another party. Since the 1976 coalition, it has been common to place ministers from different parties in the Ministries of Finance and Budget, Health and Social Affairs, and in the Ministry of

Education. Also Foreign Affairs, Labour, and Housing have had ministers from different coalition parties. These are all considered to be important and/or are ministries which have been responsible for considerable welfare spending. This suggests that the pattern is not random. Coalition parties have wanted a check on their partners in important ministries. Rather than obtaining one by placing junior ministers and ministers from different parties in the same ministry, they place a minister without portfolio in the ministry. This minister is then given the right and responsibility to prepare certain policy areas. In addition, he or she can be a useful source of information for his or her party.

In the 1995–7 period, two leading Centre Party representatives held positions in two of the Social Democratic ministries. One held a full-time position in the Ministry of Finance and the other a part-time position in the Ministry of Defence. These positions did not have the rank of junior ministers and have therefore not been included in the table above. However, the practice of giving an 'opposition' party positions within cabinet ministries is an innovation in Swedish politics. It should be seen in the context of the close cooperation that existed between the cabinet and the Centre Party. According to the then General Secretary (*partisekreterare*) of the Centre Party, this arrangement, or any of the specific policy agreements the parties have made, was not based on any formal contract. The cooperation was based on personal trust and the specifics of each separate negotiation. The main argument used to explain this cooperation is the economic problems facing the national economy and the state budget. According to the Centre Party Secretary, the two parties do not need a formal agreement in part because they share historical roots as extra-parliamentary social movements. Their long traditions of intra-party democracy are said to have served as a guarantee of the trustworthiness of their agreements (Pettersson, interview, 1996).

After the electoral setback suffered by the Social Democrats and the Centre Party in the 1998 elections, the two did no longer have the votes sufficient to guarantee a legislative victory in the parliament. The Social Democrats now turned to the Left Party and the Green Party. Without forming a formal cabinet coalition, the three parties agreed to cooperate on economic and financial issues. In a media release dated 5 October 1998 (*Statsrådsberedningen* 1998), they stated that the support arrangement is for five specific areas: economy (the state budget), employment, distributive justice, gender equality, and the environment. On other issues they have did not formally commit to cooperate but at the same time, they stated, their intention was to work together for the full electoral period.

The support arrangement of the second half of the 1990s are qualitatively different from the informal support arrangements earlier in the period. It used to be that the Social Democrats could trust the Communist Party to keep them in power without raising many specific demands for negotiated policy concessions by the Social Democrats. Instead the Social Democrats could often govern by forming *ad hoc* legislative coalitions with one or more of the non-socialist parties. After an economic and financial crisis of the early 1990s, and through the subsequent austerity measures, the Social Democrats were forced to accept a more organized form of support arrangement. The 1998 electoral setback made the apparent need for such more organized cooperation even more obvious.

But the more formalized support arrangements that have been characteristic of the second half of the 1990s have not eliminated all elements of party competition. The ease with which the Social Democrats and the Centre Party cooperated, and the relative ease of the first year of the three-party cooperation between the Social Democrats, the Greens, and the reformed Communist Party after the 1998 elections, should not obfuscate the full picture, which is that all these parties also are and have been fierce competitors. For example, from the early 1970s and until the mid-1980s, the Social Democrats and the Centre Party were led by the two main competitors for the position of prime minister, Olof Palme and Thorbjörn Fälldin. The competition between the two played a major role in the events that led to the formation of four non-socialist cabinets in the period 1976–82. The competition between them also had consequences for the duration of these cabinets. This leads over to the question of why cabinets resign and how voters judge cabinets.

COALITION TERMINATION

Table 6.7 provides basic information about why cabinets have been terminated. One reason has to do with a technicality—that is, after every general election the cabinet is classified as new. From the perspective of coalition formation theory this practice makes perfect sense. A general election changes the parties' shares of all seats in parliament, and therefore their bargaining positions. From a coalition formation perspective, this is reason enough to count a new cabinet. However, for a study of cabinet termination, these technically new cabinets are of less interest.

Other aspects are more important. Two prime ministers have died in office. In two other instances, the prime minister voluntarily retired. Once, in 1951, a cabinet resigned to make room for a voluntary enlargement of the cabinet. This was done at a time when there was widespread concern about high inflation and high interest rates. It was also done as a response to the fact that the cabinet's parliamentary basis had shrunk in the most recent election. As for the remaining resignations, three policy areas in particular have been important: social policy (public pension funds), the environment (nuclear power), and taxes.

TABLE 6.7. *Cabinet termination in Sweden, 1945–1999*

Cabinet number	Cabinet	Mechanisms of cabinet termination			
		Technical			Discretionary
		(1) Regular parliamentary election	(2) Other constitutional reason	(3) Death of Prime Minister	(4) Early parliamentary election
1	Hansson 1946			X	
2	Erlander I 1948	X			
3	Erlander II 1951				
4	Erlander III 1952	X			
5	Erlander IV 1956	X			
6	Erlander V 1957				
7	Erlander VI 1958				X
8	Erlander VII 1960	X			
9	Erlander VIIII 1964	X			
10	Erlander IX 1968	X			
11	Erlander X 1969		X		
12	Palme I 1970	X			
13	Palme II 1973	X			
14	Palme III 1976	X			
15	Fälldin I 1978				
16	Ullsten 1979	X			
17	Fälldin II 1981				
18	Fälldin III 1982	X			
19	Palme IV 1985	X			
20	Palme V 1986			X	
21	Carlsson I 1988	X			
22	Carlsson II 1991	X			
23	Bildt 1994	X			
24	Carlsson III 1996		X		
25	Persson I 1998	X			

(5) Voluntary enlargement of coalition	(7) Conflict between coalition parties		Terminal event (13) Personal event	Policy area(s)	Comments
	Policy	Personnel			
			X		Death of PM Hansson
X					Centre Party joins Social Democrats in cabinet in times of concern for national economy
	X			Social (5)	Coalition breaks up, the issue of mandatory public pension funds (ATP) is the deciding one
				Social (5)	Extra elections held, the pension fund issue is dominant
			X		PM Erlander resigns after 23 years as party leader
				Environment (9)	Social Democratic cabinet resigns after election defeat. The Swedish nuclear power programme had been the most salient issue in the election campaign
	X			Environment (9)	The three party cabinet splits over the nuclear power issue
	X			Taxes (3a, 3b)	Conservative Party leaves coalition because of disagreement over the tax-system.
			X		Death of PM Palme
				(Environment) (7)	(The leader of the Centre Party resigns in the spring, but his party stays in cabinet until the Sept. election. Disagreements over environment and procedure are behind his resignation)
			X		Voluntary resignation of PM Carlsson

In 1957–8, the most important policy struggle within the coalition was over the issue of public and mandatory pension funds (Molin 1965; Jonasson 1981; von Sydow 1978). This split began before the 1956 election. The two parties were able to continue in power together by responding to the issue by referring to future reports and consultations. The conflict was resolved only after a referendum (October 1957), an extra election, and a close vote in the Riksdag in which the parties aligned in two blocs along the left–right dimension. In part, the issue became salient because of sincere policy disagreements over the future of social politics and the public sector. However, the conflict was fuelled by the party leaders' belief that conflict would benefit their own party.

Another major policy issue that dominated the public debate for a number of years was the future of the nuclear power programme. In the early 1970s, the new leader of the Centre Party, Thorbjörn Fälldin, began to link his vision of a decentralized and ecological society to the risks associated with nuclear power. By 1976, nuclear power was the dominant environmental issue and in the election that year Fälldin campaigned in part on his personal trustworthiness on the issue. He promised that he would not compromise his ideals if he got into cabinet. But his coalition partners, the two other non-socialist parties, were both in favour of nuclear power. The three party leaders were also under strong pressure to stay together. For the first time in the post-war period, the three parties had a real chance of forming a majority government. The coalition worked out a compromise in which the fate of the nuclear power programme was made conditional on the possibility of safe storing of nuclear waste. To get this compromise, Fälldin agreed to start one more nuclear power plant. The Social Democrats argued that this showed that Fälldin's election promises had not been sincere. The issue continued to torment the coalition for two years until finally, in 1978, the dispute led to its resignation (Larsson 1986; Leijonhuvud 1979; Vedung 1979).

Later the Social Democrats and the non-socialist parties agreed to hold a referendum on nuclear power. It was held in March 1980. The outcome led to a Riksdag decision to dismantle the nuclear programme—but in the long run and with care. Nuclear power is still around, but the referendum largely removed the issue from the set of questions over which the parties fight election campaigns. In fact, the decision to hold the referendum made it possible for the three non-socialist parties to present a joint alternative in the 1979 elections. They won a one-seat Riksdag majority. In less than two years, however, this cabinet resigned as well. This time the issue that brought it down was the tax system. In 1981, to get a tax reform that would survive a change of government, the parties of the middle made a deal with the Social Democrats. The Conservatives responded by resigning from the cabinet while the two remaining parties formed a cabinet for the period until the 1982 elections (Hadenius 1981).

One resignation from cabinet is worth mentioning. It concerns an individual minister rather than a party, but the case is of general interest. In the spring of 1994, roughly six months before the next election, the leader of the Centre Party, Olof Johansson, resigned from his position as the Minster of Environment. He did so because of a conflict within the cabinet over the environmental impact of a proposed bridge between Sweden and Denmark. Yet, all other cabinet members from his party stayed in office until the election. This is in contrast to the standard Swedish practice that when a party leader leaves the cabinet, so does his party. In explaining his resignation, the party leader stated that he left because the issue of the bridge had not been handled the way that was spelled out in the coalition agreement. This was disputed by other members of the coalition. Regardless of whose version is closer to the truth, this incident illustrates both the changing importance and the changing content of coalition agreements over time. In Sweden, the general trend has been one of movement from agreements representing general policy guidelines to documents that are more comprehensive about policy. Compared to the 1950s they are also more detailed about procedural matters. The discussion surrounding the Centre Party leader's resignation reflects the growing concern with procedural matters in coalition governance and termination. The case also introduced a new distinction between the role as the head of a particular ministry versus the role as a party leader. No other party leader has been outside of a cabinet of which has party has been a member.

ELECTORAL PERFORMANCE

To draw general conclusions rather than focusing on individual PMs, we look at the electoral fortune of governments. When Swedish governments have broken up, it has generally been over genuine and important policy conflicts. Yet, parties may have additional considerations in choosing whether or not to enter or maintain a government coalition. As shown in Table 6.8, sometimes the idea of resigning is not a bad electoral strategy. It can help you win votes. For example, the Conservative Party left two coalitions in the period 1978–81. In 1978, the Conservative Party was forced out of the government by the Liberals. In 1981, the Conservatives resigned of their own choosing. Both times, this helped them increase the share of the vote in the next election. However, not all who resign are rewarded. In 1978, it was the Centre Party that left the coalition. For this, the party was not rewarded by the electorate in the following election.

In two consecutive elections, the Conservative Party gained a total of eight (8) per centage points. This success is almost unprecedented for a government party in Swedish politics. For the Conservatives, going into opposition against

TABLE 6.8. *Electoral costs/benefits of Swedish government parties, 1945–1999* (in % of votes)

Government	In office at election	Election Year	SD	Ce	CD	Li	Co	Government
SD 1945	Yes	1948	−0.6	—	—	—	—	−0.6
SD 1948	No	1952	±0	—	—	—	—	±0
SD–Ce 1951	Yes	1952	±0	−1.7	—	—	—	−1.7
SD–Ce 1952	Yes	1956	−1.5	−1.3	—	—	—	−2.8
SD–Ce 1956	No	1958	+1.6	+3.3	—	—	—	+4.9
SD 1957	Yes	1958	+1.6	—	—	—	—	+1.6
SD 1958	Yes	1960	+1.6	—	—	—	—	+1.6
SD 1960	Yes	1964	−0.5	—	—	—	—	−0.5
SD 1964	Yes	1968	+2.8	—	—	—	—	+2.8
SD 1968	Yes	1970	−4.8	—	—	—	—	−4.8
SD 1970	Yes	1973	−1.7	—	—	—	—	−1.7
SD 1973	Yes	1976	−0.9	—	—	—	—	−0.9
Ce–Li–Co 1976	No	1979	—	−6	—	−0.5	+4.7	−1.8
Li 1978	Yes	1979	—	—	—	−0.5	—	−0.5
Ce–Li–Co 1979	No	1982	—	−2.6	—	−4.7	+3.3	−4
Ce–Li 1981	Yes	1982	—	−2.6	—	−4.7	—	−7.3
SD 1982	Yes	1985	−0.9	—	—	—	—	−0.9
SD 1985	Yes	1988	−1.5	—	—	—	—	−1.5
SD 1988	Yes	1991	−5.5	—	—	—	—	−5.5
Co–Ce–CD–Li 1991	Yes	1994	—	−0.8	−3.0	−1.9	+0.5	−5.2
SD 1994	Yes	1998	−8.9	—	—	—	—	−8.9
MEANS	Yes	—	−1.5	−1.6	−3.0	−2.4	+0.5	−2.2
	No	—	+0.8	−1.8	—	−2.6	+4	−0.2
	All	—	−1.5	−1.5	−3.0	−2.4	+2.8	−1.8

Sources: *Allmänna valen 1994*: 25–6; *Från Riksdag & Departement* 1998: 13.

a government formed by one or two of the parties in the middle has been a successful vote winning strategy, more so than being in opposition against a Social Democratic government. The Centre Party 1957 resignation from the coalition helped produce a gain of similar magnitude. Otherwise, having been in government during the preceding electoral period usually means a loss of electoral support—on average 1.8 per cent at every election. It is only the Conservatives in 1979, 1982, and 1994 and Erlander's governments in 1958, 1960, and 1968 that have increased their vote support after having been in office. The Conservative gain in 1994 (0.5 per cent) was small, but still good considering the overall record of all parties in government. In the late 1950s, while remaining in government, Erlander managed to turn the pension funds conflict into an advantage for his party. His last election in 1968 was a great personal triumph, albeit that he probably got some help from international unrest (the invasion of Czechoslovakia). These cases are, however, exceptions. Generally, in electoral terms, it does not pay to be a government party in Sweden. In addition, you are generally even a bit worse off if you are in government at election time. The average loss for such a government is 2.2 per cent.

CONCLUSION

For the period as a whole, the following four features provide an explanation of the empirical record of government life cycles. They are related to each other but can be kept analytically separate. First, inter-party competition has taken place mainly, though not exclusively, on one dimension, the left–right dimension. The left–right pattern can be found in election programmes, among party activists, and among the voters. The salience of this dimension is promoted by the fact that strong organized interests are aligned along the same dimension.

Second, together with the dominance of the left–right dimension, the Social Democratic Party's electoral strength has given it an excellent bargaining position. This has been further facilitated by the fact that the party has the median position on the most salient alternative dimension as well.

The third feature has to do with the policy distances between other parties. The Social Democratic bargaining position has been strengthened by the distance between the Communist Party and the non-socialist parties. Rather than considering a coalition with a non-socialist party, the Communist Party has been willing to provide support for Social Democratic minority cabinets. Moreover, policy disagreements within the non-socialist bloc have enabled the Social Democrats to form ad hoc legislative coalitions with one or more of these parties.

The fourth feature is the constitutional arrangements. Institutional rules favour policy cohesive coalitions and do not preclude opposition parties from having an impact on cabinet policies. When cabinets are forming, the absence of a minimum size threshold facilitates formation of minority cabinets. Once they are in place, the absolute majority requirement for a declaration of no confidence helps maintain a minority cabinet.

Taken together these four characteristics provide a good account of why Swedish cabinets have so often been Social Democratic minority cabinets. The importance of the median legislator is further strengthened by the fact that the Centre Party has been a member of all Swedish cabinet coalitions (since the 1920s). A consequence of the combination of these four features is that not all combinations of parties have represented equally feasible coalitions. Formal majority coalitions and majority tolerance of minority cabinets have been forged among parties adjacent to one another in policy space.

The post-war record of coalition governance began in 1951 with the Social Democratic–Centre Party cabinet coalition. Some of the main patterns of coalition governance have remained stable since this time. Negotiations begin after elections rather than before. Coalitions are based on policy agreements, while negotiations over portfolios are taken up when progress has been made on policy content. To keep informed about what the coalition partners are up to, Swedish parties use dual ministers for one ministry rather than junior ministers from another party. Finally, coalitions do not prepare for their own demise. Their agreements do not include rules as to what will happen if the coalition fails.

Other features have changed over time. Coalition governance is associated with more elabourate arrangements today than early in the post-war era. Policy agreements are more comprehensive and the procedures for coalition coordination are set out in greater detail. The partners have more freedom in appointing their own candidates to ministry positions than they once did. This latter point is related to the fact that the Conservative Party is now accepted as a fully legitimate coalition partner by the other non-socialist parties. Until 1976, this was a controversial issue.

Setting aside technical reasons, resignations and deaths in office, cabinets resign when their election performance makes an alternative cabinet a likely outcome. They also sometimes resign over internal disagreements. In particular, three policy areas have been associated with such resignations. These are social policy, environmental policy, and taxes. Party conflict in these policy areas has not simply arisen from the social context of the parties. Parties have resigned both because of pressure from public opinion and because of strategic considerations. Moreover, public opinion has been created, at least partly, by the party leaders themselves. The pension funds, the nuclear power programme, the tax system, and even the bridge to Denmark, were all issues that party leaders decided to promote as vital issues worth fighting for and even to resign because of.

When cabinets have resigned over internal policy disagreement, Swedish voters have sometimes rewarded the parties that resigned and stayed out of the next cabinet. This happened to the Centre Party in the late 1950s, and the Conservative Party in 1979 and 1982. In the 1950s and 1960s, Prime Minister Erlander even experienced vote gains while still in office. Overall, however, Swedish voters have a habit of punishing parties who sit in cabinets.

In the second half of the 1990s, the Social Democrats once again have formed one-party minority cabinets. Again the party sought long-term support from the Centre Party in dealing with issues such as financial problems, budget deficits and social expenditures. After more than thirty-five years of a distinctive left–right split in Swedish politics, this cooperation did not lead to a formal cabinet coalition. As indicated by the cooperation between the three centre-left parties after the 1998 elections, Swedish political parties sometimes avoid formal cabinet coalitions in favour of largely informal cooperation arrangements.

It remains to be seen if the recent trend towards more formalized support arrangements will translate into formal coalitions. The chances have increased, since the conflict between a 'socialist' and a 'bourgeois' bloc seems less relevant now than in the period 1960–90. The incentives for such a coalition also hinges on the state of the national economy and the verdict of the voters. As students of coalition theory know, it will also hinge on how the parties view the consequences of a government coalition in terms of their strategic goals. The recent trend towards a decline in the importance of the left–right dimension is likely to facilitate the formation of cabinets across the blocs. It is not unlikely, that the outcome of Swedish coalition bargaining will become more similar to the outcomes in many other European countries, i.e. majority coalitions as the rule and minority governments as the exception. Nonetheless, political culture, institutions, and voter behaviour have long provided strong incentives to form minority cabinets rather than majority coalitions and will continue doing so.

INTERVIEWS

Egardt, Peter (1996). *Interview conducted on telephone by the author on 14 June*. Peter Egardt worked as the General Secretary (*Kanslichef*) at the Riksdag office of the Conservative Party in the 1980s and in the early 1990s. In the 1991–4 period, he was the junior minister in the Prime Minister's office. In both positions he worked closely with the Conservative Party leader. As a junior minister in the coalition cabinet, he prepared and administrated much of the process of cabinet coordination.

Pettersson, Åke (1996). *Interview conducted by the author on 25 May*. In the 1979–82 period, Åke Pettersson was a junior minister in the Ministry for Social Affairs. In this period he served under two coalition cabinets. Later he was the General Secretary (*Partisekreterare*) of the Centre Party. In this position, he worked closely with the leader of the Centre Party.

REFERENCES

Allmänna valen 1994. Del 1. Stockholm: Statistiska centralbyrån.
Andrén, Nils (1968a). *Modern Swedish Government*. Stockholm: Almqvist & Wiksell.
——(1968b). *Svensk Statskunskap*. Stockholm: Liber.
Arter, David (1985). 'The Nordic Parliaments: Patterns of Legislative Influence'. *West European Politics*, 8: 55–70.

Bäck, Mats and Möller, Tommy (1992). *Partier och organisationer*, 2nd edn. Stockholm: Publica.
——(1995). *Partier och organisationer*, 3rd edn. Stockholm: Publica.
Back, Pär-Erik, and Berglund, Sten (1978). *Det svenska partiväsendet*. Stockholm: Almqvist & Wiksell.
Bennulf, Martin (1992). 'En grön dimension bland svenska väljare?' *Statsvetenskaplig Tidskrift*, 95: 329–58.
——(1994). *Miljöopinionen i Sverige*. Lund: Dialogos.
Bergman, Torbjörn (1995). *Constitutional Rules and Party Goals in Coalition Formation: An Analysis of Winning Minority Governments in Sweden*. Ph.D. thesis, Department of Political Science, Umeå University.
Bergström, Hans (1987). *Rivstart?* Stockholm: Tidens förlag.
Birgersson, Bengt Owe, and Westerståhl, Jörgen (1992). *Den svenska folkstyrelsen*. Stockholm: Publica.
Bohman, Gösta (1984). *Maktskifte*. Stockholm: Bonniers.
Castles, Francis G., and Mair, Peter (1984). 'Left–Right Political Scales: Some Expert Judgments'. *European Journal of Political Research*, 12: 73–88.
Christoffersson, Ulf (1983). 'De statligt anställda i Sverige', in Lennart Lundquist and Krister Ståhlberg (eds.), *Byråkrater i Norden*. Åbo: Åbo Akademi.
Coakley, John (1987). 'The General Election in Context: Historical and European Perspectives', in Michael Laver, Peter Mair, and Richard Sinnot (eds.), *How Ireland Voted: The Irish General Election 1987*, Dublin: Poolbeg.
Erlander, Tage (1974). *1949–1954*. Stockholm: Tidens förlag.
Feldt, Kjell-Olof (1991). *Alla dessa dagar . . . i regeringen 1982–1990*. Stockholm: Norstedts.
——(1993). 'Att styra som minister: erfarenheter från 70-talets och 80-talets regeringar', in Björn von Sydow, Gunnar Wallin, and Björn Wittrock (eds.), *Politikens väsen: Idéer och institutioner i den moderna staten*. Stockholm: Tidens förlag.
Från Riksdag & Departement (1998). No. 26.
Gilljam, Mikael, and Holmberg, Sören (1993). *Väljarna inför 90-talet*. Stockholm: Norstedts Juridik.
——(1995). *Väljarnas val*. Stockholm: Norstedts Juridik (Fritzes).
Hadenius, Axel (1981). *Spelet om skatten: Rationalistisk analys av politiskt beslutsfattande*. Stockholm: P A Norstedts förlag (Lund: Studentlitteratur).
Hadenius, Stig, Molin, Björn, and Wieslander, Hans (1993). *Sverige efter 1900: En modern politisk historia*. Stockholm: Bonnier Alba.
Halvarson, Arne (1980). *Sveriges Statsskick: En Faktasamling*. Stockholm: Esselte Studium.
Hammerich, Kai (1977). *Kompromissernas koalition: Person och maktspelet kring regeringen Fälldin*. Stockholm: Rabén & Sjögren.
Holmberg, Erik, and Stjernquist, Nils (1995). *Vår författning*. Stockholm: Norstedts Juridik.
Holmstedt, Margareta, and Schou, Tove-Lise (1987). 'Sweden and Denmark, 1945–1982: Election Programmes in the Scandinavian Setting', in Ian Budge, David Robertson, and Derek Hearl (eds.), *Ideology, Strategy and Party Change: Spatial Analyses of Post-War Election Programmes in 19 Democracies*. Cambridge: Cambridge University Press.

Isaksson, Christer (1995). *Revanschen: Ingvar Carlssons väg tillbaka*. Stockholm: Ekerlids förlag.
Jonasson, Gustaf (1972). 'På väg mot koalition? Förhandlingarna mellan socialdemokrater och bondeförbundare efter 1948 års val'. *Historisk tidskrift*, 92: 355–405.
——(1981). *I väntan på uppbrott? Bondeförbundet/Centrepartiet i regeringskoalitionens slutskede 1956–1957*. Studia Historica Upsaliensa 118. Stockholm: Almqvist & Wiksell International.
Jonnergård, Gustaf (1985). *Med Gunnar Hedlund i politiken*. Stockholm: LTs förlag.
Klingemann, Hans-Dieter, Hofferbert, Richard I,. and Budge, Ian, with Keman, Hans, Pétry, François, Bergman, Torbjörn, and Strøm, Kaare (1994). *Parties, Policies and Democracy*. Boulder, Colo.: Westview Press.
Konstitutionsutskottets betänkande 1995/96: KU30 (1996). Granskning av statsrådens tjänsteutövning och regeringsärendenas handläggning. Stockholm: Riksdagen.
Larsson, Sven-Erik (1986). *Regera i koalition: Den borgerliga trepartiregeringen 1976–1978 och kärnkraften*. Stockholm: Bonniers.
Larsson, Torbjörn (1990). 'Regeringens och regerinskansliets organisationsstruktur, berednings- och beslutsformer under 150 år', in Departementshistoriekommittén, *Att styra riket—regeringskansliet 1940–1990*. Stockholm: Allmänna Förlaget.
Laver, Michael J. (1992). 'Coalition and Party Policy in Ireland', in Michael J. Laver and Ian Budge (eds.), *Party Policy and Government Coalitions*, London: MacMillan.
——and Hunt, W. Ben (1992). *Policy and Party Competition*. New York: Routledge.
——and Schofield, Norman (1990). *Multiparty Government: The Politics of Coalition in Europe*. Oxford: Oxford University Press.
Leijonhuvud, Sigfrid (1979). *Ett fall för ministären*. Stockholm: Liber Förlag.
Lewin, Leif (1992). *Ideologi och strategi*. Stockholm: Norstedts Juridik.
Mattson, Ingvar (1996). *Förhandlingsparlamentarism: En jämförande studie av riksdagen och folketinget*. Ph.D. thesis. Lund: Lund University Press.
Molin, Björn (1965). *Tjänstepensionsfrågan: En studie i svensk partipolitik*. Göteborg: Akademiförlaget.
Möller, Tommy (1986). *Borgerlig samverkan*. Uppsala: Diskurs.
Pesonen, Pertti, and Thomas, Alastair H. (1983). 'Coalition Formation in Scandinavia', in Vernon Bogdanor (ed.), *Coalition Government in Western Europe*. London: Heinemann Educational Books.
Petersson, Olof (1977). *Väljarna och valet 1976*. Stockholm: Liber.
——(1979). *Regeringsbildningen 1978*. Stockholm: Rabén and Sjögren.
Riksdagens protokoll (The Riksdag Minutes), various issues. Stockholm: Riksdagen.
Ruin, Olof (1968). *Mellan samlingsregering och tvåpartisystem*. Stockholm: Bonniers.
——(1985). 'Tvåpartisystem, samlingsregering eller vad?' I Folkstyrelsekommittén, *Makten från Folket: 12 uppsatser om Folkstyrelsen*. Stockholm: Liber.
Särlvik, Bo (1983). 'Coalition Politics and Policy Output in Scandinavia: Sweden, Denmark and Norway', in Vernon Bogdanor (ed.), *Coalition Government in Western Europe*. London: Heinemann Educational Books.
Sjölin, Mats (1993). *Coalition Politics and Parliamentary Power*. Lund: Lund University Press.
Statistisk Årsbok för Sverige 1970 (Statistical Abstract of Sweden 1970). Stockholm: Statistiska centralbyrån.

Statistisk Årsbok för Sverige 1999 (Statistical Yearbook of Sweden 1999). Stockholm: Statistiska centralbyrån.

Statsrådsberedningen 1998. 'Pressmeddelande: Samarbete mellan regeringen, vänsterpartiet och miljöpartiet'. 5 October 1998.

Strøm, Kaare (1986). 'Deferred Gratification and Minority Governments in Scandinavia'. *Legislative Studies Quarterly*, 11: 583–605.

——(1990). *Minority Government and Majority Rule*. Cambridge: Cambridge University Press.

'The Instrument of Government' (1996). in *The Constitution of Sweden 1995*. Stockholm: Swedish Riksdag.

Timmermans, Arco. 1996. *High Politics in the Low Countries: Functions and Effects of Coalition Policy Agreements in Belgium and the Netherlands*. Ph.D. thesis, European University Institute, Florence.

Vedung, Evert (1979). *Kärnkraften och regeringen Fälldins fall*. Stockholm: Raben and Sjögren.

von Heland, Erik (1969). *Optimismens och besvikelsens år 1922–1952*. Stockholm: LTs förlag.

von Sydow, Björn (1978). *Kan vi lita på politikerna: Offentlig och intern politik i Socialdemokratins ledning 1955–60*. Stockholm: Tidens förlag.

Westholm, Anders (1991). *The Political Heritage: Testing Theories of Family Socialization and Generational Change*. Uppsala: Department of Government, Uppsala University.

7

Denmark

The Life and Death of Government Coalitions

Erik Damgaard

INTRODUCTION

Single-party parliamentary majorities have not existed in Denmark since the first decade of the twentieth century. Some kind of inter-party cooperation is therefore required for decision making in legislative and governmental affairs. In the post-war period, majority coalition governments have been the exception rather than the rule, as most governments have been of the minority type (Thomas 1982). Since the early 1980s these minority governments have been coalitions, whereas previously they tended to be single-party governments (Damgaard 1992*a*).

It appears that Denmark holds the post-war record in parliamentary democracies concerning minority governance (Strøm 1984; Bergman 1995). Minority cabinets are facilitated by the 'negative' formation rule practised since the introduction of parliamentary government in 1901. Negative parliamentarism means that a government does not need a positive vote of investiture. On the other hand, a Danish government has to resign (or to call elections) if parliament adopts a motion of no confidence. Such rules imply that some parties may prefer minority to majority governments, as they can retain considerable political influence if a government of the former type is appointed and simultaneously avoid the potential costs of formal participation in government (Strøm 1986).

One way or another, minority governments have to rely on 'support' parties to form legislative majorities. Such external support for a government may be provided either ad hoc or on a more permanent basis. In the latter case, the government and the supporting party(ies) may actually function together as a quasi-majority coalition government (Damgaard 1969).

Whenever formal majority coalition governments have been formed, they have been of the minimal-winning size in the sense that the subtraction of any party would make the coalition non-winning. Thus, 'oversized' government coalitions have not occurred (apart from a short-lived all-party national liberalization coalition in 1945), but as just indicated, 'undersized' coalitions certainly do occur.

A high number of legislative parties may complicate the formation of legislative and governmental majorities, especially if it is associated with a high degree of fragmentation. In Denmark the level of parliamentary fractionalization as defined by Douglas Rae (1967) increased substantially with the 1973 election (Damgaard 1992*b*; see also Table 7.1). However, the existing high level of party cohesion in legislative voting was not affected by the increased number of parties and fractionalization (Damgaard and Svensson 1989; Mikkelsen 1994). Thus, parliamentary parties still function as cohesive building blocks in majority formation as they have done in the past.

Conclusions from empirical analyses of government formation, duration, and termination are highly dependent upon the selected definition of 'government'. This has been demonstrated in an analysis using Denmark as a test case (Damgaard 1994*b*). Different definitions may of course be used for various purposes, but any systematic comparative analysis must apply the same definition of a cabinet to all the countries involved. In this and other respects the following sections respect the conventions established by the research group producing the present volume.

This chapter first gives an overview of the Danish parliamentary party system in the post-war period, surveying the crucial actors and their strategic positions in that system. The next section describes the formal and informal rules governing the formation and termination of cabinets. The third section analyses aspects of the actual coalition formation processes in the post-war period. The fourth section focuses on aspects of coalition governance with particular emphasis on coalition agreements, norms of coalition governance, and cabinet portfolio allocations. The fifth section looks into the causes of government termination while the sixth concerns the electoral fortunes of government parties.

THE PARLIAMENTARY PARTY SYSTEM

Information on the Danish legislative party system in the post-war period may be found in various studies (e.g. Damgaard 1974; Pedersen 1987; Bille 1989; Damgaard 1992*a*; Schou and Hearl 1992). Suffice it here to note that the traditional party system, which Giovanni Sartori (1976) characterized as a system of 'limited pluralism' with four to five significant parties, in 1973 was transformed into a system of 'extreme pluralism' with six to seven significant parties. In Table 7.1 below, the Laakso–Taagepera index of the 'effective number of parties' shows the same development (Laakso and Taagepera

1979). The Danish PR electoral system, with basically a 2 per cent threshold for party representation (Elklit 1993), obviously conditions the relatively large number of parliamentary parties.

The core of the traditional system is the four 'old' parties: the Liberals, the Conservatives, the Social Democrats, and the Radical Liberals. The only major change until the 1970s was the addition in 1960 of the new Socialist People's Party as an important actor. Table 7.1 shows how the party system changed dramatically with the election of 1973 in which the voters not only punished all five parties then represented but also produced a ten-party parliament (Pedersen 1987).

The Danish legislative party system of the post-war period is probably best understood in terms of five major groupings of parties (see Table 7.1). First, there is a group of relatively small left-wing parties. To this belong at different times one, two, or even three of the following parties: the Communists, the Left Socialists, Common Course, the Unity List, and the Socialist People's Party.

Second, there is the Social Democratic Party, which has been the largest party in parliament since 1924.

Third, there is a group of relatively small centre parties. The old Radical Liberal Party has been represented all the time, accompanied by the Justice Party until 1960 and by the Liberal Centre Party for a short period in the 1960s. In the 1970s the centre space became crowded with the return of the Justice Party and the addition of two new parties: the Centre Democrats and the Christian People's Party.

Fourth, the two old moderate centre-right parties, the Liberals and the Conservative People's Party, have been represented in parliament all the time as parties of medium size.

Finally, a right-wing Independent Party was represented in the early 1960s. At the remarkable 1973-election a new Progress Party obtained surprisingly strong support as what was called a protest party. In the late 1990s the Progess Party split, with the new Danish People's Party doing best at the elections.

As indicated in Table 7.1, there have usually also been a few MPs not associated with the parties mentioned. Most of them have normally, but not always, refrained from interfering with the politics of government formation and termination.

The ordering of parties in Table 7.1 follows the expert judgements reported by Laver and Hunt (1992) on two socio-economic left–right scales, both of which appear relevant and important in a Danish political context. The Laver–Hunt data indicate the average of the reported location of party leaders on the scales of 'increase services (1) vs. cut taxes (20)' and 'pro-public ownership (1) vs. anti-public ownership (20)'. As both scales make sense in Denmark, a simple average of the two scale locations has been used for the

TABLE 7.1. Left–right placement of parties, party strength (in seats), and party composition of governments in Denmark, 1945–1999

Government	Proximity to election[a]	Com	LS	SPP	SD	CD	RL	CPP	JP	Con	Lib	PP	Other	Effective number of legislative parties	Government strength	Total number of seats
1945	FE	18	—	—	48	—	11*	—	3	26	**38**	—	5	4.5	38	149
1947	FE	9	—	—	**58**	—	10*	—	6	17	50	—	—	3.5	58	150
1950	F	7	—	—	**60**	—	12*	—	12	27	33	—	—	4.0	60	151
1950	E	—	—	—	—	—	—	—	—	**27**	**33**	—	—	4.0	60	151
1953	FE	7	—	—	62	—	13*	—	9	**26**	**34**	—	—	3.8	60	151
1953	FE	8	—	—	**75**	—	14*	—	6	30	43	—	3	3.7	75	179
1957	FE	6	—	—	**71**	—	**14***	—	**9**	30	45	Ind	4	3.9	94	179
1960	FE	—	—	11	**77**	—	**11***	—	LC	32	39	6	3	3.7	88	179
1964	FE	—	—	10	**77**	—	10*	—	4	36	38	5	3	3.6	77	179
1966	FE	—	—	20	**70***	—	13	—	—	34	35	—	3	4.1	70	179
1968	FE	—	4	11	63	—	**27***	—	—	**37**	**34**	—	3	4.3	98	179
1971	FE	—	—	17	**71**	—	27*	—	JP	31	30	—	3	4.0	71	179
1973	FE	6	—	11	47	14	20*	7	5	16	**22**	28	3	7.0	22	179
1975	FE	7	4	11	**54**	4	13*	9	—	10	42	24	3	5.5	54	179
1977	F	7	5	8	**66**	11*	6	6	6	15	22	26	1	5.2	66	179
1978	E	—	—	—	**66**	—	—	—	—	—	**22**	—	—	5.2	88	179
1979	FE	—	6	11	**69**	6*	10	5	5	22	23	20	2	4.9	69	179
1981	F	—	5	21	**60**	15*	9	4	—	26	21	16	2	5.6	60	179
1982	E	—	—	—	—	**15***	—	**4**	—	**26**	**21**	—	—	5.6	66	179
1984	FE	—	5	21	57	**8***	10	**5**	—	**42**	**23**	6	2	5.1	78	179
1987	FE	—	4	27	56	**9***	11	**4**	—	**38**	**19**	9	2	4.3	70	179
1988	FE	—	CC	24	56	9	**10***	4	—	**35**	**23**	9	2	5.4	68	179
1990	F	—	—	15	**71**	**9***	7	4	—	**30**	**30**	12	1	4.4	60	179
1993	E	—	UL	—	**71**	**9***	**7**	**4**	—	—	—	—	—	4.4	91	179

Year		Com	LS	CC	UL	SPP	SD	CD	RL	CPP	JP	LC	Con	Lib	DPP	PP	Ind	Other		
1994	F	—	6	13	63	5	8*	—	—	28	44	—	11	1	4.5	76	179			
1996	E	—	—	—	63	—	8*	—	—	—	—	DPP	—	4	—	4.5	71	179		
1998	F	—	5	13	64	8*	7	4	—	17	43	13	4	1	4.8	71	179			

[a] F = government formed immediately following an election; E = government ended by an election.

Parties

- **Com** Communists (Danmarks Kommunistiske Parti)
- **LS** Left Socialists (Venstresocialisterne)
- **CC** Common Course (Fælles Kurs)
- **UL** Unity List (Enhedslisten)
- **SPP** Socialist People's Party (Socialistisk Folkeparti)
- **SD** Social Democrats (Socialdemokratiet)
- **CD** Centre Democrats (Centrum-Demokraterne)
- **RL** Radical Liberals (Det Radikale Venstre)
- **CPP** Christian People's Party (Kristeligt Folkeparti)
- **JP** Justice Party (Danmarks Retsforbund)
- **LC** Liberal Centre (Liberalt Centrum)
- **Con** Conservatives (Det Konservative Folkeparti)
- **Lib** Liberals (Venstre, Danmarks Liberale Parti)
- **DPP** Danish People's Party (Danks Folkeparti)
- **PP** Progress Party (Fremskridtspartiet)
- **Ind** Independents (De Uafhængige)
- **Other** 1945: 4 MPs from Danish Unity Party (Dansk Samling) and 1 MP from the Faroe Islands
  1953–62: 1 MP from German Minority Party (Slesvigsk Parti) and the remaining from the Faroe Islands/Greenland
  1964–93: MPs from the Faroe Islands/Greenland
  1994: Jacob Haugaard (independent MP)
  1998: MP from Faroe Islands

Parties in **bold** formed **governments**.
* Party with median legislator.

ordering in Table 7.1. The averages run from 2.9 (Communists) to 19.3 (Progress Party). It should be noted that the rank orders of the two scales are very much alike, and that the small differences between them only concern the left-wing parties and the Justice Party.

Laver and Hunt's data refers to the parties at a certain point in time (c.1990). Therefore, three of the small Danish parties were not included in the expert survey: the Independent Party, the Liberal Centre Party and the Unity List. However, most experts will probably agree on the location of these three parties as shown in Table 7.1.

Whether the ordering of parties is valid for the whole post-war period is quite another matter. Even if the experts' judgements are accepted as true for the time when they were reported, the true rank orders could be different in previous as well as later time periods. After all, parties may change policy positions for strategic or other reasons. Furthermore, if a certain policy field is crowded with parties, even minor policy changes could easily change the rank orders. Basically, however, the socio-economic left–right ordering of Table 7.1 fits rather well with a number of previous studies (e.g. Pedersen, Damgaard, and Olsen 1971; Damgaard 1973; Damgaard and Rusk 1976; Damgaard 1977; Holmstedt and Schou 1987; Nannestad 1989; Laver and Schofield 1990: appendix B; Schou and Hearl 1992). The only major deviation is that, in the Laver and Hunt study, the Liberals and the Conservatives have exchanged locations. That probably happened during the 1980s, although appropriate data to settle the issue is not available.

Table 7.1 also contains information on the parliamentary party with the median legislator which is presumably key information on the centre of gravity in coalition formation. The table shows that one of the centre parties, most often the Radical Liberals, normally controls the balance of power in bargaining on formations of government coalitions if minimal, connected majority coalitions are to be formed along the left–right dimension. On the average, the experts placed the Centre Democrats to the left of the Radical Liberals by less than one scale point. If the ordering of the two parties had been the opposite, the dominating median position of the Radical Liberals would appear as almost crushing. According to the table, absolute parliamentary majorities along the left–right dimension could not be formed without the participation of at least one of the centre parties. Only in 1966 was it possible for the Social Democrats to form a majority with the Socialist People's Party, which was actually done although the Socialists did not formally participate in the government (Mader 1979).

A number of other policy issues, of course, also divide the parties. On the issue of European Union membership, for example, the left-wing Unity List and the right-wing Progress Party are located towards the negative end of the scale, whereas the Liberals and the Centre Democrats are located towards the positive end (Jensen 1995, reporting results from a mail questionnaire to

Danish MPs). In the Laver and Hunt (1992) material several other examples of different orderings may be found. But in all cases of possible political significance, the party locations are only marginally different from the corresponding socio-economic scale ordering. For example, the small centrist Christian People's Party is located at the far right end of the pro/anti 'permissive social policy' and anti/pro 'clerical' scales, and the Liberals are most 'rightist' in the defence of rural interests ('anti-urban'). However, compared to some other countries, these and other deviations from the main socio-economic ordering are simply not very important in Denmark. The 'new politics' issue of 'environment vs. growth' might be thought to have added a new salient dimension to the party system since the 1970s. In a sense it has, but the issue is highly correlated with the socio-economic left–right dimension, as are many other policy issues. If a party with the median legislator should nevertheless be listed after each election (since the 1970s) the Social Democrats would come out as such a party in all cases, according to the Laver–Hunt data. In sum, however, there is no point in listing the median party on a second policy dimension: Which dimension could that possibly be in the fairly small and homogeneous country of Denmark, where religious and language issues are absent?

RULES ON THE FORMATION AND TERMINATION OF GOVERNMENTS

According to the constitution of 1953, the monarch formally appoints the prime minister and the other ministers. Formally, the king or queen (which in practice means the prime minister) also determines the number of ministers and their portfolios. Apart from that, there are no positive constitutional rules on how governments are to be formed. But the constitution clearly states that no minister can remain in office if he or she has received a motion of no confidence passed by the Folketing (parliament). Furthermore, if an adopted no confidence motion concerns the prime minister, the government must resign or call elections. A government that has received such a motion, or has submitted a resignation request for other reasons, functions as a caretaker cabinet until a new government has been formed. Although the constitution is silent on the matter, governments have (in 1929 and 1983) interpreted a rejection of its budget proposal as a vote of no confidence.

To these rules of negative parliamentarism should be added that a potential government may not be formed if it is expected to receive a vote of censure as soon as it meets with the Folketing. Constitutional lawyers agree on this point (see Albæk Jensen 1989 and Germer 1988).

As the formal constitutional rules thus are very few, the actual practice as it has developed over time is crucial. It is difficult to summarize the operative rules, but elsewhere (Damgaard 1992*a*: 22–3) an attempt has been made on the basis of several studies on government formation and termination (especially works by Tage Kaarsted, and in particular Kaarsted 1988):

1. If there is uncertainty about the appointment of a new government the political parties in parliament shall advise the monarch (a so-called 'Amalienborg round' after the residence of the Queen).

2. If the advice unambiguously points to a majority government or a minority government with assured support from a majority, the monarch is bound to appoint such a government.

3. If no such majority emerges, the purpose is to appoint the minority government most likely to survive.

4. The acting prime minister, and not the monarch, is responsible for the interpretation of the possibly unclear advice given by the parties.

5. It is permissible to appoint a 'royal *informateur*' upon the advice of the parties in the first stage, or first stages, of the process. This has become a common procedure.

6. The parties are not restricted by special norms with respect to the content of the advice given.

When several parties play according to these rules, which are not all very precise, the game can become quite complicated. But the rules nevertheless constrain the behaviour of parties in the government formation process, which is therefore not a 'freestyle' bargaining exercise. Basically, the rules establish a procedure that allows and requires all parties, at one or several stages, to state their government preferences publicly at a formal visit to the monarch. They also make it clear that the head of state has no independent role in the process, as he actually had in some cases of government formation during the first decades of parliamentary government (Rasmussen 1972).

According to the constitution, the prime minister has the prerogative to dissolve the Folketing at almost any time, which obviously also affects coalition bargaining (Strøm, Budge, and Laver 1994; Laver and Schofield 1990). The only exception is that an incoming government may not call elections before it has appeared before the Folketing. This exception was introduced to ensure that the Folketing in a kind of *coup d'état* situation could retain control over political developments that might otherwise result in a very rapid dissolution of parliament.

The two single most important institutional rules with respect to government formation and termination are (1) the right of a parliamentary majority to censure the government, and (2) the right of the prime minister to dissolve parliament. Although the latter is used quite often, as will be seen below, the importance of the two rules for party behaviour is greater than can be deduced from the frequency with which they have actually been applied.

COALITION BUILDING

Governments Formed

Tables 7.1 and 7.2 show the parties forming governments in the post-war period according to the defining criteria of this volume. Of the thirty-one cabinets formed (see Table 7.3 below) only six were genuine majority coalitions in the sense that the participating parties jointly commanded an absolute majority of seats in the Folketing (the coalitions formed in 1957, 1960, 1968, and 1993), whereas a further eleven cabinets were minority coalitions. The minority coalitions formed in 1960, 1962, and 1978 were very close to having majority status and actually functioned as majority governments in many respects; those of 1960 and 1962 because a non-party MP from Greenland was appointed minister for Greenland while two other non-party MPs behaved impartially in the game on governmental office; that of 1978 because it could only be defeated if all non-governmental party MPs joined forces against the government, which only happened once in a matter of minor importance.

The remaining fourteen cabinets were of the single-party minority type. However, some of them (those formed in 1945, 1953, 1955, 1966, and 1971) enjoyed quite stable external support from opposition parties in legislative majority building, at least for a period of about two years.

It is noteworthy that ten of the seventeen coalition cabinets were formed by parties located adjacent to each other on the left–right scale presented in Table 7.1. In fact, the Social Democratic–Liberal coalition of 1978–9 is the only major deviation from the overall pattern. The two parties decided to form a coalition, which in practice had a working majority, to fight the economic difficulties of the country. The coalition was short-lived and not very successful, however. The four minority coalitions formed in the 1980s do not quite conform to the party locations on the scale, mainly because the Centre Democrats are considered more 'leftist' than the Radical Liberals (1982, 1984, 1987). On the other hand, if that placement of the two parties is erroneous, the Radical Liberals should not have formed a coalition with the Conservatives, or with the Liberals in 1988 without the Centre Democrats and the Christian People's Party! But they did so even though they were offered such a five-party coalition.

One of the lessons from these minority coalition formations is that the small centre parties have usually been able to choose coalition partners to their left (Social Democrats) or right (Conservatives and Liberals) as they thought expedient. The tables show that since 1982 the Radical Liberals, the Centre Democrats, and the Christian People's Party have in fact participated in governments with the Social Democrats, on the one hand, and the Liberals

TABLE 7.2. *Government formation in Denmark, 1945–1999*

Government	Number of parties in parliament	Number of previous bargaining rounds	Parties involved in previous bargaining rounds	Number of days required in government formation
Lib 1945	7	1	SD, RL, Lib, Con	8
SD 1947	6	2	(1) SD, RL, Lib, Con (2) Lib	16
SD 1950	6	1	SD, RL, JP	11
Lib–Con 1950	6	0		4
Lib–Con 1953	6	0		0
SD 1953	7	0		8
SD–RL–JP 1957	7	1	SD, RL, JP, Lib, Con	14
SD–RL 1960	7	0		3
SD 1964	6	1	SD, RL, Lib, Con	4
SD 1966	6	0		0
RL–Lib–Con 1968	6	0		10
SD 1971	5	1	SD, RL, Lib, Con	20
Lib 1973	10	1	all parties	15
SD 1975	10	3	(1) all except Con, LS (2) SD, RL, CD, CPP, Con (3) Con, Lib, CD, CPP, PP	35
SD 1977	11	0		0
SD–Lib 1978	11	0[a]		26[a]
SD 1979	10	0		3
SD 1981	9	1	all parties	22
Con–Lib–CD–CPP 1982	9	1	all parties	7
Con–Lib–CD–CPP 1984	9	0		0
Con–Lib–CD–CPP 1987	8	0		2
Con–Lib–RL 1988	8	2	(1) all parties (2) SD, RL, Lib, Con	24
Con–Lib 1990	8	0		6
SD–RL–CD–CPP 1993	8	0		10
SD–RL–CD 1994	8	0		6
SD–RL 1996	8	0		0
SD–RL 1998	10	0		0

[a] Informal bargaining between SD and Lib. Estimated number of days, cf. Fonsmark 1992; Thomas 1982.

or Conservatives, on the other. In various coalitions they have also cooperated with each other. Thus, the three small parties occupying the centre space of the socio-economic left–right dimension are in a sense quite interchangeable. The coalitions formed since 1987 vividly illustrate this point (see Tables 7.2 and 7.3).

Finally, no Danish government (apart from the short-lived national coalition in 1945) has ever included left- or right-wing parties as defined above. A Danish 'ad hoc' (Laver and Schofield 1990) or 'party rule' (Strøm, Budge, and

Laver 1994) constraint excludes such 'extremist' parties from formal government coalitions. But the parties in question may still exert influence on the governments to be formed and the policy decisions to be made in parliament as long as no majority coalition can be formed. The mandates of left- and right-wing parties are certainly counted as valid in the calculations of the strength behind the advice formally given to the monarch in the process of government formation. As indicated, the Social Democrats even bargained seriously with the Socialist People's Party in 1966 on a formal coalition government. Although the non-cabinet parties on the left and right have never been in office, they have often been crucial for the passing of legislation in the Folketing.

Coalition Bargaining

Whenever a cabinet has resigned for whatever reason, the rules described above on government formation apply in the game played by the parties to control the appointment of a new cabinet. The number of formation attempts listed in Table 7.2 refer to the official attempts, formally mandated by the monarch, to form a new government. It includes mandates given to *informateurs* as well as to *formateurs*, as the distinction between the two types of roles may be negligible in practice. Any other counting rule would be unreliable, as 'private' inter-party discussions or negotiations are not reported in any systematic manner. Numerous case studies show that 'private' bargaining or talks are often conducted in addition to, and frequently simultaneously with, the official rounds of government formation bargaining (the sources used here include Kaarsted 1964, 1969, 1977, 1988, 1992; Mader 1979; Fonsmark 1992; Larsen 1995; *Folketingsårbog/Folketingstidende*, various years).

According to the definition of government used in this volume, governments may turn over in a rather technical sense that has little to do with political reality. Therefore, the last column in Table 7.2 lists six governments that were formed within zero days (Lib–Con 1953, SD 1966, SD 1977, Con–Lib–CD–CPP 1984, SD–RL 1996 and 1998). Five of them are not officially counted as 'new' governments in Denmark as they were 'old' governments that just happened to survive an election, without resignation or changes with respect to party composition or prime minister. Although there was no official bargaining over government formation in these cases, it is known that there were often some private talks among party leaders, especially in 1966, to make sure that the government could continue. The sixth case (SD–RL 1996) occurred when the CD wanted to leave the coalition.

Another ten of the twenty-seven governments were formed after just one successful attempt, that is 'no unsuccessful attempts' in Table 7.2. This category includes the SD–Lib coalition 1978–9 which was formed after an estimated 26-day period of 'private' negotiations between the two parties. Aside

242   Erik Damgaard

TABLE 7.3. Danish cabinets since 1945

Cabinet number	Prime minister	Date in	Formal resignation	Maximum duration (in days)	Duration (in days)	Government composition
1	Kristensen	07 Nov. 1945	28 Oct. 1947	1,453	720	Lib
2	Hedtoft I	13 Nov. 1947	05 Sept. 1950	1,445	1,027	SD
3	Hedtoft II	16 Sept. 1950	26 Oct. 1950	1,450	40	SD
4	Eriksen I	30 Oct. 1950	21 Apr. 1953	1,406	904	Lib–Con
5**	Eriksen II	21 Apr. 1953	22 Sept. 1953	1,461	154	Lib–Con
6	Hedtoft III	30 Sept. 1953	29 Jan. 1955	1,453	486	SD
7	Hansen I	01 Feb. 1955	14 May 1957	975	833	SD
8	Hansen II	28 May 1957	19 Feb. 1960	1,447	997	SD–RL–JP
9	Kampmann I	21 Feb. 1960	15 Nov. 1960	484	168	SD–RL–JP
10	Kampmann II	18 Nov. 1960	03 Sept. 1962	1,409*	654	SD–RL
11	Krag I	03 Sept. 1962	22 Sept. 1964	754	750	SD–RL
12	Krag II	26 Nov. 1964	22 Nov. 1966	1,457	787	SD
13**	Krag III	22 Nov. 1966	23 Jan. 1968	1,461	427	SD
14	Baunsgaard	22 Feb. 1968	21 Sept. 1971	1,451	1,327	RL–Con–Lib
15	Krag IV	11 Oct. 1971	05 Oct. 1972	1,441	360	SD
16	Jørgensen I	05 Oct. 1972	04 Dec. 1973	1,101	425	SD
17	Hartling	19 Dec. 1973	09 Jan. 1975	1,446	386	Lib
18	Jørgensen II	13 Feb. 1975	15 Feb. 1977	1,426	733	SD
19**	Jørgensen III	15 Feb. 1977	30 Aug. 1978	1,461	561	SD
20	Jørgensen IV	30 Aug. 1978	23 Oct. 1979	900	419	SD–Lib
21	Jørgensen V	26 Oct. 1979	08 Dec. 1981	1,458	774	SD
22	Jørgensen VI	30 Dec. 1981	03 Sept. 1982	1,439	247	SD
23	Schlüter I	10 Sept. 1982	10 Jan. 1984	1,185	487	Con–Lib–CD–CPP
24**	Schlüter II	10 Jan. 1984	08 Sept. 1987	1,461	1,337	Con–Lib–CD–CPP
25	Schlüter III	10 Sept. 1987	10 May 1988	1,459	243	Con–Lib–CD–CPP
26	Schlüter IV	03 June 1988	12 Dec. 1990	1,437	922	Con–Lib–RL
27	Schlüter V	18 Dec. 1990	15 Jan. 1993	1,455	759	Con–Lib
28	Rasmussen I	25 Jan. 1993	21 Sept. 1994	692	604	SD–RL–CD–CPP
29	Rasmussen II	27 Sept. 1994	30 Dec. 1996	1455	825	SD–RL–CD
30	Rasmussen III	30 Dec. 1996	11 Mar. 1998	630	436	SD–RL
31**	Rasmussen IV	11 Mar. 1998		1,461		SD–RL

* The election law at the time required that elections had to be held before the month of Oct. if the previous parliament had been elected during the period of Oct.–Dec.
** According to official Danish counting rules this cabinet was not a new one. The old government just stayed in office.

from that government, the average time required for government formation in this category was only 5 days (range: 1–10 days). A further eight governments were formed after one unsuccessful official bargaining attempt. On the average, they required 12–13 days of bargaining (range: 4–22). Finally, three governments were formed after two or three unsuccessful attempts, with an average of 25 days of bargaining (range: 16–35).

Excluding the five governments formed according to purely technical criteria, the twenty-two 'real' new governments were formed after an average period of 11 days of bargaining (range 0–35 days). If the five 'technically new' governments are included, the average is only 9 days (range 0–35). For parliamentary multi-party systems with a relatively high number of parties, such figures are probably in the very low end of a 'government crisis scale'.

Table 7.2 indicates that whenever more than one bargaining attempt has taken place, the reason is that the first one or two rounds may have been purely tactical, as a fairly large number of parties have participated in most of the attempts. Typically, the possibility of a very broad coalition government is investigated, at least formally, in negotiations among the parties before the real bargaining starts. In this way, parties may claim that all possibilities of broad majority coalitions had been investigated before a more narrowly based cabinet took office.

Cabinet Durability

A previous study of Danish government formations 1945–93, in which cabinets were defined solely by their party composition, showed that majority coalitions on the average lasted three to four years and minority governments two to three years (Damgaard 1994*b*). Table 7.3 presents information on the durability of Danish cabinets defined according to the criteria of the present volume. First, it should be noted that six of the cabinets (4, 5, 6, 8, 10, 15) could not possibly have stayed in office for the full (remaining) term (see the section below on cabinet termination). Of the remaining cabinets, the two majority coalitions (14, 28) ruled for about 90 per cent of the maximum potential time. The record of minority cabinets is generally much poorer, but some minority cabinets (7, 11, 24) have actually matched majority governments in actual duration compared to maximum duration. The Hansen I (7) and the Schlüter II (25) cabinets enjoyed rather stable external support, whereas the Krag I (11) coalition almost commanded its own absolute majority in parliament.

All the other minority cabinets trail far behind the governments mentioned. The relatively short duration of these governments reflects the vulnerability of minority cabinets without stable support, on the one hand, and the prerogative of the cabinet to dissolve parliament, on the other.

COALITION GOVERNANCE

Coalition Agreements

Research on coalition governance hardly exists in Denmark, and the following is therefore a rather preliminary analysis. First, note that as there are relatively few coalitions in Denmark, there are also relatively few possible formal coalition agreements to study. But there will always be some kind of agreement between parties on policies and the distribution of cabinet offices before a cabinet coalition is formed. The agreement may, at least partially, take the form of a written document (whether published or not), but it may also be a purely informal understanding between the parties.

However, Danish constitutional rules require that any new government formed has to present its policy to the Folketing. The presentation by the prime minister is followed by a general plenary debate. In this way coalition governments are forced to agree upon a public document, viz. the speech by the prime minister which is printed in the official parliamentary records (*Folketingstidende*). In fact, such a prime ministerial statement of governmental policy has to be made at the beginning of every parliamentary year (the first Tuesday of October). Although these statements of governmental policies may often be outlined in somewhat vague and broad terms, they still constrain the activities of governmental parties. The procedure requires that coalition partners at least annually reconsider their joint policies in a comprehensive manner.

However, these opening policy statements are not considered as genuine coalition agreements in the present analysis. We shall instead look for documents in the form of formal contracts agreed upon by the parties *prior* to the public declaration of governmental policy in parliament. Even if such contracts exist, they may not be published. And whether they are published or not, they may not contain all the matters upon which the coalition partners have agreed.

Since 1945 there have been fifteen different government coalitions, i.e. multi-party cabinets with the same party composition between elections, in Denmark (see Table 7.4). If the criterion of 'between elections' is dropped, the number of coalitions is only eleven, as the coalitions of 1953, 1984, 1987, and 1998 then would have to be disregarded. A review of the literature and other information reveals only six coalition agreements as defined above, out of which four were published. None of them were pre-election agreements. For methodological reasons, the existence of additional agreements cannot be ruled out, but it is quite obvious that public coalition agreements have until recently not been very common in Denmark.

The Liberal–Conservative minority coalition of 1950 was formed very rapidly without any prior formal or detailed agreement (Kauffeldt 1966). The first post-war coalition agreement was negotiated after the election in May 1957 by the Social Democrats, the Radical Liberals and the Justice Party. The agreement (or 'government protocol' as it was called) was published in June 1957 after rumours about a 'secret protocol' (reprinted in Kaarsted 1964: 157–60).

The Social Democrats and the Radical Liberals continued to work together in government after the election of 1960. No formal agreement seems to have existed, but prior to the formation of the cabinet 'a narrow circle' of politicians from the two parties agreed upon a government programme (according to Kaarsted 1969: 29).

In 1968 the Liberals, Conservatives and Radical Liberals formed a majority coalition government. It was based on a formal agreement (*Jyllands-Posten*, 1 Feb. 1968) including at least forty-five policy issues, and informal deals on the distribution of cabinet offices. But when asked in the first parliamentary debate after the formation of the government, the prime minister denied that a real agreement had been negotiated. The agreement on government policy was never published.

The government formed in 1978 by the Social Democrats and the Liberals was surely based on party bargaining resulting in a coalition agreement. Officially, however, this agreement was presented only in the form of the prime minister's opening speech, although it is known to have included a number of other agreements between the two parties (according to information received from the Liberal (Venstre) Party Organization, 1996).

The non-socialist (or 'bourgeois' as the Danish and Nordic term is) minority government coalition formed in 1982, which survived the elections of 1984 and 1987, was not based on a formal government contract (Larsen 1995; Fonsmark 1992). Its successor, the Conservative–Liberal–Radical Liberal coalition of 1988–90, was probably partially based on a written agreement, but if so, the agreement was never made accessible to the public. In 1990, when the Radical Liberals decided to leave the coalition after an election defeat, the Liberals and Conservatives continued in government office without any formal coalition agreement.

A new pattern may have been initiated in 1993 when the first majority coalition since 1971 was formed by Social Democrats, Centre Democrats, Radical Liberals, and the Christian People's Party. The four parties negotiated and published a coalition policy agreement in January 1993 (*En ny start* 1993, 23 pages). It is known, however, that the document did not include all the deals among the four parties, as some more specific 'side papers' were mentioned in the newspapers. Without the Christian People's Party, which lost all its seats in the election of 1994, a coalition of the three remaining parties continued in office on the basis of a coalition agreement (*Fælles fremtid* 1994, 16 pages) and probably some other—not published—understandings. Having survived the election of 1998, the Social Democratic–Radical Liberal government produced a new agreement ('*Godt på vej*', 21 pages).

Generally speaking, it is quite remarkable that the few existing public coalition agreements are rarely presented as official foundations for governments in Denmark, and they never contain all the political deals and understandings of the parties involved. It almost appears as if government agreements between parties are a bit suspect. To understand this, one should probably note that the prevalence of minority governments (single-party or coalitions) in the country makes coalition agreements less essential than would be the case if majority coalitions had been prevalent.

Norms and Instruments of Governance

Danish coalition governments are not based on an 'election rule' committing the parties to an election in case the coalition breaks down (see Table 7.4). Only three cases of coalition breakdown, initiated by the government parties themselves, exist. The SD–Lib coalition was dissolved and a new election held according to a joint decision of the two parties in 1979, the Con–Lib–RL coalition was dissolved in 1993 without parliamentary dissolution, and in 1996 one of the three parties just wanted to leave the coalition. If a rule exists in this area, it is that a new election is not to be held before the end of the term, unless the coalition parties agree to have such an election. This is in fact quite an important informal rule, as the prime minister legally has the power to call elections. In 1993 Prime Minister Schlüter even refused to call elections when he resigned, disregarding the demand of his Liberal coalition partner who wanted a new election.

All Danish coalitions apply some forms of coordination and conflict management mechanisms. To these instruments always belong, apart from regular cabinet meetings, some kind of inner cabinet and a varying number of issue-specific cabinet committees (Christensen 1985; Olsen 1978). An important function of cabinet committees, especially in coalition governments, is what Grønnegaard Christensen (1985) calls 'mutual control'. But other mechanisms are often used as well, although research to document this point is unfortunately almost completely lacking. However, it appears that regular meetings of the minister in charge and the coalition parties' spokesmen in the relevant area are quite important for intra-coalition coordination and conflict resolution. A somewhat peculiar procedure was devised by the SD–Lib coalition in 1978–9, as the level of trust between the two parties was very low: Each minister was paired with a minister from the other party, and 'a minister from one party was not allowed to make a decision on an issue falling clearly within the jurisdiction of his or her department without the prior consent of his or her contact minister' (Christensen 1985: 131).

All government coalitions are based on the understanding that there will be coalition discipline in parliamentary votes on legislative proposals, and party cohesion is generally very high. Cabinet members always support the

TABLE 7.4. *Coalition governance in Denmark*

(1) Coalition	(2) Coalition agreement	(3) Agreement public	(4) Election rule	(5) Conflict management mechanisms[a]	(8) Coalition discipline in legislation	(9) Coalition discipline in other parliamentary behaviour	(10) Freedom of appointment	(11) Policy agreement	(12) Junior ministers	(13) Non-cabinet positions
1950	N	—	N	IC, CaC, PCa, O	1	1	Y	3	—	Y
1953	N	—	N	IC, CaC, PCa, O	1	1	Y	3	—	Y
1957	POST	Y	N	IC, CaC, PCa, O	1	1	Y	3	—	Y
1960	N	—	N	IC, CaC, PCa, O	1	1	Y	3	—	Y
1968	POST	N	N	IC, CaC, PCa, O	1	1	Y	3	—	Y
1978	IE	N	N	IC, CaC, PCa, O	1	1	Y	3	—	Y
1982	N	—	N	IC, CaC, PCa, O	1	1	Y	3	—	Y
1984	N	—	N	IC, CaC, PCa, O	1	1	Y	3	—	Y
1987	N	—	N	IC, CaC, PCa, O	1	1	Y	3	—	Y
1988	N	—	N	IC, CaC, PCa, O	1	1	Y	3	—	Y
1990	N	—	N	IC, CaC, PCa, O	1	1	Y	3	—	Y
1993	IE	Y	N	IC, CaC, PCa, O	1	1	Y	3	—	Y
1994	POST	Y	N	IC, CaC, PCa, O	1	1	Y	3	—	Y
1998	POST	Y	N	IC, CaC, PCa, O	1	1	Y	3	—	Y

[a] Most common conflict management mechanism: CaC for all coalitions; conflict management mechanism for the most serious conflicts for all coalitions: IC for all coalitions. O = Others, is a residual for any informal talks.

government line in parliamentary voting. It does happen that some backbench MPs deviate from the party line, but then they are required to make their position known in advance, and they risk being sanctioned by their party leadership (Damgaard 1995). Discipline is also expected in all other important matters affecting coalition unity, but there is some room for individual initiatives concerning, for example, questioning of ministers. However, members of governing parties tend to ask relatively few questions (Damgaard 1994*a*; Jensen 1994). Outside the formal parliamentary proceedings, members of government parties are much more free to state their views which may include criticism of coalition policies and actions.

In most cases, the parties joining a coalition government will be free to appoint their own ministers when the number of positions and portfolios of each party have been agreed upon. Formally, however, the prime minister must approve the ministers proposed, as they will become members of 'his' government. It is not unlikely, though, that a possible veto from other parties may in rare cases at least be anticipated when a party draws up a proposal for a list of ministers. A silent or subtle constraint on parties may exist when they propose cabinet members.

As indicated above, all coalition governments are based on some kind of policy agreement, whether it is written or not, and whether it is published or not. The opening speech of the minister can at least be regarded as a statement of government policy. In recent decades, a written legislative programme for the coming year has been attached to the oral prime ministerial presentation of government policy in parliament. In principle, the oral and written parts of the presentation of government policy cover all important policy areas. In this sense, at least, Danish coalition governments are based on comprehensive policy platforms (see Table 7.4), although they are not very detailed in every respect.

Table 7.4 also indicates that the question of junior ministers is not relevant in Denmark. The introduction of junior ministers or similar positions has been discussed for a very long time, but there are still no political appointees in government aside from the regular cabinet ministers. On the other hand, ministers can to some extent appoint people, at their own discretion, to assist them in roles that can be termed 'political'. Finally, Table 7.4 attempts to show (last column) that high-level administrative positions in the civil service and the public sector are filled according to agreements between the government parties. They are considered as governmental matters not only to be decided upon by the minister formally responsible for the appointment.

Table 7.5 describes the four published written coalition agreements mentioned above in a few quantitative terms. The table confirms some of the observations already made. The agreements are not very long documents, and policy is their main content. There are no references of any sort to distribution of offices, but some as to how certain issues should be handled by the

TABLE 7.5. *Size and content of four Danish coalition cabinets' agreements*

Coalition	Size	General procedural rules (in %)	Specific procedural rules (in %)	Distribution of offices (in %)	Distribution of competences (in %)	Policies (in %)
SD–RL–JP 1957	910	0	30	0	0	70
SD–RL–CD–CPP 1993	4,130	0	6	0	0	94
SD–RL–CD 1994	3,720	0	10	0	0	90
SD–RL 1998	5,613	0	6	0	0	93

government ('specific procedural rules'). General procedural rules, however, are not mentioned, probably because such procedures follow conventional norms of party governance in Denmark (see Table 7.4). Again it should be remembered that the four documents published are only parts of the general agreements among the parties concerned. This does not mean that they are unimportant—they certainly play a role in constraining the behaviour of parties working together in coalitions. In some situations, a reference to the formal contract is a very strong argument as to what should be done or not be done in policy making.

PORTFOLIO ALLOCATION

One of the most important aspects of government formation is the distribution of cabinet ministries. That is not included in the four coalition agreements of Table 7.5. But the results of inter-party bargaining in this respect are of course easily available for all governments. Table 7.6 shows the party distribution of ministries in the fifteen post-war coalition cabinets.

According to the constitution, the prime minister decides upon the number of ministers and upon the distribution of duties of government among them. This implies that new ministries may be established and old ones abolished at any time, and that the jurisdictions of ministries may be changed by government decree. The number of ministries has increased considerably in the post-war period as can be seen in Table 7.6 by comparing the first coalition in 1950 with the latest in the early 1990s. More important in the present context is that the number and jurisdictions of ministries may be objects for coalition bargaining among the parties. The flexible rules facilitate agreements among the parties on portfolio distribution.

Except for the Baunsgaard cabinet (number 14 in Table 7.6), the leader of the largest government party has always been appointed prime minister. The other parties have received a share of the positions in some proportion to their relative strength, but usually with a certain over-representation of the smaller parties. However, such figures do not take into account the political weights of the different ministries, and they disregard the fact that parties may have different preferences for the various cabinet positions. It is probably universally recognized that the offices of the prime minister, the minister of foreign affairs, and the minister of finance are the three most important throughout the period (Laver and Hunt 1992: 169), but no uniform rank order exists among the remaining (and changing) ministries.

Table 7.6 clearly reveals some of the party preferences with respect to portfolio allocation. Thus, the Social Democrats (when in government) have, in addition to the prime minister, always had the Ministry of Labour and almost

TABLE 7.6. *Party distribution of cabinet ministerships in Danish coalitions, 1945–1999*

Cabinet number	Cabinet	(1) Prime Minister	(2) Foreign	(3) Finance	(4) Economy	(5) Taxation	(6) Justice	(7) Interior	(8) Defence	(9) Education	(10) Church	(11) Culture
4	Eriksen I	L	C	L	—	—	L	C	L	C	L	—
5	Eriksen II	L	C	L	—	—	L	C	L	C	L	—
8	Hansen II	S	S	S	R	—	S	J	S	R	S	—
9	Kampmann I	S	S	R	R	—	S	J	S	R	S	—
10	Kampmann II	S	S	R/S	R	—	S	S	S	R	S	S
11	Krag I	S	S	S	R	—	S	S	S	R	S	S
14	Baunsgaard	R	L	C	L	L	C	C	C	R	L	R
20	Jørgensen IV	S	L	S	L	C	L	L	S	S	S	R
23	Schlüter I	C	L	L	L	C	C	L	C	L	L	CD
24	Schlüter II	C	L	L/C	L	L	C	L	C	L	L	CD/C
25	Schlüter III	C	L	C	L	L	C	L	C	L	L	C
26	Schlüter IV	C	L	C	R	L	C	L	L	L	C	R
27	Schlüter v	C	L	C	L	L	C	L	L	L	C	C
28	Rasmussen I	S	R	S	R	S	S	S	S	R	CD	S
29	Rasmussen II	S	R	S	R	S	S	S	S	R	S	S
30	Rasmussen III	S	R	S	R	S	S	S	S	R	R	R
31	Rasmussen IV	S	R	S	R	S	S	S	S	R	R	R

cont./

TABLE 7.6 Continued

Cabinet number	Cabinet	(12) Agriculture	(13) Fisheries	(14) Trade and industry	(15) Housing	(16) Public Works	(17) Labour	(18) Social Welfare	(19) Health	(20) Environment	(21) Energy	(22) Greenland	(23)[a] No portfolio
4	Eriksen I	L	L	C	C	C	C	C	—	—	—	—	—
5	Eriksen II	L	L	C	C	C	C	C	—	—	—	S	J
8	Hansen II	R	J	R	S	S	S	S	—	—	—	S	J
9	Kampmann I	R	J	S	S	S	S	S	—	—	—	MG	—
10	Kampmann II	R	R	S/R	S	S	S	S	—	—	—	MG	—
11	Krag I	R	R	R	S	S	S	S	—	—	—	R	—
14	Baunsgaard	L	R	C	C	L	R	L	—	—	—	S	S
20	Jørgensen IV	L	S	L	S	L	S	S	—	S	—	CD	—
23	Schlüter I	L	C	C	CD	CD	C	C/L/CD	—	CP	L	CD	CD
24	Schlüter II	L	C	C	CD/L	CD	C	CD	C	CP	L	CD	—
25	Schlüter III	L	C	C	CP	CD	C	CD	L	CP	L	—	—
26	Schlüter IV	L	C	C	C	C	C	R	L	R	R	—	—
27	Schlüter V	L	C	C	L	C	C	L	S	C	C	—	—
28	Rasmussen I	S	S	S/CD	CP	S	S	S/CD	S	S	CP	—	CD
29	Rasmussen II	S	S	CD	CD	S	S	S	CD	S	—	—	—
30	Rasmussen III	S	S	S	S	S	S	S	S	S	S	—	—
31	Rasmussen IV	S	S	S	S	S	S	S	S	S	S	—	—

[a] Cabinet no. 28 also had ministers for: Research: CD; Development aid: S; Communication: CD/S. Cabinets nos. 29, 30, and 31 also had ministers for: Research: S; Development aid: S. Energy and Environment were fused in Rasmussen II.

Parties
C   Conservative People's Party (Det Konservative Folkeparti)
CD   Centre Democrats (Centrum–Demokraterne)
CP   Christian People's Party (Kristeligt Folkeparti)
J   Justice Party (Danmarks Retsforbund)
L   Liberals (Venstre, Danmarks Liberale Parti)
MG   Mikael Gam (MP from Greenland)
R   Radical Liberals (Det Radikale Venstre)
S   Social Democrats (Socialdemokratiet)

always the Ministry of Social Welfare. The Liberals, with their strong links to the farming population, have always had the Ministry of Agriculture, and the Conservatives, with their ties to the business community, always the Ministry of Trade and Industry. These allocations fit well with the traditional cleavage lines in Danish politics (Elklit 1984; Damgaard 1974).

CABINET TERMINATION

A previous study of government termination in the post-war period, based on a 'Danish' conception of what constitutes a 'government' (Damgaard 1994*b*), concluded that majority coalitions always terminate because they lose their majority in the first upcoming election. Minority governments (single-party or coalition) terminate for various other reasons, as they are dependent upon the relationship with other parties. Information on cabinet termination in accordance with the design of the present volume is provided in Table 7.7.

As mentioned above, the government has the power to dissolve the Folketing at almost any time. This obviously affects the analysis of cabinet termination, at least in the sense that governments are defined to end when elections are held. But several Danish cabinets have in fact ended for technical reasons that have nothing to do with the power of dissolution. One of them (number 11 in Table 7.7) actually ruled until the end of the term, three of them (6, 8, 10) ended because of death or serious illness of the prime minister, two (4, 5) ended because elections were necessary in the process of constitutional amendment, and one (15) ended because the prime minister decided to leave politics for private reasons.

A further six cabinets (7, 9, 14, 24, 28, 30), including the three majority coalitions formed in 1960, 1968, and 1993, respectively, used the power to call early elections three to six months before the end of the term in situations that did not involve political conflict. Thus, one might argue that thirteen out of thirty cabinets terminated for reasons that were purely technical or did not involve significant inter-party conflict.

This leaves us with seventeen cabinets, all minority, that have terminated due to causes which somehow contain political conflicts or controversies. Half of them (1, 3, 13, 16, 17, 21, 23, 25) were defeated in parliamentary votes—in seven of the cases in combination with early elections as explained in Table 7.7. Four (2, 12, 18, 26) of the nine remaining cabinets ended in unsuccessful attempts to improve their bargaining position through early elections. A further two (22, 27) terminated because of voluntary resignation without dissolution of parliament, and one (29) because a party preferred to leave the coalition without withdrawing its parliamentary support. Finally, a single-party cabinet (19) was transformed into a coalition (20) in 1978, which

254 Erik Damgaard

TABLE 7.7. Cabinet termination in Denmark, 1945–1999

Cabinet number	Cabinet	Mechanisms of cabinet termination								Terminal event			Policy area(s)	Comments
		Technical			Discretionary									
		(1) Regular election	(2) Other constitutional reason	(3) Death (illness) of prime minister	(4) Early election	(5) Voluntary enlargement of coalition	(6) Cabinet defeated by opposition	(7) Conflict between coalition parties: policy	(8) Intra-party conflict	(11) International or national security	(12) Economic	(13) Personal		
1	Kristensen				X		X			X			1, 2	No confidence vote and elections due to foreign policy statements of PM (Danish/German borders)
2	Hedtoft I				X						X		3	Lack of success in fighting economic difficulties
3	Hedtoft II						X				X		3	Defeat in parliament and economic problems (voluntary resignation)
4	Eriksen I		X											Elections required in process of amending constitution
5	Eriksen II		X											Elections required in process of amending constitution

Denmark

No.	Government	C1	C2	C3	C4	Codes	Reason
6	Hedtoft III			X			Death of prime minister
7	Hansen I	X					Elections 4 months before end of term
8	Hansen II	X		X			Death of prime minister
9	Kampmann I	X					Elections 6 months before end of term
10	Kampmann II	X		X			Illness of prime minister
11	Krag I		X				End of term
12	Krag II	X				3	Elections called to improve government's bargaining position (taxation policy)
13	Krag III	X			X	3, 4, 17	Parliamentary defeat and elections (economic problems caused by British devaluation)
14	Baunsgaard	X					Elections 4 months before end of term
15	Krag IV		X		X		Prime minister decided to leave politics (non-political reasons)
16	Jørgensen I	X			X (NL)	3, 4	Defeat in parliament (taxation policy) interpreted as result of split in SD party group

256 *Erik Damgaard*

TABLE 7.7. *cont.*

Cabinet number	Cabinet	Mechanisms of cabinet termination								Terminal event			Policy area(s)	Comments
		Technical		Discretionary										
		(1) Regular election	(2) Other constitutional reason	(3) Death (illness) of prime minister	(4) Early election	(5) Voluntary enlargement of coalition	(6) Cabinet defeated by opposition	(7) Conflict between coalition parties: policy	(8) Intra-party conflict	(11) International or national security	(12) Economic	(13) Personal		
17	Hartling				X		X				X		3, 4, 5	Elections called to improve bargaining position with respect to economic crisis legislation. No confidence vote after elections
18	Jørgensen II				X						X		3, 4, 5	Election called to improve government's bargaining position (economic policy)
19	Jørgensen III					X								'Private' negotiations result in coalition of SD and Lib
20	Jørgensen IV				X			X					3, 4, 5	Election called because of conflict between coalition parties and economic policies
21	Jørgensen V				X		X						3, 4, 5	Government called election upon defeat on economic issue

Denmark   257

#	Government				Code	Reason
22	Jørgensen VI	X				Government resigned voluntarily. Could not obtain support for desired policies
23	Schlüter I		X		3, 4, 5	Budget proposal defeated. Early election
24	Schlüter II		X			Elections 5 months before end of term
25	Schlüter III		X		2	Government defeated on security policy issue. Early elections
26	Schlüter IV		X	X	3, 4, 5	Elections called to improve government's bargaining position (economic policy)
27	Schlüter V		X		6	Prime minister decided to resign (possibly anticipating defeat in parliament because of 'scandal' ('Tamilsagen')
28	Rasmussen I	X				Elections 3 months before end of term
29	Rasmussen II	X		X		CD wanted to leave the coalition
30	Rasmussen III	X				Elections 6 months before end of term

then broke down in 1979 because of inter-party policy disagreements, resulting in an early election.

The destiny of minority coalitions does not appear to differ much from that of single-party minority cabinets. Only majority coalitions have been able to avoid defeats and very early elections. On the other hand, they have never been able to retain their majority through an election.

Table 7.7 also demonstrates that severe conflicts among coalition parties, as well as intra-party conflicts, rarely terminate governments. Finally, the table illustrates that the relevant 'terminal events' are primarily related to economic policy problems and personal factors involving the prime minister, although there are also two clear cases of significant foreign policy events terminating a government.

ELECTORAL PERFORMANCE

Studies have shown that governing parties generally tend to lose votes in elections (e.g. Rose and Mackie 1983; Strøm 1990), and it has been noted that Danish majority coalitions do not survive elections. Some more detailed information is provided in Table 7.8.

Table 7.8 confirms that governing parties on the average lose votes, but the pattern is far from clear. Single-party minority governments are more often punished than rewarded at the polls, but on some occasions (1947, 1974, 1977) they have made big gains. A remarkable finding concerning coalition governments is that all the participating parties are never rewarded at the same time. The 1979 election result may seem to contradict this statement, but actually the two governing parties had already split up before the election. Maybe they were rewarded because they had brought the coalition to an end? Conversely, it does happen that coalition parties are simultaneously punished (1964, 1971), but the prevailing pattern is that they are alternately rewarded and punished by the voters. Still, the safest bet is that a party entering government will lose votes at the next election. Two-thirds of all the entries for governing parties in Table 7.8 have a negative sign.

The only major deviation from this general pattern is the electoral performance of the Liberal Party. That party actually gained votes in nine out of eleven cases. The party was particularly successful in the elections of 1947, 1974, 1990, and 1994. At the former two elections the Liberals faced the electorate as a single-party minority government, in the latter two cases as a partner in minority coalition governments. Full analyses of these interesting cases have not been carried out, but in retrospect it appears that the party benefited from taking rather strong stands on important issues. In 1947 the governing party presented itself in a nationalistic manner with respect to a possible

Denmark 259

TABLE 7.8. *Electoral costs/benefits of government parties in Denmark, 1945–1999* (% of votes)

Government	In office at time of election	Election year	SD	CD	RL	CPP	JP	Con	Lib	Government
Lib 1945–7	Yes	1947	—	—	—	—	—	—	+4.2	+4.2
SD 1947–50	Yes	1950	−0.4	—	—	—	—	—	—	−0.4
SD 1950	No	1953I	+0.8	—	—	—	—	—	—	+0.8
Lib–Con 1950–3	Yes	1953I	—	—	—	—	—	−0.5	+0.8	+0.3
Lib–Con 1953	Yes	1953II	—	—	—	—	—	−0.5	+1.0	+0.5
SD 1953–7	Yes	1957	−1.9	—	—	—	—	—	—	−1.9
SD–RL–JP 1957–60	Yes	1960	+2.7	—	−2.0	—	−3.1	—	—	−2.4
SD–RL 1960–4	Yes	1964	−0.2	—	−0.5	—	—	—	—	−0.7
SD 1964–6	Yes	1966	−3.7	—	—	—	—	—	—	−3.7
SD 1966–8	Yes	1968	−4.0	—	—	—	—	—	—	−4.0
RL–Lib–Con 1968–71	Yes	1971	—	—	−0.6	—	—	−3.7	−3.0	−7.3
SD 1971–3	Yes	1973	−11.7	—	—	—	—	—	—	−11.7
Lib 1973–5[a]	Yes	1974	—	—	—	—	—	—	+11.0	+11.0
SD 1975–7	Yes	1977	+7.1	—	—	—	—	—	—	+7.1
SD 1977–8	No	1979	+1.3	—	—	—	—	—	—	+1.3
SD–Lib 1978–9	Yes	1979	+1.3	—	—	—	—	—	+0.5	+1.8
SD 1979–81	Yes	1981	−5.4	—	—	—	—	—	—	−5.4
SD 1981–2	No	1984	−1.3	—	—	—	—	—	—	−1.3
Con–Lib–CD–CPP 1982–4	Yes	1984	—	−3.7	—	+0.4	—	+8.9	+0.8	+6.4
Con–Lib–CD–CPP 1984–7	Yes	1987	—	+0.2	—	−0.3	—	−2.6	−1.6	−4.3
Con–Lib–CD–CPP 1987–8	Yes	1988	—	−0.1	—	−0.4	—	−1.5	+1.3	−0.7
Con–Lib–RL 1988–90	Yes	1990	—	—	−2.1	—	—	−3.3	+4.0	−1.4
Con–Lib 1990–3	No	1994	—	—	—	—	—	−1.0	+7.5	+6.5
SD–RL–CD–CPP 1993–4	Yes	1994	−2.8	−2.3	+1.1	−0.4	—	—	—	−4.4
SD–RL–CD 1994–6	No	1998	+1.3	+1.5	−0.7	—	—	—	—	+2.1
SD–RL 1996–8	Yes	1998	+1.3	—	−0.7	—	—	—	—	+0.6
MEANS			−1.3	−0.9	−0.8	−0.2	−3.1	−0.5	+2.4	−0.3

[a] The election was called in Dec. 1974 but held on 9 Jan. 1975.

change of the Danish–German border, and in 1974 as the only party with a genuine plan for the solution of Denmark's severe economic problems. In the two cases of the 1990s, the Liberals emphasized 'new-right' solutions to the economic and social problems of the Danish welfare state much more than did their coalition partners. If these speculations are not wide off the mark, they suggest that a governing party may be successful if it can combine government responsibility with strong issue positions, at least if the government is of the minority type.

CONCLUSION

The fairly large number of parties in the Danish multi-party system order themselves rather nicely on a basic socio-economic left–right scale. All the parties want votes and policy influence, and most of them cabinet positions. The inter-party game on government formation is conducted according to formal and informal rules.

The two most important formal rules state that a government may be voted out of office if a parliamentary majority expresses lack of confidence in the government, and that the government at almost any time is empowered to dissolve parliament. Within this parliamentary balance-of-power system, informal rules have developed that regulate the behaviour of parties in processes of government formation.

The bargaining among parties on the formation of governments has been completed comparatively swiftly, with the small centre parties playing significant roles. In the vast majority of cases, the result has been minority governments which—since the early 1980s—have been formed by coalitions of parties rather than by single parties. There are good pragmatic and theoretical reasons for such outcomes, even if minority governments without assured support from non-governmental parties may face short lives.

Danish government coalition parties have not developed the art of signing formal, public agreements to any noticeable extent. The parties make deals in more hidden and subtle ways, and they generally want to preserve a certain freedom of action, especially if they do not command a legislative majority of their own. On the other hand, it appears obvious that quite stable norms on coalition governance have developed over time, but research in this area is very limited. In terms of portfolio allocation, however, it is not that difficult to detect what some of the parties cherish.

Apart from the cases in which governments terminate for purely technical reasons, Danish cabinets sometimes decide to call early elections three to six months before the end of the term without any observable conflict being involved. If conflicts are involved, terminations either happen because minority cabinets are defeated in parliament or because they attempt to improve their bargaining position through early elections. Although the evidence is mixed, it does show that parties in government are likely to lose votes in elections.

In many ways, the Danish parliamentary system is informal, flexible, and innovative with respect to coalition governance. If, for example, a formal majority coalition is not desired by the parties, then a minority cabinet is appointed with an obligation to create a perhaps very complex majority structure for decision making (Damgaard and Svensson 1989).

So far, coalition theory and research has not really addressed the important question of what the policy implications of the various arrangements might be, not to mention their broader consequences for representative democracy.

REFERENCES

Albæk Jensen, Jørgen (1989). *Parlamentarismens statsretlige betydning*. Copenhagen: Jurist- og Økonomforbundets Forlag.
Bergman, Torbjörn (1995). *Constitutional Rules and Party Goals in Coalition Formation*. Umeå: Department of Political Science.
Bille, Lars (1989). 'Denmark: The Oscillating Party System'. *West European Politics*, 12: 42–58.
Christensen, J. Grønnegaard (1985). 'In Search of Unity: Cabinet Committees in Denmark', in Thomas T. Mackie and Brian W. Hogwood (eds.), *Unlocking the Cabinet: Cabinet Structures in Comparative Perspective*. London: Sage.
Damgaard, Erik (1969). 'The Parliamentary Basis of Danish Governments'. *Scandinavian Political Studies Yearbook*, 4: 35–66.
——(1973). 'Party Coalitions in Danish Law-Making 1953–1970'. *European Journal of Political Research*, 1: 30–57.
——(1974). 'Stability and Change in the Danish Party System over Half a Century'. *Scandinavian Political Studies Yearbook*, 9: 103–25.
——(1977). *Folketinget under forandring*. Copenhagen: Samfundsvidenskabeligt Forlag.
——(1992a). 'Denmark: Experiments in Parliamentary Government', in Erik Damgaard (ed.), *Parliamentary Change in the Nordic Countries*. Oslo: Scandinavian University Press.
——(1992b). 'Parliamentary Change in the Nordic Countries', in Erik Damgaard (ed.), *Parliamentary Change in the Nordic Countries*. Oslo: Scandinavian University Press.
——(1994a). 'Parliamentary Questions and Control in Denmark', in Matti Wiberg (ed.), *Parliamentary Control in the Nordic Countries*. Helsinki: The Finnish Political Science Association.
——(1994b). 'Termination of Danish Government Coalitions: Theoretical and Empirical Aspects'. *Scandinavian Political Studies*, 17: 193–211.

Damgaard, Erik (1995). 'How Parties Control Committee Members', in Herbert Döring (ed.), *Parliaments and Majority Rule in Western Europe*. New York: St Martin's Press.

——and Rusk, Jerrold G. (1976). 'Cleavage Structures and Representational Linkages: A Longitudinal Analysis of Danish Legislative Behavior'. *American Journal of Political Science*, 20: 179–205.

——and Svensson, Palle (1989). 'Who Governs? Parties and Policies in Denmark'. *European Journal of Political Research*, 17: 731–45.

Elklit, Jørgen (1984). 'Det klassiske danske partisystem bliver til', in Jørgen Elklit and Ole Tonsgaard (eds.), *Valg og vælgeradfærd*. Aarhus: Forlaget Politica.

——(1993). 'Simpler than its Reputation: The Electoral System in Denmark since 1920'. *Electoral Studies*, 12: 41–57.

Folketingsårbog (yearly publication) Copenhagen: Schultz.

Folketingstidende (yearly publication) Copenhagen: Schultz.

Fonsmark, Henning (1992). *Schlüters Danmark. Historien om en politisk karriere*. Copenhagen: Børsen Bøger.

Germer, Peter (1988). *Statsforfatningsret 1*. Copenhagen: Jurist- og Økonomforbundets Forlag.

Holmstedt, Margareta, and Schou, Tove-Lise (1987). 'Sweden and Denmark 1945–1982: Election Programmes in the Scandinavian Setting', in Ian Budge, David Robertson, and Derek Hearl (eds.), *Ideology, Strategy and Party Change*. Cambridge: Cambridge University Press.

Jensen, Henrik (1994). 'Committees as Actors or Arenas? Putting Questions to the Danish Standing Committees', in Matti Wiberg (ed.), *Parliamentary Control in the Nordic Countries*. Helsinki: Finnish Political Science Association.

Jensen, Torben K. (1995). 'Partierne, Europaudvalget og europæiseringen'. *Politica*, 27: 464–79.

Jyllands-Posten (daily newspaper). Aarhus.

Kaarsted, Tage (1964). *Regeringskrisen 1957. En studie i regeringsdannelsens proces*. Aarhus: Universitetsforlaget.

——(1969). *Dansk politik i 1960'erne. Taktik og strategi*. Copenhagen: Gyldendal.

——(1977). *De danske ministerier 1929–1953*. Copenhagen: Pensionsforsikringsanstalten.

——(1988). *Regeringen, vi aldrig fik. Regeringsdannelsen 1975 og dens baggrund*. Odense: Odense Universitetsforlag.

——(1992). *De danske ministerier 1953–1972*. Copenhagen: PFA Pension.

Kauffeldt, Carl (1966). *Nye tider—nye mål 1945–1965*. Copenhagen: Nyt Nordisk Forlag.

Laakso, Markku, and Taagepera, Rein (1979). '"Effective" Number of Parties: A Measure with Application to Western Europe'. *Comparative Political Studies*, 12: 3–27.

Larsen, Dan (1995). *Et land i Europa* (Venstre i 125 år). Copenhagen: Venstres Landsorganisation.

Laver, Michael, and Hunt, W. Ben (1992). *Policy and Party Competition*. New York: Routledge.

——and Schofield, Norman (1990). *Multiparty Government*. Oxford: Oxford University Press.

Mader, Erik (1979). *SF under det røde kabinet*. Odense: Odense Universitetsforlag.
Mikkelsen, Hans C. (1994). 'Udviklingen i partisammenholdet'. *Politica*, 26: 25–45.
Nannestad, Peter (1989). *Reactive Voting in Danish General Elections 1971–1979*. Aarhus: Aarhus University Press.
Olsen, Søren-Ole (1978). 'Regeringsarbejdet og statsministeren'. *Nordisk Administrativt Tidsskrift*, 59: 55–62.
Pedersen, Mogens N. (1987). 'The Danish "Working Multiparty System": Breakdown or Adaptation?', in Hans Daalder (ed.), *Party Systems in Denmark, Austria, Switzerland, The Netherlands and Belgium*. London: Frances Pinter.
——(1988). 'The Defeat of all Parties: The Danish Folketing Election, 1973', in Kenneth Lawson and Peter H. Merkl (eds.), *When Parties Fail*. Princeton: Princeton University Press.
——Damgaard, Erik and Olsen, Peter Nannestad (1971). 'Party Distances in the Danish Folketing 1945–1968'. *Scandinavian Political Studies Yearbook*, 6: 87–106.
Rae, Douglas W. (1967). *The Political Consequences of Electoral Laws*. New Haven: Yale University Press.
Rasmussen, Erik (1972). *Komparativ politik 2*. Copenhagen: Gyldendal.
Rose, Richard, and Mackie, Thomas T. (1983). 'Incumbency in Government: Asset or Liability', in Hans Daalder and Peter Mair (eds.), *Western European Party Systems: Continuity and Change*. London: Sage.
Sartori, Giovanni (1976). *Parties and Party Systems: A Framework for Analysis*. Cambridge: Cambridge University Press.
Schou, Tove-Lise, and Hearl, Derek John (1992). 'Party and Coalition Policy in Denmark' Michael J. Laver and Ian Budge (eds.), in *Party Policy and Government Coalitions*. London: Macmillan.
Strøm, Kaare (1984). 'Minority Governments in Parliamentary Democracies'. *Comparative Political Studies*, 17: 199–227.
——(1986). 'Deferred Gratification and Minority Governments in Scandinavia'. *Legislative Studies Quarterly*, 11: 583–605.
——(1990). *Minority Government and Majority Rule*. Cambridge: Cambridge University Press.
——Budge, Ian and Laver, Michael J. (1994). 'Constraints on Cabinet Formation in Parliamentary Democracies'. *American Journal of Political Science*, 38: 303–35.
Thomas, Alastair H. (1982). 'Denmark: Coalitions and Minority Governments', in Eric C. Browne and John Dreijmanis (eds.), *Government Coalitions in Western Democracies*. New York: Longman.

8

Finland

The Consolidation of Parliamentary Governance

Jaakko Nousiainen

INTRODUCTION: FEATURES OF THE PARTY SYSTEM

The Finnish party system has been characterized by two features which are not always in good harmony: fragmentation and relative stability. For many decades the political field has been dominated, in genuine Scandinavian style, by five orientations: Conservatives, Liberals, Agrarians (Centre), Social Democrats, and Communists (the radical left). Distinctive aspects of the complexion are the strength of the agrarian centre, the clear division of the left into a moderate and a radical orientation, and its completion by a cultural and political minority movement, the Swedish People's Party.

The whole partisan field has been transformed over time with the necessary adaptation to societal change, but the unidimensional left–right scale largely holds true even today. As late as 1966 the six 'old' parties gained 96 per cent of the votes and seats in parliament. The balance was shaken only in the 1980s when new political movements directed their appeals to the socially integrating electorate. Part of those groups mobilize citizens in the spirit of new national issues, the other part challenges old parties in their established interest fields. In any event the basic partisan stability has been preserved: although around twenty parties presented their candidates for the parliamentary election in 1995, the six biggest gained 89 per cent of the votes and 94 per cent of the seats. Table 8.1 also indicates that the effective number of legislative parties has varied relatively little during the past fifty years.

Over the past five decades the centre of gravity in the party system has been moving from left to right. Up until the end of the 1960s the basic configuration consisted of three big parties (SDP, CE, and FPDU), one medium-large (CON), and a couple of small ones. From the 1970s on, the standing oppositional status gave new strength to the Conservative Party, and the loss of the appeal of Communism paved the way for a peculiar three-party system: Social Democrats, Agrarians, and Conservatives. These are today the central players in the coalition game, and all two-party combinations have been experimented with during the last fifteen years.

The disengagement of citizens from established political structures has also affected the partisan field in Finland, and since the 1960s new mobilizing and challenging movements have complemented the traditional configuration. The first of these was the populistic rural movement (FRP), which defended the interests of regional and social peripheries in the rapidly industrializing society. It was followed by the Christian Democratic movement, the breeding ground of which was based on the secularization of social life in general and of the Conservative Party in particular. The third newcomer is the mobilizing Green movement, which has stabilized its institutional support at about 5 per cent of the parliamentary seats. The main orientation of the Green movement in Finland has always been rather moderate, and in 1995 the party was adapted to the regime by entrusting its leader the portfolio of environment. However, given the deep-rooted system of collegiate government, an individual minister has rather limited opportunity for independent policy making.

A distinguishing feature of Finnish politics for almost one hundred years has been its strong centrist Agrarian Party. It has been based on the family cultivation system of small farms; the combination small farmer and lumberer used to be predominant especially in the Eastern and Northern parts of the country. Flanked by a strong leftist movement, on one side, and by liberals and right-wing forces, on the other, the Agrarian Centre has occupied the position of a median party for most of the period under consideration. It is also a fact that in this position the party was able to monopolize the coalition bargaining power until 1987. If it refused to cooperate, the only alternative on the left wing was the Social Democratic single-party cabinet. On the right wing, there were hardly any alternatives, bearing in mind the delicate foreign policy situation before the dissolution of the Soviet Union. The median position was crucial as long as the party system remained basically unidimensional and coalition building required the cooperation of adjacent parties, so that the borderline between right and left could not be crossed without its participation. The dominant coalition pattern during the period from 1937 to 1987 was the 'collaboration of workers and farmers'—the red–green coalition of SDP and the Centre Party that counterbalanced the rightist policies of the preceding period. But towards the end of the 1980s the large parties on both sides had had enough of the continuing Agrarian domination and broke the tradition in the coalition of Conservatives and Social Democrats. The solution was facilitated by the lowering of the ideological fortresses and the weakening of the Centre's parliamentary strength. Two parties representing the views of modern industrial society and defending the interests of workers and white-collar employees had found each other politically.

The new parliamentary configuration since the late 1980s reflects the fact that in the course of societal change the traditional left–right placement has

266   Jaakko Nousiainen

TABLE 8.1. *Left-right placement of parties, party strength (in seats), and party composition of governments in Finland, 1945–1999*

Government[a]	Proximity to election	FPDU	SDL	SDP	GR	CE	FRP	LIB	CHR	SW	CON	Other parties	Median party in second policy dimension	Effective number of legislative parties	Government strength	Total number of seats[b]
1945	F	49	—	50	—	49*	—	9	—	14	28	1	SDP	4.78	171	200
1946	E	49	—	50	—	49*	—	—	—	14	—	—	—	4.78	162	200
1948	F	38	—	54	—	56*	—	5	—	14	33	—	SDP	4.54	54	200
1950	—	—	—	—	—	56*	—	5	—	14	—	—	—	4.54	75	200
1/1951	E	—	—	54	—	56*	—	5	—	14	—	—	—	4.54	129	200
9/1951	F	43	—	53	—	51*	—	10	—	15	28	—	SDP	4.78	119	200
7/1953	—	—	—	53	—	51*	—	—	—	—	—	—	—	4.78	66	200
11/1953	E	—	—	—	—	—	—	—	—	—	—	—	—	4.78	0	200
5/1954	F	43	—	54	—	53*	—	13	—	13	24	—	—	4.71	120	200
10/1954	—	—	—	54	—	53*	—	—	—	—	—	—	—	4.71	107	200
1956	—	—	—	54	—	53*	—	13	—	13	—	—	—	4.71	133	200
5/1957	—	—	—	—	—	53*	—	13	—	13	—	—	—	4.71	79	200
7/1957	—	—	—	—	—	53*	—	13	—	—	—	—	—	4.71	66	200
9/1957	—	—	19	35	—	53*	—	13	—	—	—	—	—	5.59	85	200
11/1957	—	—	—	—	—	—	—	—	—	—	—	—	—	5.59	0	200
4/1958	E	—	13	38*	—	—	—	8	—	—	—	—	SDL	5.59	0	200
8/1958	F	50	—	—	—	48	—	—	—	14	29	—	—	5.32	137	200
1959	—	—	—	—	—	48	—	—	—	—	—	—	—	5.32	48	200
1961	E	—	—	—	—	48	—	—	—	—	—	—	—	5.32	48	200
1962	F	47	2	38	—	53*	—	13	—	14	32	1	SDL	5.09	112	200
1963	—	—	—	—	—	—	—	—	—	—	—	—	—	5.09	0	200
1964	E	41	7	55*	—	53*	1	13	—	14	32	—	SDP	5.09	112	200
1966	F	41	7	55*	—	49	—	9	—	12	26	—	SDP	4.96	152	200
1968	E	—	—	52	—	49	—	—	—	12	—	—	—	4.96	164	200
5/1970	F	36	—	52	—	36*	18	8	1	12	37	—	SDP	5.56	0	200
7/1970	—	36	—	52	—	36*	—	8	—	12	—	—	—	5.56	144	200
3/1971	—	—	—	52	—	36*	—	8	—	12	—	—	—	5.56	108	200
10/1971	E	—	—	—	—	—	—	—	—	—	—	—	—	5.56	0	200
2/1972	F	37	—	55	—	35*	18	7	4	10	34	—	SDP	5.51	55	200

Finland

		FPDU	SDL	SDP	GR	CE	FRP	LIB	CHR	SW	CON	Other	Gov			
9/1972	E	—	—	55	—	35*	—	7	—	10	—	—	—	5.51	107	200
6/1975	E	—	—	—	—	—	—	—	—	—	—	—	—	5.51	0	200
11/1975	F	40	—	54	—	39*	2	9	—	10	35	2	SDP	5.31	152	200
1976		—	—	—	—	—	—	—	—	—	—	—	—	5.31	58	200
1977		40	—	54	—	39*	—	9	—	10	—	—	—	5.31	152	200
1978	E	40	—	54	—	39*	—	9	—	10	—	—	—	5.31	142	200
1979	F	35	—	52	—	36*	7	4	—	10	47	1	SDP	5.21	133	200
2/1982		35	—	52	—	36*	—	—	—	10	—	—	—	5.21	133	200
12/1982	E	—	—	52	—	36*	—	—	—	10	—	—	—	5.21	98	200
1983	FE	27	2	57	—	38*	17	—	—	11	44	1	SDP	5.14	123	200
1987	F	20	4	56	—	40*	9	—	—	13	53	—	SDP	4.86	131	200
1990	E	—	—	56	—	—	—	—	—	13	53	—	—	4.86	122	200
1991	F	19	10	48	—	55*	7	—	8	12	40	—	SDP	5.23	115	200
1994	E	—	—	—	—	55*	—	1	—	12	40	—	—	5.23	107	200
1995	F	22	9	63	—	44*	1	—	7	12	39	3	SDP	4.88	145	200

[a] Month is indicated if more than one government has been formed in the same year.
[b] The theoretical maximum of the total number of votes in any parliamentary voting is only 199 because the Speaker has no right to vote.

Parties

FPDU 1944–90: Suomen Kansan Demokraattinen Liitto (Finnish People's Democratic Union) includes Finnish Communist Party; in 1987 includes also 4 seats of Demokraattinen Vaihtoehto (DEVA) (Democratic Alternative); since 1990: VAS = Vasemmistoliitto (Left Wing Alliance)

SDL 9/1957–8/1958: Sosialidemokraattinen Oppositio (Social Democratic Opposition); since 1959: TPSL = Työväen ja Pienviljelijöiden Sosialidemokraattinen Liitto (Social Democratic League of Workers and Smallholders)

SDP Suomen Sosialidemokraattinen Puolue (Social Democratic Party of Finland)

GR Vihreä Liitto (VIHR) (Green League)

CE 1906–65: Maalaisliitto (Agrarian Union); 1965–1988: Keskustapuolue (Centre Party); since 1988: KESK = Suomen Keskusta (Centre Party of Finland)

FRP 1959–66: Suomen Pienviljelijäin Puolue (Small Farmers' Party of Finland); since 1966: SMP = Suomen Maaseudun Puolue (Finnish Rural Party)

LIB 1918–51: Kansallinen Edistyspuolue (National Progressive Party); 1951–65: Suomen Kansanpuolue (Finnish People's Party); since 1965: LKP = Liberaalinen Kansanpuolue (Liberal People's Party)

CHR SKL = Suomen Kristillinen Liitto (Christian League of Finland)

SW RKP = Ruotsalainen Kansanpuolue or SFP = Svenska Folkpartiet (Swedish People's Party)

CON KOK = Kansallinen Kokoomus (National Coalition Party) (Conservatives)

Other parties Swedish Left (one seat in 1945), Liberal Union (one seat in 1962), Unity Party (one seat in 11/1975), Constitutional Party (one seat in 11/1975, 1979, and 1983), Ecological Party (one seat in 1995), and Young Finnish Party (two seats in 1995).

Parties in **bold** formed **governments**.

been effectively complemented by another policy dimension, the centre–periphery dimension, which has its roots in the juxtaposition of urban and rural values but has, in the newest development, incorporated elements of internationalism v. nationalism in terms of European politics. The SDP rather than the Centre occupies the position of the median party in this dimension.

INSTITUTIONAL BACKGROUND

There are several important institutional constraints on coalition bargaining, even though formal rules governing the cabinet formation process have been minimal. Three of these contextual factors deserve special mention.

Throughout many decades government formation was regulated by a short constitutional provision: 'The members of the Council of State, who must enjoy confidence of Parliament, shall be appointed by the President from among natural born citizens of Finland, known for their honesty and ability.' As no mechanism was indicated for immediate substantiation of the confidence, the head of state has always been the central initiating and steering force in the bargaining process. The semi-presidential system has tended to passify other actors and to impose upon the president the main responsibility for establishing a viable government in varying situations.

Government formation has been the most important presidential prerogative in the domestic field, and most presidents have used this power extensively. In a fragmented party system the president's right to select the prime ministerial candidate and to give him instructions for party negotiations has always been recognized. In the last analysis the coalition solution depends on the party leaders, but the head of state has often used pressure to include certain parties and exclude others. The latest incident came in 1987 when President Koivisto exerted decisive influence in the formation of the unprecedented coalition of Conservatives and Social Democrats and in the selection of Prime Minister Harri Holkeri.

Increasing electoral volatility tends generally to reduce the president's freedom of movement. In both 1991 and 1995 it was clear that the leader of the largest winning party was to become prime minister and that the majority coalition was shaped in negotiations presided by him.

Constitutional amendments have during the last decade tilted the balance in favour of parliament and the parties. Since 1987 parliament must be in session during the formation process, and the president is explicitly obliged to get the parliamentary parties' opinions of the situation in general and of the ministerial appointments in particular. And what is most important, a new cabinet must (since 1991) immediately present its programme to parliament and put its confidence to test.

A decisive step was taken in the new constitution that is to come into force in 2000. The reform aims at some material development of the constitutional order, especially as regards the strengthening of the element of parliamentarism in the Finnish system of government. The role of parliament in the formation of a new cabinet will be significantly increased. The prime minister will be elected by parliament and only then appointed by the president. The other ministers will be nominated by the prime minister and appointed by the president. This certainly reduces the likelihood of a minority government coming into existence with the president's support.

The second important constraint originates from legislative rules, the effective decision rules for legislation (see Strøm, Budge, and Laver 1994). Until 1992 the constitution contained a peculiar provision according to which one-third of the members of parliament—67 representatives at least—could postpone the final adoption of an ordinary law by two to four years by voting it to lie dormant. A proposal for a new state tax also had to be approved by a two-thirds majority. On the other hand, temporary exceptions from fundamental law provisions can be made by the same majority—or by a four-fifths majority in an urgent order. Especially in crisis situations such exceptions either from the constitutional division of powers or from basic rights of citizens have been habitual.

The need for qualified majorities certainly goes some way towards explaining the Finnish inclination to oversized coalitions (see Lane and Ersson 1991: 242; Laver and Schofield 1990: 71, 82). However, this is not the only, and perhaps not even the most important explanatory factor. As the predominant majority government model has been the non-bloc coalition, it has been important to build the parliamentary balance of power inside the cabinet as well. And this has presupposed the inclusion of some small bourgeois groups beyond the mere majority position. Besides, considering the actual number of MPs who belong to the parties in government, it has been rather accidental whether or not the coalitions have reached the crucial two-thirds majority. In spring 1995 Prime Minister Lipponen coaxed both the Greens and the radical left to accept government responsibility and in this way raised the support of the cabinet close to the three-quarters level in parliament, in spite of the fact that qualified majorities were no longer needed to push through economic and social policies.

The third constraint on coalition building in the post-war era was the need to maintain good or working relationships with the Soviet Union. In most cases the Soviet government did not resort to an open external veto, but Finnish presidents in the first instance anticipated its reactions. The practical result was the exclusion of the Conservatives from the coalitions—with some interruptions—until 1987. The same idea of political equilibrium legitimized the keeping of the strong Communist movement in opposition for most of the time. The official discrimination fattened the Coalition Party (the official name of the Conservatives) to such an extent that in 1987 it could no longer be disregarded. Soon after this the whole thinking that was based on balancing forces collapsed with the fall of the Soviet system.

Since the latter half of the 1980s the importance of the above-mentioned constraints has therefore considerably diminished. The party orchestra plays 'anything that goes', and Finnish practice has come closer to the coalition formation model in which 'parties shop around freely for potential cabinet partners in a world in which all possible combinations of parties represent feasible governments' (Strøm, Budge, and Laver 1994: 306). The coalition of Social Democrats, Conservatives, the Greens, and the radical left formed in 1995 indicates that the traditional bloc boundary of the party system has lost much of its importance.

It is fair to say that the forming of large heterogeneous cabinets has been made possible by the cabinet decision making rule, according to which the autonomy and responsibility of each individual minister has been, in international comparison, minimal. The principle of collective decision making, so deeply rooted in Finnish central administration, has meant that no coalition party needs to be afraid of what is happening outside the policy fields it directly controls. As long as the policy elasticity of the parties was rather restricted, they still easily broke away, waiting for a new bargaining situation in the knowledge that the breaking down of the coalition will not be punished by untimely elections.

In the newest development the situation has changed. Starting from the 1980s, in a system of 'consensual competition', parties enter the cabinet to pursue long-term national policies, not to fight over acute group interests. The substitution of pragmatic policies for ideological views has considerably increased the partners' ability to bear stress in coalition politics, and the dissolution of the cooperation will be avoided as far as possible.

It should also be noted that the electoral system in use forces small parties to form electoral alliances either with each other or with some of the big parties. The party showing the greatest compliance to alliances with right-wing groups has been the ideologically neutral Agrarian Centre. Electoral cooperation has possibly generated sympathy among partners, but for the most part electoral alliances have been understood simply as technical arrangements which do not structure the bargaining situation. In Finnish elections the parties strive to maximize their parliamentary strength, with governmental participation in mind; but pre-electoral executive commitments and agreements are practically non-existent, and coalition alternatives are not presented to the electorate.

COALITION FORMATION

The constitutional provisions concerning cabinet formation have been described above. They are complemented by established practices, parts of which were formalized in 1987 and in 1991. Until 2000 the initiative to form a new cabinet belonged to the president of the republic, who had first to establish contact with the parliamentary party groups. After a cabinet had summoned its resignation request, it was an established practice to carry out a 'presidential round': the president first summoned the speaker of parliament and then the chairmen of the parliamentary parties and discussed with them the political situation and various options in order to determine the basis for resolving the crisis. On the basis of his assessment of the situation, the president then decided who had the best chance of forming a broadly based and stable government, and nominated a prime ministerial candidate with instructions concerning the coalition base. A more prudent procedure was to nominate an *informateur* to enquire into the attitudes and options of various parties. If the architect of a government should fail in his quest, the president turned to another individual and considered other alternatives. If the formation of a majority government was impossible, it was necessary to settle for a minority coalition or even a one-party government. A non-partisan caretaker cabinet has been an extreme measure.

The latitude of presidential action was increased by the fact that a fragmented party system did not often produce a clear electoral winner. It is true that on some occasions the president had no choice: both in 1991 and 1995 the leader of the largest party became the *formateur* as a matter of course. Speculation about the president's influence is not easy because it is hard to know what goes on behind the scenes. But in general, every sitting president sought to retain his power. Even though presidents have recognized the primary importance of the party institution and have let groups reach agreement in peaceful and clear situations, presidents have none the less acted energetically in more difficult cases: they have determined which parties are 'eligible' for entrance into a cabinet, put pressure on parliamentary groups and hesitant ministerial candidates, and expressed a clear opinion concerning the coalition base—and even the government programme. Mauno Koivisto says in his memoirs that in 1983, when the time was considered to be ripe for rejecting the established phraseology, the foreign policy section of the programme was written in the president's office and accepted by party negotiators as such (Koivisto 1995: 77–8).

However, the president's role remains one of an outside overseer. Everyday negotiations are carried on by party delegations representing both the national organizations and parliamentary parties. In the first phase an agreement is reached of the composition of the coalition. In the second phase the prospective partners elaborate the outlines of a programme and divide portfolios among the parties. The nomination of individuals to specific posts is done by parties, for the most part as an internal party matter. Intra-party decision making modes on coalitions and ministers vary to some extent. Generally speaking, the party executive or party council together with the parliamentary party are formally authorized to decide. As the new parliament cannot assemble sooner than one week after election day, it can be estimated that about three weeks is the minimum time needed to construct a new coalition.

Table 8.2 contains numerical information on the post-war formation processes in Finland. As we can see, the number of parliamentary parties has increased slightly, but the figures do not reveal the latest development towards a three-party system. Some explanatory comments are in order. Since 1945 there have been seven non-partisan 'stop gap' cabinets, which have been set up when bargaining rounds have failed, or in some cases as a first measure in a crisis situation. They have been considered to be temporary solutions, and they have not always tendered a formal resignation before the installation of a new cabinet. So in these cases there was no cabinet crisis; negotiations for a partisan government were typically started during their lifetime, and according to our criteria the number of days required for government formation in these cases could be zero, assuming that the cabinet's life was not ended by an election. The same applies to cases in which we register a new coalition because one of the partners has left without any formal change of government. The question has always been one of secondary partners, and the normal solution has been to narrow down the coalition base and to divide empty portfolios among the major partners. In these cases, too, the table does not necessarily show a cabinet crisis or any period of time required for bargaining attempts. So in order to get an idea of how coalition formation typically takes place, we should look only at formal cabinet changes which take place either after parliamentary or presidential elections or when the prime minister has submitted a resignation prematurely, during a sitting parliament. The four single-party governments (two Agrarian and two Social Democratic) have been formed only after bargaining attempts between parties have failed.

The table confirms the general impression that coalition building in Finland is a complicated and time-consuming process. This follows from the above-mentioned facts that there are no compact party alliances, the government question receives only little attention during the campaign, and the election does not necessarily produce a clear winner. Many kinds of combinations and several prime ministerial candidates are possible when the bargaining game is opened after the election. Eero Murto (1994: 118–22) has calculated that in an average cabinet crisis seven or eight names have been mentioned in public speculations of the prospective *formateur*.

As regards all formally sworn-in parliamentary governments, it appears that in 1945–95 the average number of unsuccessful formation attempts has been 1.3, and that on average five or six parties have been involved in one way or another in these attempts. The number of failed bargaining attempts varies from one to six, but typically most of the parties have at some phase participated in the discussion. The periodization of the process is due either to the alteration of *formateurs* or a change in the composition of the bargaining party grouping. A certain amount of arbitrariness cannot be avoided in the quantification.

In any case, when interpreting the figures it must also be noted that the president's first assignment normally aims at a large non-bloc majority coalition—Urho Kekkonen sometimes even recommended an all-party government. The next steps are some narrower but more homogeneous combinations, the last resorts being a single-party government or a caretaker cabinet. Kaare Strøm's hypothesis of minority government as 'normal outcomes of the process of democratic party competition' applies to Finland, if at all, only for the inter-war years (Strøm 1990*b*).

Most difficult were the disorderly years of 1957–66—a period of a real parliamentary *interregnum*—whereas since the late 1970s the political scene has been restructured in the sense that it is clear after an election which party has the leading role with respect to the nomination of the prime minister and choice of coalition partners.

The number of days required for forming a new parliamentary government is on average 33—more than four weeks—but even here there is much variation. Time is needed, first, for negotiations on the partisan breadth of the cabinet and then on the government programme or agreement. The formation of a two- or three-party coalition has taken an average 27 days, the formation of a four- or five-party coalition 39 days. On the basis of what has been said above one could expect the order to be the exact opposite, and that was in fact the case until the mid-1960s (Sänkiaho and Laakso 1975: 154–5). Anyhow, minority governments have sometimes been resorted to without going through the full menu. On the other hand, the programme of a large non-bloc coalition requires long negotiations, whereas the proclamation of a right-wing minority coalition can be drawn up quickly and smoothly.

Table 8.3 provides summary data on post-war cabinets in Finland, as defined in the previous section. Of the forty-four cabinets, twenty-seven were majority coalitions, six minority coalitions, four single-party governments, and seven caretaker cabinets. The dominant type of government has been a broad surplus majority coalition involving four or five parties; in extreme cases, their parliamentary basis has exceeded 80 per cent. Minority coalitions of two or three parties have typically been built around the Agrarian Centre. Part of the short-lived caretaker cabinets have been more or less pure civil servant governments, whereas others have been composed of openly political figures, even members of parliament. The Tuomioja cabinet in 1953–4 could have been considered a right-wing minority coalition, but none of the supporting parties had formally accepted governmental responsibility.

During the last twenty years, Finnish governments have transformed from the most unstable to the most stable in the Scandinavian area. For sixty years

TABLE 8.2. *Government formation in Finland, 1945–1999*

Coalition	Number of parties in parliament	Number of previous bargaining rounds	Parties involved in the previous bargaining rounds	Number of days required for government formation
FPDU–SDP–CE–LIB–SW 1945	7	0		31
FPDU–SDP–CE–SW 1946	7	2	(1) FPDU–SDP–CE–LIB–SW (2) FPDU–SDP–CE–LIB–SW	18
SDP 1948	6	1	FPDU–SDP–CE–SW	28
CE–LIB–SW 1950	6	1	FPDU–SDP–CE–LIB–SW	16
CE–SDP–LIB–SW 1951	6	1	FPDU–SDP–CE–LIB–SW–CON	0
CE–SDP–SW 1951	6	0		80
CE–SW 1953	6	2	(1) CE–LIB–SW–CON (2) SDP–CE–LIB–SW–CON	10
Non-partisan 1953	6	2	(1) SDP–CE–LIB–SW–CON (2) SDP–CE–CON	13
SW–SDP–CE 1954	6	4	(1) SDP–CE–LIB–SW–CON (2) CE–LIB–SW–CON (3) SDP–CE–LIB–SW–CON (4) SDP–LIB–SW–CON	59
CE–SDP 1954	6	0		5
SDP–CE–LIB–SW 1956	6	0		36
CE–LIB–SW 1957	6	1	SDP–CE–LIB–SW	6
CE–LIB 1957	6	0		0
CE–SDL–LIB 1957	7	1	SDP–CE–LIB–SW–CON	0
Non-partisan 1957	7	6	(1) SDP–CE–LIB–SW–CON (2) FPDU–SDL–SDP–CE–LIB–SW–CON (3) SDP–CE–LIB–SW (4) FPDU–SDL–SDP–CE–LIB–SW–CON (5) SDP–CE–LIB–SW (6) SDL–CE–LIB–SW	42
Non-partisan 1958	7	1	SDL–SDP–CE–LIB–SW–CON	8
SDP–CE–LIB–SW–CON 1958	7	6	(1) FPDU–SDL–SDP (2) SDL–SDP–CE–LIB–SW–CON (3) SDL–SDP–CE–LIB–SW–CON (4) SDL–SDP–CE (5) FPDU–SDL–SDP–CE–LIB–SW–CON (6) SDL–SDP–CE–LIB–SW–CON	54
CE 1959	7	1	SDL–SDP–CE–LIB–SW–CON	40

Finland

Cabinet	Dur.	N	Alternatives	%
CE 1961	7			16
CE-LIB-SW-CON 1962	8	2	(1) SDL-CE-LIB-SW-CON	68
		3	(2) SDL-CE-LIB-SW-CON	
Non-partisan 1963	8	4	(1) FPDU-SDL-SDP-CE-LIB-SW-CON	1
			(2) CE-LIB-SW-CON	
			(3) CE-LIB-SW-CON	
CE-LIB-SW-CON 1964	8	1	(1) SDL-SDP-CE-LIB-SW-CON	0
		1	(2) FPDU-SDL-SDP-CE-LIB-SW-CON	68
		0	(3) CE-LIB-SW-CON	21
		3	(4) FPDU-SDL-SDP-CE-LIB-SW-CON	60
SDP-FPDU-SDL-CE 1966	8		FPDU-SDL-SDP-CE-LIB-SW-CON	0
SDP-FPDU-SDL-CE-SW 1968	8		FPDU-SDL-SDP-CE-FRP-LIB-SW-CON	
Non-partisan 1970	8	2	(1) FPDU-SDP-CE-FRP-LIB-CHR-SW-CON	0
			(2) FPDU-SDP-CE-FRP-LIB-SW	0
CE-FPDU-SDP-LIB-SW 1970	8	0	(1) FPDU-SDP-CE-FRP-LIB-SW-CON	0
		0	(2) FPDU-SDP-FRP-LIB-SW-CON	52
CE-SDP-LIB-SW 1971	8	2	(3) FPDU-SDP-FRP-LIB-CON	
Non-partisan 1971	8		(1) FPDU-SDP-CE-LIB-SW	47
SDP 1972	8		(2) FPDU-SDP-CE-LIB-SW	
SDP-CE-LIB-SW 1972	8	2	(1) SDP-CE-LIB-SW	9
			(2) SDP-CE-LIB-SW	
Non-partisan 1975	8	0	(1) FPDU-SDP-CE-LIB-SW	70
CE-FPDU-SDP-LIB-SW 1975	10	2	(2) CE-LIB-SW	12
CE-LIB-SW 1976	10	0		4
SDP-FPDU-CE-LIB-SW 1977	10	0	FPDU-SDP-CE-LIB-SW	44
SDP-FPDU-CE-LIB 1978	10	1	(1) FPDU-SDP-CE-FRP-LIB-CHR-SW-CON	69
SDP-FPDU-CE-SW 1979	9	2	(2) FPDU-SDP-CE-FRP-LIB-CHR-SW-CON	
SDP-FPDU-CE-SW 1982	9	0		24
SDP-CE-LIB-SW 1982	9	0		1
SDP-CE-FRP-SW 1983	9	1	FPDU-SDP-GR-CE-FRP-CHR-SW-CON	47
CON-SDP-FRP-SW 1987	8	1	FPDU-SDP-GR-CE-FRP-CHR-SW-CON	46
CON-SDP-SW 1990	8	0		4
CE-CHR-SW-CON 1991	9	0		40
CE-SW-CON 1994	9	0		8
SDP-FPDU-GR-SW-CON 1995	10	0		25

TABLE 8.3. *Finnish cabinets since 1945*

Cabinet number	Prime minister	Date in	Formal resignation	Maximum potential duration (in days)	Duration (in days)	Government composition
1	Paasikivi III	17 Apr. 1945	8 Mar. 1946	1,171	325	FPDU–SDP–CE–LIB–SW
2	Pekkala	26 Mar. 1946	1 July 1948	828	828	FPDU–SDP–CE–SW
3	Fagerholm I	29 July 1948	1 Mar. 1950	1,068	580	SDP
4	Kekkonen I	17 Mar. 1950	17 Jan. 1951	472	306	CE–LIB–SW
5	Kekkonen II	17 Jan. 1951	2 July 1951	166	166	CE–SDP–LIB–SW
6	Kekkonen III	20 Sept. 1951	29 June 1953	1,018	648	CE–SDP–SW
7	Kekkonen IV	9 July 1953	4 Nov. 1953	360	118	CE–SW
8	Tuomioja	17 Nov. 1953	7 Mar. 1954	229	110	Non partisan
9	Törngren	5 May 1954	14 Oct. 1954	1,523	162	SW–SDP–CE
10	Kekkonen V	20 Oct. 1954	27 Jan. 1956	1,355	464	CE–SDP
11	Fagerholm II	3 Mar. 1956	22 May 1957	856	445	SDP–CE–LIB–SW
12	Sukselainen Ia	27 May 1957	2 July 1957	405	36	CE–LIB–SW
13	Sukselainen Ib	2 July 1957	2 Sept. 1957	369	62	CE–LIB
14	Sukselainen Ic	2 Sept. 1957	18 Oct. 1957	307	46	CE–SDL–LIB
15	von Fieandt	29 Nov. 1957	18 Apr. 1958	219	140	Non partisan
16	Kuuskoski	26 Apr. 1958	6 July 1958	71	71	Non partisan
17	Fagerholm III	29 Aug. 1958	4 Dec. 1958	1,402	97	SDP–CE–LIB–SW–CON
18	Sukselainen II	13 Jan. 1959	28 June 1961	1,265	897	CE
19	Miettunen I	14 July 1961	4 Feb. 1962	352	205	CE
20	Karjalainen I	13 Apr. 1962	17 Dec. 1963	1,437	613	CE–LIB–SW–CON
21	Lehto	18 Dec. 1963	12 Sept. 1964	823	269	Non partisan

Finland

22	Virolainen	12 Sept. 1964	20 Mar. 1966	555	CE–LIB–SW–CON
23	Paasio I	27 May 1966	1 Mar. 1968	644	SDP–FPDU–SDL–CE
24	Koivisto I	22 Mar. 1968	15 Mar. 1970	724	SDP–FPDU–SDL–CE–SW
25	Aura I	14 May 1970	15 July 1970	62	Non partisan
26	Karjalainen IIa	15 July 1970	26 Mar. 1971	254	CE–FPDU–SDP–LIB–SW
27	Karjalainen IIb	26 Mar. 1971	29 Oct. 1971	217	CE–SDP–LIB–SW
28	Aura II	29 Oct. 1971	2 Jan. 1972	65	Non partisan
29	Paasio II	23 Feb. 1972	19 July 1972	147	SDP
30	Sorsa I	4 Sept. 1972	4 June 1975	1,004	SDP–CE–LIB–SW
31	Liinamaa	13 June 1975	21 Sept. 1975	100	Non partisan
32	Miettunen II	30 Nov. 1975	17 Sept. 1976	292	CE–FPDU–SDP–LIB–SW
33	Miettunen III	29 Sept. 1976	11 May 1977	225	CE–LIB–SW
34	Sorsa IIa	15 May 1977	17 Jan. 1978	247	SDP–FPDU–CE–LIB–SW
35	Sorsa IIb	2 Mar. 1978	18 Mar. 1979	381	SDP–FPDU–CE–LIB
36	Koivisto II	26 May 1979	26 Jan. 1982	976	SDP–FPDU–CE–SW
37	Sorsa IIIa	19 Feb. 1982	30 Dec. 1982	314	SDP–FPDU–CE–SW
38	Sorsa IIIb	31 Dec. 1982	20 Mar. 1983	79	SDP–CE–LIB–SW
39	Sorsa IV	6 May 1983	15 Mar. 1987	1,409	SDP–CE–FRP–SW
40	Holkeri a	30 Apr. 1987	24 Aug. 1990	1,212	CON–SDP–FRP–SW
41	Holkeri b	28 Aug. 1990	17 Mar. 1991	201	CON–SDP–SW
42	Aho a	26 Apr. 1991	20 June 1994	1,151	CE–CHR–SW–CON
43	Aho b	28 June 1994	19 Mar. 1995	264	CE–SW–CON
44	Lipponen	13 Apr. 1995		1,438	SDP–FPDU–GR–SW–CON

the average duration was only around twelve months, but since 1977 governments have *formally* resigned only after presidential or parliamentary elections and stayed in power through their full four-year electoral periods. Even if minor reconstructions may have brought about a change of cabinet in our data, the maximum duration and real duration have in any case been drawn much closer to each other. Participation in government has its costs, but in the prevailing atmosphere of reduced social tension, party leaders seem to think that the benefits of participation outweigh the costs. At least there have been no great difficulties over the past twenty years in forming and maintaining even overly large coalitions. The defection of some minor partner has never changed the majority status of the government. On the other hand, primarily due to the need for qualified majorities in legislation and the endeavour to maintain the parliamentary balance of power inside the cabinet as well, smaller parties have not been excluded from participation, as the minimum-winning hypothesis would suggest.

COALITION GOVERNANCE

Rules of the Game

As most Finnish cabinet coalitions have been rather loose conglomerates of socially and ideologically divergent groups, one would expect to see the rules of the game written expressly and in detail in every coalition agreement. This, however, is not the case. It can in fact be questioned whether it is at all legitimate in Finland to speak of coalition agreements in the proper sense of the word. Coalition partners must, of course, agree on the policy outlines at the formation phase, and all parliamentary governments have drafted a programme; but following a deep-rooted tradition it is a proclamation that concentrates on large policy issues, and detailed provisions on coalition discipline, conflict management mechanisms, or division of the spoils do not fit in with its style. As far as is known, these matters are not settled in secret protocols or in explicit verbal agreements either. The everyday procedure follows established practice or *in casu* solutions.

So the meagre information contained in Tables 8.4 and 8.5 must be complemented with more general comments about the modes of coalition governance and the contents of coalition agreements.

The long period of unstable parliamentarism established the view that after a coalition breakdown it is a legitimate and normal procedure to strive for a new cabinet in the same parliament, without going to new elections. Until 1991 the dissolution of parliament was also a presidential prerogative that was used very sparingly. It is true that two times, in 1971 and 1975, President Kekkonen resorted to this measure, after relationships between Social

TABLE 8.4. *Coalition governance in Finland*

(1) Government	(2) Coalition agreement	(3) Agreement public	(4) Election rule	(5) Conflict management mechanisms	(6) Most common management mechanisms	(7) Mechanisms for most serious conflicts	(8) Coalition discipline in legislation	(9) Coalition discipline in other parliamentary behaviour	(10) Freedom of appointment	(11) Policy agreement	(12) Non-cabinet positions
FPDU–SDP–CE–LIB–SW 1945	PRE,POST	Y	N	CaC	CaC	CaC	3	3	N	1	Y
FPDU–SDP–CE–SW 1946	IE	Y	N	CaC	CaC	CaC	3	3	N	1	Y
CE–LIB–SW 1950	IE	Y	N	CaC	CaC	CaC	3	3	N	1	Y
CE–SDP–LIB–SW 1/1951	IE	Y	N	CaC	CaC	CaC	3	3	Y	1	Y
CE–SDP–SW 9/1951	POST	Y	N	CaC	CaC	CaC	3	3	N	1	Y
CE–SW 1953	IE	Y	N	IC, CaC	CaC	IC	3	3	Y	1	Y
SW–SDP–CE 5/1954	POST	Y	N	CaC	CaC	CaC	3	3	Y	1	Y
CE–SDP 10/1954	IE	Y	N	CaC	CaC	CaC	3	3	Y	1	Y
SDP–CE–LIB–SW 1956	IE	Y	N	CaC	CaC	CaC	3	3	Y	2	Y
CE–LIB–SW 1957	IE	Y	N	IC, CaC	CaC	CaC	3	3	Y	2	Y
CE–LIB 1957 *	IE	Y	N	IC	IC	IC	3	3	Y	1	Y
CE–SDL–LIB *	IE	Y	N	IC, CaC	CaC	CaC	3	3	Y	1	Y
SDP–CE–LIB–SW–CON 1958	POST	Y	N	CaC	CaC	CaC	3	3	Y	2	Y
CE–LIB–SW–CON 1962	POST	Y	N	CaC	CaC	CaC	3	3	N	2	Y
CE–LIB–SW–CON 1964	IE	Y	N	CaC	CaC	CaC	3	3	Y	1	Y
SDP–FPDU–SDL–CE 1966	POST	Y	N	CaC	CaC	CaC	3	3	Y	2	Y
SDP–FPDU–SDL–SW 1968	IE	Y	N	CaC	CaC	CaC	3	3	Y	2	Y
CE–FPDU–SDP–LIB–SW 1970	IE	Y	N	CaC	CaC	CaC	3	2	Y	3	Y
CE–SDP–LIB–SW 1971*	IE	Y	N	CaC	CaC	CaC	2	2	Y	3	Y
SDP–CE–LIB–SW 1972	POST	Y	N	CaC, IC, PCa	CaC	PCa	2	2	Y	3	Y
CE–FPDU–SDP–LIB–SW 1975	POST	Y	N	CaC, PCa	PCa	PCa	2	2	Y	3	Y
CE–LIB–SW 1976	IE	Y	N	IC, CaC, PCa	CaC	PCa	2	2	Y	1	Y
SDP–FPDU–CE–LIB–SW 1977	IE	Y	N	IC, CaC, PCa	CaC	PCa	2	2	Y	1	Y
SDP–FPDU–CE–LIB 1978 *	IE	Y	N	IC, CaC, PCa	CaC	PCa	2	2	Y	1	Y
SDP–FPDU–CE–SW 1979	POST	Y	N	CaC, PCa	CaC	PCa	2	2	Y	3	Y
SDP–CE–LIB–SW 1982	IE	Y	N	CaC, PCa	CaC	PCa	2	2	Y	3	Y
SDP–CE–LIB–SW 1982 *	IE	Y	N	CaC, PCa	CaC	PCa	2	2	Y	3	Y
SDP–CE–FRP–SW 1983	POST	Y	N	CaC, PCa	CaC	PCa	2	2	Y	3	Y
CON–SDP–FRP–SW 1987	POST	Y	N	CaC, PCa	CaC	PCa	2	2	Y	3	Y
CON–SDP–SW 1990 *	POST	Y	N	CaC, PCa	CaC	PCa	2	2	Y	3	Y
CE–CHR–SW–CON 1991	POST	Y	N	CaC, PCa	CaC	PCa	2	2	Y	3	Y
CE–SW–CON 1994 *	POST	Y	N	CaC, PCa	CaC	PCa	2	2	Y	3	Y
SDP–FPDU–GR–SW–CON 1995	POST	Y	N	CaC, PCa	CaC	PCa	2	2	Y	3	Y

* The rules of the game and the coalition agreement remained valid under a changed party composition of government.

TABLE 8.5. *Size and content of coalition agreements in Finland, 1945–1999*

Coalition	Size	General procedural rules (in %)	Specific procedural rules (in %)	Distribution of offices (in %)	Distribution of competences (in %)	Policies (in %)
FPDU–SDP–CE–LIB–SWE 1945	448	0	0	0	0	100
FPDU–SDP–CE–SWE 1946	418	0	0	0	0	100
CE–LIB–SWE 1950	248	0	0	0	0	100
CE–SDP–LIB–SWE 1951	268	0	0	0	0	100
CE–SDP–SWE 1951	413	0	0	0	0	100
CE–SWE 1953	224	0	0	0	0	100
SEW–SDP–CE 1954	354	0	0	0	0	100
CE–SDP 1954	561	0	0	0	0	100
SDP–CE–LIB–SWE 1956	225	0	0	0	0	100
CE–LIB–SWE 1957	242	0	0	0	0	100
CE–LIB 1957	242	0	0	0	0	100
CE–SDL–LIB 1957	751	0	0	0	0	100
SDP–CE–LIB–SWE–CON 1958	1,415	0	0	0	0	100
CE–LIB–SWE–CON 1962	1,103	0	0	0	0	100
CE–LIB–SWE–CON 1964	404	0	0	0	0	100
SDP–FPDU–SDL–CE 1966	777	0	0	0	0	100
SDP–FPDU–SDL–CE–SWE 1968	841	0	0	0	0	100
CE–FPDU–SDP–LIB–SWE 1970	1,723	0	0	0	0	100
CE–SDP–LIB–SWE 1971	1,723	0	0	0	0	100
SDP–CE–LIB–SWE 1972	1,936	0	0	0	0	100
CE–FPDU–SDP–LIB–SWE 1975	204	0	0	0	0	100
CE–LIB–SWE 1976	2,222	0	0	0	0	100
SDP–FPDU–CE–LIB–SWE 1977	512	0	0	0	0	100
SDP–FPDU–CE–LIB 1978	512	0	0	0	0	100
SDP–FPDU–CE–SWE 1979	1,118	0	0	0	0	100
SDP–FPDU–CE–SWE 1982	1,025	0	0	0	0	100
SDP–CE–LIB–SWE 1982	1,025	0	0	0	0	100
SDP–CE–FRP–SWE 1983	1,788	1	0	0	0	99
CON–SDP–FRP–SWE 1987	2,861	*	0	0	0	100
CON–SDP–SWE 1990	2,861	0	0	0	0	100
CE–CHR–SWE–CON 1991	2,697	0	0	*	0	100
CE–SWE–CON 1994	2,697	0	0	*	0	100
SDP–FPDU–GR–SWE–CON 1995	4,541	0	0	0	0	100

Democrats and the Centre inside the cabinet deteriorated beyond repair. Unscheduled elections now require the prime minister's initiative, but as a consequence the mechanism has become more rigid rather than more sensitive.

There has never existed a formal and separate mechanism of conflict management. In narrow coalitions the members of the influential inner circle are picked up on the basis of their personal capacities, but in large coalitions the political weight of individuals is the decisive factor. Supposing that party chairmen accept portfolios—which is currently the rule—they can settle divergent views in standing ministerial committees or in informal meetings outside them. The dominant pair in some governments of the 1970s was formed by the powerful leaders Kalevi Sorsa (SDP) and Johannes Virolainen (Centre Party). Other suitable arenas for conflict management are the informal evening meetings of the whole cabinet, as well as various *ad hoc* working groups of interested ministers (see Nousiainen 1992: 153–60). Since the beginning of the 1970s heads of the coalition parties' parliamentary groups have attended the weekly informal policy meeting. Collective policy making in a broad coalition is a slow and incremental process of negotiations and compromises, and conflict resolution is an integral part of it, a highly variable and flexible mechanism.

For many decades coalition discipline was rather weak and impossible to impose on ministerial party groups and parliamentary parties. Internal conflicts, the resolution of which was often sought through formal votes in the cabinet, became audible to the large public. This for its part intensified the propensity to deviate from the line among the members of parliament. Only in the 1970s, as their position strengthened, did the prime ministers begin authoritatively to pay attention to the integrity and internal solidarity in the government.

Cabinet solidarity has a weaker and a stronger criterion (Nousiainen 1988). According to the weaker criterion open disagreements and majority decisions taken by vote are possible; but after the decision has been reached ministers in the minority must comply with the majority stand, so that the cabinet is able to appear united vis-à-vis parliament, and they have also to use pressure on their party groups to keep them in line. According to the stronger criterion, the cabinet does not show its dissensions to the outer world but makes its decisions in central policies with at least apparent unanimity. In a heterogeneous government this presupposes negotiations and arbitration behind closed doors and effective discipline within parliamentary parties; it might also cause a delay in decision making and the narrowing down of the cabinet agenda.

When assuming the leadership in spring 1977 of his second government, a broad peoples' front coalition, Kalevi Sorsa reminded his colleagues of the bad experiences of the preceding cabinets and announced that the cabinet will not take votes on central policy issues. Prime Minister Koivisto repeated this principle in 1979. In those governments, in which the recalcitrant radical left also participated, this norm created many difficulties. The strong, divergent attitudes of the Communist group repeatedly threatened to pull the cabinet apart.

After these experiences Sorsa presented in 1983 his fourth cabinet as a stronger standard of parliamentarism: 'Prime minister Sorsa and leaders of all cabinet groups repeated that the cabinet purports to sit the whole four-year electoral period. Sorsa took it for granted that the cabinet makes its decisions in all central issues on the basis of unanimity' (*Helsingin Sanomat*, 10 May 1983, p. 8). In the following cabinets, chaired by Harri Holkeri (CON), Esko Aho (CE), and Paavo Lipponen (SDP), the same standard has been followed without major problems. The latest coalitions have been based on the understanding that the cabinet shall appear to the outside world as a united body and that there will be coalition discipline in parliament on all policies except those explicitly exempted. Religion and various 'moral' issues have traditionally formed an area within which the members of parliament have been allowed much freedom of movement.

Offices

As was mentioned above, the nomination of specific persons to assigned ministerial posts is for the most part an internal party affair. Only an experienced and strong *formateur* can use a veto to block the candidacy of an unsuitable person. Kalevi Sorsa has summarized his multiple experiences as follows (Murto 1994: 234):

The parties themselves must be able to select capable and politically suitable persons. This is the baseline situation. But of course during the bargaining process the *formateur* will talk with party delegates about their ministerial candidates, and he can also present his own views because he must, in addition to the ministers' individual competence, also consider the cabinet's atmosphere and ability to concerted action.

The foreign minister and minister of defence form a special category; their nomination presupposes the consent of the president of the republic. At times President Kekkonen also tried to influence other ministerial nominations, sometimes by suggesting specific individuals or, what happened more often, by presenting lists of persons whom he would not accept (Murto 1994: 238).

The parties will want to have politically strong personalities in coalitions, the prime minister for his part politically loyal individuals. However, because of the collective tradition of the cabinet, the formal jurisdictions of individual ministers have not been sufficient for autonomous policy making. The effective policy of a government may be made dependent on arrangements at three levels: the appointment of individual politicians to the leadership of policy sectors; the allocation of portfolios between participant parties; and the total partisan structure of the coalition. It seems that Finnish cabinet policies in different issue areas are conditioned primarily through the partisan structure of the coalition, less through the allocation of portfolios between parties, and least of all through the appointment of individual politicians (Nousiainen 1994: 103).

Table 8.6 shows the distribution of portfolios among parties. According to established practice, from five to seven important portfolios are reserved for each of the two leading coalition partners, and the minor parties have to be contented with what is left. The best indication of the permanent links between parties and policy sectors is the strong representation of the Centre Party in the Ministry of Agriculture. But generally, the distribution of portfolios among four or five parties is such a complicated process that the parties have not been able permanently to 'colonize' the ministries within their areas of interest; portfolios change partisan hands. Since the 1970s ministers of labour have represented Communists, Social Democrats, Agrarians, centrist populists, and Conservatives; their policy objectives have varied, but the coalition lathe has smoothed off the rough edges.

The structure of the Finnish cabinet is uncomplicated in the sense that it does not include any junior ministers. But the problem of 'divided portfolios' is relevant in the sense that it is an established practice to appoint two full ministers to the most important ministries, who regularly come from different parties. They have their own jurisdictions within which they basically operate independently of each other. However, they are of course able to watch each other very carefully and to report the doings of their colleague to the party and to the coalition leadership. Table 8.6 gets rather complicated because of the multiple ministers per department and redistribution of portfolios among parties.

No government programme has touched upon the question of distribution of civil service offices or other positions in the public sector. However, the allocation of jobs—both at the national and the provincial level—on party-political grounds remains the most visible form of cabinet patronage in Finland. Throughout the whole period in office the partners jealously watch each other and agree on the balanced distribution of offices. The practice is facilitated by the fact that many offices in both the central and provincial administration are filled by the cabinet or by the president of the republic on the recommendation of the cabinet. In earlier years the Social Democrats and Agrarians used to agree on major appointment packages to preserve the mutual balance; this task was specifically assigned to one of the party ministers. Even though President Kekkonen once threatened to open such a package and even though the most recent governments have promised to drop the practice, it still exists.

TABLE 8.6. Distribution of cabinet ministerships in Finnish coalitions, 1945–1999

Cabinet number	Cabinet	(1) Prime Minister	(2) Finance	(3) Foreign	(4) Interior	(5) Social Affairs	(6) Trade and Industry	(7) Justice
1	Paasikivi III	N	LIB/SW,SDP	N,FPDU,N	FPDU,CE	SDP,SDP/CE,SDP,FPDU	N,/SDP	CE
2	Pekkala	FPDU	SW,SDP	N,/FPDU,SDP	FPDU,CE	FPDU,CE/SDP	SDP	FPDU
3	Fagerholm I	SDP	SDP,SDP	N,SDP	SDP,SDP	SDP,SDP,SDP	SDP,/SDP	SDP
4	Kekkonen I	CE	CE,SW	N,LIB	CE,CE	SW,CE,CE/LIB	LIB	LIB
5	Kekkonen II	CE	SDP,SW	N	CE	CE,SDP,SDP	SDP	LIB
6	Kekkonen III	CE	SDP,CE	N/CE,/SW	CE	SW/SDP,CE,SDP	SDP	SW
7	Kekkonen IV	CE	CE,SW	SW	CE	N,CE	N	SW
8	Tuomioja	N	N,N	N,N	N	N,N,N	N,N	N
9	Törngren	SW	CE,CE	CE	SDP	SDP,CE,SDP	SDP	N
10	Kekkonen V	CE	SDP,CE	CE	SDP	SDP,SDP,SDP	SDP	N
11	Fagerholm II	SDP	SDP,CE	SW	SDP	LIB,SDP,SDP	CE	SDP/N
12	Sukselainen Ia	CE	SW,CE	CE	LIB	LIB	LIB	N
13	Sukselainen Ib	CE	CE,CE	CE	LIB	LIB,LIB	LIB	N
14	Sukselainen Ic	CE	CE,LIB	CE	N	SDL,SDL	LIB,N	N
15	von Fieandt	N	N,N	N	N	N,N	N	N
16	Kuuskoski	N	N	N	N	N	N	N
17	Fagerholm III	SDP	CON,CE	CE/	CE	SDP,SDP	SDP,CON	SW
18	Sukselainen II	CE	CE,CE	N/CE	CE	CE,CE	CE/N	N/CE
19	Miettunen I	CE	CE,CE	CE	CE	CE,CE	N	CE
20	Karjalainen I	CE	CON,N/CE	LIB,/N	CE	N,CON	CON	SW
21	Lehto	N	N,N	N	N	N,N	N,N	N
22	Virolainen	CE	LIB,CON	CE	CE	LIB,N	CON	SW

Finland

#	Cabinet							
23	Paasio I	SDP	SDP,FPDU	CE	SDP	FPDU,CE	SDP	SDL
24	Koivisto I	SDP	SDP,FPDU	CE	SDP	FPDU,CE	SW,SDP	SDL
25	Aura I	N	N	N	N	N,N	N	N
26	Karjalainen IIa	CE	SW,SDP	SDP	CE	FPDU,CE	LIB,SDP	FPDU
27	Karjalainen IIb	CE	SW,SDP	SDP	CE	SDP,CE	LIB,SDP	SDP
28	Aura II	N	N,N	N,N	N	N	N	N
29	Paasio II	SDP	SDP,SDP	SDP	SDP	SDP,SDP	SDP,SDP	SDP
30	Sorsa I	SDP	CE,SDP,/N	CE	N	SDP,CE	SW,SDP	SDP
31	Liinamaa	N	N,N	N	N,N	N,N	N,N	N
32	Miettunen II	CE	SDP,N	SDP	SDP,FPDU	LIB,SDP	SDP,N	SW
33	Miettunen III	CE	N,CE	CE	CE	LIB,CE	LIB,SW	SW
34	Sorsa IIa	SDP	SDP,N	CE	CE	SDP,CE	SDP	LIB
35	Sorsa IIb	SDP	SDP,N	CE	CE	SDP,CE	SDP	LIB
36	Koivisto II	SDP	CE,SDP	CE	CE,SDP	SDP,CE	SDP,N	SW
37	Sorsa IIIa	SDP	CE,SDP	SW	SDP,CE	SDP,CE	CE,N	SW
38	Sorsa IIIb	SDP	CE,SDP	SW	SDP,CE	SDP,CE	CE,LIB	SW
39	Sorsa IV	SDP	CE,FRP	CE	SDP,SDP/	CE,SDP	SDP,SDP	SW
40	Holkeri a	CON	SDP,CON	SDP	SDP	CON,SDP	CON,CON	SDP
41	Holkeri b	CON	SDP,CON	SDP	SDP	CON,SDP	CON,CON	SDP
42	Aho a	CE	CON	CE,CHR	CE	CE	CE,CON	CE
43	Aho b	CE	CON	CE/N	CE	CE	CE,CON	CE
44	Lipponen	SDP	CON,SDP	SDP	SW,SDP	SDP,FPDU	SDP,SW	CON

TABLE 8.6 cont.

Cabinet number	Cabinet	(8) Defence	(9) Education	(10) Agriculture	(11) Public Works and Transport	(12) Labour	(13) Supply	(14) Environment	(15) Minister at the Prime Minister's Office
1	Paasikivi III	FPDU	FPDU	CE,CE	SDP,FPDU,/CE,/SDP	—	CE,SDP,SDP/SDP	—	FPDU,/SDP/,/SDP
2	Pekkala	SDP,FPDU	FPDU/CE	CE,CE	CE,SDP	—	CE,FPDU,SDP	—	SDP/FPDU
3	Fagerholm I	SDP	SDP	SDP,SDP	SDP,SDP,/SDP	—	SDP/,SDP/	—	SDP/
4	Kekkonen I	CE	CE	CE,CE	CE,CE,CE	—	—	—	
5	Kekkonen II	SDP	CE	CE,SDP	SDP,CE,SDP	—	—	—	CE
6	Kekkonen III	SDP	SDP	CE,SDP,CE	SDP,CE,SDP	—	—	—	
7	Kekkonen IV	CE	CE	CE	N,CE	—	—	—	
8	Tuomioja	N	N	N,N	N,N	—	—	—	
9	Törngren	SDP	CE	CE,SDP	CE,SDP	—	—	—	
10	Kekkonen V	SDP	CE	CE	CE,SDP	—	—	—	
11	Fagerholm II	SDP	CE	CE,CE	CE,SDP	—	—	—	CE
12	Sukselainen Ia	CE	CE	CE,SW	CE,SW	—	—	—	SW
13	Sukselainen Ib	CE	CE	CE	CE,CE	—	—	—	LIB
14	Sukselainen Ic	LIB	CE	CE,SDL	CE,SDL	—	—	—	SDL
15	von Fieandt	N	N	N	N,N	—	—	—	N
16	Kuuskoski	N	N	N,N	N,N	—	—	—	N
17	Fagerholm III	CON	LIB	CE,CON	CE,SDP	—	—	—	
18	Sukselainen II	CE	CE	CE,CE	CE,CE	—	—	—	
19	Miettunen I	CE	CE	CE,CE	CE/CE	—	—	—	
20	Karjalainen I	CE	LIB	CE,SW	CE,N/CE	—	—	—	

Finland

21	Lehto	N	N	N	N	—	—	—	N/
22	Virolainen	CE	CON	CE,CE	SW,CE	—	—	—	—
23	Paasio I	CE	SDP	CE,SDP	FPDU,CE	—	—	—	SDP
24	Koivisto I	CE	CE	CE	FPDU,SDP	—	—	—	—
25	Aura I	N	N	N	N	—	—	—	N
26	Karjalainen IIa	SW	LIB,SDP	CE	FPDU	N	—	—	N
27	Karjalainen IIb	SW	LIB,SDP	CE	SDP	SDP	—	—	—
28	Aura II	N	N,N	N	N	SDP	—	—	SDP
29	Paasio II	SDP	SDP,N	SDP	SDP	N	—	—	—
30	Sorsa I	SW	SDP/N/SDP,CE	CE	LIB	SDP	—	—	—
31	Liinamaa	N	N	N	N	SDP	—	—	N
32	Miettunen II	SW	CE,FPDU	CE	FPDU	N	—	—	CE
33	Miettunen III	LIB	CE	CE	SW	FPDU	—	—	CE
34	Sorsa IIa	CE	SW,FPDU	CE	FPDU	CE	—	—	—
35	Sorsa IIb	CE	LIB,FPDU	CE	FPDU	FPDU	—	—	—
36	Koivisto II	CE	SW,FPDU	CE	FPDU	FPDU	—	—	—
37	Sorsa IIIa	CE	FPDU,SDP	CE	FPDU	FPDU	—	—	—
38	Sorsa IIIb	CE	SDP,SDP	CE	SDP	SDP	—	—	—
39	Sorsa IV	CE	SDP,SW	CE	SDP	FRP	—	/SDP	—
40	Holkeri a	SW	SW,SDP	CON	FRP	SDP	—	SDP	—
41	Holkeri b	SW	SW,SDP	CON	SDP	SDP	—	SDP	CON
42	Aho a	SW	CON,CE	CE	SW	CON	—	CON,CON	—
43	Aho b	SW	CON,CE	CE	SW	CON	—	CON,CON	—
44	Lipponen	CON	CON	N	CON	SDP	—	GR	—

Policies

The published government programme only includes items dealing with coalition policies. It has changed considerably during the period under consideration, briefly from a vague policy proclamation towards an explicit policy agreement. The programmematic development can be roughly divided into three phases.

Before World War II, government programmes were typically vague and circuitous declarations written by routine administrators. They contained few innovations and had only little directing importance for governmental operations.

After the war, programmes originated as compromises and adjustments between big interests, and contained in varying melanges new and recurrent agenda items, mostly focusing on the economic and social security field. As they often reflected more the hopes of participants than real potentialities, they tended to boil down into pseudo-agendas which were used to assuage frustrations of constituency groups.

Since the mid-1960s the tone of politics became more peaceful and rational, and increased tax revenues improved the prospects of innovative policies. Government programmes were formulated more carefully than before, written as detailed and concrete documents striving to outline comprehensively and authoritatively public policies for the coming years. A centrally coordinated monitoring system was added at the beginning of the 1980s. Political motives could also be seen behind the latest turn. With the rise of the SDP as a leading force, Agrarians had fears with regard to governmental policy, and they insisted on making more detailed advance agreements on policy lines and the goals of coalitions. But irrespective of party politics, the change was brought about primarily by an enormously accentuated technocratic-administrative thinking in an atmosphere of excessive optimism with regard to chances of successful social planning. This was indicated by the fact that basic value-laden goals were almost totally dropped from these documents, while the technocratic tone of the contents was decisively strengthened (Koskiaho 1973: 193–218).

But even today, the effective cabinet agenda is not confirmed in the coalition agreement. As non-participation in long-lasting governments has a high cost, the party leaders' 'area of tolerance' in the bargaining process is broad. The leaders are willing to compromise on their objectives and to limit their decisive preferences to those principles that are of the greatest concern to their party (Luebbert 1986: 44–53). This strategic thinking sets the tone of the coalition agreement: it is not a detailed listing of measures to be implemented but a collection of mutually agreed-upon principles, good purposes, and broad goals. These principles are later raised on the concrete agenda for operationalization and specification that takes place on different arenas of the coalition system.

Finnish practice comes close to this model. Even the most recent coalition agreements are a mixture of action programmes and declarations. These documents, running up to about 15 to 20 pages, are prepared in a 'something-for-everybody' mode and do not yet include implementation schedules, cost estimates, or draft bills. So agenda formation is a process that continues throughout a cabinet's life. At best the government programme provides a topic for discussion and general direction for a particular project, but details have to be ironed out on the basis of varying party preferences in a complicated negotiation and mediation process. Party leaders are well aware that the real settlement of the issues takes place later; by including many kinds of items in the declaration they seek tentative assurance of voice in that settlement. It will be very difficult for the cabinet partners to come up with new policy innovations concerning social or economic reforms, if these are not already agreed upon during the bargaining process. In this sense the programme has a good deal of steering power in shaping future visions of politics (Wiberg 1991: 39).

Mutual dependence prevails between the tone of the coalition agreement and constitutional collectivism, but it is difficult to say exactly what is cause and what is effect. The relative vagueness of points in the government programme necessitates collective treatment of the problems that need to be solved. On the other hand, party leaders may be content with general formulations—in this way they save time and effort in the government formation phase—because they know that all costly and politically sensitive issues have to be processed on the collective arena in any case.

Traditionally the proclamation has been entered in the minutes of the Council of State at some of the first meetings of a new cabinet, and published in the newspapers. Following the new constitutional requirement the Lipponen cabinet presented in 1995 its programme to parliament, but the procedure did not have any immediate impact on the form or substance of the document. Its various policy items were, however, soon operationalized more carefully than before to form a governmental 'project portfolio' for coming years.

CABINET TERMINATION

Table 8.6 includes all cabinet terminations since 1945. As far as the seven caretaker cabinets are concerned it suffices to say that in accordance with their initial purpose they have remained in office only until such time as a new partisan government has been negotiated. In three cases this has required extraordinary elections.

The habitual and largely valid model for explaining the dissolution of governments in Finland is a combination of the structural attributes approach

TABLE 8.7. *Cabinet termination in Finland, 1945–1999*

Cabinet number	Cabinet	Mechanisms of cabinet termination					Terminal events					Policy area(s)	Comments
		Technical		Discretionary									
		(1) Regular parliamentary election	(2) Other constitutional reason	(3) Early parliamentary election	(5) Voluntary enlargement of coalition	(6) Cabinet defeated by opposition in parliament	(7) Conflict between coalition parties: policy	(8) Intra-party conflict in coalition party or parties	(9) Elections (non-parliamentary)	(12) Economic event	(13) Personal event		
1	Paasikivi III		X						X				Presidential election
2	Pekkala	X											
3	Fagerholm I		X						X				Presidential election
4	Kekkonen I				X								New majority coalition formed
5	Kekkonen II	X											
6	Kekkonen III						CE,SPD					2	Lowering of cost of production
7	Kekkonen IV					X							Housing policy
8	Tuomioja			X									Early election to solve parliamentary deadlock
9	Törngren						SW,SDP					2	Stabilization policy
10	Kekkonen V		X						X				Presidential election
11	Fagerholm II						CE,SPD	SDP;L				2	PM Fagerholm defeated in party convention
12	Sukselainen Ia						SW,CE			X		2,5	Swedish ministers resigned
13	Sukselainen Ib				X								Minority coalition enlarged
14	Sukselainen Ic					X	CE,LIB					2	Interpellation on economic policy
15	von Fieandt					X							Dissatisfaction with a non-partisan government
16	Kuuskoski	X											

#	Cabinet						Coalition	#	Event
17	Fagerholm III						CE,SDP	3	Crisis in Finno–Soviet relationships
18	Sukselainen II		X			X			PM Sukselainen sentenced for malfeasance
19	Miettunen I		X						Soviet note, parliament dissolved
20	Karjalainen I						CE,CON	2	Conflict over increased taxation
21	Lehto	X							New partisan coalition formed
22	Virolainen	X							
23	Paasio I	X							Presidential election
24	Koivisto I	X			X				
25	Aura I	X							New partisan government formed
26	Karjalainen IIa						FPDU,CE	2	Price decontrol
27	Karjalainen IIb						CE,SDP	2,10	Agricultural policy
28	Aura II	X							Early election to solve parliamentary deadlock
29	Paasio II	X			X				Single–party government replaced by a coalition
30	Sorsa I						CE,SDP	2	Regional policy
31	Liinamaa	X							Early election to solve parliamentary deadlock
32	Miettunen II	X							Budget
33	Miettunen III						FPDU,SDP	2	Minority coalition enlarged
34	Sorsa IIa		X						
35	Sorsa IIb		X			X			Presidential election
36	Koivisto II					X			Presidential election
37	Sorsa IIIa						FPDU,SDP		Defence budget
38	Sorsa IIIb	X							
39	Sorsa IV	X						2,8	
40	Holkeri a		X						
41	Holkeri b		X				FRP,CON	2,5	Conflict over budget
42	Aho a		X						
43	Aho b	X					CHR,CE	3	EU membership

Finland 291

and the 'critical events' approach. According to this model cabinet durability in the sense of an 'inherent amount of stability' is low because of the fragmented party system and the life of a coalition can be predicted to be very risky even at the time of its formation. The participants' ability to bear stress is low, and various problems in the policy arena sooner or later generate insurmountable conflicts which destroy the willingness of at least one governing partner to continue the partnership (cf. Browne, Frendreis, and Gleiber 1986: 94).

It is also true that about half of the twenty-seven majority coalitions have dissolved—or changed shape without formally resigning—before regular elections because of policy conflicts between coalition parties. The cause of the conflict in these cases has not been an individual exogenous event in the coalition's environment but closely linked with the cabinet's decision making process. An insignificant policy issue could cause the partners to drift apart, as they are already bored with each other. Conflicts have most often been generated in economic and welfare policies (cf. Nousiainen 1993). It is not surprising to find that the longer the maximum duration of a cabinet, the greater is the risk of conflictual dissolution of the coalition. In our data the average maximum duration of cabinets whose life terminated in internal conflicts was thirty-six months.

As far as 'technical mechanisms' of cabinet termination are concerned, it is to be noted that it has been a well-established habit to submit the cabinet's resignation after every presidential election, even when the same person is re-elected. The president accepts the resignation, and a new bargaining process is set into motion. Only President Koivisto, who promoted the aims towards a genuine parliamentary system, ended this practice after his re-election in 1988 (see Koivisto 1994: 350). Later on, in 1994, the Aho cabinet remained in office in spite of a new head of state being elected, and the new president Martti Ahtisaari was reconciled to this. At the time the president's own party SDP was the main opposition group.

The minority governments' termination profile is notably different. Their position as temporary solutions is reflected in the fact that only one of them has persisted until the next regular election. Only two of them have been defeated by opposition and two have been dissolved internally. They have met their fate because of varying external events—economic, international, personal, etc.—that they have been unable to control. On two occasions the president has proclaimed unscheduled elections in order to facilitate the formation of a majority coalition, and similarly in two cases a minority government has resigned in favour of a new majority coalition without any external push.

During the last two decades, Finland has been governed by broad and relatively stable majority governments. The restructuring of the latest Sorsa, Holkeri, and Aho governments has been insignificant, because the portfolios remaining vacant after the withdrawal of an individual splinter party have been filled from within the coalition, and the numerical status of the cabinet in parliament has not changed. The stability of the basic coalition structure means that the policy elasticity of the parties has considerably increased but their coalition elasticity during the constitutional inter-election period has correspondingly diminished (Nousiainen 1988: 245–6).

The concepts of policy elasticity and coalition elasticity refer to the ways in which government parties respond to internal coalition stress: they either vary governmental policies or coalition structure (which means easy dissolution of coalitions and a new bargaining process). Beginning from the 1980s, parties have stayed in the government, which means that they are forced to compromise on policies more than before.

The importance of the 'electoral consideration' for the coalition behaviour of parties has paradoxically diminished during the period under consideration. In the hectic years of the short-pulsating parliamentarism, the parties deliberated the government question very carefully, always bearing in mind the reactions of the electorate and the perpetual policy compromising. They knew they would not be in opposition for very long and that they would soon be in a new bargaining situation. The approach of a new election caused extra strain and tension in the cabinet and very easily a total rupture of cooperation on secondary policy issues.

In the prevailing system of consolidated parliamentary governance there is a real crush to the government: party leaders want to get involved in effective decision making rather than staying in an unprofitable opposition for four years. This is true in spite of the propensity among the voters to react negatively to cabinet participation and the fact that the cost of participation in this sense has increased.

ELECTORAL PERFORMANCE

The prime minister and the cabinet cannot decide on new elections at their own discretion, but they must have an aim to constitutionally ordained elections. The cabinet can, however, manipulate the electoral situation. Recent research has also revealed a clear election cycle in the cabinets' economic policies (Paloheimo, Wiberg, and Koiranen 1993). There has been a very conscious effort to buy votes by manipulating the economy. Ever since the late 1970s, there has been a budget deficit every time there has been a general election. Also, income distribution between the public and the private sector has fluctuated in relation to elections. In the private sector, the proportion of disposable national income has always increased in election years. Between general elections, the government proportion of national disposable income has

TABLE 8.8. *Electoral costs/benefits of government parties in Finland, 1945–1999 (in % of votes)*

Government	In office at time of election	Election year	FPDU	SDL	SDP	CE	FRP	LIB	CHR	SWE	CON	Government
FPDU–SDP–CE–LIB–SWE 1945–6	N	1948	–3.5	—	+1.2	+2.9	—	—	—	–0.2	—	–0.9
FPDU–SDP–CE–SWE 1946–8	Y	1948	–3.5	—	+1.2	+2.9	—	—	—	–0.2	—	+0.4
SDP 1948–50	N	1951	—	—	+0.2	—	—	—	—	—	—	+0.2
CE–LIB–SWE 1950–1	N	1951	—	—	—	–1.0	—	+1.8	—	–0.1	—	+0.7
CE–SDP–LIB–SWE 1951	Y	1951	—	—	+0.2	–1.0	—	+1.8	—	–0.1	—	+0.9
CE–SDP–SWE 1951–3	N	1954	—	—	–0.3	+0.9	—	—	—	–0.6	—	0
CE–SWE 1953	N	1954	—	—	—	+0.9	—	—	—	–0.6	—	+0.3
NON-PARTISAN 1953–4	Y	1954	—	—	—	—	—	—	—	—	—	—
SWE–SDP–CENT 1954	N	1958	—	—	–3.0	–1.0	—	—	—	–0.3	—	–4.3
CE–SDP 1954–6	N	1958	—	—	–3.0	–1.0	—	—	—	—	—	–4.0
SDP–CE–LIB–SWE 1956–7	N	1958	—	—	–3.0	–1.0	—	–2.0	—	–0.3	—	–6.3
CE–LIB–SWE 1957	N	1958	—	—	—	–1.0	—	–2.0	—	–0.3	—	–3.3
CE–LIB 1957	N	1958	—	—	—	–1.0	—	–2.0	—	—	—	–3.0
CE–SDL–LIB 1957	N	1958	—	+1.7	—	–1.0	—	–2.0	—	—	—	–1.3
NON-PARTISAN 1957–8	N	1958	—	—	—	—	—	—	—	—	—	—
NON-PARTISAN 1958	Y	1958	—	—	—	—	—	—	—	—	—	—
SDP–CE–LIB–SWE–CON 1958–9	N	1962	—	—	–3.7	–0.1	—	+0.4	—	–0.3	–0.3	–4.0
CE 1959–61	N	1962	—	—	—	–0.1	—	—	—	—	—	–0.1
CE 1961–2	Y	1962	—	—	—	–0.1	—	—	—	—	—	–0.1
CE–LIB–SWE–CON 1962–3	N	1966	—	—	—	–1.8	—	+0.2	—	–0.4	–1.2	–3.2

Finland

NON-PARTISAN 1963–4	N	1966	—	—	—	—	—	—	—	—
CE–LIB–SWE–CON 1964–6	Y	1966	—	—	—	—	—	—	−1.2	−3.2
SDP–FPDU–SDL–CE 1966–8	N	1970	−4.4	−1.2	−3.8	−1.8	—	—	—	−13.5
SDP–FPDU–SDL–CE–SWE 1968–70	Y	1970	−4.4	−1.2	−3.8	−4.1	—	−0.4	—	−13.9
NON-PARTISAN 1970	N	1972	—	—	—	−4.1	—	−0.4	—	—
CE–FPDU–SDP–LIB–SWE 1970–1	N	1972	+0.4	—	+2.4	−0.7	—	−0.2	—	+1.1
CE–SDP–LIB–SWE 1971	N	1972	—	—	+2.4	−0.7	—	−0.2	—	+0.7
NON-PARTISAN 1971–2	Y	1972	—	—	—	—	—	—	—	—
SDP 1972	N	1975	—	—	−0.9	—	—	—	—	−0.9
SDP–CE–LIB–SWE 1972–5	N	1975	—	—	−0.9	+1.2	—	−0.4	—	−1.0
NON-PARTISAN 1975	Y	1975	—	—	—	—	—	—	—	—
CE–FPDU–SDP–LIB–SWE 1975–6	N	1979	−1.0	—	−1.0	−0.3	—	−0.5	—	−3.4
CE–LIB–SWE 1976–7	N	1979	—	—	—	−0.3	—	−0.5	—	−1.4
SDP–FPDU–CE–LIB–SWE 1977–8	N	1979	−1.0	—	−1.0	−0.3	—	−0.5	—	−3.4
SDP–FPDU–CE–LIB 1978–9	Y	1979	−1.0	—	−1.0	−0.3	—	—	—	−2.9
SDP–FPDU–CE–SWE 1979–82	N	1983	−4.4	—	+2.8	+0.3	—	+0.4	—	−0.9
SDP–FPDU–CE–SWE 1982	N	1983	−4.4	—	+2.8	+0.3	—	+0.4	—	−0.9
SDP–CE–SWE 1982–3	Y	1983	—	—	+2.8	+0.3	—	+0.4	—	+3.5
SDP–CE–FRP–SWE 1983–7	Y	1987	—	—	−2.6	0	−3.4	+0.7	—	−5.3
CON–SDP–FRP–SWE 1987–90	N	1991	—	—	−2.0	—	−1.5	+0.2	−3.8	−7.1
CON–SDP–SWE 1990–1	Y	1991	—	—	−2.0	—	—	+0.2	−3.8	−5.6
CE–CHR–SWE–CON 1991–4	N	1995	—	—	—	−5.0	—	−0.4	−1.4	−6.9
CE–SWE–CON 1994–5	Y	1995	—	—	—	−5.0	—	−0.4	−1.4	−6.8
MEANS			−2.6	+0.3	−0.9	−0.7	−2.5	−0.4	−0.1	−0.2	−1.7	−2.8

increased. The money supply has also increased above the trend during election years.

The rigidity of the party system as a whole and the popular affiliation to it is reflected in the fact that up until the 1980s, there was no regularity with respect to electoral costs or benefits of government participation. In most elections the relative strength of parties did not change to any significant extent. The parliamentary election in 1970 was exceptional as the populistic Rural Party gained in strength in both the social and geographical peripheries of society and caused losses to all government parties.

The situation changed profoundly in the 1980s. Along with the bridging of the old ideological cleavages, the juxtaposition between the government and opposition emerged in the minds of many people as the crucial question, and in the three last elections government parties have suffered a clear defeat. The changes in the shares of votes and seats do not compare with what happens in majority elections; but the reaction of the electorate has been clear enough to bring about a fundamental change in the coalition structure. So there is an apparent contradiction in the latest development: while parties are much keener than before to participate in government, governing is less rewarding from an electoral point of view than in the immediate post-war period.

CONCLUSION

Finland represents among Western European parliamentary systems a variant which is characterized by a fragmented party system and a permanent minority situation. The proportional electoral system has always precluded the possibility that one of the parties could alone command a parliamentary majority. In these circumstances coalition-building is the rule and the formation of single-party cabinets a rare exception, justified only by a complete deadlock. Because the accepted rules of parliamentary behaviour demand majority governments, minority coalitions are also understood as stopgap solutions that will have to do because there is no better option.

The analysis has indicated, however, that within this general frame the mode of parliamentary governance has changed essentially. Up until the 1970s everyday practice followed the traditional model according to which ideological and policy differences between parties and party families were sharp and most salient, and the policy pursuit motive was a major factor in government formation, functioning, and termination. This meant a careful selection of cabinet partners, an easy withdrawal from the bargaining process, as well as a minimal ability to tolerate stress, manifested in the tendency for coalitions to dissolve in the face of even minor difficulties. It is indeed a more general observation that ideological diversity within governments is a significant determinant of cabinet survival rates in Western European regimes (Warwick 1994: 146). Office-seeking behaviour as such was not the first concern as the visibility of top politicians was relatively poor, and opportunities to influence policy making in the legislative process outside the government were exceptionally good. The pursuit of votes did not presuppose the use of huge resources because the parties' electorates were stable and the number of marginal voters was small.

In certain respects the recent development is paradoxical if we think of vote-seeking, office-seeking, and policy-seeking as three independent and mutually conflicting forms of behaviour (Strøm 1990a). Electoral party competition has intensified and the importance of vote-seeking behaviour has consequently increased. But at the same time office-seeking behaviour has increased to such an extent that in the last coalition formation cases practically all parliamentary parties were willing to enter the government and cooperate with anyone. As has been indicated, the inter-party bargaining situation is much less constrained than before. The main task of the *formateur* party is to exclude part of the desirous, not to induce parties to join in order to build a majority. The propensity of coalition partners to yield and compromise in policy issues is reflected in the considerable growth of actual cabinet durations. But electoral volatility has at the same time increased, and during the last two decades government participation has included clear electoral costs.

In the new parliamentary arrangement the control of political office certainly produces direct and independent benefits. In a political society dominated by the mass media, parties are profiled largely through their leaders, and they require everyday visibility. In consequence, for the smallest parties the holding of cabinet portfolios has a considerable electoral value. Office-seeking and policy-seeking goals do not necessarily contradict each other. Parties, of course, pursue office instrumentally, as a precondition for policy influence. In a consensus-oriented society the cabinet is in many ways in the nucleus of national problem-solving and conflict management, and the parties want to be where effective decisions are made. Partisan policy strategies have transformed from abrupt and forced changes towards a more incremental approach that calls for cooperation and long-range participation.

A separate explanation is needed for the contradiction between vote-seeking pursuit and office-seeking pursuit, which have both been accentuated in the latest development. The question, briefly, is how to weigh safe benefits in the short term and perhaps very large but uncertain costs in the long term. The strategic thinking of parties apparently puts the main stress on the former. As there no longer are very many fixed ideological commitments involving difficult compromising but as the tremendous increase in electoral volatility makes the future unpredictable in any case, it seems wise to secure the short-term realization of certain policy goals in the negotiation process of a broad coalition. The losses suffered in proportional elections are not necessarily disastrous and do not completely exclude a party from the future coalition formation process. So it is quite possible that in pursuing office a party also maximizes its effect on public policy. Following Strøm's (1990a) terminology, the systemic office benefit differentials and policy influence differentials between governing and opposition parties seem to have become merged.

And finally: How can we explain the transformation of closed ideological party behaviour to pragmatic consensual politics within such a short space of time? A good answer requires an extensive historical and sociological analysis of Finnish society. Here reference is made only to some apparent crucial factors. First, for many decades there prevailed a forced national unanimity in one of the most important policy sectors, i.e. foreign policy, and the foreign policy factor also largely determined coalition building. Second, the neocorporatist policy making mode that became established in the 1960s, notably in the form of extensive incomes policy agreements between the government and organized labour market interests, attenuated the traditional conflict lines and helped to generate pragmatic behaviour among the actors. Third, the centrality of a large agrarian party has always bridged the cap between the right and the left and prevented bloc division as seen in Sweden, for instance. And last, the structural change from agrarian to industrial society in the 1960s and 1970s was probably faster than in any other Western European country. It destroyed, at a single stroke, many old structures and loyalties and took the political parties by surprise. The process resulted in a sudden endeavour to political renewal and a rush towards the political and geographical centre. Here the expanding middle class forms a large electoral base and politically visible and effective interest-bound policies can be made.

REFERENCES

Browne, Eric C., Frendreis, John B., and Gleiber, Dennis W. (1986). 'Dissolution of Governments in Scandinavia: A Critical Events Perspective'. *Scandinavian Political Studies*, 9: 93–110.
Koivisto, Mauno (1994). *Kaksi kautta I. Muistikuvia ja merkintöjä 1982–1994*. Helsinki: Kirjayhtymä.
——(1995). *Kaksi kautta II. Historian tekijät*. Helsinki: Kirjayhtymä.
Koskiaho, Briitta (1973). 'Hallitusohjelma ei ole puu', in Harto Hakovirta and Tapio Koskiaho (eds.), *Suomen hallitukset ja hallitusohjelmat 1945–1973*. Helsinki: Gaudeamus.
Lane, Jan-Erik, and Ersson, Svante O. (1991). *Politics and Society in Western Europe*. London: Sage.
Laver, Michael J., and Schofield, Norman (1990). *Multiparty Government: The Politics of Coalition in Western Europe*. Oxford: Oxford University Press.

Luebbert, Gregory M. (1986). *Comparative Democracy: Policymaking and Governing Coalitions in Europe and Israel*. New York: Columbia University Press.

Murto, Eero (1994). *Pääministeri*. Helsinki: Painatuskeskus.

Nousiainen, Jaakko (1988). 'Bureaucratic Tradition, Semi-Presidential Rule and Parliamentary Government: The Case of Finland'. *European Journal of Political Research*, 16: 229–49.

——(1992). *Politiikan huipulla: Ministerit ja ministeristöt Suomen parlamentaarisessa järjestelmässä*. Juva: WSOY.

——(1993). 'Decision-Making, Policy Content and Conflict Resolution in Western European Cabinets', in Jean Blondel and Ferdinand Müller-Rommel (eds.), *Governing Together: The Extent and Limits of Joint Decision-Making in Western European Cabinets*. London: Macmillan.

——(1994). 'Finland: Ministerial Autonomy, Constitutional Collectivism, and Party Oligarchy', in Michael Laver and Kenneth A. Shepsle (eds.), *Cabinet Ministers and Parliamentary Government*. Cambridge: Cambridge University Press.

Paloheimo, Heikki, Wiberg, Matti, and Koiranen, Hannu (1993). 'Hallitus ostaa ääniä—ja kansa maksaa', *Politikka*, 35: 77–93.

Sänkiaho, Risto, and Laakso, Seppo (1975). 'Ministeristöjen muodostaminen ja eroaminen', in *Valtioneuvoston historia 1717–1966*. Helsinki: Valtion painatuskeskus.

Strøm, Kaare (1990a). 'A Behavioral Theory of Competitive Political Parties'. *American Journal of Political Science*, 34: 565–98.

——(1990b). *Minority Government and Majority Rule*. Cambridge: Cambridge University Press.

——Budge, Ian, and Laver, Michael J. (1994). 'Constraints on Cabinet Formation in Parliamentary Democracies'. *American Journal of Political Science*, 38: 303–35.

Warwick, Paul V. (1994). *Government Survival in Parliamentary Democracies*. Cambridge: Cambridge University Press.

Wiberg, Matti (1991). *Analysis and Politics*. Turku: Turun yliopisto.

9

Belgium

On Government Agreements, Evangelists, Followers and Heretics

Lieven De Winter, Arco Timmermans and Patrick Dumont

INTRODUCTION

Belgium undoubtedly has the most complex coalition bargaining system in Western Europe. Its party system is the most fragmented, with the highest average number of parties in government (De Winter, Della Porta, and Deschouwer 1996), and an extremely long government formation process. Electoral responsiveness is very low, with parties taking office more often after electoral losses than after electoral success. In order to reduce the high potential of uncertainty and shirking, political parties have developed a multifaceted and sophisticated set of coalition maintenance mechanisms. They evidently do not suffice, as cabinet instability approximates the pathological Italian case. Yet, in practice, some aspects of coalition formation are rather simple. As the pivotal and usually largest party family, the Christian Democrats are typically the driving force in the formation process, usually choosing its coalition partners between Socialists and Liberals. Thus, the party has been in power from 1958 to 1999, and in that period has had to yield the prime ministership to another party for one year only.

THE PARLIAMENTARY PARTY SYSTEM

The post-war Belgian party system underwent dramatic changes in the 1970s. Still reflecting in the 1950s and early 1960s the form it had at the introduction of general male suffrage in 1919, it in a relatively short period of time became the most fragmented European party system. The number of parties represented in parliament (Lower House) rose from four in 1949 to fourteen in 1981. Since then, despite a slight decrease in the number of parties (11 in 1995), the degree of fragmentation has not declined, as reflected in the effective number of parties (see Table 9.1a). The Belgian party system started out as a two-party system in the nineteenth century, with Catholics and Liberals basically opposed on the issue of the religious neutrality of the state. After the breakthrough of the Socialists at the end of that century and the politicization of the socio-economic left–right cleavage, Belgium had a clear-cut example of a two-and-a-half-party system (the Liberals being the smaller party) until at least 1965 (De Winter and Dumont 1999). The three 'traditional' parties, Christian Democrats (CVP/PSC), Socialists (PSB/BSP), and Liberals (PRL/VLD), alternated in government in different coalition combinations. The Communists only scored significant electoral gains in the period just after World War II.

In the 1960s and the 1970s the number of parties represented in parliament rose drastically (see Tables 9.1a and 9.1b). First the ethno-regionalist parties broke through: the Volksunie (VU) in Flanders, the Rassemblement Wallon (RW) in Wallonia, and the Front Démocratique des Francophones (FDF) in the Brussels region. The growing saliency of the linguistic and regional cleavage internally divided the Christian Democrat, Liberal, and Socialist parties, and each traditional party split into organizationally and programmatically independent Flemish- and French-speaking branches (in 1968, 1972, and 1978, respectively). At the end of the 1970s, the party system once again expanded with the emergence of the Flemish separatist and anti-migrant Vlaams Blok (VB), the poujadist Union Démocratique pour le Respect du Travail (UDRT), and the Green parties (AGALEV in Flanders and ECOLO in the Francophone areas). Thus, by 1981, fourteen parties were represented in parliament. During the 1980s, the Communists, the RW and the UDRT lost their representation, and thus a small reduction of the party system occurred. However, the 1991 general election introduced the latest lasting (representation gained for two elections in a row) newcomer, the Francophone extreme-right Front National (FN). Hence, one crucial feature of the Belgian party system is that there are no 'Belgian' parties any more! All parties are homogeneously Flemish or Francophone, and only present themselves in the Flemish or Francophone constituencies.[1] In fact, although the formats are quite similar, Belgium has two quasi-autonomous party systems, each with a different balance of power between the main parties, and a different evolution of their electoral fortunes (De Winter and Dumont 1999).

---

[1] With the exception of the bilingual Brussels-Halle-Vilvoorde constituency in which the Flemish and francophone systems overlap.

TABLE 9.1a. *Left–right placement of parties and party strength (in seats) in Belgium: House of Representatives, 1945–1999*

Year elections	Proximity to elections	PCB/KPB	BSP/PSB SP PS	A	E	RW	FDF[a]	CVP/PSC CVP PSC	VU	PVV/PLP VLD PRL	UDRT	FN	VB	Other[b]	Effective number of legislative parties	Median party second dimension[c]	Median party third dimension[d]	Government strength	Total of seats
1946	F	23	69	—	—	—	—	92*	—	17	—	—	—	1	2.9	PVV/PLP	PVV/PLP	69	202
1946	—	23	69	—	—	—	—	—	—	17	—	—	—	—	—	—	—	109	
1947	E	—	69	—	—	—	—	92*	—	—	—	—	—	—	—	—	—	161	
1949	FE	12	66	—	—	—	—	105*	—	29	—	—	—	—	2.8	PVV/PLP	PVV/PLP	134	212
1950	FE	7	77	—	—	—	—	108*	—	20	—	—	—	—	2.5	CVP/PSC	CVP/PSC	108	212
1954	FE	4	86	—	—	—	—	95*	1	25	—	—	—	1	2.6	PVV/PLP	PVV/PLP	111	212
1958	F	2	84	—	—	—	—	104*	1	21	—	—	—	—	2.5	PVV/PLP	PVV/PLP	104	212
1958	E	—	—	—	—	—	—	104*	—	21	—	—	—	—	—	—	—	125	
1961	FE	5	84	—	—	—	—	96*	5	20	—	—	—	2	2.7	PVV/PLP	PVV/PLP	180	212
1965	F	6	64	—	—	2	3	77*	12	48	—	—	—	—	3.6	PVV/PLP	PVV/PLP	141	212
1966	E	—	—	—	—	—	—	77*	—	48	—	—	—	—	—	—	—	125	
1968	FE	5	59	—	—	5	7	50 * 19	20	47	—	—	—	—	5.0	PVV/PLP	PVV/PLP	128	212
1972	F	5	61	—	—	14	10	47* 20	21	20 14	—	—	—	—	5.9	RW	BSP/PSB	128	212
1973	E	—	61	—	—	—	—	47* 20	22	20 14	—	—	—	—	—	—	—	162	
1974	F	4	59	—	—	13	9	50* 22	22	21 9	—	—	—	3	5.8	RW	BSP/PSB	102	212
1974	—	—	—	—	—	13	—	50* 22	—	21 9	—	—	—	—	—	—	—	115	
1977[e]	E	—	—	—	—	10	—	50* 22	—	21 12	—	—	—	—	—	—	—	105	
1977	FE	2	62	—	—	5	10	56* 24	20	17 14	1	—	—	2	5.2	FDF	BSP/PSB	172	212
1979	F	4	26 32	—	—	4	11	57* 25	14	22 14	1	—	1	1	6.8	FDF	SP	151	212
1980	—	—	26 32	—	—	—	—	57* 25	—	22 15	—	—	—	—	—	—	—	140	
1980	E	—	26 32	—	—	—	—	57* 25	—	22 15	—	—	—	—	—	—	—	177	
1980	E	—	26 32	—	—	—	—	57* 25	—	22 15	—	—	—	—	—	—	—	140	
1981	FE	2	26 35	2	2	2	6	43* 18	20	28 24	3	—	1	—	7.7	VLD	SP	113	212
1985	FE	0	32 35	4	5	0	3	49* 20	16	22 24	1	—	1	—	7.0	VLD	SP	115	212
1988	F	0	32 40	6	3	0	3	43* 19	16	25 23	0	—	2	—	7.2	VLD	SP	150	212
1991	E	—	32 40	—	—	—	—	43* 19	—	—	—	—	—	—	—	—	—	134	212
1992	FE	0	28 35	7	10	0	3	39* 18	10	26 20	0	1	12	3	8.4	VLD	SP	120	212
1995	F	0	20 21	5	6	0	—	29* 12	5	21 18	0	2	11	—	8.1	VLD	SP	82	150

cont./

TABLE 9.1a. *cont.*

ᵃ The party still existed in 1995, but in a federation with the French–speaking Liberals. The 'new party' is named PRL–FDF.

ᵇ From 1973 to 1979, the Brussels federation of the Liberal Party (PVV/PLP) seceded and changed the name of the Brussels PLP into PLPD (Parti Libéral Démocrate et Pluraliste—Liberal Democratic and Pluralistic Party). It was further renamed PL/LP (Parti Libéral/Liberale Partij) in June 1974. Their MPs (three in 1974, two in 1977, and one in 1978) did not support the three Tindemans' governments in which the Walloon and Flemish Liberals were part. The Brussels Liberals reunited the Walloon Liberals in May 1979 when the PRL was created.

ᶜ The second policy dimension is based on the older cleavage opposing Catholic to non–Catholic interests: from the Catholic pole to the non–Catholic one, we find the VB, CVP, PSC, VU, A, E, FDF, RW, VLD, PRL, SP, PS and then the PCB/KPB. There are less reasons to worry about the respective positions of the VLD and the PRL around the centre of this dimension, for there is a higher proportion of Catholic MPs and voters in VLD than in the PRL, partly due to the sociological differences between Flanders and Wallonia.

ᵈ The third policy dimension that opposes Flemish to French–speaking interests progressively became acute since World War I and the creation of the first nationalist parties in the inter–war years. Before 1965, we found, starting from the Flemish interests pole, the VU (which entered parliament in 1954), the CVP/PSC, PVV/PLP, PCB/KPB, and the BSP/PSB. In 1965 the first RW and FDF MPs were elected. Between 1968 and 1978, all three traditional parties split along linguistic lines. The Flemish Liberals became fiercer defendants of Flemish interests than the Socialists after their split. The first VB MP was elected in Dec. 1978. Hence, from 1979 onwards we find the VB, VU, CVP, VLD, SP, A, PCB/KPB, E, PSC, PRL, PS, RW, FDF.

ᵉ In Nov. 1976, the PLP was renamed PRLW (Parti des Réformes et de la Liberté de Wallonie, Reforms and Freedom Party of Wallonia, which became PRL in 1979), and three MPs from the RW joined the party. Hence, when in Mar. 1977 the RW was ejected from the Tindemans II government, the number of seats controlled by the next government (Tindemans III) went down to 105 instead of 102 as the Tindemans I government controlled, even though these two governments consisted of the same coalition of parties. In effect, the number of MPs of the PRLW was then 12 instead of 9 (without any election being held) and the number of remaining RW MPs was 10.

Parties

As a convention throughout the chapter and the tables, we first give the name (abbreviation) of the party in Dutch, followed by its name (abbreviation) in French for the unitary period of the three traditional parties. As in 1965 (the last election in which all traditional parties were still unitary parties), respectively 70, 48, and 42% of the Catholics', Socialists', and Liberals' votes came from Flemish constituencies, for respectively 21, 40, and 37% from strictly French–speaking constituencies (Wallonia), and respectively 7, 12, and 20% in the balanced bilingual Brussels–Halle–Vilvoorde constituency, and that 6 out of 10 Belgian voters were Flemish speakers throughout the period, this seems to be reasonable.

PCB/KPB   Parti Communiste Belge/Kommunistische Partij België (Belgian Communist Party). The Communists presented lists in about all constituencies, but never had an MP elected in Flemish constituencies. This is the reason why the French name of the party is here listed first.

BSP/PSB   Until 1978 the Flemish and French–speaking Socialist parties (SP and PS) were united in the unitary Belgian Socialist Party (BSP/PSB)

SP   Socialistische Partij ([Flemish] Socialist Party). The party was called 'Belgian' Socialist Party (BSP) until the 'B' was dropped in Mar. 1980, a bit more than one year after the split of the Belgian Socialist Party (BSP/PSB)

PS   Parti Socialiste ([French–speaking] Socialist Party). The party was called 'Belgian' Socialist Party (PSB) until the 'B' was dropped in Dec. 1978, when the unitary Belgian Socialist Party (BSP/PSB) split

A   AGALEV = the acronym is based on the contraction of the three words 'Anders Gaan Leven' (Another Way of Living) forming the name of the ecologist movement that gave birth to the party (Flemish ecologists)

E   ECOLO = the acronym is based on the six first letters of the word 'Ecologie' (Ecology), as 'Wallonie Ecologie' was the first list presented by French–speaking ecologists

TABLE 9.1a. *cont.*

RW	Rassemblement Wallon (Walloon Rally)
FDF	Front Démocratique des Francophones (French–speakers' Democratic Front)
CVP/PSC	Before 1968 the Flemish and the French–speaking Christian Democratic parties (CVP and PSC) were united in the unitary Belgian Christian Democratic Party (CVP/PS)]
CVP	Christelijke Volkspartij (Christian People's Party [Flemish])
PSC	Parti Social–Chrétien (Christian Social Party [French–speaking])
VU	Volksunie (People's Union [Flemish Nationalists])
PVV/PLP	Before 1972 the Flemish and the French–speaking Liberal parties (VLD and PRL) were united in the unitary Belgian Liberal Party (PVV/PLP). Before 1961 the Liberals used to be called LP/PL (Liberale
VLD	Vlaamse Liberalen en Democraten (Flemish Liberals and Democrats [Flemish Liberals]), known as the PVV=Partij voor Vrijheid en Vooruitgang (Freedom and Progress Party) from 1972 to1992
PRL	Parti Réformateur Libéral (Liberal Reform Party [French-speaking Liberals]), known as the PLP=Parti de la Liberté et du Progrès (Freedom and Progress Party) from 1972 to 1976, then PRLW (Parti des Réformes et de la Liberté de Wallonie [Reforms and Freedom Party of Wallonia]) from November 1976 to May 1979 when the PRL was created
UDRT	Union Démocrate pour le Respect du Travail (Democratic Union for the Respect of Work [Poujadist Party])
FN	Front National (National Front)
VB	Vlaams Blok (Flemish Block)

Left–right placement

Belgium is clearly a multidimensional party system. It includes a common left–right salient (since the end of the nineteenth century), but also a clear and older opposition between Catholics and anti-clerical forces, and the more recent regional/linguistic dimension. On the socio-economic dimension, we find, consistently since 1945, the Communists at the left pole, followed by the Socialists, the Christian Democrats, and the Liberals. The newcomers have fluctuated considerably.[2] Until the mid-1960s, the VU tended more towards the centre-right, then after 1968 it moved to the centre-left, to arrive at a centre position at the end of the 1970s. At the end of the 1980s, the VU adopted a 'liberal-left' profile. However, since the arrival of the latest president (1992), the party has made a definite move to the left, to a position somewhere between the ecologist party AGALEV and the Flemish Socialists (Hearl 1992; De Winter 1994: 30).

The FDF moved from the centre in the 1960s, to the centre-left in the 1970s and 1980s, and since its collaboration with the Francophone Liberals, to the centre-right in the 1990s. As the RW grew out of the Socialist trade union, it was clearly to the left of the FDF, and on some issues (e.g. workers' self-management of enterprises) also to the left of the Parti Socialiste (PS). Like the FDF, it was neutral on denominational conflicts. The Greens, although they often refuse to place themselves on a left–right continuum, have shifted

[2] A survey amongst MPs presents a snapshot of the positions of the three regionalist parties in 1983 (De Winter 1991: 154). It situates the parliamentary parties as follows: PCB, PS, SP, RW, VU, FDF, PSC, CVP, PVV, PRL.

TABLE 9.1b. *Left–right placement of parties and party strength (in seats) in Belgium: Senate, 1945–1999*

Year	Proximity to elections	PCB/ KPB	BSP/PSB SP PS	A	E	RW	FDF[a]	CVP/PSC CVP PSC	VU	PVV/PLP VLD PRL	UDRT	VB	Other[b]	Effective number of legislative parties	Median party second dimension	Median party third dimension	Government strength	Total of seats
1946	F	17	**55**	—	—	—	—	83*	—	12	—	—	—	2.7	PVV/PLP	PVV/PLP	55	167
1946	—	**17**	**55**	—	—	—	—	—	—	**12**	—	—	—				84	
1947	E		**55**	—	—	—	—	**83***	—		—	—	—				138	
1949	FE	6	53	—	—	—	—	92*	—	24	—	—	1	2.6	CVP/PSC	CVP/PSC	116	175
1950	FE	3	62	—	—	—	—	90*	—	19	—	—	1	2.5	CVP/PSC	CVP/PSC	90	175
1954	FE	2	72	—	—	—	—	78*	—	22	—	—	1	2.6	PVV/PLP	PVV/PLP	94	175
1958	F	1	65	—	—	—	—	90*	—	18	—	—	1	2.4	CVP/PSC	CVP/PSC	90	175
1958	E			—	—	—	—	**90***	—	**18**	—	—					108	
1961	FE	1	73	—	—	—	—	81*	2	17	—	—	1	2.1	PVV/PLP	PVV/PLP	154	175
1965	F	4	52	—	—	—	1	76*	5	40	—	—	—	2.0	PVV/PLP	PVV/PLP	128	178
1966	E			—	—	—		**76***		**40**	—	—					116	
1968	FE	2	53	—	—	8	—	46* / 18	14	37	—	—	—	4.7	PVV/PLP	PVV/PLP	117	178
1972	F	1	49	—	—	12	7	42* / 19	19	13 / 16	—	—	—	5.8	RW	BSP/PSB	110	178
1973	E		**49**	—	—			**42*** / **19**		**13** / **16**	—	—					139	
1974	F	1	50	—	—	10	8	48* / 18	16	15 / 12	—	—	3	5.5	RW	BSP/PSB	93	181
1974	—			—	—	**10**		**48*** / **18**		**15** / **12**	—	—					102	
1977[c]	E		52	—	—	5	6	48* / 19	—	15 / 17	—	—	4	—	—	—	99	
1977	FE	1	**21** / **32**	—	—	7	**8**	49* / **21**	17	14 / 10	—	—	2	5.2	FDF	BSP/PSB	147	181
1979	F	2	**21** / **32**	—	—	6	**9**	51* / **22**	11	18 / 8	1	—	1	6.3	VLD	SP	135	181
1980	—		**21** / **32**	—	—			**51*** / **22**			0	—					126	
1980	E		**21** / **32**	—	—			**51*** / **22**	—	**18** / **9**	—	—					153	
1981	F	1	21 / 29	1	4	2	6	40* / 16	17	23 / **20**	—	—	—	7.4	VLD	SP	99	181
1985	F	0	28 / 33	3	3	0	2	42* / 18	12	19 / **23**	—	—	—	6.7	VLD	SP	102	183
1988	F		29 / 36	5	3	2	—	39* / 16	**13**	18 / 21	—	1	—	6.9	VLD	SP	143	183
1991	E		**29** / **36**					**39*** / **16**									120	
1992	FE	—	26 / 30	8	11	—	2	36* / 16	8	22 / 18	0	6	1	8.1	VLD	SP	108	184
1995	F	—	9 / 11	2	3	—	—	12* / 7	3	10 / 9	0	5	—	8.4	VLD	SP	39	71

cont./

TABLE 9.1b. cont.

ᵃ The party still exists, but in a federation with the French-speaking Liberals. The 'new party' is named PRL–FDF.
ᵇ From 1973 to 1979, the Brussels federation of the Liberal Party (PVV/PLP) seceded and changed the name of the Brussels PLP into PLPD (Parti Libéral Démocrate et Pluraliste—Liberal Democratic and Pluralistic Party). It was further renamed PL/LP (Parti Libéral/Liberale Partij) in June 1974. Their Senators (three in 1974, two in 1977 and one in 1978) did not support the three Tindemans' governments in which the Walloon and Flemish Liberals were part. The Brussels Liberals reunited the Walloon Liberals in May 1979 when the PRL was created.
ᶜ In Nov.1976, the PLP was renamed PRLW (Parti des Réformes et de la Liberté de Wallonie, Reforms and Freedom Party of Wallonia, which became PRL in 1979), and five Senators from the RW joined the party. In the course of the life of the Tindemans II government, one Senator of the FDF turned to the PSC and another Senator of the FDF decided to seat as an independent. Hence, when in Mar. 1977 the RW was ejected from the Tindemans II government, the number of seats controlled by the next government (Tindemans III) went down to 99 instead of 93 as the Tindemans I government controlled, even though these two governments consisted in the same coalition of parties. In effect, the number of Senators of the PRLW was then 17 instead of 12, the number of PSC Senators 19 instead of 18 (without any election being held), and thus only the remaining five RW Senators went to the opposition.

Note: Elections were held in 1971, 1978, 1987, and 1991, but the cabinets that formed after the elections took office respectively in 1972, 1979, 1988, and 1992.

from the centre-left to a position closer to the Socialists, sometimes bypassing them on the left (Swyngedouw 1993: 91; Claeys and Desmarez 1994: 131). Finally, the anti-migrant populists clearly define themselves on the right, although they do not have a well-developed programme on socio-economic issues (Spruyt 1995).

Hence, two main problems complicate the identification of the party with the median legislator. First, the fluctuation of the regionalist parties around the centre occupied by the Christian Democrats. Second, as the centrist Christian Democrats themselves split in a Flemish and a Francophone branch (each fluctuating around the centre), it is difficult to decide whether to place the median legislator in the CVP or in the PSC. Yet, if one ignores the ethno-regionalist parties, one can safely state that in the entire period the median legislator has been a Christian Democrat, whether CVP or PSC (in Table 9.1a and 9.1b, we based our identification of the CVP as the party containing the median legislator on the higher probability of finding him/her in the largest of these two parties located in the same place on the left–right continuum). This explains the quasi-permanent presence of these parties in the post-war governments.

Finally, we should not forget that in order to explain coalition building, the denominational and linguistic/regional dimensions should be fully taken into account. As is the case of the left–right divide, some parties have shifted position substantially.[3] For reasons of space and simplicity, we only reproduced

[3] For instance, the Liberals dropped their anti-clericalist attitude in the beginning of the 1960s while all traditional parties shifted from a rather Belgicist position at the time of the unitary parties to much more polarized positions on regional/linguistic matters since the 1970s.

snapshots of the positions the main parties occupied before and after the linguistic divide of the three traditional parties in the notes of Table 9.1a, and identified the median party on these second and third dimensions in two distinct columns (see Tables 9.1a and 9.1b). On the denominational dimension, especially salient until the 1960s, we found at the 'clerical' pole—until the breakthrough of the VB—the Christian Democrats, and at the opposite end the Communists (since 1985 the Socialists, as the PCB/KPB has no representatives anymore). On the linguistic/regional divide, the VU and the CVP represented the strongest defenders of Flemish linguistic and regional interests (since 1979, the VB has become the 'Flemish pole'), with the RW/FDF and the PS at the Francophone-Walloon end. Hence, the strongest party in each party system was and is still situated rather at the extreme, which explains the centrifugality of electoral competition. On this dimension, the Belgian party system hence represents a case of Sartori's (1976) 'polarized pluralism' (De Winter and Dumont 1999).

INSTITUTIONAL BARGAINING CONSTRAINTS

A large number of soft and hard institutional constraints determine the government formation process. Some reduce the excessively high number of potential coalitions, others further complicate the bargaining process (Strøm, Budge, and Laver 1994).

Coalition Size

Belgium features a number of institutional constraints that induce the parties to form large majorities. One is the positive investiture rule (Bergman 1993; De Winter 1995): the government has to gain the confidence of a majority of the valid votes (excluding blank votes), with a quorum of half of the members present. The impact of the congruent and symmetrical bicameral system (Lijphart 1984) that Belgium had until 1995 was that each cabinet had to win an investiture vote in each chamber, including the Senate, in order to assume office (see Table 9.1b). Although parties' strengths in the two chambers are highly correlated, the occasional inter-cameral difference has sometimes been enough to render a particular coalition unviable. Until 1995, a vote of no confidence in either chamber, or a negative vote on a government bill, would have brought the cabinet down.[4] Hence, parties strove to build coalitions with some numerical cushion, as a few rebels could provoke fatal accidents and parliamentary dissolution as well.

[4] Since 1995, the government is only accountable to the House of Representatives. In 1995 the governmental declaration (summary of the coalition agreement) was not even read in the Senate anymore.

Two-thirds majorities are required for reforming the constitution. As institutional reform has dominated the governmental agenda since the early 1960s, any government with the ambition of tackling this issue has to control a two-thirds majority in parliament. Apart from constitutional revisions, there are the 'special majority laws' concerning the implementation of constitutional rules regarding the communities and the regions in those matters explicitly enumerated in the constitution (modifying borders/competencies/statutes of the provinces, the linguistic communities and regions). Unlike 'ordinary' laws, those bills must be passed by a majority in each linguistic group in each house (with a majority of members of each linguistic group being present). Moreover, the total number of favourable votes in both linguistic groups taken together must constitute two-thirds of the votes cast.

The Formation Process

Before the government seeks the investiture by parliament (and before the nomination of ministers), the national party conferences of the respective coalition parties approve the coalition programme and composition. Hence, in each party, a majority of the conference delegates have to vote in favour of the agreement; and a veto by any of the coalition party congresses means the end of the coalition bargaining attempt. Behind the scenes, the monarch plays a relatively active role in the formation process, especially with regard to the nomination of government *formateurs* and *informateurs*. The monarch will sometimes give some broad indications about the type of coalition that he finds desirable.[5] He also sometimes takes decisions that, at this stage, differ from the recommendations of the *informateur*.

Cabinet Composition and Operational Rules

The cabinet (Council of Ministers) operates according to a parity rule: it must have an equal number of Flemish- and French-speaking members, when the PM and the junior ministers (secretaries of state) are not taken into account. Moreover, although this is not constitutionally mandated, a very large majority of ministers are recruited from parliament.[6] Within this constraint, *formateurs* aim at a fair representation of Representatives and Senators, but also of different provinces and the sexes. Under the doctrine of collective cabinet responsibility, most matters decided by individual ministers are subject to cabinet oversight. Moreover, coalition parties have a large set of instruments giving

---

[5] The Belgian King sometimes expresses preference for a government relying on a two-thirds majority to reform the constitution and solve the country's recurrent institutional problems. For an overview of the role of the Belgian monarchs in the formation process, see the special issue of *Res Publica* (1991, no. 1), Stengers (1992).

[6] 87% in the 1945–84 period, 94% in the 1970–84 period (De Winter 1991, 1995).

them effective veto power over policies proposed by ministers of other parties (see coalition maintenance). Belgian parties are thus better placed than those in some other countries to check individual cabinet members from other parties. The effect may be to reduce the risks involved in joining coalitions.

COALITION FORMATION

General Procedures

Government formation in Belgium is subject to a large number of formal or informal rules. The first general rule is that the largest party, if interested, takes the initiative. Formally, the making of a new cabinet starts with the King's consultations of the parties represented in parliament. The King then appoints a *formateur*, or more often first an *informateur*, or sometimes a mediator in case the political situation is exceptionally difficult.[7]

From an analytical point of view, there are four stages in the formation process: (1) the making of a party combination, (2) negotiations on policy and (3) the distribution of portfolios, followed by (4) the appointment of ministers. Policy negotiations may also precede definitive decisions on the coalition composition (Laver and Budge 1992: 415). The policy negotiations take most of the time of cabinet formation, and therefore this process constitutes a policy making arena par excellence (Peterson et al. 1983; Peterson and De Ridder 1986). Since the early 1970s, negotiations take place between gradually extending party delegations and it has become customary to concentrate discussions in work groups, each dealing with a number of policy fields.

The term 'stage' may however not give an adequate picture of the formation process, as the making of party combinations and policy negotiations often cannot be separated. Sometimes, one or more parties agree to start negotiations and subsequently elaborate a joint policy programme. More commonly, however, a general programme is first produced by a *formateur* or *informateur*, which is then submitted to a number of parties. This programme may vary from a summary list of items to be discussed to a lengthy and

---

[7] Mediators have been used only four times. In 1979, after the failed missions of a first *informateur* and a first *formateur*, the situation was so extremely confused that the King asked Mr Claes and Mr Nothomb, a Flemish and a francophone, to undertake 'more than an information mission but less than a formation mission' or 'a particular (instead of general) information mission and a preliminary for a formation mission'. The King had already asked particular information missions in 1968 and 1972. They included deeper conversations than in a normal information mission and even the composition of working groups drafting solutions likely to be part of a coalition agreement. In 1979, however, the mediation mission aimed to establish the conditions of a dialogue between the parties and to restore a minimum of trust between the representatives of the two linguistic communities. Mr Claes was asked to carry out another mission of the same type in 1988 (with the title of 'Royal negotiator') after the mission of a first *informateur* had failed.

comprehensive piece of prose. At that moment, parties may still join or leave the negotiations. Occasionally, two- or three-party families reach agreement on a number of issues first before one or more additional parties are invited, the condition for participation being acceptance of the preliminary agreement as the basis for further negotiations.

Many other matters are negotiated. First, until 1995, when the number of ministers was constitutionally restricted, the coalition negotiators decided the size of the cabinet. The number of cabinet members varied considerably, depending on the number of parties and party factions included in the coalition (Frognier 1993). Second, the governments' hierarchical structure and its methods of coordination (the composition of standing cabinet committees, for example) are also usually decided at that moment. Third, since the early 1970s, allocation of patronage resources has been included. Fourth, coalition building at the national and regional level is strongly intertwined, as until 1999 the national and regional legislatures were elected at the same time. Parties involved in coalitions at the national level usually also demand inclusion at the regional level, and vice versa. Fifth, the role of parliament in policy making is set. Some coalition agreements stipulate that certain delicate policy issues (like abortion or institutional reform) should be decided by parliament autonomously, without government initiatives or interference. On other issues, the government sometimes reserves the right of initiative (gatekeeping powers) and asks the majority parliamentary groups not to raise the matter until the government has introduced a relevant bill (De Winter, Frognier, and Rihoux 1996). Finally, sometimes agreements are made about the duration of the coalition formula.[8]

The coalition composition becomes definitive when the results of the negotiations are submitted to the party conferences or congresses. Though party support is often far from unanimous, no party ever rejected the negotiation results and thus decided to stay outside the cabinet (see below). The extent of party support may be seen as a measure of commitment to the new coalition.

The portfolio distribution is more clearly the final stage in the formation process, but since many negotiators are 'ministrables', bargaining over cabi-

[8] During the formation of the Tindemans IV government (1977), the leaders of the five coalition parties decided to maintain this particular coalition for a period of two legislative terms, i.e. eight years. In fact, the institutional plan designed in the coalition agreement implied a number of constitutional reforms whilst the preceding parliament had not voted a constitutional reform declaration. Such a declaration that lists the various articles of the constitution that are open for modification in the subsequent legislature must be passed with a simple majority of MPs before any reform is possible. Thus, the Tindemans IV coalition had first to deal with its coalition agreement that did not trigger any changes in the constitution, then let the parliament draft and pass a constitutional reform declaration (the passing of which automatically dissolves the parliament and leads to general elections) in order to allow the subsequent parliament to amend (with a two-thirds majority) the constitution. Hence, the coalition parties promised to remain faithful for two legislatures instead of one.

net portfolios also cannot be seen in isolation from what has gone on before. Parties may and often do claim particular cabinet portfolios. Though it is conventional that the largest party takes the office of prime minister, and it has become a tradition that certain parties obtain certain portfolios (Budge and Keman 1990: 101–5), the allocation of portfolios nonetheless involves inter-party bargaining.

Once the portfolio distribution is completed and the cabinet has taken office, there is an official investiture that takes place in the House of Representatives and, until 1995, also in the Senate. Since 1945, all cabinets except one (the Spaak I single-party minority government in 1946) have cleared this hurdle. Notwithstanding the usual broad support amongst majority MPs, the investiture vote may indicate the support the new cabinet draws from the parliamentary parties.

COALITION COMPOSITION

It is important to realize that in coalition bargaining, the relevant parties in Belgium are driven by policy as much as by office goals (Budge and Laver 1986, 1992). We can approach these concerns by considering the main dimensions of inter-party competition.

Dimensions of Party Competition

Although the left–right dimension is important, a one-dimensional representation leads to a distorted picture of inter-party relationships in the cabinet making process in Belgium. Since 1970, when language parity in the cabinet became a constitutional requisite, it is constitutionally required to take language into account in coalition formation. Furthermore, the religious cleavage has influenced party and coalition politics, in particular in the 1950s. As Table 9.1a demonstrates, not all governments have contained parties that were adjacent on the left–right dimension. One outstanding example of an 'unconnected' coalition is the Socialist–Liberal government of 1954. For this two-party coalition and for the Catholic single-party government succeeding it in 1958, the main *raison d'être* was the 'school war' between the Catholics and the secular parties. While in this case one cleavage dominated coalition politics for some time, usually several dimensions are salient at once. In combination with the presence of up to nine coalitionable parties, bargaining becomes quite complex.

Pre-Electoral Exclusion

Party strategies may reduce this complexity. Party strategies are behavioural constraints in coalition formation which decrease the number of viable alternatives. To begin with, the Communists were banned from the coalition formation table in 1947. In the late 1940s and the 1950s, the Catholics and the Socialists pursued strategies of polarization in which they tried to reach parliamentary majorities (the Catholics alone, the Socialists in combination with the Liberals) (Dewachter 1987: 291–2). The signing in 1958 of the School Pact by the three main parties marked the end of this period of 'adversarial politics', and both secular parties became more prepared to accommodate with the CVP/PSC. It was however also the beginning of a period of more antagonism between the Socialists and the Liberals given their diverging socio-economic positions. These parties maintained a mutual veto until the early 1970s, when cooperation between the three traditional party families came to be seen as one of the few ways in which institutional reforms could be carried out, given the need for a two-thirds majority in parliament. This led to (short-lived) 'tripartite' cabinets made of the three traditional party families in 1973 and 1980.

It was also in the early 1970s that the regionalist parties became coalitionable. Whether previously the pariah status of the VU, RW, and FDF was self-imposed or stemmed from the traditional parties has been a source of debate among students of Belgian politics. In either case, the participation of any of these parties in government was systematically excluded for many years. By the end of the 1980s, pre-electoral exclusions had largely disappeared, and since then the coalition preferences of the main players in the game must be seen in more relative terms.

Bargaining Rounds

One reason why coalition formation lasts long is that often several bargaining rounds take place. In some cases, the appearance of successive bargaining rounds may simply reflect conventional procedures such as the appointment of a *formateur*, often the prime minister designate, after one or more *informateurs* have completed their preparatory work. Nonetheless, it is quite common that several bargaining rounds are inconclusive before parties arrive at the point of allocating cabinet portfolios to 'ministrables'. Such inconclusive bargaining rounds may involve the same parties or different parties, and bargaining rounds may remain without success because the parties sincerely fail in their efforts to reach agreement, or because one or more of the participating parties does not really want to take office with its discussion partners or is not seriously considered to be an attractive partner by the others (see Table 9.2).

The average for the period 1946–95 is 1.3 bargaining rounds. If we consider only the cabinets preceded by elections, the average increases to 2.1 bargaining rounds. Thus, when the voters have their say, formation is more complicated. When no elections are held, it takes only 0.5 bargaining rounds on average. Mid-term formations often constitute (successful) bargaining rounds at reviving the sitting coalition, and therefore the number of parties taken into consideration while trying to form a new government tends to be smaller than in post-election formation.

The number of inconclusive bargaining rounds has risen over time (from, on average 1 in the 1946–66 period, to 1.5 in the 1968–95 period). Calculated only on the basis of post-elections formations, the increase in inconclusive bargaining rounds is more dramatic, from on average 1.1 in the 1946–66 period to 2.7 in the 1968–95 period. Hence, the year 1968 (which coincides with the splitting up of the first traditional party CVP/PSC, and the first profound government crisis over a linguistic issue, the splitting of the Catholic University of Louvain) constitutes a turning point in the process of government formation, a qualitative jump away from the rather simple logic of government formation in a two-and-a-half-party system.

Parties Involved

There are often more parties at the coalition bargaining table than eventually at the cabinet table. More parties have become involved since the mid-1970s, due to the fragmentation of the party system. Also, the number of formation-relevant parties has tripled, largely due to the split of the traditional parties and the fact that the regionalist parties have become coalitionable. The regionalist parties have participated in cabinets since 1974, but these parties have also particularly commonly been involved in negotiations without going into office.

Successive bargaining rounds usually involve trying out different party combinations consecutively. Of the 76 bargaining rounds altogether (successful or not), 12 were reconstructions of the previous one, and in 1949 and 1979 multiple successive attempts with the same parties were made. Sometimes, negotiations are started by a particular set of parties which is reduced in one or more bargaining rounds. The constant factor is the presence of the Christian Democrats in all bargaining rounds except in 1946 and 1954 (which were successful) and in one inconclusive bargaining round in 1992. Although coalition formation is a selection process, it does not necessarily follow that the ensuing coalition is less preferred or less viable than the combinations discussed previously. Sometimes the opposite is even true: it may take different attempts to find a viable combination that also meets particular criteria such as a two-thirds majority in parliament.

TABLE 9.2. *Government formation in Belgium, 1945–1999*

Government	Parties in House of Representatives	Number of previous bargaining rounds	Parties involved in previous bargaining rounds	Number of days required for government formation
BSP/PSB 1946 1	5	2	(1) CVP/PSC–BSP/PSB–PVV/PLP (2) BSP/PSB–PVV/PLP–PCB/KPB	23
BSP/PSB–PVV/PLP–PCB/KPB 1946 2	5	0		11
BSP/PSB–PVV/PLP–PCB/KPB 1946 3*	5	2	(1) BSP/PSB–PVV/PLP–PCB/KPB (2) BSP/PSB–CVP/PSC	25
CVP/PSC–BSP/PSB 1947	5	1	BSP/PSB–CVP/PSC–PVV/PLP–PCB/KPB	7
CVP/PSC–PVV/PLP 1949	4	3	(1) CVP/PSC–BSP/PSB–PVV/PLP (2) CVP/PSC–BSP/PSB–PVV/PLP (3) CVP/PSC–BSP/PSB–PVV/PLP	45
CVP/PSC 1950	4	0		1
CVP/PSC 1950*	4	0		5
CVP/PSC 1952*	4	0		6
BSP/PSB–PVV/PLP 1954	6	0		10
CVP/PSC 1958 1	5	1	CVP/PSC–BSP/PSB–PVV/PLP	21
CVP/PSC–PVV/PLP 1958 2	5	0		2
CVP/PSC–BSP/PSB 1961	6	0		29
CVP/PSC–BSP/PSB 1965	7	2	(1) CVP/PSC–BSP/PSB–PVV/PLP (2) CVP/PSC–BSP/PSB–PVV/PLP	64
CVP/PSC–PVV/PLP 1966	7	3	(1) CVP/PSC–BSP/PSB–PVV/PLP (2) CVP/PSC–BSP/PSB (3) CVP/PSC–BSP/PSB–PVV/PLP	36
CVP–PSC–BSP/PSB 1968	8	4	(1) CVP–PSC–PVV/PLP (2) CVP–PSC–PVV/PLP–BSP/PSB (3) CVP–PSC–BSP/PSB (4) CVP–PSC–PVV/PLP–BSP/PSB	77
CVP–PSC–BSP/PSB 1972	9	1	CVP–PSC–BSP/PSB	74
BSP/PSB–CVP–PSC–VLD–PRL 1973	9	1	CVP–PSC–BSP/PSB–VLD–PRL	64

Belgium

Cabinet		Composition	
CVP-PSC-VLD-PRL 1974 1	9	5	(1) CVP-PSC-VLD-PRL	45

CVP-PSC-VLD-PRL 1974 1	9	5	(1) CVP-PSC-VLD-PRL	45
			(2) CVP-PSC-BSP/PSB-VLD-PRL	
			(3) CVP-PSC-BSP/PSB-VLD-PRL	
			(4) CVP-PSC-BSP/PSB	
			(5) CVP-PSC-VLD-PRL-VU-RW-FDF	
CVP-PSC-VLD-PRL-RW 1974 2	9	1	CVP-PSC-VLD-PRL-RW-VU-FDF	1
CVP-PSC-VLD-PRL 1977 1	9	0		2
CVP-PSC-BSP/PSB-VU-FDF 1977 2	9	1	CVP-PSC-BSP/PSB-VLD-PRL	46
PSC–CVP-BSP/PSB-VU-FDF 1978*	9	0		9
CVP-PSC-PS-SP-FDF 1979	12	7	(1) CVP-PSC-PS-SP-VU-FDF	106
			(2) CVP-PSC-PS-SP-VU-FDF	
			(3) CVP-PSC-PS-SP-FDF	
			(4) CVP-PSC-PS-SP-VU-FDF	
			(5) CVP-PSC-PS-SP-VU-FDF	
			(6) CVP-PSC-PS-SP-VU-FDF	
			(7) CVP-PSC-PS-SP-VU-FDF-VLD-PRL	
CVP-PSC-PS-SP 1980 1	12	0		7
CVP-PSC-PS-SP-VLD-PRL 1980 2	12	0		39
CVP-PSC-PS-SP 1980 3	12	0		15
CVP-PSC-PS-SP 1981 1*	12	0		4
CVP-PSC-VLD-PRL 1981 2	14	3	(1) CVP-PSC-PS-SP	39
			(2) CVP-PSC-VLD-PRL	
			(3) CVP-PSC-VLD-PRL-PS-SP	
CVP-PSC-VLD-PRL 1985	12	0	(1) CVP-PSC-VLD-PRL-PS-SP	45
CVP-PSC-PS-SP-VU 1988	11	3	(2) CVP-PSC-PS-SP	148
			(3) CVP-PSC-PS-SP	
CVP-PSC-PS-SP 1991	11	0	(1) VDL-PRL-PS-SP	0
CVP-PSC-PS-SP 1992	13	3	(2) CVP-PSC-PS-SP	103
			(3) CVP-PSC-VLD-PRL-PS-SP	
CVP-PSC-PS-SP 1995	11	0		33

* No new government according to the definition used throughout this volume, but a new cabinet.

Formation Duration

As far as the overall duration of bargaining is concerned, Table 9.2 indicates a gradual but rather erratic increase over time. If we include only the formations that took place after a general election, a situation in which the bargaining set is most likely to be different from the previous government, the increase is more linear.[9] The duration of government formation has gone up considerably since the end of the 1960s, due to a number of new constraints (imposed since the end of the 1960s), as well as to party system fragmentation (De Winter 1995).

This growing complexity of coalition formation explains the dramatic growth in duration of the formation process. In fact, in the period before formation became so complex, the process consumed less than half the time it took afterwards: from an average of 20.4 days in the 1946–66 period, it rose to an average of 45.1 for formations that took place between 1968 and 1995 (the average for all post-war formations is 34.6 days). Again, the increase is clearer for post-electoral formations: an average of 27.6 days between 1946 and 1966; for 71.6 days in the subsequent period (average for the whole 1946–95 period: 53.5 days). The contrast with mid-term formations is evidently striking, as for the latter formation duration was almost stable throughout the whole period (14.6 days in the 1946–95 period; 13.1 between 1946 and 1966 and 15.6 between 1968 and 1995). Table 9.2 also indicates that before 1968, the mean number of parties in government was 1.8. In the 1968–95 period, it was 4.3 (overall mean 3.2).

Coalition Membership

The Belgian Christian Democrats have been present in every cabinet from 1958 to 1999, notwithstanding the erosion of their electoral base by half. The Socialist Party family has lost in all successive elections between 1958 and 1985, but nonetheless the PS and SP participated in seven of the nine cabinets preceded by elections in this period, and in six of the eleven cabinets formed without preceding elections.

Belgian cabinets have been either minimal-winning or oversized. The latter can be explained by the constitutional constraints, stipulating that constitutional reform bills require a two-thirds majority in both Houses. Hence, given the fact that since the mid-1960s institutional reform has been high on the governmental agenda, two classical tripartite coalitions (or hexapartites, e.g. Leburton, Martens III) were formed with that objective. We also find several quintapartites (Tindemans IV and Vanden Boeynants II that were composed

---

[9] This is not the case when a government stumbles over a bill, and decides to continue to go on with some modifications, like dropping a minor coalition partner, or when a PM is replaced but all other characteristics of the sitting cabinet remain intact.

of five different parties as at that time the Socialist Party was still unitary, Martens I and Martens VII) and one bipartite (Harmel) with a two-thirds majority that aimed at constitutional reform. On the other hand, the Spaak II and Lefèvre governments did not aim at constitutional reform, but were the result of the strength of the Christian Democrats and Socialist parties in that period. Of the thirty-three cabinets under consideration, nine controlled a two-thirds majority in the House of Representatives (and twelve in the Senate).

Another reason for the large number of oversized governments is the practice of double symmetry in coalition membership. First, traditional parties belonging to the same family have up until now always been together in government or opposition, in spite of the fact that since the 1970s they have become fully autonomous. This means that often a coalition included a surplus party of relatively small size, which was the linguistic sister party of a main party of the other side of the linguistic border (especially the PSC and SP vis-à-vis the *incontournable* CVP and PS, respectively). Hence, since the splitting of the traditional parties, we find a few surplus coalitions amongst those that did not attain a two-thirds majority: Eyskens IV (1968–71) and V (1972), Martens II (1980 1), IV (1980 3), and M. Eyskens (1981 1) (the latter three had a two-thirds majority in the Senate), and Martens VIII (1991).[10] Of thirty-three cabinets, technically twelve were surplus majorities (both in the House of Representatives and in the Senate).

Second, as far as numerically possible, coalitions at the regional level also include the same parties as the national-level coalition. As the negotiators at both levels are often identical (party presidents, some top party leaders, and party experts), they usually manage to link the formation of executives at different levels and force the entry of their party at all levels.

Notice that we also find a few minority cabinets. The first one did not outlive its investiture vote (Spaak I in 1946), while the Eyskens II (1958) and Tindemans I (1974) minority cabinets were formed while attempts were being made to enlarge the coalition in order to reach a majority, which in fact happened some months later. Another minority cabinet was Tindemans III (1977), formed after the RW ministers were revoked by the prime minister.

Do the actual coalitions conform to the predictions made in coalition theories that take policy into account? In recent work based on the Manifesto Project, the observation has been made that coalitions in Belgium are not often connected on the left–right dimension (Budge and Laver 1992: 416), and are also not often minimum connected winning.[11] The far less restrictive

---

[10] In the period before the first split of traditional parties (1945–68), not a single surplus majority was formed.

[11] However, non-connectedness on the left–right scale was common in the 1944–58 period. Afterwards, all coalitions did contain traditional parties that were connected on the first dimension. The fluctuating positions of the regionalist parties around the centre explain the apparent non-connectedness of some coalitions.

prediction that coalitions contain the median party has been the most successful proposition derived from a one-dimensional representation of coalition politics for Belgium (Hearl 1992: 259; Budge and Laver 1992: 416). In the present analysis, the participation of the median party on the first (left–right) dimension is verified in 86.7 per cent of the cases (thirty cabinets, as we exclude the three cabinet formations that took place in a single-party majority context, between 1950 and 1954), and in all post-1958 cases.

Several authors (Hearl 1992; Budge and Laver 1992) have argued that multidimensional models are more successful in predicting the composition of coalitions in Belgium. From Tables 9.1a and 9.1b, we notice that the median party on the denominational dimension participated in 40 per cent of the cases, and more often when this denominational question was salient (62.5% of the cases preceding the School Pact of 1958), whilst the median party on the linguistic divide entered the cabinet in 63.3 per cent of all cases, and here again more often when this dimension became especially salient (68.4% of the cases in the 1968–95 period).[12] When we analyse coalition formation with a 'doubled version' of the median party thesis, expecting that the median parties on the two most salient dimensions (the left–right cleavage throughout the period, the denominational one from 1946 to 1958, replaced by the linguistic divide as the other salient dimension from 1958 to 1995)[13] will both enter the coalition, we find that although in 96.7 per cent of the cases, there was at least one of these two median parties in the actual cabinet that was formed, the two median parties participated both in 57 per cent of the cases (excluding all single-party cabinets and the cabinets in which the same party family was median on both dimensions).[14] This is not an impressive result, given the fact that the CVP/PSC (or the CVP on its own) was always the median party in the left–right dimension, participated in 89 per cent of these coalition cabinets, and always chose its junior partner between the two other traditional parties (or even chose both of them). Therefore, even if in these cabinets containing two median parties (57% of all coalition cabinets) there was no other supplementary party (than the party family counterparts) in 43.7 per cent of the cases, meaning that the doubled version of the median thesis predicts the exact composition of the coalition (in terms of party families)

---

[12] This analysis was based on the House of Representatives only. The Senate displayed very similar levels (62.1% of all median parties participated to cabinets, for 63.3% in the House of Representatives) and evolutions.

[13] As the median party on the second and third dimensions was the same from 1946 to 1968, the results are the same if we take 1968 as the year where the saliency of the linguistic cleavage bypassed the religious one. The only cabinet for which this hypothesis was not verified was the single-party minority cabinet of 1946 (that failed to pass the parliamentary investiture vote).

[14] In our analysis, the same party family actually never controlled the median position on both dimensions, except of course in the 1950–54 legislature during which the CVP/PSC held the absolute majority of seats in parliament.

in about one-quarter of all coalition cabinets, this is not a great improvement from a simple model predicting that the CVP(/PSC) (either because it is the largest party or because it has the median position on the left–right unidimensional spectrum) will choose one of the two other traditional party families to form a coalition.

Another multidimensional proposition, stipulating that the coalition will contain the predominant party (the one with most median positions on a wider range of issues), was tested by Hearl (1992: 261–3) in the Belgian context over twenty disaggregated dimensions constructed on manifesto data. In 93 per cent of the cases from 1946 to 1981, the hypothesis was verified (but did not say anything about the coalition partner), as the CVP/PSC was always predominant except in 1946. Even if, according to Schofield (1993: 26–7), it is difficult for one party in a multidimensional system to maintain this position over time, the post-1981 practice seems to continue the trend highlighted by Hearl: despite the gradual erosion of the electoral strength of the CVP(/PSC), it remained the core of coalition politics in terms of membership, leadership, and policy (Klingemann et al. 1994). Table 9.3 provides more detailed information on Belgian cabinets.

COALITION GOVERNANCE: ENFORCING AGREEMENTS

Coalition bargaining in Belgium is a complex and highly institutionalized process. Yet, the most crucial step is coalition governance: the implementation and enforcement of the coalition agreements into public policy. As with so many other facets of Belgian coalition politics, governance is both particularly challenging and regulated in a great number of respects. This process starts with a central product of the formation process: the government agreement. The party composition and the distribution of portfolios among 'ministrables' may already indicate what policies the new cabinet is likely to pursue. The more substantive link between the formation and cabinet policies is, however, provided by the coalition agreement.

The Central Role of Agreements

The joint programme containing coalition policy is generally considered to be important. It is typically drafted before the cabinet takes office. Coalition agreements are often mixed with the 'courtship' part of coalition formation, the forming of party combinations, and this means that the drafting of coalition agreements is not always a linear, cumulative process. Coalition agreements are meant to provide part of the policy agenda and to prevent the occurrence of conflict within the coalition (Timmermans 1996). Parties tend

TABLE 9.3. *Belgian cabinets since 1945*

Cabinet number	Cabinet	Date in	Formal resignation	Maximum potential duration	Duration	Government composition
1	Spaak	13 Mar. 1946	20 Mar. 1946	1,495	7	BSP/PSB
2	Van Acker III	31 Mar. 1946	9 July 1946	1,477	100	BSP/PSB–PVV/PLP–PCB/KPB
3	Huysmans	3 Aug. 1946	13 Mar. 1947	1,352	222	BSP/PSB–PVV/PLP–PCB/KPB
4	Spaak II*	20 Mar. 1947	27 June 1949	1,123	830	BSP/PSB–CVP/PSC
	Spaak II/2*	26 Nov. 1948	27 June 1949	[506]	[213]	BSP/PSB–CVP/PSC
5	Eyskens	11 Aug. 1949	18 Mar. 1950	1,473	219	CVP/PSC–PVV/PLP
6	Duvieusart	8 June 1950	11 Aug. 1950	1,515	64	CVP/PSC
7	Pholien	16 Aug. 1950	9 Jan. 1952	1,446	511	CVP/PSC
8	Van Houtte	15 Jan. 1952	12 Apr. 1954	929	818	CVP/PSC
9	Van Acker IV	22 Apr. 1954	2 June 1958	1,508	1,502	BSP/PSB–PVV/PLP
10	Eyskens II	23 June 1958	4 Nov. 1958	1,497	134	CVP/PSC
11	Eyskens III	6 Nov. 1958	27 Mar. 1961	1,361	872	CVP/PSC–PVV/PLP
12	Lefèvre	25 Apr. 1961	24 May 1965	1,489	1,490	CVP/PSC–BSP/PSB
13	Harmel	27 July 1965	11 Feb. 1966	1,454	199	CVP/PSC–BSP/PSB
14	Van den Boeynants I	19 Mar. 1966	7 Feb. 1968	1,219	690	CVP/PSC–PVV/PLP
15	Eyskens IV	17 June 1968	8 Nov. 1971	1,388	1,239	CVP–PSC–BSP/PSB
16	Eyskens V	21 Jan. 1972	23 Nov. 1972	1,444	307	CVP–PSC–BSP/PSB
17	Leburton	26 Jan. 1973	19 Jan. 1974	1,073	358	BSP/PSB–CVP–PSC–VLD–PRL
18	Tindemans	25 Apr. 1974	11 June 1974	1,473	47	CVP–PSC–VLD–PRL

19	Tindemans II	11 June 1974	4 Mar. 1977	1,426	997	CVP–PSC–VLD–PRL–RW
20	Tindemans III	6 Mar. 1977	18 Apr. 1977	427	43	CVP–PSC–VLD–PRL
21	Tindemans IV	3 June 1977	11 Oct. 1978	1,472	495	CVP–PSC–BSP/PSB–FDF–VU
22	Van den Boeynants II	20 Oct. 1978	18 Dec. 1978	968	59	PSC–CVP–BSP/PSB–FDF–VU
23	Martens I	3 Apr. 1979	16 Jan. 1980	1,412	288	CVP–PSC–PS–SP–FDF
24	Martens II	23 Jan. 1980	9 Apr. 1980	1,117	77	CVP–PSC–PS–SP
25	Martens III	18 May 1980	7 Oct. 1980	1,001	142	CVP–PSC–PS–SP–VLD–PRL
26	Martens IV	22 Oct. 1980	2 Apr. 1981	854	162	CVP–PSC–PS–SP
27	M Eyskens	6 Apr. 1981	21 Sept. 1981	690	168	CVP–PSC–PS–SP
28	Martens V	17 Dec. 1981	14 Oct. 1985	1,432	1,397	CVP–PSC–VLD–PRL
29	Martens VI	28 Nov. 1985	14 Dec. 1987	1,473	746	CVP–PSC–VLD–PRL
	Martens VI/2*	21 Oct. 1987	14 Dec. 1987	[781]	[54]	CVP–PSC–VLD–PRL
30	Martens VII*	9 May 1988	29 Sept. 1991	1,371	1,238	CVP–PSC–PS–SP–VU
31	Martens VIII*	29 Sept. 1991	25 Nov. 1991	133	57	CVP–PSC–PS–SP
32	Dehaene I	7 Mar. 1992	21 May 1995	1,415	1,170	CVP–PSC–PS–SP
33	Dehaene II	23 June 1995		1,486		CVP–PSC–PS–SP
	MEAN DURATION			520		

* The Spaak II/2 and Martens VI/2 do not have a cabinet number (first column) for they are not considered as cabinets according to the definition (three criteria) used in this volume, and thus are not analysed separately from the cabinet preceding them. We nevertheless wanted to report the existence of two important reshuffles that are usually considered as distinct cabinets in Belgian political literature because a formal resignation of the preceding cabinet was accepted by the King: the reshuffle of Spaak II (referred as Spaak II/2 in the table but known in Belgium as Spaak III) and the reshuffle of Martens VI (here noted as Martens VI/2), a caretaker cabinet aimed at voting a constitutional reform declaration. Hence, as the Martens VI/2 cabinet is known in Belgian conventional numbering as Martens VII, the two following cabinets (Martens VII and VIII) are in fact known as Martens VIII and IX under that rule of counting. While reading this chapter and the tables, one can bear in mind that the definition of cabinet used throughout this volume causes a slight deformation from national cabinet counting conventions.

to pre-cook concrete policy decisions. Sometimes they are less ambitious and just place certain matters on the agenda, something that is reflected in the agreement. Particularly on issues that appeared to be controversial during coalition formation, the conflict prevention function is important. This too is reflected in the different types of arrangements; the parties can piece together specific compromises or instead agree to disagree, resulting in the specification of procedural rules of the game.

The Morality of Duty: pacta sunt servanda

Coalition agreements contain rules of the game, which have in common that they concern the moral aspect of commitments. Agreements are, after all, not contracts and are thus not legally binding. It is, however, not only in coalition formation that the moral commitment to the agreement is made explicit. Often, this is one of the central topics of the parliamentary debate preceding the vote of investiture. Once in office, party leaders, ministers, and parliamentary parties legitimize their policy positions and initiatives (or lack of) by referring repeatedly to the stipulations of the coalition bible.

Party Investiture

Since 1961, nearly all parties have conventions or statutory rules that require that the government composition and policy agreement has to be approved by the national congress, the supreme decision making body of each party, which formally makes binding decisions for all party members (Dewachter 1987: 332). These congresses are made up of representatives selected at the level of the communal or constituency party organization. In practice, all top- and mid-level party elites are amongst those selected. The decisions of the parties' most sovereign decision-body bind the entire party (rank-and-file members, the parliamentary group, the party executive, and the party leader) to the coalition contract, and therefore constitute a central element in coalition maintenance. Any critique on the policy of ministers of other parties voiced by these internal party actors can be condemned by the party's leadership and ministers as a breach of party discipline, as long as this policy is covered by the coalition agreement. Hence, coalition agreements tie not only coalition parties to each other, but also all bodies within each coalition party. Hence, these congresses constitute a crucial moment in the formation process.

Table 9.4 indicates that in practice, no party conference has ever rejected a coalition agreement.[15] The votes taken indicate a usually large consensus on government composition and agreement, with some notorious exceptions.

---

[15] Apart from the Brussels francophone Liberal splinter party in 1974, which should be considered as a party faction, rather than an autonomous party.

TABLE 9.4. *Party vote on governmental agreement in Belgium, 1961–1999*

Cabinet number	Cabinet	SP	PS	RW	FDF	CVP	PSC	VU	VLD	PRL	Mean
12	Lefèvre	82.5					78.5				
13	Harmel	64.5					97.5				
14	Van den Boeynants I						100			90	
15	Eyskens IV	69				85	77				
16	Eyskens V	91				87	100				
17	Leburton	57				60	94				73
18	Tindemans					99	93				98
19	Tindemans II		99.5			99	na				
20	Tindemans III										
21	Tindemans IV	96			70	75	83.5	67			78
22	Van den Boeynants II				67						
23	Martens I	88	87			71	93.5				81
24	Martens II	100	82.5			99	100				95
25	Martens III	77	66			94	77		77	96	81
26	Martens IV	93	87			80	99				90
27	M Eyskens						na				
28	Martens V					98	93		98	99	97
29	Martens VI					99	98		99	100	99
30	Martens VII	95	60			91	66	87			80
31	Martens VIII										
32	Dehaene	97.3	98.3			61.8	94.5		93	60	88
33	Dehaene II	99.5	95			100	99.8		100	100	98.5

na = not available

Note: Some means were not calculated on purpose, for it appeared irrelevant to draw conclusions on party support to governments if a party organ that voted the approbation was a non–representative body. Only congresses or councils comprising at least 100 members have been taken into account.

This large consensus is due not only to the attractiveness of the policies the new government promises to implement, or the brilliance with which the party negotiators present their deal to the rank-and-file. It is also due to the fact that a large number of conference participants have—directly or indirectly—an interest in their party gaining or maintaining power. First, most top party leaders are appointed to the cabinet, to which every normal MP aspires. Second, MPs support the government because participation facilitates their individual and collective constituency service. Third, the party intelligentsia is awarded with positions in the *cabinets ministériels* and with promotions into the highly politicized public sector (see below). Fourth, intra-party factions not only find a government favourable to their demands, but also often can nominate the ministers relevant to their interest, and appoint trustees in the relevant cabinets and administrations. Finally, most constituency party organizations can put some of their administrative personnel on state payroll by 'parking' them in the *cabinets ministériels* (De Winter, Frognier, and Rihoux 1996). Hence, it is not at all surprising that party congresses usually approve government participation by overwhelming majorities.

Parliamentary Investiture

Parliamentary votes of investiture of a new cabinet are characterized by a high level of voting discipline. In the entire post-war period, in each chamber, on the average only 0.6 per cent of the majority MPs voted against the government at the investiture vote. Since the coalition programme and configuration are approved by the national congress of the respective coalition parties before the government seeks the investiture by parliament, a negative vote by majority MPs would openly defy the decisions of the party's supreme decision making body. Thus, during the vote of confidence debate, majority MPs do occasionally criticize governmental intentions contained in its programme, but rarely dare they follow up with a negative vote.

Yet, at times a large number of majority MPs fail to show up for or participate in the investiture vote. If we exclude the first government (Spaak I), which was never invested, nearly one out of ten majority MPs (8.7%) have failed to vote in favour of the government. This discrepancy between the actual vote in favour of the government and the theoretical number of coalition seats can be explained in several ways. In several coalitions based on a large parliamentary majority (Lefèvre, Leburton, Martens I, Martens III), a larger-than-average gap may reflect neglect of parliamentary duties rather than rejection of the coalition bargaining result. In these cases, individual MPs may have remained absent because they believed the government's majority would be so overwhelming that their absence would not make a difference. Conversely, cabinets with very narrow theoretical majorities often manage to marshal a very high proportion of their representatives (Van

Acker III and IV, Duvieusart, Pholien, Martens V and VI).[16] Another category consists of several governments with a less than overwhelming majority, which managed to mobilize less than average support (Martens II, IV, VIII, and M. Eyskens). All these were centre-left governments that were particularly unpopular among Christian Democratic backbenchers (De Winter 1989).

Cabinets and Ministerial Discretion

Most matters decided by individual ministers fall under the doctrine of collective cabinet responsibility. However, coalition parties have a large set of instruments that give them effective veto power against unwelcome policies proposed by ministers of other parties. In fact, since 1985, internal cabinet rules stipulate that every ministerial decision that can jeopardize the stability of the coalition must be approved by the full cabinet collectively. Hence, if a single party or minister opposes a certain policy proposal, the full cabinet may be forced to consider the matter and decide by consensus. In addition, on any matter that may involve the government as a whole, ministers should consult the relevant cabinet committee or the Council of Ministers. Also, ministers may not make declarations about matters that do not belong to their colleagues' competencies that could embarrass the latter. Yet, even within their own jurisdictions, ministers should be extremely discreet as long as the matter has not been decided by the government! Finally, ministers should not make any declaration or take any action expressing their personal point of view if that would question the governmental agreement (Alen and Dujardin 1986: 532–4). Hence, Belgian ministers are not at all policy dictators in their respective jurisdictions (Timmermans 1994: 116–19). Every policy initiative of any relevance has to be scrutinized and approved by the cabinet by consensus.

The Watchdog Role of Junior Ministers

The position of junior ministers has existed since 1960. The coalition negotiators collectively decide the number and competencies of junior ministers, and two types of arrangements have existed. Until 1991 junior ministers often did not belong to the same party (or to the same linguistic wing of the former unitary parties). In this case, a junior minister tended to operate as a watchdog over his minister. His decision making autonomy *vis-à-vis* his minister was often relatively large, depending on the overall balance of power in the

---

[16] However, other large majorities have been able to mobilize an average number of majority MPs (and in the case of Tindemans IV more than average).

coalition. This system led to enough conflicts between ministers and their juniors that since 1991 junior ministers have belonged to the same party as the minister. Moreover, the most recent governments (Dehaene I and II) have dramatically reduced the number of junior ministers.

The incidence of inter-party control by junior ministers can be measured by the proportion of junior ministers who belong to a different party than the minister to whom they are attached (for traditional parties before their linguistic split, junior ministers belonging to a different linguistic wing of the same party as their ministers are not considered watchdogs). In cabinets with junior ministers (1960–95), more than one out of five (21.5%) ministers had a junior minister from a different party. In two cabinets (Leburton and Martens VI), more than half the ministers were controlled by junior ministers of other parties. This oversight device was especially common in the classical 'tripartite' coalition and other surplus governments (an average of almost one out of three ministers checked this way). But even a number of more homogeneous 'simple' four-party coalitions have had high proportions of 'watchdog' junior ministers (Martens V and VI were both above a 40% watchdog/minister ratio).

Ministerial Political Staff

The Belgian government has large ministerial staffs of political appointees, ranging from several dozen to over two hundred members (De Winter, Frognier, and Rihoux 1996). In the traditional parties, the party organization appoints most of these individuals. This is true even at the highest level, including the *chef de cabinet,* the main aide to the minister.[17] The party leadership thus has its trusted servants serving as monitoring and information agents in the ministers' immediate entourage. The members of the *ministerial cabinet* spend a considerable time following the government's conduct of business at the level of the Council of Ministers and in the cabinet committees of which the minister is a member. They prepare the ministers' interventions in these meetings as well as in parliament. Evidently, they also prepare with particular care the minister's own projects, which often require numerous consultations with the administration and with the political appointees of other ministers. These consultations may be organized formally, for instance in inter-cabinet groups, or informally. In some cases, political appointees specialize in the jurisdiction of another department. This is usually the case for particularly salient policy areas in which the party does not control a minis-

---

[17] Evidently, the minister has his say, esp. with regard to the refusal of some candidates. Yet, usually they can only appoint themselves a small number of collaborators at the superior level, but have more leeway for the lower levels.

ter or secretary of state.¹⁸ The task of these 'shadow staff members' or 'policy cells' is to scrutinize every policy declaration, proposal, or intention of the relevant minister.¹⁹

Cabinet Committees and Vice-Prime Ministers

Usually each coalition party has one vice-prime minister in charge of a large department.²⁰ In addition, vice-PMs serve as the *chef de file*, the cabinet leader of their party's ministers, and, with the other vice-PMs and the PM, constitute the so-called *Kerncabinet* (core cabinet). This is a cabinet committee that meets quite regularly and resolves major conflicts between the coalition parties. Its final decisions are later only formally ratified by the full cabinet. For their cabinet leadership role, these vice-PMs are equipped with a special *'ministerial cabinet* for general policy' of about seventy staff members, whose main tasks are to follow the decision making of the other ministers in the government and to safeguard the party's interest.²¹

The regular subject cabinet committees (foreign affairs, social policy, economy, etc.) consist not only of ministers competent in the subject field. Usually, each coalition party will have a representative in each cabinet committee. Thus, each party is fully informed about the decisions prepared by every cabinet committee.

Intra-Party Summits

In all Belgian parties, nearly all ministers by now regularly attend the weekly meeting of their party executive.²² In addition, in all parties ministers and secretaries of state meet with the chairman of the party (who by definition is not

---

¹⁸ Parties also drop in the *cabinets ministériels* MPs who were not re-elected or young wolves in order to acquire some political or governmental apprenticeship. Cabinet members recruited amongst the civil service use their passage through a ministerial cabinet as a way to ensure their promotion in the civil service.

¹⁹ An important part, esp. those at lower levels, is engaged in running the clientelist machinery, esp. for the minister's electoral constituency. Some superior level collaborators ('phantoms') work directly and exclusively for the party, and hardly ever show up at the cabinet's offices.

²⁰ Usually with exclusion of the party which provides for the PM.

²¹ In addition to this ministerial cabinet for general affairs, they can rely on a cabinet for each ministerial portfolio they have. Thus, these vice-PMs often have more than two hundred personal collaborators, as they often have three cabinets.

²² The impact of the party executive on ministers' behaviour varies between parties. In the CVP, PSC, PVV, and PRL, the ministers play a dominant role. They inform the executive about cabinet matters, and only on matters crucial to the party can the executive exert some corrective power. In contrast, the executives of the PS and the SP do have a more significant influence. Discussions are reported to be fierce, ministers often receive 'marching orders', and on important matters ministers generally have to consult their party executive (De Winter 1993).

a member of the cabinet) the day before the cabinet meeting. These meetings carefully scrutinize the cabinet agenda and define the positions to be defended by the ministers the following day. In all parties, these meetings with the party chairman and other party leaders exert a stronger influence on the positions of ministers than do meetings with the party executive. Informal and ad hoc contacts are important as well. For instance, when important issues or new facts are unexpectedly evoked in the cabinet, the meeting is sometimes suspended to allow ministers to phone their party leader for advice, or the matter is postponed until the next meeting.

Inter-Party Summits, Pacts, and Package Deals

Coalition parties also influence cabinet decision making through direct formal and informal contacts between leaders of the parties outside government (and outside the parliamentary arena). Decisions that are reached are binding for cabinet members. Often these summits reach compromises by adding a large number of conflictual issues to the logroll. This solves the problem of shirking, which is particularly relevant when a large number of coalition parties have to vote on a number of bills sequentially. The more these bills are decoupled and spread out over time, the stronger this temptation may be. Hence, on major conflictual issues, like linguistic and denominational matters and mass subsidies to declining industrial sectors, compromises are reached through comprehensive logrolls. Sometimes these decisions acquire the status of political pacts, amendable neither by the cabinet nor by the parliamentary majority.

This type of coalition maintenance became extremely visible in the 1970s with regard to federalization. During Tindemans IV, party leaders had often come to the aid of a gridlocked cabinet, while trying to implement the government agreement on institutional reform. It was clear that in this policy area the six party presidents were making the most important decisions outside the cabinet. Yet, in the 1981–8 period, most parties have appointed their real leaders as vice-PMs to redefine the power relationship between cabinet and parties. Thus, in that period the cabinet once again became the most prominent arena of coalition maintenance. The Belgian experience suggests that whether the real leaders of the coalition parties serve in the cabinet is a key determinant of the prominence of this form of coalition maintenance.

COALITION AGREEMENTS

The joint programme containing coalition policy is, as mentioned above, typically drafted before the cabinet takes office. Since the late 1960s this accord is referred to as the 'coalition agreement' which is usually published as an appendix to the official 'government declaration' in parliament. Agreements have also emerged at sub-national level, during the formation of regional and community executives as well as local executives (Ackaert 1996). Coalition agreements are essentially policy packages and hardly ever deal with matters such as portfolios or patronage appointments. Coalition agreements are meant to provide part of the coalition policy agenda and to prevent the occurrence of conflict within the coalition (Timmermans 1996). The conflict prevention function is particularly important on issues that proved to be controversial during coalition formation.

Table 9.5 reports whether or not a coalition agreement was reached and made public. The practice of writing down policy agreements into a protocol before portfolios are distributed dates back to 1958 (Eyskens 1993: 462). While at that time agreements remained secret, a few years later they became public. This has meant a greater pressure on the coalition parties not to 'lose face' before the party militants as well as the broader public, as journalists are keen to find leaks in the coalition boat. The size of coalition agreements has certainly grown, as can be seen in Table 9.6. Until 1958 the government declaration, which was presented in both houses of parliament, was the only written document. In the early 1960s, the party leaders began to write down the results of the negotiations earlier in the formation process, though these results (the 'technical ordinances') were published only after the cabinet was sworn in or not at all (Neels 1975: 2394). In the 1970s, policy negotiations became more institutionalized and coalition agreements were published immediately after the negotiators had signed. The agreement is now often referred to, somewhat irreverently, as the 'coalition bible'. They also became longer than the government declaration, which increasingly was used to outline the agreement. The longest agreements have been issued when the Socialists have participated, which may have something to do with the traditionally programmatic character of this party family.

Policies

The increased length of coalition agreements and the policy content suggest that these documents are evolving into comprehensive programmes. Different kinds of factors such as the broadening scope of government activities and the complex internal structures of parties may require that all areas of government activity be included, but the number of really controversial issues in coalition formation usually seems to be between five and ten, though the scarcity of information and the absence of agreements in written form makes it difficult to be precise about the period before 1965.

The multidimensional character of the important issues in most coalition agreements has become evident since the mid-1960s. It is precisely in the

TABLE 9.5. Coalition governance in Belgium, 1946–1999

(1) Government	(2) Coalition agreement	(3) Agreement public	(4) Election rule	(5) Conflict management mechanisms	(6) Most common management mechanisms	(7) Mechanism for most serious conflicts	(8) Discipline in legislation	(9) Discipline in other parliamentary behaviour	(10) Freedom of appointment	(11) Policy agreement	(12) Junior ministers	(13) Non-cabinet positions
BSP/PSB–PVV/PLP–PCB/KPB 1946 2	N	NA	N	CaC	CaC	CaC	2	4	Y	1	N	Y[c]
BSP/PSB–PVV/PLP–PCB/KPB 1946 3*	N	NA	N	CaC	CaC	CaC	2	4	Y	1	N	Y[c]
CVP/PSC–BSP/PSB 1947	N	NA	N	CaC,PS	CaC	PS	2	4	Y	1	N	Y[c]
CVP/PSC–PVV/PLP 1949	N	NA	N	CaC	CaC	CaC	2	4	Y	1	N	Y[c]
BSP/PSB–PVV/PLP 1954	N	NA	N	CaC,PS	CaC	PS	2	4	Y	1	N	Y[c]
CVP/PSC–PVV/PLP 1958 2	IE	N	N	CaC,PS	CaC	PS	2	4	Y	1	Y	Y[c]
CVP/PSC–BSP/PSB 1961	POST	N	N	IC,CaC,PS	IC	PS	2	4	Y	3	N	Y[c]
CVP/PSC–BSP/PSB 1965	POST	Y	N	IC,CaC,PS	IC	PS	2	4	Y	3	Y	Y[c]
CVP/PSC–PVV/PLP 1966	IE	Y	N	IC,CaC	IC	IC	2	4	Y	3	Y	Y[c]
CVP–PSC–BSP/PSB 1968	POST	Y	N	IC,CaC,PS	IC	PS	2	4	Y	3	Y	Y[c]
CVP–PSC–BSP/PSB 1972	POST	Y	N	IC,CaC,PS	IC	PS	2	4	Y	3	Y	Y[c]
PSB/BSP–CVP–PSC–VLD–PRL 1973	IE	Y	N	IC,CaC,PS	IC	PS	2	4	Y	3	Y	Y[d]
CVP–PSC–VLD–PRL 1974 1	POST	Y	N	IC,CaC	CaC	IC	2	4	Y	3	Y	Y[d]
CVP–PSC–VLD–PRL–RW 1974 2	IE	Y	N	IC,CaC	CaC	IC	2	4	Y	2[b]	Y	Y[d]
CVP–PSC–VLD–PRL 1977 1	IE	NA	N	IC,CaC	CaC	IC	2	4	Y	0	Y	Y[d]
CVP–PSC–BSP/PSB–VU–FDF 1977 2	POST	Y	N	IC,CaC,PS	IC	PS	2	4	Y	3	Y	Y[d]
PSC–CVP–BSP/PSB–VU–FDF 1978*	N	N	N	IC,CaC,PS	IC	PS	2	4	Y	3	Y	Y[d]
CVP–PSC–PS–SP–FDF 1979	POST	Y	N	IC,CaC,PS	IC	PS	2	4	Y	3	Y	Y[d]
CVP–PSC–PS–SP–VLD–PRL 1980 1	NA	NA	N	IC,CaC,PS	IC	PS	2	4	Y	3	Y	Y[d]
CVP–PSC–PS–SP–VLD–PRL 1980 2	IE	Y	N	IC,CaC,PS	IC	PS	2	4	Y	3	Y	Y[d]
CVP–PS–SP 1980 3	IE	Y	N	IC,CaC,PS	IC	PS	2	4	Y	3	Y	Y[d]
CVP–PS–SP 1981 1*	IE	Y	N	IC,CaC,PS	IC	PS	2	4	Y	3	Y	Y[d]
CVP–PSC–VLD–PRL 1981 2	POST	Y	N	IC,CaC	CaC	IC	2	4	Y	3	Y	Y[d]
CVP–PSC–VLD–PRL 1985	POST	Y	N	IC,CaC	CaC	IC	2	4	Y	3	Y	Y[d]
CVP–PSC–PS–SP–VU 1988	POST	Y	N	IC,CaC,PS	IC	PS	2	4	Y	3	Y	Y[d]
CVP–PS–SP 1991	POST	Y	N	IC,CaC,PS	IC	PS	2	4	Y	1	Y	Y[d]
CVP–PS–SP 1992	POST	Y	N	IC, CaC,PS	IC	PS	1	4	Y	3	Y	Y[d]
CVP–PS–SP 1995	POST	Y	N	IC,CaC,PS	IC	PS	1	4	Y	3	Y	Y[d]

* New cabinet, but no new government.
(Decl) Government declaration presented to both Chambers.
[a] The inner cabinet (*kerncabinet*) is officially abolished but in practice it still exists.
[b] Extension of the previous agreement after the RW joined the government.
[c] Sectoral and punctual.
[d] Global.

TABLE 9.6. *Size and content of coalition agreements in Belgium, 1966–1999*

	Size	General rules of the game (in %)	Specific rules of the game (in %)	Distribution of offices (in %)	Distribution of competences (in %)	Policy (in %)
CVP/PSC–PVV/PLP 1966	3,150	1	8	0	0	91
CVP/PSC–BSP/PSB 1968	6,150	4	7	3	3	83
CVP–PSC– BSP/PSB 1972	12,050	0	1.5	0	0.5	98
BSP/PSB–CVP–PSC–VLD–PRL 1973	21,000	5	4	1	1	89
CVP–PSC–VLD–PRL 1974 1	7,350	0	1	0	0	99
CVP–PSC– VLD–PRL–RW 1974 2	10,400	3	3	1	0	93
CVP–PSC– VLD–PRL 1977 1	nnca					
CVP–PSC–BSP/PSB–VU–FDF 1977 2	12,600	3	12	1	1.5	84
PSC–CVP–BSP/PSB–VU–FDF 1978*	nnca					
CVP–PSC–PS–SP–FDF 1979	15,500	0	14	1	1	84
CVP–PSC–PS–SP 1980 1	nnca					
CVP–PSC–PS–SP–VLD–PRL 1980 2	21,800	0	14	1	0	85
CVP–PSC–PS–SP 1980 3	13,900	1	1	0	0	98
CVP–PSC–PS–SP 1981 1*	nnca					
CVP–PSC–VLD–PRL 1981 2	6,950	0	0	0	1	99
CVP–PSC–VLD–PRL 1985	13,500	0	3	0	0	97
CVP–PSC–PS–SP–VU 1988	43,550	0	7	0	0	93
CVP–PSC–PS–SP 1991	nnca					
CVP–PSC–PS–SP 1992	7,500	1	3	0	0	96
CVP–PSC–PS–SP 1995	17,350	1	1	0	1	97

* new cabinet, but no new government
nnca = no new coalition agreement

coalition agreement that the salience of different policy dimensions becomes most visible, provided that conflicts on a particular dimension do not prevent the formation of the coalition in the first place. One policy area that has become important in coalition bargaining and the subsequent agreements is cultural autonomy and the regionalization of socio-economic competencies for the French-speaking and the Dutch-speaking communities. These matters have caused the fall of many coalitions. A particularly thorny issue has been the drawing of the boundaries of Brussels, which was to become the country's third region next to Flanders and Wallonia. Especially when such issues were prominent on the agenda and large coalitions were thought to be necessary, heterogeneity on other issues increased. And the more parties participate, the greater the likelihood of policy conflict. This has induced parties to make accords on economic and financial issues, on school policy, as well as on morality issues such as abortion. More recent matters of general salience are nuclear policy and environmental issues.

Procedural Rules and Competencies

Coalition agreements also contain procedural rules and statements on competencies, though both are clearly less prominent. Changes in ministerial jurisdictions, however, usually fall outside the scope of coalition agreements (hence the low percentages mentioned in Table 9.5). The main reason why the coalition agreement is called the coalition bible may be the often-felt need for an exegesis of the document. But even if arrangements are detailed and clear-cut, they still need enforcement mechanisms within and between coalition parties. Coalition parties have to enforce this agreement in such disparate fora as the parliamentary party, the party's ministers, the party executive and president, and the national congress. How, then, can coalition agreements be enforced between and within coalition parties? A large and sophisticated set of coalition maintenance mechanisms has been developed over time.

The general rules of the game stress the 'morality of duty' of coalition partners, to remain loyal and faithful to the substantive or procedural arrangements in the coalition agreement. Initially these rules concerned the coalition agreement. Such references can be positive, if the argument is that the bible explicitly includes the proposed policy, or negative, if nothing in the bible precludes the initiative. From 1991 to 1999, this latter strategy was obsolete, as coalition agreements concluded with the formula that 'also for all matters not included in the coalition agreement the majority parties have agreed to observe the classical rule of consensus within the cabinet and in parliament' (see below). This meant that according to the agreement, majority MPs and ministers could only launch new policies when their initiative had been explicitly approved by the other majority parliamentary parties or by the full cabinet. Hence, for individual MPs and ministers, the clause meant 'the bible and nothing but the bible', unless all coalition parties agreed to modify or expand it. A second category of written rules detail how parties will deal with specific policy areas, in particular controversial ones such as language and community policy. Often, such procedures are 'agreements to disagree' that postpone the issue or refer it to some external committee of experts. When these issues have been high on the political agenda, coalition agreements have contained extensive procedural arrangements for dealing with them (1968, 1977, 1979, 1980, and 1988).

Allocation of Cabinet and Junior Ministerships

With the growing number of governing parties and the complexity of institutional constraints, the allocation of cabinet and junior ministerships is ruled by detailed arrangements. First, each position has a specific weight. The '3-2-1' counting rule, installed in 1980, accords three points for the position of prime minister, two for a minister, and one for a secretary of state. To this package are added the presidents of the House and the Senate (each worth 2 points). As constitutionally the number of Flemish and Francophone ministers must be equal, the party leaders first negotiate the number of points for each linguistic community. They then allocate points to the specific parties according to their numerical strength. In a first round each party president then chooses his most preferred portfolio(s), starting with the president of the strongest coalition party and ending with the weakest partner.[23] Once the portfolios are distributed amongst the players, they evaluate the initial result, which can sometimes be less than optimal for all parties. If this is the case, new bilateral and multilateral negotiations occur, until a new equilibrium is reached. These secondary bargaining rounds sometimes require the augmentation of the number of portfolios, or the moving of certain competencies from one portfolio to another. Pay-offs at the level of the regional and community executives may also be negotiable. Even the Belgian seat in the European Commission is (as in 1988) included in the negotiations. Hence, during the stage of portfolio distribution, many scenarios may be tried out before one arrives at a final solution. The combination of the linguistic parity constitutional provision and this recent arithmetic practice restricts the role of the *formateur* even more, but it impinges on the parties' discretion as well.

Finally, each party president decides who will occupy the party's positions in government. Even for the ministers of his own party, the PM is only the

---

[23] For instance, in the formation bargaining process of 1995, the PSC could claim six points, and had thus to 'choose' between three ministers or two ministers and a federal Assembly President. As the PS wanted to keep its five ministers and that altogether the French-speaking partners had to respect the linguistic parity in the Council of Ministers, the PSC finally had no choice at all and received the same 'package' as before, two ministers and the Chair of the House of Representatives.

coordinator of this complex allocation process. His own personal influence on the distribution of portfolios between parties and aspirants is severely restricted by the party presidents, at least since the 1960s. Yet, party presidents are evidently not entirely free in nominating those who they personally prefer. Former ministers will demand to be reappointed, politicians representing strong constituency parties or intra-party factions will demand ministerial representation, ministerial appointments have to fairly represent the provinces and constituency parties, the sexes, and the two chambers. In addition, a party president's discretion depends strongly on his power within his party, as well as on his personal resources and background. Finally, the King has discreetly managed to promote some candidates and reject some others (Waleffe 1971).

In order to calculate the degree of proportionality between each party's share of portfolios and its relative (that is to say, within the coalition) share of parliamentary seats, we summed the differences between the proportions of parliamentary seat (within the coalition) and the proportions of ministerial portfolios, and divided by two.[24] The overall disproportionality is often quite high, in nine cases even 10 percentage points or more. Yet, as mentioned above, many other positions are added to the coalition bargain, which may account for some of the discrepancies. Hence, if we take into consideration the '3-2-1' rule and include the chamber presidents and the secretaries of state, disproportionality decreases in twenty-three out of thirty-three cases. Still, nine cases exhibit disproportionality indices of 10 points or more even under this counting rule. Do some parties systematically get more than their proportional share of portfolios, and if so, why? During the period in which the traditional parties were still united, the CVP/PSC usually got less than their share in seats, the PSB/BSP were always cut short except once, while the PVV/PLP nearly always got a better than proportional deal. First, in other words, the small Liberal Party got a better share than the two major parties.[25] This could be explained in several ways. In the period considered, there was strong clerical–anti-clerical opposition, and the Liberals were the pivotal party on that dimension. Second, for the Liberals, as a party of notables, portfolios may have been more important than policies. Hence, maybe Socialists and Christian Democrats made portfolio sacrifices for policy concessions. Finally, especially early in that period disproportionality is affected by the nomination of non-partisan technicians.

[24] Portfolios given to non-partisan technicians have been counted in the calculation of the basis from which proportions of portfolios have been calculated. Thus, the sum of parliamentary seat shares may in some cases be larger than the sum of portfolio shares held by the coalition parties.

[25] In his memoirs, Gaston Eyskens (1993: 461) writes in fact that usually the Liberals were asking more posts than the number they could claim for given their parliamentary strength.

For the period after the parties split up along regional lines, the biggest party, the CVP, has always been under-represented, along with the Flemish Socialists and Liberals. The constitutional rule of linguistic parity amongst ministers causes an over-representation of the francophone parties, for which the exclusion from this rule of the secretaries of state,[26] the 'linguistic neutrality' of the PM, the '3-2-1' counting rule, and the inclusion of the chamber presidents do not compensate. Of the francophone parties, the PSC (except once) and the PRL have always been over-represented, while the PS has usually drawn its share. Finally, of the other parties, only the FDF has consistently received more than its share, while the VU, the RW, and the Communists have been under-represented. Hence, apart from the poor share of the Flemish parties, there has been no clear pattern after the traditional parties split. Only the PSC has been over-represented among the pivotal parties, and only the FDF among the surplus parties indispensable for a two-thirds parliamentary majority. Nor have parties returning to power after a long opposition period been over-represented in compensation for their meager years in the opposition.

With regard to the degree of 'partisan ownership' of particular departments, some departments have been nearly monopolized by one party, while some parties have been systematically excluded from others. The CVP, in addition to the prime ministership, has usually controlled Agriculture, as the Boerenbond (Farmers' League) is one of the three CVP factions.[27] Also, Public Health is a Catholic 'property',[28] along with Flemish Culture and Environment. On the other hand, until 1999, Foreign Affairs never went to the Liberals, who have also been rare occupants in Interior. They have even more clearly been excluded from all the social departments (Social Affairs, Pensions, Labour, and Employment) and some of the large public employment departments, such as Transports and Telecommunications and Civil Service. Finance has usually gone to a Catholic in centre-left coalitions, to a Liberal in centre-right coalitions, and only once to a Socialist. Defence and Middle Classes have also rarely been given to Socialists, who, however, often occupied the Ministry of Economy. Before 1999, the non-traditional parties are often found on peripheral departments like Scientific Policy, Development Aid, and Foreign Trade. Only once has one of them won an important traditional department (Budget by the VU). The FDF got the Brussels Affairs post in the three governments it entered, and the RW the

---

[26] From 1968 (the first split of a traditional party) to 1995, for a total amount of 142 posts, 83 secretaries of state were Flemish (nearly 60%). Hence, only at the level of secretary of state, are the Flemish parties represented in proportion to their parliamentary strength.

[27] In the 1946–95 period, 26 out of 33 Ministers of Agriculture were CVP, three were PSC, the four other the result of the party being out of power.

[28] 19 Catholic ministers in the 25 coalitions they entered (19 out of 21 in the 1949–88 period), due to the predominance of Catholic pillar organizations in the Health sector (De Winter 1992).

Table 9.7. Distribution of cabinet and junior ministerships in Belgium, 1945–1999 (1)

Cabinet number	Cabinet	Number of ministers and junior ministers (secretaries of state)	(1) Prime Minister	(2) Vice-Prime Minister	(3) Finance, Budget	(4) Economy, Energy, Planning	(5) Foreign, European Affairs	(6) Defence
1	Spaak	16 = 11S + 5T	S1		T	S	S1	T
2	Van Acker III	19 = 7S + 6L + 4CO + 2T	S1		S,S	L,S1	S2	T
3	Huysmans	19 = 7S + 6L + 4CO + 2T	S		T,S	L	S1	T
4	Spaak II	19 = 8S + 9C + 2T	S1		C,S	C,S,S	S1	T
5	Eyskens	17 = 9C + 8L	C		L	C1	C2	L
6	Duvieusart	15 = 15C	C		C	C1	C2	C
7	Pholien	16 = 15C + 1T	C		C	C3	C	T
8	Van Houtte	16 = 15C + 1T	C		C	C2	C	T
9	Van Acker IV	16 = 9S + 7L	S		L	L	S	S
10	Eyskens II	15 = 15C	C		C	C	C	C
11	Eyskens III	19 = 12C + 7L	C		C	L	C	C
12	Lefèvre	18 = 11C* + 7S;1c* + 2s	C1	S1	C + s	S,C1	S1	C
13	Harmel	20 = 12C + 8S;3c + 4s	C1	S1	C + s	S1	S2	C
14	Van den Boeynants I	19 = 12C + 6L + 1T;1c + 3l	C1	L1	T, L1	L	C,C3	L
15	Eyskens IV	27 = 15C + 12S;1c + 1s	CN	S1F	CF,SF	S1F	CF	CN
16	Eyskens V	19 = 10C + 9S;5c + 5s	CN	S1F	CN, S1F + s1n	SF	CF + s2n + s1f	CF
17	Leburton	22 = 9S + 9C + 4L;4s + 6c + 4l	S1F + cf**	L1N,C1N	L1N,C1N + cf	S2N	CN + s1f + l1n	CF
18	Tindemans I	19 = 13C + 6L.3c + 3l	C1N		LN,cm	CF	C2N + cf	C2F
19	Tindemans II	21 = 14C + 6L + 1RW.;2c + 2l + 2rw	C1N		LN,cm	CF + rwf	C3N	C2F
20	Tindemans III	25 = 16C + 9L;1c + 2l	CN		LN,C3N	C5F,LF	C1N	C2F
21	Tindemans IV	23 = 10C + 9S + 2FDF + 2VU;2c + 3s + 1fdf + 1vu	CN	C1F,S1F	CN,c1n	SN	SF	C1F
22	Van den Boeynants II	22 = 9C + 9S + 2FDF + 2VU;2c + 3s + 2fdf + 2vu	C1F	C2N,S1F	CN,C1F + c1n	SN	S2F	C1F
23	Martens I	25 = 12C + 11S + 2FDF;4c + 3s + 1fdf	CN	S1F,C1F,S1N	CN,S1F	S3N	SF	C1F
24	Martens II	24 = 13C + 11S;4c + 4s	CN	S1 F,C1F,S2N	CN,S1F	S2N	SF	C1F
25	Martens III	27 = 12C + 10S + 5L;3c + 2s + 4l	CN	S1F,L1N	LF + sn,CN	SN,C1F	CF	LF
26	Martens IV	25 = 13C* + 12S;6c* + 2s	CN	S1F,C1F,S2N	CN,S4F	S2N,C1F	CF	CN

27	M Eyskens	25 = 13C* + 12S;6c* + 2s		S2F,C1F,S1N	CN,S2F	S1N,C1F	CF	CN
28	Martens V	15 = 8C + 7L;5c + 5l	CN	L1F,C1F,L2N	L2N,C4F	CN+1f,C4F	C3N	LN
29	Martens VI	15 = 8C + 7L;8c + 5l	C1N	L2F,C4F,L1N	CN,L1N	CF+cn,L1N	C3N	L3F
30	Martens VII	19 = 8C + 9S + 2VU;5c + 7s + 1vu	CN	VU1N,C2F,C1N,S1F,S2N	CF+c1n,VU1N	S2N+sf	CN	SF
31	Martens VIII	17 = 8C + 9S;4c + 5s	CN	C2F,S1F,C1N,S2N	CF,C3N	S2N+sf	CN	SF
32	Dehaene I	15 = 7C + 8S;1s	CN	C1F,S2F, S1N	CF,CN	C1F	S1N	CN
33	Dehaene II	15 = 7C + 8S;1c + 1s	CN	C2N,S2F,C1F,S1N	C1F,C2N	S2F	SN	CF

Notes

The first figure (before =) is the total number of cabinet ministers. Next the column reports the number of ministers per party (S = socialists, T = technician, CO = communists, C = catholics, L = liberals). Finally, the column reports the number of secretaries of state per party (s = socialists, t = technician, co = communists, c = catholics, l = liberals).

After the linguistic issue has become relevant, the table not only identifies the ministers' and junior minister's party affiliation:

C/c   Catholics
L/li   Liberals
RW/rw Rassemblement Wallon
FDF/fdf Front Démocratique des Francophones
VU/vu Volksunie
Co/co Communists
S/s   Socialists
T/t   Technician

but also their linguistic group:

F   francophone
N   dutchspeaking

The party affiliation always comes first, followed by linguistic group, for instance CN for a Dutch-speaking minister of the Catholics or sf for a French-speaking junior minister of the Socialists. Ministers holding several portfolios are identified by their party family, the linguistic affiliation and a number, which is repeated for each portfolio under their command. For instance, for the Dehaene II cabinet, the Vice-PM of the CVP is labeled C2N (dutch-speaking Catholic), who also held the portfolio of budget (where he appears again as C2N). In particular the Vice-PMs often hold multiple portfolios.

If there is more than one entry of a minister in a cell (separated by commas), this means that at this time two departments existed, e.g. a Ministry of Budget and a Ministry of Finance.

* One of the members of these cabinets is a genuine minister and a watchdog junior minister for another minister at the same time. As they share two different roles, they are identified by an asterisk rather than a number.

** Secretary of State for the German Community and Tourism, helps the prime minister.

338 De Winter, Timmermans, and Dumont

TABLE 9.7. Continued

Cabinet number	Cabinet	(7) Justice	(8) Interior	(9) Education	(10) Social Affairs, Pensions	(11) Labour, Employment, Equal Opportunities	(12) Health, Family	(13) Public Works, Housing, Infrastructure
1	Spaak	S	S	S	S2	S2	T	S
2	Van Acker III	L	L	S	S3	S3	CO	CO, CO
3	Huysmans	L	L	S	S2	S2	CO	CO, CO
4	Spaak II	C	S	S	S2	S2	C	C, C
5	Eyskens	L	C	L	C3	C3	L	L, L
6	Duvieusart	C	C	C	C3	C3	C	C, C
7	Pholien	C	C	C	C1	C1	C	C, C
8	Van Houtte	C	C	C	C1	C1	C	C, C
9	Van Acker IV	L	S	S	S1	S1	S	L1
10	Eyskens II	C	C	C	C1	C1	C	C2
11	Eyskens III	L	L	L	C	C	C	L1
12	Lefèvre	S	C2	S+c*	S	C	C	S
13	Harmel	C	S	S	S, C	C	C, C2	C, C2, S
14	Van den Boeynants I	C2	L	L	C	C	C, C4	C, C4
15	Eyskens IV	SN	SF	SF, SN	CN	SN	SF, S2N	CN, S2N
16	Eyskens V	SN	CN	SF, SN	SF	SN	CF	CN + sn + cf
17	Leburton	LN	SF	LF, SN	SN	SF	CN	CF + cn + sn + sf
18	Tindemans I	LN	CF	CF, LN	CN	CF	CN	LF, cln, llf
19	Tindemans II	LN	CF	CF, LN	CN, CF	C6F	CN	LF, C6F + cln
20	Tindemans III	LN	CF	CF, LN	c2f, s2n, vuln	C6F	CN	LF, C6F
21	Tindemans IV	CN	SN	CF, SN	c2f, s2n, vuln	SF	C2N	S2F
22	Van den Boeynants II	C2N	SN	SF, SN	CF	SF	C5N	S2F
23	Martens I	CN	C2F	SF, SN	CF	SF	C4N	SF
24	Martens II	CN	C2N	SF, SN	CN, L2N	SN	C4N	SF
25	Martens III	L1N	S2F	SF, SN + cm*	C3N, CF	SN	C2F	CN
26	Martens IV	S5F	S4F	SF, SN + cm*	C4N, CF	SN	C3N	C2N
27	M Eyskens	S3F	S4F	S4F, SN + cm*	C2N + cf	SN	C4N	C2N
28	Martens V	L1F	C1F	LF, CN	C2N + cf	CF	—	LF
29	Martens VI	L2 F	C4F	LF, CN	SF, SF + sn	CF	cn	LF
30	Martens VII	C2F	S3N	SF, S2N	SF, SF + sn	SN	sf	CN
31	Martens VIII	C2F	S1N	S1F, S2N	SF, SN	CN	sf	—
32	Dehaene I	C1F	S3N	—	SF, SN	CN	SF	—
33	Dehaene II	CN	S1N	—	SF, S3N	CN	SN	—

Belgium 339

Cabinet number	Cabinet	(14) Transports, Telecom	(15) Agriculture, Small and Medium-sized Enterprises	(16) Middle Classes	(17) Trade, Foreign Aid Development	(18) Culture	(19) Science Policy	(20) Civil Service
1	Spaak	S	S	—	T, S	—	—	—
2	Van Acker III	S	L	—	S2, L	—	—	—
3	Huysmans	S	L	—	S1, L	—	—	—
4	Spaak II	S	C	C	C, C	—	—	—
5	Eyskens	C	C	C1	C2, C	—	—	—
6	Duvieusart	C	C	C1	C2, C	—	—	—
7	Pholien	C	C	C3	C, C	—	—	—
8	Van Houtte	C	C	C2	C, C	—	—	—
9	Van Acker IV	S	L	C	S, L	—	—	—
10	Eyskens II	C	C	C	C	—	—	—
11	Eyskens III	C	C	C	L, C	C	C1	L
12	Lefèvre	C, S	C	C	C	C*	C1	C2
13	Harmel	C, S	C	C	S2 + c	—	C1	C1 + s
14	Van den Boeynants I	C	C	C	L	C2F, C3N	C1	c
15	Eyskens IV	CN, SN	CF	CF	SN, CF	CF, CN	CN	CF
16	Eyskens V	SF, SN	C2N	C2N	s2n, s1f	CF, CN	C1N	C1N + cf
17	Leburton	SN + ln	CN	LF	l1n, s1f	SF, C3N	CF	S1F + cn
18	Tindemans I	CN	CN	LF	LF, C2N	CF, C4N	C1N	C1N + ln
19	Tindemans II	CN	CN	LF	LF, C3N	CF, C4N	C1N	C1N + ln
20	Tindemans III	CN	CN	LF	LF, C1N	CF, C4N	C3N	LN
21	Tindemans IV	CN, FDF1F	C3F	C3F	VUN, FDFF	SF + fdff, C4N + vuln	VUN	S1F
22	Van den Boeynants II	CN, FDF1F	C6F	C6F	VUN, FDFF	SF + fdff, C4N + vuln	VUN	S1F
23	Martens I	CN, SF	C3N	C3N	FDF1F, CN	—	FDF1F	S2N
24	Martens II	CN, SF	C3N	C3N	SF,CN	—	C2N	—
25	Martens III	S2F, L2N	C3N	C3N	SF, CN	—	C1F	CF
26	Martens IV	S1F, SN	CN	C1F	SF, CN	—	C5F	C5F
27	M Eyskens	SF, SN	CN	C1F	SF, CN	—	C5F	C5F
28	Martens V	LN + cn	cn	L3F	L2N, C3N + lf	—	C4F	C1F + lf
29	Martens VI	C1N, L4N	cn	LN + lf	L4N + lf, C3N + ln	—	L1N	C4F + ln, C1N + cf
30	Martens VII	C1N, SN	cn	C2F + cn	SF, VUN	—	VU1N + sn	CF
31	Martens VIII	C1N, SN	cn	C2F + cn	SF, SN	—	C3N + sn	CF
32	Dehaene I	S2F	CN	—	SF, sn	—	SF	S3N
33	Dehaene II	S2F	CN	—	C1F, cn	—	SF	—

TABLE 9.7. Continued

Cabinet number	Cabinet	(21) Environment	(22) Institutional Reforms	(23) Brussels	(24) Wallonia	(25) Flanders	(26) French Community	(27) Flemish Community	(28) Regional Economy	(29) War Recovery
1	Spaak	—	—	—	—	—	—	—	—	T, S
2	Van Acker III	—	—	—	—	—	—	—	—	CO, T, L
3	Huysmans	—	—	—	—	—	—	—	—	CO, S, L
4	Spaak II	—	—	—	—	—	—	—	—	T, S, T
5	Eyskens	—	—	—	—	—	—	—	—	—
6	Duvieusart	—	—	—	—	—	—	—	—	±
7	Pholien	—	—	—	—	—	—	—	—	—
8	Van Houtte	—	—	—	—	—	—	—	—	—
9	Van Acker IV	—	—	—	—	—	—	—	—	—
10	Eyskens II	—	—	—	—	—	—	—	—	—
11	Eyskens III	—	—	—	—	—	—	—	—	—
12	Lefèvre	—	—	—	—	—	—	—	—	—
13	Harmel	—	—	—	—	—	—	—	C1 + l	—
14	Van den Boeynants I	—	—	—	—	—	—	—	cn, sf	—
15	Eyskens IV	—	—	—	—	—	—	—	S1F + cn	—
16	Eyskens V	—	—	—	—	—	—	—	S2N + cn + lf	—
17	Leburton	C2N	C1N, S1F + lf	SF	CF	C3N	—	—	cln, llf	—
18	Tindemans I	C1N + ln	RWF,CN	CF	C6F	C4N	—	—	cln, rwf	—
19	Tindemans II	C1N + ln	LF,CN	C2F	C6F	C4N	—	—	C5F, cln, lln	—
20	Tindemans III	lln	sf, cn	C2F + ln	C6F	C4N + lln	—	—	cln, slf	—
21	Tindemans IV	C2N	sf, cn	FDF1F + vuln	S2F + c2f	C4N + s2n	—	—	cln, slf	—
22	Van den Boeynants II	C5N	C2F, S2N	FDF1F + vuln	S2F + c2f	C4N + s2n	—	—	—	—
23	Martens I	C4N	C2N	FDFF + sf + sn	SF + cf	SN + cn + cn	CF + fdff	CN	—	—
24	Martens II	C4N	S2F,L1N	CF + sf + sn	SF + cf	SN + cn + cn	CF + sf	CN	—	—
25	Martens III	C2F	—	CF + ln + sf	SF + cf + lf	—	CF + lf	LN, SN, CN + ln + cn + cn	—	—
26	Martens IV	C5F	S5F, C2N	SF + cf + sn	SF + cf	—	CF	CN*, SN	—	—
27	M Eyskens	C5F	S3F, C2N	SF + cf + sn	SF + cf	—	CF	CN*, SN	—	—
28	Martens V	—	L1F, C2N	L3F + cf + ln	—	—	—	—	—	—
29	Martens VI	cn	L2F, C2N	L3F + cf + ln	—	—	—	—	—	—
30	Martens VII	cn	S1F, C1N + sn	S1F + cf + vun	—	—	—	—	—	—
31	Martens VIII	cn	C1N, S1F + cn	S1 F	—	—	—	—	—	—
32	Dehaene I	S5F	—	—	—	—	—	—	—	—
33	Dehaene II	sn	—	—	—	—	—	—	—	—

portfolio 'without department' of Institutional Reforms, which were small portfolios but central to the parties' programmes. The Communists have never won a politically important department. Given these poor office rewards, the surplus parties presumably have joined coalitions because they were offered more specific policy rewards, which fits with their nature as single-issue parties.

Patronage Agreements

Belgian parties have developed sophisticated arrangements for monitoring agreements on job patronage. Together with Italy and Austria, Belgium constitutes one of the Western European countries in which government patronage over the public sector, which employs nearly one-quarter of the working population, is particularly wide and deep (De Winter 1996). Recruitment to normal positions within the national administration is effectuated by the Permanent Secretariat for Recruitment. Appointments are based on exams, and little or no patronage is possible. However, political patronage is made possible by circumventing these normal provisions, through a variety of measures.[29] Parties exert an even stronger influence on public sector promotions. Until the end of the 1980s, the majority parties controlled the promotion of university trained civil servants through two types of inter-party concertations. The cabinet itself decides the distribution of top civil service positions and evidently takes coalition party preferences into full consideration. For the lower ranks of university trained civil servants, an unofficial inter-party committee, chaired by a collaborator of the PM, was established in the 1970s.

The parties' grip on Belgian society does not end there. The recruitment and promotion of judges was until very recently nearly completely based on party patronage, and similarly the promotion of public broadcasting personnel. Finally, in most other sectors in which parties are influential, such as public education, public, semi-public, and quasi-autonomous enterprises and services, local government, etc., parties (and trade unions) interfere with the recruitment and promotion of personnel, from the janitor in a public kindergarten to the chairman of the board of directors of SABENA. Thus, public sector patronage is a very pervasive phenomenon in Belgium, and all traditional parties participate. However, as Liberals and Socialists are not always in power (contrary to the Christian Democrats), they regularly have to try to catch up to compensate for their inability to promote their clientele while in

---

[29] Among these are the abuse of a rule which permits the recruitment of outside candidates of unique value to the civil service, the recruitment of temporary personnel or personnel for newly created departmental services, and the 'regularization' of temporary personnel (De Winter 1981; Hondeghem 1990).

[30] According to D'Hondt (1993: 128), Liberal and Socialist parties always demand a catch-up operation. The need for this seems real, as for instance data for 1990 indicates that

opposition.[30] Although as early as the 1950s, almost all public jobs were subject to governmental patronage (De Winter 1981), it is only since 1973 that the parties conclude, during coalition bargaining, a secret pact specifying party patronage quotas in different public and semi-public agencies.[31] Recently, however, patronage has declined considerably, at least in the federal government (Hondeghem 1996). Since 1988, the secret coalition agreements have therefore also included items on the depolitization of recruitment and promotions in the public sector.

CABINET TERMINATION

Termination Rules

Belgian cabinets were until 1995 subjected to a negative resignation rule: a simple majority voting in favour of a motion of censure or not supporting a motion of confidence could bring the government down (De Winter 1995). In addition, a government would also step down after a defeat on a major bill, even if it was constitutionally not obliged to and even if the government did not turn this vote into a matter of confidence.[32] Therefore, Belgian governments needed to be assured of a permanent unconditional support by the parliamentary majority.

When a PM tenders his government's resignation of to the King, the latter

---

six out of ten higher civil servants belong to the Christian Democratic ticket (Tegenbos 1992). However, the figures published by De Winter (1981: 69), Hondeghem (1990), and Tegenbos (1988) suggest that Liberal and Socialist parties do not manage to recuperate too much of the ground lost in opposition, and that the quotas agreed upon correspond closely to the parties' parliamentary strength.

[31] Before 1973, periodically, large patronage agreements were concluded, for instance following the conclusion of the School Pact (1958), and the creation of the Belgian Radio and Television (BRT-RTB) (1960), representatives of the three main parties (i.e. with the Socialists in opposition) concluded an agreement on the division of the top nominations. For the other nominations, each minister had a certain discretionary power, but within each party, a watchdog closely followed the nominations made and would interfere if he felt that the party's interests were threatened in that matter.

[32] The constitutional reform of 1993 reduces the already limited role of parliament in government resignation. When the House rejects a motion of confidence introduced by the government and manages to introduce the name of a new prime minister within three days, the acting government has to resign. If the House does not manage to name a new prime minister, the chambers will be dissolved. The House can also take the initiative itself to unseat the government, by voting a motion of censure, whereby at the same moment a new prime minister is named ('positive vote of censure'). If it does not manage to name an alternative PM, the government can continue or even ask the monarch to dissolve the House. Finally, when a government resigns for other reasons, the monarch can also dissolve the House if a majority in the House agrees. The dissolution of the House causes also the dissolution of the Senate.

will usually first order the demissionary PM to verify whether a reconduction of the old coalition is possible. If this is not the case, an entirely new formation process can be launched, or general elections called. The head of state will then ask the demissionary government to remain as a caretaker and attend to 'current affairs' (but no politically important matters) until a new government can be sworn in. Often, the time between resignation and election date is artificially prolonged to give both Houses time to declare certain constitutional articles open for revision, as a new parliament can only change constitutional articles declared amendable by the previous parliament. This may create a strategic dilemma, as few parties are sure to be included in the next government. Hence, the constitutional articles they declare amendable may be changed by a different majority. Parties that fear that they might be relegated to the opposition will therefore tend to maintain the constitutional status quo.

Cabinet Composition and Stability

With thirty-three cabinets between 1946 and 1995, or an average duration of 1.42 years (or 520 days), Belgium comes close to the 'pathological' Italian case of cabinet instability (see Table 9.3). On the average, post-war cabinets have only survived during 42 per cent of their theoretical maximum duration, calculated as the proportion of the number of days a cabinet lasted (from its investiture by the head of state until its resignation) compared with the total number of days that lie between the date of the investiture and the normal date for the following general elections.[33] Yet one should not overestimate the degree of instability. Over about half of the period we cover (26 years), Belgium was governed by only seven cabinets: four that completed (or nearly completed) their full four years, two that called elections during their fourth year to reinforce the parliamentary strength of the incumbent coalition, and

---

[33] Formally, there is no maximum duration for a cabinet. The electoral code stipulates that elections are held the latest four years after the final composition of the Senate. Until 1995 the Senate was composed of directly elected members, elected at the same date as the members of the House, of provincially co-opted senators, co-opted upon proposal of the nine provincial council (elected at the same moment as the members of the House), and finally these two types of senators co-opted some 'national co-opted' senators, upon proposal of the parliamentary groups in the Senate. Although the provincial councils have to appoint their candidates for co-optation into the Senate the latest three weeks after the general elections, the Senate statutory rules do not include any timetable with regard to the formal inclusion of these provincial senators, and the selection of the 'national co-opted' senators. Hence, in practice, especially if the formation of a new cabinet takes its time, the senate often takes several weeks before arriving at its full composition. This explains why in some cases the period between two election dates exceeds more than four years (between the election of 11 Apr. 1954 and 1 June 1958 (1,502 days), and between 25 Mar. 1961 and 23 May 1965 (1,519 days)). Hence, as a practical rule, we used as 'theoretical' maximum duration the practical maximum duration, i.e. the longest period between elections that ever occurred, namely 1,519 days (between 1961 and 1965).

one cabinet that lasted nearly three years. The low overall stability is caused by the large number (9) of cabinets that lasted less than six months, often due to an ill-conceived departure (like the attempts to form the Spaak 1946 minority cabinet), to the imminent enlargement of the coalition (1958, 1974), or to an attempt to resurrect a virtually dead coalition (1977, 1978, 1980, and 1991).

Minority cabinets have been the shortest lived, followed by the two-thirds majority coalitions. Of the 32 cabinets between 1946 and 1995, the four minority cabinets ruled on average only 58 days, the nine cabinets with a two-thirds majority (in the House) on average 567 days, while the nineteen other cabinets were on average 596 days in power, which is not much more than the former.[34] Cabinet instability also has varied substantially over time. During post-war reconstruction and the settlement of war-related issues (terminated by the settlement of the King's Question), cabinets were extremely unstable (8 cabinets in the Sept. 1944–July 1950 period). In the following period (Aug. 1950–June 1968), cabinets were relatively stable (8 cabinets in 18 years). The splitting of the traditional parties, the inclusion of regionalist parties in coalitions, and the primacy of regional/community problems then provoked high cabinet instability (June 1968–Dec. 1981: 13 cabinets in 13 years). Analyses of intra-cabinet conflicts indicate that cabinets that tried to proceed with institutional reform were also the most conflictual (Eeckhaut 1990).

The growing stability of Belgian cabinets since late 1981 (5 cabinets in 13 years)[35] does not primarily reflect a fading of (regional) conflicts, but rather the drastically increased bargaining complexity. As regional/community conflicts have become increasingly salient and difficult, cabinet formation has become such a difficult enterprise that parties that support the government have become less eager to provoke a crisis. Moreover, since asymmetrical majorities (a national government supported by a different coalition in the North than in the South) are more likely to occur in the future, no party can any longer be sure to be included in a new coalition. Finally, the explosion of public debt, fuelled by cabinet instability over the institutional problems of the 1970s and early 1980s, convinced the political elites that cabinet stability is a precondition for solving the country's deep budgetary crisis.[36]

[34] The short-lived Martens II, Martens IV, and M. Eyskens cabinets for which the two-thirds majority was not attained in the House of Representatives (contrary to the Senate), mainly cause this small difference. For the former two cases, this situation arose after the loss of coalition partner(s) that allowed the preceding cabinet to pass constitutional amendments with a special majority.

[35] If one excludes Martens VIII (1991) cabinet, which was a very short-lived and futile attempt at reviving the coalition without one of its partners, stability is quite high. Of the 1981–95 period, 11 years were completed by three cabinets only.

[36] Public debt is currently around 122% of the GNP. The size of this debt increasingly cripples the federal government in budgetary terms. Around 40% of the annual federal budget is allocated to the payment of interest on this debt (currently 38%, with a peak of 44% in 1993).

Finally, Table 9.4 indicates that some cabinets got only a lukewarm welcome (70% or fewer favourable votes) at their respective party congresses. This was the case in the PSB/BSP in 1965,[37] 1968, and 1973; the PS in 1980 and 1988; the CVP in 1973 and 1991; the PSC in 1988; the PRL in 1973; the VU in 1977; and in the FDF in 1977 and 1979. Especially some oversized cabinets have been only weakly supported by one or more coalition partners (Tindemans IV, 1977–8; Leburton, 1973–4; Martens VII, 1988–91). The first two lasted only one year. Of the eight cabinets cited above, the average duration (relative to maximum potential) was 47 per cent, against an average of 42 per cent. Hence, weak initial party support does not necessarily jeopardize a coalition's chances for survival. Yet, this surprising result is basically due to the long duration of Eyskens VI, Martens VII, and Dehaene I, while the lifespans of the five others were quite short.

Causes of Termination

Table 9.8 indicates that about two-thirds of Belgian coalition cabinets have been dissolved due to policy conflict between coalition parties (17 out of 27). Only six times have these breakdowns been followed by anticipated elections, the second most important reason for termination (11 out of 27). More often, the coalition was reconducted or a coalition change was negotiated. This illustrates once again the low degree of electoral responsibility of Belgian government, as the voter is hardly ever called upon to indicate which parties should govern when a government breaks down. As far as the parties involved in policy breakdowns are concerned, each of the three regionalist parties has once defected.[38] In each case, the other coalition parties have continued in government. Most often, the policy conflict has involved the CVP and the PS, the strongest party of each linguistic community. Only three times has an intraparty conflict, in each case in the CVP, led to a cabinet breakdown. Twice a minority cabinet has been enlarged (Eyskens II in 1958 and Tindemans I in 1974), according to the original intention of the PM. Only once has a cabinet stepped down because it lost a vote of confidence/censure (Spaak I in 1946). And only three times parliament has been indirectly involved. Following the principle of cabinet solidarity Van Acker III (1946) and Spaak II (1947) cabinets stepped down after heavy parliamentary criticism of the Minister of Justice. The plan for regionalization introduced by Martens II in 1980 failed to

---

[37] Only a majority of the Walloon federations voted in favour (36%). Therefore, the agreement was accepted only due to the large support in the Flemish and Brussels federations (93% and 73%, respectively).

[38] Twice they were 'revoked': in 1977 the RW—by refusing to vote parts of the budget—wanted to force the government to speed up the regionalization process. Upon PM Tindemans' proposal, the King revoked the RW ministers. In 1980 the King revoked the FDF ministers on Martens' proposal.

346 De Winter, Timmermans, and Dumont

TABLE 9.8. *Cabinet termination in Belgium, 1946–1999*

Cabinet number	Cabinet	Mechanisms of cabinet termination									Terminal Events	Policy areas	Comments
		Technical		Discretionary									
		(1) Regular elections	(2) Other constitutional reason	(3) Early parliamentary elections	(5) Voluntary enlargement of government	(6) Cabinet defeated by opposition	(7) Conflict between coalition parties		(8) Intraparty conflict in coalition	(10) Popular opinion shocks		
							Policy	Personnel				
1	Spaak					X						Did not pass investiture vote in the Lower House
2	Van Acker III							X			7	Parliament vote against Minister of Justice (politics interference in the Judiciary), dismissal and cabinet solidarity
3	Huysmans						PCB/KPB: the rest				4	Conflict over coal prices and governmental decisions overmining industry led to Communist ministers' resignation
4	Spaak II			X			X				7, 10	Early dissolution due to internal dissensions, after different conflicts: referendum on King's question in and Minister of Justice policy over repression leading to a reshuffle in 1948, and finally dissensus between partners over financing of unemployment benefits
5	Eyskens I			X			X				8	Cabinet crisis after the referendum over the King's question. A first government resignation had been refused in order to dissolve parliament

Belgium

#	Prime Minister	C1	C2	C3	C4	C5	Coalition	Ref	Reason
6	Duvieusart	X							Leopold III resigns (because of violent demonstrations), his son Baudouin becomes Royal Prince
7	Pholien						CVP/PSC:L	7	The CVP decided to change their Prime Minister
8	Van Houtte	X							End of term
9	Van Acker IV	X							End of term
10	Eyskens II			X					Enlargement of minority government
11	Eyskens III	X						4, 17	General strike and Congo crisis
12	Lefèvre	X							End of term
13	Harmel	X							Health insurance policy
14	Van den Boeynants I	X					CVP/PSC	12, 9	Language issue, transfer of the French-speaking section of the University of Louvain out of Dutch-speaking territory
15	Eyskens IV	X							Expectations of good electoral result for outgoing coalition
16	Eyskens V		X					8	Language issue in a small commune (Fourons)
17	Leburton	X	PSB: the rest					4	State intervention in industry
18	Tindemans I			X					Enlargement of minority government (joining of the RW)
19	Tindemans II	X				RW: the rest (esp. CVP)		22	The process of federalisation is too slow for the RW ministers
20	Tindemans III	X							Caretaker cabinet
21	Tindemans IV	X						22	Egmont Pact: Regionalization, conflict over the status of Brussels
22	Van den Boeynants II	X							Caretaker cabinet
23	Martens I					FDF: the rest		22	Conflict over regionalization (Brussels in particular). The FDF ministers have to leave the cabinet

TABLE 9.8. cont.

Cabinet number	Cabinet	Mechanisms of cabinet termination									Terminal Events	Policy areas	Comments
		Technical		Discretionary									
		(1) Regular elections	(2) Other constitutional reason	(3) Early parliamentary elections	(4) Early parliamentary elections	(5) Voluntary enlargement of government	(6) Cabinet defeated by opposition	(7) Conflict between coalition parties		(8) Intraparty conflict in coalition	(10) Popular opinion shocks		
								Policy	Personnel				
24	Martens II							X		CVP;LNL		22	Regions' financial autonomy
25	Martens III							X				4, 6	Economic and defence (missiles crisis) policies
26	Martens IV							PS				4	Economic recovery plan
27	M. Eyskens			X				X				4	Crisis over state support to steel industry in Wallonia. The PS ministers went on strike in order to force their partners to allow these subsidies
28	Martens V	X										8, 9	Heysel drama and the foreseen education federalization
29	Martens VI			X				X				8	Language issue in a small commune (Fourons)
30	Martens VII							VU				17	Arms trade leads to dismissal of VU Ministers
31	Martens VIII	X						(X)				22	Federalization (Regions and Communities' competencies), resignation refused by the King and caretaker Government before constitutional revision and regular election
32	Dehaene I			X									Expectations of good electoral result for outgoing coalition

reach the two-thirds Senate majority because a few CVP senators rejected a single article. Finally, technical causes for termination have been uncommon, as only five of the sixteen general elections have not been anticipated.

As far as terminal events are concerned, only one dissolution has been due to the destabilizing effects of popular opinion pressure. Duvieusart resigned because his solution to the King's question was contested by an important part of the population, which resulted in riots with several casualties. As this is the only example of this type of terminal event, the coalition system seems rather immune to outside critical events. In fact, hardly ever has a foreign policy conflict led to termination. Domestic policy conflicts resulting in cabinet termination include six cases of institutional matters on which Flemish and francophone parties have been opposed. Six of the conflicts classified under other departmental competencies have also been of a regional/linguistic character.[39] Seven terminal policy conflicts have been related to the economy, and one general strike has terminated a cabinet.

Hence, most cabinet dissolutions are not related to critical events or technical causes, but rather to conflicts on the most salient Belgian cleavages: regional/linguistic and socio-economic issues. The fact that the denominational divide has never directly been the cause of a cabinet termination indicates that the School Pact effectively pacified this cleavage by removing it from the cabinet agenda and referring it to the all-party School Pact Commission. For several reasons, such pacification has not yet occurred for linguistic/regional issues, which only became predominant when the traditional parties split along linguistic lines. This increased the number of feasible coalition partners and therefore triggered higher instability. In a polity with two linguistically autonomous party systems, there is less danger that a party may be sanctioned by its voters for blowing up a cabinet for linguistic reasons. 'When a linguistic problem comes up, parties feel a lot of pressure to be radical, and eventually to leave or kill the coalition, and not so much pressure to try to find any compromise in order to save the coalition. The separation of the national Belgian parties has built a strong mechanism to shorten the life of coalitions' (Deschouwer 1994: 46). This kind of electoral insulation is not equally present on religious issues, on which parties therefore have a greater incentive to act cooperatively.

ELECTORAL PERFORMANCE

Table 9.9 presents the electoral costs/benefits of governmental participation. As far as the parties in power at the time of elections are concerned, Table 9.9

[39] Vandenboeynants I (1966–8), Eyskens V (1972), M. Eyskens (1981), Martens V (1981–5), VI (1985–8), and VII (1988–91).

TABLE 9.9. *Electoral costs/benefits of government parties in Belgium, 1945–1999*

Government	Government in office	Election year	CVP	PSC	SP	PS	VLD	PRL	FDF	RW	VU	PCB/ KPB	Government Mean
1946 1	No	1949											−1.1	+0.2
1946 2	No	1949			−1.8							**−4.8**	−0.2	±0
1947	Yes	1949	+1.1		−1.8		+6.4						−0.7	−6.6
1949	Yes	1950	**+4.1**		**−1.8**		**−4.1**						±0	−1.3
1950	Yes	1954	−6.6										−6.6	
1954	Yes	1958			−1.5		−1.1						−2.6	−1.85
1958 1	No	1961	−5										−5	−7.2
1958 2	Yes	1961	**−5**				+1.3						−3.7	
1961	Yes	1965	−7		−8.4								−15.4	−1.3
1965	No	1968	**−2.8**										−3.1	−0.8
1966	Yes	1968	**−2.8**		−0.3		−0.7						−3.5	
1968	Yes	1971	**−0.4**	**−1.2**	**−0.8**								−2.4	+0.3
1972	No	1974	**+1.4**	+0.9	−0.5								+1.8	
1973	Yes	1974	**+1.4**	+0.9	−0.5								+1.5	
1974 1	No	1977	+2.9	+0.7				−1.2					+3.5	+0.1
1974 2	No	1977	+2.9	+0.7				+1.8					+0.6	−0.8
1977 1	Yes	1977	**+2.9**	+0.7				+1.8					+3.5	
1977 2	Yes	1978	−0.1	+0.3		−1.6		+1.8	+0.2	−2.9	−3		−4.2	
1979	No	1981	−6.8	−3	±0	−0.3			−3.1				−13.2	−2.5
1980 1	No	1981	−6.8	−3	±0	−0.3							−10.1	+0.6
1980 2	No	1981	−6.8	−3	**±0**	**−0.3**	**+2.5**						−5	−0.45
1980 3	Yes	1981	−6.8	−3	±0	−0.3							−10.1	
1981	Yes	1985	+2	**+0.9**			−2.2	+1.6					+2.3	−2.1
1985	Yes	1987	−1.8	**±0**			+0.8	−0.8					−1.8	−0.15
1988	No	1991	−2.7	−0.3	−2.9	−2.2					−2.2		−10.3	−1.5
1991	Yes	1991	−2.7	−0.3	**−2.9**	**−2.2**							−8.1	
1992	Yes	1995	+0.4	±0	+0.6	−1.6							−0.6	
		MEANS	−0.6	−0.2	−0.8	−1.4	±0	+0.8	−1.5	−2.9	−2.6	−4.8	−3.5	
	1945–1995:		−1.5		−2.1		+0.6							

Note: The parties that decided to leave the cabinet a short time before the elections are represented in italics, and the parties responsible for governmental downfalls are represented in bold. We calculated the means for the parties which effectively ran the elections as incumbent coalition partners (excluding the ones that 'jumped off the sinking ship'). We also distinguished the unitary periods of the traditional parties from the elections they ran separately before calculating the means for the entire post–war era for the 'families'.

indicates that in most cases they lose votes, and sometimes a quite considerable percentage. Only six cabinets could increase the aggregate vote share of the government parties. In contrast, twenty cabinets faced losses, partly substantial ones. The average losses of government parties are 3.5 per cent. Only the three governments of the early 1970s, the Tindemans centre-right coalition (1976–7), and the Martens V centre-right coalition (1981–5) improved their standing through the elections. Yet, only in the last of these cases did political elites adhere to the principle of never changing a winning team, as more often a losing team was maintained (1965, 1971, 1978, 1991, 1995). In fourteen out of twenty-four cases, some parties in the coalition won, while others lost.

The averages for the individual parties are mostly negative. The Christian Democrats have lost the greatest number of post-war elections (8 out of 16), often spectacularly, and compensated only by relatively small recuperations (7 out of 16). Interestingly, the electoral fortunes of the Flemish and the francophone Christian Democrats run quite parallel after their split in 1968 (Pearson's r = 0.82). On the average, in nine centre-left cabinets (Christian Democrats, Socialists, and sometimes a regionalist party), the Christian Democrats lost 2.24 per cent. In these elections, the Socialists lost on average nearly as much: 2.20 per cent. In centre-right cabinets that went to the polls (with the Liberals and sometimes a regionalist party), however, the Christian Democrats lost on the average only 0.17 per cent, whereas the Liberals on average neither lost nor gained. Notice also that since their split, the Flemish and francophone Liberal parties have always been sanctioned differently by their respective electorates. The federalist parties usually have suffered badly from their government participation. Finally, Table 9.9 does not allow us to conclude that the 'breaker pays', that the voters systematically punish the parties responsible for breaking up the incumbent cabinet.

CONCLUSION

Since the early1970s, Belgium has become undoubtedly the Western European country with the most complex coalition bargaining system. The formation process has also become the most critical policy decision making stage. The complexity and centrality of the formation process are primarily due to the extreme fragmentation of the party system resulting from at least three salient cleavages. When one adds the recurrent necessity of forming two-thirds majority coalitions in both chambers, it is no surprise that Belgium also features the highest average number of parties in government. As a consequence, the formation process is one of the longest in Western Europe, involving a high number of formation attempts, *informateurs* and *formateurs*, often with different bargaining actors. With parties taking office more often after electoral losses than after electoral success, electoral responsiveness is very low. In addition, a large number of other matters are decided during the formation process (sub-national coalition, political patronage, the autonomy of parliament, etc.).

A large number of soft and hard institutional constraints reduce the excessively high number of potential coalition compositions, while others further complicate the bargaining process. The coalition size is affected by positive investiture vote rules, congruent and symmetrical bicameralism, two-thirds majorities required for adapting the constitution and other special majorities needed for reforming laws regarding the organization of the competencies of communities and regions. Yet, in practice, from 1958 to 1999, the coalition composition question was rather simple. As the pivotal and usually largest party family, the Christian Democrats were the main driving force in the formation process, usually choosing their coalition partner between Socialist and Liberal. When special majorities were required, tripartite coalitions amongst the three traditional political families were formed, or bipartite coalitions enlarged with regionalist parties. Therefore, Christian Democrats have been in power from 1958 to 1999 and have only had to yield the prime ministership to another party for one year in this period.

To reduce the high potential for uncertainty and shirking, political parties have developed a multifaceted and sophisticated set of coalition maintenance mechanisms. Comprehensive and detailed coalition agreements streamline the policies the cabinet will pursue. These agreements, which are endorsed by the party congresses, bind the entire party (ministers, executive, parliamentary group, rank-and-file) to the coalition. Portfolio allocation, which is decided at the very end of the formation process, generally conforms to the rule of proportionality within the constraints of the constitutionally guaranteed parity between Flemish and French-speaking ministers. Internal cabinet decision rules and conventions point to a high degree of collectiveness in decision making. Belgian ministers are not at all policy dictators: every policy initiative of any relevance has to be scrutinized and approved by the full cabinet by consensus. In addition, the inner cabinet, the vice-PMs staff for general policies, the balanced cabinet committees, junior ministers acting as watchdogs over senior ministers, inter-party summits, package deals, and political pacts all serve to enforce loyalty to the government agreement. Party leaders maintain their ministers' loyalty through intra-party summits and by posting party leadership agents in the *cabinets ministériels*.

Yet, all these coalition maintenance arrangements do not suffice, as cabinets are very unstable. They usually break down due to inter-party conflicts over issues related to the linguistic/regional divide. When coalitions survive to face the voters, in most cases the parties on the government benches lose votes, and sometimes a quite considerable percentage. Electoral responsiveness is very low. In sum, the coalition formation process is rather immune to outside critical events, technical causes of dissolution or electoral shifts. In order to understand better the underlying determinants of this process and its effect on policy, we need further in-depth analysis of the motivations, goals, and constraints of the different actors on the Belgian stage.

REFERENCES

Ackaert, Johan (1996). 'De kiezers delen de kaarten uit, de partijen spelen ermee ...', in Jo Buelens and Kris Deschouwer (eds.), *De dorpstraat is de Wetstraat niet*. Brussels: VUB Press.
Alen, André, and Dujardin, Jean (1986). *Caseboek Belgische grondwettelijk recht*. Gent: Story and Scientia.
Bergman, Torbjörn (1993). 'Formation Rules and Minority Governments'. *European Journal of Political Research*, 23: 55–66.
Budge, Ian, and Keman, Hans (1990). *Parties and Democracy*. Oxford: Oxford University Press.
——and Laver, Michael J. (1986). 'Office Seeking and Policy Pursuit in Coalition Theory'. *Legislative Studies Quarterly*, 11: 485–506.
————(1992). 'The Relationship between Party and Coalition Policy in Europe: An Empirical Synthesis', in Michael J. Laver and Ian Budge (eds.), *Party Policy and Government Coalitions*. New York: St Martin's Press.
Claeys, Paul-Henri, and Desmarez, Pierre (1994). 'L'Électorat francophone et l'axe gauche-droite', in André-Paul Frognier and Anne-Marie Aish-Van Vaerenbergh (eds.), *Elections: la fêlure? Enquête sur le comportement électoral des Wallons et des Francophones*. Brussels: De Boeck.
Deschouwer, Kris (1994). 'The Termination of Coalitions in Belgium'. *Res Publica*, 36: 43–55.
Dewachter, Wilfried (1987). 'Changes in a Partycracy: The Belgian Party System from 1944 to 1986', in Hans Daalder (ed.), *Party Systems in Denmark, Austria, Switzerland, the Netherlands and Belgium*. London: Frances Pinter.
De Winter, Lieven (1981). 'De partijpolitisering als instrument van de particratie. Een overzicht van de ontwikkeling sinds de Tweede Wereldoorlog'. *Res Publica*, 23: 53–107.
——(1989). 'Parties and Policy in Belgium'. *European Journal for Political Research*, 17: 707–30.
——(1991). 'Parliamentary and Party Pathways to the Cabinet', in Jean Blondel and Jean-Louis Thiebault (eds.), *The Profession of Government Minister in Western Europe*. London: Macmillan.
——(1992). 'Christian Democratic Parties in Belgium', in Lieven De Winter et al., *Christian Democracy in Europe*. Barcelona: Institut de Ciènces Politiques et Socials.
——(1993). 'The Links between Cabinets and Parties and Cabinet Decision-Making,. in Jean Blondel and Ferdinand Müller-Rommel (eds.), *Governing Together: The*

Extent and Limits of Joint Decision-Making in Western European Cabinets. London: Macmillan.

——(1994). 'Regionalist Parties in Belgium: The Rise, Victory and Decline of the Volksunie', in Lieven De Winter (ed.), *Non-state-wide Parties in Europe*. Barcelona: Institut de Ciènces Politiques et Socials.

——(1995). 'The Role of Parliament in Cabinet Formation and Resignation', in Herbert Döring (ed.), *Parliaments and Majority Rule in Western Europe*. New York: St Martin's Press.

——(1996). 'Party Encroachment on the Executive and Legislative Branch in the Belgian Polity'. *Res Publica*, 48: 325–52.

——and Dumont, Patrick (1999). 'The Belgian Party System(s) on the Eve of Disintegration', in David Broughton and Mark Donovan (eds.), *Changing Party Systems in Western Europe*. London: Pinter.

——Della Porta, Donnatella, and Deschouwer, Kris (1996). 'On the Comparison between the Italian and Belgian Partitocracies: Definitions, Methods and Similarities'. *Res Publica*, 48: 215–36.

——Frognier, André-Paul, and Rihoux, Benoît (1996). 'Belgium', in Jean Blondel and Maurizio Cotta (eds.), *Party and Government*. London: Macmillan.

D'Hondt, Paula (1993). *Green dienaar van de macht*. Brussels: Dedalus.

Eeckhaut, Laurence (1990). *Modes de régulation des conflits au sein du Conseil des Ministres dans la politique belge de 1961 à 1985*. Dissertation. Département des Affaires Publiques et Internationales, Université Catholique de Louvain.

Eyskens, Gaston (1993). *De memoires*. Tielt: Lannoo.

Frognier, André-Paul (1993). 'The Single Party/Coalition Distinction and Cabinet Decision-Making', in Jean Blondel and Ferdinand Müller-Rommel (eds.), *Governing Together. The Extent and Limits of Joint Decision-Making in Western European Cabinets*. London: Macmillan.

Hearl, Derek John (1992). 'Policy and Coalition in Belgium', in Michael J. Laver and Ian Budge (eds.), *Party Policy and Government Coalitions*. New York: St Martin's Press.

Hondeghem, Annie (1990). *De loopbaan van de ambtenaar: Tussen droom en werkelijkheid*. Katholieke Universiteit Leuven.

——(1996). *Inleiding tot de bestuurskunde*. Leuven: Vervolmakingscentrum voor overheidsmanagement en beleid.

Klingemann, Hans-Dieter, Hofferbert, Richard, Budge, Ian, et al. (1994). *Parties, Policies, and Democracy*. Boulder, Colo.: Westview.

Laver, Michael J., and Budge, Ian (1992) (eds.). *Party Policy and Government Coalitions*. New York: St Martin's Press.

——and Hunt, W. Ben (1992). *Policy and Party Competition*. New York: Routledge.

Lijphart, Arend (1984). *Democracies*. New Haven: Yale University Press.

Neels, Leo (1975). 'Regeringsverklaringen en Regeerakkoorden als Documenten van Toenemend Publiekrechtelijk Belang. Een nieuwe bron van het publiek recht?' *Rechtskundig Weekblad*, 38: 2369–2410.

Peterson, Robert L., and De Ridder, Martine M. (1986). 'Government Formation as a Policy-Making Arena'. *Legislative Studies Quarterly*, 11: 565–81.

————Hobbs, J. D., and McClellan, E. F. (1983). 'Government Formation and Policy Formulation: Patterns in Belgium and the Netherlands'. *Res Publica*: 25: 49–82.

Sartori, Giovanni (1976). *Parties and Party Systems*. Cambridge: Cambridge University Press.
Schofield, Norman (1993). 'Political Competition and Multiparty Coalition Governments'. *European Journal of Political Research*, 23: 1–33.
Spruyt, Marc (1995). *Grove Borstels*. Leuven: Van Halewyck.
Stengers, Jean (1992). *L'Action du Roi en Belgique depuis 1831: Pouvoir et influence*. Paris: Duculot.
Strøm, Kaare, Budge, Ian, and Laver, Michael (1994). 'Constraints on Cabinet Formation in Parliamentary Democracies'. *American Journal of Political Science*, 38: 303–35.
Swyngedouw, Mark (1993). 'Nieuwe breuklijnen in de Vlaamse politiek?' in Mark Swyngedouw, Jaak Billiet, An Carton, and Roeland Beerten (eds.), *Kiezen is Verliezen. Onderzoek naar de politieke opvattingen van Vlamingen*. Leuven: Acco.
Tegenbos, Guy (1988). 'Van benoemingen 15 t.h. gedepolitiseerd'. *De Standaard*, 30 Aug.
——(1992). 'Politieke benoemingen in België en Vlaanderen'. *Streven*, 553–60.
Timmermans, Arco (1994). 'Cabinet Ministers and Parliamentary Government in Belgium: The Impact of Coalitional Constraints', in Michael Laver and Kenneth A. Shepsle (eds.), *Cabinet Ministers and Parliamentary Government*. Cambridge: Cambridge University Press.
——(1996). *High Politics in the Low Countries: Functions and Effects of Coalition Policy Agreements in Belgium and the Netherlands*. Doctoral Dissertation. European University Institute, Florence.
Waleffe, Bernard (1971). *Le Roi nomme et révoque ses ministres: La Formation et la démission des gouvernements en Belgique depuis 1944*. Bruxelles: Bruylant.

10

The Netherlands

Still the Politics of Accommodation?

Arco Timmermans and Rudy B. Andeweg

INTRODUCTION

In the summer of 1994, three parties negotiating the formation of a new Dutch government agreed to draft legislation that would introduce a referendum at national and local level. This intention was included in the coalition agreement, the policy package that was approved by the PvdA (Social Democrats), the VVD (Liberals), and the Liberal Democrats (D66) and that was to form the programmatic basis of the ensuing three-party government. The issue was raised by D66, a party that has always advocated institutional and electoral reforms. The PvdA and especially the VVD were not too keen on introducing a referendum, but as part of a broader coalition policy package they could accept the announcement of legislation on this subject.

In the course of 1995, the government indeed drafted legislation on the referendum. While thus far the process of implementing the coalition agreement on this issue had been relatively smooth, problems occurred when the leader of the VVD in the First Chamber (Senate) stated that his party's support of the bill would depend on what compensations were offered. Alarm! cried the leader of D66 in the Second Chamber (Lower House), who stressed that these compensations already existed in the form of the coalition agreement. 'If the VVD cooperates on this issue', thus this parliamentary leader, 'my party will do the same on other policies included in the coalition agreement. But the more the VVD questions elements of the agreement, the less we will cooperate in realizing the compensations' (*De Volkskrant*, 27 Nov. 1995; translation by the authors). In June 1997 the dispute was temporarily resolved. In this context the representative of the VVD remarked that his party's loyalty 'has everything to do with the coalition agreement' and 'nothing with our opinion on this bill' (*De Volkskrant*, 26 June 1997).

This example contains two elements which are central to Dutch coalition politics. First, the formation of governments is not only about the question of which parties will join, but it also involves negotiations on policies. Each of the parties participating in these negotiations introduces the points that are salient to it. As a consequence, the results of the government formation process are twofold: a new government and, usually even before this government is formed, an agreement on coalition policy, which since the 1960s is written and has increased in size. This agreement is not just a document drafted by a *formateur* with the tacit agreement of parties, but it often requires several rounds of bargaining between party leaders.

Second, the enforcement of the coalition agreement is an important element in the coalition game. Enforcement of policy intentions made up to four years before they are really on the cabinet agenda is by no means a mechanical process. Time and circumstances, but also party competition and other political forces encroach upon the implementation of the coalition agreement within government coalitions.

This chapter deals with these two central aspects of coalition politics in the Netherlands. We begin by drawing up the main features of the party system. As the context of coalition politics also involves institutional factors, we mention a number of central institutional rules in section two. In section three we move on to the procedures and empirical processes of coalition formation. The emphasis in this chapter is on coalition governance, which is discussed in section four. Though we deal with coalition termination and duration in a separate section, it will appear from the discussion of this subject that it relates strongly to the central features of coalition governance. In the conclusion, we sum up the main points of our argument and see to what extent the character of Dutch coalition politics has changed over time.

FEATURES OF THE PARTY SYSTEM

Since political parties were formed at the end of the nineteenth century, the Netherlands has a multi-party system. The introduction of proportional representation in 1917 has been an important institutional reason for the continuous presence of Catholics, Protestants, social democrats, and liberals, and it also facilitated the entry of new parties into the Tweede Kamer, the Dutch lower house of parliament.

If we confine ourselves to the period after 1945, the number of parties represented in parliament has varied from seven parties in 1946 to fourteen parties in 1971, with an average of ten parties since the early 1980s. Changes in the number of parties in parliament have been the result of elections, but also of party splits and fusions, of which the merging of the three major religious parties into the CDA in 1977 is the most significant. A more recent political event which cannot be left unmentioned is the 'shock' elections of May 1994, which no doubt will be high in the European top 10 on electoral volatility. In these elections, the CDA suffered the greatest loss (from 54 down to 34 seats) since the introduction of proportional representation, and one party (D66) made a gain of 12 seats, the greatest success a party has ever had since 1945.

What seems to be most relevant in the present study, however, is not the number of parties in parliament as such but the number of effective parties (Laakso and Taagepera 1979). As can be seen in Table 10.1, the 'effective number of legislative parties', a measure of the size of the bargaining system, has varied between four and six parties.

In the literature on coalition theory, the Netherlands is classified as a multipolar or as a fragmented system (Laver and Schofield 1990; Schofield 1993). In both types of systems, there are three or four parties with relatively limited differences in electoral strength, and individual parties rarely obtain more than about one-third of the seats in parliament, something that can be seen in Table 10.1. The difference between multipolar and fragmented is that in the second type, there are not only several large or medium-sized parties but also a number of small parties. Given the parliamentary strength of the parties with coalition potential over time, the Dutch bargaining system has been multipolar rather than fragmented, except perhaps for the early 1970s when some new small parties were accepted as coalition partners.[1]

The one-dimensional representation of Dutch parties given in Table 10.1 is a standard way of locating parties and this has the advantage of comparability. Especially when speaking of bargaining relationships, however, this unidimensional picture about the Dutch party system is a simplification which leaves out important elements. Even if coalitions would be formed on the basis of left–right positions, other dimensions may still be relevant in coalition bargaining, especially over policy. Although much depends on how a policy dimension is defined, inter-party relationships have often involved at least one other dimension, something that is also acknowledged generally in the literature (see e.g. Luebbert 1986; Laver and Hunt 1992; Tops and Dittrich 1992; Laver 1995).

Matters on which parties have been most clearly related to each other in a way different from their usual left–right ordering are issues that relate to the

---

[1] An argument against this qualification as a multipolar system is that the Netherlands is often characterized as a country with one central party, the KVP, since 1977 the CDA. This can be seen in Table 10.1, where the KVP and CDA are located in the centre of the left–right dimension, taking the median position after almost all elections since 1945. Literally, 'multipolar' means that there are more than two 'poles' within the bargaining system (otherwise we should speak of a unipolar or bipolar system). The KVP and the CDA seem to have attracted (and repelled) other parties on both of its sides, rather than that several parties have strong 'magnetic fields'. It is only since the 1994 elections that the other main parties have become serious competitors to the CDA in all respects of coalition politics (including exclusion from office) and the bargaining system has become truly multipolar.

TABLE 10.1.[a] *Left–right placement of parties,[b] party strength (in seats),[c] and party composition of governments in the Netherlands, 1946–1999*

Government	Proximity to election	SP	CPN	PSP[d]	EVP	PPR	PvdA	AOV	Unie 55+	D66	ARP	KVP[e]	CHU
1946	FE	—	10	0	—	0	**29**	—	—	—	13*	**32**	8
1948	FE	—	8	—	—	—	**27**	—	—	—	13	**32**	**9**
1952	FE	—	6	—	—	—	**30**	—	—	—	**12**	**30***	**9**
1956	F	—	7	—	—	—	**50**	—	—	—	**15**	**49***	**13**
1958	E	—	—	—	—	—	—	—	—	—	**15**	**49***	**13**
1959	FE	—	3	2	—	—	48	—	—	—	**14**	**49***	**12**
1963	F	—	4	4	—	—	43	—	—	—	**13**	**50***	**13**
1965	—	—	—	—	—	—	**43**	—	—	—	**13**	**50***	—
1966	E	—	—	—	—	—	—	—	—	—	**13**	**50***	**12**
1967	FE	—	5	4	—	—	37	—	—	7	**15**	**42***	**12**
1971	F	—	6	2	—	2	39	—	—	11	**13**	**35***	**10**
1972	E	—	—	—	—	—	—	—	—	—	**13**	**35***	**10**
1973	F	—	7	2	—	**7**	**43**	—	—	**6**	**14***	27	7
1977	FE	—	2	1	—	3	53	—	—	8	—	**49***	—
1981	F	—	3	3	—	3	**44**	—	—	**17**	—	**48***	—
1982	E	—	—	—	1	—	**47**	—	—	**17**	—	**48***	—
1982	FE	—	3	3	—	2	47	—	—	6	—	**45***	—
1986	F	—	—	1	—	2	52	—	—	9	—	**54***	—
1989	FE	—	—	6	—	—	**49**	—	—	12	—	**54***	—
1994	FE	2	—	5	—	—	**37**	6	—	**24***	—	34*	—
1998	F	5	—	11	—	—	**45**	—	1	**14***	—	29*	—

TABLE 10.1. cont.

Government	DS70	NMP	CP/CD	GPV	RPF	SGP	KVP/RKPN	VVD	BP/RVP	Median party in second policy dimension[f]	Effective number of legislative parties[g]	Government Strength	Total number of seats[h]
1946	—	—	—	—	—	2	—	6	—	CHU	4.5	61	100
1948	—	—	—	—	—	2	1	8	—	CHU	4.7	76	100
1952	—	—	—	—	—	2	2	9	—	CHU	4.6	81	100
1956	—	—	—	—	—	3	—	13	—	CHU	4.1	127	150
1958	—	—	—	—	—	—	—	—	—	CHU	4.1	77	150
1959	—	—	—	—	—	3	—	**19**	—	CHU	4.2	94	150
1963	—	—	—	1	—	3	—	**16**	3	CHU	4.5	92	150
1965	—	—	—	—	—	—	—	—	—	CHU	4.5	106	150
1966	—	—	—	—	—	—	—	—	—	CHU	4.5	63	150
1967	—	—	—	1	—	3	—	**17**	7	BP	5.5	86	150
1971	**8**	2	—	2	—	3	—	**16**	1	VVD	6.4	82	150
1972	6	—	—	—	—	—	—	**16**	3	VVD	6.4	74	150
1973	6	—	—	2	—	3	1	22	3	VVD	6.4	97	150
1977	1	—	—	1	2	3	—	**28**	1	VVD	3.7	77	150
1981	—	—	—	1	2	3	—	26	—	VVD	4.3	109	150
1982	—	—	1	1	2	—	—	—	—	VVD	4.3	65	150
1982	—	—	0	1	1	3	—	**36**	—	VVD	4.0	81	150
1986	—	—	1	2	1	3	—	**27**	—	VVD	3.5	81	150
1989	—	—	—	2	3	3	—	22	—	VVD	3.8	103	150
1994	—	—	3	2	3	2	—	**31**	—	VVD	5.4	92	150
1998	—	—	—	2	3	3	—	**38**	—	VVD	4.9	97	150

TABLE 10.1. cont.

[a] Thanks to Martijn Kuit for his assistance.

[b] Based on Laver and Hunt's (1992: 263) and Laver's (1995: 22) 'pro public ownership vs. anti public ownership' scale. The 'increase services vs. cut taxes' scale produces a similar but not identical ordering of the parties. The two sources refer to the sitiuation in 1989 and 1994, respectively. They do not include the three separate parties, KVP (Catholics) and ARP and CHU (both Protestant) that merged into the CDA. Nor is DS70 included, a right-wing splinter from the PvdA as well as a number of very small and usually short-lived parties. These parties have been ordered on the basis of the authors' analysis of the respective paries' manifestos. The ARP and the CHU are ordered to the left and the right of the KVP, respectively, but in a number of elections this ordering has been different.

[c] That is, in the Second Chamber. Formally, the indirectly elected First Chamber (Senate) has also the right to censure a government, but it has never done this. The numbers of seats reflect the situation immediately after the relevant election for the Second Chamber, ignoring occasional mid-term split-offs.

[d] In 1989 CPN, PSP, EVP, and PPR merged into Groen Links.

[e] In 1977, KVP, ARP, and CHU merged into the CDA.

[f] Although some country experts prefer to see the Dutch party system as unidimensional, and although those who do discern a second dimension are not always in agreement as to the nature of this second dimension, most would agree that a religious-secular dimension has been of paramount importance in the past, and is still significant. Laver and Hunt (1992: 263–4) and Laver (1995: 23–4) present two relevant scales: 'promote permissive policies on abortion and homosexuality vs. oppose permissive policies on abortion and homosexuality' and 'strongly anti-clerical vs. strongly pro-clerical'. They produce similar but not identical party orderings. We prefer the first, as (anti-) clericalism is not much of an issue in Dutch politics. If we add parties not mentioned in the two sources on the basis of our analysis of the manifestos, the ordering (from 'promote permissive policies' to 'oppose permissive policies'): PSP, PPR, CPN (now GL), D66, PvdA, DS70, VVD, SP, AOV, Unie 55+, EVP, CHU, KVP, ARP (these three now CDA), NMP, CD, BP/RVP, GPV, RPF, SGP, RKPN. This ordering was used to calculate which party contained the median legislator in the religious-secular dimension.

[g] The effective number of parties (Nv) as reported for the period 1946–72 in Laakso and Taagepera (1979:11) and as calculated by the authors for later years.

[h] In 1956 the number of seats was increased to 150. For this year, both the old and the new seat shares are given.

Parties
SP   Socialistische Partij (Socialist Party)
CPN   Communistische Partij Nederland (Communist Party of the Netherlands)
PSP   Pacifistische Socialistische Partij (Pacifist Socialist Party)
EVP   Evangelische Volks Partij (Evangelical People's Party)
PPR   Politieke Partij Radicalen (Radical Party)
GL   Groen Links (Green Left)
PvdA   Partij van de Arbeid (Labour Party)
AOV   Algemeen Ouderen Verbond (General Pensioners' Leage)
Unie 55+ (Union 55+)
D66   Democraten 66 (Liberal Democrats)
ARP   Anti Revolutionaire Partij (Anti-Revolutionary Party)
CHU   Christelijke Historische Unie (Christian Historical Union)
CDA   Christen-Democratisch Appel (Christian Democratic Appeal)
DS70   Democratische Socialisten 70 (Democratic Socialists 1970)
NMP   Nederlandse Middenstands Partij (Dutch Retailers' Party)
CP   Centrum Partij (Centre Party)
CD   Centrum Democraten (Centre Democrats)
GPV   Gereformeerd Politiek Verbond (Reformed Political League)
RPF   Reformatorische Politieke Federatie (Reformed Political Federation)
SGP   Staatkundig Gereformeerde Partij (Political Reformed Party)
KVP   Katholieke Volks Partij (Catholic People's Party)

TABLE 10.1. cont.

RKPN   Rooms-Katholieke Partij Nederland (Roman Catholic Party of the Netherlands)
VVD   Volkspartij voor Vrijheid en Democratie (People's Party for Freedom and Democracy)
BP   Boerenpartij (Farmers' Party)
RVP   Rechtse Volkspartij (Rightwing People's Party)

Parties in **bold** formed **governments**.
* Party with median legislator.
In 1994 and 1998 no median legislator can be identified on the left–right dimension.

religious cleavage. These have set apart the Christian Democrats and the two main secular parties, the PvdA and VVD, in particular. This is not surprising, as the religious cleavage has been an important *raison d'être* of the Catholic and Protestant parties, and since these parties exist, issues relating to this dimension have been on the agenda, but it must be noted that these 'morality' issues are usually not religious issues in a narrow sense. In Table 10.1, the median party on this second dimension is given for each election, and it appears clearly that, since the early 1970s, this is always a secular party, the VVD. Furthermore, when defined as major policy themes, other 'dimensions' in coalition bargaining, such as foreign policy, nuclear policy, and the environment have been or are still salient next to socio-economic and morality issues. While here the ordering of the traditional parties is less distinct from that on the left–right dimension in an 'objective' sense, the parties' *perceptions* of their relative positions have often influenced coalition bargaining.[2]

INSTITUTIONAL RULES AND CONVENTIONS

Although both the formation and the functioning of Dutch governments are highly institutionalized, surprisingly little is codified in the written constitution or in any other document with a legal status. The only reference in the constitution to the formation of governments is that 'The Prime Ministers and the other Ministers shall be appointed by Royal Decree' (Art. 43), which replaces an earlier text stating that 'Ministers shall be appointed and dismissed at the King's pleasure'. The new text (1983) is more accurate, but it tells us little about the actual formation of governments. The standardized procedure is that, shortly after the election outcome is announced, the Queen invites the parliamentary leader of each party in the Second Chamber to give his or her views about the options for forming a new government. The Queen then usually appoints one or more *informateurs* first, and a *formateur* (customarily the prime minister designate) later. The *informateur* tends to be a

[2] This point is elaborated by Laver and Hunt (1992).

party prominent who is somewhat aloof from day-to-day party politics, a condition for obtaining the confidence of other parties.

Formally (as far as this term applies), the *informateur*'s task is to collect information about various potential coalitions, while a *formateur* is assigned to lead the negotiations that should result in a new cabinet. In practice, however, the two offices overlap, and usually an *informateur* is replaced by a *formateur* only when the prospective coalition parties have reached agreement and all that is left to do is nominating the new ministers (on the suggestion of the respective party leaders) to the Queen. The Queen's instruction is usually to form or investigate the possibilities of forming 'a government that can look forward to fruitful cooperation with the States General'. There is no formal limit to the period of government formation, but some time pressure is felt during this process. There are no legal obstacles to forming minority governments and there is no formal investiture in parliament. Yet, with the exception of caretaker cabinets, no minority coalitions have been constructed and this apparent reluctance to form minority governments is an aspect of Dutch coalition politics that still awaits an explanation.

The doctrine of collective responsibility, which may be anticipated during coalition bargaining, is an institutional factor that may induce parties to build ideologically compact coalitions (Strøm, Budge, and Laver 1994: 313). Another possible constraint is that parties make the policy scope of their collective responsibility explicit before being committed to it by participating in the new government.

Once a government is sworn in, it is assumed to have the support of a parliamentary majority until it is proven otherwise. There is nothing in the written constitution pertaining to votes of investiture or (no) confidence. It is all understood to be implied in the following article: 'The ministers, and not the King, shall be responsible for acts of government' (Art. 42.2). As a result, any vote in parliament can be a vote of no confidence if it is interpreted as such by the government. This may lead to confusion; in 1966, for example, the government resigned after a parliamentary vote on a motion, even though the MP who had tabled the motion still maintains that it was never intended to bring down the government.

The government's power to dissolve parliament is acknowledged in the written constitution, which mentions no restrictions. It has become generally accepted, however, that parliament cannot be dissolved twice over the same issue. The two primary reasons for dissolving parliament have not been conflicts between the government and parliament, but constitutional revisions[3] and cabinet crises. In the past, after a coalition fell apart, a new government was sometimes formed without early elections. In the mid-1960s,

[3] After a proposal to change the constitution has been accepted by both houses, the procedure requires a dissolution and another vote by at least a two-thirds majority in the newly elected houses.

three different coalitions were formed on the basis of one election (1963), and severe criticism of this 'undemocratic practice' resulted in the unwritten rule that new governments should be formed only after parliament is dissolved and new elections are held. This unwritten election rule has been observed in those cases where the government terminated well before the end of its constitutional term (in 1972, 1982, and 1989).

Another important rule pertaining to the relationship between the government and parliament is that, except for the duration of government formation negotiations, an MP cannot be also a minister or junior minister (Art. 57.2). This rule reflects the desire for some separation of powers. Even before it was written into the constitution in 1938, it was extremely rare for a Dutch MP to hold on to his seat in parliament after being appointed to a ministerial portfolio. This rule has allowed *formateurs* and *informateurs* as well as party leaders to widen the base for recruiting ministers: between 1848 and 1990 only 42 per cent of the Dutch cabinet ministers had parliamentary experience when they were first appointed, though there has been a clear trend to more political experience, especially since the 1960s (Secker 1991: 198).

THE COALITION FORMATION PUZZLE

'Dutch elections suffer from a structural lack of results', a PvdA party leader once complained. He was referring to the phenomenon that major parties may win the elections but lose the subsequent game of government formation. Statistically, this complaint is true: for the parties with government potential, electoral gains can even be inversely related to the incidence of subsequent government participation. Only once, in 1977, did the ensuing government consist of parties that had all gained seats. Especially for the KVP and CDA, and for the PvdA, there has been a comparatively low level of electoral responsiveness. A situation of perfect responsiveness is one in which only parties that have gained in the most recent election are among those that form governments (Strøm 1990). In the Netherlands, however, electoral gainers have often been excluded from the cabinet and losers included. This has been the situation in half of the cases of government formation for the Christian Democrats and in more than half of the cases for the Social Democrats, which may explain why it was a prominent representative of the latter party that made the complaint. It would be too simple to say that the Social Democrats often ended up in opposition *because* they had won the elections, but the relationship between electoral results and the composition of the government clearly is an indirect one, in which bargaining relationships are the intermediate variable.

As the 'who's in and who's out' question is usually not answered immediately after the elections, the emphasis is on the process of coalition building in the Netherlands. In this section, we first deal briefly with coalition formation procedures. We then move on to characteristics of the actual coalition formation processes since 1945.

Procedures in Coalition Formation

As mentioned in the previous section on institutional rules, the 'coalition making machine' is set in motion when the Queen consults the parliamentary leaders. The party leaders' initial recommendations are made public, but the actual consultations take place in utmost secrecy; a logical consequence of the principle that the Queen bears no political responsibility. The ensuing negotiations are presided over by one or more *informateurs* or *formateurs*. The absence, with some exceptions, of pre-electoral coalitions is one reason why first an *informateur* is often appointed to consult party leaders and explore different coalition alternatives.

There are different answers to the question of which party may supply the first *formateur* or *informateur* and thus takes the initiative in building a new government. One informal rule known as the 'plebiscitary principle' is that the party that has gained most parliamentary seats should first be instructed to form a government, provided that this party has government potential. In theory, this principle could make elections more 'responsive' to electoral results, but it has been used only occasionally. Another and more common rule is that the largest party supplies the first *formateur* or *informateur*. The KVP (or later, the CDA) and the PvdA have often been close competitors for this status.

The three main subjects of negotiation in coalition formation are (1) the choice of a party combination that is supported by a parliamentary majority, (2) the policy programme of the coalition, and (3) the allocation of portfolios to cabinet ministers and junior ministers from the participating parties. Although these matters may be analytically distinct, they cannot always be separated in reality. Often, there are changes in the party configuration during policy negotiations, and in 1977 the PvdA even withdrew from coalition bargaining with the CDA in the final stage, when the portfolio distribution was nearly completed.

While formerly coalition formation was the privilege of party leaders, policy area specialists from within the parliamentary groups became involved in the early 1970s. Since then, discussions are held between party delegations, the size of which has varied. Moreover, since 1971, policy negotiations sometimes take place in working groups that each cover a broad policy area. In 1998, for instance, three working groups were set up, on Employment and Income issues, on Taxation, and on Policy Intensifications and Retrenchments, with four subgroups reporting to this last working group. Each group consisted of two representatives from each of the three prospective governing parties. Usually, however, the leaders of the parliamentary groups control the agenda and deal with the most important and controversial issues. Government formation is a policy making arena par excellence (Peterson *et al.* 1983).

Although there does not seem to be a single particular convention on this which has persisted over time, the organization of the process is also important, as it may influence the overall results. As far as the often scanty information about the period 1945–60 allows us to make observations about coalition bargaining, party leaders either respectfully awaited the programme as it was drafted by the *formateur*, or discussed the big issues one by one. In more recent years, the approach has often been 'concentric', which means that a general round of discussions is held first, followed by rounds of negotiations on the real issues on which parties have strong and conflicting preferences, a sort of funnel approach. Issues are not always discussed sequentially, however. Especially when working groups are formed, negotiations are also parallel, and this way of proceeding seems to facilitate package deals across different policy areas.

Changes in party statutes due to calls for internal party democratization have meant that the results of coalition formation must be approved formally by particular party organs such as the congress or the parliamentary party. While in theory this is the moment supreme for the party rank and file to put their mark on government formation, party leaders have only in exceptional cases gotten into serious trouble at this point. The party with the most turbulent history in this respect is the PvdA, which, like most Social Democratic parties in Europe, has a powerful extra-parliamentary party. In the early 1970s, decentralization efforts within the party gave the party congress more power with respect to the electoral list, the party manifesto, and on the approval of government participation. The contrasting case is the Liberal VVD, the leader of which is sometimes given carte blanche in coalition formation. In this party, authority traditionally rests with the parliamentary party, whereas the extra-parliamentary party plays a very limited role compared to other parties. In the CDA, decisions concerning cabinet participation have traditionally been made by the party council, and there have been no important statutory changes with respect to coalition formation.

Bargaining Relationships and their Consequences

If election results lack a direct and unambiguous effect, procedures and conventions alone do not determine coalition formation outcomes either. Two key variables that are expressed in the bargaining process are the stakes and the strategies of parties. The first section of this chapter gave a general picture of party positions and inter-party relationships. As noted there, the number of parties with direct relevance in coalition bargaining is smaller than the wide array of parties represented in parliament. None the less, the presence of four or five relevant parties may make coalition bargaining complex. This is even more so as Dutch parties advance not only demands for office, but also, and vigorously, policy priorities. This may be seen in connection with the salience of different policy 'dimensions' in party competition. On closer inspection of Table 10.1, we find that several coalitions have consisted of parties that were not each other's neighbours on the left–right dimension. Generally, such 'disconnected' coalitions are more common in multipolar systems, such as the Netherlands, than in other types of bargaining systems (Timmermans 1996: 16).[4]

It was said earlier that perceptions, the subjective positioning of parties by parties, are important. They are important because such perceptions form the basis of party strategies. Party strategies are behavioural constraints, formed and changed within the bargaining system, and they may be more or less institutionalized. Parties may base their actions on a strategy for a certain length of time, and provided that this really becomes manifest in party behaviour, the strategy also influences the expectations of others.

No doubt the most debated example of a party strategy in the Netherlands is the manœuvring of the KVP and later the CDA in the centre, where it is seen to have alternated consciously between the Social Democrats and the Liberals as its coalition partner. Another view is that the Catholics have opted for cooperation with the Social Democrats only when this party was needed for a majority, a situation referred to as one of 'absolute necessity' (Daudt 1982). Both views have been criticized for ascribing too much power to the Christian Democrats (Daalder 1986; De Jong and Pijnenburg 1986). In any case, what may have strengthened the ability of the Catholics and later the CDA to choose between the two major secular parties is that the PvdA and the VVD have excluded each other mutually since 1959, and it is only recently that this 'policy based' mutual veto has been withdrawn. Moreover, from the late 1960s until the mid-1980s, the PvdA pursued a strategy of polarization, which the party hoped would yield a majority of the Left in the Tweede Kamer. The tragedy of this strategy is that its failure as an electoral strategy (the majority was never reached) had dramatic consequences for the party's bargaining relationships. In 1971 and 1973 the PvdA formed a pre-electoral coalition with D66 and the small PPR, but only in 1973 did these three 'progressive' parties manage to 'break into' the Christian Democratic camp and form a coalition with two of the three Christian Democratic parties. In 1977

---

[4] This conclusion is based on an asessment of types of governments in which, for this specific question, single-party and minority governments are excluded. It must be noted that in coalitions that are connected on the left–right dimension, other dimensions may be relevant as well. This only does not become visible if the ordering of the governing parties on all dimensions is identical. In the Dutch case, however, the ordering of parties on the second salient dimension is different from that on the left–right dimension.

and in 1982, the Social Democrats suffered the trauma of a 'defeat in a victory': the PvdA become the largest party in the elections, but lost the subsequent coalition formation. It was only in the late 1980s that, in the view of the CDA, the PvdA became really coalitionable again. Finally, D66, the party that has always profiled itself as being more pragmatic, has refused persistently to form a coalition with the CDA and the VVD at the same time (1977, 1981, 1989, 1994).

Tops and Dittrich (1992: 286) have shown that due to structural and behavioural constraints (among which explicit party strategies), the number of possible winning coalitions is reduced from several hundreds to less than ten, and sometimes even to just one or two viable alternatives, as was the situation in 1971, 1972, and 1981. The very limited number of viable alternatives does not mean, however, that the path towards a new government is straight and smooth. Bargaining can be quite complex even when the set of actors is more limited. This may be seen in combination with the variation in policy areas and issues that are central in coalition formation. For the period 1956–66, Luebbert (1986: 274–9) mentions fiscal policy, housing, real estate policy as well as education, broadcasting, and equality issues as dominating the agenda of coalition negotiations. In the period 1967–90, the impact of international economic developments was such that financial and economic issues, especially those in which fundamental party principles were expressed, were high on the government formation agenda. Attention was also given to other matters such as education, broadcasting, and equality issues, as well as nuclear policy and morality issues such as abortion and euthanasia (Timmermans 1996: 64). The salience of 'immaterial' policy in coalition formation sustains the view that coalition bargaining in the Netherlands takes place in a multidimensional policy space. Discussions of the coalition's policy programme usually take most of the time in government formation, even though real bargaining takes place on a limited number of controversial issues, usually between five and ten (Timmermans 1996: 61).

Two symptoms of bargaining complexity are the number of inconclusive bargaining rounds and the duration of government formation. These are closely related, for the obvious reason that more attempts usually take more time. Different attempts may concern the party configuration or the policy profile of the coalition. In 1977, the PvdA withdrew from coalition bargaining during the portfolio distribution phase; this exit was followed by new policy discussions between the CDA and the VVD. Table 10.2 gives information about the previous bargaining rounds and the parties involved in these attempts in all cases of coalition formation between 1946 and 1994.

The number of inconclusive bargaining rounds and the duration of the formation process indicate that Dutch coalitions are certainly not made overnight. More often than not, the first attempt to form a new government fails, and frequently there are two or more inconclusive bargaining rounds,

TABLE 10.2. *Government formation in the Netherlands, 1945–1999*

Government	Parties in Second Chamber	Number of previous bargaining rounds	Parties involved in previous bargaining rounds	Number of days required for government formation
KVP–PvdA–ARP 1945	—	?	?	?
KVP–PvdA 1946	7	0	—	47
PvdA–KVP–CHU–VVD 1948	8	2	(1) PvdA–KVP–CHU–VVD (2) same	31
PvdA–KVP–CHU–VVD 1951** PvdA–KVP–CHU–VVD	8 50	4	(1) PcdA–KVP–CHU–VVD (2) same (3) PvdA–KVP–CHU–ARP–VVD (4) same	
PvdA–KVP–CHU–ARP 1952	8	3	(1) PvdA–KVP–CHU–ARP (2) same (3) same	69
PvdA–KVP–CHU–ARP 1956	7	6	(1) PvdA–KVP–CHU–ARP–VVD (2) same (3) same (4) same (5) KVP–CHU–ARP–VVD (6) PvdA–KVP–CHU–ARP–VVD	122
KVP–ARP–CHU 1958	7	0	—	10
KVP–ARP–CHU–VVD 1959	8	4	(1) KVP–PvdA–CHU–ARP–VVD (2) same (3) KVP–CHU–ARP–VVD (4) KVP–PvdA–CHU–ARP–VVD	68
KVP–ARP–CHU–VVD 1963	10	3	(1) KVP–PvdA–CHU–ARP–VVD (2) same (3) KVP–CHU–ARP–VVD	70
KVP–PvdA–ARP 1965	10	2	(1) KVP–CHU–ARP–VVD (2) PvdA–KVP–CHU–ARP	46
ARP–KVP 1966*	10	2	(1) KVP–PvdA–ARP (2) same	38
KVP–ARP–CHU–VVD 1967	11	1	KVP–PvdA–CHU–ARP–VVD	48
ARP–KVP–CHU–VVD–DS70 1971	14	1	ARP–KVP–CHU–VVD–DS '70	69
ARP–KVP–CHU–VVD 1972*	14	0	—	22
PvdA–D66–PPR–KVP–ARP 1973	14	3	(1) KVP–CHU–ARP–VVD–DS '70 (2) PvdA–D66–PPR–KVP–ARP–CHU (3) PvdA–D66–PPR–KVP–ARP	163
CDA–VVD 1977	11	5	(1) PvdA–CDA–D66 (2) same (3) same (4) same (5) same	208
CDA–PvdA–D66 1981	10	3	(1) CDA,PvdA,D66 (2) same (3) same	108
CDA–D66 1982*	10	0	—	17
CDA–VVD 1982	12	1	PvdA,CDA,VVD,D66	57
CDA–VVD 1986	8	0	—	52
CDA–PvdA 1989	9	1	CDA–PvdA–D66	61
PvdA–VVD–D66 1994	12	2	(1) PvdA,VVD,D66 (2) PvdA,CDA,VVD,D66	111
PvdA–VVD–D66 1998	9	0	—	87

* Caretaker government   ** No new government as defined in this volume, but new cabinet.

especially in cases following immediately after parliamentary elections. As can be seen in Table 10.2, different attempts are between the same parties or involve changes in the configuration of parties, particularly since the 1960s. The average length of the government formation process is some three months, with a variation between 31 days and 208 days for normal (i.e. not caretaker) governments.

It is important to realize that alternatives tried in a second or subsequent attempt are not necessarily less preferred than the alternative tried first. Nor are they necessarily less viable, as Table 10.3 demonstrates. In fact, the failure of an attempt may indicate that the alternative tried in that attempt lacked viability.[5] In 1982, for example, the PvdA emerged from the elections as the largest party, and an *informateur* was nominated from its ranks, but it needed CDA to obtain a parliamentary majority and that party had no intention to team up with the Social Democrats. Thus, discussions between CDA and PvdA were little more than a ritual dance before negotiations between CDA and VVD were started. When speaking of the duration of coalitions we will see that the outcomes of multiple attempts are not 'pathological' coalitions, at least not in terms of life expectancy. Apart from changes in the party composition, restarts have been made also by the same parties; in 1981, for example, negotiations between PvdA, CDA, and D66 were broken off several times when policy discussions ended in stalemate, but were restarted after new *informateurs* had been appointed. Another point to appreciate is that the complexity of bargaining is determined also by what happened during the previous government.

There are two or perhaps three reasons why parties may try alternatives that are actually unfeasible. First, the convention is that the largest party receives instructions to form a government, but twice when PvdA had this status, cooperation with either CDA or VVD was politically impossible (1977, 1982). Second, sometimes an attempt was made to reinstall a coalition that broke down, but conflict proved to be too intense (1959, 1973). Third, a party may adopt the strategy of first talking to a party to demonstrate to advocates of a coalition with this party among its own MPs or party members that no basis for cooperation exists, and then turning to the party it really prefers to govern with (the CDA is often said to have behaved this way, but it applies also to the PvdA, which then chose opposition).

---

[5] This contrasts with the view of Laver and Schofield, who argue that the number of failed attempts is an indication of the number of viable alternatives (1990: 162; for a discussion of this point, see Timmermans 1996: 13).

TABLE 10.3. *Dutch cabinets since 1945*

Cabinet number	Prime minister	Date in	Formal resignation	Maximal potential duration (in days)	Duration (in days)	Government composition
1	Schermerhorn	24 June 1945	17 May 1946	327	327	KVP–PvdA–ARP
2	Beel I	3 July 1946	7 July 1948	735[a]	735	KVP–PvdA
3	Drees I[b]	7 Aug. 1948	24 Jan. 1951	1,418	900	PvdA–KVP–CHU–VVD
4	Drees II	15 Mar. 1951	25 June 1952	468	468	PvdA–KVP–CHU–VVD
5	Drees III[c]	2 Sept. 1952	13 June 1956	1,380	1,380	PvdA–KVP–CHU–ARP
6	Drees IV	13 Oct. 1956	12 Dec. 1958	1,339	790	PvdA–KVP–CHU–ARP
7	Beel II*	22 Dec. 1958	12 Mar. 1959	80	80	KVP–CHU–ARP
8	De Quay[d]	19 May 1959	15 May 1963	1,457	1,457	KVP–CHU–ARP–VVD
9	Marijnen	25 July 1963	27 Feb. 1965	1,391	584	KVP–CHU–ARP–VVD
10	Cals	14 Apr. 1965	15 Oct. 1966	761	549	KVP–PedA–ARP
11	Zijlstra*	22 Nov. 1966	15 Feb. 1967	85	85	ARP–KVP
12	De Jong	5 Apr. 1967	28 Apr. 1971	1,484	1,484	KVP–ARP–CHU–VVD
13	Biesheuvel I	6 July 1971	20 July 1972	1,392	358	ARP–KVP–CHU–VVD–DS70
14	Biesheuvel II*	9 Aug. 1972	28 Nov. 1972	132	132	ARP–KVP–CHU–VVD
15	Den Uyl	11 May 1973	22 Mar. 1977	1,474	1,411	PvdA–PPR–D66–KVP–ARP
16	Van Agt I	19 Dec. 1977	27 May 1981	1,254	1,254	CDA–VVD
17	Van Agt II[e]	11 Sept. 1981	12 May 1982	1,353	243	CDA–PvdA–D66
18	Van Agt III*	29 May 1982	9 Sept. 1982	102	102	CDA–D66
19	Lubbers I	4 Nov. 1982	21 May 1986	1,296	1,296	CDA–VVD
20	Lubbers II	14 July 1986	2 May 1989	1,409	1,151	CDA–VVD
21	Lubbers III	7 Nov. 1989	3 May 1994	1,638	1,638	CDA–PvdA
22	Kok I	22 Aug. 1994	5 May 1998	1,355	1,355	PvdA–D66–VVD
23	Kok II	3 Aug. 1998		1,373		PvdA–D66–VVD

* Caretaker government.

[a] The Beel (1946–8) government could have served for four years, but it introduced an urgently needed constitutional revision and for this reason had to dissolve parliament and call early elections.
[b] In the conventional counting this is the Drees–Van Schaik government (Van Schaik was the leader of KVP's group of ministers). The subsequent Drees governments are known as Drees I, II and III, respectively.
[c] The Drees (1952–6) government tendered its resignation on 17 May 1955 which was revoked on 2 June 1955 after a successful mediation by a *formateur*.
[d] The De Quay government tendered its resignation on 23 Dec. 1960 but this was revoked after a successful mediation by an *informateur* on 2 Jan. 1961.
[e] The Van Agt (1981–2) government tendered its resignation on 16 Oct. 1981, but it was revoked on 4 Nov. 1981 after two *informateurs* had mediated successfully.

COALITION GOVERNANCE: HOW PARTIES ARE KEPT ON THE TRACK

The results of coalition formation are some form of agreement on policy and a particular allocation of portfolios among parties and to 'ministrables' within these parties. This coalition agreement and the distribution of cabinet portfolios also form the link between the formation and the life of coalition governments. In recent theoretical work, Laver and Shepsle (1990, 1994) argue that portfolio allocation affects the credibility of policy commitments made during government formation. In their view, portfolio allocation between, and to an extent also within, parties constrains government policy making, even if parties have agreed on a particular policy package before the portfolios were distributed. In this section, we consider both coalition policy agreements and the allocation of portfolios, as both are related to coalition governance. Table 10.4 shows whether a written policy agreement was issued, either before or after parliamentary elections, and the table also contains a number of key variables relating to coalition governance. Table 10.5 gives more detailed information about the coalition agreements since 1963.

Coalition Agreements as Policy Containers

In 1963, the first written coalition agreement was issued. Typically, coalition agreements are reached and approved by the prospective coalition parties before the government takes office. They should be distinguished from government declarations, which are made later and are read by the prime minister when the government officially presents itself to parliament (although, as said, there is no investiture in the formal sense). If government declarations are made by governments, coalition agreements usually are made for them, although those obtaining a cabinet portfolio may have been involved in drafting the agreement.

Policy negotiations among the party leaders did exist before coalition agreements were written down and made public, but the scope of such discussions was limited and the status of the (verbal) results was not clear. As one parliamentary leader declared in 1951: 'we have reached agreement on a number of matters, but this does not change the fact that there should be complete freedom for members of parliament in the elaboration and implementation of this agreement' (Duynstee 1966: 51). Since 1963, when agreement on a number of issues was codified and published for the first time, coalition agreements have grown in size, scope, and specificity. This may directly reflect the changes in the political climate in the 1960s, which brought more competition and mistrust in the interaction between parties, expressed in part in party strategies. The longest agreement to date was produced in 1998 by the

TABLE 10.4. *Coalition governance in the Netherlands, 1945–1999*

(1) Coalition	(2) Coalition agreement	(3) Agreement public	(4) Election rule	(5) Conflict management mechanisms	(6) Most common management mechanisms	(7) Mechanisms for most serious conflicts	(8) Coalition discipline in legislation	(9) Coalition discipline in other parliamentary behaviour	(10) Freedom of appointment	(11) Policy agreement	(12) Junior ministers	(13) Non-cabinet positions
1945	N	NA	N	Parl	Parl	Parl	2	4	Y1	1	N	N
1946	N	NA	N	Parl	Parl	Parl	2	4	Y	1	N	N
1948	N	NA	N	Parl	Parl	Parl	2	4	Y	1	N	N
1951	N	NA	N	Parl	Parl	Parl	2	4	Y	1	Y	N
1952	N	NA	N	Parl	Parl	Parl	2	4	Y	1	Y	N
1956	N	NA	N	Parl	Parl	Parl	2	4	Y	1	Y	N
1958	N	NA	N	Parl	Parl	Parl	2	4	Y	1	Y	N
1959	N	NA	N	Parl	Parl	Parl	2	4	Y	1	Y	N
1963	POST	Y	N	Parl	Parl	Parl	2	4	Y	2	Y	N
1965	IE	N	N	Parl	Parl	Parl	2	4	Y	2	Y	N
1966	N*	—	N	Parl, IC	IC	Parl	2	4	Y	—	Y	N
1967	POST	Y	Y	Parl, IC	IC	Parl	2	4	Y	2	Y	N
1971	POST	Y	Y	Parl, IC, CoC[b]	IC	CoC	2[c]	4	Y	3	Y	N
1972	N*	—	Y	Parl, IC, CoC	IC	CoC	2	4	Y	—	Y	N
1973	N[d]	Y	Y	Parl, IC, CoC	IC	CoC	2	4	Y	0	Y	N
1977	POST	Y	Y	Parl, IC, CoC	IC	CoC	2	4	Y	3	Y	N
1981	POST[e]	Y	Y	Parl, IC, CoC	IC	CoC	2	4	Y	3	Y	N
1982	N*	—	Y	Parl, IC, CoC	IC	CoC	2	4	Y	—	Y	N
1982	POST	Y	Y	Parl, IC, CoC	IC	CoC	2	4	Y	3	Y	N
1986	POST	Y	Y	Parl, IC, CoC	IC	CoC	2[f]	4	Y	3	Y	N
1989	POST	Y	Y	Parl, IC, CoC	IC	CoC	2	4	Y	3	Y	N
1994	POST	Y	Y	Parl, IC, CoC	IC	CoC	2	4	Y	3	Y	N
1998	POST	Y	Y	Parl, Ic, CoC	IC	CoC	2	4	Y	3	Y	N

cont./

TABLE 10.4. cont.

* Caretaker government.

[a] Since 1945 parties have always appointed their own ministers, with the exception of a few cases in which a candidate was vetoed by another party.

[b] From 1971 onwards, this resolution mechanism could also have been coded Pca in terms of its composition. As it consisted of parliamentary leaders rather than ordinary MPs, the code CoC was used.

[c] Three issues were exempted explicitly from discipline: legislation on games of chance, the fixing of an electoral threshold, and legislation on the forming of regions.

[d] Before the Den Uyl government was formed, the PvdA, D66, and PPR had formed a pre-electoral coalition in which they had also made a 'coalition agreement'. The three parties continued to see this document as the coalition agreement when the government, containing two additional parties, had taken office. In the formation of this government, the five parties had failed to reach a real coalition agreement.

[e] The coalition agreement was renegotiated during the life of the cabinet, during a short internal cabinet crisis that did not result in a formal resignation. The renegotiated coalition agreement was made public.

[f] Exempted from coalition discipline was legislation on euthanasia.

second 'purple' coalition of PvdA, D66, and VVD. It contained some 36,000 words (almost three times the length of this chapter).

It is often thought that the length of coalition agreements is directly associated with the length of the formation process, but this is a misunderstanding. Recall that the number of bargaining attempts is closely related to formation duration. Given the fact that long durations and multiple attempts often involve changes of the parties involved, coalition formation should not

TABLE 10.5. *Size and content of coalition agreements in the Netherlands, 1963–1999*

Government	Size	General rule of the game (in %)	Specific rules of the game (in %)	Distribution of offices (in %)	Distribution of competences (in %)	Policies (in %)
KVP–ARP–CHU–VVD 1963	3,350	16	29	3	0	52
KVP–PvdA–ARP 1965	3,600	5	0	0	0	95
ARP–KVP 1966*						
KVP–ARP–CHU–VVD 1967	3,100	7	0	0	0	93
ARP–KVP–CHU–VVD–DS70 1971	6,100	2	5	0	0	93
ARP–KVP–CHU–VVD 1972*						
CDA–VVD 1977	7,900	0	2	0	0	98
CDA–PvdA–D66 1981	15,900	1	1	0	4	94
CDA–D66 1982*						
CDA–VVD 1982	20,300	1	2	0	9	88
CDA–VVD 1986	15,500	0	2	0	9	89
CDA–PvdA 1989	28,450	0	2	0	1	97
PvdA–VVD–D66 1994	16,250	0	1	0	2	97
PvdA–VVD–D66 1998	36,000	0	1	0	1	98

* Caretaker cabinet

be envisaged as a process in which programmatic agreements simply accumulate. The formation in 1981 of the CDA–PvdA–D66 government, for example, took more than three months and resulted in a coalition agreement of some 16,000 words. The coalition agreement of the next government, composed of the CDA and the VVD, was longer even though it was produced in less than two months of negotiations, the shortest coalition formation since 1967. Indeed, the attempt involving the two parties that really formed the government took just over one month. Moreover, before 1963, government formation was often protracted, but policy agreements were brief, if anything was written down at all.

Be this as it may, today the coalition agreement is eagerly awaited not only by backbenchers in parliament but also by the top and middle-level civil servants within government departments (notably the spending departments), local governments, interest groups, and the media. The officially published version becomes a national bestseller within a few weeks, and ministers are sometimes reported to have the document on their bedside table. What is it that these ministers read in coalition agreements?

Rules of the Game

Parties are not only constrained by general rules that are given in the process of coalition formation or at any moment during the life cycle of a coalition government. They may also create rules specifically for the coalition they form. These 'rules of the game' spell out behavioural norms to be observed by each coalition member, as well as procedures for resolving conflicts. In addition, there may be procedures which are designed for single issues, for instance those that were dealt with during government formation but on which substantive agreement could not be reached. Such rules of the game may be made at any time, but here we consider only those rules of the game that are incorporated in coalition agreements. Table 10.5 presents the percentages of the contents of coalition agreements devoted to these two types of rules: general and issue-specific.

As the table shows, since 1971 issue-specific procedural rules are used more often than general ones. In the first coalition agreements (1963, 1965), general rules were used to indicate the nature of commitments made on policy intentions included in the coalition agreement. Since the 1970s, these general rules of the game are more implicit in coalition politics, and specific procedural arrangements have become a more important way to deal with controversial issues. Controversial issues, however, form only a part of the contents of coalition agreements, and the proportion of procedural arrangements on controversial issues is likely to be higher than the percentages mentioned in Table 10.4. In the agreement of the Van Agt II government (1981–2), for example, 20 per cent of the arrangements on conflictual issues were of a procedural nature (Timmermans 1996: 126).

Policy Arrangements

Policy intentions invariably constitute the bulk of coalition agreements, which are therefore primarily policy documents. As different dimensions or areas are salient in party competition and thus often in coalition bargaining, these documents are broad in scope and may become extremely detailed, though this varies between policy areas. The typical arrangement on substantive issues is a compromise, which may be specific or general, explicit or implicit (Luebbert 1986: 62–3). Explicit compromises contain clear concessions and are fairly 'doable', whereas implicit compromises consist of general goals that no one can reasonably disagree with or that are so vague that they hardly constitute any real commitment.[6] In terms of text length, socioeconomic policy is the predominant policy area included in coalition agreements. This type policy agreement tends to contain relatively specific compromises, whereas on 'immaterial policy', implicit compromises are relatively more frequent (Timmermans 1996: 64, 173).

The portfolio allocation was included in the coalition agreement only in 1963, as Table 10.4 shows, but the distribution of competences is sometimes an important element. If this theme is included in the coalition agreement, it is often due to departmental reorganizations. In fact, large departmental reorganizations, in which departmental units are set up or are transferred from one ministry to another, are nearly always decided during government formation (1981, 1982, 1989, 1994). Such reorganizations are not always purely 'technical' in character. In 1981, for instance, the Ministry of Social Affairs became the Ministry of Social Affairs and Employment to express the ambitious intentions of the Social Democrats to pursue an active employment policy in the new government, which was a highly controversial issue.

Functions of Coalition Agreements

The different types of arrangements included in coalition agreements indicate that, in the perception of parties, these documents may have a variety of functions (Timmermans 1996: 36–40). One function of coalition agreements is to provide (part of) the government agenda. This agenda may be more or less specific, varying from complete draft bills to statements which merely announce that an issue is to be dealt with by the government. Apart from this function as a blueprint for legislation or a reference document, agreements may also have a negative agenda function in case parties agree on procedures to prevent issues from rising to the government agenda for some time or perhaps for the government's whole term in office (as has happened, for example, on euthanasia).

---

[6] Luebbert (1986) distinguishes further between implicit compromises on the substance of matters and procedural agreements, which in the present chapter are called issue-specific rules of the game. If such procedures are made, this is often because parties are unable to agree on the substance of issues.

A second function is to prevent conflict within the coalition, especially on issues that were contentious during the formation process. The idea that negotiations on a coalition agreement may help reduce the conflict potential within the government is remarkably widespread among the major parties. Consider the following statement taken from the introduction to the 1989 CDA–PvdA coalition agreement: 'Two major parties intending to form a new and cohesive coalition must first pay attention to agreements that bridge differences in viewpoints. Substantive and procedural agreements form the point of departure of the government' (translation by the authors) Procedural arrangements such as the postponement of substantive decisions (specific rules of the game) relate to this conflict prevention function, but explicit and detailed compromises may also cement the coalition internally and streamline policy making by the government and by the governmental majority in parliament.

'Portfoliology'

The other link between coalition formation and coalition life is the allocation of portfolios. As said, this is a subject dealt with in government bargaining after the parties have concluded a coalition agreement, though obviously parties will have various expectations concerning portfolios during the prior stage. Parties have freedom of appointment of cabinet ministers and, more recently, also of junior ministers (*staatssecretarissen*). Table 10.6 lists the partisan allocation of cabinet ministers and junior ministers.

Generally speaking, the allocation of portfolios to the major Dutch parties is as could have been expected given the particular portfolio preferences of these parties. Budge and Keman (1990) have found that in case no other party with competing preferences is involved, the Social Democrats (PvdA) take Labour, Health, and Social Affairs in 88 per cent of the cases, and the Liberals (VVD) take at least one portfolio from the set of Economy/Finance and Justice in 75 per cent of the cases. For the Christian Democrats (CDA) the picture is less clear (Budge and Keman 1990: 122–8).

Partisan composition remains stable for the duration of the government; any resignation of a minister from a particular party is followed by the appointment of someone else from the same party. An interesting exception occurred during the Lubbers III coalition (1989–94) after scheduled elections were held and the government was outgoing. Parliament criticized the two police ministers (Justice and the Interior) so severely over their handling of the prosecution of organized crime that both decided to step down immediately. For the few weeks that were left they were succeeded by their junior ministers, in both cases a member of the other party. This constituted an unintended cabinet reshuffle of sorts.

It is argued sometimes that junior ministers, where they exist, serve as a party's watchdogs over the minister of a different party. The Dutch prime

378 Arco Timmermans and Rudy B. Andeweg

TABLE 10.6. Distribution of cabinet and junior ministerships in the Netherlands, 1945–1999

Cabinet number	Cabinet	(1) Prime Minister	(2) Foreign	(3) Justice	(4) Interior	(5) Education	(6) Social Work	(7) Public Health	(8) Housing	(9) Finance
1	Schermerhorn	P	X	K	K	P	—	—	—	P
2	Beel I	K	X	K	K	K	—	—	P	P
3	Drees I	P	V,p	K	K	P	—	—	P	P
4	Drees II	P	V,p	U	K	K	—	—	P	P
5	Drees III	P	X	P	K	K	K	—	K	P,x
6	Drees IV	P	K,p	P	K	K	K	—	K	P
7	Beel II	K	K	K	K	K	K	—	K	A
8	De Quay	K,k	K,v	U	V,k	K,c	K	—	A	A,x
9	Marijnen	K	K,v	U	V	K,a	V	—	K	V,x
10	Cals	K	K,p	P	A,p	A	P	—	K	P,k
11	Zijlstra	A	K	K	A	A	K	—	A	A
12	De Jong	K	K,v	V	U	K,a	K	—	A	V,k
13	Biesheuvel I	A	K	K,a	V,s	V,k	K,v,s	K	V,k	K,v
14	Biesheuvel II	A	K	K	V	K	K,v	K	V,k	K,v
15	Den Uyl	P	P,a,d	K,d	A,p	P,a	R,p	P,k	D,p,p	P,k,d
16	Van Agt I	C	V,c	C	V	V,c	C,v	V	C	C
17	Van Agt II	C	O,c	C,d	P,c	P,c	P,c	C,d	P	C,p
18	Van Agt III	C	C	C,d	D,c	C	C	C,d	D	C
19	Lubbers I	C	C,v	V,c	V,c	C,v	C	—	V,c	C,v
20	Lubbers II	C	C	V,c	C	C,v	C,v	—	V,c	C,v
21	Lubbers III	C	C,p	C/P,p	P/C,c	P	P	—	P,c	P,c
22	Kok I	P	D,v	D,p	V,p,d	P,d	D,v	—	P,d	V,p
23	Kok II	P	V,p	V,p	P,v	V,p,p	D,p	—	P,v	V,p

The Netherlands

TABLE 10.6. cont.

Cabinet number	Cabinet	(10) Defence	(11) Navy	(12) Transport	(13) Public Works	(14) Agriculture	(15) Social Affairs	(16) Colonies	(17) Economic Affairs	(18) Without portfolio	(19) Without portfolio
1	Schermerhorn	A	X	K	X	P	P	P	P	X	—
2	Beel I	K	X	P	X	P	P	P	K	X	—
3	Drees I	U,k,v	—	K	—	P	P,x	K	K	K	X
4	Drees II	U,k,v,	—	X	—	P	P,x	K,x	K	K	K
5	Drees III	U,k,p	—	A	—	P	P,x	U	A,k	K	K
6	Drees IV	U,k,p	—	A	—	P	P	U	A,k	K	K
7	Beel II	U,k	—	A	—	U	P	U	A,k	—	—
8	De Quay	V,k	—	V	—	K	K,a	—	U,k	—	—
9	Marijnen	K,a,c,v	—	A,v	—	A	K	—	V,a	K	—
10	Cals	K,a,x,	—	P	—	A	K	—	P,z	K	—
11	Zijlstra	K,a,x,x	—	K	—	A	K	—	A,k	K	—
12	De Jong	V,k,a	—	A,v	—	K	A,v	—	K	A	S
13	Biesheuvel I	V,a	—	S,v	—	K	A,v	—	V,k	A	—
14	Biesheuvel II	V,a	—	U	—	K	A,v	—	K	A	—
15	Den Uyl	P,k	—	K,r	—	K	A,k	—	K	P	R
16	Van Agt I	C,v	—	V	—	C	C	—	V,c	C	C
17	Van Agt II	D,p,c	—	D,p	—	C	P	—	D,c	C	—
18	Van Agt III	D,c	—	D	—	C	C	—	D,c	C	—
19	Lubbers I	C,v	—	V	—	C,v	C,v	—	V,c	V	—
20	Lubbers II	V,c	—	V	—	C	C	—	V,c	C	—
21	Lubbers III	P,c	—	C	—	C	C,p	—	C	P	—
22	Kok I	V	—	V	—	C	P,v	—	D,p	P	—
23	Kok II	V	—	P,v	—	D,p	P,v,d	—	V,d	P	D

P/p = PvdA   C/c = CDA   R/r = PPR
K/k = KVP   V/v = VVD   X/x = non-partisan
A/a = ARP   D/d = D66
U/u = CHU   S/s = DS70

minister usually has no junior minister (only De Quay in 1965 asked for one, to make up for his self-perceived lack of economic expertise). The Ministry of Agriculture housed a junior minister only twice, during the Lubbers I and Kok II governments. Transport is another ministry with few junior ministers. In contrast, the ministries of Foreign Affairs and Social Affairs have almost invariably had a junior minister since that office was introduced in 1948. Moreover, some ministries, such as Education and Defence, often have more than one junior minister.

For most departments, the appointment of junior ministers is dictated by political factors (the need to create an overall partisan balance within the government) as much as by the departmental workload that the portfolio entails. As regards the 'watchdog hypothesis', it is true that junior ministers often serve under a minister from a different party. Table 10.6 mentions junior ministers only when they are from a party other than that of the department's cabinet minister. This is the case for two-thirds of the total of 228 junior ministers that were appointed from the Drees I government (1948–51) through the Kok II government in 1998. In only one government (Van Agt I, 1977–81) were most junior ministers assigned to ministers from their own party (10 out of a total of 16). When interviewed about this exception, some cabinet ministers thought it was merely a coincidence, but others did see the absence of 'watchdogs' as an indicator of the relative trust that existed between the CDA and the VVD at that time. They often referred to the preceding Den Uyl coalition (1973–7) as the contrasting case. In that government, just 3 out of 17 junior ministers were from the same party as their respective minister. Some of the evidence for the watchdog hypothesis indeed comes from this government, which had the reputation of displaying an exceptional level of mistrust and suspicion. What makes this example even more interesting is that the Den Uyl government had no real coalition agreement (see Tables 10.4 and 10.5). The participant parties may have wanted to compensate for the absence of this source of inter-party control by the specific allocation of portfolios to junior ministers.

Yet, even of this cabinet one of its junior ministers has remarked that all the watchdogs turned into guide dogs over time. This is even more true of other cabinets. In most post-war governments the ministers were allowed to select their junior minister(s) themselves. Even in cases where junior ministers did get watchdog appointments, they seem to have acted more as a sort of *postillon d'amour* between their department and their party, for example in the regular Thursday meeting of their party's group of ministers (see below).

Coalition Policy Making

The more or less extensive attempts to make policy commitments during coalition bargaining, as well as the allocation of portfolios, establish a potential for coalition policy making. Let us now turn to the way in which this potential is or is not used during the life of coalition governments. First, we consider briefly a number of rules that apply to decision making within the cabinet, the most central policy making body in Dutch politics. Next, we deal more specifically with the enforcement of coalition agreements.

Cabinet Decision Making Rules

The constitution mentioned neither a prime minister nor a cabinet until 1983. It is now recognized that a council of ministers (*ministerraad*) exists to 'consider and decide upon overall government policy and (to) promote the coherence thereof', and that 'the prime minister shall be the chairman of the council of ministers' (Art. 45). The constitution further allows for ministers without portfolio. In practice, however, this is a misnomer, as ministers without portfolio are responsible for a particular policy area (such as development cooperation), but not for a department. Junior ministers are also recognized by the constitution, but they are only allowed to attend cabinet meetings when an item is relevant to their portfolio. Until 1998, they were not even allowed to substitute for their respective ministers in the event of the minister's illness or other absences.

The standing orders of the council of ministers provide most of the rules that apply during the lifetime of a cabinet. It spells out the voting procedures: by ordinary majority of all ministers present; a second vote in case of a tie and if the tie remains unbroken, the prime minister casts the deciding vote. Formal cabinet votes are rare, however, and they tend to be seen more as a last resort in a situation of stalemate than as an efficient decision making mechanism. The usual mode of decision making is what Steiner and Dorff (1980) have labelled 'decision by interpretation'. Nevertheless, the codification of decision making by majority, in 1850, is regarded as the introduction of collective ministerial responsibility. The standing orders also establish a system of cabinet committees, but their infrequent meetings and lack of formal powers have prevented these committees from becoming significant decision making arenas (Andeweg, 1985, 1997). More importantly, the standing orders spell out in detail what should be decided by the full cabinet: all bills, all orders in council, specified appointments, and in general anything that is politically controversial or involves major government spending. Given this nearly exhaustive list, the prime minister has little discretion in setting the agenda. He is given the power to arbitrate disputes of competence between ministers, but lacks the formal powers to give instructions to ministers, to dismiss ministers, or even to reshuffle his government. If the Dutch prime minister has become more than a *primus inter pares*, it is because his external role has increased (European summits, the cabinet's spokesperson *vis à vis* the media), and because in the last decade or so there has been a growing demand for coordination (Andeweg 1991).

It should be emphasized that most of the formal rules, whether in the constitution or in the standing orders, regulate the Dutch council of ministers as a board of heads of departments. How the cabinet operates as a body of prominents speaking on behalf of their respective parties seems to be left to precedent and coincidence. This second role of the cabinet is discussed in the next paragraphs.

Enforcement of Coalition Agreements

'We open the Holy Agreement and read Part III, Verse 1'. This caricature was once given of the beginning of a cabinet meeting during the Lubbers I coalition (1982–6). The Lubbers I government was known for its comprehensive and detailed coalition agreement, and at the time, the general opinion was that individual ministers had little discretion in policy making. In the view of interviewed ministers, the agreement came to be seen as 'something like a law' (Andeweg and Bakema 1994: 64).

Coalition agreements, however, are not laws nor even contracts, and they are thus not legally binding. This means that the implementation of anything written in these agreements must be enforced from within the coalition rather than from outside by some third party. This enforcement does not come by itself. Indeed, it is the key problem with regard to coalition agreements during the life of governments.

In bargaining during coalition formation, different issues are often linked, and policy arrangements on issues may thus be included in logrolls. Even when parties focus on the most important and controversial policies, such logrolls make it easier for individual parties to concede on specific issues. This may mean that positions on specific issues do not command majority support within the coalition. Still, at the time of government formation, such logrolls may be approved by the coalition parties. When the government has taken office, however, issues will often be dealt with separately. The more such issues are dealt with in isolation from other matters, the more parties that made important concessions during government formation may be tempted to try to reopen negotiations. The typical excuse is that 'external circumstances have changed'.

The containment of such centrifugal tendencies involves both coalition 'machinery' and 'mentality'. The coalition machinery concerns formal or more often informal decision making structures within the coalition that may facilitate enforcement (Timmermans 1996: 45–51). Such enforcement powers may be vested in the core executive or in the more peripheral institutions surrounding it.

One structural factor that may facilitate the implementation of coalition agreements is the presence of former negotiators within the government. Ministers with this background are more likely to feel committed to the coalition agreement; they may be able to read between the lines; and they know what were the costs of negotiating it. This may apply especially to the prime minister, who has usually been the *formateur*, and who may be expected to act as guardian of the agreement and do this either as an activist or as an arbitrator over conflicts within the cabinet (Blondel and Müller-Rommel 1993: 14–15). In contrast, ministers (and prime ministers) who have not been involved in the negotiations may lack this commitment to the coalition agreement and may even perceive it as an infringement on their policy making discretion.

In the governments formed between 1963 and 1998, the proportion of senior or junior ministers involved actively in the negotiations on the coalition agreement has varied from one-third to about three-fourths. Equally important are the specific portfolios these negotiators obtained. A former negotiator who is 'ministrable' does not automatically obtain the portfolio in the field he or she helped negotiate during coalition bargaining. One reason for this is that policy areas in coalition bargaining tend to be broader (and certainly defined less strictly) than the jurisdiction of ministerial portfolios. Obviously, three or four party spokespersons involved in discussions within a particular area cannot all take the related cabinet portfolio (although the creative use of 'subportfolios' at junior ministerial level may help parties cope with this problem). Most cabinet discussions over coalition policy usually take place within informal committees (rather than formal cabinet committees), and key issues have since the 1970s been dealt with by what is essentially an inner cabinet (although the term itself is carefully avoided in Dutch politics). At the same time, however, the Dutch cabinet is still a body in which collective decision making is relatively important when compared to other countries (Andeweg 1988, 1997).

One mechanism for enforcing coalition agreements outside the government consists, since the early 1970s, of the weekly consultations between ministers and their party's parliamentary leader and, since the early 1980s, of similar consultations between the prime minister, the deputy prime minister(s), and the parliamentary leaders of the coalition parties. Each Thursday evening, all the ministers (cabinet and junior) from the coalition parties meet with their parliamentary leaders, the party presidents, and occasionally other participants to prepare the next day's cabinet agenda. In this informal arena, junior ministers represent the departments where a party has no cabinet minister. It is here that ministers seek support from their own parliamentary party for their departmental plans. Matters of high politics are discussed mostly in the Wednesday luncheon meetings called 'the turret consultation' (*torentjeoverleg*, so named after the small semi-detached tower near the houses of parliament which serves as the prime minister's personal office). This is essentially a coalition committee, containing the prime minister, the deputy prime minister(s), and the leaders of the parliamentary groups in the Second Chamber. When the situation calls for their participation, specialized MPs may attend. As a regular participant in the turret meetings of the Kok government explains: 'it is a kind of follow up on government formation, and real negotiations take place. But the coalition agreement serves as the big stick; if we cannot agree, the coalition agreement remains fully in force' (*Vrij Nederland*, 4 May 1996: 27; authors' translation).

Coalition structures such as these may facilitate the implementation of coalition agreements, in that in informal arenas the possibilities for 'invisible politics' are larger than in the parliamentary arena, where backbenchers and the electorate carefully watch the moves made by their party's spokespersons. Yet, structures alone do not seem to be sufficient. Another important factor relates to the nature of the game that is played within the formal and informal arenas.

As we saw, in the 1960s, agreements contained general rules of the game, and these concerned mostly the moral aspect of commitments made on policy intentions. In 1963, the agreement stated that a moral commitment between the government and the affiliated groups in parliament is in the nature of the agreement. The notion of moral obligation may also be felt when it is not written down explicitly. When interviewed about this subject, ministers from the Lubbers I government (1982–6), for example, recalled that they 'promised to honour the coalition agreement . . . and all felt that the agreement was not something to be forgotten so easily' (Van Tijn and Van Weezel 1986: 62–3; translation by the authors). Earlier, we mentioned that the agreement is sometimes jokingly referred to in cabinet meetings as the Holy Book. Even if this is an exaggeration, it testifies to the coalition agreements' moral status in Dutch coalition culture.

Related to this moral factor is a general 'norm' of discipline in the parliamentary behaviour of coalition parties (see Table 10.4) as well as discipline within parties (coalition discipline requires internal party discipline). For most of the post-war period, the norm has been that the coalition parties support legislation originating from within the coalition, certainly if this legislation is based directly on the coalition agreement. This implies also that legislative adventures with opposition parties are not tolerated, at least not if these are on politically important issues. The governmental majority in parliament is thus extremely important in the practice of coalition politics (Timmermans 1991). The only condition under which the norm of coalition discipline is relaxed is if it is mentioned explicitly in advance that particular issues will be the subject of a free vote in parliament. In 1971, for example, increasing the electoral threshold and legislation on games of chance were considered to be matters of personal conscience. Individual coalition parties are less constrained in exercising the general control functions of parliament, as long as this control does not develop into a direct threat to the continuation of the coalition. Since the existence of coalition agreements, only one coalition has ended because of an apparent lack of confidence from a parliamentary majority (in 1966, when coalition agreements were still a new phenomenon; the end of the Lubbers II cabinet in 1989 could also be a case in point, but it never came to a vote in parliament). It has been less exceptional, but still uncommon for individual cabinet ministers to be forced to resign, which is largely because in the logic of Dutch coalition politics this implies the resignation of the minister's colleagues from the same party, followed inevitably by the resignation of the government as a whole.

Within parties, discipline may be established by the threat of sanctions. Recalcitrant MPs may risk sanctions which are damaging to their political career. Similarly, at the inter-party level, it may be not only moral principles that determine the way in which the game is played. The mechanism of reciprocal control is of particular importance here. Taking that individual compromises contain unequal pay-offs and that individual parties are relative losers on one issue and relative winners on another (if one party were always the losing party the coalition agreement probably would never have been approved in the first place), a case of 'unfaithfulness' by one party may be followed by a similar action by another party. Moreover, facing the choice between unilaterally breaking an agreement and remaining loyal, a party must take its credibility as a future coalition partner into account. Calculations about expected benefits from breaking or shirking must thus include the possible costs in the longer term.

Are Coalition Agreements Observed?

For obtaining a full answer to this question, it is necessary to make a detailed study of policy making within all coalitions that had a coalition agreement, and in such an exercise it would not be sufficient to trace only the positive substantive decisions. Procedural arrangements, for example, usually are meant to prevent certain decisions from being taken during the coalition's term in office. In such cases it is rather the absence of substantive decisions which would indicate that parties have observed the coalition agreement.

This point underlines that coalition agreements may be seen as a feature of the politics of accommodation, which involves more party competition since the 1960s, when new parties and issues had appeared on the political scene. For this reason, the effects of coalition agreements should be seen in terms of the two possible functions of coalition agreements: agenda formation and conflict prevention. One effect may be that coalition agreements streamline policy making, the results in such cases being substantive policies on which no new conflicts have occurred. These results may be based on specific compromises or follow after the elaboration of general intentions. Another potential effect of coalition agreements is that no substantive decisions are taken during the term of the coalition, this being the price for the coalition's continuity in office, or at least for the absence of conflict over particular issues. Yet another possibility is that controversial issues are still allowed on the cabinet agenda, but the condition for substantive decisions being that the process of bargaining is continued.

The results of a study of functions and effects of coalition agreements indicate that in the Netherlands these documents are important in different respects, one of which (but only one) is the implementation of feasible policy intentions (Timmermans 1996, 1998). Case studies of the Van Agt II government in 1981–2 (a story of failure) and the 1982–6 Lubbers I government (more but not entirely a story of success), found that different types of arrangements on the most central and controversial issues in coalition formation have had rather different effects. Relatively specific compromises and especially procedural arrangements appeared to have given rise to conflict less frequently than general and often ambiguous compromises. If the outcome was a substantive policy approved by the government that had set out to formulate this policy during government formation, a crucial intervening variable was the specific area in which arrangements were made. Substantive success was more frequent in the field of financial and socio-economic policy than in the field of 'immaterial policy', including issues such as school reform, broadcasting, and morality issues like euthanasia and abortion (Timmermans 1996: 183–4).

There are both technical and political reasons for the variation in the extent to which the policy intentions of coalition parties are accomplished during the life of these coalitions. In part, this depends on the different factors relating to enforcement by the government for which the agreement was made. Apart from the moral factor, coalition and cabinet structures may be favourable or unfavourable conditions for enforcement. Perhaps most importantly in a country where parties are motivated by the pursuit of policy, it depends on the actual pay-offs that the coalition parties obtain after they have taken office. If a party feels that it has not achieved much of its plans in the negotiations, and if it expects few substantive pay-offs from continuing the coalition, this party's willingness to cooperate in the implementation of the coalition agreement is likely to be reduced considerably. Indeed, it may even be a reason to give up cooperation altogether, as happened for example in May 1982 when the Van Agt II government was just eight months into its four-year term. This coalition, however, was an exceptionally conflictual one and certainly not exemplary for the way coalition agreements are dealt with in Dutch governments. The subsequent coalitions seem to have been more successful in enforcing the agreement, be it that this involved many interparty conflicts. Clearly, peace and policy do not always go together in coalition cabinets.

THE END OF GOVERNMENT COALITIONS: NOT EARLY AND YET OFTEN PREMATURE

The paradox about the end of coalition governments in the Netherlands is that governments have a comparatively long duration while the causes of termination are often the same as in countries with much shorter lived governments (Belgium, Finland, Israel, Italy, and these countries have all a multipolar bargaining system, see Laver and Schofield 1990: 159; Timmermans 1996: 10–16). The maximum time between parliamentary elections is four years, with elections taking place in the spring. If a dissolution necessitates early elections at another time of the year, the period until the next elections can be longer, but it should not exceed five years, so that the usual timing of elections can be restored again in the spring. This exception is taken into account in Table 10.3. Between 1945 and 1998 there have been twenty-two governments, lasting an average of 27 months, but if we exclude the governments that were intended for a short period only (to prepare new elections), the average increases to nearly three years.

Causes of Termination

Table 10.7 shows the causes of government termination. The two main reasons why governments end are regular elections and inter-party conflicts. Inter-party conflicts have been particularly important since the 1960s, when the political climate in the Netherlands became more polarized and competition between the major parties was intensified. The areas where most 'terminal' inter-party confrontations occurred are related to 'material' policy: fiscal policy, housing, real estate, cutbacks. The coalition crisis on broadcasting (1965) is an exception, but what the conflicts in these areas all have in common is that central party principles were involved.

Strategic calculations about how early elections can benefit individual parties do not seem to be as important as in some other countries, and this may relate to the low degree of responsiveness of government formation to electoral results noted earlier in this chapter. Moreover, the early elections mentioned in Table 10.7 were mostly on the instigation of one of the parties in the government preceding the government that called these elections. This was the case when caretaker governments called early elections after the previous government had broken down. In these cases early elections were called technically by a caretaker or interim cabinet, but the political (and real) reasons for the early election are to be found in the preceding (normal) cabinet that ended prematurely. Thus, the Beel II, Biesheuvel II and Van Agt III cabinets mentioned in Table 10.7 called the early elections that were provoked by parties in the preceding cabinets. Only the Lubbers II cabinet called the early elections itself after a political incident.

The frequency of inter-party conflict (nearly always over coalition policy) since the 1960s, in combination with the occurrence of written coalition agreements suggests that when push comes to shove, agreements are not effective as conflict preventing devices. The problem with this conclusion is of course that we cannot tell how the governments of this period would have

TABLE 10.7. *Cabinet termination in the Netherlands, 1945–1999*

Cabinet number	Cabinet	Mechanisms of government termination							Terminal events	Policy area(s)	Comments
		Technical		Discretionary						
		Regular election	Other constitutional reason	Early election	Defeat in parliament	Inter-party policy conflict	Intra-party conflict	National/ international security event		
		(1)	(2)	(4)	(6)	(7)	(8)	(11)		
1	Schermerhorn	X								
2	Beel I		X							
3	Drees I							X	16	Nieuw-Guinea crisis
4	Drees II	X					V:L			
5	Drees III	X			(X)ᵃ		(P,K:L)		(8,9)	(Rent policy)
6	Drees IV					X			9	Fiscal policy
7	Beel II			X						
8	De Quay	X			(X)ᵇ	(X)	(A:L)		(8,9)	(Housing policy)
9	Marijnen					X			6	Broadcasting
10	Cals				X	X			9,15	Tax policy, expenditures

11	Zijlstra	X			
12	De Jong	X			
13	Biesheuvel I		X	9	Financial policy
14	Biesheuvel II				Caretaker government
15	Den Uyl		X	3,14	Real estate policy
16	Van Agt I	X			
17	Van Agt II		X	9,15,17	Expenditures
18	Van Agt III		X		Caretaker government
19	Lubbers I	X			
20	Lubbers II		X	V:L	
21	Lubbers III	X		12	Fiscal policy
22	Kok I	X			

[a] The Drees III government was defeated in parliament in May 1955 after a part of the PvdA group in parliament refused to support government policy on rents. The government was however reinstalled and remained in office until the regular elections of 1956.
[b] The De Quay government was defeated in parliament on housing policy in December 1960, but its resignation was revoked and the government retained office until the regular elections of 1963.

Note: As a cause of termination, inter-party and intra-party may occur at the same time. This is because the distinction cuts across the cabinet and the parliamentary arena. A minister may be in conflict with his parliamentary group, for example on a motion, while the coalition parties in parliament are also divided in their support for the motion.

done without a coalition agreement. Something that can be said with more certainty is that only once, shortly after the introduction of written coalition agreements, a government has been defeated in parliament (this was in 1966). Given the fact that political problems among coalition parties were so important that they frequently led to a coalition crisis, the absence of terminal political conflicts between the government and parliament seems to indicate that coalition agreements have committed the parliamentary groups of the coalition parties especially.[7] Parliamentary leaders who distance themselves from what the coalition does are warned frequently not to 'pass the limit', and an upsurge of activism within the First Chamber (Senate) during the Lubbers III government, involving severe criticism of government policy, immediately reactivated an old debate about the disadvantages of bicameralism.

Features of Relative Government Stability

The number of coalition formation attempts and the length of the government formation process were mentioned as indicators of bargaining complexity. These variables, however, are not related to coalition duration in the way they are sometimes assumed to be. Excluding caretaker and interim governments, which are usually formed in a single attempt but are intended to be in office for a short period only, coalitions formed after many attempts and in a long process do not appear to have a shorter life than coalitions that are formed relatively quickly. As we argued above, coalitions formed after several inconclusive bargaining rounds are not necessarily less preferred (and therefore less viable). When comparing the five governments with the longest duration (1,380 days or more, see Table 10.3) with the five the were most short lived (584 days or less), we find that on average both involved 2.4 inconclusive bargaining rounds, and the group with a long term in office took even more days to be formed (82 days) than the group of short-lived governments (69 days).

The most prominent explanation for the relative government stability is given by the theory of consociational democracy. Until the 1960s, Dutch society was characterized by a strong segmentation or pillarization (*verzuiling*). Catholics, Protestants, social democrats, and to a lesser extent the liberals formed clearly identifiable subcultures, each with its own infrastructure of social organizations (schools, health organizations, mass media, political party), isolated from and relatively hostile towards each other. According to Arend Lijphart (1975), the Dutch elites realized the dangers inherent in the deep religious and socio-economic cleavages, and acted to compensate for

[7] As all coalitions except caretaker governments controlled a majority, a defeat in parliament would require that at least one coalition party, or a group within such a party, votes with the opposition. It is the self-restraint of coalition parties in their legislative behaviour that indicates the commitment to the coalition agreement.

centrifugal forces at the mass level by what was coined a 'politics of accommodation' at the elite level. Cooperation within the government was one of the ways in which the leaders of the various social groups tried to stabilize what seemed to be an inherently unstable political situation. According to others, the old Dutch tradition of bargaining and compromise, grown during the days of the confederal Dutch Republic (eighteenth century) are now applied to a new political situation. Whatever the correct explanation may be, until the 1960s the result was 'government above politics', protected as it were against the heat of party conflict. This was expressed in the adage 'the closer to the throne, the less partisan'. Since the 1960s, the government has also become an arena of inter-party conflicts, but the absence of a decline in the duration of governments points to the development of successful conflict management mechanisms as discussed in the previous section.

Incumbency and Electoral Performance

Just as the effects of electoral performance on government formation are rather mixed, so are the effects the other way around. Table 10.8 shows that the vast majority of governments since 1945 lost as a whole, but for individual coalition parties incumbency has not always led to electoral punishment; out of the 67 cases of electoral performance (the cumulative number of parties in the 21 coalition governments of which electoral performance has been recorded is 67), there were 26 cases in which a party gained seats and 41 cases in which incumbency proved to be a liability. Some of these 67 election results, however, are counted more than once, when a party participated in several coalitions between two elections. If we exclude those cases, and only count each election result for a party that has governed during the preceding parliamentary period once (as we did when calculating the means in the bottom row of Table 10.8), we have a total of 50 election results of which 20 were gains and 30 were losses. If we further confine the analysis to those parties who were actually in office at the time of the elections we have 44 election results of which 17 were gains and 27 were losses.

Narud and Irwin (1994) present a roughly similar pattern, in which they also include a category for incumbent parties who experienced only very small gains or losses. They conclude: 'with the exception of the VVD, it would seem that Dutch parties need not fear that incumbency will necessarily lead to a loss of votes' (Narud and Irwin 1994: 268). True, but Dutch parties do well to remember that the probability that incumbency results in electoral losses is greater than the probability that it leads to gains at the polls. And any optimism may be further dampened if they realize that the average losses tend to be much bigger than the average gains, even if we leave the exceptional landslides of 1994 out of the analysis. The bottom row of Table 10.8 shows that the mean incumbency effect for the post-war period has been negative.

TABLE 10.8. *Electoral costs/benefits of government parties in the Netherlands, 1945–1999 (in % of votes)*

Government	In office at time of election	Election year	PPR	PvdA	D66	ARP	KVP	CHU	CDA	DS70	VVD	Government
PvdA–KVP 1946–8	Yes	1948	—	−1.7	—	—	+0.2	—	—	—	—	−1.5
PvdA–KVP–CHU–VVD 1948–52	Yes	1952	—	+3.4	—	—	−2.3	−0.3	—	—	+0.9	+1.7
PvdA–ARP–KVP–CHU 1952–6	Yes	1956	—	+3.7	—	−1.4	+3.0	−0.5	—	—	—	+4.8
PvdA–ARP–KVP–CHU 1956–8	No	1959	—	−2.3	—	−0.5	−0.1	−0.3	—	—	—	−3.5
ARP–KVP–CHU 1958–9	Yes	1959	—	—	—	−0.5	−0.1	−0.3	—	—	—	−0.9
ARP–KVP–CHU–VVD 1959–63	Yes	1963	—	—	—	−0.7	+0.3	+0.5	—	—	−1.9	−1.8
ARP–KVP–CHU–VVD 1963–5	No	1967	—	—	—	+1.2	−5.4	−0.5	—	—	+0.4	−4.3
PvdA–ARP–KVP 1965–6	No	1967	—	−4.4	—	+1.2	−5.4	—	—	—	—	−8.6
ARP–KVP 1966–7	Yes	1967	—	—	—	+1.2	−5.4	—	—	—	—	−4.2
ARP–KVP–CHU–VVD 1967–71	Yes	1971	—	—	—	−1.3	−4.7	−1.8	—	—	−0.4	−8.2
ARP–KVP–CHU–DS70–VVD 1971–2	No	1972	—	—	—	+0.2	−4.1	−1.5	—	+1.8	+4.1	+0.5
ARP–KVP–CHU–VVD 1972–3	Yes	1972	—	—	—	+0.2	−4.1	−1.5	—	—	+4.1	−1.3
PPR–PvdA–D66–ARP–KVP 1973–7	Yes	1977	−3.1	+6.5	−1.2	—	—	—	+0.6	—	—	+2.8
CDA–VVD 1977–81	Yes	1981	—	—	—	—	—	—	−1.1	—	−0.6	−1.7
PvdA–D66–CDA 1981–2	No	1982	—	+2.1	−6.8	—	—	—	−1.4	—	—	−6.1
D66–CDA 1982	Yes	1982	—	—	−6.8	—	—	—	−1.4	—	—	−8.2
CDA–VVD 1982–6	Yes	1986	—	—	—	—	—	—	+5.2	—	−5.7	−0.5
CDA–VVD 1986–9	Yes	1989	—	—	—	—	—	—	+0.7	—	−2.8	−2.1
PvdA–CDA 1989–94	Yes	1994	—	−7.9	—	—	—	—	−13.1	—	—	−21.0
PvdA–D66–VVD 1994–8	Yes	1998	—	+5.0	−6.5	—	—	—	—	—	+4.7	+3.2
MEANS	—	—	−3.1	+0.5	−4.8	−0.4	−1.6	−0.6	−1.5	+1.8	−0.1	−3.0

However, the fact that, occasionally, a governing party also wins votes in Dutch elections, has prompted Rose and Mackie (1983) to place the Netherlands in the 'continental' category where the 'split pendulum' dominates, i.e. where one governing party loses while another wins in the same elections. The question then arises why incumbency has this differential effect. One explanation could be that incumbency is not the only variable affecting election outcomes. In fact, it is impossible to disentangle how the parties would have fared without the incumbency or opposition factor. Especially for the Christian Democrats it is difficult to assess how much of their losses during the 1970s can be put to their continuous participation in government, and how much to the secularization of Dutch society. Other potential explanations refer to the governing coalition itself. It is popularly assumed that the party of the prime minister receives a 'bonus', as the prime minister gets most media coverage, and as he may rise statesmanlike above the partisan conflicts within the coalition. This factor does seem to play a role. We saw that incumbent parties lose more often than that they gain, but the party of the prime minister at the time of the elections has gained votes in 9 out of 15 elections. Finally, according to a Dutch political adage, in elections that follow a government crisis *'qui casse, paie'* (the breaker must pay). On the basis of Table 10.8 the evidence is inconclusive. Sometimes the party responsible for the crisis seems to be punished (such as the VVD in 1989), but sometimes a party seems to profit from bringing an unpopular coalition to an end (such as the PvdA in 1982). In order to ascertain to which party voters assign responsibility for a government crisis, and how this affects their voting intentions, Narud and Irwin have analysed public opinion data in addition to election results. They conclude that there are exceptions, but that on the whole 'everybody loses in a '"divorce"' (Narud and Irwin 1994: 270).

CONCLUSION

In coalition systems, a fundamental tension exists between the formulation of joint policies and the preservation of a distinct identity by each of the governing parties. This tension is of particular relevance in the Netherlands, where parties are motivated strongly by policy intentions. The context in which the formation and maintenance of Dutch government coalitions takes place consists of four to six relevant parties, referred to as a multipolar bargaining system. The complexity of coalition formation relates to the number of relevant ('coalitionable') players, but lies also, and perhaps even more, in the salience of different policy dimensions. The two most relevant dimensions defining the space in which Dutch parties interact are the left–right dimension and the religious dimension, which includes matters of 'immaterial' policy and especially morality issues.

Policy preferences and the mutual perceptions of these result in a puzzle which is seldom solved by parliamentary elections, except perhaps for the convention that the largest party takes the initiative. Other institutional rules are important, but these determine more the general procedures than the specific direction of the outcomes. A much more important factor to coalition formation outcomes is the nature of bargaining relationships, and these relationships are in part formed by party strategies of cooperation or exclusion. Pre-electoral coalitions, however, are more exceptional than exclusions, which have even been mutual. Yet coalition building often involves several attempts that fail; as a matter of fact, inconclusive bargaining rounds are often also the result of party strategies. In such cases, it is only in the second (or third) attempt that serious bargaining within a viable party combination starts.

The two most tangible results of coalition formation are a written policy agreement and a particular allocation of portfolios. These two kinds of results are the links between the formation and the actual life of coalition governments. Written coalition agreements occur since the mid-1960s, and they have increased in scope and in specificity. Their potential relevance for coalition governance is that they contain policy intentions which may form part of the cabinet agenda and, when issues were controversial in government formation, general and specific rules of the game which indicate how thorny issues are to be dealt with. The portfolio distribution at the level of cabinet ministers is mostly in line with the size and the specific preferences of parties, be it that the granting of an individual party's wishes depends on which other parties have joined the coalition. The allocation of 'miniportfolios' to junior ministers is in part a matter of political compensation. Although they usually serve under a minister from another party, creating divided portfolios, they do not seem to be political 'spies', except in the exceptional case when there is profound mistrust between the parties and a real policy agreement is lacking.

The growing attention of parties for coalition agreements does not mean that the tension between coalition policy and party policy has disappeared. As a matter of fact, the more comprehensive and detailed the agreement, the more this tension may become manifest during the course of a government's term. There are different sources of commitment of parties to the joint policy intentions of the coalition. Next to what could be called the 'morality of duty', the most relevant general enforcement mechanism seems to be reciprocal control; as in one of Hobbes' Laws of Nature, a party may be prevented from acting against the agreement by the threat of similar behaviour of another party. This is what the parliamentary leader of D66 was referring to in the example with which we began this chapter. In that same example, the talk of 'compensations' relates to another point, which is that the linking of issues may reduce the pains for individual parties in the same way as this is often done in government formation. The coalition machinery that may facilitate this faithful and disciplined behaviour can be found within the government and outside the government, of which the regular informal meetings of prominents from different party branches have become most important.

Yet these mechanisms are not a guarantee of enforcement. In part this is because intentions in Dutch coalition agreements, especially those on immaterial policy, are sometimes so vague that they can hardly be considered constraints. Another reason is that parties make periodical evaluations of their pay-offs from those things that are accomplished and the expectations that they have about policy pay-offs during the remainder of the government's term. During the term of the government, the possibilities for controlling the agenda and for making deals across issues that are satisfactory to all parties are more limited than during government formation. This is because the formal legislative process takes time and policy making is constrained by the formal budgetary process, and both may increase the impatience of parties that want to receive concrete benefits from being in office. In a number of cases, the perspective of *not* continuing cooperation turned out to be more attractive to one party, even if the electoral fortune of such behaviour was highly uncertain.

Still, the conclusion need not be that coalition agreements always cease to have substantive effects when the coalition is no longer in office. Especially with regard to issues that are politically delicate, the agreement is one element in a continuous process of policy formulation. Whether or not this process of policy making on individual issues is cumulative depends in part on the party composition of the next government.

Given these different aspects of coalition dynamics, one feature of the Dutch system of coalition governments that stands out is its relative stability over time. This is expressed in the longevity of governments compared to other countries with a multipolar bargaining system and a high effective number of parties. This is remarkable, as the Netherlands is often characterized as a country with a strong and stable system of societal and political pillars which however started to decompose in the 1960s. This change has been noted also in this chapter.

On the face of it, the process of depillarization could be expected to have produced important changes in coalition politics. Since the 1960s, polarization increased, expressed in party strategies which were aimed at reaching an absolute majority (attempts by the PvdA to contain the Christian Democrats, which failed) or consisted of exclusions from cooperation in a coalition (PvdA, VVD, D66). As we saw, the cabinet has become an arena of interparty conflicts, which led to coalition collapse from within the government more often than before the 1960s. Electoral volatility also increased, reaching its height in the elections of 1994. The phenomenon discussed at length in this chapter is the occurrence of written coalition agreements since 1963.

Have these changes meant the end of the 'politics of accommodation'? The increase in party competition has surely affected the style of politics; coalition agreements for example are essentially a codification of mistrust. However, notwithstanding the depillarization process, the Netherlands is still a country of political minorities; even the merger of the three religious parties into the CDA in 1977 has not prevented the size differences between the main parties from gradually decreasing, especially in the 1994 elections. At the same time, proposals to increase the decisiveness of elections through electoral reform have never been implemented. The Kok I government, excluding the Christian Democrats for the first time since 1918, would 'change the style of policy making' as it was put in the coalition agreement of 1994, but during the first half of this government's term, a reform-oriented party like D66 became increasingly frustrated about the non-implementation of reform plans (*De Volkskrant*, 30 May 1996). Perhaps most important to the process of coalition governance, the development of coalition agreements and the mechanisms for enforcement and for conflict management may be seen as a sort of adaptation to the changes that have taken place. The drafting of coalition agreements and the implementation of these documents is still to a large extent an affair of the political elites. In fact, the pacts made between political leaders that Lijphart saw as a typical aspect of consociational democracy have the same essential features as coalition agreements, even though coalition agreements have evolved into fully fledged government programmes. The development of what we called the coalition 'machinery', from meetings between parliamentary leaders to different institutionalized informal circuits (inner cabinet, coalition committee) may be seen as a way in which coalition parties try to cope with the centrifugal forces that are implicit in the increased party competition. This machinery has continued to produce compromises and postponements as typical modes of conflict resolution in the Netherlands (Timmermans and Bakema 1990). In reflecting on developments since the 1960s, Lijphart (1989) concludes that despite the increased antagonism between parties, the Netherlands is still a country of the politics of accommodation. Our findings in this chapter sustain this conclusion.

REFERENCES

Andeweg, Rudy B. (1985). 'The Netherlands: Cabinet Committees in a Coalition Cabinet', in Brian Hogwood and Thomas T. Mackie (eds.), *Unlocking the Cabinet: Cabinet Structures in Comparative Perspective*. London: Sage.
——(1988). 'Centrifugal Forces and Collective Decision-Making: The Case of the Dutch Cabinet'. *European Journal of Political Research*, 16: 125–51.

——(1991). The Dutch Prime Minister: Not Just Chairman, Not Yet Chief?', *West European Politics*, 14 (2): 116–32.
——(1997). 'Collegiality and Collectivity: Cabinets, Cabinet Committees, and Cabinet Ministers', in Patrick Weller, Herman Bakvis, R. A. W. Rhodes (eds.), *The Hollow Crown: Countervailing Trends in Core Executives*. London: Macmillan.
——and Bakema, Wilma (1994). 'The Netherlands: Ministers and Cabinet Policy', in Michael Laver and Kenneth A. Shepsle (eds.), *Cabinet Ministers and Parliamentary Government*. New York: Cambridge University Press.
Blondel, Jean, and Müller-Rommel, Ferdinand (1993). 'Introduction', in Jean Blondel and Ferdinand Müller-Rommel (eds.), *Governing Together: The Extent and Limits of Joint Decision-Making in Western European Cabinets*. Basingstoke: MacMillan.
Budge, Ian, and Keman, Hans (1990). *Parties and Democracy: Coalition Formation and Government Functioning in Twenty States*. Oxford: Oxford University Press.
Daalder, Hans (1986). 'Changing Procedures and Strategies in Dutch Coalition Building'. *Legislative Studies Quarterly*, 11: 507–31.
Daudt, H. (1982). 'Political Parties and Government Coalitions in the Netherlands since 1945'. *Netherland's Journal of Sociology*, 10: 1–23.
De Jong, Jan, and Pijnenburg, Bert (1986). 'The Dutch Christian Democratic Party and Coalitional Behaviour in the Netherlands', in Geoffrey Pridham (ed.), *Coalitional Behaviour in Theory and Practice: An Inductive Model for Western Europe*. Cambridge: Cambridge University Press.
Duynstee, F. J. F. M. (1966). *Kabinetsformaties 1945–1966*. Deventer: Kluwer.
Laakso, Markku, and Taagepera, Rein (1979). '"Effective" Number of Parties: A Measure with Applications to Western Europe'. *Comparative Political Studies*, 12: 3–27.
Laver, Michael (1995). 'Party Policy and Cabinet Portfolios in the Netherlands, 1994: Results from an Expert Survey'. *Acta Politica*, 30: 3–28.
——and Hunt, W. Ben (1992). *Policy and Party Competition*. New York: Routledge.
——and Schofield, Norman (1990). *Multiparty Government: The Politics of Coalition in Europe*. Oxford: Oxford University Press.
——and Shepsle, Kenneth A. (1990). 'Coalitions and Cabinet Government'. *American Political Science Review*, 84: 873–90.
————(1994) (eds.). *Cabinet Ministers and Parliamentary Government*. New York: Cambridge University Press.
Lijphart, Arend (1975). *The Politics of Accommodation: Pluralism and Democracy in the Netherlands*. Berkeley: University of California Press.
——(1989). 'Consociational or Adversarial Democracy in the Netherlands', in Hans Daalder and Galen A (eds.), *Politics in the Netherlands: How Much Change?*, Irwin. London: Cass.
Luebbert, Gregory M. (1986). *Comparative Democracy: Policymaking and Governing Coalitions in Europe and Israel*. New York: Columbia University Press.
Narud, Hanne Marthe, and Irwin, Galen A. (1994). 'Must the Breaker Pay? Cabinet Crises and Electoral Trade-offs'. *Acta Politica*, 29: 265–84.
Peterson, Robert L., and De Ridder, Martine M. (1986). 'Government Formation as a Policy-Making Arena'. *Legislative Studies Quarterly*, 11: 565–81.
——Hobbs, J. D., and McClellan, E. F. (1983). 'Government Formation and Policy Formulation: Patterns in Belgium and the Netherlands'. *Res Publica*, 18: 49–82.

Rose, Richard, and Mackie, Thomas T. (1983). 'Incumbency in Government: Asset or Liability?' in Hans Daalder and Peter Mair (eds.), *Western European Party Systems: Continuity and Change*. London: Sage.

Schofield, Norman (1993). 'Political Competition and Multiparty Coalition Governments'. *European Journal of Political Research*, 23: 1–33.

Secker, W. P. (1991). *Ministers in beeld: De sociale en functionele herkomst van de Nederlandse ministers 1848–1990*. Leiden: DSWO Press.

Steiner, Jürg, and Dorff, Robert H. (1980). 'Decision by Interpretation: A New Concept for an Often Overlooked Decision Mode'. *British Journal of Political Science*, 10: 1–13.

Strøm, Kaare (1990). *Minority Government and Majority Rule*. Cambridge: Cambridge University Press.

——Budge, Ian, and Laver, Michael J. (1994). 'Constraints on Cabinet Formation in Parliamentary Democracies'. *American Journal of Political Science*, 38: 303–35.

Timmermans, Arco (1991). 'Königreich der Niederlande', in Winfried Steffani (ed.), *Regierungsmehrheit und Opposition in den Staaten der EG*. Opladen: Leske und Budrich.

——(1996). *High Politics in the Low Countries: Functions and Effects of Coalition Policy Agreements in Belgium and the Netherlands*. Doctoral Dissertation. Florence: European University Institute.

—— (1998). 'Policy Conflicts, Agreements, and Coalition Governance'. *Acta Politica*, 33: 409–32.

——and Bakema, W. E. (1990). 'Conflicten in Nederlandse kabinetten', in R. B. Andeweg (ed.), *Ministers en Ministerraad*. 's-Gravenhage: SDU.

Tops, Pieter, and Dittrich, Karl (1992). 'The Role of Policy in Dutch Coalition Building 1947–81', in Michael J. Laver and Ian Budge (eds.), *Party Policy and Government Coalitions*. New York: St Martin's Press.

Van Tijn, Joop, and van Weezel, Max (1986). *Inzake het kabinet Lubbers*. Amsterdam: Sijthoff.

11

Luxembourg

Stable Coalitions in a Pivotal Party System

Patrick Dumont and Lieven De Winter

Coalition formation in Luxembourg, usually following general elections when a legislature has lasted its full term, is a well-structured process. The Grand-Duke straight away asks the leader of the largest party to form a new government (an information mission is exceptional). This party's main decision making body then asks its *formateur* to start talks with a particular party, usually a potential partner that has done well in the election. Alternative coalition formation attempts are hardly ever made. After about a month, negotiations conclude with the signing of a comprehensive and detailed government agreement, while portfolio distribution and ministerial appointments are the last questions to be settled. Only a summarized version of the coalition agreement is presented for the parties' (and parliament's) approbation, and the full document remains secret. Each coalition party's vote of approval is a *condicio sine qua non* for a new government. The investiture vote on the government declaration, though not constitutionally required, routinely takes place after the Grand-Duke has officially accepted the new cabinet.

POLITICAL BACKGROUND AND PARTY SYSTEM EVOLUTION

The Formation of a Pivotal Party System

Structured party competition dates from 1848, when the Grand-Duchy of Luxembourg became a unified constitutional monarchy with a parliamentary

---

We thank former Prime Minister Pierre Werner for his answers to our questions and for his comments. We are also thankful to Mrs Baustert, head of the documentation services of the Chambre des Députés, for her competence and kindness, and to Foreign Affairs Minister Jacques Poos for according us an interview.

form of government.[1] Catholics (the 'Catholic Action Committee') opposed the then predominant Liberals along the church-state divide. The industrial revolution of the 1880s added a second divide, with a first 'socialist' MP elected before the turn of the century. In 1921 the Communist Party (Kommunistesch Partei Lëtzebueurg, KPL) formed as a split-off from the Social Democrats. After the turn of the century, the Christian Democrats (Chrëschtlech-Sozial Vollekspartei, CSV, formerly Party of the Right) adopted a more pronounced 'social' stance by addressing a wide, social-Christian message to all social classes, which enabled them to become the strongest party in parliament as soon as 1917.

The four-party system after World War II strongly reflects the pre-war two-dimensional cleavage structure, with the newer socio-economic class cleavage superimposed upon the older clerical/anti-clerical one (Hearl 1987: 254). On the socio-economic divide, the CSV is situated between the Socialists (Lëtzebuerger Sozialistesch Aarbechterpartei, LSAP), the post-war second party, and the Liberals (Demokratesch Partei, DP), the third party. Still, the three parties are not very far apart on the left–right dimension (Laver and Hunt 1992).[2] With regard to the old church–state divide, and on newer ethical issues such as abortion or homosexuality, the CSV is markedly to the right of the DP and the LSAP, but this divide lost most of its saliency even before World War II. Curiously for a multilingual country, language has never emerged as a conflictual issue.

As a consequence of its stable two-dimensional policy position, the CSV was not only the numerically predominant party throughout the post-war period, it also controlled the median legislator, and was, predictably, almost permanently in government. With the introduction of universal adult suffrage in 1919, the Christian Democrats started dominating Luxembourg's politics. They only left prime ministership from 1925 to 1926 and from 1974 to 1979. Apart from one Catholic single-party majority government (1921–5), and two

[1] Unlike the previous constitution granted by the Grand-Duke William II in 1841, the 1848 constitution was drafted by a constitutional assembly consisting of the elected Council of States and the government, with no interference from the head of state. The Grand-Duke, considering the European wave of revolutionary ideas of the period, himself initiated this revision and gave his full powers to the *Constituante*. Most of the new text was inspired by the 1831 Belgian constitution. By the 1867 Treaty of London, the Grand-Duchy became a fully independent, neutral country under the guaranteed protection of the Great Powers, and its personal union with the Dutch Crown came to an end in 1890.

[2] Dodd (1976) and Morgan (1976) placed the Christian Democrats to the left of the Liberals, while Inglehart and Klingemann (1976) found them more rightist than the DP. In a more recent country-specific factor analysis of party manifestos, Hearl (1992) comes to the same conclusion. He argues that since the late 1960s, the Liberals have clearly been shifting from the Right to the Centre in order not to be 'trapped' at the end of the spectrum, with no coalition alternative to being junior partner to the Christian Democrats. According to Hearl, today's DP more closely resembles its British and German cousins than the rest of the (more rightist) continental liberal parties.

'national union' experiences, each after a World War, the Christian Democrats always governed with either the Socialists or the Liberals, with a clear preference for centre-left coalitions. In fact, in the 1945–99 period, the CSV formed five cabinets with the DP (with a total duration of 7,178 days) and eight with the LSAP (8,084 days).[3]

Hence, since World War II, Luxembourg's four-party system shared all the characteristics of Sartorian moderate pluralism (Sartori 1976: 173), in that (1) only coalition governments materialized; (2) centripetal competition favoured the most centrist party which governed in coalition with one of the two other main parties;[4] (3) since the end of the Communist experience in government (1945–7), only this small anti-system party has been excluded from any new coalition negotiation (and thus lost its governing relevance), and the small ideological distance between the relevant parties has enabled all other possible coalition formulae (CSV–LSAP, CSV–DP, but also DP–LSAP in 1974) to form.

The electoral oligopoly of the these four traditional parties began to erode in 1974, and their overall electoral score dropped from an astonishing 99.6 per cent in 1968 to 80.2 per cent in 1989. The first non-traditional party that successfully contested two consecutive elections (1974 and 1979) was the SDP (Sozialdemokratesch Partei, Social Democratic Party) a right-wing breakaway from the LSAP, but in 1984 the two remaining SDP representatives joined the CSV, and the party was dissolved soon thereafter. The Greens emerged in 1984 and fought the 1989 elections on two separate tickets. They reunited in 1993 and did well in 1994. The Aktiounskomitee fir Demokratie a Rentegerechtegkeet (ADR) was created in 1987 as a pressure group lobbying for the modification of the private sector pensions. They presented candidates for the 1989 as well as the 1994 elections and fared relatively well for a single-issue protest party.[5]

Hence, apart from the SDP interlude, since 1947 there have been only three relevant parties, even though the number of parties in parliament rose to seven in 1979 and 1989. Table 11.1 shows that the effective number of parties has followed the same trend, from an average of three before the 1970s to its peak value in 1974 (4.05). The 1995 figure is 3.9.

---

[3] As in Jan. 1999 the Juncker cabinet was still in office, the figures mentioned do not include the latter cabinet's duration (only pre-1995 cabinets are computed). Hence, there is only a small difference in days between the two most common formulas, as three pre-1995 CSV–LSAP cabinets were very short (Bech 1953, Frieden 1958, and Santer 1994).

[4] For each coalition in Luxembourg, there is a plausible alternative. Yet, this does not mean that a particular coalition formula cannot be maintained in power, as was proved by the four consecutive CSV–LSAP governments from 1951 to 1959 and from 1984 up until 1999, or even by the two CSV–DP cabinets in the 1947–51 period).

[5] In the 1994 general elections, the remaining KPL representative was not re-elected.

TABLE 11.1. *Left–right placement of parties and party strength (in seats) in Luxembourg, 1945–1999*

Government	Proximity to election	KPL	LSAP	SDP	GLEI[a]	Déi Gréng	GAP[a]	CSV	DP	ADR	EF	SI	MIP	PIE	Median party in second policy dimension[b]	Effective number of parties	Number of government seats	Total number of seats
1945	F	5	11	—	—	—	—	25*	9	—	—	—	—	1	DP	3.05	50	51
1947	E	—	—	—	—	—	—	25*	9	—	—	—	—	0	DP	—	34	51
1948	FE	5	15	—	—	—	—	22*	9	—	—	—	—	0	DP	3.19	31	51
1951	F	4	19	—	—	—	—	21*	8	—	—	—	—	0	DP	3.06	40	52
1954	F	3	17	—	—	—	—	26*	6	—	—	—	—	0	DP	2.68	43	52
1959	FE	3	17	—	—	—	—	21*	11	—	—	—	—	0	DP	3.14	32	52
1964	FE	5	21	—	—	—	—	22*	6	—	—	—	—	0	DP	3.17	43	56
1969	FE	6	18	—	—	—	—	21*	11	—	—	—	2	0	DP	3.4	32	56
1974	FE	5	17	5	—	—	—	18*	14	—	—	1	0	0	DP	4.05	31	59
1979	FE	2	14	2	—	—	—	24*	15	—	1	0	0	0	DP	3.46	39	59
1984	FE	2	21	0	2	—	2	25*	14	—	0	0	0	0	DP	3.22	46	64
1989	FE	1	18	0	2	—	2	22*	11	4	0	0	0	0	DP	3.77	40	60
1994	F	0	17	0	—	5	—	21*	12	5	0	0	0	0	DP	3.9	38	60

[a] In 1993 the GLEI and the GAP merged in an electoral alliance.
[b] The second policy dimension is based on the older cleavage opposing Catholic to non-Catholic interests. According to expert judgements, we find on this cleavage respectively the CSV, ADR, DP, Déi Gréng, LSAP, and the KPL.

cont./

TABLE 11.1. *cont.*

Parties

KPL	Kommunistesch Partei Lëtzebuerg (Communists)
LSAP	Lëtzebuerger Sozialistesch Aarbechterpartei (Socialists)
SDP	Sozialdemokratesch Partei (right-wing breakaway from the LSAP formed in 1968)
GLEI	Gréng Lëscht Ekologesch Initiativ (Left-wing splinter party from the Alternative Greens, formed by Mr Jup Weber, a GAP deputy unhappy with the internal democracy of his party).
Déi Gréng	An electoral alliance of the GLEI and GAP formed in the North constituency for the 1989 election which has become a national alliance, the Greens, in Jan. 1993
GAP	Gréng Alternativ Partei (Alternative Greens Party)
CSV	Chrëschtlech-Sozial Volleksparteï (Christian Democrats)
DP	Demokratesch Partei (Liberals). Until 1951, the party was called Groupement Patriotique et Démocratique before turning to Groupement Démocratique. It finally changed to DP in 1954
ADR	Aktiounskomitee fir Demokratie a Rentegerechtegkeet (known as Aktionskomitee 5/6 in 1989, they formed lists of candidates in order to put pressure on the government. They are claiming that private sector pensions should be raised to the five-sixths of final salary paid to former public sector employees)
EF	Enrôlés de Force ('forcibly enlisted'), a list formed by a pressure group claiming compensation for Luxembourg citizens forcibly enlisted into the German Army during World War II
MIP	Mouvement Indépendant Populaire. (Independent Popular Movement). One of their two deputies joined the CSV and the rest of the party merged with the DP immediately before the 1968 election
SI	Socialistes Indépendants (Independent Socialists)
PIE	Parti des Indépendants de l'Est (Party of the Eastern Independents)

Parties in **bold** formed **governments**.
* Party with median legislator.

THE INSTITUTIONAL FRAMEWORK

Electoral System

Elections to the Luxembourg parliament are to be held at least every five years, and early elections are rare.[6] Luxembourg is divided into four electoral districts, and each voter has as many votes as there are seats in his district.[7] Nowadays the industrial South elects 23 MPs, the Centre 21, the North 9, and the East only 7. Seats are allocated within the four districts, not nationally. This feature of the electoral system has important implications for portfolio allocation.

A voter may cast all his votes for a single party list in which there is no pre-ordered ranking of candidates (in which case each of the candidates is awarded one vote), but he or she may alternatively choose specific candidates either from the same party or from several parties. This *panachage* both determines each

---

[6] Until 1954, half the chamber was elected every three years, as elections were held alternatively in two of the four constituencies.

[7] Voting is compulsory for all citizens aged 18 or older.

party's representation and selects individual MPs from the parties' list of candidates. Voters may cast at most two votes for the same candidate. Hence, this system 'not only ensures party proportionality but also makes every successful candidate's seat dependent upon his or her personal vote rather than upon party preferment' (Hearl 1987: 256). Such *panachage-capital* (a candidate's capacity to attract personal votes) is crucial as it determines who gets elected and who can claim a portfolio in case his or her party enters the government. Hence, the electoral system fosters a certain degree of clientelism, or at least localism, among MPs competing for personal votes (Hearl 1987: 256).

CONSTRAINTS ON COALITION BARGAINING

A number of constraints on coalition bargaining reduces the number of potential coalitions. The small number (four) of actual coalition formulae tested since 1945 testifies to the effectiveness of these institutional constraints in shaping coalition outcomes.

Size Constraints

Investiture

Although not constitutionally required, the debate on the government declaration in parliament is concluded by an investiture vote, which the government must win by a simple majority (more positive than negative votes and with a quorum of at least half of the MPs). This vote is considered as a preliminary survival test for the government, as each year the approval of the budget is also turned into a customary vote of confidence.

Constitutional Majorities

Constitutional reforms require two-thirds majorities with a quorum of three-quarters of the MPs present. Given the long legislative term and the rigidity of the system (a declaration of revision specifying the constitutional clauses subject to change has to be adopted by a majority in the Chamber before its dissolution in order to allow the next legislature to revise these clauses), potential government parties tend to anticipate future needs for constitutional reform. To play it safe, they pass such a revision declaration concerning most clauses potentially ripe for reform. Hence, in the event that the subsequent cabinet bargaining process were to produce a two-thirds majority coalition, it can be assured the opportunity to launch constitutional reforms. In fact, eight constitutional revision declarations have been made in the post-war period; and ten out of sixteen governments have controlled a two-thirds parliamentary majority.

Formation Procedures

Party Ratification

The most crucial phase of the formation process is the approval of the government agreement by the coalition parties' respective supreme decision making bodies (usually an extraordinary national party congress). The leaders of the respective negotiation teams must defend their results in front of the party rank and file, who must endorse it with a positive vote. A veto by any coalition party congress means the end of the bargaining attempt.

The European Parliament and External Duties

Usually, several ministers of the outgoing government are part of the negotiation teams if their parties are included in bargaining. Not only are they in charge of current affairs in their ministries, however, they also have to continue to represent the outgoing government abroad. Due to the traditional June European summits, formation negotiations that fall in that month are suspended for a few days.[8] More importantly, given the decision to hold general and European elections simultaneously, since 1979 the aim is to finish negotiations before the first meeting of the European Parliament. As leading politicians often contest and win seats in both assemblies, they have to choose between the two constitutionally incompatible mandates. If they opt for the European one, which is more prestigious than the national mandate, they have to give up their ministerial ambitions. Hence, negotiators try to conclude the formation process before the first meeting of the Strasbourg's Assembly in order to allow *ministrables* to make the best-informed choice they can.

Electoral Responsiveness in the Choice of the Junior Partner

The electoral fortunes of the outgoing government parties are the best predictor of membership in the next government. Typically, when a party suffers an electoral catastrophe, it is either not considered by the *formateur* as a priority partner, or in the unique case of CSV in 1974, decides itself to undertake an 'opposition cure' in order to regenerate itself. The permanent presence in government of the biggest party (with the exception due to the electoral defeat just mentioned), and the overall electoral responsiveness (in the choice of the junior partner) clearly constrain coalition bargaining. Pre-electoral pacts are the exception rather than the rule. The only example goes back to 1969, when Prime Minister Werner asked the electorate to reconfirm his outgoing CSV–LSAP coalition. Eventually, he failed to re-establish this coalition.

---

[8] Obligations following from local mandates or Luxembourg's National Day (23 June) further extend the overall formation bargaining period.

The ban on the anti-system parties imposed by the traditional parties further reduces the *formateur*'s discretion. Since 1947, the Communists, overtly Stalinist and the most pro-Soviet party in Western Europe, have never been considered in coalition bargaining. Today, a protest, single-issue party such as ADR is also far less likely to enter a government than the numerically equivalent Greens.

CABINET FORMATION

In discussing the process by which cabinets form, we concentrate on post-electoral formations, since they represent three-quarters of the post-war cases. Of the four formations in-between elections, three have been mere coalition renegotiations with a different prime minister.

Formateurs *and* Informateurs

The making of a new cabinet starts when the previous one resigns the day after the elections. The incumbent prime minister is then charged by the monarch to deal with *affaires courantes*. On the very same day, the Grand-Duke tries to get a full picture of the new political situation by consulting first the former chairman of the Chamber, then the president of the Council of State,[9] and finally the chairpersons of the parties represented in the new parliament, starting with the largest party and ending with the smallest. If the new parliamentary constellation differs sufficiently from the previous one but the electoral outcome does not dictate any obvious coalition formula, the Grand-Duke will not take the risk of appointing a *formateur* directly. Instead, he will appoint an *informateur* in order to identify the parties that are willing to collaborate.

Informateurs have been designated in 1959 (Bech), 1969 (Werner), 1974 (Vouel), in 1979 (Dupong), and 1984 (Werner). This has occurred when elections have triggered major changes in the parliamentary balance of powers, and it has usually also provoked a shift in coalitions. There has, however, been no clear trend towards or away from such processes over time. The information stage obviously lessens the Grand-Duke's role in designating the party leader who is to spearhead the coalition formation process. It therefore leads to more informal, 'freestyle', bargaining between the *regierungsfähige*

---

[9] The Council of State consists of 21 members plus the members of the Grand-Duke's family. Appointment to the Council of State is by the Grand-Duke, with the Grand-Duke (*de facto* the cabinet) filling each first vacancy, and the parliament and the Council of State itself making proposals, respectively, and for each second and third vacancy. Members of the Council of State remain in office until they are 72 years old.

parties, at least prior to the appointment of a *formateur* (Hearl 1992: 226). Hence, the role of the *informateur* is, on the one hand, to ascertain whether the outgoing coalition is still available, and if not, to test the viability of alternative coalition formulae. As in practice all *informateurs* have belonged to the CSV, it is highly implausible that they have tested formulae from which the CSV was absent. Hence, even for information missions, the set of formulae considered has been highly restricted. Therefore, if we consider the entire post-war period, coalition bargaining in Luxembourg is not freestyle but on the contrary very formal. Finally, with or without the *informateur* stage, the role of the Grand-Duke in selecting the *formateur* is usually insignificant. With the exception of the DP–LSAP coalition in 1974, post-war *informateurs* and *formateurs* have always come from the largest party, the CSV (provided it wanted to govern). Yet, contrary to the *formateur*,[10] the information mission has often—but without success—been claimed by the party that had made the largest gain in parliamentary seats.

Early Party Interventions

Party executives usually analyse the results right after the elections and make their comments known in the media. In the most recent cabinet formations, the claims of the different parties—and even the remarks of party leaders to the monarch—have been made public by the media. The monarch's final decisions on a *formateur* or *informateur* suggest that the advice of the chairman of the largest party carries more weight than that of others.

When an *informateur* has been appointed, party executives tend to convene rather informally while the official mission is in progress. These executives discuss their willingness and conditions for participation before the *informateur* formally inquires into these questions. Some *informateurs* have done so by sending a list of questions to be answered by the parties.

Concerning the choice of potential coalition parties, CSV *formateurs* receive formal marching orders—indicating which party to talk to first—from the CSV's main decision making body, usually the National Council but sometimes the enlarged National Committee,[11] which also confirms the party

---

[10] The 1964 electoral results raised a touchy question: the LSAP gained 0.2% more popular votes than the CSV but one seat less. Which party should under these circumstances take the initiative in forming a government? By appointing a Christian Democratic *formateur*, the monarch confirmed the tradition that only the balance of power in Parliament counts.

[11] The National Council counts around 70–80 members, including the National Committee, MPs, and cabinet members, representatives of the districts, and the Catholic youth, women, and trade union. The National Committee of 15 persons consists of the chairman, vice-chairpersons, treasurer, a few other members elected by the Congress and the chief editor of the largest Luxembourg newspaper, the *Luxemburger Wort,* which is ideologically close to the party. This Committee is enlarged by the parliamentary group.

executive's proposal concerning the party's delegation to the coalition negotiations. In the DP, the Comité Directeur designates the party delegation.[12] When in 1974 the CSV decided to go into opposition, the Liberal *formateur* Thorn sought this committee's approval for his inevitable decision to start talks with the Socialists. In the LSAP, the General Council (around 60 members) usually accepts the party delegation proposed by the executive and thus endorses negotiations with the *formateur*'s party. In the LSAP main decision making bodies, the Socialist Trade Union also has a significant influence in matters of coalition formation. This has occasionally led to unsuccessful bargaining attempts.[13]

Negotiation Teams and Procedures

Negotiation teams have gradually grown in size: from four members per party in 1947 to nine in 1994. They are led by the most influential party personality, who is not always the party chairman but rather the *Spitzenkandidat* (the candidate who headed the party's lists) from the elections. The *formateur*, who is expected to become prime minister, has usually been his party's *Spitzenkandidat*. His party delegation is usually headed by the party chairman or an outgoing minister. Negotiation teams regularly include former ministers, the parliamentary group leader (who act as backbenchers' watchdogs in the bargaining process), and each party's parliamentary secretary (who collectively draft the minutes of the negotiations and polish the final text), plus some MPs that are *ministrables* and/or policy specialists.

When parties conclude a coalition agreement, the leaders of the party delegations—and the *formateur*—always get a portfolio. Given the size of the negotiation teams relative to cabinet positions, not all negotiators are rewarded with a cabinet position, particularly the party or parliamentary secretaries who only perform administrative tasks during the negotiations. Despite their prominence in the party organization and the negotiation team, even outgoing parliamentary group leaders are often 'bypassed' for cabinet office by backbenchers. Party leaders typically try to convince parliamentary group leaders to remain in their positions to assure well-disciplined and faithful support in parliament.

[12] The DP Comité Directeur of more than 40 members consists of the national chairman and vice-chairpersons, the regional chairmen, the General Secretary, two deputy secretaries, the presidents of the 4 regional committees, 2 delegates per region, 16 members delegated by the National Committee, DP national MPs, and MEPs, members of the national government and of the European Commission, 3 representatives of the democratic youth, 3 co-opted members, and the former national chairmen. In 1947 the parliamentary group proposed the names and the National Council ratified the composition.

[13] In 1959 the DP finally broke off negotiations with the LSAP because they feared excessive trade unionist demands. In 1969 the pressure the Socialist Trade Union put on their delegation caused the latter to desert, against the will of the Socialist Party executive!

In recent times, the first meeting between the negotiation teams has been procedural. Delegations are divided into working groups responsible for drafting proposals in a more or less homogeneous policy area. The working groups meet according to a schedule established during this first round. Sometimes specialized MPs or party experts are added to the negotiation teams. Whenever the working group is ready, a plenary session is held in order to hear and endorse or amend its proposals.

Negotiation schedules have varied over time. Although the first item on the agenda has usually been policy, sometimes overall government structure or even the numerical distribution of portfolios between the parties, has taken temporal priority. In these few cases, one or two conflictual matters have been left for the end of the deal. Sometimes, potential disagreements have been pre-empted by a pact (so-called 'disagreement protocols') aimed at preventing the most cherished but isolated party policies from dooming the coalition attempt to failure. For instance, in 1979 the CSV and the DP decided to put the abortion issue 'on ice' and continue their negotiations.

Party Investitures

A critical phase of the formation process is the endorsement of the coalition agreement by the party rank and file. Although negotiation team leaders keep regular contact with their respective party executives during the entire bargaining process, they still have to defend to their members the policy and personnel compromises they had to make.

Generally, this internal ratification of the coalition agreement is done by an extraordinary party congress called especially for the occasion. The Socialist Party has given its members this veto power throughout the post-war period. Party congresses have sometimes shown a certain degree of discontent, as in 1954 when 47 per cent of the members opposed the coalition deal. Following a trend towards greater transparency and media scrutiny of the coalition negotiations, by the end of the 1960s the CSV members were granted this right as well. Still, the members' delegates in the LSAP retained a greater say than their opposite numbers in the CSV. For a long time, the CSV congress only voted on the results of the policy agreement and the numerical portfolio distribution, while the designation of CSV ministers was left to a much smaller body (the national committee or the national council). Since the end of the 1960s, this body meets just before the congress, and the latter approves the policy programme as well as personnel appointments. The LSAP congress always first dedicates a session to the presentation and approval of the policy agreement. It is then interrupted in order to let the general council deliberate and vote on the personnel distribution. Then the list of LSAP ministers is proposed to the congress delegates for approval. If it is rejected as a whole, a separate vote is held on each name on the list. In theory, if one of the proposed candidates is rejected, other names can be proposed and endorsed. In practice, the general council's proposed list has never been rejected. The Liberals, on the other hand, so far have never given their congress the opportunity to approve a coalition agreement. In 1979, the last time they entered a government, only the 34 members of the Comité Directeur were asked to endorse the DP's government participation.

Dissent is rare in these party proceedings, which usually focus more on personnel appointments than on the policy agreement. The average rate of approval for the 1984, 1989 and 1994 party ratifications was 96 per cent, with only 1 per cent voting against the deal. Here the LSAP congresses were more cohesive than their CSV counterparts (98% vs. 92.6% favourable votes, respectively).

Parliamentary Investiture

Although constitutionally not required, a parliamentary vote of investiture follows the Grand-Duke's official appointment of all the members of the cabinet. The government declaration read by the prime minister is only a summary of the coalition agreement, and sometimes differs from the version approved by the respective coalition parties, as the latter tends to focus on specific policies cherished by the parties' rank and file. In some cases, the government declaration is more specific than the coalition agreement itself: the 1969 coalition agreement was so vague that the first cabinet had to redraft it before presenting it to parliament.

The investiture debate usually lasts two days or more. The chairmen of the majority parliamentary groups first address the House and comment on the negotiation process and its results from the point of view of their respective teams. Then the opposition parties are given the floor. During these debates, majority MPs seize the occasion to voice their possible discontent or reservations about specific provisions of the coalition agreement, though party discipline does not tolerate that dissent is reflected in votes. Opposition MPs usually criticize the government declaration in detail. The investiture vote that concludes these debates always follows the 'majority vs. opposition' pattern, with very few abstentions. As a result, all post-war governments have received a vote of confidence by a majority of the MPs.

Bargaining Attempts and Formation Duration

Table 11.2 shows the partisan composition of post-war governments, the number of parties in parliament, the parties involved in inconclusive bargaining rounds, and the overall duration of formation processes. The rather long formation processes cannot be explained by the number of bargaining attempts. The 1945–99 average of 0.5 inconclusive bargaining rounds is very

TABLE 11.2. *Government formation in Luxembourg, 1945–1999*

Government	Number of parties in parliament	Number of previous bargaining rounds	Parties involved in previous bargaining rounds	Number of days required for government formation
CSV–LSAP–DP–KPL 1945	5	0		20
CSV–DP 1947	5	1	CSV–LSAP–DP–KPL	0
CSV–DP 1948	4	1	CSV–LSAP–DP	37
CSV–LSAP 1951	4	1	CSV–DP	29
CSV–LSAP*	4	0		6
CSV–LSAP 1954	4	0		29
CSV–LSAP*				0
CSV–DP 1959	4	3	(1) CSV–LSAP–DP (2) LSAP–CSV (3) LSAP–DP	28
CSV–LSAP 1964	5	0		37
CSV–DP 1969	4	1	CSV–LSAP	52
DP–LSAP 1974	5	0		19
CSV–DP 1979	7	0		35
CSV–LSAP 1984	5	0		32
CSV–LSAP 1989	7	0		25
CSV–LSAP 1994	5	0		30
CSV–LSAP 1995*	5	0		6

* No new government according to the definition used throughout this volume, but a new cabinet.

low compared to the duration average (29 days). If we consider only formations preceded by elections (thus ignoring the 1947 CSV–DP government formation), mean duration increases to 31 days. This is quite normal, since elections often change the relative balance of power between parties. This effect is even more obvious when we consider cabinet formations that have taken place after early elections: although we only have two examples (1959 and 1969), mean duration jumps to 40 days while the number of inconclusive bargaining rounds reaches 2. Clearly, with parliamentary seats reshuffled and the tensions that provoked early elections, the formation process becomes more open and difficult.

The number of parties in parliament does not seem to affect the number of inconclusive bargaining rounds. In fact, the largest number of failures (3) occurred in 1959, when the number of parties was at its lowest (4). Moreover, when parliament contained seven parties (in 1979), no bargaining round was inconclusive. Note also that in the end, Luxembourg's *formateurs* have always been successful: up until now, every *formateur* has become prime minister, even though in some cases several attempts have been required.

The relation between inconclusive bargaining rounds, formation duration, and the actual partisan composition of the cabinet reveals some interesting patterns. Coalitions with the Liberals have been the second choice for the Christian Democrats (in 1947, 1949, 1959, and 1969), who have first tried another formula, usually a bipartite coalition with the Socialists. Due to their second choice status, the mean CSV–DP post-electoral formation duration is higher (38 days) than for the CSV–LSAP alternative (30.5 days). This pattern further confirms the position of the LSAP as the favourite partner of the CSV, but also the relevance of the veto power of the Socialist congress and anxillary organizations vis-à-vis their leadership's eagerness to participate in government.

There is also a (rather weak) relation between formation duration and shifts in coalition composition. Coalitions composed of incumbent parties take on the average 30 days to form, new coalitions an average of 33 days (excluding here the 1945 national union government and its successor). This is mainly due to the fact that outgoing partners first try to renegotiate the old coalition, as long as the election outcome does not force a coalition shift (in 1951, 1959, and 1969). The excessive policy and portfolio appetite of the main opposition party when it is invited back to the negotiation table may also slightly lengthen the negotiations.

Finally, although overall formation duration seems high for a simple party system like Luxembourg's, the real time spent around the negotiations table is relatively short, given the fact that European and local duties make negotiators lose almost a week.

COALITION GOVERNANCE

Coalition Agreements

Considering the efforts made by the Luxembourg government to politically inform its citizens (the most spectacular one being the frequent mailing, since 1883, of summaries or, since 1979, full text of parliamentary debates to every single home), the secrecy of government agreements is surprising. Coalition agreements are, and always remain, top secret documents. Only the ministers and the parties' archives receive a copy. Since 1945, only one government agreement has been published by a newspaper close to the opposition (in 1984). The actual coalition agreement is the combination of, on the one hand, the reports from the negotiations sessions (the *Sitzungsprotokolle*) that include an analysis of the political situation and the different policy positions, and, on the other hand, the negotiated documents (the *Verhandlungsdokumente*), which contain policy decisions, rules of the game, and the allocation between parties of ministerial portfolios and extra-cabinet positions.

TABLE 11.3. *Cabinets in Luxembourg since 1945*

Cabinet number	Prime Minister	Date in	Formal resignation	Maximum potential duration (in days)	Duration (in days)	Government composition
1	Dupong I	14 Nov. 1945	1 Mar. 1947	1,075	472	CSV–LSAP–DP–KPL
2	Dupong II	1 Mar. 1947	7 June 1948	603	464	CSV–DP
3	Dupong III	14 July 1948	4 June 1951	1,058	1,055	CSV–D
4	Dupong IV	03 July 1951	23 Dec. 1953	1,066	904	CSV–LSAP
5	Bech I	29 Dec. 1953	31 May 1954	156	153	CSV–LSAP
6	Bech II	29 June 1954	29 Mar. 1958	1,797	1,369	CSV–LSAP
7	Frieden	29 Mar. 1958	2 Feb. 1959	428	310	CSV–LSAP
8	Werner I	2 Mar. 1959	8 June 1964	1,925	1,925	CSV–DP
9	Werner II	15 July 1964	29 Oct. 1968	1,789	1,567	CSV–LSAP
10	Werner III	6 Feb. 1969	27 May 1974	1,936	1,936	CSV–DP
11	Thorn	15 June 1974	11 June 1979	1,822	1,822	DP–LSAP
12	Werner IV	16 July 1979	18 June 1984	1,799	1,799	CSV–DP
13	Santer I	20 July 1984	19 June 1989	1,795	1,795	CSV–LSAP
14	Santer II	14 July 1989	13 June 1994	1,796	1,795	CSV–LSAP
15	Santer III	13 July 1994	20 Jan. 1995	1,796	191	CSV–LSAP
16	Juncker	26 Jan. 1995		1,599		CSV–LSAP

Note: Maximum potential duration has been calculated on the basis of a 5-year term (4 times 365 and 366 days) from 1945 to 1954, as the parliamentary term was then 6 years long, but the renewal of half the Chamber occurred every 3 years and triggered the formation of a new government. In each case, formation duration was taken away from this figure. For the two legislatures that extended beyond the normal term, as consequences of the only two examples of early elections in Luxembourg (1959 and 1969), the practical duration was taken as maximum potential duration, in order not to get percentages over 100%. In three other occasions (1974, 1979, and 1984), we had to apply the same logic for these legislatures exceeded, due to calendar reasons in the choice of elections dates, by a few days their normal term. Calendar reasons refer to the rule that elections are to be held on the first Sunday of June (Art. 105 of the electoral law). If the latter is the With Sunday (Pentecost), then elections are held on the last Sunday of May (1974). If the following election date does not fall on Pentecost Sunday, they are held on the first Sunday of June. This explains why the actual duration can exceed the theoretical maximum potential duration of 1,826 days (four times 365 and one time 366 days). Moreover, since 1979, when European elections are to be held in the same year as national ones, they are held jointly on the day chosen by Grand Ducal decree. This was always the case since 1979. Elections were held on the second Sunday of June in 1979 and 1989, and on the third Sunday in 1984. These are the reasons why these parliaments lasted one (1979–84) or two (1974–9) weeks more than five years. In the remaining case (1984–9) parliament lasted only one day longer as a result of two leap years (366 days) instead of one in the same period.

TABLE 11.4. Coalition governance in Luxembourg, 1945–1999

(1) Government	(2) Coalition agreement	(3) Agreement public	(4) Election rule	(5) Conflict management mechanisms	(6) Most common management mechanisms	(7) Management mechanisms for most serious conflicts	(8) Coalition discipline in legislation	(9) Coalition discipline in other parliamentary behaviour	(10) Freedom of appointment	(11) Policy agreement	(12) Junior ministers	(13) Non-cabinet positions[a]
CSV–LSAP–DP–KPL 1945	POST	N	N	—	—	—	2	4	Y	3	N	Y
CSV–DP 1947	IE	N	N	—	—	—	2	4	Y	3	N	Y
CSV–DP 1948	POST	N	N	—	—	—	2	4	Y	3	N	Y
CSV–LSAP 1951	POST	N	N	—	—	—	2	4	Y	3	N	Y
CSV–LSAP 1953*	POST	N	N	—	—	—	2	4	Y	3	N	Y
CSV–LSAP 1954	POST	N	N	—	—	—	2	4	Y	3	Y	Y
CSV–LSAP 1958*	POST	N	N	—	—	—	2	4	Y	3	Y	Y
CSV–DP 1959	POST	N	N	—	—	—	2	4	Y	3	N	Y
CSV–LSAP 1964	POST	N	N	CoC, PS	CoC	PS	2	4	Y	3	N	Y
CSV–LSAP 1969	POST	N	N	CoC, PS	CoC	PS	2	4	Y	3	N[b]	Y
DP–LSAP 1974	POST	N	N	CoC, PS	CoC	PS	2	4	Y	3	Y	Y
CSV–DP 1979	POST	N	N	CoC	CoC	CoC	2	4	Y	3	Y	Y
CSV–LSAP 1984	POST	N	N	CoC, PS	CoC	PS	2	4	Y	3	Y	Y
CSV–LSAP 1989	POST	N	N	CoC	CoC	CoC	2	4	Y	3	Y	Y
CSV–LSAP 1994	POST	N	N	CoC	CoC	CoC	2	4	Y	3	Y	Y
CSV–LSAP 1995*	POST	N	N	CoC	CoC	CoC	2	4	Y	3	Y	Y

* No new government according to the definition used throughout this volume, but a new cabinet.
[a] At least the Chairman of the House, and since the 1950s, European positions.
[b] In the 1969–71 period.

Coalition agreements are not only secret, they are long and detailed documents. The scarce information gathered from newspaper articles and interviews indicates a gradual evolution towards longer texts. The 1974 agreement was 71 pages long, while the 1994 one contained over 200 pages (while the 1984 and 1989 agreements count 128 and 190 pages, respectively).

Given the general unavailability of coalition agreements, a content analysis of these documents has been impossible. Nevertheless, the government declarations present an approximate picture of the content of the *Verhandlungsdokumente*. Government declarations usually begin with an analysis of the new political situation (following either elections or a government crisis) and a justification of the party composition of the new government. The prime minister also reports on the coalition negotiations. These introductory paragraphs reflecting the general political context and climate of the formation process are followed by an enumeration of the government's intentions in a wide range of policy areas. Depending on the composition of the coalition, the political agenda, and the priorities of government partners for the forthcoming term, the discussion of some policy areas will be quite detailed, whereas others will not even be mentioned.

Even though policy constitutes the main part (probably over 90%) of both the coalition agreement and the government declaration, sometimes internal government organization is also discussed, e.g. in the case of the creation or splitting of ministries.[14] Inner cabinet rules are rarely mentioned in the declaration. The most important such references have been to the sacrosanct status of coalition agreements: in 1954 Prime Minister Bech insisted that the implementation of (and thus the faithfulness to) the common programme was his government's first goal. He added that the government could also deal with questions not included in the agreement, but only contingent on the respective parties' approval. Other declarations have explicitly mentioned subjects that coalition partners agree not to raise: in 1945, under Prime Minister Dupong, a ban on controversial or irritating questions about church–state relations between the partners of the National Union; in 1974, under the Thorn DP–LSAP government, the taxation of large fortunes; and in 1979, under the CSV–DP coalition, abortion. Hence, on these issues, the coalition parties gave notice that they did not agree and that an agreement in the near future would be highly unlikely. Still, they agreed to govern together despite their policy divergences.

Finally, nominations for top political positions are always negotiated during the formation process and can thus be found in the secret document. These include European positions (Luxembourg's seat in the European

---

[14] For instance, in the 1964 declaration Prime Minister Werner explained the rationale for splitting the Finance and Economy departments.

Commission and Cour des Comptes) as well as the Speaker of the House, and are taken into account in the portfolio allocation between the coalition partners.

Coalition Maintenance

Enforcing the coalition agreement is at the core of governance in Luxembourg. Efforts are made to assure the loyalty of the majority parties to the coalition agreement at the cabinet, the parliamentary, and the party level. Yet, mechanisms of coalition maintenance are less numerous and sophisticated than elsewhere (e.g. Belgium).

Intra-cabinet Mechanisms

As members of their party's negotiation team, ministers have participated in all plenary bargaining sessions and thus can recall the discussions on specific topics. As a consequence, they can understand the spirit of any policy intention, as well as specific formulae (or even words) that have been carefully chosen in drafting. When in doubt, cabinet members can go back to the *Sitzungsprotokolle* where they can find the original context of all drafted policies. Violations of the coalition agreement, even involuntary ones, can destroy a minister's career (cf. the fate of minister Fischbach in 1966, *infra*). Coalition agreements are not renegotiable because coalition partners fear that the general equilibrium between partisan demands fixed in the joint programme could be seriously endangered by the renegotiation of a section of the agreement, whatever its importance. The rigidity of coalition agreements thus help enhance their credibility in bargaining. Ministers and their parties do not want to risk provoking a veto from the party congresses, which have to ratify major modifications of the programme. Hence, even though *ministrables* are in charge of negotiations and could try to use their influence to include in the coalition agreement policies they personally favour, they cannot be considered 'policy dictators' (Laver and Shepsle 1996). This is because they do not know in advance which portfolio they will receive, and they will not always have had a decisive say in negotiating the policies which they will eventually be asked to implement. Thus, cabinet members are mere executors of a collectively defined and controlled policy programme.

The guardians of ministers' loyalty to the policy programme are the leaders of the respective party ministers, namely the prime minister and his counterpart, the vice prime minister. They scrupulously verify whether all ministerial proposals respect the agreement's stipulations. Furthermore, either the prime minister or the vice prime minister (acting on behalf of the prime minister) may bring up for discussion in the cabinet any departmental project (or any project involving more than one department) if they feel that the issue could undermine the coalition's cohesion. Given this prior control of the cabinet, individual ministerial responsibility therefore lies only in the management and implementation of their department's policies.[15]

Given the low number of parties and ministers in Luxembourg cabinets, it is no surprise that there is no institutionalized inner cabinet. However, there are sometimes informal contacts between the prime minister and the vice prime minister. Permanent cabinet committees do not exist, but sometimes specialized ministerial committees are convoked (though only on very pragmatic grounds).

Finally, junior ministers do not serve as political 'watchdogs', monitoring ministers of other parties. Instead, they provide strictly a form of day-to-day assistance to ministers in charge of large or highly compartmentalized departments. No junior minister has belonged to a different party from the minister to whom he or she was attached. Hence, before the creation of a specific conflict management mechanism in the 1960s (the inter-fractional parliamentary meetings), coalition conflicts were mainly dealt with in the plenary cabinet meetings. Given the small number of cabinet members (a maximum of eight until 1964), this was a very efficient mechanism.

The Inter-fractional Parliamentary Meetings

Coalition governance is also effectuated through 'inter-fractional meetings', the most original feature of Luxembourg's coalition maintenance mechanisms. These contacts between majority parliamentary groups *(Fraktionen)* have in recent times become more and more important and frequent. Although never formally institutionalized, the 'inter-fractionals' include each partner's parliamentary group.[16] In ordinary meetings, held every month or so, the core of the inter-fractional session is composed of the party chairmen, the prime minister and vice prime minister, and the most active MPs. As the agenda varies from one meeting to another, the pertinent ministers and specialized MPs are added to the core group of participants. The main task of these ordinary meetings is to verify whether all government projects follow the coalition agreement to the letter. The meetings are also authorized to reject any parliamentary initiative that would run counter to the coalition programme. Although majority MPs have a right of initiative in legislation, they must present all proposals to their parliamentary group secretary. The latter will always refer the proposal to the inter-fractional before introducing it in parliament. Hence, a majority MP's bill that has not been cleared by the inter-fractional will not be debated, let alone passed. Hence, the necessity of

---

[15] Note that even if it is always sought, consensus is not required in the Council of government, where decisions are made by majority vote. Members of the government who opposed a particular decision can disclaim collective responsibility. Their personal disagreement is then stated in the Council's written report (Royal Decree of 9 July 1857).

[16] The composition of Luxembourg's parliamentary groups is rather peculiar, since they include not only national MPs, but also MEPs, ministers, and the party chairman.

coalition maintenance and strict voting discipline has shifted the individual MP's right to initiate legislative to the inter-fractional (at least on sensitive issues). Moreover, even when a proposal accords with the common agreement and gets a go-ahead, the politically interesting ones are most often appropriated and introduced by the government, which thus erases the parliamentary origin of the proposal.

Inter-fractional meetings may also be held at the prime minister's request. These 'extraordinary' sessions have been rare in recent times (according to Vice Prime Minister Poos, about two or three per government term). These have had to deal with the interpretation of the coalition agreement in the light of the priorities of the day, cabinet positions on particularly 'hot' topics (civil servants' pension system reform, for instance), or they have simply been held when a conflict could not be solved in the cabinet. Extraordinary inter-fractional meetings were particularly commonly convened in times of government crisis in the late 1960s, when they were nicknamed 'the fire brigade'. Ordinary or not, inter-fractionals were very often used throughout the 1970s, when cabinets could not rely on comfortable parliamentary majorities. Prime Minister Thorn in particular had to use this technique in order to avoid defections in plenary votes (the DP–LSAP coalition controlled only 31 of the 59 seats in parliament).

Coalition Maintenance within Parties

We already noted that (at least in recent times) the early party investitures have played a major role in committing all the party bodies of each coalition partner. Ordinary members, the party executive, and the whole range of elected representatives from communal councillors to national MPs, united in their most sovereign decision making body, have examined and endorsed the coalition programmes. As the party chairman, party ministers, and MPs also attend fractional and inter-fractional meetings, the leading members of each party thus have a constant grip on intra-party coalition governance. Moreover, parliamentary group meetings serve to assure coalition discipline in legislation (*Fraktionszwang*).

The relative importance of the different party components may also suggest how coalition maintenance is assured by the partners. At the top of party hierarchy, we invariably find the party's cabinet members. Over the years, an increasing number of parliamentary generalists considered to be party leaders have received cabinet portfolios. With all the 'heavyweights' in the cabinet, the role of the party leadership outside the executive has been severely reduced. The clearest example of this shift of power towards the party in government was Mr Juncker's cumulation of offices in the early 1990s: the CSV chairman was at the same time Minister of Finance and Labour.[17]

[17] Nevertheless, CSV ministers, deputies, and members considered Prime Minister Santer as their real leader.

Luxembourg's central party organizations are very poor both in terms of financial and personnel resources in comparison to their parliamentary group.[18] In 1965, the Chamber of Deputies' statutory rules formally recognized the *Fraktionen*, which then finally received financial support from the state for offices and staff.

PORTFOLIO ALLOCATION

Luxembourg's government features only a very small number of political appointments. As 'ministerial cabinets' do not exist and other patronage resources are scarce, parties entering a government cannot promise jobs to their intelligentsia or to their most active members.

The cabinet must consist of at least three members, whereas the constitution does not stipulate a maximum. In fact, the number of cabinet positions has ranged from six in 1951 to twelve in 1995. Since 1959, the leader of the junior coalition partner has been accorded the title of vice prime minister. Apart from regular ministers, political appointments include the secretaries of state.[19]

Although portfolio allocation usually comes last in the bargaining process, matters like the general structure of the cabinet, the creation of new ministries, and partisan distribution have sometimes been discussed in between negotiation rounds over policy. On the other hand, the selection of individuals for these cabinet portfolios remains the unique responsibility of each party. While Article 77 of the constitution formally gives the monarch total freedom to appoint and dismiss his or her ministers, he in fact only chooses the prime minister. Since World War I, he has never intervened in the selection of regular cabinet ministers, a matter in which each party is sovereign.

Although this is not constitutionally prescribed, cabinet members have a parliamentary, or at least political, background. The last 'technician' minister dates from 1945. Electoral results are good predictors of ministerial appointments. The MPs with the best personal poll results are almost sure to become ministers if their party enters the coalition. In recent times, geographical representation has become more and more important. Up until the 1960s, with a very low number of cabinet members (from six to twelve), a fair

---

[18] Political parties do not have legal status, as they are neither officially recognized by the constitution nor by law or regulation. As a result, it has been impossible for the government to finance party central offices or, conversely, to control their resources.

[19] The creation of these positions triggered a cabinet crisis. Prime Minister Bech, who was also responsible for Foreign Affairs, felt he was too often abroad and therefore needed a secretary of state in order to assist him in his foreign tasks. Facing a constant refusal by his coalition partner, he resigned as prime minister in 1958. The position of secretary of state was finally created by the following government.

representation of the four very unevenly populated electoral districts was impossible to reach within each party's team of ministers. Given the very small number of MPs of the Eastern district (in 1995 seven seats divided amongst four parties), ministerial delegations have at times failed to include a minister from the East. Hence, party leaders usually choose the best known politicians of the Centre and, to a lesser degree, of the South.

Rules for intra-party portfolio allocation vary between parties. As a result of the internal democratization of every party, the weight of the local delegates in the party investiture bodies has recently become a bigger constraint. In 1989, for instance, delegates of the East district decided to leave the LSAP general council meeting because the East was not awarded the sixth and last socialist portfolio.

Finally, incumbent ministers who were not sanctioned by the electorate get served first (though their departmental competencies may change). By now, each cabinet contains at least one female minister.[20] Personal competencies and professional or parliamentary specialization are also taken into account for intra-party portfolio allocation.

Throughout the post-war period, the prime minister has tended to hold multiple portfolios, but this phenomenon has decreased since the early 1980s. Prime ministers always had other key competencies in their hands.[21] Pierre Werner was almost the first 'full time' prime minister in 1979, as he added only culture to his premiership, but Prime Minister Santer in 1984 once again combined the prime ministership with a major portfolio (Finance). Finance has in fact been the key portfolio most commonly held by prime ministers since 1945. While vice prime ministers usually also have accumulated portfolios, this office has not grown into a full-time responsibility.

The Christian Democrats—whenever they have been part of a coalition—have always led the cabinet, and apart from the prime ministership, have until 1999 had the key portfolio of Finance, but also Education and Agriculture, two ministries highly salient for traditional Christian Democratic electorates. The policy areas of Social Housing and Urban Areas, which belonged to different ministries, have also been headed exclusively by Christian Democrats. Thus the Christian Democrats have always controlled at least one department relevant to rural as well as urban areas. Since 1951, all Family ministers have been Christian Democrats as well. Apart from these real monopolies, the CSV has only had to leave Labour to its partner once since 1959, while Interior has been conceded only twice in the past forty years. Finally, the

---

[20] The first female cabinet member was Mrs Frieden in 1969, who resigned in 1972. From 1980 to 1984, Colette Flesch was vice-PM. From 1989 onwards, cabinets have always included a woman.

[21] Prime Minister Thorn even held Foreign Affairs, Trade, Economy, and Middle Classes.

TABLE 11.5. *Distribution of cabinet ministerships and junior ministerships in Luxembourg, 1945–1999*

Cabinet number	Cabinet	Number of ministers[a]	(1) Prime Minister	(2) Vice Prime Minister	(3) Finance	(4) Foreign/ Trade/Aid	(5) Interior	(6) Justice	(7) Social Affairs/ Labour and Mines
1	Dupong I	8	CSV1	—	CSV1	CSV2	DP	LSAP2	KPL1, LSAP1
2	Dupong II	7	CSV1	—	CSV1	CSV2	DP1	DP1	CSV1
3	Dupong III	7	CSV1	—	CSV1	CSV2	DP1	DP1	CSV1
4	Dupong IV	6	CSV1	—	CSV1	CSV2	CSV3	LSAP2	LSAP1
5	Bech I	6	CSV1	—	CSV2	CSV1	CSV3	LSAP2	LSAP1
6	Bech II	7+1ss	CSV1	—	CSV2	CSV1	CSV3	LSAP2	LSAP1
7	Frieden	7+1ss	CSV1	—	CSV3	CSV2	CSV1	LSAP2	LSAP1
8	Werner I	7	CSV1	DP1	CSV1	DP1	CSV4	CSV1	CSV2
9	Werner II	8+2ss	CSV1	LSAP1	CSV1	CSV1+CSV4[b]	LSAP1	CSV1	LSAP2
10	Werner III	7	CSV1	DP1	CSV1	DP2	DP1	DP1	CSV2
11	Thorn	8+2ss	DP1	LSAP1	LSAP1	DP1	LSAP2	LSAP3	LSAP4
12	Werner IV	9+2ss	CSV1	DP1	CSV3	DP1	CSV4	DP1	CSV3
13	Santer I	9+3ss	CSV1	LSAP1	CSV1	LSAP1	CSV3	LSAP3	LSAP2, CSV4
14	Santer II	9+2ss	CSV1	LSAP1	CSV4	LSAP1	CSV3	CSV5	LSAP2, CSV4
15	Santer III	11+1ss	CSV1	LSAP1	CSV2	LSAP1	CSV3	CSV6	LSAP5, CSV2
16	Juncker	11+1ss	CSV1	LSAP1	CSV1	LSAP1	CSV3	CSV6	LSAP5, CSV1

cont./

TABLE 11.5. cont.

Cabinet number	Cabinet	(8) Health	(9) Defence	(10) Education/ Culture and Sciences	(11) Agriculture/ Rural Areas[c]	(12) Transports, Mail, Telecom/ Public Works	(13) Economy	(14) Family Population/ Women, Handicapped	(15) Sports/ Youth
1	Dupong I	KPL1	CSV1	CSV3	CSV3	LSAP2	?	—	—
2	Dupong II	DP2	CSV4	CSV3	CSV3	DP3	CSV4	—	—
3	Dupong III	DP2	CSV1	CSV3	CSV4	DP3	CSV4	—	—
4	Dupong IV	CSV3	CSV2	CSV3	CSV1	LSAP2	LSAP3	CSV3	—
5	Bech I	CSV3	CSV2	CSV3	CSV1	LSAP2	LSAP3	CSV3	—
6	Bech II	CSV4	CSV2	CSV3	CSV4	LSAP2	LSAP3	CSV3	—
7	Frieden	CSV4	CSV3	CSV1	CSV4	LSAP2	LSAP3	CSV1	—
8	Werner I	CSV2	DP1	CSV3, CSV4	CSV3	CSV4, DP2	DP3	CSV3	DP2
9	Werner II	LSAP2	CSV4	CSV2	CSV3	LSAP3	LSAP4	CSV3	LSAP1
10	Werner III	CSV4	DP1	CSV2, CSV4	CSV3	DP3, CSV3	DP3	CSV4	DP2, CSV4
11	Thorn	DP3	DP3	LSAP3	DP4	DP2, DP4	DP2	LSAP4	DP1
12	Werner IV	DP2	DP2	CSV5, CSV1	CSV2	DP3, DP4	DP1	CSV4	DP2
13	Santer I	LSAP2	CSV5	CSV2, LSAP3	CSV5	LSAP4	LSAP1	CSV3	CSV5, CSV2
14	Santer II	LSAP2	LSAP1	CSV5, CSV1	CSV6	LSAP3	LSAP3	CSV2	LSAP2
15	Santer III	LSAP2	LSAP4	CSV4, CSV1	CSV	LSAP5, LSAP3	LSAP3	CSV	LSAP4
16	Juncker	LSAP2	LSAP4	CSV4	CSV5	LSAP5, LSAP3	LSAP3	CSV2	LSAP4

Cabinet number	Cabinet	(16) Middle Classes/ Tourism	(17) Budget	(18) Social Solidarity	(19) Civil Service	(20) Energy	(21) Environment	(22) Social Housing/ Urban Areas	(23) Reconstruction
1	Dupong I	—	—	—	—	—	—	—	LSAP1
2	Dupong II	—	—	—	—	—	—	—	—
3	Dupong III	—	—	—	—	—	—	—	DP3
4	Dupong IV	—	—	—	—	—	—	—	LSAP3
5	Bech I	—	—	—	—	—	—	—	LSAP3
6	Bech II	—	—	—	—	—	—	—	—
7	Frieden	—	—	—	—	—	—	—	—
8	Werner I	DP3	—	—	—	—	—	—	—
9	Werner II	CSV4, LSAP1	LSAP4	CSV3	CSV2	LSAP4	—	—	—
10	Werner III	DP3	—	CSV4	DP2	DP3	—	—	—
11	Thorn	DP2	—	LSAP4	DP3	DP2	—	LSAP4	—
12	Werner IV	DP1, CSV5	—	CSV4	DP4	DP3	DP3	CSV4	—
13	Santer I	LSAP1, CSV2	CSV4	CSV3	CSV5	LSAP4	LSAP3	CSV3	—
14	Santer II	CSV2	CSV	CSV2	CSV5	—	LSAP4	CSV3	—
15	Santer III	CSV5	CSV	—	CSV	LSAP3	LSAP2	CSV5	—
16	Juncker	CSV5	CSV6[d]	—	CSV3	LSAP3	LSAP2	CSV5	—

[a] This column gives the number of cabinet ministers (first number) and junior ministers (second number, with ss meaning state secretaries). All junior ministers belonged to the sema party as the respective cabinet minister.

[b] Werner (C1) was PM and Foreign Affairs Minister. Fischbach (C4) was Minister of Middle Classes, Minister of Defence and 'Assistant-Minister' for Foreign Affairs.

[c] The same Minister has had (or has at the moment) both of these competences.

[d] The Minister of Budget in charge in January 1999 was also responsible for the relations with the Parliament.

Notes

Each minister has a code (his or her party acronym plus a number) to identify the portfolio combination. For instance, in the last government, the Vice-PM (LSAP1) is also responsible for Foreign Affairs, Trade, and Aid.

The table represents the typical combination of portfolios, in the hands of single ministers. However, there were periods where these competences were split between two or three different ministers. We then follow the order used in the heading of the column: in the last government, Socialist Minister LSAP5 is in charge of Social Affairs (not of Labour and Mines which are CSV1's responsibilities), and also of Transports, Mail, and Telecom (while LSAP3, is in charge of Public Works. LSAP 3 is also minister for Energy, on his own).

Christian Democrats have held the Foreign Office and Defence uninterruptedly until 1959.

Social Affairs has always been controlled by Socialist ministers when the LSAP has been in power, except for the 1945 national union government, when it was left to the Communists. The Socialists have always had the three ministries of Economy, Transports, and Public Works package, except during their coalition with the Liberals. Justice has also often been held by the LSAP. In the four most recent governments, they have shown a particular interest in Foreign Affairs.

During their six government participations from 1954 to 1999, the Liberals have always had: Transports and Public Works, Middle Classes, Civil Service, and Energy, while four times they have headed the Foreign Office, Health, and the Ministry of Economy. Surprisingly, the DP has never held Finance, despite the importance of tax policy in the party programme. The complete absence of Liberals in Education, and the failure of the Socialists to obtain this ministry in the most recent governments, are also remarkable, given both parties' emphasis on the interests of public vs. Catholic schools. More logical is the absence of Liberals in ministries which include 'social solidarity' or 'social housing' on their names. Surprisingly, Civil Service has never been given to a Socialist, the defenders of a large public sector.

Thus, selective portfolio holding is the rule in Luxembourg. The parties' portfolio appetites are determined by their ideology, by the interests of specific components of their electorate, and by the visibility and spending power of the ministries. Our analysis basically confirms Laver and Budge's (1992: 413) observation: parties in Luxembourg are slightly more office-seeking than policy-driven when they enter a government coalition. However, they do not pursue office for its own sake, but rather as a means to advance policy.

CABINET TERMINATION

Cabinet Stability

Luxembourg's post-war governments have proved remarkably stable. Most cabinets have lasted the entire legislature.[22] Until 1999 (excluding the latest

---

[22] Table 11.3 shows that two cabinets exceeded the normal maximum life expectancy. These cases were the results of early elections (1959 and 1969). According to Art. 56 of the constitution, MPs are elected for a 5-year term, and their mandate normally lasts until the end of the fifth ordinary session of the chamber. If a parliamentary dissolution occurs before the end of the legislature, the newly elected MPs remain in parliament until the year following the opening of the fifth ordinary session, when new ordinary elections are to be held. As ordinary sessions start on the second Tuesday of Oct., any session opened at a different date must be considered as extraordinary. Thus, under these circumstances, MPs

one headed by Juncker), seven out of the eight cabinets have completed their full term, and the only exception was caused by Prime Minister Santer's nomination as head of the European Commission in 1995, an event completely exogenous to Luxembourger politics. Since 1945, mean duration of governments is thus 1,170 days (a bit more than 3.2 years) and average cabinet survival rate is 83.3 per cent, the record in Western Europe.[23]

The exceptionally stable CSV–DP cabinets (average survival rate: 95.3%) have been the most durable coalition type. With less than 50 per cent, the 1945 National Union cabinet had the worse survival rate until 1995, when Prime Minister Santer was forced to resign after only 191 days in order to head the European Commission. Even without taking this very low score into account, the average survival rate of CSV–LSAP cabinets is 'only' 88.4 per cent, which is still lower than CSV–DP or DP–LSAP figures (the unique Liberal-Socialist coalition completed its term). The comparative instability of CSV–LSAP (78.7% *in globo*, i.e. including the short-lived Santer III cabinet) cabinets has basically been due to policy conflicts between the two partners (*infra*).

Only the 1951–9 period, with four cabinets, can be considered unstable. Curiously enough, they all had the same composition and (apart from the 1945 national union government) the broadest parliament support of the entire post-war period (see Tables 11.1 and 11.3). This paradoxical situation shows that coalition size is irrelevant to cabinet stability in Luxembourg. To understand cabinet stability, one should turn to the concrete reasons for their termination.

Causes of Cabinet Termination

Accountability rules in Luxembourg are of a 'negative' type (De Winter 1995). In order to bring a government down, a simple majority of those voting (with a quorum of half of the MPs) in the Chamber has to vote for a motion of no confidence, or against a government proposal to which the government has linked its survival. In the post-war era, parliament has never formally used this power to unmake government. Table 11.6 shows that the most common reason for cabinet termination has simply been the completion of the legislature's constitutional term (nine cases out of fifteen governments, taking the partial elections into account). The other 'technical' terminations

who enter parliament following early elections spend their entire constitutional 5-year mandate term plus the extra-months of the extraordinary session. Therefore, as cabinet maximum life expectancy is the longest time possible spent by MPs between their election and the next dissolution, we cannot put that it is always limited to 5 years.

[23] We have estimated maximum potential duration on the basis of a 5-year term (4 times 365 plus 366 days) since 1954, and on a 3-year term basis in the 1945–54 period, when MPs were elected for 6 years, but the renewal of half the chamber occurred every 3 years and triggered the formation of a new government.

TABLE 11.6. *Cabinet termination in Luxembourg, 1945–1999*

Cabinet number	Cabinet	Mechanisms of cabinet termination							Terminal events	Policy area(s)	Comments
		Technical			Discretionary						
		(1) Regular parliamentary election	(2) Other constitu-tional reason	(3) Death of PM	(4) Early election	(7) Conflict between coalition parties		(8) Intra-party conflict	(13) Personal event		
						Policy	Personnel				
1	Dupong I		X					LSAP, LNL		12	Socialist Trade Union aimed at breaking the coalition. The railway issue opposed CSV and LSAP
2	Dupong II	X[a]									
3	Dupong III	X[a]									
4	Dupong IV			X							
5	Bech I	X									
6	Bech II		(X)				CSV; LSAP				PM Bech overworked, wanted a secretary of state to help him. LSAP ministers refused. Bech decided to quit. Voluntary resignation
7	Frieden		X		X	CSV; LSAP				12	CSV deputies voted with the opposition against LSAP Transports Minister Bodson. LSAP ministers decide to leave the government
8	Werner I	X									
9	Werner II		X		X	X				7, 13	Financing of revised pensions schemes
10	Werner III	X									
11	Thorn	X									
12	Werner IV	X									
13	Santer I	X									
14	Santer II	X									
15	Santer III		X						X		PM Santer quit to become European Commission President. Voluntary resignation.

[a] Until 1954, partial elections were held. The Parliament was renewed by half each three years.

have been the death of Prime Minister Dupong in 1953 and the nomination of Prime Minister Santer as President of the European Commission in 1995.

Hence, behavioural motives account for only four resignations out of fifteen. During the period of post-war reconstruction and the settlement of war-related issues such as Nazi collaboration, Dupong's national union government was constantly under popular pressure. His former cabinet in exile was reputed to have been very benevolent towards the occupants. After the death of Pierre Krier, socialist Minister of Labour and highly influential party personality, more conflicts reached cabinet level. Socialist rank and file began to put pressure on the ministers while the Socialist trade union openly tried to break the all-inclusive coalition. As a consequence, cooperation between coalition partners became impossible. The final clash between the two main parties occurred in 1947 over the railway issue, eventually leading to a shift in coalition. In 1958, the CSV–LSAP cabinet fell over the question of the creation of a secretary of state, aimed at aiding the prime minister. The LSAP refused, and as a surprise to all observers, Prime Minister Bech decided to quit.

The two remaining crises have been the longest and deepest ones in Luxembourg's post-war history. Both triggered early elections and a change of partners. In 1959, Prime Minister Frieden resigned because the LSAP members withdrew from the cabinet, due to several small but cumulative conflicts that had poisoned the coalition from within. The final clashes between the coalition partners concentrated on issues related to Minister Bodson's competences, Justice and Transports. The first source of conflict had to do with a very minor question of whether to introduce new rules concerning lorries' overtaking and a generalized system of periodical technical inspections of cars. The second was a case of civil service corruption in the Ministry of Justice that Mr Bodson had not reported to the judicial authorities. Given the already bad atmosphere in the cabinet, this was the last straw. The Liberals launched a motion of no confidence against Minister Bodson. Catholic MPs supported that motion together with the opposition. The Minister of Justice and Transports had to resign, but, as an act of solidarity with its minister, the whole socialist team seized this opportunity to leave the government. So even if parliament (and in particular the opposition) triggered the downfall of the government by sanctioning a minister, the government resigned due to rather insignificant inter-party policy conflicts.

The last such cabinet crises occurred under the 1964–8 CSV–LSAP coalition. A simple reshuffle put an end to the 1966 conflict over conscription. Since World War II, military service had been compulsory in Luxembourg. Even though popular opinion was clearly favourable, a return to the previous voluntary service system was regarded as a defeat for any government in this founding member of the North Atlantic Treaty Organization. Each time they have been out of government, Socialists and Liberals have alternated as champions of voluntary service. The CSV was considered the staunchest defender of conscription, although internally this position was contested, especially by the party youth. The issue was put on the agenda, and negotiations were held between Luxembourg's government and NATO in order to find the best possible solution. In a speech to the Chamber of Deputies, Catholic Defence Minister Fischbach wanted to confirm that a reform schedule was in progress, when he was so vehemently interrupted by the leader of the opposition that he took the initiative and came forward with a proposal to end conscription. The government felt betrayed by this declaration, and Prime Minister Werner, together with the cabinet members present, left the parliament with a sibylline statement (*'le gouvernement se retire'*) indicating his cabinet's resignation.

The same coalition remained in power until 1968, when parliament was dissolved early to avoid deep conflicts between the coalition partners. At the end of the 1960s, the Grand-Duchy was suffering an economic recession. Given a government budget deficit, all ministers intended to be very cautious about costly policy initiatives. Socialist Vice Prime Minister Cravatte nevertheless thought that even under these economic circumstances a pension reform was possible. Together with other financial issues, this question soon became a source of conflict between coalition partners. Rather than systematically trying to outbid one another on expenditures, the coalition leaders, Prime Minister Werner and Vice Prime Minister Cravatte, preferred to dissolve parliament. They also clearly committed themselves to a reconduction of the coalition after the elections. Sitting on the same couch, Werner and Cravatte appeared on television to inform the population of their common arrangement (the episode was subsequently denounced as 'canapé politics' by the Liberals). Having suffered a severe electoral defeat, the LSAP (although contacted as a first choice by the CSV) subsequently was prevented from entering the new government by its trade union.

In short, Luxembourg has had very stable governments in the post-war period: eleven of the fifteen terminations have had technical causes, whereas only four have been terminated for other reasons. The latter have invariably been inter-party cabinet conflicts, either in terms of policies or of personnel. Such coalition breakdowns, however, have only occurred under CSV–LSAP cabinets and never under different coalitions.

ELECTORAL PERFORMANCE

Table 11.7 clearly illustrates the negative effect of government participation on subsequent electoral results for incumbent parties. Of all parties that have been in power at the time of elections, Table 11.7 reveals that only one coalition (1954) has as a whole benefited from its incumbency. The social reforms[24] of both the Dupong cabinet of 1951–3 and its successor Bech (1953–4) account for this positive result, as the latter premier continued, with the same team, the task Prime Minister Dupong had undertaken before his death. The coalition as a whole was confirmed and the principle of 'never changing a winning team', was respected although one coalition partner, the Socialists, lost some seats.

TABLE 11.7. *Electoral costs/benefits of government parties in Luxembourg, 1945–1999* (in % of votes)

Government	In office at time of election	Election year	LSAP	CSV	DP	KPL	Government
CSV–LSAP–DP–KPL 1945–47	No	1948	+13,1	–4,8	–0,7	–1,8	+5,8
CSV–DP 1947–48	Yes	1948	—	–4,8	–0,7	—	–5,5
CSV–DP 1948–51	Yes	1951	—	–6	–2,6	—	–8,6
CSV–LSAP 1951–54	Yes	1954	–0,9	3,1	—	—	+2,2
CSV–LSAP 1954–59	Yes	1959	0,1	–6,3	—	—	–6,2
CSV–DP 1959–64	Yes	1964	—	–3,2	–8,1	—	–11,3
CSV–LSAP 1964–69	Yes	1968	–4,9	+2	—	—	–2,9
CSV–DP 1969–74	Yes	1974	—	–7,6	+5,3	—	–2,3
DP–LSAP 1974–79	Yes	1979	–4,5	—	–1,4	—	–5,9
CSV–DP 1979–84	Yes	1984	—	+0,2	–1,5	—	–1,3
CSV–LSAP 1984–89	Yes	1989	–5,6	–4,2	—	—	–9,8
CSV–LSAP 1989–94	Yes	1994	–0,8	–2,1	—	—	–2,9
MEANS	—	—	–0,5	–2,9	–1,5	–1,8	–4,1

Note: Because the number of votes at the disposal of each elector varies with the number of deputies in a constituency, it is not possible to calculate a national party vote by simply summing the four (South, North, Centre, and East) constituency-level vote totals. In order to estimate a national vote, each constituency vote is firstly divided by the number of seats in the constituency and the four quotients summed. For this reason and because some voters do not use all the votes to which they are entitled, this total sum (called theoretical number of voters) is not only lower than the total number of people requested to vote, but also to the total number of valid votes, which are the number of valid ballot papers cast.

Thus, from 1954 to 1999, incumbent governments have never come out strengthened from any elections. Note also that governments as a whole have been more heavily sanctioned by the electorate than any of their members taken separately (the average loss for cabinet that have been in at time of elections, 5%, exceeds the mean losses of any individual party). Usually, at least one of the members of the coalition has lost heavily in favour of opposition parties. As a consequence, the principle 'do change a losing team' was con-

---

[24] The major reforms in question were towards a better social security system. Important laws extended the scope of pensions and family benefits to new professional categories like liberal professions, both the public and private sectors were also better protected than by the former system. The income policy of these governments reintroduced the indexation of wages.

stantly applied from 1959 to 1989. Even the CSV–DP coalition's marginal loss of 1.3 per cent in 1979 sufficed to provoke a coalitional change, given the fact that in opposition the Socialists had gained more than 9 per cent. Hence, at least in the choice of the junior partner, the electoral responsiveness of the coalition formation process has over thirty years been very high. However, from 1989 to 1999, losing teams have tended to stay in power.

All types of coalitions have tended to lose at the polls. On average, CSV–LSAP governments have done slightly better (–3.9% losses) than CSV–DP coalitions (–5.8%), and the unique DP–LSAP cabinet (–5.9%). However, coalition composition does affect the electoral fortune of the pivotal party: on average, the CSV has lost more in coalition with the Liberals (–4.3%) than with the Socialists (–1.5%). This may to a certain extent explain the overall preference of the CSV for coalitions with the LSAP, as well as their recent willingness to maintain the same coalition, even after considerable electoral defeats (1989 and 1994).

On average, the Socialists lose more than their partners, whatever the party (with the CSV a mean loss of –0.9%, and with the DP –3.1%) while the DP always does better than its outgoing partner (2.6% better than the CSV and 4.5% better than the LSAP). Thus, with an average shift of –1.5 per cent, the Liberals have suffered least from government participation,[25] the LSAP coming second with –2.8 per cent, very close to the CSV, the party most sanctioned by its electorate (–2.9%). The poor record of the Christian Democrats is mainly due to the wear and tear of long-term incumbency: their quasi-permanence in office and the general negative impact of government status on electoral results has triggered a long decline. For the Socialists, on the other hand, excessive policy compromises are the likely explanation of why they tend to lose so much. In fact, Laver and Budge (1992) indicate that the coalition programmes in Luxembourg are usually far to the right of the electoral manifestos of the participating parties—Luxembourg even holds the record in that respect. The same analysis suggests that the LSAP may more willingly accept substantive policy concessions than its coalition partners, for it shows that in the 1951–79 period the LSAP received by far the worst policy pay-offs of the three traditional parties in terms of the distance between electoral manifestos and government programmes. Conceivably then, the LSAP electorate sanctions this ideological 'treason' by the party leadership at the end of the government's term. That has effectively been the case in the pertinent elections (1954, 1959, 1964, 1968, 1974, 1979, and 1984): when in power, the LSAP has lost an average of –2.5 per cent while the CSV and the DP have done clearly better with average outcomes of –2 and –1.2 per cent, respectively. On average, for the period analysed by Laver and Budge, the DP did

---

[25] The DP is the only party that has gained a considerable proportion of votes (+5.3% in 1974) after participating in a government.

better in policy pay-offs and electoral performance than the two others, with the CSV second and the LSAP third.

CONCLUSION

Post-war coalition government in Luxembourg has been very stable in partisan composition as well as in duration. The close-to-permanent presence of the Christian Democrats in government since 1945 has been due to the informal rule of giving the initiative of forming a new cabinet to the strongest party in parliament. Although *formateurs* have been highly successful, their discretion is limited by structural and behavioural constraints: positive formation rule, electoral responsiveness of the choice of the junior partner, and the restriction of *Regierungsfähigkeit* to the three traditional parties only.

During the entire lifetime of a cabinet, the increasingly comprehensive and detailed coalition agreements remain the 'contract' between the party rank and file, the parliamentary party, the party executive, and the ministers. Through the endorsement by its 'supreme' party congresses, each coalition party is in effect bound from top to bottom to the joint programme. Yet, only cabinet members and party leaders know the detailed contents of the full agreement, for these texts are kept secret. Day-to-day coalition maintenance is concentrated in the hands of the cabinet, and more particularly the prime minister and vice prime minister. The inter-fractional meetings constitute the second conflict management arena. Together the members make sure that the coalition contract is not violated and assure well-disciplined support in parliament. These maintenance mechanisms have proved very effective, for most of Luxembourg's governments have lasted the full term of the legislature. Only in four cases has an inter-party conflict triggered the downfall of a cabinet.

In practice, each party is free to designate its cabinet personnel. Many departments have turned to *chasses gardées*. Government participation in Luxembourg has a negative effect on coalition parties' subsequent electoral results, especially on those of the Socialists.

Thus, the birth, life, and death of Luxembourg coalition governments are governed by a wide range of highly structured phases, sophisticated mechanisms, and self-imposed behavioural rules that are often thought to be typical of only the bigger or more politically complex states. Therefore, although often neglected, Luxembourg offers one of the best possible introductions to the world of coalition politics.

REFERENCES

Als, Nicolas, and Philippart, Robert L. (1994). *La Chambre des Députés: Histoire et lieux de travail*. Luxembourg: Chambre des Députés du Grand-Duché de Luxembourg.
Delvaux, Michel, and Hirsch, Mario (1976). 'Le Grand-Duché de Luxembourg: Aspects de sociologie politique'. *Res Publica*, 1: 101–13.
De Winter, Lieven (1995). 'The Role of Parliament in Cabinet Formation and Resignation', in Herbert Döring (ed.), *Parliaments and Majority Rule in Western Europe*. New York: St Martin's Press.
Dodd, Lawrence C. (1976). *Coalitions in Parliamentary Government*. Princeton: Princeton University Press.
Hearl, Derek J. (1987). 'Luxembourg 1945–1982: Dimensions and Strategies', in Ian Budge, David Robertson, and Derek Hearl (eds.), *Ideology, Strategy and Party Change*. Cambridge: Cambridge University Press.
——(1992). 'Party and Coalition in Luxembourg', in Michael Laver and Ian Budge (eds.), *Party Policy and Government Coalitions*. New York: St Martin's Press.
Inglehart, Ronald, and Klingemann, Hans-Dieter (1976). 'Party Identification, Ideological Preferences and Left–Right Dimension among Western Mass Publics', in Ian Budge, Ivor Crewe, and Dennis Farlie (eds.), *Party Identification and Beyond*. London: Wiley.
Keman, Hans (1996). 'The Low Countries', in Josep Colomer (ed.), *Political Institutions in Europe*. London: Routledge.
Laver, Michael, and Budge, Ian (1992) (eds.). *Party Policy and Government Coalitions*. New York: St Martin's Press.
——and Hunt, W. Ben (1992). *Policy and Party Competition*. New York: Routledge.
——and Shepsle, Kenneth A. (1996). *Making and Breaking Governments*. Cambridge: Cambridge University Press.
Majerus, Pierre (1990). *L'Etat Luxembourgeois: Manuel de droit constitutionnel et de droit administratif*. Luxembourg: Imprimerie Saint-Paul.
Morgan, Mary-Jane (1976). 'The Modelling of Governmental Coalition Formation: A Policy-Based Approach with Interval Measurement'. Ph.D. thesis. University of Michigan.
Roemen, Rob (1995). *Aus Liebe zur Freiheit: 150 Jahre Liberalismus in Luxemburg*. Luxembourg: Imprimerie Centrale.
Sartori, Giovanni (1976). *Parties and Party Systems: A Framework for Analysis*. Cambridge: Cambridge University Press.
Waha, Robert (1992). *Le Fonctionnement de la démocratie au Grand-Duché de Luxembourg*. Dissertation. Département des Sciences politiques et sociales, Université Catholique de Louvain-la-Neuve.

Numerous leaflets edited by the *Service Information et Presse du Gouvernement*.
Newpaper articles on day-to-day reports of coalition negotiations for all post-war government formations taken from *Luxemburger Wort*.

12

Italy

From 'Constrained' Coalitions to Alternating Governments?

Luca Verzichelli and Maurizio Cotta

INTRODUCTION

The making of governments in Italy after World War II, which has ordinarily meant coalition governments, has been very visibly affected by the durable features of 'polarised multipartism' (Sartori 1976). Only recently has the breakdown of that system opened the door to new and unexplored territory (Cotta and Isernia 1996; Bartolini and D'Alimonte 1998). The Italian democratic experience after the fall of Fascism can be broken down into three periods: two transitional ones and a longer period of 'normality'. The first transitional period (1944–47) immediately followed the fall of Fascism and was dominated by the problems of democratic reconstruction. The second transitional period, the duration of which is still uncertain, began in 1992 with the crisis of the traditional governing parties. Between the two transitions, there was a relatively long period of stable conditions which in predictable ways governed the making of coalition governments.

The Period of Anti-Fascist Coalitions

The first transitional period was that of the 'anti-Fascist' coalitions, which are largely explained by the special conditions of the immediate post-war period. Among the factors that made a grand coalition of all the six original parties[1]

Maurizio Cotta is particularly responsible for sections on the party system and institutional rules and for the conclusion, Luca Verzichelli for the remaining sections and for the data collection. The writing of this chapter has been possible thanks to the support of the Italian Ministry for Scientific Research and Technology (*fondi ex 40%, Co-finanziamento 1997*) and of the Foundation Monte dei Paschi di Siena.

[1] The six original parties were from left to right: the Communist Party (PCI), the Socialist Party (PSIUP, later PSI), the liberal-socialist Action Party (PdA), the Christian Democracy (DC), the moderate Labour Democracy (DdL), and the rightist Liberal Party (PLI).

TABLE 12.1. *Phases of coalition government in Italy*

Government formula	Years	Parties involved*	Number of cabinets	Sub-phases and prime ministers	Major policy issues
Democratic instauration	1945–7	DC–PCI–PSI–PLI–PRI	4	Parri 1945 De Gasperi 1946	Constitutional setting
Centrism	1947–60	DC–PLI–PSDI–PRI	13	• Preparation: De Gasperi 1947 • Central period: De Gasperi 1948–53 • Crisis: De Gasperi 1953, Pella 1953, Fanfani 1954 • New stabilization: Scelba 1954, Segni 1955 • Final crisis: Zoli 1957, Fanfani 1958, Segni 1959, Tambroni 1960	International alliances, economic reforms
Centre-left	1960–75	DC–PSI–PSDI–PRI	17	• Preparation: Fanfani 1960–2, Leone 1963 • Central period: Moro 1964–8 • Crisis: Leone 1968, Rumor 1968–70 • New stabilization: Colombo 1970 • Attempts to change the coalition: Andreotti 1972–3 • Decline and final crisis: Rumor 1973, Moro 1974–6	Nationalizations, enlargement of the public sector
National solidarity	1976–9	DC–PCI–PSI–PSDI–PRI–PLI	3	• Preparation and central period: Andreotti 1976–8 • Crisis: Andreotti 1979	Economic crisis, terrorist emergency
Five-party	1980–92	DC–PSI–PSDI–PRI–PLI	14	• Preparation: Cossiga 1979–80 Forlani 1980 • Central period: Spadolini 1981–2, Fanfani 1982, Craxi 1983–6 • Crisis and renegotiation: Craxi 1986, Fanfani 1987, Goria 1987, De Mita 1988 • New stabilization: Andreotti 1989–91 • Final crisis: Amato 1992	Correction of the state intervention public debt—European 'costs'—inflation
First transitional cabinet	1993–4	DC–PSI–PSDI–PLI (PDS–Greens–PRI–LN)	1	Ciampi 1993	Economic crisis, institutional reforms
Centre-right attempt	1994–5	FI–AN–LN–CCD	1	Berlusconi 1994	Institutional reforms, federalism privatizations
Second transitional cabinet	1995–6	PDS–PPI–LN (FI–CCD–AN)	1	Dini 1995	Institutional reforms
Centre-left government	1996–	PDS–PPI–Greens–RIN	2	Prodi 1996–8, D'Alema 1998	European policies, reform of the welfare state

* Not necessarily in each cabinet.

desirable and possible were opposition to the past regime and to the German occupation of part of the country (which had followed Mussolini's fall in 1943 and the Italian reversal of international alliances), the lack of a dominant party, the need to write a new constitution, plus a common interest among the parties in regaining control over the making of the new democracy from the monarchy and the occupying armies (Pasquino 1987). The cabinets formed before the first democratic elections (1946) gave equal representation to all the six coalition parties. This original equality of representation could not, however, last very long. Already at the end of 1945, the pivotal position of Christian Democracy (DC) between left and right gave this party the opportunity to capture the prime ministership. The Constituent Assembly elections of 1946 established beyond doubt the greater strength of three parties: Communists (PCI), Socialists (PSI), and Christian Democrats, vis-à-vis all the others. This fact plus the birth of new parties outside the anti-Fascist coalition (especially on the right with the Monarchists, the rightist populists of the Uomo Qualunque, and the neo-Fascists of the Movimento Sociale Italiano, MSI) initiated a coalition crisis. The Liberal Party (PLI) was the first to leave; and soon the three main parties were left to govern alone. The next step was the break among the latter ones. The political isolation of the MSI, which represented continuity with the past regime, was a lasting legacy of this period. It was overcome only in 1994, with the birth of a centre-right coalition guided by Forza Italia (FI), the new political movement of the TV tycoon Berlusconi, and which included the MSI, transformed into a new party (Alleanza Nazionale, AN), after burning the bridges with its former neo-Fascist tradition.

The Great Divide between Government and Opposition

The breakdown of the anti-Fascist coalition was definitively sealed by the great confrontation brought about by the Cold War and by the ensuing linkage between international and domestic conflict. The 1948 elections, which were fought as a battle between two unreconcilable camps, between 'pro-system' (where 'system' meant the West, competitive democracy, and a market economy) and 'anti-system' forces, shaped in a lasting way party and political systems. The victory of the pro-Western side meant that the other side was since then confined to permanent opposition. The 'political battle' of 1948 had a further consequence: it very significantly strengthened the leading parties of the two camps (Christian Democrats and Communists, respectively). Intermediate forces were squeezed between these two giants. The political identities of the two major parties were as a result heavily influenced by the cleavage that was to a large extent responsible for their success. This success was obviously greater for the DC, which was on the winning side; but it was significant also for the PCI, which lost the battle for the government

TABLE 12.2a.[a] Left–right placement of parties,[b] party strength (in seats), and party composition of governments in Italy, 1945–1999: Lower Chamber[c]

Government election	Proximity to	Extr. Left[d]	PCI/ PDS[e]	Indep Left[f]	Greens[g]	PR	PSIUP[h]	PSI	PSDI	DC	PRI	LN	PLI	Mon[i]	MSI[j]	Effective number of legislative parties	Median party in second policy dimension[k]	Government seats[l]	Total number of seats
1946	F		104					115		207*	23		57		30	4.8	DC	449	556
1947			104					115		207*	23		57		30	4.8	DC	426	556
1947			104					115		207*	23		57		30	4.8	DC	264+23	556
1948	F		131					52	33	306*	10		15	13		2.9	DC	364	574
1950			131					52	33	306*	10		15	13		2.9	DC	349	574
1951			131					52	33	306*	10		15	13		2.9	DC	316	574
1953	F		143					75	19	262*	6			14	29	4.2	DC	262	590
1953**			143					75	19	262*	6			14	29	4.2	DC	262+25	590
1954**			143					75	19	262*	6			14	29	4.2	DC	262+6	590
1954			143					75	19	262*	6			14	29	4.2	DC	287+6	590
1957	E		143					75	19	262*	6			14	29	4.2	DC	262	590
1958	F		141					88	17	273*	7		18	20	24	3.8	DC	290+7	596
1959			141					88	17	273*	7		18	20	24	3.8	DC	273	596
1960**			141					88	17	273*	7		18	20	24	3.8	DC	273+42	596
1962	E		141					88	17	273*	7		18	20	24	3.8	DC	297	596
1963	F		166					62	32	260*	5		38	8	27	4.2	DC	260	630
1963			166					62	32	260*	5		38	8	27	4.2	DC	359	630
1968	F		171				23	91		265*	9		31	6	24	3.6	DC	265	630
1968			171				23	91		265*	9		31	6	24	3.6	DC	365	630
1969			171				23	91		265*	9		31	6	24	3.6	DC	265+91	630
1970	E		171				23	91		265*	9		31	6	24	3.6	DC	365	630
1972	F		171				23	91		265*	9		31	6	24	3.6	DC	265+31	630
1972			175					61	30	265*	15		20		55	3.6	DC	315+15	630
1973			175					61	30	265*	15		20		55	3.6	DC	371	630

Italy

Government	Year	Proximity to election	RC	PdCI	Left DS	Other Left	PPI	RI	CCD CDU	UDR	LN	FI	AN	Effective number of legislative parties	Median party in second policy dimension	Government strength	Total number of seats
	1974				175		61	30	265*	15		20	55	3.6	DC	356+15	630
	1974	E			175		61	30	265*	15		20	55	3.6	DC	280+91	630
	1976	F			175		61	30	265*	15		20	55	3.6	DC	265+30	630
	1976				222	6	57	15	262*	14		5	34	3.1	PRI	262	630
	1978**				222	6	57	15	262*	14		5	34	3.1	PRI	262+308	630
	1979				222	6	57	15	262*	14		5	34	3.1	PRI	291	630
	1979	F			193	6	61	20	262*	16		9	29	3.4	PRI	291	630
	1980				193	17	61	20	262*	16		9	29	3.4	PRI	339	630
	1980				193	17	61	20	262*	16		9	29	3.4	PRI	359	630
	1981				193	17	61	20	262*	16		9	29	3.4	PRI	368	630
	1982				193	17	61	20	262*	16		9	29	3.4	PRI	352	630
	1983	E			177	11	73	22	226*	29		16	42	4.0	PRI	366	630
	1987	F			177	11	73	22	226*	29		16	42	4.0	PRI	226	630
	1987	E			157	12	94	17*	234	21		11	35	4.1	PRI	377	630
	1991	F	20		157	12	94	17*	234	21		11	35	4.1	PSDI	356	630
	1991	E	20	13	107	6	92	16	206*	27	55	17	34	5.7	PSDI	331	630
	1992	F	35	13	107	6	92	16	206*	27	55	17	34	5.7	DC	331	630
	1993^m	E	35	16	107	6	92	16	206*	27	55	17	34	5.7	DC	331^n	630
Berlusconi	1994	F	39	—	143	—	33	—	27	—	117*	112	109	5.7	PPI	365	630
Dini	1995	E	39	—	143	—	33	—	27	—	117*	112	109	5.7	PPI	—	630
Prodi	1996°	F	34	—	197	—	67	26*	30	—	58	123	92	5.9	PPI	324	630
D'Alema	1998	—	14	21	166	26	66	26*	15	27	55	110	91	6.4	RI	332	630

cont.

TABLE 12.2a. cont.

a   This table reports changes in government (i.e. elections and changes in the party composition of government). In addition to this the table also reports changes in the external support of government. These lines are marked with ** after the year. Some of them were very important.

b   We adopt the Laver and Hunt's 'increase services vs. cut taxes' scale but with a significant correction: the neo-Fascist party (MSI), is located at the extreme right of the scale rather then at the left of DC. In this way we preserve the position of this party, traditionally isolated from the anti-Fascist coalition and considered the prototype of the anti-system party (Sartori 1976). This manipulation could be dangerous if we look to the development of some policies (for instance the welfare sector) but, under the point of view of the government formation, it is correct to keep the three 'classical poles' of the party system (left opposition, centre-left, and right opposition) separated.

c   The sum of the single-party groups is not equal to the total number of MPs because we do not consider other small parties.

d   Extreme left: Proletarian Democracy (DP) 1976–92; Proletarian Unity for Communism (PDUP) 1979–87; Refounded Communist Party (RC) 1992.

f   Elected at the list of the Communist Party (PCI).

g   In 1992 the seats of Greens and those of La Rete—Movimento per la democrazia are counted together.

h   The PSIUP (Partito socialista di unità ploretaria) was created from a split of PSI in 1963.

i   Monarchist parties: 1953–1963 National Monarchist Party (PNM); 1958–1972 Monarchist Party for National Unity (PDIUM).

j   This column also includes the seats of UQ (Uomo qualunque), a movement of the right created in 1946.

k   The second relevant policy dimension is the 'pro friendly relations USSR vs. anti' (Laver and Hunt 1992).

l   The number after + is the strength of the government's external support. A party is counted as an external support party if it declared during cabinet formation that it would support the government in parliament and supported the government in the investiture vote.

m   The Ciampi cabinet is reported here because of the presence of technical ministers. Initially, also the PDS and the Greens participated in this government, but they withdrew before the government went through the investiture vote. However, the PDS and Greens supported the Ciampi cabinet throughout the legislative term.

n   The PDS and Greens supported the Ciampi cabinet throughout the legislative term. However, according to our defintion (see Note 12) they have not been counted as external support parties.

o   Despite the fact that there had been no elections, the distribution of seats changed significantly with the change from the Prodi to the D'Alema cabinets. Many MPs changed their party affiliation and new parliamentary parties were established. After the decisions of the RC to revoke the external support of the cabinet, a group of its MPs broke away and founded the new Party of the Italian Communists (PdCI) which entered the new D'Alema Cabinet, while the RC is in the opposition. The federal left group was transformed in the official parliamentary group of the Democratic Left Party (DS, the former PDS). The Other Left comprises MPs from parties externally supporting the cabinet, like the Greens or the new socialist party (Italian Democratic Socialists, SDI), which did not join the new DS. In the centre the UDR (National Union for the Republic) was established. It resulted from the fusion of the CDU and a faction of the CCD, plus some former FI and AN MPs. This party provides external support for the D'Alema cabinet.

Party names

DP (1976–92)	Democrazia Proletaria	Proletarian Democracy
PDUP (1979–87)	Partito di Unità Proletaria per il Comunismo	Proletarian Unity for Communism
RC (since 1992)	Partito della Rifondazione Comunista	Refounded Communist Party
PCI (1946–92)	Partito Comunista Italiano	Italian Communist Party
PDS (since 1992)	Partito democratico della Sinistra	Democratic Left Party independents (elect under PCI umbrella)

Greens (since 1987)	Federazione Nazionale delle liste Verdi	National Federation of Greens
La Rete (1992–94)	La Rete: movimento per la Democrazia	The Net: movement for democracy
PR (1976–94)	Partito Radicale	Radical Party
PSIUP (1968–72)	Partito Socialista di Unità Proletaria	Socialist Party for Proletarian Unity
PSI (1946–94)	Partito Socialista Italiano	Italian Socialist Party
PSDI (1948–94)	Partito Socialista Democratico Italiano	Italian Social Democratic Party
DC (1946–94)	Democrazia Cristiana	Christian Democracy
PPI (since 1994)	Partito Popolare Italiano	Italian Popular Party
CCD (since 1994)	Centro Cristiano Democratico	Christian Democratic Centre
CDU	Cristiani Democtatici Uniti	United Christian Democats
RI	Rinnovamento Italiano	Italian Renewal
UDR	Unione Democratica per la Repubblica	Democratic Union for the Republic
PRI (1946–1994)	Partito Repubblicano Italiano	Italian Republican Party
LN (since 1992)	Lega Nord	Northern League
PLI (1946–94)	Partito Liberale Italiano	Italian Liberal Party
FI (since 1994)	Forza Italia	Forza Italia
PNM (1953–63)	Partito Nazionale Monarchico	National Monarchist Party
PDIUM (1948–72)	Partito di Unità Monarchica	Monarchist Party for National Unity
AN (since 1994)	Alleanza Nazionale	National Alliance
UQ (1946–8)	Uomo Qualunque	List of the Common People
MSI (1948–94)	Movimento Sociale Italiano	Italian Social Movement
PdA (1946–8) (cabinet only)	Partito d'Azione	Action Party
PdL (1946–8) (cabinet only)	Partito del Lavoro	Work Party

but won that for the leadership of the Left. The incentives to replicate the political 'pièce' that had proved so successful in 1948 were so strong that the communist/anti-communist divide would dominate the long political cycle from 1948 to 1992 (Cotta and Isernia 1996).

PARTIES AND POLICY POSITIONS

From 1948 to 1992 the configuration of the party system remained fairly stable (see Tables 2a and 2b). Seven parties (PCI, PSI, PSDI, PRI, DC, PLI, MSI) enjoyed relatively stable support throughout this period. A few more small parties appeared and disappeared mainly as a result of splits and fusions. Along a left–right dimension, the PCI was conventionally placed at the extreme left and the MSI at the extreme right. The perceived left–right dimension was not strictly economic, however, since the MSI would then have been to the left of the Liberals and perhaps also of the Republicans (PRI). The communist/anti-communist dimension was undoubtedly also a major component of this perception.

TABLE 12.2b. *Left–right placement of parties, party strength (in seats), and party composition of governments in Italy, 1945–1999: Senate[a]*

Government	Proximity to election	Extr. left[b]	PCI-PDS[c]	Greens[d]	PR	PSIUP	PSI	PSDI	DC	PRI	LN	PLI	MPN[e]	MSI	Effective number of legislative parties	Median party in second policy dimension	Government strength	Total number of seats
1948	F		42				29	12	131*	6		10	4		2.7	DC	159	237
1950			42				29	12	131*	6		10	4		2.7	DC	149	237
1951			42				29	12	131*	6		10	4		2.7	DC	137	237
1953	F		53				29	4	113*	2		3	16	9	3.9	DC	113	237
1953**			53				29	4	113*	2		3	16	9	3.9	DC	113+5	237
1954**			53				29	4	113*	2		3	16	9	3.9	DC	113+2	237
1954			53				29	4	113*	2		3	16	9	3.9	DC	120+2	237
1957	E		53				29	4	113*	2		3	16	9	3.9	DC	113	237
1958	F		59				36	5	123*			4	7	8	3.6	DC	128	246
1959			59				36	5	123*			4	7	8	3.6	DC	123	246
1960**			59				36	5	123*			4	7	8	3.6	DC	123+7	246
1962	E		59				36	5	123*			4	7	8	3.6	DC	128	246
1963	F		85				44	14	129*	4		19	3	14	3.7	DC	129	315
1963			85				44	14	129*	4		19	3	14	3.7	DC	191	315
1968	F		89			12	46		135*	2		16	2	11	3.2	DC	135	315
1968			89			12	46		135*	2		16	2	11	3.2	DC	181	315
1969			89			12	46		135*	2		16	2	11	3.2	DC	135+46	315
1970			89			12	46		135*	2		16	2	11	3.2	DC	183	315
1972	E		87			7	33	11	135*	2		16		11	3.2	DC	135+16	315
1972	F		87			7	33	11	135*	5		11		26	3.0	DC	157+5	315
1973			87			7	33	11	135*	5		11		26	3.0	DC	184	315
1974			87			7	33	11	135*	5		11		26	3.0	DC	179+5	315
1974			87			7	33	11	135*	5		11		26	3.0	DC	140+44	315
1976	E		116				29	7	135*	6		3		15	2.8	DC	135+11	315
1976	F		116				29	7	135*	6		3		15	2.8	DC	135	315
1978**			116				29	7	135*	6		3		15	2.8	DC	135+158	315
1979			104	2			32	9*	138	6		2		13	3.0	PRI	148	315
1979	F	3	104	2			32	9*	138	6		2		13	3.0	PRI	149	315
1980		3	104	2			32	9*	138	6		2		13	3.0	DC	176	315

Italy

	Proximity to election	RC	PdCI	PDS	Greens[g]	SDI	PSI-RI	PPI	UDR	LN	CCD	FI	AN	Effective number of legislative parties	Median party in second policy dimension	Government strength	Total number of seats
1980						32	9*	138	6					3.0	DC	185	315
1981						32	9*	138	6					3.0	DC	187	315
1982	E					32	9*	138	6					3.0	DC	181	315
1983	F					38	8	120*	11					3.7	PRI	183	315
1987	E					38	8	120*	11					3.7	PRI	120	315
1987	F					42	8	125*	9					3.9	PRI	189	315
1991	E					42	8	125*	9					3.9	PRI	180	315
1992	F					49	3	107*	10	25				4.9	DC	163	315
1993[f]	E					49	3	107*	10	25				4.9	DC	163+71[g]	315

1994–1999[h]

Government		Proximity to election	RC	PdCI	PDS	Greens[g]	SDI	PSI-RI	PPI	UDR	LN	CCD	FI	AN	Effective number of legislative parties	Median party in second policy dimension	Government strength	Total number of seats
Berlusconi	1994[h]	F	18		76	13	10		34		60	12	36	48	5.4	PPI	156	315
Dini	1995	E	18		76	13	10		34		60	12	36	48	5.4	PPI		315
Prodi	1996	F	11		99	14	11		31*		27	25	47	44	5.4	PPI	166	315
D'Alema	1998	E	4	6	105	14	4	7	31*	20	24	12	40	41	6.1	PPI	187	325

** No new government as defined in this volume but a relevant change in the external support of the government.

[a] The first legislature begins in 1948, after the election of 18 Apr.

[b] Extreme left: Proletarian Democracy (DP), 1976–92; Proletarian Unity for Communism (PDUP) 1979–17; Refounded Communist Party (RC) 1992.

[c] PDS from 1992.

[d] The group was composed of the senators of the Rete and the Greens.

[e] Monarchist parties: 1953–63 National Monarchist Party (PNM); 1958–72 Monarchist Party for National Unity (PDIUM).

[f] The Ciampi cabinet is reported here because of the presence of technical ministers. Initially, also the PDS and the Greens participated in this government, but they withdrew before the government went through the investiture vote. However, the PDS and Greens supported the Ciampi cabinet throughout the legislative term.

[g] The PDS and Greens supported the Ciampi cabinet throughout the legislative term. However, according to our definition (see Note 1 to Table 12.2a) they have not been counted as external support parties.

[h] During the short duration of the 13th legislature so many changes were produced in the structure of the parliamentary groups. See note o of Table 10.2a for the details.

The existence of a big and heterogeneous centrist party, the DC, made it difficult to decide the relative location of some of the small parties (like the Republicans and Social Democrats, PSDI). Their position would in most policy areas (except on issues related to religion) be inside the range of the DC.

During this period the cabinet formation process worked under very strict political constraints which seriously limited the *Koalitionsfähigkeit* of several parties. The MSI to the right and the PCI to the left were systematically excluded from government. Attempts to overcome this condition did indeed take place, as shown by a few cases in which these parties provided external government support (the MSI in the late 1950s, the PCI in the late 1970s). But such attempts never had any lasting success, and the two parties reverted to permanent opposition. Only the deep crisis of the governing parties in the 1990s would produce the favourable conditions that enabled the two (transformed) parties to become full players in the governmental game.

The existence of a relatively high number of small centrist parties was a typical feature of the Italian party system during this period. The fairly low threshold of parliamentary representation provided by a proportional electoral system (particularly in the case of the lower chamber, the Camera dei Deputati), and the persistence of a number of traditional political cleavages which could not be completely erased by or included in the communist/anti-communist divide, are the main explanations. Except for the elections of 1948, the Christian Democratic Party was never able to win a parliamentary majority, and although by far the largest party of the anti-communist camp, it always needed to build coalitions with some of those smaller parties. As a result, the governing anti-communist camp always included both socialist and bourgeois parties, both clerical and anti-clerical parties, and so on.

Within the confines of the 'long cycle' the coalition game was affected by three main forms of competition: (1) competition among parties of the anti-communist camp; (2) factional competition within the DC; and (3) interconnections between these two levels of competition. At the centre of the governing camp, the DC has faced competition from both the left and the right. It has generally attempted to reduce the negative effects of this situation by incorporating parties from both sides within the coalition. Centre-left and centre-right parties have typically had opposite interests. In order to face competitors further to their left or right they have generally striven to give to the coalition a more clearly leftist or rightist orientation. The Socialist Party, once it had broken its previous close alliance with the PCI and moved into the governing camp, had to protect itself against competition from the Communists; the Liberal Party similarly against Monarchists and neo-Fascists. To further complicate things, there has been always a very significant degree of competition between the three parties of the centre-left (Socialists, Social Democrats, and Republicans) for the limited political space available between the two giants (PCI and DC). Finally, various competing factions within the DC have often worked at cross-purposes in pushing different alliances.

Within this long political cycle, the complicated political game of coalition building produced a number of short-term political cycles characterized by the predominance of one coalitional formula. The short cycles are (see Table 12.1): (1) centrist coalition (*centrismo*), (2) centre-left coalition (*centro-sinistra*), (3) national solidarity (*solidarietà nazionale*), and (4) five-party coalition (*pentapartito*). The main difference among formulae (except for the third) has been the inclusion or exclusion of one or the other of the smaller parties. While the lasting features of the party system and of the long cycle have had very much to do with the original polarization between the two largest parties and with the pro-system/anti-system cleavage, shorter-term changes have rather been influenced by the strength and strategies of the other parties.

The Transition of the 1990s: Adieu to the First Republic or What?

Between 1992 and 1994 the First Republic unravelled at great speed. A crucial aspect of the crisis, which cannot be discussed here in detail (see Cotta and Isernia 1996), was undoubtedly the implosion of the old party system and more specifically of its 'centre'. A mutually reinforcing combination of electoral losses, judicial prosecutions on grounds of misuse of public money, party splits, and the effects of a new 'semi-majoritarian' electoral system[2] brought very quickly the traditional governing parties to their knees. For the first time after nearly fifty years they lost control of the executive. Technical or semi-technical governments (the Amato and Ciampi cabinets) made their appearance between 1992 and 1994. At the same time new or previously excluded parties captured a significant part of the political space that the centre parties had controlled with great success for well over forty years (Morlino 1996). The implosion of the centre parties coincided with the end of the double exclusion of the communist left and the extreme right. Suddenly, all the parties gained a reasonable expectation to win access to the government. In the new political landscape a bipolar competition developed between two broad alliances of the left and right respectively. The 1994 election was won by the centre-right camp, which combined in a rather heterogeneous alliance Forza Italia, the Northern League—the regionalist/separatist movement of Umberto Bossi born in the 1980s—and Alleanza Nazionale. But the difficult

---

[2] The reform of the electoral system was triggered by a 'bottom up' process demanding a majoritarian system. In 1991 a first referendum opposed by the main governmental parties had abolished the multiple preference vote in lower chamber elections. In the spring of 1993 another referendum erased the entire 'proportional mechanism' in the electoral system for the Senate, forcing the parliamentary parties to reform the whole electoral legislation.

coexistence among these forces, in particular between FI and the League which were competing for the same votes in the regions of Northern Italy, determined, a few months later, the fall of the Berlusconi cabinet and the rise of another 'technical government' (the Dini cabinet). After an early dissolution the elections of 1996 were fought mainly by two large competing coalitions each with a well identifiable leader and prime ministerial candidate. The Northern League was isolated. This time, the centre-left coalition won and its leader, Romano Prodi,[3] could govern for a longer period, achieving important political goals, like the inclusion of Italy in the first group of countries participating in the European Monetary Union (May 1998). But the 'majoritarian miracle' was not without problems: in the autumn of 1998 Rifondazione Comunista (the New Communist Party), the leftist split of the former Communist Party, which provided external support to the cabinet, provoked a crisis, forcing Mr Prodi to resign. The cabinet that followed can also be defined as a 'centre-left' government, but some important differences must be underlined. The new prime minister, Mr. D'Alema, is not the leader of the electoral coalition but the chairman of the biggest party of the majority (the DS, formerly PDS). His designation to this position was not the result of a prime ministerial candidature in the electoral process but of a negotiation among parliamentary groups. Moreover the majority supporting the government is partially different from the electoral cartel (the Ulivo) that had won the election of 1996. It includes two new formations both on the extreme left and at the centre of the political spectrum: the Partito dei Comunisti Italiani (Party of the Italian Communists), born from the split of the New Communist Party during the crisis, and the Democratic Republican Union (UDR), a parliamentary fraction created by the former head of state, Mr. Cossiga and comprising a number of MPs who had been elected in the centre-right coalition. The difficult consolidation of the new party system is thus making the stabilization of the new method of government formation by victorious electoral coalitions uncertain.

INSTITUTIONAL RULES

The Italian constitution of 1948 adopted more or less the ordinary rules of parliamentary democracy. A proposal to introduce a presidential system received only limited support, and efforts to strengthen the executive did not go beyond a very limited 'rationalization' of the motion of no confidence. For an understanding of the actual process of government building, a strictly for-

---

[3] When Romano Prodi was nominated, he was a former Christian Democratic minister who had not been too much involved in party life and had a reputation of technical competence.

mal reading of the legal rules is generally of little help. Their practical interpretation is more important.

Government Nomination

The power to nominate the prime minister is vested in the president of the Republic (Art. 92). In practice, prime ministers were until 1992 chosen on the basis of the suggestions of the parties which had agreed to coalesce, or from the DC in the case of single-party cabinets. However, given the complicated process of coalition making, the head of state has on occasion been able to exert a certain degree of influence over the choice of prime minister and even over some other aspects of the coalition (e.g. appointing 'technical' ministers in certain portfolios). In general, heads of state belonging to one of the smaller parties have attempted to strengthen their party's chances to participate in the coalition.[4] Christian Democratic presidents have sometimes taken part in the factional games inside their party. The prime minister, following the indications of the coalition parties, chooses the ministers who are then nominated by the president (Art. 92). Once the composition of the government has been decided the government is sworn before the president of the Republic.

Parliamentary Investiture (Vote of Confidence)

According to the constitution, an incoming government has to receive a positive roll-call vote of confidence (*scrutinio per appello nominale*) in both chambers. Majority of the members attending is required. The standing orders of the Chamber of Deputies count abstentions as favourable votes, while in the Senate they are counted as negative votes. Therefore, in the Senate parties or individual senators who want to enable the government to form, but who do not want to support it explicitly, have to leave the house at the moment of the vote instead of abstaining. Since the two chambers may have different majorities (a possibility which the electoral reform of 1993 has not eliminated), the bicameralism of the Italian constitution can be seen as a factor encouraging larger than minimal coalitions.

Votes of No Confidence

The vote of no confidence of a single chamber suffices to bring down a government. One source of such an event is a no confidence motion proposed by the opposition, which has to be signed by at least one-tenth of the members of the chamber and cannot be put to a vote until three days after its presentation (Art. 94). Another possibility is that the government itself asks for a parliamentary vote of confidence and fails to obtain a majority. Such an initiative, the purpose of which is to discipline the majority, typically occurs

---

[4] This applies in particular to Luigi Einaudi and the PLI, Giuseppe Saragat and the PSDI, and Alessandro Pertini and the PSI.

within the law-making process or during final deliberation on the budget. Voting is, as in the case of no confidence motions, by roll call. Ordinary parliamentary votes against the government do not entail either a formal or an informal obligation to resign.

The Impact of Electoral Rules

The PR electoral system existing until 1993 provided no incentive for pre-electoral coalitions. In 1952, after an extremely harsh parliamentary battle, the majority had been able to pass an electoral law that awarded a 'majority bonus' to any party or coalition that gained an absolute majority of votes, thus creating an incentive for pre-electoral coalitions. But in the 1953 elections, the centrist coalition narrowly missed the 50% + 1 threshold and the majority bonus. Soon afterwards the new electoral system was abolished and PR re-established. In the 1980s, however, similar proposals were once again put forward by the DC and the PCI. The PSI, on the other hand, proposed the direct election of the president of the Republic. In 1993, following a referendum against the existing electoral system of the Senate, the parliament approved a reform of the electoral systems of both chambers. The new electoral systems of the two chambers, although different on a number of dimensions, are both mixed: 75 per cent of the seats are allocated through a plurality system in single-member constituencies and 25 per cent on the basis of compensatory PR (D'Alimonte and Chiaramonte 1995; Katz 1996). While the new electoral systems have not substantially reduced the number of parliamentary parties, they have encouraged the formation of pre-electoral cartels of parties which have presented common candidates in the single-member districts (but not for the proportional seats). These cartels have also projected themselves as potential government coalitions and designated (implicitly in 1994, more explicitly in 1996) their prime ministerial candidates.

GOVERNMENT FORMATION

From the immediate post-war Parri cabinet through the D'Alema cabinet, in office since 21 October 1998, Italy has had by our counting rules fifty-one different cabinets.[5] This is a larger number than any of the other countries in this volume and it indicates the highest rate of cabinet turnover in Western

---

[5] Our counting rules yield a slightly lower number of cabinets than Italian conventions, since we do not count a new cabinet when the same prime minister returns with a coalition of the same parties, and without the intervention of a general parliamentary election. Thus, our Moro I would by Italian conventions consist of Moro I, II, and III; Spadolini would be Spadolini I and II; and Craxi would be Craxi I and II. Our numbering of Moro's later cabinets consequently also deviates from Italian practice.

Europe over this period. In discussing government formation in Italy, we will have to keep in mind a more general point: the varying political significance of cabinets.

The formal rules concerning government formation have not changed in the fifty years of the Republic. In any case, the constitution has little to say about the details of the process. According to custom, the formation process begins with consultations held by the head of state, who meets with the former presidents of the Republic and then with the party leaders. At the end, a *formateur* is officially designated to begin the real negotiations with those parties that seem ready to reach an agreement. Sometimes during this process one of the potential coalitional parties refuses to cooperate. This could lead to a new round of negotiations, or the *formateur* may even relinquish his mandate, whereupon the president would make a new selection.[6] Once a basic agreement is reached, the prime minister designate reports the results of his consultations to the president and receives the official mandate to form a government. Now it is time to negotiate the policy platform and, when a compromise has been reached, he can begin to select his ministers.

Bargaining Attempts and Duration

This procedure makes it relatively easy to determine the number of bargaining attempts before each new cabinet. Italy has experienced failed bargaining attempts on a number of occasions, most frequently during the crisis of the centre-left (1968–76), but as early as 1947 and as late as 1989 as well. The process has included two or more failed attempts on no fewer than ten occasions. The record is three failed attempts, which has happened on three different occasions and during distinct coalition formulae: at the beginning of centrism in 1947, during the final disintegration of the centre-left in 1974, and during the crisis of the five-party coalition in 1987. A particularly long process, in terms both of failed bargaining attempts and temporary cabinets, occurred at the dawn of the centre-left (1960–3), as well as at the beginning of the five-party coalition. Moreover, complicated crises have occurred that have occasioned a coalition renegotiation under the centre-left and also, as noted above, in the five-party coalition following the 1987 election, when both policies and portfolios were once again up for grabs.

---

[6] In order to solve an intricate situation, the president may occasionally give an experienced politician a so-called 'exploratory mandate', to find out and evaluate the possibility of creating a majority. When these attempts, even if there has been no change of *formateur*, have had the explicit aim of changing or enlarging the majority, they have been coded as new bargaining attempts. Examples include the attempt by Ugo La Malfa in 1979 (an attempt to enlarge the cabinet majority without losing the external support of the PCI) and the attempt by Oscar Luigi Scalfaro in 1983 (when it seemed possible to form of a cabinet without socialists but with a large majority of abstentions). These politicians were not *informateurs* because they themselves had the chance to form a cabinet.

A number of party system or intra-party transformations have caused a high number of inconclusive bargaining attempts and/or weak cabinets (Mershon 1994). Most changes in coalitional formula have entailed at least one failed attempt to form a cabinet. Moreover, the number of parties involved in the bargaining attempts has often varied, because of the strategic behaviour of the small centre parties, which could switch from full cooperation to external support, to abstention during the parliamentary vote of confidence, or even to what used to be called 'constitutional opposition' (to distinguish it from that of the anti-system parties). But the most evident indicator of bargaining difficulty is the duration of the crisis. Paradoxically, it is much more difficult to define exactly how long it takes to form a new coalition. Sometimes, in fact, a minority or otherwise transitional cabinet has been formed with the sole purpose of preparing the agreement for a new coalition.[7] Such a cabinet could be viewed as a bargaining attempt towards the next full coalition cabinet. Before every 'full' coalition formula there has been at least one provisional coalition or a single-party cabinet with a limited mandate. The reason is clear. The birth of a new coalition is always complicated by conflicts among the parties (over the reforms demanded by a new coalitional partner, or the allocation of cabinet portfolios) and within one or more parties (resistance within the old governmental parties to the enlargement of the coalition, refusal to accept the coalition in some segments of the new party involved). A transitional cabinet may help solve such problems.

Given our counting rules, the time required to form a new cabinet has almost always exceeded a week and has commonly extended to one or several months. The record is the 126 days it took Cossiga to put together his first cabinet in the formative stages of the five-party coalition, but two other cabinets have exceeded 100 days as well. Given the notoriously low duration of Italian cabinets, these figures are particularly striking. They reflect the fact that since World War II Italy has spent more time in transitions from one cabinet to the next than any other European country. The duration of cabinet crises has tended to increase over time, at least up until the five-party coalition. No cabinet crisis lasted more than three weeks until the 1960, but during the centre-left, month-long crises became the rule rather than the exception (Battegazzorre 1987).

Crisis duration has been particularly significant just prior to the formation of cabinets that have inaugurated a 'new' coalitional formula. During the early stages of an alliance, in fact, cabinet formation is particularly slow and 'incremental'. If reaching agreement on an 'organic' coalition has taken too much time, a more limited (both in coalition size and programmatic scope)

---

[7] The *convergenza democratica* cabinets led by Fanfani (1960–3) have to be seen as transitional cabinets towards the new coalitional formula. Something similar can be said about the *governi ponte* of Leone (1963 and 1968) and the Rumor cabinet in 1969.

provisional government has often formed while party leaders continue to work towards a broader political pact.[8]

On the other hand, when a cabinet falls but a coalitional formula and its policy guidelines are still supported, the process of cabinet formation can be faster. In fact, it may often result in the retention of the former PM and of most of the ministers. This was the case with De Gasperi during centrism, Moro and Rumor during the centre-left, Andreotti during the national solidarity, and (albeit with more complicated bargaining) Spadolini and Craxi during the five-party coalition.[9]

Towards the end of a coalition phase, cabinet formation is generally particularly delicate and problematic, because of the appearance of conflicting coalition alternatives. The most evident example is the phase from 1958 to 1960 (the end of centrism), when attempts to create a new coalition with the Socialist Party coexisted with an official project to reconsolidate the previous coalition and a more or less evident attempt to include the rightist parties in the governmental majority. The normal outcome during the decay of a coalitional formula is the loss of some coalitional actors; a good example are the many quasi centre-left cabinets during the 1970s, or the four-party coalition of 1991, when the PRI left the *pentapartito*). Even in these cases the bargaining process has often been long, since the PM designate has first tried to revive the old formula, then had to verify the support for a new coalition, and finally start the 'ordinary' bargaining process towards a new distribution of ministerial and sub-ministerial posts.

Historically, internal conflicts within the largest governmental party have been a recurrent source of difficulties during coalition building. The equilibrium among the DC *correnti* (factions) has always been a major concern for the nominators (officially the head of state, but in practice the party leaders) of a new PM and then for the *formateur* himself. The factionalized structure of the largest party has typically complicated two aspects of the bargaining process in particular: the choice of a new prime minister and the distribution

---

[8] Sometimes, however, there is no way to solve the crisis with a provisional compromise and, if it is impossible or inconvenient to call an early election, the crisis drags on without any way of escape (*crisi al buio*). This was the case in the dramatic crisis after the 1976 election before the first cabinet of national solidarity, and in 1979 before the five-party coalition.

[9] None the less, even when the same PM has been reinstated, there has been, in most cases, some slight difference in the composition of the next cabinet. Only four cabinets have had the same leader and exactly the same majority as the one that preceded it: two of them were led by Moro (1964 and 1966), one by Spadolini (1982), and one by Craxi (1986). According to the criteria adopted here, these administrations have not been counted as separate cabinets. Along these lines, the fourth Andreotti cabinet (1978) is Andreotti IIIb. Yet, we have decided to list the Andreotti IIIb cabinet separately in the tables because of differences in the legislative support coalitions: to stress the passage from a parliamentary coalition based on PCI abstention to the full national solidarity formula based on the explicit parliamentary support from the Communists.

TABLE 12.3. *Government formation in Italy*

Government	Number of parties in parliament	Number of previous bargaining rounds	Parties involved in previous bargaining rounds	Number of days required for government formation
PdA–DC–PCI–PLI–PSIUP–PdL 1945		0		8
DC–PCI–PSI–PdA–PdL–PLI 1945		0		16
DC–PCI–PSI–PRI 1946	16	0		12
DC–PCI–PSI 1947	16	1	DC–PCI–PSI	13
DC–PLI–tec 1947	16	3	(1) DC–PCI–PSI–PRI (2) DC– PCI–PSI–(PRI) (3) DC– PLI–PRI	18
DC–PSDI–PLI–PRI 1948	10	0		11
DC–PSDI–PRI 1950	10	0		15
DC–PRI 1952	10	0		10
DC 1953	10	0		17
DC 1953*	10	1	DC	20
DC 1954*	9	0		10
DC–PSDI–PLI 1954	9	0		11
DC 1957	9	2	(1) DC–PSDI–PLI–PRI (2) DC– PSDI–PLI	13
DC–PSDI 1958	11	0		12
DC 1959	11	0		20
DC 1960*	11	0		7
DC–PSDI–PRI 1962	11	0		19
DC 1963	9	1	DC	36
DC–PSI–PRI–PSDI 1963	9	0		20
DC 1968	9	1	DC	19
DC–PSI–PRI 1968	9	1	DC–PSI–PRI	23
DC 1969	9	2	(1) DC–PSI–(PRI) (2) DC–PSI–PRI	31
DC–PSI–PSDI–PRI 1970	9	0		48
DC 1972	8	2	(1) DC–PSI–PSDI–PRI (2) DC–PSI–PSDI	33
DC–PSDI–PLI 1972	8	0		121
DC–PSI–PSDI–PRI 1973	8	0		30
DC–PSI–PSDI 1974	8	0		12
DC–PRI 1974	8	2	(1) DC–PSI–PSDI–PRI (2) DC–PSI–PRI	51
DC 1976	9	1	DC	36
DC 1976	9	0		90
DC 1978*	9	0		55
DC–PSDI–PRI 1979	9	2	(1) DC–PSDI–PRI–PLI (2) DC–PSDI–PLI	48
DC–PSDI–PLI 1979	10	2	(1) DC–PSDI–PRI–PLI (2) DC–PSDI–PLI	126
DC–PRI–PSI 1980	10	0		16
DC–PSI–PRI–PSDI 1980	10	0		20
PRI–DC–PSI–PSDI–PLI 1981	10	0		33
DC–PSI–PSDI–PLI 1982	10	0		18
PSI–DC–PRI–PSDI–PLI 1983	11	0		101
DC–Tec 1987	12	3	(1) DC–PSI–PSDI–PRI–PLI (2) DC–(PSI)–PSDI–PRI–PLI (3) DC–PSDI–PRI–PLI	46
DC–PSI–PRI–PSDI–PLI 1987	12	0		11
DC–PSI–PSDI–PLI 1991	12	0		14

Government	Number of parties in parliament	Number of previous bargaining rounds	Parties involved in previous bargaining rounds	Number of days required for government formation
PSI–DC–PLI–PSDI 1992	13	0		47
Tec–DC–PSI–PSDI–PLI 1993	13	0		7
FI–LN–AN–CCD 1994	13	0		48
Tec 1995	13	0		1
PDS–GRE–PPI–RI–RC 1996	13	0		11
DS–PPI–GRE–RI–PdCI–SDI–UDR 1998	14	1	DS–PPI–GRE–RI–PdCI–SDI–RC–PR–UDR	12

* No new government as defined in this volume but a relevant change in the external support of the government (see Table 12.2a).

Note: Parties in parentheses: With these parties explicit negotiations were conducted about external support for the government.

of cabinet portfolios among the factions.[10] Moreover, some coalitional partners have been able to object to the presence of a Christian Democratic minister considered unfriendly to that party, or to demand that a given ministry not fall into the hands of a specific DC faction. Although factions have been particularly important in the DC, the behaviour of other coalitional partners has often been similarly influenced by internal conflicts.[11]

With the passing of time, failures or delays in bargaining have increasingly been due to the resistance of the smaller parties. Especially during the 'centre-left', the smaller parties often alternated in participating in the coalition, and the same happened when the 'five-party coalition' formula was forming in the early 1980s. It was particularly in the 1980s that a new balance of power in coalition politics became evident, which most importantly entailed the end of the Christian Democratic monopoly on the prime ministership, and a different distribution of ministerial and junior-ministerial positions (Table 12.6a). This shift was caused by the entrance of the mid-sized PSI into the coalition. To this should be added the progressive diminution of the pivotal role of the most important coalitional party: during the 1970s the DC lost the pivotal position in parliament on what we have defined here as a second significant policy dimension during the long cycle of the First Republic: foreign policy (pro- or anti-Soviet Union) (Cotta and Isernia 1996). Furthermore, during

[10] DC intra-party conflicts were in evidence during the 1950s, at the time of the different attempts by Fanfani, and during the 1960s, with the Tambroni cabinet and the veto against Scelba's participation in the centre-left.

[11] The Socialist Party was for a long time internally divided over government collaboration with the DC. To a lesser extent, the Social Democratic Party has also been factionalized. The PRI and the PLI were traditionally more cohesive, and elites' conflicts were more easily solved through governmental or sub-governmental patronage.

the 1980s the DC lost its central position in the political spectrum even on the first policy dimension (see Tables 12.2a and 12.2b).

Cabinet Composition

This complicated game of coalition building has produced a number of short-term political cycles characterized by the predominance of one coalitional formula. The main difference among formulae (except for the third one) has been the inclusion or exclusion of one or the other of the smaller parties. The short cycles include (see Table 12.1):

(1) Centrist coalition (*centrismo*)
(2) Centre-left coalition (*centro-sinistra*)
(3) National solidarity (*solidarietà nazionale*)
(4) Five-party coalition (*pentapartito*)
(5) The transition of the 1990s and a new centre-left coalition

The first four political cycles have typically had a preparatory phase of experimentation, often without the full engagement of all the political partners, a central period of more durable cabinets, and a period of decline characterized by growing instability, shorter cabinets, the disengagement of some partners, and attempts to renegotiate the alliance (Marradi 1982). During most of these cycles an intermediate crisis has taken place, but after a period of instability a second stabilization has been possible. Only the national solidarity coalition was not restabilized after the initial crisis. This was in any case the most unusual of the coalition cycles, since the attempt to involve the Communist Party in the government clashed with long-term constraints which had not yet lost all of their strength.

Over the course of the various coalitional phases, a slow but sufficiently evident transformation can be noticed. The typical pattern during the first phase of the Republic (the 1950s and 1960s) was an incremental inclusion of all the 'potential actors' of the coalition (meaning, all the governmental parties and all the representative factions of the main party). This process took time and very often created problems for the stability of individual cabinets. The use of external support was a typical temporary solution to ensure a majority during phases of coalition renegotiation. The result was the alternation between full-fledged cabinets (representing the entire coalition of each phase) and transitional ones (either single-party minority cabinets or cabinets based upon incomplete coalitions).

The internal dynamics of coalition cycles followed a recurrent pattern. 'From great hopes (and promises) to disillusionment' is probably the formulation that best captures this pattern. At the beginning of each coalition cycle there is always a fairly significant redefinition (or at least the perception of it) of the ideological and/or policy image of one or more parties within or outside the previous coalition pattern. Such redefinition aims at placing the party in question in a more competitive position to play the electoral and also the coalition game (which are obviously connected in important ways). A more clearly defined political profile for the DC and for the splinter Social Democrats was the crucial factor at the beginning of centrism; the Socialist Party's move towards the centre played the same role for the centre-left and again for the five-party coalition; and the increasing moderation of the PCI for the national solidarity period. The new political profile of one or more parties enables new coalition partners to find common ground and therefore facilitates agreements on possible policy initiatives. The beginning of a new coalition formula typically heralds a period of 'reforms' (which are proclaimed in the programmes of the new governments). But the road from promises and hopes to concrete legislation and to its implementation generally proves much more difficult than expected. The cumbersome and heterogeneous nature of coalitions in which many partners are often internally divided is one of the foremost causes of government troubles. It is true that while agreement on significant reforms is difficult to come by, distributive policies and patronage are more easily accessible and can to some extent compensate for the failures at the higher level (Cotta 1996; Cotta and Verzichelli 1996). But in the end the political gains derived from the coalition game are generally lower than expected. Only very rarely is there a net electoral gain for the coalition as a whole (Table 12.8); moreover there is always at least one party which has not profited and is unhappy with the coalition. With few exceptions, only short-lived, transitional cabinets are put in place after elections. The coalition parties require some time before they are able to digest the electoral results. 'Summer holidays governments' (elections in Italy typically take place at the end of the spring), which generally do not enjoy the full support of all the coalitions partners, take care of current affairs until the parties are able to reach a more stable agreement.

The lack of electoral success, bargaining difficulties on significant policy issues, and increasing distributive conflicts progressively induce one or more of the coalition partners to take a more rigid stance *vis-à-vis* the others. In order to face external competition, some parties find it more politically profitable to shift to a position of external support or abstention. After some time the coalitional formula may be renewed, maybe on the basis of a renegotiated agreement and a re-equilibration of the roles of the coalition partners. Otherwise, the coalition will draw to an end and a new political scenario will follow.

With the political earthquake that started in 1992, the selection and role of prime ministers began to change. Giuliano Amato in 1992 was still a 'party nominated' candidate,[12] but he seemed to enjoy greater discretion in the

---

[12] After the 1992 elections, the Socialist Party again had the chance to obtain the prime ministership, but the first revelations about *Tangentopoli* made Craxi's candidacy unacceptable. The delegation of the Socialist group, during the official negotiations with the head of state, provided three names: De Michelis, Martelli, and Amato. Amato, who was perceived as the most autonomous from the previous leadership, was accepted by the other parties and was probably pushed by the president of the Republic himself.

TABLE 12.4. *Italian cabinets since 1945*

Cabinet number	Cabinet	Date in	Formal resignation	Maximum potential duration (in days)	Duration (in days)	Government composition	External support
1	Parri	9 Dec. 1945	24 Nov. 1945		156	PdA–DC–PCI–PLI–PSIUP–PdL	
2	De Gasperi I	13 July 1946	1 July 1946	645	203	DC–PCI–PSI–PdA–PdL–PLI	
3	De Gasperi II	2 Feb. 1947	20 Jan. 1947	441	191	DC–PCI–PSI–PRI	
4	De Gasperi III	31 May 1947	13 May 1947	323	100	DC–PCI–PSI	
5	De Gasperi IV	23 May 1948	12 May 1948	323	323	DC–PLI–tec	
6	De Gasperi V	21 Jan. 1950	12 Jan. 1950	1,841	599	DC–PSDI–PLI–PRI	
7	De Gasperi VI	26 July 1951	16 July 1951	1,233	541	DC–PSDI–PRI	
8	De Gasperi VII	16 July 1953	29 June 1953	682	682	DC–PRI	
9	De Gasperi VIII	17 Aug. 1953	28 July 1953	1,774	12	DC	PRI
10	Pella	18 Jan. 1954	15 Jan. 1954	1,742	151	DC	PRI, PLI, PNM
11	Fanfani I	10 Feb. 1954	30 Jan. 1954	1,588	12	DC	
12	Scelba	22 July 1955	6 July 1955	1,565	527	DC–PSDI–PLI	PRI
13	Segni I	19 May 1957	16 May 1957	1,054	680	DC–PSDI–PLI	PRI
14	Zoli	1 July 1958	19 June 1958	371	371	DC	MSI, PNM
15	Fanfani II	15 Feb. 1959	26 Jan. 1959	1,762	209	DC–PSDI	PRI
16	Segni II	25 Mar. 1960	24 Feb. 1960	1,533	374	DC	PLI
17	Tambroni	26 July 1960	19 July 1960	1,129	116	DC	MSI
18	Fanfani III	21 Feb. 1962	12 Feb. 1962	1,006	566	DC	PRI, PSDI
19	Fanfani IV	21 June 1963	16 May 1963	431	431	DC–PSDI–PRI	PSI
20	Leone I	4 Dec. 1963	5 Nov. 1963	1,794	137	DC	
21	Moro I[a]	24 June 1968	15 June 1968	1,628	1,628	DC–PSI–PRI–PSDI	
22	Leone II	12 Dec. 1968	19 Nov. 1968	1,790	148	DC	
23	Rumor I	5 Aug. 1969	15 July 1969	1,619	215	DC–PSI–PRI	
24	Rumor II	27 Mar. 1970	17 Feb. 1970	1,383	196	DC	
25	Rumor III	6 Aug. 1970	16 July 1970	1,149	111	DC–PSI–PSDI–PRI	
26	Colombo	17 Feb. 1972	15 Jan. 1972	1,017	527	DC–PSI–PSDI–PRI	
27	Andreotti I	26 June 1972	26 Feb. 1972	457	9	DC	
28	Andreotti II	7 July 1973	12 June 1972	1,776	351	DC–PSDI–PLI	PRI
29	Rumor IV		2 Mar. 1974	1,400	238	DC–PSI–PSDI–PRI	

Italy

#	Cabinet	Start date	End date	Days	Composition	Notes
30	Rumor V	14 Mar. 1974	3 Oct. 1974	203	DC–PSI–PSDI	PRI
31	Moro II[b]	23 Nov. 1974	7 Jan. 1976	410	DC–PRI	PSDI
32	Moro III[c]	12 Feb. 1976	30 Apr. 1976	78	DC	PSDI
33	Andreotti IIIa[d]	29 July 1976	16 Jan. 1978	536	DC	
	Andreotti IIIb*	11 Mar. 1978	31 Jan. 1979	326	DC	PCI, PSI, PSDI, PRI
34	Andreotti IV[e]	20 Mar. 1979	31 Mar. 1979	11	DC–PSDI–PRI	
35	Cossiga I	4 Aug. 1979	19 Mar. 1980	228	DC–PSDI–PLI	
36	Cossiga II	4 Apr. 1980	28 Sept. 1980	177	DC–PRI–PSI	
37	Forlani	18 Oct. 1980	26 May 1981	220	DC–PSI–PRI–PSDI	
38	Spadolini[f]	28 June 1981	7 Aug. 1982	487	PRI–DC–PSI–PSDI–PLI	
39	Fanfani V	1 Dec. 1982	22 Apr. 1983	142	DC–PSI–PSDI–PLI	
40	Craxi[g]	04 Aug. 1983	27 July 1986	1,088	PSI–DC–PRI–PSDI–PLI	
41	Fanfani VI	17 Apr. 1987	28 Apr. 1987	11	DC–tec	
42	Goria	28 July 1987	11 Mar. 1988	227	DC–PSI–PRI–PSDI–PLI	
43	De Mita	13 Apr. 1988	19 May 1989	401	DC–PSI–PRI–PSDI–PLI	
44	Andreotti V[h]	23 July 1989	29 Mar. 1991	614	DC–PSI–PRI–PSDI–PLI	
45	Andreotti VI[i]	13 Apr. 1991	24 Apr. 1992	358	DC–PSI–PSDI–PLI	
46	Amato	28 June 1992	22 Apr. 1993	298	PSI–DC–PLI–PSDI	
47	Ciampi	29 Apr. 1993	13 Jan. 1994	259	DC–PSI–PSDI–PLI–tec	
48	Berlusconi	11 May 1994	22 Dec. 1994	225	FI–LN–AN–CCD	
49	Dini	17 Jan. 1995	07 Jan. 1996	355	Tec	Centre-left parties[j]
50	Prodi	18 May 1996	09 Oct. 1998	874	PDS–GR–PPI–RI	RC
51	D'Alema	21 Oct. 1998		912	DS–PPI–GR–RI–SDI–UDR–PdCI	

* No new cabinet according to the definition used in this volume but a relevant change in the cabinet's external support ('historic compromise').

[a] According to conventional Italian numbering this cabinet is divided into three cabinets: Moro I (4 Dec. 1963–26 June 1964), Moro II (22 July 1964–21 Jan. 1966), and Moro III (23 Feb. 1966–19 May 1968).

[b] According to conventional Italian numbering this cabinet is Moro IV.

[c] According to conventional Italian numbering this cabinet is Moro V.

[d] According to conventional Italian numbering this cabinet is Andreotti III and IV.

[e] According to conventional Italian numbering this cabinet is Andreotti V.

[f] According to conventional Italian numbering this cabinet is divided into two cabinets: Spadolini I (28 June 1981–7 Aug. 1982) and Spadolini II (23 Aug. 1982–13 Nov. 1982).

[g] According to conventional Italian numbering this cabinet is divided into two cabinets: Craxi I (4 Aug. 1983–27 July 1986) and Craxi II (1 Aug. 1986–3 Mar. 1987).

[h] According to conventional Italian numbering this cabinet is Andreotti VI.

[i] According to conventional Italian numbering this cabinet is Andreotti VII.

[j] The parties supporting Dini were the centre-left (PDS, Greens, Socialists, *La Rete*) and PPI and LN.

formation of his cabinet. During the last part of his mandate, the cabinet had lost a good deal of its 'partyness' (Cotta and Verzichelli 1996). This was even more pronounced in the next cabinet, which was headed for the first time by a 'technician' without a parliamentary background, the former governor of the Bank of Italy, Carlo Azelio Ciampi. The role of the president of the Republic in choosing the prime minister and then, together with the latter, the cabinet ministers (a great number of whom were not politicians) increased very significantly, while the parties were seriously weakened. The adoption since 1994 of a new (partially majoritarian) electoral system, and the consequent restructuring of the party system, led to further important changes. With the electoral victory of a cartel of parties, the candidate for the position of prime minister is immediately clear (Berlusconi in 1994, Prodi in 1996). The strong role recently acquired by the president has shrunk again. The cabinet formation process becomes much simpler and, without any change in constitutional procedures, the PM designate gains a significant strength in the bargaining *vis-à-vis* the other party leaders. This new pattern of government formation is, however, still far from consolidated (Fabbrini 1998; Morlino 1996). Both the centre-right and the centre-left coalitions, in 1994 and 1996, respectively, showed some evident difficulties in the consolidation of the prime ministerial prerogative during the life of the legislature. Above all, the premature end of the Berlusconi cabinet and the formation of a new technical government in 1995 (the Dini cabinet), but also the crisis of October 1998 which brought the downfall of Prodi, showed that as soon as the electoral majority becomes unstable, the fragmented party system can win back the control of cabinet formation, and the president of the Republic can regain a substantial influence.

COALITION GOVERNANCE

Cabinet formation negotiations in Italy generally support the view that stresses the dominance of office distribution motivations. The allocation of ministries usually takes more time and receives more attention than the definition of policy platforms, and the pervasive partyness of government appointments goes hand in hand with the weakness of policy platforms (Vassallo 1994; Cotta 1996; Pasquino 1997). Yet, it would be an exaggeration to say that policy issues are irrelevant in coalition bargaining. First, it is obvious that some 'high policy' issues determine which parties can enter government coalitions and which not. And empirical analysis of government programmes has shown that a set of policy issues have provided the general guidelines for coalition making since World War II (Mastropaolo and Slater 1992). Moreover, one should distinguish between coalition phases and individual cabinets. A new coalition phase typically entails a more substantial redefinition of policy platforms than is the case for an ordinary change of cabinets. During a coalition phase some broad policy guidelines will remain relatively stable. During the formation of individual cabinets only more specific policy issues will be negotiated.

The general model of coalition governance which characterized Italy between 1945 and the early 1990s is summarized in Table 12.5. At least until the beginning of the current transition (1992), the main features can be described as follows:

1. There has generally been no official written agreement of the coalition parties on a common policy platform. The formal definition of the government platform has been delegated to the prime minister designate, who after contacting the party delegations would write the draft text of the government programme to be presented in parliament. While the text originally proposed by the PM could be relatively detailed, the final result, the government programme, has usually been rather general and vague (Mastropaolo and Slater 1992; Guagnano 1996). Contrary to, for instance, the case of Belgium (De Winter 1989), this document would not become a strict guide for the cabinet's policy agenda. On only two occasions have we been able to ascertain the existence of a formalized, although not officially reported, 'coalition agreement'. The first case was at the beginning of the centre-left[13] and the second before the full national solidarity cabinet.[14] No formal resolution mechanism has been provided for bringing the coalition to an end in case of government failure to implement the programme (see Table 12.5). The inter-ministerial committees, established during the 1960s to coordinate the activity of the cabinet in specific policy sectors, did not cover this function, with the only partial exception of the CIPE (Inter-ministerial Committee for Economic Planning). However, a reform in 1977, determining the creation of some new formal *Comitati*, further reduced the role of CIPE as an instrument to regulate inter-party relations within the coalition (Hine 1993: 221). The second case is a particularly interesting episode in Italian post-war history: in June 1976 a DC *monocolore* government was formed which obtained the confidence of parliament thanks to the abstentions of PCI, PSI, PSDI, PRI, and PLI. After one year (July 1977), during the life of the same government, the parties supporting the government agreed to sign a joint document. This pact can be seen as

[13] This document was not recorded in any official document, but it was distributed by the Christian Democratic Party. It included a short political introduction and a policy chapter, mainly devoted to economic problems.

[14] The reference here is to the document signed by DC, PCI, PSI, PRI, PSDI, and PLI in July 1977. This cannot be considered the official agreement for the next cabinet (Andreotti IIIb), formed in Mar. 1978, but a necessary step towards a full national solidarity government. Paradoxically, it was a document developed mainly to limit the political implications of the cabinet (the Christian Democratic executive referred to it as a pure policy agreement but refused the label 'coalition pact').

TABLE 12.5. *Coalition governance in Italy, 1946–1998*

(1) Coalition	(2) Coalition agreement	(3) Agreement Public	(4) Election rule	(5) Resolution mechanism	(6) Most common management mechanisms	(7) Mechanisms for most serious conflict	(8) Coalition discipline in legislation	(9) Coalition discipline in other parliamentary behaviour	(10) Freedom of appointment	(11) Policy agreement	(12) Junior ministers	(13) Non-cabinet positions
1946	N	N	N	CoC	CoC	CoC	2	3	Y	1	Y	Y
1947	N	N	N	CoC	CoC	CoC	2	3	Y	1	Y	Y
1947	N	N	N	CoC	CoC	CoC	2	3	Y	1	Y	Y
1948	N	N	N	CoC	CoC	CoC	2	3	Y	1	Y	Y
1950	N	N	N	CoC	CoC	CoC	2	3	Y	1	Y	Y
1952	N	N	N	CoC	CoC	CoC	2	3	Y	1	Y	Y
1954	N	N	N	CoC	CoC	CoC	2	3	Y	1	Y	Y
1958	N	N	N	CoC	CoC	CoC	2	3	Y	2	Y	Y
1962	N	N	N	CoC	CoC	CoC	2	3	Y	2	Y	Y
1963	IE	N	N	CoC,PS	CoC	CoC	2	3	Y	2	Y	Y
1968	N	N	N	CoC,PS	CoC	CoC	2	3	Y	2	Y	Y
1970	N	N	N	CoC,PS	CoC	CoC	2	3	Y	2	Y	Y
1972	N	N	N	CoC,PS	CoC	CoC	2	3	Y	2	Y	Y
1973	N	N	N	CoC,PS	CoC	CoC	2	3	Y	2	Y	Y
1974	N	N	N	CoC,PS	CoC	CoC	2	3	Y	2	Y	Y
1974	N	N	N	CoC,PS	CoC	CoC	2	3	Y	2	Y	Y
1978*	(IE)	(N)	(N)	CoC,PS	PS	PS	(2)	(3)	(Y)	(2)	(Y)	(Y)
1979	N	N	N	CoC,PS	PS	PS	2	3	Y	2	Y	Y

Italy

Year											
1979	N	N	N	CoC,PS	PS	2	3	Y	1	Y	Y
1980	N	N	N	CoC,PS	PS	2	3	Y	1	Y	Y
1980	N	N	N	CoC,PS	PS	2	3	Y	1	Y	Y
1981	N	N	N	CoC,PS	PS	2	3	Y	1	Y	Y
1982	N	N	N	CoC,PS	PS	2	3	Y	1	Y	Y
1983	N	N	N	CoC,PS	PS	2	3	Y	1	Y	Y
1987	N	N	N	CoC,PS	PS	2	3	Y	1	Y	Y
1991	N	N	N	CoC,PS	PS	2	3	Y	1	Y	Y
1992	N	N	N	CoC,PS	PS	2	3	Y	1	Y	Y
1993	N[a]	N[a]	N	CoC,PS	CoC	2	3	Y	1	N	N
1994	N[b]	N[b]	N	CoC,PS	PS	2	3	N	1	Y	Y
1995	N[a]	N[a]	N	CoC,PS	CoC	2	3	Y	1	N	N
1996	N[b]	N[b]	N	CoC,PS	CoC	2	3	Y	2	Y	Y
1998	N	N	N	CoC,PS	CoC	2	3	Y	1	Y	Y

* The 1978 Andreotti cabinet was a single-party one. It is nevertheless worth mentioning in this context, since it was inaugurated after all parties had signed an agreement on 'national solidarity' some months before. However, this agreement was not a fully-fledged parliamentary coalition agreement.

[a] Due to their technical nature, the Ciampi and Dini cabinets could hardly be based on a public coalition agreement between parties.

[b] The centre-right government in 1994 (Berlusconi) is somehow based on an unwritten agreement of the electoral double-sided cartel winning the election in March (Forza Italia and Lega Nord in the North, Forza Italia and Alleanza Nazionale in the South). Similarly, the *Tesi dell'Ulivo* (a pre-electoral programme which was hammered out when Prodi accepted the candidature as prime minister in case of a victory of the left) can be interpreted as a kind of agreement. However, it was still far from a fully-fledged coalition agreement.

an important step towards the formation of the next cabinet (Andreotti IIIb), born in March 1978, which received a positive vote of confidence from all the parties of the pact. The meaning of that pact was in a sense twofold: on the one hand, it was obviously a formalization of the inter-party agreement. On the other hand, its purpose was also to limit the discretion of the cabinet and of the DC, the only party inside it.

2. The distribution of government offices has followed a proportionality norm, which has been applied not only to ministerial positions but also to junior ministerships and other sub-governmental offices (see below).

3. The birth of a new cabinet has not usually produced expectations of strong coalition discipline in parliament (Table 12.5). This clearly has to do with the nature of coalition agreements. The 'normal' agreement has been a weak and often ambiguous set of compromises (partly negative commitments to exclude some policies, and partly positive ones to promote others) concerning a number of short-term and specific policies (e.g. conjunctural measures concerning the economy, state finances, and welfare policies) and, more rarely, guidelines about more wide-ranging reforms. In general, new cabinets have not tended to present comprehensive and enforceable policy platforms.

The weakness of coalition discipline becomes easily apparent as soon as we examine the law-making process. The high proportion (40% to 50%) of government bills that are not passed by parliament, the frequent bargains struck with the opposition, and the large number of parliamentary amendments accepted by the government suggest that the cohesiveness of the majority has been far from assured (Di Palma 1977). Governments generally have expected discipline in parliamentary votes on their legislative proposal but have not been able to take it for granted. Whenever coalition discipline has failed, the government has had to accept either a defeat or a compromise that might involve the opposition. This lack of discipline has not directly endangered the life of the cabinet, unless the PM or another party leader has explicitly asked for parliamentary compliance. In any case, in policy areas where a clear cleavage has divided the governing parties (e.g. on issues like private education, divorce, or abortion), no coalition discipline has been possible and the government has simply refrained from taking positions. Despite some variations in coalition discipline, this general view is more or less applicable to all coalitions considered here (Table 12.5). Especially early on and during the 'golden age' of each coalition phase (Table 12.1), discipline has generally been stronger.

Mechanisms of Conflict Management

Some of the conflicts that have emerged within Italian cabinets have been solved through the use of informal mechanisms such as the coalitional summit, which confirms the need for continuous bargaining among governing parties (Criscitiello 1994; Hine 1993). Otherwise, coalitional problems have sometimes been solved by a slight change in portfolio allocation[15] or with a short governmental crisis which has enabled the parties to renegotiate some aspects of policy without endangering the coalition itself.[16] During the decay of a coalitional formula or the transitional periods cohesion among allied parties has declined and discipline has become much more uncertain.

During the late 1970s and the 1980s cabinet stability increased slightly (Battegazzorre 1987, Mershon 1996), and since then a number of minor reforms have been made to strengthen the institutional roles of the executive and of the prime minister. Particularly after the end of the 'national solidarity' phase, which had been based on a parliamentary grand coalition, the new governmental coalition tried to bring back into the hands of the Cabinet control over decision making. The effects of these attempts were at best ambiguous. An empirical study of a typical feature of the last two decades, the 'majority summits',[17] shows that this instrument had mixed effects: on the one hand, it strengthened the executive (by providing an instrument for reaching decisions), on the other hand, it constrained cabinet autonomy (by removing from its hands crucial decisions) (Criscitiello 1994). The 'majority summits', semi-formal meetings between cabinet and parties, which are not a pure mechanism for agenda setting or for cabinet conflict resolution, but which produce extraordinary and incremental changes of the cabinet's policy orientation, are a peculiar character of Italian governance. It is interesting that this practice makes a comeback in the coalitional cabinets of the 1990s, after having disappeared in the phase of 'technical governments' (Criscitiello 1996: 384).

In general, no formal rule has been able to provide for very strict control upon the members of the coalition. And because of their weakness and ambiguity, coalition agreements have not been able to substitute for such rules. The same can be said about the rules concerning the dissolution and formation of a new coalitional formula.

---

[15] There have been at least ten partial substitutions of ministerial personnel which did not affect the partisan composition structure of the coalition. This procedure, called *rimpasto* (reshuffle), was used, esp. during the centre-left period, to pacify party influentials (particularly in the DC) or to cover positions left by ministers of a party faction which had become hostile to the government. In the latter case (for example, in the replacement of the ministers of the left DC faction, who in 1990 had left the cabinet because of a disagreement about new television legislation), the *rimpasto* has the same political meaning as a 'normal' crisis.

[16] As is the case of some cabinet crises not counted here (those during the government led by Moro in the 1960s) or even the crisis of the third Andreotti cabinet (1978). All those crises were triggered by one or more of the coalition parties with the purpose of renegotiating the structure of the cabinet or enforcing its policy agenda.

[17] The summits were typically a meeting of the party leaders with the prime minister and possibly other ministers and experts. They could be devoted to one specific issue or to a broader review of the political agenda of that moment.

As many observers have noted, the willingness and ability of different cabinets to respect and implement their official agreements have varied greatly. For example, the 'centre-left' cabinets of the 1960s and 1970s are thought to have been quite different in this respect (Amato 1981). Similarly, coalitional cohesion underwent important changes during the 'five-party' era. Early on, with efforts to strengthen the cabinet and to introduce majoritarian provisions, the parties seemed engaged also in the building of a more ambitious policy platform that included broad economic and institutional reforms. The fact that Christian Democrats were for the first time willing to relinquish the prime ministership to another coalition party (first the Republican Party and then the Socialists) was another clear sign of change. But practical results were much less significant than originally expected, and with the passing of time the coalition became more and more 'office-seeking and policy-controlling'.[18] This turn became particularly clear with the crisis of the Craxi cabinet, when the struggle over the prime ministership gained pre-eminence, and the search for a compromise to ensure the alternance between PSI and DC premiers (the famous *patto della staffetta*) overshadowed any policy discussion.

Did coalition governance change significantly during the transition following the crisis of the traditional governing parties? Since 1992, technocratic and political cabinets alternated in power (Table 12.1). The two cabinet types faced somewhat different problems, but the weakening of the old parties and the uncertain consolidation of the new ones, plus the volatility of inter-party behaviour, in all cases prevented strong and comprehensive coalition agreements. The three major parties of the winning coalition of 1994 developed their own pre-electoral programmes, though the common document was little more than a double preamble on the rationale for the electoral coalitions (FI–LN in the north, FI–AN in the south). In 1996, more clearly defined electoral platforms were proposed by the winning alliance (L'Ulivo), as well as by the losing side (Polo per le libertà). But also in this case the coalitional behaviour has been quite unpredictable, above all because of the political instability among the forces of the electoral cartel. From this point of view, governance has not been too dissimilar from the past. The main new element has been the enhanced role of the president, who has frequently dictated cabinet guidelines from the outside. To an extent, the president has substituted for the party leaders in providing external guidance for the cabinet.

---

[18] The decade of five-party coalition could be divided into two periods: the rise and consolidation of a politically ambitious project (the cabinets led by Spadolini and Craxi), and a long decay, from the renegotiation of the coalition under the weak Goria cabinet, to the failure of de Mita, to the leadership of Andreotti. On the five-party coalition, see Pasquino (1994) and Cotta and Isernia (1996).

PORTFOLIO ALLOCATION

In putting together his cabinet, the prime minister chooses the ministers who are then nominated by the president (Art. 92). In practice, the nomination of ministers has been done on the basis of indications provided by each party or by within-party factions (where they are important, as it was the case in the DC). The prime minister in reality chooses the ministers (and only those assigned to his party or faction) only when he is the leader of his party or of his faction. Otherwise his role is not very different from that of other party influentials. Prime ministers of technical governments have probably had somewhat greater discretion over ministerial selection. In these cases, the head of state has also played a very significant role. The number of ministers is not fixed. While a law is needed to establish a new ministerial department, ministers without portfolio can easily be appointed. The choice of undersecretaries takes place in the first cabinet meeting and follows the same informal rules discussed for the ministers: the nominations, though presented by the individual ministers, are in reality made by the parties. The only effect that may result from prime ministerial intervention or bargaining inside the cabinet is to shift some nominee from one assignment to another. However, the President of the Council (PM) has always had a certain autonomy in choosing a 'personal' undersecretary (the junior minister of the Presidency of the Council with the function of secretary of the cabinet meetings).

Portfolio allocation has followed a proportionality (parity) norm, which has been applied not only to ministerial positions but also to junior ministerships and other sub-governmental offices. In 1982 the number of ministerial posts assigned to the DC was for the first time lower than that given to the other coalition partners combined. From this moment onward, the bargaining relationship between the DC and the Socialist Party came to be nearly 'paritetical' (Verzichelli 1992). Looking at the historical trend of the portfolio allocation one can see the efforts of the major governmental parties to control some 'crucial' positions: for the DC it was particularly important to keep some ministries like Interior, Education, and Agriculture, while the Socialist Party since its first entrance in the cabinet explicitly asked for an economic ministry. The competition for posts has taken place not only between parties: the representation of different Christian Democratic factions has generally been a major concern in the formation process, and it has very often been the main cause of cabinet termination (see below). In the DC, for example, the Ministry of Labour was traditionally assigned to the 'unionist faction' while the Agriculture portfolio was controlled by politicians close to the influential small farmers' association (*Coldiretti*).

Once the quota of offices for each party or faction has been determined, party and faction leaders have been relatively free to decide the 'names'.

Before the 1980s, the ministers were essentially nominated by a small party elite which generally remained outside the cabinet (Dogan 1989). Some change took place during the 1980s, when party leaders increasingly moved inside the cabinet and cumulated the two positions (Verzichelli 1992). This was particularly evident for the smaller parties, while in the DC competition among faction leaders made it more difficult to combine the positions of party and cabinet leader.

Tables 12.6a, 12.6b, and 12.6c report in detail on the partisan distribution of governmental (and sub-governmental) positions. If the names of the ministers were added, one would see that while a high level of cabinet turnover has prevailed, an inner circle of relatively long-lasting ministers has assured a somewhat more stable pattern of governance in some crucial ministries[19] (Calise and Mannheimer 1982).

The dominance of office distribution concerns in the traditional government formation process does not mean that the parties have not been interested in the policies pertaining to different ministries. On the contrary, the persistent control by one party (and particularly the DC) over particular ministries, and the intense struggle over a number of others, are proof of the importance parties and factions have attributed to the control over specific areas of policy and patronage. Although it is difficult to determine to what extent these conflicts were about policies (between leftist or 'social' factions, on the one hand, and conservative ones, on the other) or simply about the internal allocation of government positions, it is sufficiently clear that the second element was always very important. The struggles over portfolio allocations were particularly evident among Christian Democrats during the 'golden age' of centrism and the centre-left, when the DC could control more than half of the cabinet portfolios. At that time, coalition parties and factions employed an informal code of proportional distribution, commonly known as the 'Cencelli handbook'. This code took into account both the 'number' and the 'weight' of ministerial positions. But even the smaller parties faced challenges over internal office distribution, in that they sometimes had to solve internal ideological differences,[20] or simply to balance and pacify individual ambitions within the party elite (for instance, by giving a ministry to the leader of the inner opposition).

---

[19] The Socialist Party leaders Giolitti (Finance) and Nenni (Foreign Affairs) are good examples of long-serving ministers. The same applies to La Malfa (PRI) in the Department for Economics. DC ministers have generally not held specific portfolios for a very long period.

[20] The most prominent case was perhaps the request of an economic ministry by the left socialists in the first centre-left experience.

Italy 465

TABLE 12.6a. *Distribution of cabinet ministerships (with portfolio) in Italian coalitions, 1945–1999* (at the beginning of the cabinet)

Cabinet number	Cabinet	(1) PM	(2) Vice-PM	(3) FOR	(4) INN	(5) JUS	(6) BUD	(7) FIN	(8) ECO	(9) DEF	(10) SCH	(11) PUB	(12) AGR
1	Parri	PdA	PLI,PSI	DC	PdA	PCI	PLI	PCI	—	DC	PLI	PSI	PCI
2	De Gasperi I	DC	PSI	DC	PSI	PCI	PLI	PCI	—	PLI	PdL	PLI	PCI
3	De Gasperi II	DC	—	DC	DC	PCI	PLI	PCI	—	PRI	DC	PSI	DC
4	De Gasperi III	DC	—	PRI	DC	PCI	DC	DC	—	PdL	DC	DC	DC
5	De Gasperi IV	DC	PRI,PSLI	PRI	DC	PLI	PLI	DC	DC	DC	DC	DC	DC
6	De Gasperi V	DC	DC,PLI	PRI	DC	PLI	DC	DC	DC	PRI	DC	DC	DC
7	De Gasperi VI	DC	—	PRI	DC	DC	DC	DC	DC	PRI	DC	DC	DC
8	De Gasperi VII	DC	DC	DC	DC	DC	DC	DC	DC	PRI	DC	DC	DC
12	Scelba	DC	PSDI	DC	DC	DC	DC	DC	DC	DC	PLI	PSDI	DC
13	Segni I	DC	PSDI	PLI	DC	DC	DC	PSDI	DC	DC	PSDI	PSDI	DC
15	Fanfani II	DC	DC	DC	DC	DC	DC	DC	DC	DC	DC	DC	DC
19	Fanfani IV	DC	DC	DC	DC	DC	DC	DC	PSDI	DC	DC	DC	DC
21	Moro I	DC	PSI	PSDI	DC	PRI	PSI	PRI	DC	DC	DC	PSI	DC
23	Rumor I	DC	PSI	PSI	DC	DC	PSI	PRI	DC	DC	DC	PSI	DC
25	Rumor III	DC	PSI	DC	DC	PRI	PSI	PSDI	DC	PSDI	DC	PSI	DC
26	Colombo	DC	PSI	DC	DC	DC	PSI	PSDI	DC	PSDI	DC	PSI	DC
28	Andreotti II	DC	PSDI	DC	DC	DC	DC	DC	PLI	PSDI	DC	DC	DC
29	Rumor IV	DC	—	DC	DC	PSI	PSI	PSDI	PRI	PSDI	DC	PSI	DC
30	Rumor V	DC	—	DC	DC	PSI	PSI	DC	PRI	PSDI	DC	PSI	DC
34	Andreotti IV	DC	PRI	DC	DC	DC	PRI	DC	DC	DC	PRI	PRI	DC
35	Cossiga I	DC	—	DC	DC	DC	DC	TEC	DC	DC	PLI	PSDI	DC
36	Cossiga II	DC	—	DC	DC	DC	PRI	PSI	DC	PSI	DC	PRI	DC
37	Forlani	DC	—	DC	DC	DC	PRI	PSI	DC	PSI	DC	PSDI	DC
38	Spadolini I	PRI	—	DC	DC	DC	PRI	PSI	DC	PSI	DC	PSDI	DC
39	Fanfani V	DC	—	DC	DC	DC	DC	PSI	DC	PSI	DC	PSDI	DC
40	Craxi	PSI	DC	DC	DC	DC	PSDI	PRI	DC	DC	DC	PSDI	DC
42	Goria	DC	PSI	DC	DC	PSI	DC	DC	PSI	DC	DC	PSDI	DC

TABLE 12.6a. cont.

Cabinet number	Cabinet	(1) PM	(2) Vice-PM	(3) FOR	(4) INN	(5) JUS	(6) BUD	(7) FIN	(8) ECO	(9) DEF	(10) SCH	(11) PUB	(12) AGR
43	De Mita	DC	PSI	DC	DC	PSI	DC	DC	PSI	DC	DC	PSDI	DC
44	Andreotti V	DC	PSI	PSI	DC	PSI	DC	PSI	DC	DC	DC	DC	DC
45	Andreotti VI	DC	PSI	PSI	DC	PSI	DC	PSI	DC	DC	DC	DC	DC
46	Amato	PSI	—	DC	DC	PSI	PSI	DC	DC	PSI	DC	DC	DC
47	Ciampi	TEC	—	DC	DC	TEC	TEC	TEC	DC	PSI	DC	DC	DC
48	Berlusconi	FI	AN,LN	FI	LN	FI	LN	TEC	TEC	FI	CCD	FI	AN
50	Prodi	PPI	PDS	RI	PDS	TEC	TEC	PDS	TEC	PPI	PDS	TEC	PPI
51	D'Alema	DS	PPI	RI	PPI	PdCI	—	DS	TEC	UDR	DS	TEC	TEC

Cabinet number	Cabinet	(13) TRA	(14) PT	(15) IND	(16) WOR	(17) EXT	(18) MAR	(19) PAR	(20) HEA	(21) TUR	(22) CUL	(23) ENV	(24) UNI
1	Parri	PdA	DC	DC	PSI	PdA	—	—	—	—	—	—	—
2	De Gasperi I	PSI	DC	DC	PSI	PSI	—	—	—	—	—	—	—
3	De Gasperi II	PCI	DC	PSI	PSI	DC	DC	—	—	—	—	—	—
4	De Gasperi III	PCI	PSI	PSI	PSI	DC	DC	—	—	—	—	—	—
5	De Gasperi IV	TEC	DC	DC	DC	TEC	—	—	—	—	—	—	—
6	De Gasperi V	TEC	DC	PSDI	DC	TEC	—	—	—	—	—	—	—
7	De Gasperi VI	PSDI	DC	DC	DC	PSLI	—	—	—	—	—	—	—
8	De Gasperi VII	DC	DC	DC	DC	PRI	DC	—	—	—	—	—	—
12	Scelba	DC	DC	PLI	PSDI	DC	DC	—	—	—	—	—	—
13	Segni I	DC	DC	DC	PSDI	DC	DC	PSDI	DC	—	—	—	—
15	Fanfani II	DC	PSDI	DC	PSDI	DC	DC	—	—	—	—	—	—

19	Fanfani IV	DC	DC	DC	PSDI	PSDI	PRI	DC	DC	DC	—	—	—
21	Moro I	DC	DC	DC	DC	DC	DC	DC	PSI	PSI	—	—	—
23	Rumor I	PSI	DC	PSI	PSI	DC	PSI	DC	DC	DC	—	—	—
25	Rumor III	DC	DC	DC	DC	PSI	DC	DC	PSI	PSDI	—	—	—
26	Colombo	PSI	DC	DC	DC	PSI	DC	DC	PSI	PSDI	—	—	—
28	Andreotti II	PLI	DC	PSDI	DC	PSDI	PSDI	DC	DC	PLI	—	—	—
29	Rumor IV	PSDI	DC	DC	PSI	PSDI	PSI	DC	DC	DC	—	—	—
30	Rumor V	PSDI	DC	DC	PSI	PSDI	DC	DC	DC	DC	—	—	—
31	Moro II	DC	DC	DC	DC	DC	DC	DC	DC	DC	PRI	—	—
34	Andreotti IV	PSDI	DC	PSDI	DC	DC	PSDI	DC	DC	PSDI	DC	—	—
35	Cossiga	PSDI	DC	DC	DC	DC	DC	DC	PLI	DC	PSDI	—	—
36	Cossiga II	PSI	DC	DC	DC	PSI	DC	PSI	PSI	DC	PRI	—	—
37	Forlani	PSI	PSDI	DC	DC	PSI	PRI	PSI	PSI	DC	PRI	—	—
38	Spadolini I	PSI	DC	DC	PSDI	PSI	DC	PSI	PLI	DC	DC	—	—
39	Fanfani V	PSI	DC	DC	DC	PSI	PSDI	PSI	PLI	DC	DC	—	—
40	Craxi	PSI	DC	PLI	PSI	PSI	DC	DC	DC	PSI	DC	—	—
42	Goria	DC	PRI	PRI	PSI	PSI	DC	DC	DC	PSI	PSDI	PSI	—
43	De Mita	DC	PRI	PRI	PSI	PSI	DC	DC	DC	PSI	PSDI	PSI	—
44	Andreotti V	DC	PRI	PRI	DC	PSI	PSDI	DC	PLI	PSI	PSDI	PSI	PSI
45	Andreotti VI	DC	PSDI	DC	DC	DC	PSDI	DC	PLI	PSI	DC	PSI	PSI
46	Amato	DC	PSDI	DC	DC	DC	—	DC	PLI	PSI	TEC	PSI	DC
47	Ciampi	PLI	PSDI	TEC	PSI	TEC	—	—	DC	—	TEC	PSI	TEC
48	Berlusconi	AN	AN	LN	CCD	FI	—	—	FI	—	AN	AN	FI
50	Prodi	PDS	PPI	PDS	RI	RI	—	—	PPI	—	PDS	GR	PDS
51	D'Alema	RI	UDR	DS	DS	DS	—	—	PPI	—	DS	GR	PPI

TABLE 12.6a. *cont.*

Abbreviations used in the Tables 12.6a, 12.6b, and 12.6c.

Ministries

PM	Prime Minister	SCH	Education	MAR	Mercantile marine
FOR	Foreign Affairs	PUB	Public works	PAR	State participation
INN	Interior Affairs	AGR	Agriculture	HEA	Health
JUS	Justice	TRA	Transports	TUR	Tourism
BUD	Budget[a]	PT	Communications	CUL	Culture
FIN	Finance[a]	IND	Industry	ENV	Environment
ECO	Treasury[a]	WOR	Labour	UNI	University and Research
DEF	Defence	EXT	Foreign Trade		

Parties

AN	National Alliance	PCI	Communist Party
CCD	Christian Democratic Centre	PdA	Action Party (left liberal)
CDU	Unified Christian Democrats	PdCI	Party of the Italian Communists
DC	Christian Democracy	PdL	Work Party (Reformed Socialists)
DS	Left Democrats (after 1998)	PDS	Democratic Party of the Left (1991–8)
FI	Forza Italia	PLI	Liberal Party
GR	Greens	PPI	Italian Popular Party
LN	Northern League	PRI	Republican Party
		PSDI	Social Democratic Party (1968–70)
		PSU	Unified Socialist Party
		PSI	Socialist Party (1948–51)
		PSIUP	Unified Proletarian Socialist Party (original Socialists)
		PSLI	Social Democrats (1948–51)
		RI	Italian Renewal
		SDI	Italian Social Democrats
		UDR	Democratic Union for the Republic

Other

TEC   Technicians

[a] The Minister of Budget (*Bilancio*) usually takes care of the expenditures. The Minister of Finance looks after the taxation system, while the Minister of the Treasury is in charge of the preparation of financial policy in general and, in the end, is the leading actor in the budgetary process.

TABLE 12.6b. *Distribution and number of cabinet ministerships (without portfolio) in Italian coalitions, 1945–1999* (at the beginning of the cabinet)

Cabinet number	Cabinet	Number of ministers without portfolio	(1) South	(2) Public administration	(3) Parliamentary	(4) Sport	(5) Scientific research	(6) Special office	(7) Regions
1	Parri	0	—	—	—	—	—	—	—
2	De Gasperi I	1	—	—	TEC	—	—	—	—
3	De Gasperi II	0	—	—	—	—	—	—	—
4	De Gasperi III	0	—	—	—	—	—	—	—
5	De Gasperi IV	1	—	—	DC	—	—	—	—
6	De Gasperi V	2	—	PSDI	PLI	—	—	—	—
7	De Gasperi VI	3	DC	PRI	DC	—	—	—	—
8	De Gasperi VII	1	—	PRI	—	—	—	—	—
12	Scelba	4	DC	DC	PLI	DC	—	—	—
13	Segni I	3	DC	DC	PLI	—	—	—	—
15	Fanfani II	3	DC	DC	DC	—	—	—	—
19	Fanfani IV	4	DC	DC	DC	—	DC	—	—
21	Moro I	5	DC	PSI	DC	—	DC	DC	—
22	Leone II	4	DC	DC	DC	—	—	DC	—
23	Rumor I	6	DC	DC	DC	DC	PSI	DC	—
24	Rumor II	5	DC	DC	DC	DC	—	DC	—
25	Rumor III	6	DC	DC	DC	—	PSI	DC	DC
26	Colombo	6	DC	DC	DC	—	PSI	PSDI	DC
28	Andreotti II	6	DC	DC	PLI	—	PSDI	—	PSDI
29	Rumor IV	9	DC	DC	DC	—	PRI	PSDI	DC
30	Rumor V	6	PSI	DC	DC	—	—	PSDI	—
31	Moro II	4	—	DC	—	—	—	DC	—
34	Andreotti IV	1	PRI	PSDI	—	—	—	—	—
35	Cossiga I	4	PSDI	TEC	DC	—	DC	—	—
36	Cossiga II	7	PSI	TEC	DC	—	PSI	DC	DC
37	Forlani	6	PSI	DC	DC	—	PSDI	—	DC
38	Spadolini I	7	PSI	PSDI	DC	—	DC	—	PSI
39	Fanfani V	7	PSI	PSDI	DC	—	PSDI	—	PSI
40	Craxi	8	DC	DC	PRI	—	DC	—	PSDI
41	Fanfani VI	4	DC	TEC	TEC	—	DC	—	—
42	Goria	8	—	DC	DC	—	PSI	DC	PRI
43	De Mita	9	DC	DC	DC	—	PSI	DC	PRI
44	Andreotti V	8	DC	DC	PLI	—	—	DC	PRI
45	Andreotti VI	9	DC	DC	PLI	—	—	DC	DC
46	Amato	3	—	—	—	—	—	DC	—
47	Ciampi	4	—	TEC	TEC	—	—	TEC	—
48	Berlusconi	6	—	LN	TEC	—	—	—	FI
49	Dini	0	—	—	—	—	—	—	—
50	Prodi	3	—	—	—	—	—	—	PDS
51	D'Alema	6	—	SDI	UDR	—	—	—	PdCI

TABLE 12.6b. cont.

Cabinet number	Cabinet	(8) Youth	(9) Environment	(10) Culture	(11) European Affairs	(12) Civil protection	(13) Urban areas	(14) Immigration	(15) Social affairs	(16) Women
1–27		No ministers without portfolio in these areas.								
28	Andreotti II	DC	—	—	—	—	—	—	—	—
29	Rumor IV	DC	PSI	PSI	—	—	—	—	—	—
30	Rumor V	DC	PSDI	—	—	—	—	—	—	—
31	Moro II	DC	PRI	—	—	—	—	—	—	—
34–35		No ministers without portfolio in these areas.								
36	Cossiga II	—	—	—	DC	—	—	—	—	—
37	Forlani	—	—	—	DC	—	—	—	—	—
38	Spadolini I	—	—	—	DC	DC	—	—	—	—
39	Fanfani V	—	—	—	PLI	PSI	—	—	—	—
40	Craxi	—	PLI	—	PSI	DC	—	—	—	—
41	Fanfani VI	—	—	—	—	—	—	—	—	—
42	Goria	—	—	—	TEC	DC	PSI	—	—	—
43	De Mita	—	—	—	TEC	DC	PSI	—	—	—
44	Andreotti V	—	—	—	PSDI	DC	PSI	—	—	—
45	Andreotti VI	—	—	—	PSDI	PSI	PSI	PSI	—	—
46	Amato	—	—	—	—	PSDI	PSI	—	—	—
47	Ciampi	—	—	—	TEC	—	—	—	—	—
48	Berlusconi	—	—	—	LN	—	—	TEC	FI	—
49	Dini	—	—	—	—	—	—	—	—	—
50	Prodi	—	—	—	—	—	—	PDS	PDS	—
51	D'Alema	—	—	—	PPI	—	—	—	DS	GRE

COALITION TERMINATION

Cabinet termination has been a common occurrence in Italy. Only one cabinet (Moro I) has lasted for more than three years, and even this achievement is in some sense an artefact of our counting rules (the Moro I of this book is counted by Italian standards as three different cabinets). Mean cabinet duration is less than one year, even under our permissive counting rules. The causes and events associated with cabinet termination vary across 'termination types': from cabinet terminations that close a coalitional period, to those that help inaugurate a new coalitional formula, to those that simply reflect the renegotiation of limited aspects of a coalition. In a word, the termination of a cabinet is a political tool that can be used with very different aims by different coalitional actors.

Constitutional lawyers generally differentiate between government crises on procedural grounds; in particular whether they resulted from a parliamentary vote of no confidence or if the cabinet resigned without such a vote. Most Italian crises have been of the second type ('extra-parliamentary crises') (Carducci 1989; Ruggeri 1990). Behavioural explanations of cabinet crises are however much more complicated. Quite often crises involve both party and sub-party actors, and sometimes, formally or informally, the head of state or

Italy   471

TABLE 12.6c. *Distribution of junior ministerships in Italian coalitions, 1945–1999 (at the beginning of the cabinet)*

Cabinet number	Cabinet	(1) PM	(2) FOR	(3) INN	(4) JUS	(5) BUD	(6) FIN	(7) ECO	(8) DEF	(9) SCH	(10) PUB	(11) AGR
1	Parri	PLI PCI	PCI PLI	DC	PdL	PdL	PdL	—	PdA	DC TEC	PdA	DC
2	De Gasperi I	PLI PCI	PCI PLI	DC	PdL	PdA	PdA	—	DC	DC	DC PdL	DC
3	De Gasperi II	—	PCI PSI	PSI	DC	DC	DC PCI	—	DC	PRI	DC	—
4	De Gasperi III	PCI	DC PSI	PSI	DC	—	PCI DC	—	DC DC PCI PSI	PSI	—	PCI
5	De Gasperi IV	—	DC DC DC	—	—	—	DC DC PLI	—	—	—	PSLI PRI	PSLI PSDI
6	De Gasperi V	—	DC DC	—	DC	—	DC DC	PSDI	DC	PLI PLI	PSLI PRI	PSDI
7	De Gasperi VI	—	DC DC	—	—	—	DC DC	PSDI	DCDC	PSDI	PRI	PSDI
8	De Gasperi VII	—	—	—	—	—	DC DC	—	PRI PSDI	—	PRI DC	—
12	Scelba	—	PLI	—	—	—	DC PLI	—	PSDI	DC DC DC	DC	PLI
13	Segni I	—	DC DC	—	—	—	DC DC	PSDI	PSDI	DC	DC	PLI
15	Fanfani II	PSDI	—	—	—	—	DC	—	—	—	PSDI	PSDI
19	Fanfani IV	—	PSDI PSI DC	PSDI PSI PSDI	— DC	PSDI DC	DC PSI DC DC	DC PSI	— —	— PSI	PSDI PSDI DC	PRI PRI PSI
21	Moro I	—										
23	Rumor I	PSI PSI PSI	DC DC	PSI	PSI	DC DC	DC DC DC DC	PSI	PSII	PRI PSI	DC	PSI

TABLE 12.6c. cont.

Cabinet number	Cabinet	(1) PM	(2) FOR	(3) INN	(4) JUS	(5) BUD	(6) FIN	(7) ECO	(8) DEF	(9) SCH	(10) PUB	(11) AGR
25	Rumor III	PSI PSI	PSDI	PSI PSDI	PSI DC	DC	DC DC PSI	PSI PSDI	DC	PRI PSI PSDI	DC	PSDI PSI
26	Colombo	PSI PSDI	PSDI	PSI PSDI	PSI	DC	DC DC PSI	PSI	PSI	PRI PSI PSDI	DC DC	PSDI PSI
28	Andreotti II	—	DC DC	PLI PSDI	PLI	—	PLI PSDI DC DC	DC DC DC PSDI	DC DC DC	PSDI PLI	PSDI	PLI PSDI
29	Rumor IV	PRI PSI	PSI	PSI PSDI	DC	DC	DC DC PSDI PSI	DC DC DC PSDI PSI	PSI DC DC	PSDI PSI	PSDI	PSDI PRI PSI
30	Rumor V	—	PSI	PSI PSDI	DC	DC	PSDI PSI DC	PSDI PSI PSDI	PSI	PSDI PSI	DC PSDI	PSI
31	Moro II	PRI	PRI	—	DC	DC	DC DC DC	—	—	—	DC	—
34	Andreotti IV	—	PRI	PSDI	—	—	DC DC PSDI	PRI	PSDI	DC DC DC	DC DC	—
35	Cossiga	PSDI	— PLI	— —	— PLI	— —	PSDI DC PSDI	— PLI	— PSDI	—	— DC DC	— —
36	Cossiga II	PSI	PSI PRI	PSI	IND	DC	DC DC PSI	PSI PRI	DC DC PRI	PSI	DC DC PSI	PSI

#	Government	1	2	3	4	5	6	7	8	9	10	11
37	Forlani	—	PSI / PSDI / PRI	PSI	IND	DC	PSI / PSDI / DC	PSI / PRI	PRI / DC / PSDI	PSI	DC / PSI	PSI / PSDI
38	Spadolini I	DC / DC	PSI / PSDI / PLI	IND	PSI	DC	DC / DC / PSI / PSDI	PRI	DC / DC / PSDI	PSI / PLI	DC / PSI	PSI
39	Fanfani V	—	PSI / PSDI / PLI	IND	PSI	—	PSI / PSDI / DC / DC / PSDI	PSI	DC / DC / PSDI	PSI / PLI	PSI / DC	PSI
40	Craxi I	DC	PRI / PSDI / PSI / PSI	PSI / PRI	PSI / PSDI	DC	PSI / PSDI / DC / DC / DC	PSI / PRI	PRI / PSI	PLI / PSI	DC / PRI	PSI
42	Goria	—	PSI / PSDI / PSI / PSI	PLI / PSI	PSI	PSI	PSI / DC / DC / DC / PSI / PLI	—	PSI / PSDI	PSI / PLI	DC / DC / PLI	PSI
43	De Mita	PRI	PRI / PSDI / PSI	PSI / PLI	DC / DC	PSI	PSI / DC / DC / PSI / PSI / PLI	PSI	PSI / PRI	PSI / PLI	DC / DC / PLI	PSI
44	Andreotti V	PSI / PRI	PRI / DC	PLI / PSI	DC / DC	—	DC / DC / DC / DC / DC / PLI	PSI	PSI / PRI / PLI	PSI / PLI	PSI / PRI	PSI / PSDI
45	Andreotti VI	PSI	DC / DC / DC	PSI / PLI	DC / DC	PSI	DC / PSI / PSDI / PLI / DC / DC	PSI	PSI / PRI / PLI / PSDI / PLI	PSI / PLI	PSI / PSI	PSI / PSDI

474 Luca Verzichelli and Maurizio Cotta

TABLE 12.6c. cont.

Cabinet number	Cabinet	(1) PM	(2) FOR	(3) INN	(4) JUS	(5) BUD	(6) FIN	(7) ECO	(8) DEF	(9) SCH	(10) PUB	(11) AGR
46	Amato	—	PSI	PLI PSI	DC DC	DC DC	DC PSDI PLI	PSI PSDI	DC PSDI	PLI	PSI	PSI
47	Ciampi	TEC	PSI	PSI PLI	—	DC DC	DC PSDI PLI	PSI PSDI	DC DC	PSI	PSI	PSI
48	Berlusconi	CCD	LN AN	FI FI AN	LN AN	FI AN	LN FI AN	LN FI CCD AN	AN LN	AN LN	LN AN	FI
50	Prodi	TEC TEC PPI PDS	PDS PDS PPI	PPI PPI	PPI GR PDS	PDS PDS	RIN PDS	TEC PDS PPI	RIN PDS	GR PPI	GR PDS	PDS
51	D'Alema	PPI	UDR DS DS	UDR DS SDI DS	DS GRE UDR RI	—	UDR DS	RI PPIR TEC UD	DS RI PPI PdCI	UDR GRE PPI	DS GRE UDR	DS PPI

Cabinet number	Cabinet	(12) TRA	(13) PT	(14) IND	(15) WOR	(16) EXT	(17) MAR	(18) PAR	(19) HEA	(20) HEA	(21) TUR	(22) CUL	(23) ENV	(24) UNI
1	Parri	PCI	TEC	PLI	DC	—	—	—	—	—	—	—	—	—
2	De Gasperi I	PCI	TEC	PLI PdL	DC	—	—	—	—	—	—	—	—	—
3	De Gasperi II	DC	PCI	DC PCI	DC	PRI	PCI	—	—	—	—	—	—	—
4	De Gasperi III	DC	DC	DC	DC	PCI	PSI	—	—	—	—	—	—	—
5	De Gasperi IV	DC	PRI	—	PRI	TEC	PSLI	—	—	—	—	—	—	—

Italy

6	De Gasperi V	DC	—	—	DC	—	—	—	—	—	—	—
7	De Gasperi VI	DC	—	PSDI	DC	PRI	—	—	—	—	—	—
8	De Gasperi VII	—	—	—	DC	DC	—	—	—	—	—	—
12	Scelba	PSDI	—	—	PSDI	DC	PLI	—	—	—	—	—
							PSDI					
13	Segni I	PSDI	—	—	PSDI	PSDI	—	—	—	—	—	—
15	Fanfani II	PSDI	DC	—	—	—	—	DC	—	—	—	—
18	Fanfani III	DC	DC	—	DC	DC	DC	DC	DC	DC	DC	—
		DC	DC		DC				DC	DC	DC	
19	Fanfani IV	PSDI	—	—	DC	DC	DC	—	—	—	—	—
21	Moro I	PSI	PSI	PSI	—	—	—	—	DC	DC	DC	—
				PSDI								
23	Rumor I	DC	PSI	DC	PSI	DC	DC	PSI	PSI	PSI	PSI	—
		PRI		DC		DC						
25	Rumor III	—	PSDI	PSI	PRI	PSI	PSI	PSI	PSI	PSI	PSI	—
			PSI									
26	Colombo	DC	PSDI	—	PSDI	DC	DC	—	PSI	PSI	PSI	—
		DC	PSI		PSI		DC					
			PRI									
28	Andreotti II	PSDI	PSDI	PSDI	DC	DC	DC	PSDI	PLI	PSDI	PSDI	—
		DC			DC				DC			
		DC			PLI							
29	Rumor IV	PSI	PSDI	DC	PSDI	PSI	PSI	PSI	PSI	PSI	PSI	—
		DC	PSI	DC	PSI	DC			DC			
				DC								
30	Rumor V	DC	PSDI	PSDI	PSDI	PSI	PSI	PSI	—	PSI	—	—
			PSI	PSDI	PSI	DC						
				DC								
				DC								

476 *Luca Verzichelli and Maurizio Cotta*

TABLE 12.6c. *Continued*

Cabinet number	Cabinet	(12) TRA	(13) PT	(14) IND	(15) WOR	(16) EXT	(17) MAR	(18) PAR	(20) HEA	(21) TUR	(22) CUL	(23) ENV	(24) UNI
31	Moro II	—	—	—	—	—	—	PRI	PRI	—	DC	—	—
34	Andreotti IV	DC	—	DC	PSDI	PRI	—	PRI PSDI	PSDI	DC	—	—	—
35	Cossiga I	DC DC DC	PSDI	DC PSDI	PSDI	—	—	PSDI	DC DC	—	DC	—	—
36	Cossiga II	DCI PR	PSI PRI	PSI	DC PSI	DC	PSI	DC	DC	PSI	DC	—	—
37	Forlani	PSDI DC	PSI PRI DC	PSDI PSI	PSI	DC	PSI DC	DC	DC	PSI	DC	—	—
38	Spadolini I	PSDI DC	PRI PSI	PSI	DC DC DC PSI	DC	PSI	DC DC	DC PSI	PSI	—	—	—
39	Fanfani V	DC	PSI	PSI	DC DC PSI	DC	PSI DC PSDI	DC DC PSI	DC PSI PLI	PSI	PSDI	—	—
40	Craxi	DC DC PLI	PRI PSI	DC DC PSI DC	DC DC PSDI DC DC	DC DC	—	—	—	DC	PRI	—	—
41	Fanfani VI	DC	—	DC	—	DC	—	—	—	DC	—	DC	—
42	Goria	PSI PSDI	DC DC PSI	DC DC DC PSI	DC DC PSDI	DC PRI	PSI	PSI	PSI	DC	DC	DC	—
43	De Mita	PSDI PSI	DC DC PSI	DC PSI DC DC	DC DC PSDI	PRI DC	PSI	PSI	PSI	DC	DC	DC	—

Italy 477

44	Andreotti V	PSI	DC DC PSI	DC DC DC PSI	PSI PSDI	DC DC	—	DC PSI	DC PSI PSDI	DC	DC	DC DC
45	Andreotti VI	PSI	DC DC PSI	DC DC PSI	PSI PSDI	—	—	DC PSI	DC PSI PSDI	PSI	DC	DC DC
46	Amato	—	DC DC PSI	DC PSI	PSI	—	—	—	DC	—	DC	PSI
47	Ciampi	PSI PSDI	DC DC	DC	DC PSI	DC PSI	—	—	PSI	AN	DC	DC
48	Berlusconi	LN FI	LN	FI AN	FI AN	—	—	—	AN	—	FI	LN
49	Dini	TEC TEC	TEC TEC	TEC TEC	TEC TEC	TEC	—	PPI	TEC	TEC	TEC	TEC
50	Prodi	PPI UDR DS	PDS DS PPI	—	PDS PdCI RI PPI	PPI	—	—	PDS DS RI	—	—	PDS DS PdCI
52	D'Alema											

other institutional actors. The actors who initiate the crisis may intend to leave the coalition or simply to change their role inside it. Cabinet crises have most commonly been initiated when a party has threatened to leave the cabinet. On many occasions, this has led directly to the resignation of the prime minister, or, more rarely, to a parliamentary vote of confidence. Very rarely has one of the coalition parties explicitly requested a confidence vote, though parliamentary actors may occasionally wish to have a highly publicized debate in parliament.[21] The prime minister can use different strategies (immediate acceptance of the crisis or attempts to resist and request a formal confidence vote in parliament) to enhance his chances of heading the next cabinet.

A general overview of cabinet termination shows the importance of 'non-technical' causes. Even prior to 1968, when every parliament completed its regular term, the instability of the centrist and centre-left coalitions produced cabinets with different life expectancies during every parliamentary term. This had very much to do with the phase of the coalition formula, whether it was that of the preparation, consolidation, or crisis of that coalition. Intra-party conflicts often terminated transitional single-party cabinets during this period, and there was a strong relationship between the duration of the crisis and coalition stability (Battegazzorre 1987).

The history of cabinet termination during the long cycle of the First Republic can be subdivided into two periods: the first extending from the end of the anti-Fascist coalition (1947) to the end of the first 'centre-left' phase (1974–6), and the second from the mid-1970s to 1992 (Table 12.7). During the first period constitutional and 'technical' causes of termination had greater importance since four legislatures reached their natural end. However, three cabinets coded here as having resigned because of regular elections (Zoli in 1958, Fanfani in 1962, and Moro in 1968), had in fact lost their parliamentary support some time before the election and been 'invited' by the head of state to stay in office until the new parliament would be in place. In the end most cabinets were pushed to resign because of a parliamentary crisis (loosely defined) following a government defeat in the legislature. During this period the behaviour of the smaller coalition parties (Liberals, Republicans, and Social Democrats during 'centrism'; Socialist, Republicans, and Social Democrats during the 'centre-left') was relatively coherent and predictable, particularly during the early and stable years of the centre-left (1964–8). Throughout this period, and especially during the 1950s conflicts within the predominant government party (the DC) over policies or simply (and more commonly, perhaps) over portfolio allocation, were one of the most

[21] The parliamentary debate has always been a crucial moment in coalition crises. In many cases, the PM has attempted to solve the crisis before it would come to a confidence vote either by proposing some government reshuffle (the so-called *rimpasto*) or by announcing his willingness to continue even if a minor party would leave the coalition. In some cases (Zoli, Cossiga, and, recently, Dini), the PM preferred to present his resignation to the president before a formal vote of no confidence took place.

TABLE 12.7. *Cabinet termination in Italy, 1945–1999*

Cabinet number	Cabinet	Mechanisms of cabinet termination							Terminal events					Policy area(s)	Comments
		Technical				Discretionary			Conflict between coalition parties		(8) Intra-party conflict in coalition party or parties	(9) Elections non-parliamentary	(10) Popular opinion shocks	(11) International or national security events	(13) Personal events		
		(1) Regular parliamentary election	(2)	(3)	(4) Early parliamentary election	(5) Voluntary enlargement of government	(6) Cabinet defeated by opposition in parliament	(7) Policy	Personnel							
1	Parri									PdA,L						Split in the party of the prime minister
2	De Gasperi I									PSI,L						Crisis determined by the split inside PSI
3	De Gasperi II							DC, PSI		PSI,L					1, 12	Policy conflicts on agrarian reform
4	De Gasperi III							DC, PSI	DC,PSI PCI						1, 12	Voluntary resignation to accelerate the exclusion of the left parties
5	De Gasperi IV	X														
6	De Gasperi V					X				PSDI, L						During the life of the cabinet the PSLI decided to leave the coalition. The cabinet resigned voluntarily to recuperate the coalition partner
7	De Gasperi VI							DC, PSDI		PSDI,L					8	Again troubles inside PSDI and conflicts with the largest coalition party about social reforms
8	De Gasperi VII	X														

TABLE 12.7. *cont.*

Cabinet number	Cabinet	Mechanisms of cabinet termination							Terminal events					Policy area(s)	Comments
		Technical		Discretionary											
		(1) Regular parliamentary election	(4) Early parliamentary election	(5) Voluntary enlargement of government	(6) Cabinet defeated by opposition in parliament	(7) Conflict between coalition parties Policy	(7) Personnel	(8) Intraparty conflict in coalition party or parties	(9) Elections nonparliamentary	(10) Popular opinion shocks	(11) International or national security events	(13) Personal events			
9	De Gasperi VIII				X									8	The cabinet did not pass the investiture vote (lower chamber)
10	Pella							DC,L							Resignation after a negative negotiation with the parliamentary groups of the DC. The cabinet did not pass the investiture vote (lower chamber)
11	Fanfani I				X										
12	Scelba				X	DC, PLI		DC,L						1, 8	Again troubles among the DC factions, and conflicts about economic policy (with PLI)
13	Segni I				X			DC,L						12	Conflict between the government and the PRI and PSDI over agrarian reform
14	Zoli	(X)						DC,L							The minority cabinet keeps on to the end of Legislature, but it formally resigns before (because of internal conflicts inside DC)

15	Fanfani II		DC,PRI	PSDI,L	Split in the PSDI and personal conflicts between Fanfani and the PRI leaders
16	Segni II	X			7,1 The PLI withdraws its external support mainly because of different opinions about economic policy
17	Tambroni			DC,L	The MSI's support for the cabinet caused social tensions and conflicts inside the DC (three ministers resigned)
18	Fanfani III	X			*Convergenza democratica* cabinet, before the DC congress which decided the enlargement of the coalition to include the PSI
19	Fanfani IV	X			
20	Leone I	X		DC,L	*Bridge cabinet* to take time before a fully-fledged centre-left coalition
21	Moro I	X	X	DC,L	Mechanism: Defeat in parliament (over a decree about the private schools). This was also a pause for the coalition required because of intra-party conflicts (DC) and even the need of a renegotiation after the local electoral test (Sicily)

TABLE 12.7. cont.

Cabinet number	Cabinet	Mechanisms of cabinet termination								Terminal events				Policy area(s)	Comments
		Technical		Discretionary											
		(1) Regular parliamentary election	(4) Early parliamentary election	(5) Voluntary enlargement of government	(6) Cabinet defeated by opposition in parliament	(7) Conflict between coalition parties Policy	(7) Personnel	(8) Intra-party conflict in coalition party or parties	(9) Elections non-parliamentary	(10) Popular opinion shocks	(11) International or national security events	(13) Personal events			
22	Leone II			X											Transitory cabinet to re-negotiate the coalition
23	Rumor I					PSI,PSDI	DC,L								Problems among DC factions all along the cabinet's duration. The cause of termination was the resignment of three minister from PSDI after the new split
24	Rumor II				X										Tension between the DC and the secular parties (especially the PSI) over the divorce issue did not allow the cabinet to face parliament
25	Rumor III							DC,L PSI,L	X						Impact of local election results and formation of local coalitions between the PCI and PSI
26	Colombo					DC,PRI								7, 8	Conflict between PRI and DC on economic policy

27	Andreotti I	X								The cabinet did not pass the investiture vote (Senate). This event caused early elections
28	Andreotti II			DC, PRI		DC,L			14	
29	Rumor IV			PSI, PRI	PSI,PRI				6, 8	Personal conflict between two ministers who were supported by their respective parties
30	Rumor V			PSI, PSDI	DC,PSI, PSDI				1, 6	One party (PSDI) asked for the end of the coalition with a number of policy criticism. Personal conflicts were also visible
31	Moro II			DC, PSI			X		6, 8	Victory of the left in the local elections (1975). Formal mechanism: The PSI withdrew its external support, criticizing the economic policy of cabinet
32	Moro III	X		DC, PSI				X	6, 8, 1	Again troubles over economic policy; effects of the final battle on divorce (the 1974 referendum), plus the effect of the Loockeed Scandal caused early elections
33	Andreotti IIIa		(X)			DC,L				In one sense it was a voluntary enlargement (from the abstention to the external support of the PCI). On this point the DC was divided what was also the reason of the crisis

TABLE 12.7. cont.

Cabinet number	Cabinet	Mechanisms of cabinet termination						Conflict between coalition parties		(8) Intra-party conflict in coalition party or parties	Terminal events				Policy area(s)	Comments
		Technical Discretionary														
		(1) Regular parliamentary election	(2)	(3)	(4) Early parliamentary election	(5) Voluntary enlargement of government	(6) Cabinet defeated by opposition in parliament	(7) Policy	Personnel		(9) Elections non-parliamentary	(10) Popular opinion shocks	(11) International or national security events	(13) Personal events		
	Andreotti IIIb*						X								1, 7, 8	The support of the PCI remained safe only during the terrorist emergency. Among the new policy divisions the most important was the question of the entrance in the European Monetary System
34	Andreotti IV				X					DC,L						The cabinet did not pass investiture vote (Senate)
35	Cossiga					X				DC,L						Prime minister resignation without parliamentary vote and immediate reappointment, in order to include the PSI in the coalition after the intra-party agreements within the DC (new secretary) and the PSI (now ready to return to government)

Italy

#	Cabinet								Description
36	Cossiga II	X	DC, PSI, PRI					6, 7, 8	Parliamentary cabinet defeat (lower chamber) on the economic decree. But signs of dissension even before that
37	Forlani				DC,PSI	X			Mechanism: The PSI leaders did not attend a crisis summit of the party leaders, what was perceived by the prime minister as their willingness to terminate the cabinet. But the effect of the abortion battle (referendum lost by Catholics) and the involvement of some ministers in the P2 scandal determined the crisis
38	Spadolini I		DC, PSI,PRI		DC,PSI			6, 7	Retirement of PSI ministers after the defeat of a decree signed by a PSI minister. Personal conflicts among ministers and more complicated games about micro budgeting
39 40	Fanfani V Craxi I	X	PRI, PSI	X	DC,PSI			1, 9	Technical reason: defeat of cabinet on its decree about local finance. Before that a policy conflict in foreign policy (Sigonella affair) and the beginning of the personal duel between Mr Craxi and the DC secretary

TABLE 12.7. cont.

Cabinet number	Cabinet	Mechanisms of cabinet termination								Terminal events				Policy area(s)	Comments
		Technical		Discretionary											
		(1) Regular parliamentary election	(4) Early parliamentary election	(5) Voluntary enlargement of government	(6) Cabinet defeated by opposition in parliament	(7) Conflict between coalition parties Policy	Personnel	(8) Intra-party conflict in coalition party or parties	(9) Elections non-parliamentary	(10) Popular opinion shocks	(11) International or national security events	(13) Personal events			
41	Fanfani VI		X				DC,PSI								The cabinet did not pass investiture vote (lower chamber)
42	Goria				X	DC, PSI								1, 8	Defeat of the financial bill (already delayed out of the financial year). A number of criticisms about different policies between the DC and PSI
43	De Mita						PSI,DC								Extra-parliamentary crisis determined at the end of the PSI congress
44	Andreotti V					DC,PRI, PSI	DC,L								First reason of crisis: conflict within the DC about the TV regulation. After the replacement of some ministers a number of personal conflicts among parties and ministers
45	Andreotti VI	X													

Italy 487

46	Amato	PSI, DC, PSDI, PLI	X	Mechanism: voluntary resignment of the prime minister after the results of referenda (which meant, impossibility to put a majority together on different issues). But a real cause is also the dramatic decline in legitimacy of the political class (*mani pulite* etc.)
47	Ciampi		X	*Governo a termine*: cabinet formed only to produce the electoral and economic reform before a new early election
48	Berlusconi	AN,FI FI,LN		The conflict was mainly personal (between the leader of Northern League, who withdrew his party's ministers from cabinet) and Mr Berlusconi. There was also a conflict between LN and AN about the federal reform
49	Dini		X	Temporary cabinet to complete some reforms before the early elections
50	Prodi	PDS-RC	X	After the decision of PRC to revoke the support to the cabinet, the prime minister asks a confidence vote which fails for one vote

important sources of cabinet instability. Inter-party and intra-party (within the DC) conflicts were particularly intense during the preparation of the centre-left coalition, the so-called 'opening to the left'. Strong policy conflicts existed between the DC and the PLI, a former governing party which refused the new alliance with the PSI, but also inside the Christian Democratic Party.

After 1972 the scenario of government termination had clearly changed: no legislature was able to reach its regular end and early elections were always called.[22] Inter-party conflicts dominated. Inside the coalition both policy and pure personnel conflicts were always present, but generally personal battles among ministers of different parties and/or among party leaders increased compared to the past. Especially during the 1980s a frequent consequence of such conflicts was that one of the coalitional partners would ask for a reassessment (*verifica*) of the state of the coalition (generally using a majority summit for this purpose) in order to defend the actions of its ministers and to discuss or attempt to discipline its coalition partners. This was, most of the time, the first step towards a cabinet crisis.

We have coded most of these terminations as caused by a 'personnel conflict', though most cases were not purely about personalities. Rather, the real issue has typically been the allocation of executive power between the leading groups of each coalition party. Most 'five-party coalition' cabinets during the 1980s were forced to resign because of a struggle between party leaders which had much less to do with substantive policy issues than with competition for supremacy within the coalition, or with contrasting interpretations of the agreement by which the DC and the PSI would hold the prime ministership alternately (the so-called *patto della staffetta*). Thus, personnel conflicts (often instrumentally interwoven with policy conflicts or with a symbolic issue, such as a vague call for reform) have been, in the last twenty years, the typical cause of cabinet termination and the most significant constraint on the five-party coalition. These include personal battles between ministers (for example in the two crises under Spadolini, coded here as one cabinet) or the much more publicized struggles between party leaders, such as the De Mita–Craxi duel in the mid-1980s. This conflict directly or indirectly affected the termination of at least five cabinets: two Craxi cabinets (here coded together), the Fanfani cabinet in 1987, Goria (1987), and De Mita (1988).

---

[22] We have coded the termination of the Andreotti VI cabinet (1992) as due to an 'early parliamentary election'. While it is true that the parliament had only two months left in its term and the government had not lost its majority, the early parliamentary election was due to the polemical resignation of the head of state, President Cossiga. The termination of this cabinet was clearly caused by Cossiga's resignation, which was a political act designed to bring about a governmental crisis, and not by the end of the legislature. The decision by parties and parliament when to call the early election was a technical one intended to leave time for the complex procedure of electing a new president of the Republic. But, since the early elections were not caused by the lack of a parliamentary majority, we do not consider this as a discretionary cause of cabinet termination.

In sum, the Italian experience with cabinet termination suggests two different points. First, cabinet crises have been used assiduously as a tool for solving different coalitional problems. For example, while some DC leaders have been considered at a given moment the 'natural' prime ministerial candidates for a specific type of coalition,[23] others could lead temporary cabinets in order to win time and overcome inter-party and intra-party conflicts. During each coalition cycle, situations have occurred in which party strategies for preserving the existing coalitional formula or promoting new ones could conflict with the personal strategy of the incumbent prime minister or of other potential government leaders.[24]

Second, cabinet termination has resulted both from intra-party conflict and from external events. Most of the terminations here coded as 'intra-party conflicts' followed splits inside one of the coalitional parties or at least important changes in internal leadership. The most important type of external event has surely been 'mid-term' local elections. It is obviously quite difficult to compare the importance of such different causes, but there are good reasons to think that the effects of troubles not directly related to the previous coalitional platform could be greater than in other countries. Among the latter there are, for instance, changes in the leadership of just one of the coalition parties, which in turn may lead to new conflicts between the parties, or purely personal conflicts. The abundant and fragmented set of coalitional actors (parties, factions, and individual leaders) could find many incentives to utilize cabinet crises to improve their bargaining positions.

In recent decades the impact of those external and intra-party events has had less to do with the equilibrium inside the largest coalition party (DC) and much more with the 'inter-party' balance. The decline of the 'predominant party' and the increasing weight of its coalitional partners also explain the greater need for collegiality that seems to have characterized this period: as many as nineteen majority summits have since 1970 been called to discuss the possibility of cabinet termination, and most of those meetings in fact determined the effective termination of an administration (Criscitiello 1996). In other words, changes in the party system during the 1980s (and in particular the enlargement of the effective set of coalitional actors) have affected the nature of cabinet crises more than their frequency.

The weakness of the prime minister, who, unlike many government heads, is unable to call new general elections, explains the rest (Ieraci 1996): despite attempts to strengthen government leadership, Italian cabinet instability

---

[23] Moro, for example, was the natural leader of the centre-left, Andreotti at first for the centre-right cabinets and later for the national solidarity coalition.

[24] This was the case of the crisis of the Andreotti IIIb cabinet, but also of a crisis not coded here, but extremely important, in 1987. The Craxi cabinet resigned because of conflicts with the DC (see above), and difficult negotiations followed. At the end, Craxi obtained a mandate for a new five-party cabinet, but only after an agreement which defined the maximum duration of the cabinet and the coalition's agenda.

remains high, and this seems to hold true even after the recent major electoral reforms. The Berlusconi cabinet, born after the 'revolutionary' election of 1994, lasted only 225 days and fell because of a typical intra-coalitional conflict. The Dini cabinet was designed to be a temporary caretaker cabinet with the tasks of producing some economic reforms and a reform of the television system before the next election, but disagreement among the parties over the timing of the election prolonged Dini's tenure and expanded the cabinet's agenda. As for the Prodi cabinet it fell at the end of an exhausting discussion with its 'external supporter', the neo-Communist Party, but also because of the lack of cohesion of the rest of the coalition. Paradoxically enough, the PM, in spite of having received a clear electoral legitimation, had suddenly to recognize his weakness in the parliamentary arena. He was, in fact, the first PM who had to leave his office because of the negative result of a confidence request. In the end, if the quasi-direct election of prime ministers resulting from the new majoritarian competition has created a new situation, two 'classic' causes of cabinet instability—party system fragmentation and institutional weakness of the executive—are still at work.

ELECTORAL PERFORMANCE

By and large, Italian elections from the late 1940s to the early 1990s showed a high degree of aggregate stability. The Christian Democrats were the largest party throughout this period, the Communists generally came in second, and there was little change in the support of any of the traditional parties from one election to the next. It is consistent with this stability that the electoral costs or benefits of governing Italy have generally been small. As Table 12.8 reveals, the mean electoral performance of Italian cabinet parties (when treated as a bloc) is a loss of 1.7 per cent of the popular vote. Only three cabinets, however, have experienced aggregate electoral shifts of greater than 10 per cent (in either direction) in the next election, and two of those cabinets had actually been terminated before the elections (those of 1953 and 1994, respectively) took place. The modest average cost of governing has been shared by most parties. Of the long-standing parties, only the Social Democrats and the Republicans have made net gains, in both cases minuscule, after they have been in office. All the other traditional parties have tended to lose, though on average only slightly. The parties on the left, and particularly the Socialists, have lost more than those on the right. In general, the tendency for government incumbency to be an electoral liability became noticeable after the opening to the left in the late 1950s. One more observation of note is that when we examine the electoral costs of governing relative to party size, the smaller parties have clearly been more susceptible than the DC.

Italy 491

TABLE 12.8. *Electoral costs/benefits of government parties in Italy* (in % of votes)

Government	In office at time of election	Election year	PCI[a]	PSI[a]	PSDI[a]	DC	PRI	LN	PLI	FI	AN	Government
DC–PCI–PSI–PRI 1946[b]	No	1948	−9.4	[+7.1]	+13.3	−1.9	—	—	—	—	+9.0	—
DC–PCI–PSI 1947	No	1948	−9.4	—	+13.3	—	—	—	—	—	+3.9	—
DC–PLI–Tec. 1947	Yes	1948	—	—	—	+13.3	—	—	+1.0	—	—	+14.3
DC–PSDI–PLI–PRI 1948	No	1953	—	—	−2.6	−8.4	−0.9	—	−0.9	—	—	−12.8
DC–PSDI–PRI 1950	No	1953	—	—	−2.6	−8.4	−0.9	—	—	—	—	−11.9
DC–PRI 1952	Yes	1953	—	—	—	−8.4	−0.9	—	—	—	—	−9.3
DC 1953	No	1958	—	—	—	+2.2	—	—	—	—	—	+2.2
DC–PSDI–PLI 1954	No	1958	—	—	+0.1	+2.2	—	—	+0.5	—	—	+2.8
DC 1957	Yes	1958	—	—	—	+2.2	—	—	—	—	—	+2.2
DC–PSDI 1958	No	1963	—	—	+1.4	−4.0	—	—	—	—	—	−2.6
DC 1959	No	1963	—	—	—	−4.0	—	—	—	—	—	−4.0
DC–PSDI–PRI 1962	Yes	1963	—	—	+1.4	−4.0	±0	—	—	—	—	−2.6
DC 1963	No	1968	—	—	—	+0.8	—	—	—	—	—	+0.8
DC–PSI–PRI–PSDI 1963	Yes	1968	—	−5.4	+0.8	+0.6	—	—	—	—	−4.0	+0.5
DC 1968	No	1972	—	—	—	+0.5	—	—	—	—	—	+0.5
DC–PSI–PRI 1968	No	1972	—	+0.2	+0.5	+0.9	—	—	—	—	+1.6	+0.5
DC 1969	No	1972	—	—	—	+0.5	—	—	—	—	—	+0.5
DC–PSI–PSDI–PRI 1970	No	1972	—	+0.2	+0.5	+0.9	—	—	—	—	+1.6	+0.5
DC 1972	Yes	1972	—	—	—	+0.5	—	—	—	—	—	+0.5
DC–PSDI–PLI 1972	No	1976	—	—	−1.7	±0	—	—	−2.6	—	—	−4.3
DC–PSDI–PRI 1973	No	1976	—	±0	−1.7	±0	+0.2	—	—	—	—	−1.5
DC–PSI–PDSI 1974	No	1976	—	±0	−1.7	±0	—	—	—	—	—	−1.7
DC–PRI 1974	No	1976	—	—	—	±0	+0.2	—	—	—	—	+0.2
DC 1976	Yes	1976	—	—	—	±0	—	—	—	—	—	±0
DC 1976	No	1979	—	—	—	−0.5	—	—	—	—	—	−0.5
DC–PSDI–PRI 1979	Yes	1979	—	—	+0.4	−0.5	−0.1	—	—	—	—	−0.2
DC–PSDI–PLI 1979	No	1983	—	—	+0.3	−5.3	—	—	+1.0	—	—	−4.0

Cont./

TABLE 12.8. cont.

Government	In office at time of election	Election year	PCI[a]	PSI[a]	PSDI[a]	DC	PRI	LN	PLI	FI	AN	Government
DC–PRI–PSI 1980	No	1983	—	+1.6	—	−5.3	+2.1	—	—	—	—	−1.6
DC–PRI–PSI–PSDI 1980	No	1983	—	+1.6	+0.3	−5.3	+2.1	—	—	—	—	−1.3
PRI–DC–PSI–PSDI–PLI 1981	No	1983	—	+1.6	+0.3	−5.3	+2.1	—	+1.0	—	—	−0.3
DC–PSI–PSDI–PLI 1982	Yes	1983	—	+1.6	+0.3	−5.3	—	—	+1.0	—	—	−2.4
PSI–DC–PRI–PSDI–PLI 1983	No	1987	—	+2.9	−1.2	+1.4	−1.4	—	−0.8	—	—	+0.9
DC 1987	Yes	1987	—	—	—	+1.4	—	—	—	—	—	+1.4
DC–PSI–PRI–PSDI–PLI 1987	No	1992	—	−0.7	−0.2	−4.6	+0.7	—	+0.7	—	—	−4.1
DC–PSI–PSDI–PLI 1991	Yes	1992	—	−0.7	−0.2	−4.6	—	—	+0.7	—	—	−4.8
PSI–DC–PSDI–PLI 1992	No	1994	—	−11.5	−2.7	−18.6	—	—	−2.8	—	—	−35.6
Tec–DC–PSI–PSDI–PLI 1993[c]	Yes	1994	—	—	—	—	—	—	—	—	—	—
FI–LN–AN–CCD 1994	No	1996	—	—	—	—	—	+1.7	—	−0.4	+2.2	+3.5
Tec. 1995	Yes	1996	—	—	—	—	—	—	—	—	—	—
MEANS			−4.7	−1.9	0.1	−1.9	0	+1.7	−0.5	−0.4	+2.2	−1.7

[a] The PCI and PSI run a common list (National Front) in the 1948 elections. The PSI and PSDI run a common list (Unified Socialists, PSU) in the 1968 elections. In calculating the means for the parties gains and losses have been equally divided between the parties of the common list.
[b] During the De Gasperi II cabinet the PSDI split from the PSI. For a few days ministers from both parties were represented in the cabinet. Given the origin of the PSDI, both the PSI and PSDI are considered as 'government parties' in 1948.
[c] We do not consider the electoral performance of the parties included in the 1993 cabinet (Ciampi) because the technical nature of the executive. The few 'political' ministers from DC, PSI, PSDI, and PLI participated as individuals rather than party representatives.

CONCLUSION

Coalition government and its problems have dominated the Italian political scene since the fall of Fascism. Even the deep transformations resulting from the crisis of the early 1990s have not altered this basic feature. But coalition government is obviously not enough to explain the functioning and performance of the Italian executive. In spite of great internal turbulence coalitions exhibit a long-term continuity lasting basically until the early 1990s. Although some significant changes (for instance the end of the DC monopoly over the prime ministership, and a more frequent fusion of the positions of prime minister and of party leader) had already begun in the 1980s, the great acceleration of change began only after the elections of 1992.

The fragmented party system with no less (but often more) than seven parliamentary parties and the long-term persistence (albeit with a progressively declining intensity) of the pro-system/anti-system cleavage, combined until the early 1990s to produce a durable pattern of complicated, quarrelsome, and scarcely cohesive, but at the same time fundamentally irreplaceable coalitions. The lack of real alternatives (disregarding here the alternation among the smaller centre parties) has contributed significantly to the 'stable instability' of Italian governments. Short-lived cabinets have been based on coalitions which mostly have changed very little from one cabinet to the next. Hence, an important distinction can be drawn between 'cabinet' and 'coalition', which typically correspond to time periods of different length. Except in a minority of cases, the making of a cabinet and the making of a coalition are phenomena that cannot be equated. Normally a cabinet, from its birth to its death, has been but one of a series of such political episodes within a longer-term coalition formula. This fact goes a long way towards explaining the limited ability of the cabinet as an institution to 'govern' political life. Through the making and unmaking of governments, party leaders, who have typically stayed outside the cabinet, have to a significant extent governed underneath and beyond the cabinet.

The description of typical patterns of government formation in Italy confirms this view. The time required for government formation, the number of attempts to create a new majority, and the number of designated prime ministers are very different over the time. But they always follow the 'golden rule' of external party dominance: when the coalition is 'ready' in parliament or somewhere else (for instance after a party congress which determines a new equilibrium within the respective party elite) the time for a normal 'positive' investiture can be relatively short. But even if a minor change happens the delicate equilibrium inside the coalition has to be affected from it and different effects can be created (reshuffles, change of cabinet, change of governmental coalition). The instability of the cabinets of 'centrismo' age (in the 1950s) gives a clear picture of this incremental process of government formation (and of coalition transformation), but the main indicators tell us this pattern has never been abandoned.

The separation of responsibilities between parties and government has encouraged party leaders to pursue party goals without paying too much attention to the constraints (e.g. budgetary) which governments typically have to face. At the same time and as a consequence, party leaders have not been able to exploit the institutional prestige and legitimation that they would have gained from a more direct involvement in government responsibilities. The strong anti-party feelings which have prevailed in Italian public opinion may have had to do with this phenomenon. The attempts of Craxi and De Mita during the 1980s to overcome the separation between party and government leadership were probably in part motivated by these party leaders' concerns about this problem. But in the end the tough competition for the coalition leadership between the two largest parties (DC and PSI) caused the failure of any attempt to change the relationship between parties and cabinet.

The performance of the Italian coalition government helps explain the crisis of the 1990s. The limited ability of weak governments to innovate and thus successfully to solve political challenges such as controlling public expenditures and government debt, and thus to fulfil the requirements for participation in European monetary integration, seriously affected the political credibility of the traditional governing parties. Moreover, after the fall of the Berlin Wall and the transformation of the Communist Party into the post-communist PDS (Democratic Party of the Left), the remaining legitimation of the governing parties as the bastions of the 'anti-communist dam' was waning. It is against this background that a limited prosecution of political corruption, as 'clean hands' originally was, could snowball into a global process against the political class that had ruled the country after Fascism.

A few years after the political earthquake of 1992–4, the consolidation of a new political system is yet far from accomplished. Uncertainty about its structure and functioning is necessarily still significant. Yet some important changes are already apparent, such as the end of the permanent exclusion of some parties from the government. With the collapse of the old (permanent) governing parties (and in particular the DC), all the surviving parties of the First Republic, plus the newly created ones, have acquired the legitimacy to play the government game. This, together with the new electoral system, has created the conditions for alternative coalitions of the left and of the right (each of which incorporates bits of the old centre). This is clearly an important change from the past, when government coalitions were always dominated by the centre. This heightened electoral competitiveness has gone hand in hand with a transformation of the political role of the prime minister, who now combines more clearly the role of cabinet leader with that of leader of the coalition. In fact, with pre-electoral coalitions being established, the latter role becomes the foundation for the former.

The significantly changed party system and the largely renovated political class (elected under a new electoral system) of the 1990s have not meant automatically a strengthened role of the cabinet. As we show above (Table 12.5), it is clear that the central problem for coalitional government in Italy remains the lack of a real responsiveness which would make a government stronger, the MPs more disciplined, and the parties less litigious. Today, like yesterday, the rules of governance seem to reflect a quite flexible and general framework of limited government. There is no formal agreement and/or a list of 'real' priorities provided directly by the coalition for the cabinet's agenda. On the contrary, the evaluation of the cabinet activity is done by a formal confidence vote, based on the generic investiture 'speech' and on a number of not formalized external mechanisms (first of all the majority summits). Moreover, party discipline had not increased recently, and also the 'proportional principles' from the 1970s are still the most governing parliamentary rules of procedure. Clear perspectives of change have still to be seen, both in the constitutional and legal framework and in the practice of government.

The events of the past two years have demonstrated that this is still not enough to create stable governments and strong prime ministers. The reasons are pretty clear. Party system fragmentation together with the unstable electoral basis and spatial positions of some parties explain the rapid failure of the first coalition governments of the new period, and can impose the persistence of temporary solutions like the 'technical cabinets' with a less clearly defined political agenda. On the other hand, also a mixed (and very discussed) electoral system, like the one adopted in 1993, had already determined two majoritarian miracles (Bartolini and D'Alimonte 1998): the emergence of a clear governmental majority (both in 1994 and 1996) and that alternation which was considered for a long time the main missing character of the Italian system. The linkage between elections and government formation seems to have been accepted as the 'normal' feature of the new politics. The further evolution of the new party system, and in particular the consolidation and spatial strategies of the new parties, will critically affect the life of coalitions and the stability and performance of governments.

REFERENCES

Amato, Giuliano (1981). 'Il primo centro-sinistra: Ovvero, l'espansione della forma di governo'. *Quaderni Costituzionali*, 1: 293–311.

Bartolini, Stefano, and D'Alimonte, Roberto (1998). 'Majoritarian Miracles and the Question of Party System Change'. *European Journal of Political Research*, 34: 151–69.

Battegazzorre, Francesco (1987). 'L'Instabilità di governo in Italia'. *Rivista Italiana di Scienza Politica*, 17: 285–317.
Calise, Mauro, and Mannheimer, Renato (1982). *Governanti in Italia: Un trentennio repubblicano*. Bologna: Il Mulino.
Carducci, Michele (1989). *L'accordo di coalizione*. Padova: Cedam.
Cotta, Maurizio (1996). 'La crisi del governo di partito all'italiana', in Maurizio Cotta and Pierangelo Isernia (eds.), *Il gigante dai piedi di argilla: La crisi del regime partitocratico in Italia*. Bologna: Il Mulino.
——and Isernia, Pierangelo (1996) (eds.). *Il gigante dai piedi di argilla: La crisi del regime partitocratico in Italia*. Bologna: Il Mulino.
——and Verzichelli, Luca (1996). 'Italy: Sunset of a Particracy', in Jean Blondel and Maurizio Cotta (eds.), *Party and Government*. London: Macmillan.
Criscitiello, Annarita (1994). 'The Political Role of Cabinet Ministers in Italy', in Michael Laver and Kenneth A. Shepsle (eds.), *Cabinet Ministers and Parliamentary Government*. Cambridge: Cambridge University Press.
——(1996). 'Alla ricerca della collegialità di governo: I vertici di maggioranza dal 1970 al 1994'. *Rivista Italiana di Scienza Politica*, 26: 365–89.
D'Alimonte, Roberto, and Chiaramonte, Alessandro (1995). 'Il nuovo sistema elettorale italiano: Quali opportunità?', in Stefano Bartolini and Roberto D'Alimonte (eds.), *Maggioritario ma non troppo: Le elezioni del 27 marzo 1994*. Bologna: Il Mulino.
De Winter, Lieven (1989). 'Party and Policy in Belgium'. *European Journal of Political Research*, 17: 707–30.
Di Palma, Giuseppe (1977). *Surviving Without Governing*. Berkeley: University of California Press.
Dogan, Mattei (1989). 'How to Become Minister in Italy: Unwritten Rules of the Political Game', in Mattei Dogan (ed.), *Pathways to Power: Selecting Rulers in Pluralistic Democracies*. Boulder, Colo.: Westview Press.
Fabbrini, Sergio (1998). 'Chi guida l'esecutivo? Presidenza della Repubblica e Governo in Italia (1996–1998)' *Siena, CIRCaP Occasional Paper*, no. 2.
Guagnano, Giuseppina (1996). 'Fenomenologia del comportamento dei governi', in Massimo Villone e Alberto Zuliani (eds.), *L'attività dei governi della repubblica italiana*. Bologna: Il Mulino.
Hine, David (1993). *Governing Italy: The Politics of Bargained Pluralism*. Oxford: Oxford University Press.
Ieraci, Giuseppe (1996). 'Perchè cadono i governi? La stabilità di Governo nelle democrazie parlamentari dell'Europa Occidentale (1945–1995)'. *Quaderni di Scienza Politica*, 3: 43–82.
Katz, Richard S. (1996). 'Electoral Reforms and the Transformation of Party Politics in Italy'. *Party Politics*, 2: 31–53.
Marradi, Alberto (1982). 'Italy: From "Centrism" to Crisis of Centre-Left Coalition', in Eric C. Browne and John Dreijmanis, (eds.), *Government Coalitions in Western Democracies*. New York: Longman.
Mastropaolo, Alfio, and Slater, Martin (1992). 'Party Policy and Coalition Bargaining in Italy, 1948–1987: Is There Order Behind the Chaos?', in Michael J. Laver and Ian Budge (eds.), *Party Policy and Government Coalitions*. New York: St Martin's Press.

Mershon, Carol A. (1994). 'Expectations and Informal Rules in Coalition Formation'. *Comparative Political Studies*, 27: 40–79.
——(1996). 'The Costs of Coalition: Coalition Theories and Italian Governments'. *American Political Science Review*, 90: 534–54.
Morlino, Leonardo (1996). 'Crisis of Parties and Change of Party System in Italy'. *Party Politics*, 2: 5–30.
Pasquino, Gianfranco (1987). 'Party Government in Italy. Achievements and Prospects', in Richard S. Katz (ed.), *Party Government and Its Alternatives*. Berlin: De Gruyter.
——(1994). 'Le coalizioni di pentapartito 1980–1991: Quale governo dei partiti?', in Mario Caciagli, Franco Cazzola, Leonardo Morlino, and Stefano Passigli (eds.), *L'Italia tra crisi e transizione*. Roma: Laterza.
——(1997). 'No Longer a Party State? Institutions, Power and the Problems of the Italian Reforms'. *West European Politics*, 20: 34–53.
Ruggeri, Andrea (1990). *La crisi di governo tra ridefinizione delle regole e rifondazione della politica*. Milano: Giuffrè.
Sartori, Giovanni (1976). *Parties and Party Systems*. Cambridge: Cambridge University Press.
Vassallo, Salvatore (1994). *Il governo di partito in Italia*. Bologna: Il Mulino.
Verzichelli, Luca (1992). 'The Recruitment of Ministers and Party Leaders in Italy'. Paper presented at the workshop on the relations between government and supporting parties in Europe, European University Institute, Florence, June 1992.

13

France

Forming and Maintaining Government Coalitions in the Fifth Republic

Jean-Louis Thiébault

THE CONTEXT: THE PARLIAMENTARY PARTY SYSTEM

The French parliamentary party system has undergone important changes under the Fifth Republic, with equally significant consequences for the way the country is governed. The aim of this section is to identify the factors imposed by the French parliamentary party system in which government coalitions have been formed. The two factors that most decisively determine a party's bargaining power are its share of parliamentary seats and its spatial location vis-à-vis the other parliamentary parties.

At the end of the Fourth Republic, France was saddled with a fragmented party system. The period between 1958 and 1962 was one of transition from a fragmented multi-party system without stable coalitions towards a bipolar party system with lasting coalitions. But since 1962, the presidential structuring of party competition has led to a decrease in the number of parties in parliament (National Assembly) from seven in 1958 to four in 1993. The development of two opposing electoral blocs, each consisting of two rival but allied parties (the Communists and the Socialists on the left, the Gaullists and the moderate Conservatives on the right) has facilitated the creation and maintenance of governing majority coalitions. The pattern of government in France has become one of comparatively stable majority coalitions.

More precisely, the French party system has presented two models since the beginning of the Fifth Republic. First it was a system of coalitions with a dominant party, during two specific periods:

During the 1962–74 period, the Gaullist Party (UNR, then UDR), which had been created by General de Gaulle's supporters, occupied a dominant position within the French parliamentary party system. Its dominance was reflected in a high percentage of votes in legislative elections (about 35–40%) and a large number of seats in the National Assembly (a plurality in 1962,

TABLE 13.1. *Left–right placement of parties, party strength (in seats) and party composition of governments in France, 1959–1999*[a]

Government	Proximity to election[b]	Communist party	Socialist party	Centre-left parties	Centre-right parties	Moderate conservative parties	Gaullist party	Unity of the republic	Extreme right party	Non-registered deputies[c]	Effective number of legislative parties	Government strength[d]	Real government strength[e]	Total number of seats
1959	FE	—	44	**39**	**56**	118	216*	47	—	32	5.4	429	453	552
1962	F	41	66	39	55	**35**	**233***	—	—	13	4.8	268	268	482
1965	E	41	66	39	55	**35**	**233***	—	—	13	4.8	268	268	482
1967	FE	73	121	—	41	42*	**200**	—	—	10	4.5	242	261	487
1968	F	34	57	—	33	61	293*	—	—	9	3.5	354	354	487
1969	E	34	57	—	**33**	**61**	**293***	—	—	9	3.5	387	354	487
1973	F	73	102	**34**	**30**	**55***	**183**	—	—	13	5.3	268	270	490
1974	E	73	102	**34**	**30**	**55***	**183**	—	—	13	5.3	302	270	490
1978	F	86	115	—	—	**123***	**154**	—	—	13	4.3	277	260	491
1981	E	86	115	—	—	123*	154	—	—	13	4.3	115	201	491
1981	F	**44**	**285***	—	—	63	88	—	—	11	3.3	329	302	491
1984	E	44	**285***	—	—	63	88	—	—	11	3.3	285	302	491
1986	F	35	212	—	—	**131***	**155**	—	35	9	4.3	286	292	577
1988	E	35	**212**	—	—	131*	155	—	35	9	4.3	212	212	577
1988	FE	26	**272***	—	41	91	131	—	—	16	4.1	272	—	577
1993	F	23	57	—	—	**215***	**258**	—	—	24	3.4	473	457	577
1995	E	23	57	—	—	**215***	**258**	—	—	24	3.4	473	457	577
1997	F	**36**	**250***	**33**	—	113	140	—	—	5	5.1	319	297	577

[a] In France the definition of a government differs from the one used in the other chapters by taking into account both parliamentary elections (1962, 1967, 1968, 1973, 1978, 1981, 1986, 1988, 1993, 1997) and presidential elections (1959 [by an electoral college], 1965, 1969, 1974, 1981, 1988, 1995) as terminating a government.
[b] In France this relates to both parliamentary and presidential elections.
[c] Among the 36 non-registered deputies in 1958, there were 10 communist deputies. In 1993, 23 of the 24 non-registered deputies constituted the group Republique et Liberté. In 1997 this category includes one deputy of the extreme right.
[d] Number of seats held by the government parties. This column equals the corresponding column of Table 1 in other chapters.
[e] This column reports the pro-government votes in the first confidence vote on the government's programme or the votes in favour of a general policy declaration by the government. Sometimes, when the first confidence vote is held just after the government formation, some ministers are no longer MPs but not yet replaced by their substitutes in the National Assembly. This is the main reason why actual support of government occasionally is smaller than 'government strength'.

cont./

TABLE 13.1. cont.

Parties	
Communists (C)	Parti Communiste (PC) (Communist Party) 1958–
Socialists (S)	Section Française de l' Internationale Ouvrière (SIFO) (French Section of the Socialist International) 1958–62
	Fédération de la Gauche Démocratique et Socialiste (FGDS) (Federation of the Democratic and Socialist Left) 1967–8
	Parti Socialiste (PS) (Socialist Party) 1973–
	Mouvement des Radicaux de Gauche (MRG) (Movement of the Left Radicals) 1978–
Centre Left Parties (CL)	Parti Radical-Socialist (Radical Party) and Entente Démocratique (ED) (Democratic Entente) 1958–62
	Mouvement Réformateur (Movement of Reformers) (Réf.) 1973
	Radical, Citoyen, Vert (RCV) (Radicals, Citizens, Greens) 1997
Centre Right Parties (CR)	Mouvement Republicain Populaire (MRP) (Popular Republican Movement) (Christian democrats) and Centre Démocratique (CD) (Democratic Centre) 1958–62
	Centre Democrate (CD) (Centre of Democracy) 1967
	Progrès et Démocratie Moderne (PDM) (Progress and Modern Democracy) 1968
	Centre Democratie et Progres (CDP) (Centre for Democracy and Progress) 1973
	Union du Centre (UC) (Centre Union) 1988
Moderate Conservative Parties (MC)	Centre National des Indépendants (CNI) 1958
	Fédération National des Républicains Indépendants (FNRI) (National Federation of Republicans) 1962–73
	Union pour la Démocatie Française (UDF) (Union for French Democracy) 1978–
Gaullist Parties (G)	Union pour la Nouvelle République (UNR) (Union for the New Republic) 1958–62
	Union Démocratique pour la 5e République (UDVe) (Democratic Union for the 5th Republic) 1967
	Union des Démocrates pour la République (UDR) (Union of Democracy for the Republic) 1968–73
	Rassemblement pour la République (RPR) (Rally for the Republic) 1978–
Unité de la République	(Unity of the Republic) (deputies from Algeria and Sahara) 1958
Extreme Right Parties	Front National (FN) (National Front) 1986

1967, and 1973, and an absolute majority in 1968). As a governing party, it was loyally supported by a part of the moderate and conservative right which had been gathered, in a small parliamentary group (RI), around V. Giscard d'Estaing. This support was necessary to create a majority coalition. The only exception was the 1968 election, when the Gaullist Party gained the absolute majority of parliamentary seats but maintained the coalition with the small moderate parliamentary group to respect the electoral alliance. The French parliamentary electoral system, which is two-ballot (run-off) majority, provides strong incentives towards electoral alliances between parties which are politically and ideologically close to each other, at least for the second ballot. For most of the Fifth Republic, the Gaullist Party has maintained an electoral agreement with the small party of the moderate and conservative right to field a single candidate in most of the electoral districts on the first ballot. The maintenance of this coalition is the result not only of the habit of governing with one another, but also of the necessity of building electoral alliances.

During the 1981–6 and 1988–93 periods and since June 1997, the Socialist Party dominated the parliamentary party system, but in four different ways. From 1981 to 1984, it held an absolute majority of parliamentary seats but nevertheless formed a government coalition with the Communists because of their electoral alliance. Since 1962, Socialists and Communists had agreed on an electoral alliance committing them to mutual withdrawal on the second ballot of legislative elections, then from 1972 on to a common manifesto. From 1984 to 1986, the Socialist Party continued to hold an absolute majority of seats in the National Assembly, but lost the Communists' support for its policies. The Communists left the government coalition in 1984 to gradually act as an opposition party to the Socialist single-party government. From 1988 to 1993, the Socialist Party had only a plurality of seats and formed minority governments which faced a double opposition: from the right-wing alliance RPR–UDF, consisting of three parliamentary party groups (Gaullist, centrists, and moderates), and from the Communists. The Socialist governments survived for five years because of institutional mechanisms intended to enhance governmental stability. These cabinets relied on the mechanisms of government political accountability before parliament, provided by Article 49 of the constitution (Huber 1996).[1] Finally, since 1997 the Socialists have led a government that embraces the entire spectrum of the left, including the Communists and Greens. The Greens had joined the Socialist-led electoral alliance before the 1997 parliamentary elections. The parliamentary elections of 25 May (first round) and 1 June 1997 (second round), which had been caused by president Chirac's decision to dissolve the National Assembly nearly a year before its five-year term ended, had produced a majority of the left.

The French party system has also been a system of bipolarization, during three specific periods:

1. During the 1974–81 period, the system of bipolarization gradually evolved into a *quadrille bipolaire* (Duverger 1985). The 1974 presidential

---

[1] This means that the cabinet may make any bill a confidence question in the National Assembly. 'In this case, the bill is considered adopted unless a motion of censure, introduced within the next 24 hours, is adopted' (Art. 49.3, quoted from Huber 1996: 3).

election, won by V. Giscard d'Estaing, led to the formation of a new conservative majority which was rejuvenated with the addition of opposition centrists. Within the majority coalition a new internal reshuffle took place through the transformation of UDR into RPR under the leadership of J. Chirac and with the creation of the smaller UDF out of all the small centrist and moderate formations which wished to balance the RPR in the centre-right majority. Giscard's attempt to create a new balance within the majority did not work for the 1978 legislative election, as the RPR maintained a numerical superiority. The contest for the supremacy within the majority weakened it, but not sufficiently to prevent it from governing. The divided left-wing parties first made up a united opposition around the common manifesto between the Communists and the Socialists in 1972. But they then parted during the process of updating this electoral programme, because the Communist Party wanted to maintain its supremacy which was threatened by F. Mitterrand.

2. The 1986–8 period witnessed a first experiment in power-sharing ('cohabitation') between the Socialist president of the Republic, F. Mitterrand, and a narrow parliamentary majority of RPR–UDF. The government coalition was directed by J. Chirac, the leader of the main party within this majority, the Gaullist RPR.

3. During the 1993–5 period, there was a second experiment of power-sharing ('cohabitation') after the electoral alliance RPR–UDF won the 1993 legislative elections. The government coalition was directed by E. Balladur, one of the RPR leaders, whereas the party president, J. Chirac, prepared himself for the 1995 presidential election. This election put an end to the experiment in power-sharing. It resulted in J. Chirac's success against the Socialist candidate, L. Jospin, and in the appointment of A. Juppé as head of government, with the same coalition maintained since 1993 between RPR and UDF.

France represents a clear example of a unidimensional party system, in which the left–right placement of parties provides a meaningful representation of the policy space. At the beginning of the Fifth Republic, there was a strong disagreement between Gaullist and anti-Gaullist parties over the political regime. But in the 1970s, the return of the traditional left–right cleavage intervened. The presidential and parliamentary elections gradually engendered two opposing coalitions: the left comprises the Communists and the Socialists and the right is composed of the Gaullists and the moderate conservative parties. The terms 'left' and 'right' are gradually used to indicate positions on the socio-economic divide, with the rightist coalition representing the conservative pole and the Communists and the Socialists representing the progressive pole. The right-wing parties also stand for defending the Catholic religion and its interests, whereas the left-wing parties take an anti-clerical stand. The Gaullist Party and the Socialist Party were for a long time located towards the centrist end of their respective blocs, but now the moderate conservative UDF has taken the median position.

INSTITUTIONAL BACKGROUND

The constitution of the Fifth Republic is a mixed system that grafts a popularly elected president with extensive constitutional powers onto a more or less conventional parliamentary system in which the prime minister and the cabinet are responsible to the popularly elected legislative chamber, the National Assembly. This institutional background constitutes a strong constraint on coalition formation. Political parties may be forced to consider the relevance of political institutions as given facts on coalition formation, governance, and termination.

The initiative to form a new government belongs to the president of the Republic, who must first establish contact with a party leader. He plays an active role in the selection and the appointment of the prime minister. He decides who has the best chance of forming a government. The latitude of presidential action is, however, limited by the result of legislative elections. But the government is really formed by the prime minister, who has just been appointed by the president of the Republic. This became most clear under the present 'cohabitation', when Lionel Jospin was standing alone on the steps of the Elysée Palace, announcing his own appointment as prime minister.

The new prime minister moves into the Hotel Matignon shortly after his predecessor has formally passed his responsibilities to him. He immediately starts working and consulting on the formation of the government. He is visited by some majority politicians (leaders of majority political parties, chairmen of parliamentary party groups, and political friends) and consults very much by telephone. He reports on his consultations to the president of the Republic. The president does not remain inactive and proceeds to his own consultations. The result of these consultations comes rapidly: the new government is formed after only one or two days. A longer bargaining process would surprise the media. The conclusion of these consultations comes after the prime minister's last visit to the president of the Republic. The composition of the new government is then made public by the general secretary of the Presidency of the Republic who speaks to cameras and microphones waiting on the steps of the Palais de l'Elysée, ideally right in time for the eight o'clock television evening news programme, so as to be broadcast live.

There is no appointment of an *informateur* specifically designated by the president of the Republic to carry out a first consultation: the single *formateur* is the prime minister nominated by the president of the Republic. If we only include the formation process which takes place after a general election, the duration of government formation is short. One of the reasons is that only one formation attempt is made. Coalition formation in France has rarely taken repeated efforts. Table 13.2, which contains numerical information on the formation process in France, shows that the initial attempt at cabinet formation has failed in only three cases. In 1973 the right-wing majority parties failed to agree with the centrist opposition. In 1984 Socialists and Communists failed to resuscitate their coalition. In 1988 Rocard's initial attempt to bring the centrists into his government failed. All others governments, however, have formed on their first attempt. Coalition bargaining has not taken much time.

As Table 13.2 shows, there have been only two cases in which coalition bargaining has taken more than one week, namely 1962 and 1973. All other government formations have only taken from one to three days. Coalition building in France is not a complicated and time-consuming process. The only topic of discussion is portfolio allocation.

TABLE 13.2. *Government formation in France, 1959–1999*

Government	Number of parties in parliament	Number of previous bargaining rounds	Parties involved in previous bargaining rounds	Number of days required for government formation
UNR–CNI–CD–ED 1959	6	0		1
UNR–FNRI 1962	6	0		10
UNR–FNRI 1966	6	0		1
UNR–FNRI 1967	5	0		1
UDR–FNRI 1968	5	0		1
UDR–FNRI–PDM 1969	5	0		1
UDR–FNRI–UC 1973	6	1	UDR–FNRI–UC–Réf.	11
UDR–FNRI–UC–Réf. 1974	6	0		2
RPR–UDF 1978	4	0		3
PS 1981	4	0		2
PS–PC 1981	4	0		2
PS 1984	4	1	PS–PC	2
RPR–UDF 1986	5	0		1
PS 1988	5	0		2
PS 1988	5	1	PS–UC	5
RPR–UDF 1993	4	0		1
RPR–UDF 1995	4	0		2
PS–PC–RCV 1997	5	0		2

The Relevance of Political Institutions on Coalition Formation: Investiture Rules

The president of the Republic retains important constitutional powers in the process of coalition government formation. He plays an active role as the main initiating and steering force. First of all he selects the prime minister and appoints him. The other government members are also appointed by him, but on the prime minister's proposal. In fact, his position varies. When the president of the Republic is supported by a parliamentary majority that is close to his political conceptions or belongs to the same political family, the president can freely select the person of his choice as prime minister. In practice, as pointed out by Duhamel (1980), the president tends to appoint a 'political' head of government during the first part of his term and then to choose a more 'technician' head of government or somebody who is closer to him for the second part. Then the president of the Republic lets the prime minister select the other government members though he closely scrutinizes who is in charge of the portfolios associated with his own responsibilities (external affairs and defence in particular).

The situation is different in a period of power-sharing ('cohabitation'). The president of the Republic has no parliamentary majority at his disposal: the majority is even hostile to him. The head of state cannot even choose the prime minister freely. He has to appoint the leader or one of the leaders of the majority. His room for manoeuvre is reduced, because the majority parties have come to a previous agreement on the head of government. The president of the Republic is not free to choose the other cabinet members, either. He exercises no more control, even if he may try with more or less success to influence the choice for some portfolios which are related to his own powers (external affairs, defence).

According to the constitution, the prime minister and the government members are appointed by the president of the Republic. The government officially exists from the presidential act of appointment. A parliamentary investiture no longer exists. The newly appointed prime minister presents his programme before the deputies, but is not obliged to seek a vote of confidence on this programme. He only does so if he has a broad majority in the National Assembly. If not, he abstains. However, in a period of power-sharing, a vote of confidence allows the head of government to show that it can rely on sufficient support in parliament to govern without presidential support. Prime ministers Chirac (in 1986), Balladur (in 1988), and Jospin (in 1997) therefore have initiated votes of confidence when facing parliament at the beginning of their term.

Governance Institutions: Cabinet Decision-Making Rules

The cabinet (Council of Ministers) is a place where decisions taken somewhere else are formally ratified. There are no votes to identify any majority and opposition within the government, which is supposed to take collective decisions. In fact, there are no real discussions during the Council. These discussions take place in the multiple inter-ministerial councils, committees, and meetings, prior to the Council of Ministers, and the conflicts are resolved by the prime minister or, in the case of serious contestation, by the president of the Republic.

Decision Rules in the Legislature

Legislative bills (ordinary laws or budgets) are passed by a majority of all members present and voting. However, motions of censure deposited by the opposition parties have to win an absolute majority of all members of the National Assembly. The discipline of parliamentary parties means that we should not expect governments to be defeated. To reach this point would necessarily mean a serious break in party discipline, or a split within majority parliamentary party groups. But even in that case the government still has an emergency tool at its disposal: it may engage its political accountability on a bill through the Article 49.3 procedure. This procedure allows for a bill to be passed without any vote except in the case when a question of censure has been proposed. Therefore, the government is entitled to decide upon a policy without risking any unfavourable vote from its parliamentary majority. This system may protect a fragile government coalition from being tested too vigourously (see Huber 1996).

CABINET FORMATION

The constitutional provisions regulating the post-1958 coalition formation processes, which have been described above, are complemented by a set of established practices. The three main stages in coalition formation are: (1) the construction of a party combination supported by a parliamentary majority, (2) negotiations over policy, and (3) the distribution of portfolios among cabinet ministers.

Coalition Membership

A French government emerges not as the result of real bargaining during the formation process. It occurs after a simple process, and therefore quickly. This formation process is rapid for several reasons. First there are no discussions on the coalition composition, because the parties involved belong to the presidential and/or parliamentary majority and are linked by an electoral alliance. One cleavage has dominated coalition politics and bargaining under the Fifth Republic: the left–right dimension. All governments have contained parties that were adjacent on this dimension—there is no example of an 'unconnected' coalition. Party strategies have also functioned as political constraints and reduced the number of viable coalition alternatives. After 1958, the right pursued a strategy of polarization, and the left was banned from the government formation.

Most the French cabinets have been minimal winning. The practice of constructing coalitions even if a single party has an absolute majority has also

TABLE 13.3. French cabinets since 1959

Cabinet number	Prime minister	Date in	Formal resignation	Maximum potential duration (in days)	Duration (in days)	Government composition
1	Debré	8 Jan. 1959	14 Apr. 1962	1,909	1,191	UNR–CNI–CD–ED
2	Pompidou I	14 Apr. 1962	5 Oct. 1962	353	173	UNR–CNI–CD–ED
3	Pompidou II	28 Nov. 1962	8 Jan. 1966	1,577	1,136	UNR–FNRI
4	Pompidou III	8 Jan. 1966	1 Apr. 1967	449	448	UNR–FNRI
5	Pompidou IV	6 Apr. 1967	10 July 1968	1,822	461	UNR–FNRI
6	Couve de Murville	10 July 1968	20 June 1969	1,909	345	UDR–FNRI
7	Chaban Delmas	20 June 1969	5 July 1972	1,564	1,111	UDR–FNRI–PDM
8	Messmer I	5 July 1972	28 Mar. 1973	271	266	UDR–FNRI–PDM
9	Messmer II/1	2 Apr. 1973	27 Feb. 1974	1,826	420	UDR–FNRI–UC
	Messmer II/2	27 Feb. 1974	27 May 1974			
10	Chirac	27 May 1974	25 Aug. 1976	1,771	821	UDR–FNRI–UC–Réf.
11	Barre I/1	25 Aug. 1976	29 Mar. 1977	590	583	UDR–FNRI–UC–Réf.
	Barre I/2	29 Mar. 1977	31 Mar. 1978			
12	Barre II	3 Apr. 1978	13 May 1981	1,825	1,136	RPR–UDF
13	Mauroy I	21 May 1981	22 June 1981	1,046	31	PS
14	Mauroy II/1	22 June 1981	22 Mar. 1983	1,759	1,121	PS–PC
	Mauroy II/2	22 Mar. 1983	17 July 1984			
15	Fabius	17 July 1984	20 Mar. 1986	989	611	PS
16	Chirac	20 Mar. 1986	10 May 1988	1,838	782	RPR–UDF
17	Rocard I	10 May 1988	14 June 1988	1,423	35	PS
18	Rocard II	23 June 1988	15 May 1991	1,756	1,057	PS
19	Mme Cresson	16 May 1991	2 Apr. 1992	687	321	PS
20	Beregovoy	2 Apr. 1992	29 Mar. 1993	365	360	PS
21	Balladur	29 Mar. 1993	10 May 1995	1,828	772	RPR–UDF
22	Juppé 1	17 May 1995	7 Nov. 1995	1,051	746	RPR–UDF
	Juppé 2	7 Nov. 1995	2 June 1997			
23	Jospin	2 June 1997		1,825		PS–PC–RCV

Note: The cabinets with both roman and arabic numbers (e.g. Messmer II/1) ended by a formal resignation and represent the conventional counting of cabinets in France. They do not fulfil the three criteria for counting a new cabinet applied in this volume, (1) new Prime Minister, (2) change in party composition, (3) parliamentary election.

contributed to the formation of some oversized (surplus majority) governments. One reason that such governments have formed is that parties have respected their electoral alliances and refrained from reneging on them even when they could have governed alone. Decisions on coalition party composition are therefore in reality taken long before the legislative elections. The parties agree to start negotiations and subsequently select candidates and elaborate a joint policy programme.

Policy Negotiations

Negotiations over policy also occurs before the legislative elections. During the Fifth Republic, the history of such bargaining over policy programmes can be roughly divided into two phrases. The beginning of the Fifth Republic was characterized by the absence of coalition agreements negotiated before going into government collaboration. Right-wing parties had their own electoral programmes, but they were only linked by the great options defended by the different presidents (General de Gaulle, G. Pompidou, and V. Giscard D'Estaing), during presidential campaigns. The rules of the games were not written expressly or in any detail into a coalition agreement.

The first case of a coalition agreement comes from the left-wing opposition, more particularly from the FGDS's manifesto, in July 1966, which adopted the principle of 'contrat de législature', matched with the principle of automatic dissolution in the case of government crises (Duhamel 1980). The second example is the 'programme commun de gouvernment' signed on 27 June 1972 by PCF and PS (text given as an appendix in Chagnollaud and Quermonne 1996). In response, the right-wing majority (UDR, Républicains Indépendants and Centre Démocratie et Progrès) produced no written coalition programme, but only a common list of candidates which campaigned under the label 'Union des républicains de progrès' (URP), after an agreement signed on 12 December 1972. The outgoing majority received a coalition programme from the hands of Prime Minister P. Messmer, who delivered a speech on 7 January 1973, before the legislative elections, in Provins. The so-called 'programme de Provins' contained policy commitments, but no reference to a procedure of conflict resolution between the different parties which made up the outgoing majority, nor did it make reference to a procedure of distributing government portfolios or other offices within the future government.

The outgoing right-wing majority was also unable to agree on a coalition programme for the 1978 legislative elections. The president of RPR, J. Chirac, suggested a 'pacte majoritaire' on 18 May 1977. He sent a letter to the leaders of the other majority parties (PR, CDS, Parti Radical, and CNI), on 24 June 1977, in order to hold a top meeting with their leaders. On 19 July 1977, the RPR leader proposed to his partners, who accepted it, a 'pacte électoral'. This agreement, which consisted of a majority 'code de bonne conduite', was adopted to solve the cases where a single candidacy could not be negotiated for individual electoral districts. On 14 September 1977, the 'manifeste de la majorité' was published. J. Chirac, opposed to any unitary initiative which could jeopardize the autonomy of his party, asked that the preamble of this document not refer to the role of the prime minister and that the text in question not be considered as a 'programme commun de la majorité'. The preamble also said: 'This document is not a government programme, for we refuse the model of party government, contrary to the spirit of our institutions.' This manifesto decided upon the stakes for the elections and delineated some orientations: a society of liberty, a society of justice, and independence (*Le Monde* 1978: 67). But within this majority, the competition between RPR and UDF prevented the adoption of a real coalition programme. It was again the prime minister, R. Barre, who presented, on 7 January 1978, the 'programme de Blois'. This programme gave a list of thirty 'objectives of action for liberties and justice', gathered under the following themes: 'liberated citizens', 'economic progress at the service of employment', and 'solidarity at the service of social justice' (*Le Monde* 1978: 24–7). But it contained nothing on the procedure of conflict-solving between the parties of the outgoing majority or on the allocation of government portfolios.

The fact that the Socialists came to power in 1981 has modified the practice. The Socialist governments (Mauroy and Fabius) were linked by the great options defended by F. Mitterrand at the time of the 1981 presidential election. The '110 propositions' manifesto had been ratified by the Socialist conference convened in Créteil on 24 January 1981 (the '110 propositions' are also published as an appendix in Chagnollaud and Quermonne 1996). On 5 May 1981—between the first and second ballot of the presidential elections—F. Mitterrand announced that he would form a government with those which had approved the options of his presidential campaign. On 10 May 1981 Mitterrand was elected president. On 22 May 1981 a government which contained only Socialists was formed under the direction of Pierre Mauroy. The new first secretary of PS, L. Jospin, specified the conditions of an agreement with the Communists before a conference of his party on 25 May 1981. First, not 'to abandon any of our principles and any of our fundamental positions' (followed the enumeration of the main subjects of controversy with the PCF) and, then, to obtain 'a clear commitment of solidarity in governmental action'. On 2 June 1981 the delegations of the two parties gathered, and on 4 June issued a declaration noting some 'convergences' between them, notably on a list of enumerated social measures. It referred also to 'disagreements', without specifying them. The declaration further established the possibility of agreement on reciprocal withdrawal on the second ballot of the 1981 legislative elections, which would allow the constitution of a government majority 'decided to do everything possible to participate in the application of the new policy that the French have chosen with the election of F. Mitterrand' (*Le Monde* 1981: 19). However, the superiority of the May 1981 presidential election was emphasized clearly. The presidential programme of Mitterrand constituted the reference point for the programme of the left parties for the parliamentary elections on 14 and 21 June 1981. Their agreement also emphasizes the PCF's commitment of support. At the Council of Ministers on 3 June 1981, the new president specified that the commitments made during the presidential campaign and approved in the presidential elections on 10 May 1981 'constitute the charter of the governmental action' (*Le Monde* 1981: 35). On 22 June 1981 the Prime Minister P. Mauroy offered his resignation and, immediately reappointed, formed the new government whose composition was published on 23 June 1981. The question was obviously about the participation of PCF, which the same day had signed an agreement with the PS in which the two parties decided to promote the new policy in the National Assembly 'as part of the majority it belongs to', but also in the government, 'in a solidarity without flaw', in the local and regional authorities, and in the firms (*Le Monde* 1981: 136).

The presence of Communists in the government implied that the PCF fully committed itself to the solidarity expressed in the agreement of 23 June 1981. But there were some difficulties. The common declaration on 23 June 1981 did not contain any problem-solving procedures. L. Jospin and G. Marchais conducted a meeting of the two party delegations which ended up, on 8 January 1982, on 'convergences' and 'differences', and among the latter was the Polish question. The economic and social difficulties also grew as a test on majority solidarity. A meeting of the top leaders of the two parties took place on 1 December 1983. The prime minister twice even had to involve the government's political accountability by making use of Article 49.3 of the constitution to proceed to a 'clarification' with the Communists, in order to constrain them to approve a wage policy involving the end of wage indexation, as well as industrial reorganization in the coal-mining, shipbuilding, and steel industries. The resignation of P. Mauroy, who had been a partner for the PCF and a protector of the left-wing unions, put into question the future of the alliance. Laurent Fabius was appointed as the new prime minister on 17 July 1984, but the Communist leaders made the decision not to participate in the new government.

On 10 April 1985 an 'accord pour gouverner ensemble' was signed by RPR and UDF. It was followed by the 'plate-forme commune', adopted on 16 January 1986. The preamble of this manifesto proclaimed that 'socialism has been a failure' and that the country needs 'to break with dirigism'. The text also proposed a number of political, economic, cultural, and social objectives (*Le Monde* 1986: 42–5). On 17 March 1986, after the legislative elections, RPR and UDF published a communique in the form of an ultimatum to the head of state, warning him that any member of the new majority parties must be agreed by them before he or she can accept any government responsibility. The come-back of traditional parliamentary practice was confirmed when, after his visit to the Elysée on 18 March 1986, the prime ministerial candidate, J. Chirac, spent a whole day consulting with his associates before he gave the head of state a list of government members. All the leaders of the parties that composed the majority coalition found a seat in the government, while they retained their party functions. The common declaration of 16 January 1986 once again provided no mechanisms of conflict resolution between the alliance parties.

The 1988 presidential election resulted in F. Mitterrand's re-election, on the basis of the proposals for action contained in his 'Lettre aux Francais'. He appointed Michel Rocard as his prime minister. This appointment was understood by the centrists as a signal of openness. But the Rocard government expressed less openness than announced and expected. The president of the Republic dissolved parliament, but the next assembly did not yield the parliamentary majority to complement his presidential majority. The PS gained neither an absolute majority nor reliable support. The new Rocard government, formed after the 1988 legislative elections, was a minority one-party government, not a coalition, which had to seek collaboration from the Communists or the centrists.

Hoping for a quick return to power, UDF and RPR created a committee for concertation, the Union pour la France (UPF), on 26 June 1990. For the preparation of 1993 legislative elections, in mid-November 1992, the UDF proposed to the RPR a text entitled 'Un nouveau pacte social' which expressed six commitments for the alternance of power. On 13 January 1993 the RPR and the UDF reached an agreement concerning parliamentary candidacies. On 10 February 1993 the two parties presented the 'projet de l'Union pour la France'. As a result of their victory in the 1993 legislative elections, the president of the Republic appointed the nominee of the right, E. Balladur, as prime minister. The latter proceeded to form a team restricted to thirty members, politically balanced. This cabinet's coalition agreement provided no mechanisms of conflict resolution. The victory of J. Chirac in the 1995 presidential election did not modify the balance within the right-wing majority. The new A. Juppé government, formed after the 1995 presidential election, was also based on the same political balance between the RPR and the UDF.

Long before the 1997 parliamentary elections, on 22 January 1997, the Socialist Party and the Greens had reached a programatic agreement and formed an electoral alliance that meant fielding joint candidates. On 29 April 1997 the Socialist Party and the Communist Party made a joint strategy declaration, following summit talks between the party leaders. This joint declaration was described as a joint electoral manifesto. The Communists agreed to put off the question of participation in a government of the left until after the second round of the parliamentary elections on 1 June 1997. After the victory of the left, the Communist national committee voted unanimously for the principle of Communist participation in the Jospin government. The national council of the Greens also voted for government participation. Hence the government of the 'plural' left was established.

COALITION GOVERNANCE

The central theme of this section is the role of agreements in coalition governance. Table 13.4 shows for each coalition whether or not a coalition agreement was reached. The coalition agreements are presented before the legislative elections as policy documents indicating the joint policy platform of the parties involved. Coalition agreements are to be distinguished from government declarations, which are presented by the prime minister in the first meeting of the parliament. Coalition agreements constitute the basis for such government declarations.

As Table 13.5 shows, the pre-electoral coalition agreements deal exclusively with policy matters and provide part of the policy agenda. These programmes are more often a summary list of mutually agreed-upon principles, good purposes, and broad goals to be discussed, rather than a detailed list of measures to be implemented. These items are later raised in the concrete agenda for operationalization and specification. At best, the coalition agreement provides a topic for discussion and general direction for a particular project. Since 1981, coalition programmes have been more carefully formulated than previously. They are becoming documents outlining policies for the coming years.

As can be seen in Table 13.5, coalition agreements are generally short. They contain arrangements on economic and social issues. The socio-economic part of these programmes is important. The 1981 common declaration between Socialist and Communist party leaders enumerated social measures and foreign policies (*Le Monde* 1981: 35 and 136). The 1986 common platform between RPR and UDF proposed political, economic, and social objectives (*Le Monde* 1986: 42–5). The 'projet pour l'Union de la France' was presented by RPR and UDF with political, social, and economic commitments. These pre-electoral coalition programmes are submitted to a special party conference or the party congress of the respective coalition parties for approval long before the legislative elections. Generally, party congresses approve coalition agreements by overwhelming majorities.

Apart from policy, coalition agreements contain no 'rules of the game' concerning decision making procedures and any particular inter-party (or intra-party) conflict resolution mechanisms, especially on issues that appeared to

TABLE 13.4. *Coalition governance in France, 1959–1999*

(1) Coalition	(2) Coalition agreement	(3) Agreement public	(4) Election rule	(5) Conflict management mechanisms[a]	(6) Most common management mechanisms[a]	(7) Mechanisms for the most serious conflicts[a]	(8) Coalition discipline in legislation	(9) Coalition discipline in other parliamentary behaviour	(10) Freedom of appointment	(11) Policy agreement	(12) Junior ministers	(13) Non-cabinet positions
1959	N	–	Y	CaC, Pr	CaC	Pr	4	4	N	0	N	N
1962	N	–	Y	CaC, Pr	CaC	Pr	2	2	N	0	N	N
1966	N	–	Y	CaC, Pr	CaC	Pr	2	2	N	0	N	N
1967	N	–	Y	CaC, Pr	CaC	Pr	2	2	N	0	N	N
1968	N	–	Y	CaC, Pr	CaC	Pr	2	2	N	0	N	N
1969	N	–	Y	CaC, Pr	CaC	Pr	–	–	–	–	–	–
1973	N	–	Y	CaC, Pr	CaC	Pr	2	2	N	0	N	N
1974	N	–	Y	Cac, Pr	Cac	Pr	2	2	N	0	N	N
1978	N	–	Y	CaC, Pr	CaC	Pr	2	2	N	0	N	N
1981	PRE-POST	Y	Y	CaC, PS, Pr	CaC	Pr	2	2	Y	2	N	N
1986	PRE	Y	Y	CaC, CoC	CaC	CoC	2	2	N	2	N	N
1993	PRE	Y	Y	CaC, CoC	CaC	CoC	2	2	N	2	N	N
1995	PRE	Y	Y	CaC, CoC, Pr	CaC	Pr	2	2	N	2	N	N
1997	PRE-POST	Y	Y	CaC, PS	CaC	PS	2	2	Y	2	N	N

[a] In France there is one conflict management mechanism not used and coded in other countries: conflict resolution by decision of the President of the Republic (Pr).

TABLE 13.5. *Size and content of coalition agreements in France, 1959–1999*

Government	Size	General procedural rules (in %)	Specific procedural rules (in %)	Distribution of offices (in %)	Distribution of competences (in %)	Policies (in %)
PS–PC 1981	530 / 870[a]	9.4 / 5.1	0	0	0	90.6 / 94.9
RPR–UDF 1986	2,060	0	0	0	0	100
RPR–UDF 1993	1,780	0	0	0	0	100
PS–PC–RCV 1997						
—PS–PC	1,930	0	0	0	0	100
—PS–Greens	1,460	0	0	0	0	100

[a] The first coaltion agreements (530 words) was pre-electoral, the second post-electoral.

be controversial during coalition formation. They also do not contain provisions on coalition discipline. Concerning coalition discipline, no rule exists as regards voting on legislation or other parliamentary behaviour. Party discipline is now high in the French National Assembly, and it is common for the parliamentary party groups to vote together as a bloc on important issues. On votes of confidence regarding the installation of a new cabinet, the data indicate that few majority deputies fail to show up or to vote. Coalition agreements do not provide mechanisms of government conflict-solving through formal contacts between party leaders outside the government. But the prime minister routinely gathers the majority leaders for an informal weekly lunch at Matignon. The various inter-ministerial meetings or even the Council of Ministers are also arenas of conflict resolution. Government solidarity is very strong. After cabinet decisions have been reached, ministers must comply with the prime ministerial stand. The French government thus appears as a united body.

PORTFOLIO DISTRIBUTION

In France, portfolio distribution is the only important stage in the formation process. It typically occurs after the legislative elections. The allocation of portfolios involves constrained inter-party bargaining. Such matters as the number of ministers, the government's hierarchical structure, the size of the government, and the methods of coordination are not decided by some coalitions actors, but by the prime minister after consultations with parties and politicians. Often two parties are involved in the portfolio distribution. But more than parties, this process involves individual politicians. The governments of the Fifth Republic often include 'technician' ministers, the existence of whom testifies to a presidential preference for non-partisan recruitment.

TABLE 13.6. *Distribution of cabinet and junior ministership in French coalitions, 1959–1999 (1)*

Cabinet number	Cabinet	(1) PM	(2) Justice	(3) Foreign Office	(4) Interior	(5) Defence	(6) Finance	(7) Budget	(8) Consumer
1	Debré	G,np,np	G	NP,g	CL,g/G	NP	MC/NP/MC	—	—
2	Pompidou I	NP,mc,g,g,g	G	NP,g	G	NP	MC,g,g	—	—
3	Pompidou II	NP,mc,g,g	G	NP,g	G	NP	MC,g	—	—
4	Pompidou III	G	G	NP,g,mc	G	NP	G,cm	—	—
5	Pompidou IV	G	G	NP,g,mc/G	G/MC,g	NP	G,np	—	—
6	Couve de Murville	G,mc	G	G	MC,g	G	G	—	—
7	Chaban Delmas	G,mc	CR	G/MC,g	MC,g	G	MC,g,g,g	—	—
8	Messmer I	G,mc	CR	NP,mc,g	MC	G	MC,g	—	—
9	Messmer II/1	G,mc	G	NP,mc,g	MC,g	G	MC,g,g	—	—
9	Messmer II/2	G	G	NP,mc,g	G	G	MC,g	—	—
10	Chirac	G,cl,cl,np	CR,mc	NP,mc	MC	G	MC,g	—	—
11	Barre I/1	NP,g,mc	G	NP,mc	MC	G	CL,g,mc	—	—
12	Barre I/2	NP,g,mc	G	NP,mc	MC,g	G	G,cr	—	mc
14	Barre II	NP,mc,g	G,mc	NP,g,mc	MC,g	G	CR	G	S
14	Mauroy II/1	S	NP	NP	S	S	S	S	—
16	Mauroy II/2	S,c	NP	NP	S	S	S	—	—
21	Chirac	G,np	G	NP,mc	G,mc	NP	G	G	—
22	Balladur	G	MC	G	G	MC	MC	G	—
22	Juppé 1	G,np	G	MC,g/mc	G	MC	MC,g/MC,g	—	—
23	Juppé 2	G,np	G	MC,cr	G	MC	MC	MC	—
23	Jospin	S	S	S	CL,s	S	S,cl,np	np	—

cont./

516 Jean-Louis Thiébault

TABLE 13.6. Continued (2)

Cabinet number	Cabinet	(9) Education	(10) Public Works	(11) Industry	(12) Agriculture	(13) Labour	(14) Health	(15) Housing	(16) European Affairs
1	Debré	NP	CR	cr,g	MC	CR	NP/CR	NP	—
2	Pompidou I	NP	CR,g/G	G	[CL^a]	CR/G	CR/MC	G	—
3	Pompidou II	G	G	G	[CL^a]	G	MC	G	—
4	Pompidou III	G	G	MC	G	—	—	—	—
5	Pompidou IV	G,np,cr	—	G	G	—	—	—	—
6	Couve de Murville	G	—	MC	G	—	—	—	—
7	Chaban Delmas	G	—	G	CR,g	CR,g	G,cr	—	—
8	Messmer I	CR,g	—	G	G	—	G,cr	—	—
9	Messmer II/1	CR	—	G	G	G	MC,cr	—	—
9	Messmer II/2	CR,g,g	—	G	MC	G	MC,cr	—	—
10	Chirac	NP,cr	mc	MC	MC	CL,mc	NP	—	—
11	Barre I/1	NP	—	MC	MC,cr	NP,mc,mc	NP	—	—
11	Barre I/2	NP	—	CR	CR,mc	NP,g,mc	NP,g	cr	—
12	Barre II	NP,cl	—	NP,cl	CR,mc	G,mc,mc	NP,cr	—	—
14	Mauroy II/1	S	—	NP/S	S	S	C	S	S
14	Mauroy II/2	S	—	S	S	C	—	S	—
16	Chirac	MC,g,g	—	MC	NP	—	G	—	—
21	Balladur	MC	—	MC	MC	G	NP/MC	MC	MC
22	Juppé 1	MC,g,np	—	MC	MC	MC	G	G	G
22	Juppé 2	MC	—	G	MC	G	—	G	G
23	Jospin	S	—	—	S	S	cl	s	S

TABLE 13.6. Continued (3)

Cabinet number	Cabinet	(17) Cooperation	(18) Overseas Territories	(19) Veterans	(20) Relations with Parliament	(21) Culture	(22) Electric or atomic power	(23) Posts and Telecommunication	(24) Research and Technology
1	Debré	CR,g/G	G/MC/mc	G	—	NP	NP	G	—
2	Pompidou I	CR/G	MC	G	G	NP	G	G	—
3	Pompidou II	—	G	G	—	NP	G	G	—
4	Pompidou III	—	G	G	G	NP	G	G	—
5	Pompidou IV	—	G	G	G	NP	G	G/MC	—
6	Couve de Murville	—	—	G	G	NP	G	G	—
7	Chaban Delmas	—	G	G	G	G/CR	—	G	—
8	Messmer I	—	—	G	G	CR	—	G	—
9	Messmer II/1	—	G	G	G	NP	—	G	—
	Messmer II/2	—	—	—	G	G	—	G	—
10	Chirac	CR	G	g	—	np	—	cr	—
11	Barre I/1	G	g	g	G	np	—	mc	—
	Barre I/2	G	g	g	g	MC	—	mc	—
12	Barre II	G	—	g	—	MC	—	mc,g	—
14	Mauroy II/1	S	—	S	S	S	—	S	S
	Mauroy II/2	S	—	—	S	S	—	S	—
16	Chirac	G	G	g	MC	MC	—	—	—
21	Balladur	G/G	G	MC	MC,G	G	—	G	—
22	Juppé 1	G	G	G	G	MC	—	G	—
	Juppé 2	G	G	G	G	MC	—	G	—
23	Jospin	s	s	s	S	S	—	—	—

518 Jean-Louis Thiébault

TABLE 13.6. Continued (4)

Cabinet number	Cabinet	(25) Planning	(26) Information Communication	(27) Training	(28) Social Affairs	(29) Transports	(30) Public Works	(31) Environment	(32) Sea	(33) Youth and Sport
1	Debré	CR	G	—	—	—	—	—	—	—
2	Pompidou I	—	G	—	—	—	—	—	—	—
3	Pompidou II	—	G	—	—	—	—	—	—	g
4	Pompidou III	—	—	—	NP	—	CL,[a]g,mc	—	—	G
5	Pompidou IV	MC/G	G	—	NP,g/G	MC	G,np	—	—	G
6	Couve de Murville	G	—	—	G,cr	MC	G	—	—	—
7	Chaban Delmas	MC	—	—	—	MC	G,mc	G	—	—
8	Messmer I	—	G	—	G	G	G,mc	G	—	—
9	Messmer II/1	—	G	—	—	G	G,mc,mc	G	—	—
9	Messmer II/2	—	G	—	—	—	G,mc,mc	G,mc	—	—
10	Chirac	CR	—	—	—	—	G,cr	G,cl,mc	—	—
11	Barre I/1	—	—	—	np	mc	MC,cr	G,mc,mc	—	mc
11	Barre I/2	—	MC	—	np	mc	MC	MC	—	MC
12	Barre II	—	S	C	S	G	—	MC	—	S
14	Mauroy II/1	S	—	C	S	C	—	S	—	S
14	Mauroy II/2	—	—	—	—	C,s	—	—	S	—
16	Chirac	—	MC	—	G,mc,mc	MC	MC	G	mc	—
21	Balladur	MC	G/G	—	NP	—	MC	G	—	G
22	Juppé 1	MC	—	—	G	—	G,mc	NP	—	G
22	Juppé 2	MC	—	—	MC,g	—	G,mc	NP	—	G
23	Jospin	—	—	S	—	—	C,s	CL	—	C

France 519

TABLE 13.6. Continued (5)

Cabinet number	Cabinet	(34) Leisure	(35) Civil Service	(36) Women	(37) Commerce	(38) Universities	(39) Tourism	(40) Algeria	(41) Administrative Reforms	(42) Refugees	(43) Foreign Trade
1	Debré	—	—	—	—	—	—	—	—	—	—
2	Pompidou I	—	—	—	—	—	—	NP	—	G	—
3	Pompidou II	—	—	—	—	—	—	—	NP	G	—
4	Pompidou III	—	G	—	—	—	—	—	NP	—	—
5	Pompidou IV	—	—	—	—	—	G	—	—	—	—
6	Couve de Murville	—	—	—	—	—	—	—	NP	—	—
7	Chaban Delmas	—	—	—	—	—	—	—	G	—	—
8	Messmer I	—	—	—	G	—	—	—	—	—	—
9	Messmer II/1	—	MC	—	G	—	—	—	G	—	—
9	Messmer II/2	—	—	—	G	—	—	—	—	—	—
10	Chirac	—	—	—	G	mc	—	—	—	—	mc
11	Barre I/1	—	—	—	CL	mc	—	—	—	—	CR
11	Barre I/2	—	mc	—	CR,g,mc	mc	mc	—	—	—	CR
12	Barre II	—	—	—	CR	MC	—	—	—	—	MC
14	Mauroy II/1	S	C	S	S	—	—	—	—	—	NP
14	Mauroy II/2	—	—	S	S	—	—	—	—	—	S
16	Chirac	—	—	—	—	G	—	—	—	mc	G
21	Balladur	—	MC	—	MC	—	—	—	—	—	—
22	Juppé 1	—	MC	—	MC	—	G	—	MC	—	MC
22	Juppé 2	—	G	—	MC	—	—	—	—	—	—
23	Jospin	—	CL	—	s	—	c	—	—	—	cl

520   Jean-Louis Thiébault

TABLE 13.6. Continued (6)

Cabinet number	Cabinet	(44) Privatization	(45) Security	(46) Francophony	(47) Elderly people	(48) City	(49) Humanitarian action
1	Debré	—	—	—	—	—	—
2	Pompidou I	—	—	—	—	—	—
3	Pompidou II	—	—	—	—	—	—
4	Pompidou III	—	—	—	—	—	—
5	Pompidou IV	—	—	—	—	—	—
6	Couve de Murville	—	—	—	—	—	—
7	Chaban Delmas	—	—	—	—	—	—
8	Messmer I	—	—	—	—	—	—
9	Messmer II/1	—	—	—	—	—	—
9	Messmer II/2	—	—	—	—	—	—
10	Chirac	—	—	—	—	—	—
11	Barre I/1	—	—	—	—	—	—
11	Barre I/2	—	—	—	—	—	—
12	Barre II	—	—	—	—	—	—
14	Mauroy II/1	—	—	—	—	—	—
14	Mauroy II/2	—	—	—	—	—	—
16	Chirac	G	G	—	—	—	—
21	Balladur	—	—	—	—	NP	G
22	Juppé 1	—	cr	—	—	G,mc	—
22	Juppé 2	—	np	—	—	G	—

[a] Individual politicians who did not represent their party.

Notes: Some ministries (small letters only) are not always directed by a cabinet minister. In these cases a junior minister is in charge of the ministry but remains under the oversight of a cabinet minister.

Ministers
G = gaullist   MC = moderate conservative   CR = centre-right   CL = centre-left   S = socialist
C = communist   ECO = ecologist   NP = non-partisan
Secretaries of state
g   mc   cr   cl   s
c   eco   np

The nomination of individuals to specific ministerial posts is not done by the parties, but by the prime minister. He has to select capable and politically suitable persons. The president of the Republic has also tried to influence ministerial nominations by suggesting specific individuals. The Minister of Foreign Affairs and the Minister of Defence form a special category: their nomination presupposes the consent of the president. The distribution of portfolios among parties shows the permanent links between parties and policy sectors. But the parties have not generally been able permanently to 'colonize' the ministries within their areas of interest. No coalition programme has touched upon the question of distribution of civil services offices and other positions in the public sector. Once portfolio distribution has been completed, the government takes office. Very often, there is no official investiture in the National Assembly.

COALITION TERMINATION

The traditional rules of cabinet accountability to the parliament (questions of confidence and motions of censure) no longer play any real part in the French parliamentary game. This is because of the discipline of the majority parliamentary party groups and the solidity of electoral alliances. Instead, many cabinets have been defeated because of a very specific aspect of the French semi-presidential regime: the conflicts between the president of the Republic and the prime minister. Indeed, the president is sometimes forced to part with a prime minister he has appointed, because he thinks the prime minister's personality no longer accords with the new political orientation that the president intends to bring to his action. Although the formal constitution gives the president no such power, some prime ministers have had to resign at the president's request. We must also note that the prime minister traditionally offers the resignation of his government after the election of a new Assembly or a new president of the Republic. This resignation is regular, when it coincides with a new parliamentary or presidential majority. In these cases a new prime minister will take over. But it happens in any case, even when the same majority is re-elected.

J. Chirac was the first president of the Fifth Republic who, on 21 April 1997, dissolved the National Assembly for 'his own convenience'. He announced early parliamentary elections in an attempt to minimize the expected losses of the Gaullist-led majority and hence to provide himself with a working parliamentary majority for the remainder of his term as president. This would have allowed him to lead France into the European economic and monetary union, free of short-term electoral constraints.

The emergence of bipolarization has contributed to the disappearance of real cabinet accountability before parliament. The existence of a stable, coherent, and disciplined majority has prevented the overthrow of governments. The government can be censured only by the vote of an absolute majority, that is to say, by the majority of the total membership of the National Assembly (as opposed to a majority of the deputies voting). The only example happened at the beginning of the Fifth Republic: the fall of the first Pompidou government in October 1962. It was defeated on a motion of censure. The majority elected in November 1958 was unstable and undisciplined. The settling of the Algerian conflict had exacerbated this indiscipline. A majority of deputies refused General de Gaulle's proposal to elect the president of the Republic by direct universal suffrage. The majority coalition ended because Pompidou lost a censure vote in the National Assembly. The overthrow of the government allowed General de Gaulle to dissolve the National Assembly. The 18 and 25 November 1962 legislative election results favoured the formation of a stable and coherent majority coalition and the emergence of bipolarization. Parliament now plays only a weak role in the termination of coalitions.

More than the parliament, the president of the Republic has been responsible for many cabinet terminations. Constitutionally, the president of the Republic cannot revoke the mandate of the prime minister. In practice, however, there are many examples of government terminations at the request of the president. The latter, for example, may ask the prime minister to resign because his popularity in the public opinion has become so low that it weakens the government. This situation characterized the termination of the Messmer II, Barre I, Mauroy III, Mme. Cresson cabinets (this also applies to Juppé 1, which is not counted as a cabinet according to the counting rules of this volume). The president can also ask the prime minister to resign because of an economic policy change. In 1983, F. Mitterrand wanted such a change of economic policy. He therefore asked Prime Minister Pierre Mauroy to resign. But the president hesitated over the policy to follow and over the name of the prime minister's successor (Jacques Delors). Finally, he recalled P. Mauroy as the head of the government.

The termination of a cabinet can also be the result of a conflict with the president of the Republic. This type of conflict is the most important cause of government termination. Four such conflicts can be inventoried since the beginning of the Fifth Republic. In April 1962 General de Gaulle, in order to distance himself politically from Michel Debré, asked him to leave, after the settling of the Algerian conflict. In July 1972 J. Chaban-Delmas left at the request of President G. Pompidou shortly after he had received a vote of confidence in the National Assembly. In contrast, in August 1976, it was Prime Minister J. Chirac who himself decided to leave. He blamed President V. Giscard d'Estaing for not granting him the means to govern. This conflict culminated in the dramatic resignation of the prime minister. Finally, as a last example, in May 1991, F. Mitterrand decided to part with M. Rocard and

TABLE 13.7. Cabinet termination in France, 1959–1999

| Cabinet number | Cabinet | Mechanisms of cabinet termination ||||| Terminal events ||||| Policy area(s) | Comments |
| | | Technical || Discretionary ||| | | | | | | |
		(1) Regular parliamentary election	(2) Other constitutional reason	(4) Early parliamentary election	(6) Defeated by parliamentary opposition	(7) Conflict between coalition parties: policy	(9) Conflict between President and prime minister	(10) Elections (non-parliamentary)	(11) Popular opinion shocks	(13) Economic event	(14) Personal event		
1	Debré								X				Conflict on dissolution
2	Pompidou I				X		L						Constitutional reform and dissolution
3	Pompidou II	X	X										Presidential election
4	Pompidou III	X						X					Legislative election
5	Pompidou IV			X					X				May 1968 events
6	Couve de Murville		X					X					Presidential election
7	Chaban Delmas										X		Conflict on prime minister's powers
8	Messmer I	X					L						Legislative election
9	Messmer II/1								X				Internal majority conflict
9	Messmer II/2		X			X	L	X					Presidential election
10	Chirac										X		Conflict on prime minister's powers
11	Barre I/1						L	X					Internal majority conflict; municipal elections
11	Barre I/2	X				X							Legislative election
12	Barre II		X					X					Presidential election
13	Mauroy I			X					X				Dissolution
14	Mauroy II/1									X		6	Internal majority conflict

TABLE 13.7. cont.

Cabinet number	Cabinet	Mechanisms of cabinet termination							Terminal events				Policy area(s)	Comments
		Technical		Discretionary										
		(1) Regular parliamentary election	(2) Other constitutional reason	(4) Early parliamentary election	(6) Defeated by parliamentary opposition	(7) Conflict between coalition parties: policy	(9) Conflict between President and prime minister	(10) Elections (non-parliamentary)	(11) Popular opinion shocks	(13) Economic event	(14) Personal event		
14	Mauroy II/2					X	L		X			9	Internal majority conflict
15	Fabius	X				X	L						Legislative election
16	Chirac		X					X					Presidential election
17	Rocard I			X					X				Dissolution
18	Rocard II										X		Internal majority conflict
19	Mme Cresson					X	L		X				Internal majority conflict
20	Beregovoy	X				X	L						Legislative election
21	Balladur		X					X					Presidential election
22	Juppé 1								X				Internal majority conflict
22	Juppé 2			X		X	L			X			Dissolution

asked him to hand in his resignation, after the prime minister had made clear his desire to continue in office.

The last major cause of cabinet termination lies in the results of legislative or presidential elections. Traditionally, in France, the day after these elections, the prime minister resigns as a matter of protocol. The president accepts the resignation and a new bargaining process is set into action. The legislative elections have put an end to the functions of nine cabinets (Pompidou III and IV, Messmer I, Barre II, Mauroy I, Fabius, Rocard I, Bérégovoy, and Juppé). Three of these cases coincided, however, with defeats of the outgoing majority (Fabius, Bérégovoy, and Juppé). Presidential elections have led to the departure of six cabinets (Pompidou II, Couve de Murville, Messmer III, Barre III, Chirac, Balladur). Three of these resignations corresponded with majority changes: (1) R. Barre's resignation in May 1981 is linked to the defeat of V. Giscard d'Esteign and to the victory of F. Mitterrand in the 1981 presidential election; (2) J. Chirac's resignation in May 1988 was the consequence of his own defeat and the success of F. Mitterrand in the 1988 presidential election; (3) E. Balladur's resignation also corresponded with his own defeat and with the victory of J. Chirac in the 1995 presidential election, as well as with the end of Mitterrand's second seven-year term.

Electoral Performance

Government participation has some effects on electoral performance. Table 13.8 shows the gains and losses (in votes) of incumbent parties between 1958 and 1997. In most cases, the incumbency effect is negative. Only the moderate conservative parties have a positive overall balance and even they have experienced more elections with losses than gains when they faced the voters as government parties. However, there is interesting variation over time. The Gaullist Party has been the leading force and core of a stable governing coalition for a long period and did well in the elections of 1962, 1968, and 1978. From 1958, in almost each parliamentary election, it increased its share of the total vote. The UN–CNI–CD–ED coalition in 1962, the UN–RI coalitions in 1967 and 1968 and the RPR–RI–UC–Réf coalition in 1978 came strengthened out of the elections. Since the 1980s, however, the burden of government has produced considerable negative electoral effects for all parties.

CONCLUSION

Under the Fifth Republic, the institutional background with a semi-presidential system constitutes a strong constraint on coalition formation,

TABLE 13.8. *Electoral costs/benefits of government parties in France, 1959–1999* (in % of votes)

Government	In office at time of election	Election year	PC	S	CL	CR	MC	G	Government
UNR–CNI–CD–ED 1959–62	Yes	1962	—	—	−2.4	−3.2	−6.1	+13.8	+2.1
UNR–FNRI 1962–7	Yes	1967	—	—	—	—	+27.0	−0.3	+26.7
UNR–FNRI 1967–8	Yes	1968	—	—	—	—	+2.0	+5.9	+7.9
UDF–FNRI 1968–9	No	1973	—	—	—	—	−1.8	−14.0	−15.8
UDR–FNRI–PDM 1969–73	Yes	1973	—	—	—	−6.6	−1.8	−14.0	−22.4
RPR–FNRI–UC[a] *1973–4*	*(No)*	*(1978)*	—	—	—	*(+1.3)*	*(+3.9)*	*(+1.1)*	*(+6.3)*
RPR–FNRI–UC–Réf.[a] 1974–8	Yes	1978	—	—	—	+1.3	+3.9	+1.1	+6.3
RPR–UDF 1978–81	Yes	1981	—	—	—	—	−2.2	−1.6	−3.8
PS 1981	*(Yes)*	*(1981)*	—	*(+13.2)*	—	—	—	—	*(+13.2)*
PS–PC 1981–4	No	1986	−6.4	−5.5	—	—	—	—	−11.9
PS 1984–6	Yes	1986	—	−5.5	—	—	—	—	−5.5
RPR–UDF 1986–8	Yes	1988	—	—	—	—	—	−4.3	−4.3
PS 1988	*(Yes)*	*(1988)*	—	*(+5.6)*	—	—	—	—	*(+5.6)*
PS 1988–93	Yes	1993	—	−16.2	—	—	—	—	−16.2
RPR–UDF 1993–97	Yes	1997	—	—	—	—	−4.9	−4.7	−9.8
MEANS[b]			−6.4	−10.8	−2.4	−2.8	+2.6	−0.5	−3.9

[a] In the 1978 parliamentary election the Réf. was part of the CDS, which belonged to the UDF. (The UDF falls in the category of Moderate Conservative (MC) parties.) The 1973–4 government therefore has not been included as a separate government when calculating the means.

[b] The mean does not include the performance of the PS in 1981 and 1988. In both cases the PS governments were appointed by the newly elected or re-elected president—François Mitterrand—only a few weeks before the elections. The electoral results indicate the popularity of the president and his party at the beginning of a government term, rather than its end.

governance, and termination. France represents a variant of coalition building in which the president retains important powers in the process of coalition government formation. In this semi-presidential system, coalition government formation tends to be the most important presidential prerogative. Most presidents have used their power intensively to select the prime ministerial candidate and to give him instructions for party negotiations. The second aspect is the existence of the two-ballot electoral system which induces parties to form second-ballot coalitions.

The beginning of the Fifth Republic is characterized by the absence of coalition policy agreements. The right-wing parties rejected party government as contrary to the primacy of the presidency and to the spirit of the constitutional framework. They were only linked together by the great options defended by the different presidents during their presidential campaigns. The rules of the game are not written expressly in a coalition agreement. The fact that the Socialists came to power in 1981 has modified this practice. Negotiations on policy now occur before the legislative elections. The coalition programmes are formulated more carefully than before. They structure the bargaining situation more rigorously. The French case is therefore much less distinctive than previously: the government is now more coalitional and less presidential.

REFERENCES

Avril, Pierre (1987). *La Ve République: Histoire politique et constitutionelle*. Paris: Presses Universitaires de France.
Chagnollaud, Dominique, and Quermonne, Jean-Louis (1996). *Le Gouvernment de la France sous la Ve République*. Paris: Fayard.
Cohendet, Anne-Marie (1993). *La Cohabitation*. Paris: Presses Universitaires de France.
Colombani, Jean-Marie, and Portelli, Hugues (1995). *Le Double Septennat de François Mitterrand*. Paris: Grasset.
Duhamel, Olivier (1980). *La Gauche et la Vème République*. Paris: Presses Universitaires de France.
——(1991). *Le Pouvoir politique en France*. Paris: Le Seuil.
Duverger, Maurice (1985). *Le Système politique francais*. Paris: Presses Universitaires de France.
Fournier, Jacques (1987). *Le Travail gouvernemental*. Paris: Presses de la Foundation Nationale des Sciences Politiques-Dalloz.
Gicquel, Jean (1999). *Droit constitutionel et institutions politiques*. Paris: Montchrestien.
Huber, John D. (1996). *Rationalizing Parliament: Legislative Institutions and Party Politics in France*. Cambridge: Cambridge University Press.

Mény, Yves (1991). *Il système politique français*. Paris: Montchrestien.
Le Monde, Dossiers et documents: Les Élections législatives de mars 1978.
Le Monde, Dossiers et documents: Les Élections législatives de juin 1981.
Le Monde, Dossiers et documents: Les Élections législatives de mars 1986.
Le Monde, Dossiers et documents: Les Élections législatives de juin 1988.
Le Monde, Dossiers et documents: Les Élections législatives de mars 1993.
Le Monde, Dossiers et documents: Les Élections législatives de mai–juin 1997.
Plouvin, Jean-Yves (1980). 'Le Conseil des Minstres, institution seconde'. *Revue Administrative*, 33: 485–92.
Portelli, Hugues (1994). *La Vème République*. Paris: Hachette, Le Livre de Poche.
Pougnaud, P. (1993). *Les Rouages de l'état*. Paris: Eska.
Suleiman, Ezra N. (1980). 'Presidential Government in France', in Richard Rose and Ezra N. Suleiman (eds.), *Presidents and Prime Ministers*. Washington, DC: American Enterprise Institute.
Thiébault, Jean-Louis (1988). 'France: Cabinet Decision Making under the Fifth Republic', in Jean Blondel and Ferdinand Müller-Rommel (eds.), *Cabinets in Western Europe*. London: Macmillan Press.
——(1994). 'The Political Autonomy of Cabinet Ministers in the French Fifth Republic', in Michael Laver and Kenneth A. Shepsle (eds.), *Cabinet Ministers and Parliamentary Government*. Cambridge: Cambridge University Press.
Tricot, Bernard, Hadas-Lebel, Raphael, and Kessler, Denis (1995). *Les Institutions politiques françaises*. Paris: Presses de la Fondation Nationale des Sciences Politiques-Dalloz.

14

Portugal

The Rationale of Democratic Regime Building

José M. Magone

INTRODUCTION

Portugal is a latecomer to the club of democracies, and from the beginning democratic government was constrained by a lack of historical experience with genuine democracy based on universal secret and equal suffrage. The Portuguese parliamentary system was in flux from 1976 to 1987. It became consolidated only after the absolute majority of Anibal Cavaco Silva (PSD) in the elections of 19 July 1987. In the early consolidation period, this fledgling democracy had some experiences with coalition government, yet over time they have remained exceptions to the rule. The importance of the coalition experience lies in the fact that it was important for the consolidation of the political system.

From 1976 to 1985, Portuguese democracy was characterized by several distinctive features. First, coalition governance took place under high ideological polarization after a turbulent democratic transition. The three parties that were the actors in the coalition game belonged to different ideological blocs, and yet in spite of their ideological divergences, they entered into various coalitions with each other. Second, ideological, personalistic, or policy divergences very often led to an early break-up of the coalitions, the average duration being only fifteen months. Third, coalition formation was a freestyle bargaining process without the differentiation between *informateur* and *formateur* that can be found in, for example, Belgium or the Netherlands. Fourth, coalition formation was, as a rule, minimal winning. Fifth, coalition governance increased the set of feasible government constellations, and in promoting the learning of the rules of the democratic game contributed to the consolidation of the new political system. Sixth, coalition governance was until 1982 constrained by the role of the president. The semi-presidentialist role assumed by President Ramalho Eanes led to a growing antagonism between the parties and the presidency (see Duverger 1980).[1] This situation changed with the first constitutional revision in 1982, which reduced the powers of the president in government formation and dissolution. Seventh, the legacy of the revolution was a major contextual factor constraining coalition governance. Until 1982, the Movement of the Armed Forces (Movimento das Forças Armadas, MFA) had the right to supervise the new democracy through the Council of the Revolution (Conselho da Revolução, CR). The CR was abolished in 1982 and replaced by a Constitutional Court (Tribunal Constitucional), thus completing the 'civilianization' of the political system.

THE PARLIAMENTARY PARTY SYSTEM

The genesis of the Portuguese political and party systems during the revolutionary period of 1974–5 makes this case distinctive from other Western European democracies. Apart from the Communist Party (Partido Comunista Português, PCP) and the Socialist Party (Partido Socialista, PS), the main parties of resistance to the authoritarian regime, all the main parliamentary parties emerged only during the revolutionary process.

The Constituent Assembly elections of 25 April 1975 created a new party system of four main parties and some smaller ones. The four main parties are the PS, the PCP, the PSD and the CDS.[2] These four parties have in the past two decades been able to accumulate over 90 per cent of the vote, thus preventing party system fragmentation. The tendency towards the four-party system has generally become more salient from election to election. In spite of a proportional representation system based on the d'Hondt method, smaller parties have had little representation in the new parliament.

The PS has been the pivotal party of the new party system and indeed of Portuguese politics. Although a Socialist Party existed as early as 1878 and attempts to revitalize it were undertaken after 1945, the new party was not founded until 17 April 1973, in Bad Münstereiffel, West Germany. This cadre party had to build party structures during the revolutionary era. Yet, its leading figure, Mário Soares, successfully forged the PS into one of the major forces of this period. After the elections of 25 April 1975, Soares clearly committed himself to preventing a development towards Communist or extreme-left government. During the constitutional period (i.e. after November 1975),

---

[1] The Portuguese case tends to semi-presidentialism in times of crisis or absolute majority. This was practised particularly by President Ramalho Eanes, who in 1978–9 nominated prime ministers without the approval of the parliamentary parties.

[2] We follow here the Laver and Hunt (1992: 292–3) positioning of the Portuguese political parties. This is similar to that of other authors such as Bruneau and Macleod (1986). This is confirmed by the leading Portuguese party system specialist Aguiar (1989: 232–3).

TABLE 14.1. *Left–right placement of parties, party strength (in seats) and party composition of governments in Portugal, 1975–1999*

Year	Proximity to elections	UDP	MDP/CDE	PCP	PS	PRD	PSD	PSN	PPM	CDS	Median party in second policy dimension	Effective number of legislative parties	Government strength	Total number of seats
1975[a]	—	1	5	30	116*	—	80	—	—	16	PS	4,75	—	250
1976	F	1	—	40	107*	—	73	—	—	42	PS	4,96	107	263
1978	F	—	—	—	107*	—	—	—	—	**42**	PS	4,96	149	263
1978	F	—	—	—	—	—	—	—	—	—	—	—	—[b]	263
1978	F	—	—	—	—	—	—	—	—	—	—	—	—[b]	263
1979	F	—	—	—	—	—	—	—	—	—	—	—	—[b]	263
1979	FE[c]	1	—	47	74	—	80*	—	**4**	**44**	PSD	6,23	128	250
1980	FE	1	—	47	71	—	82*	—	**5**	**47**	PSD	6,21	134	250
1983	FE	—	—	44	101*	—	75	—	—	30	PS	5,35	176	250
1985	FE	—	—	38	57	45*	88	—	—	22	PRD	6,49	88	250
1987	FE	—	—	31	60	7	148*	—	—	4	PS	3,76	148	250
1991	FE	—	—	17	72	—	135*	1	—	5	PS	4,25	135	230
1995	F	—	—	15	112*	—	88	—	—	15	PS	4,21	112	230

[a] Elections to the constituent assembly during the transition period.
[b] These were caretaker governments invested by President Ramalho Eanes without support in the parliament. This is the main reason why they do not have a long cabinet life.
[c] The elections of Dec. 1979 were considered as interim, so that the complete period of the first legislature could be completed, before the second legislature could be started in 1980. After this intercalating legislative session completing the first legislature, new elections were held in Oct. 1980, leading to the victory of the AD.

Parties

UDP   Uniao Democratica Popular (Democratic Popular Union)
MDP/CDE Movimento Democratico Popular–Comissão Democratica Eleitoral (People's Democratic Movement –Electoral Democratic Commission)
PCP   Partido Comunista Portugues (Portuguese Communist Party)
PS   Partido Socialista (Socialist Party)
CDS   Partido do Centro Democratico Social (Party of the Democratic Social Centre)
PRD   Partido Renovador Democrático (Democratic Renewal Party)
PSD   Partido Socialdemocrata (Social Democratic Party)
PSN   Partido de Solidariedade Nacional (Party of National Solidarity)
PPM   Partido Popular Monarquico (Monarchic People's Party)

the PS had difficulties achieving party cohesion (Corkill 1995: 73). Ideologically, the party was now dominated by technocrats. Their main aim was electoral success, rather than a rigid commitment to socialism. Such pragmatism was heavily criticized by the so-called *historicos* around Mário Soares (Cruz 1995: 143–7). The Socialist Party's status as one of the parties of government has clearly caused major problems for the consolidation of the party structures (Panebianco 1988: 34–6).

The PPD/PSD (Partido Popular Democrático/Partido Social Democràta) was founded in May 1974 by prominent figures critical of the former authoritarian regime, the main leader being Francisco Sá Carneiro. The 1975 elections made it the second largest party and paved the way for a crucial role in the 1980s. The creation of the Democratic Alliance (Aliança Democrática, AD) with the CDS in 1979 led to a formation of an intra-bloc coalition government. Yet, this strong majority was weakened by constant factionalism inside the PSD and the CDS and broke down at the end of 1982 (Stock 1989*b*). The PSD became more cohesive after 1985, when Cavaco Silva was elected party leader at the XII congress in Figueira da Foz. Factionalism persisted, but Cavaco Silva geared the party's attention towards his technocratic modernization programme for Portugal, which until October 1995 was supported by structural funds from the European Community. Cavaco Silva stepped down as president of the party in February 1995 and the party returned to factionalist politics, at least for the time being.

The third coalitional party is the CDS (Partido do Centro Democrático Social). This Christian Democratic Party founded by Freitas do Amaral, Amaro da Costa and Basilio Horta shortly after the *coup d'état*, on 25 April 1974, consisted of former notables from the Caetanist/Salazarist regime and was attacked by the extreme left groups during the revolution. In the elections of 25 April 1975, it became the fourth largest party of the new party system (Pinto 1989). The party can be described as a 'coalition of politicians' (Laver and Schofield 1990: 20). Personalities play an important role in building party cohesion. During the late 1970s, the CDS maintained a rigid ideological opposition to the new constitution, which was highly influenced by Marxism. The party's decline during the Cavaco Silva governments was reversed in the most recent elections, when new leader Manuel Monteiro, using very populist language, succeeded in more than doubling the CDS vote, from 4 to 9.08 per cent. The party was renamed the People's Party (Partido Popular, PP) and became an anti-Maastricht party. Whilst supporting European integration, it vehemently opposes the Treaty on the European Union as a major constraint on national sovereignty. Monteiro's populist message appealed to social groups who have not been able to profit from European integration, such as fishermen and farmers (Magone 1996*b*: 150).

The PCP is the oldest party of the new system. It was founded in 1921 and became the most important force against the authoritarian regime. At the start of the revolution, the PCP was the only party with an organization, and it spread very quickly by creating a network of party branches all over the country (Ferreira 1982: 89–90). Moreover, the party steadily gained control over the media and parts of the state apparatus, a process Mário Soares regarded as a major danger and countered. From this moment on, the PCP became more isolated within the party system. After 1976, it remained the main defender of the achievements of the revolution, but was nevertheless ostracized from the national decision making structures (Lopes and Barroso 1980: 152).

Portugal then experienced a situation similar to the Italian experience of *'bipartitismo imperfetto'* (Galli 1966), which implied the exclusion of the Communist Party from government. In the Portuguese case, in which the PCP has never been considered as a coalition partner because of its role during the revolutionary process, one may label it 'imperfect multi-partyism' (*pluripartidarismo imperfeito*) (Stock 1989*b*: 157). Ideologically, the PCP maintains its Marxist-Leninist identity (*Expresso*, 12 Dec. 1992: 12R–13R). The party's strategy has always been to seek an intra-bloc coalition government with the PS, which, although a possibility in 1978, has never materialized. Since the late 1970s, the PCP has formed electoral coalitions with smaller parties such as the Portuguese Democratic Movement/Electoral Democratic Commission (Movimento Democràtico Português/Comissão Democrática Eleitoral, MDP/CDE), until 1987 called the Unitary People's Alliance (Alianca Popular Unitária, APU), and the ecological party of the Greens (Partido Ecologista 'Os Verdes', PEV), later called the Unitary Democratic Coalition (Coligação Democràtica Unitária, CDU). In spite of this electoral coalition strategy, the PCP has declined considerably to slightly more than 9 per cent of the vote (1995). The party membership is quite old, and the ideology has proven unattractive to younger voters (Pereira 1987: 11; Costa e Sousa 1983: 529).

For a recent democracy, the parties in the Portuguese system have been very stable (Aguiar 1985), and the system has neither fragmented nor defragmented markedly. In 1985 a new party, called the Democratic Renewal Party (Partido Renovador Democrático, PRD) and founded by President Ramalho Eanes, gathered 17.92 per cent of the vote. After two years, however, this party vanished almost completely from the political scene. The main reason seemed to be that its search for an identity in the Portuguese Assembly led to a very radical opposition to the PSD minority government, which alienated its electorate. The PRD folded in 1991.

This stability of the number of parties and fragmentation of the vote is counterbalanced by various forms of party system fluidity. On the one hand, there is a high level of inter-bloc electoral volatility between the PS and the PSD, which is responsible for the different electoral configurations since 1975. On the other hand, intra-bloc volatility is also quite strong between the

CDS and the PSD, and to a lesser extent between the PCP and the PS (Morlino 1995: 318 and 320).

The four-party system is dominated by the two main parties of the centre: the PS and the PSD. Whereas until 1985 they had to search for working majorities by creating several coalition options, this changed considerably afterwards. The period prior to 1985 was characterized by ideological rigidity among the four parties leading to tensions within them. The period of coalition government after 1976 was one of experimentation and political learning within the new institutional framework set up by the constitutional settlement. This experimentation also served to overcome ideological inter- and intra-bloc rigidities, thus broadening the options available to the parliamentary actors. At the same time, it helped consolidate the four-party system and reduce vote fragmentation.

INSTITUTIONAL BACKGROUND

Two major factors constrained coalition government in Portugal during the early period of democracy. First, the new constitution included some institutions that were created during the revolutionary period and which significantly influenced policy formulation. Second, due to the instability of the parties and the new parliamentary institutions, the president of the Republic was dominant in the first six years of the young democracy.

Until the first revision of the 1976 constitution, Portuguese governments were heavily constrained by the political presence of the military through the so-called Council of the Revolution (Conselho da Revolução, CR). The CR was founded on 19 May 1975 during the radical phase of the revolution by the Assembly of the MFA (Assembleia do MFA) (Assembleia do MFA 1976: 132–4). This was the main institution created during the revolutionary period, and it had been enshrined in the constitution as a means to control the democratization process for a further five years. Its core project was the 'Alliance People's-MFA' (Alianca Povo-MFA), which was intended to foster a political structure based on popular institutions emerging spontaneously during the revolution. The CR would remain the military element of the new constitution until it was abolished in the constitutional revision of 1982 (Domingos 1980: 127–32).

Through its Constitutional Commission, the CR scrutinized the laws approved by the government and the Assembly of the Republic (Assembleia da República, AR). It could send bills that it deemed to be unconstitutional to the Constitutional Commission. In this sense, it had powers similar to those of the president of the Republic. In reality, the CR was quite moderate, and its formal competence was not used very frequently. It sent 35 bills to the

Constitutional Commission and 29 to the president of the Republic. Together these 64 bills represented no more than 1.5 per cent of the total number of bills (4,060) sent to the president of the Republic for his signature (Mendes 1989: 936). Nevertheless, the potential constraint of the revolutionary legacy was always there, because Article 147 of the constitution stipulated that the CR acted to guarantee fidelity to the spirit of the Portuguese revolution, which was defined in Article 2 as 'to assure the transition to socialism through the creation of conditions for the democratic exercise of power by the working classes'. This was one of the main reasons for the formation of the AD in 1979, which was geared towards constitutional reform, and which collapsed soon after this had been achieved.

The second main constraint on coalition formation has been the head of state. The president is elected by universal suffrage, which gives him democratic legitimacy to play an active political role. The election of General Ramalho Eanes on 27 June 1976 with 61.59 per cent of the votes, established him in a strong position to influence the political process. The most important constraint in relation to government formation is probably the president's ability to nominate and discharge the prime minister and his government. Moreover, he can dissolve the Assembly of the Republic. During the period of coalition government between 1976 and 1985, General Ramalho Eanes was a major constraint on coalition bargaining. His fidelity to the Constitution of 1976 and close relationship to the MFA made him a difficult actor to deal with. In this period of economic disarray, government policies had to be geared towards economic austerity.

Although Eanes was supported during the presidential elections by the PS, the PSD, and the CDS, all three parties had a difficult relationship with him. The inherent semi-presidentialism in the Portuguese institutional framework came to the fore because the parties in the Assembly of the Republic were not able to build a working majority (Domingos 1980: 161–76). The collapse of the PS–CDS coalition government in 1978 can be considered the apex of presidential power. Eanes discharged Prime Minister Mário Soares from office, and after consulting all relevant political parties, he decided to appoint an independent as Soares' successor. Between late August 1978 and December 1979 three 'presidential' caretaker governments consisting of independents were installed, in spite of the opposition of the two main parties (Ferreira 1985: 705).

This contributed to a worsening of the relationship between the parties and the president. The negative relationship became evident when Ramalho Eanes asked for the support of the political parties for his re-election. From the start, Sá Carneiro, leader of the Democratic Alliance after its victory of the interim elections of December 1979 and 5 October 1980, declared that he would support General Soares Carneiro against Eanes. He presented a 'parliamentarist' position against the 'presidentialist' one of Ramalho Eanes. His motto was: 'one government, one majority, one president.'

Ramalho Eanes was more successful with the Socialist Party. Yet, the PS asked a high price for its support in that Eanes was forced to sign a pact in anticipation of the upcoming constitutional revision. The pact was signed in November 1980. The PS committed itself to support the re-election of Ramalho Eanes and to prevent a diminution of his constitutional powers. Eanes was forced to abandon the accumulated position as Commander of the Armed Forces, and agreed not to present any personal project for a constitutional revision and not to use the referendum as a means to introduce limits to the revision of the constitution. Moreover, he was asked to respect constitutional norms relating to the nomination of governments, the acceptance of minority governments, and respect for the role of the parties in democracy (Cruz 1994: 249).

The death, in a tragic aviation accident on 4 December 1980, of Sá Carneiro, who supported General Soares Carneiro against Ramalho Eanes, was a severe blow to the PSD. President Eanes was re-elected on 7 December 1980 with a comfortable majority of 56.44 per cent. During his second term, he reverted to an expansionist vision of the presidency. Until the constitutional revision of 1982, the president committed himself to fostering consensus between the two main parties: the PS and the PSD. This ran against the PSD's strategy of bipolarization (Cruz 1994: 250). Between 1980 and 1982, the AD under Francisco Pinto Balsemão continued this policy of bipolarization. It was joined later by the PS, when Mário Soares was able to regain the party leadership and no longer felt committed to the pact signed in November 1980. The constitutional revision considerably reduced the powers of the president in the government investiture process. The adoption of a National Law of Defence further consolidated the steady civilianization of the Portuguese political system (Bruneau and Macleod 1986: 122–3). Nevertheless, the instability of the AD government, which collapsed six months after the constitutional revision, and later on of the PS/PSD central bloc government, continued to assure a pivotal role for the president. Ramalho Eanes called early elections in 1983 and 1985, when no workable majority was achieved.

Mário Soares's first term as president of the Republic was characterized by cooperation with the Cavaco Silva governments. This changed after Soares's re-election in 1991. He became a major critic of the Cavaco Silva government, refusing to ratify several bills, and sending them instead to the Constitutional Court. He thus became a major constraint on the PSD government.

COALITION FORMATION

Since 1976 Portugal has had six coalition cabinets, four single-party cabinets, and three caretaker cabinets. The process of cabinet formation can be characterized as freestyle bargaining. There is no distinction between the *informateur*, who sounds out the potential coalition partners before the negotiations, and the *formateur*, the actual broker of the coalition. No pure *informateur* has been used, and a *formateur* is appointed only after the parties have reached a bargaining solution. Coalition government was quite prevalent in Portugal between 1978 and 1985.

This section will focus predominantly on the coalition government between the PS and the CDS in 1978, the AD-governments between 1979 and 1983, and the Central Bloc government formed by the PS and the PSD between 1983 and 1985. In general terms, each of them conditioned the subsequent ones, closing the options available for working majorities. Portuguese coalition formation has been relatively simple: it has included no more than three parties, and only once has there been more than one bargaining attempt. None the less, coalition governments have needed more time to form than single-party ones (see Table 14.2).

TABLE 14.2. *Government formation in Portugal, 1976–1999*

Government	Number of parties in parliament	Number of previous bargaining rounds	Parties involved in previous bargaining rounds	Number of days required for government formation
PS 1976	6	0		14
PS–CDS 1978	6	1	PS, PCP	45
Nobre da Costa 1978	6	0		31
Mota Pinto 1978	6	0		37
Pintassilgo 1979	6	0		50
AD (PSD–CDS–PPM) 1979	6	0		7
AD (PSD–CDS–PPM) 1980	6	0		1
Bloco Central (PS–PSD) 1983	4	0		45
PSD 1985	5	0		30
PSD 1987	5	0		30
PSD 1991	5	0		25
PS 1995	4	0		30

All three coalitions can be characterized as minimal winning and have been very unstable. This has been exacerbated by intra-party factionalism leading to the split of MPs from the parliamentary groups. Moreover, in the Portuguese case, there has been no differentiation between the roles of *informateur* and *formateur* (as in the Belgian and Dutch cases). On the contrary, freestyle bargaining (as in the Irish case) is a more appropriate description of the Portuguese experience. Coalition formation procedures have been created on an *ad hoc* improvisational basis.

The PS–CDS Coalition of 1978

The case of the PS–CDS coalition government was overshadowed by a severe economic crisis. The need to negotiate a package of austerity measures with the International Monetary Fund (IMF) led to the collapse of the PS minority government on 9 December 1977. After a failed motion of confidence in the AR, Soares was confirmed in his position as prime minister by his party and he started parallel negotiations with both the PCP and the CDS. Both negotiations were kept secret from each other until the last minute. The negotiations with the PCP were held in December 1977 and early January 1978. They failed because of the demands the PCP placed on the PS. The Communists wanted more concessions to preserve a vast area of the agrarian reform in the southern province of Alentejo. The PCP, which had a vast clientele who worked in the so-called collective units of production (unidades colectivas de produção-UCPs), wanted to assure that a potential coalition government would protect these collective farms. In the end, the PS decided to go no further in the negotiations, so that a strengthening of the Communist-dominated UCPs could be prevented. The first PS government opposed the expansion of the Communist influence in Alentejo and started a policy of counter-action. Some measures had been approved together with the PSD during 1977 (Vester 1984: 497–500).

The negotiations with the CDS started on 17 January 1978. This highly sensitive rapprochement of two ideological distinctive parties was kept secret from the public. In the end, the formula was a PS government integrating some CDS members. In the National Commission of the PS, the new government was accepted with an overall majority. It was confronted with a *fait accompli*. If the National Commission would not support the new government, the alternative was to give Eanes the decision to form a new government or to call for early elections. The main task was to stabilize the economy by implementing the IMF standby credit. Mário Soares was nominated as the new prime minister on 23 January 1978, and the new government took office on 30 January. The coalition did not last long due to general disagreements between the PS and the CDS. It was terminated after six months (Rother 1985: 254).

The AD Cabinets 1980–1982

The AD government was of a different kind. It was Francisco Sá Carneiro, charismatic PSD leader, who decided to develop a strategy of bipolarization of the right-wing bloc against the left. A first attempt to bring all the democratic parties under the same umbrella was the so-called Democratic Convergence (Convergência Democratica) formed between the PSD and the CDS in May 1977, with the objective of articulating the positions of both parties in parliament. Interestingly, the PS was also invited to join the democratic convergence (Gomes 1982: 30). At the end of 1977 the Soares government collapsed, prompting negotiations with the CDS and the PCP. After the collapse of the PS–CDS government in July 1978, Sá Carneiro started to build up the Democratic Alliance (Aliança Democrática, AD) between the PSD, the CDS, and the Monarchic People's Party (Partido Popular Monárquico, PPM) (Gomes 1982: 30–1). In its agreement the AD committed itself to dialogue with other democratic parties, but excluded cooperation with future PS governments. Ultimately, the AD intended to change the highly Marxist constitution. Both the CDS, the PSD, and the PPM saw this as the common denominator of the coalition. In spite of the death of Sá Carneiro and the re-emergence of factionalism inside the PSD, this alliance strategy was preserved until the cabinet of Pinto Balsemão II resigned in late 1982.

At the inception of the AD government, there was only one bargaining attempt and three parties involved. The coalition agreement was already in place before the elections of 2 December 1979. This electoral coalition changed the nature of cabinet formation, governance, and duration. As already mentioned, the semi-presidentialism inherent in the political system was a further inducement towards this strategy of bipolarization, as Sá Carneiro intended to enhance the power of parliament. Yet, the coalition was plagued by instability, and factionalism in the PSD and the CDS caused problems for the government. In the end, in the period between 1979 and 1982 Portugal experienced three AD cabinets: one under Sá Carneiro which would last until his death on 4 December 1980, and two under the premiership of media tycoon Francisco Pinto Balsemão.

The 'Central Bloc' Cabinet 1983–1985

The genesis of the 'Central Bloc' government between 1983 and 1985 goes back to the position of Ramalho Eanes, who during his second presidential term tried to foster a policy of consensus between the PS and the PSD (Cruz 1994: 250). In 1980 such a broad coalition was pre-empted by the bipolarization strategy of the AD. But the collapse of the AD in late 1982 led to early elections on 25 April 1983. In the pre-electoral period, the main parties were already discussing the governmental options. Between January and April 1983, the PS decided to follow Mário Soares's strategy of compromise, which aimed at achieving a working majority, and which in the case of a plurality prescribed cooperation with the PSD. Soares had to contend with resistance inside his party from the 'ex-secretariat', which had had close ties to President Eanes.[3]

---

[3] The ex-secretariat consisted of the members of the secretariat that negotiated an agreement to support Ramalho Eanes for re-election. Soares left the party leadership in protest, because he thought that the party should not support Eanes. The fourth party congress in 1981, at which Soares won a majority of delegates, increased the power of the secretary general and abolished the secretariat. However, the members of the secretariat had rallied

TABLE 14.3. *Portuguese cabinets since 1974*

Cabinet number	Cabinet	Date in	Formal resignation	Maximum potential duration (in days)	Duration (in days)	Government composition
1	Palma Carlos	16 May 1974	11 July 1974	55	55	Provisional
2	Goncalves I	18 July 1974	30 Sept. 1974	72	72	Provisional
3	Goncalves II	30 Sept. 1974	11 Mar. 1975	161	161	Provisional
4	Goncalves III	26 Mar. 1975	8 Aug. 1975	132	132	Provisional
5	Goncalves IV	8 Aug. 1975	12 Sept. 1975	34	34	Provisional
6	Pinheiro de Azevedo	19 Sept. 1975	22 July 1976	303	303	Provisional
7	Soares I	23 July 1976	9 Dec. 1977	1,440	474	PS
8	Soares II	23 Jan. 1978	28 July 1978	966	185	PS–CDS
9	Nobre da Costa	29 Aug. 1978	15 Sept. 1978	771	18	Presidential
10	Mota Pinto	22 Nov. 1978	11 June 1979	753	189	Presidential
11	Pintassilgo	31 July 1979	27 Dec. 1979	564	147	Presidential
12	Sá Carneiro I	3 Jan. 1980	5 Oct. 1980	365	272	AD (PSD + CDS + PPM)
13	Sá Carneiro II	5 Oct. 1980	9 Jan. 1981	1,440	96	AD (PSD + CDS + PPM)
14	Balsemão 1	9 Jan. 1981	14 Aug. 1981	1,380	691	AD (PSD + CDS + PPM)
	Balsemão 2	4 Sept. 1981	23 Dec. 1982			AD (PSD + CDS + PPM)
15	Soares III	9 June 1983	12 July 1985	1,440	794	Bloco Central (PS + PSD)
16	Cavaco Silva I	6 Nov. 1985	17 Aug. 1987	1,440	510	PSD
17	Cavaco Silva II	17 Aug. 1987	31 Oct. 1991	1,440	1,506	PSD
18	Cavaco Silva III	31 Oct. 1991	28 Oct. 1995	1,440	1,440	PSD
19	Guterres	28 Oct. 1995		1,440		PS

Nevertheless, at the beginning of the year Soares preferred to be open to all kinds of coalitions. From March, it became evident that the PS would exclude an alliance with the PCP (Stock 1989*b*: 158–9). It reflected Mario Soares's anti-communist stand, which had been shaped by his experiences during the revolutionary period. The position of the PCP was similar, as it prepared a campaign arguing that a vote for the Socialist Party was a vote for the right (*Avante!* 5 May 1983). This antagonistic relationship indicated that Soares already had a preference for the 'Central Bloc' solution. However, the PS leadership had not yet accepted a coalition with the CDS, which was regarded as a right-wing party.

After the resignation of Pinto Balsemão, the new CDS leadership consisted of Eurico de Melo, Mota Pinto, and Nascimento Rodrigues. In the end, Mota Pinto would become the new leader. In this pre-campaign period the PSD seemed to search for a coalition with the CDS. The main aim was to restore the AD coalition government. In May, Mota Pinto advocated the strategy that the PSD would govern alone if it achieved an absolute majority, and return to opposition if the results were worse than those of 1979. In case of a plurality, it would first approach the CDS, and afterwards, if trends in the electorate so indicated, the Socialists (Stock 1989*b*: 158–9).

As it turned out, the 1983 elections gave the PS a plurality and a major boost. For Mota Pinto, one of the architects of the *Bloco Central* government, there were now only four alternatives. The first was for the PSD not to support any motion of rejection; the second, to seek an agreement of mere parliamentary incidence; the third, to return to the opposition benches; and the fourth, to form a government coalition with the PS. In the end, he opted for the latter in spite of resistance from a strong minority of the party. Meanwhile, Mário Soares organized a referendum among the PS members and was able to gather the support of approximately 80 per cent for the PS/PSD coalition, as against the alternative of joining with the communist coalition APU. Among PS leaders there was general approval of the coalition, so long as it would not fall into the past anti-communist and anti-Eanist rhetoric of the AD.

Negotiations between the PS and the PSD started on 26 April, one day after the elections. The Permanent Commission of the PS and the Political Commission of the PSD met jointly to discuss official positions. In the PSD, the opening of negotiations was approved by the National Council on 8 May. The majority of 31 to 14, with 9 abstentions, mirrored the internal divergences over the coalition.[4] Continuing internal disagreements in the PSD imposed a

one-third of conference delegates behind them, and infighting between the 'Soaristas' and the group now known as the ex-secretariat continued until the general elections of April 1983 (Gallagher 1989: 21–2).

[4] Both parties have a similar organizational structure. In both parties the congress is the most important decision making body. The interim decision making body elected by the

major constraint on the coalition negotiations and persisted even after the government agreement had been signed on 4 June 1983. The new government was invested by President Eanes on 9 June. Yet for all its promise, the government lasted only until October 1985. Intra-party factionalism in the PSD and the debate concerning Mário Soares's candidacy for the presidency of the Republic revealed its instability (Stock 1989b: 160-1).

COALITION GOVERNANCE

The Portuguese case shows that coalition government during early democratic consolidation can be very tightly constrained by external factors. Consequently, coalition governance procedures have been very unstable. And although coalition agreements are carefully drafted, they are seldom adhered to.

Coalition Agreements

The few existing coalition agreements are not very structured or detailed documents. Between 1978 and 1985 the coalition agreements were quite diverse: some were written during legislative terms, long before the elections (PS-CDS in 1978), some were pre-electoral coalition agreements reached shortly before the elections (AD 1979-83), and some were post-electoral coalition agreements (PS-PSD 1983-5). The genuine coalition agreements are small in size and dedicate most of their wording to policy issues and secondarily to general and procedural rules. In the two-party coalition agreements the general and specific procedures of inter-party cooperation and consultation are well defined. In the AD governments, the 'political cabinet' institution played a role in defining positions in relation to the opposition. All three coalition agreements include formal or informal rules of discipline in the initiation of legislation in the Assembly of the Republic.

The PS–CDS Coalition of 1978

The coalition agreement between the PS and the CDS in 1978 was geared to the need to negotiate an austerity programme with the IMF, so that the

congress and acting between congresses in the PS is the National Comission (Comissão Nacional) and in the PSD is the National Council (Conselho Nacional). A more flexible commission manages the daily aspects of party administration. In the PS this is called the Permanent Commission (Comissão Permanente) and in the PSD is the National Political Commission (Comissão Political Nacional). These two commissions negotiated the coalition agreement and submitted a motion of approval to the respective interim decision making bodies. In the PS alone, there was a survey among the members about the different coalition options.

TABLE 14.4. *Coalition governance in Portugal*

(1) Coalition	(2) Coalition agreement	(3) Agreement public	(4) Election rule	(5) Conflict management mechanisms	(6) Most common management mechanisms	(7) Mechanisms for most serious conflicts	(8) Coalition discipline in legislation	(9) Coalition discipline in other parliamentary behaviour	(10) Freedom of appointment	(11) Policy agreement	(12) Junior ministers	(13) Non-cabinet positions
1978 PS–CDS	IE	Yes	No	CoC, PS	CoC	PS	3	3	Yes	3	No	No
1979 AD (PSD–CDS–PPM)	PRE	Yes	No	CaC, PS	CaC	PS	2	3	Yes	3	No	No
1980 AD (PSD–CDS–PPM)	PRE	Yes	No	Cac, PS	CaC	PS	2	3	Yes	3	No	No
1983 Bloco Central (PS–PSD)	POST	Yes	No	CoC, PS	CoC	PS	2	3	Yes	3	Yes	No

Portuguese economy could be stabilized. The final document was devoted mainly to the government's economic policy. It was intended to shift national economic policy from a directive role to a more corrective and advisory one. Henceforth, economic policy should be designed not to influence developments inside the enterprises. The main guideline for economic policy was the 'opening of the market to the outside world and continuing austerity policy within the country' (Rother 1985: 255). This, Soares held, was justified in that the PS and the CDS wanted to overcome the financial crisis without ideological prejudices. This programme complemented PS policy from 1977 on, which was based on the premiss that economic improvement could be achieved only through the conquest of new export markets.

TABLE 14.5. *Size and content of coalition agreements in Portugal, 1978–1985*

Coalition	Size	General procedural rules (in %)	Specific procedural rules (in %)	Distribution of offices (in %)	Distribution competences (in %)	Policies (in %)
PS–CDS 1978[a]	4,476	39	0.6	0	0	60.4
1979 AD (PSD–CDS–PPM)[b]	34,300	0	0	0	0	100
Bloco Central (PS–PSD)[c]	2,461	10.4	14.2	4.5	0	70.9

[a] Acordo Político PS–CDS; Anexo I ao acordo PS/CDS: Programa Economico de Estabilizacao para 1978. Anexo II ao acordo PS–CDS: Plano de Desenvolvimento a Médio Prazo (Lopes 1978: 61–72).
[b] Aliança Democrática, *Programa Eleitoral de Governo* (Lisboa: PSD, 1979). This coalition agreement continued to be in force under the 1980 AD government.
[c] Acordo Político, parlamentar e do Governo celebrado entre o PSD e o PS (*Povo Livre*, 8 June 1983, 2–4).

At the same time, the new government decided to eliminate import restrictions. These liberalization policies caused, as a matter of course, limits to public spending on social transfers and investments. The consequences were a lingering high unemployment rate, a decline in real wages, and the strong dependency of small and medium-sized enterprises. The low growth policies were intended to be in place for three years only, to be replaced by a policy of economic expansion. This economic package closely met the demands of the IMF stabilization programme. But more than that, the Socialist government itself saw this as a necessary precondition to stabilizing the Portuguese economy. The Democratic Social Centre was integrated to achieve a broader basis in parliament, so that these unpopular measures could be successfully implemented (Rother 1985: 255–7; Ferreira 1985: 699–704).

Other policy issues mentioned in the agreement became of secondary priority: compulsory education for all 6-year-olds, a National Health Service created and financed by the state, the development of a central apparatus of social insurance, some increases in social transfers such as pensions and sickness grants, administrative reform to enhance the implementation of laws, a revised abortion law, and legislation to protect citizens' rights ('Acordo' 1978: 61–2).

It was agreed that eleven ministers should go to the PS and three to the CDS (Foreign Affairs, External Trade, and Administrative Reform), with two independents (Minister of Agriculture Saias and Defence Minister Firmino Miguel). Only five ministers from the previous government retained seats in the new cabinet (Rother 1985: 257–8).

The coalition agreement also included several general procedural rules and a few specific ones. 'The Political Agreement PS/CDS' ('Acordo Politico PS/CDS') was defined as an 'inter-partisan political agreement, of parliamentary understanding and governmental incidence'. The agreement would be valid until the end of the ongoing legislature (1980). The agreement would be terminated if one of the members were to violate it, or if the political situation changed considerably.

The government should be understood essentially as a socialist government including non-PS personalities and counting on a stable parliamentary majority. This implied that the CDS was not allowed to undermine the government in the Assembly of the Republic. For its part, the government had to keep the CDS informed about the principal sectors of government policy. This was achieved by regular meetings between the prime minister and the president of the CDS, as well as between the ministers and the respective spokespersons of the CDS.

The ministers were selected entirely by the prime minister, as defined in the agreement ('Acordo' 1978: 62–3). The agreement also stipulated that there should be previous consultations in the Assembly of the Republic in relation to several policy areas such as media policy, laws related to the exercise of the rights, freedoms, and guarantees of citizens, local and regional policy, laws related to interest groups, labour policy, and education policy. Moreover, inter-party cooperation should extend to issues related to the organization and functioning of the Assembly of the Republic, particularly concerning elected offices. This should be monitored through inter-partisan cooperation. At the extra-parliamentary level, there should be cooperation in the area of administrative reform, in the National Council of Planning (Conselho Nacional do Plano), and in the sector of the Council of Information (Conselho de Informacão) ('Acordo' 1978: 65–6).

Although the coalition tried to pursue its programme until July 1978, a general divergence began to appear in relation to the agrarian reform in the southern province of Alentejo. The CDS wanted a faster return of expropriated land estates to the owners, while Agriculture Minister Saias wanted to follow a more moderate approach. In the end, the junior partner asked for the dismissal of Saias, which was vehemently opposed by the PS. The coalition was also under pressure from the president, who criticized the political class as a whole for their inability to deliver on their promises (Domingos 1980: 186; *Diario de Noticias*, 27 Apr. 1978). Moreover, protests from different social groups impeded the implementation of the agreed policies.

The AD Cabinets 1980–1982

The AD administration presented as its priority in its electoral programme, and later in its government programme, the establishment of the 'state of democratic law' and the return to governability after years of government instability and transition. Such statements by Sá Carneiro appealed to the population. These priorities were to occupy a large part of all the three government programmes. In economic policy, the government sought to liberalize by strengthening the private sector.

Central to this strategy was the commitment to the integration into the European Community. In relation to the agrarian reform, the alliance was unanimous in speeding up the return of confiscated land estates to former landowners and in weakening the power base of the Communist Party. As a concession to the third partner of the coalition, the PPM, a special chapter on the improvement of the quality of life was included in the programme. On the question of national defence the AD saw the necessity to establish the civil powers over the armed forces. This agreement among the three parties was maintained unaltered throughout the coalition period (Gomes 1982: 31–2). This can be verified by an analysis of the three governmental programmes between 1980 and 1982 (DAR II, 11, 12 Jan. 1980; DAR II, 20, 17 Jan. 1981; DAR II, 101, 15 Sept. 1981). Although during Sá Carneiro's government the AD was able to improve the level of governability, this declined after his death. The new Prime Minister Pinto Balsemão had to deal with the resistance of factions inside his party. In particular, Eurico de Melo, Helena Roseta, and Cavaco Silva wanted a stronger commitment to economic liberalization. Balsemão was able to keep the AD was together until late 1982 because of the upcoming revision of the constitution.

The pre-electoral coalition agreement is in its entirety devoted to policy formulation. Office distribution is not a major item in coalition agreements. Informally, several cabinet members indicated that it was very much up to the prime minister to choose persons that enjoyed his personal confidence for the cabinet. The appointment of non-cabinet positions was not regulated in these documents.

In the AD governments the 'political cabinet' (*gabinete politico*), consisting of the prime minister and the vice-prime minister, the associate minister (*ministro adjunto*), the Minister of Defence, and the associate secretary of state (*secretario de estado adjunto*, junior minister), was the most important decision making body. In this political cabinet, strategies towards the parliamentary opposition were discussed, and the impact of individual policies was analysed (Portas and Valente 1990: 344–5).

The programmes of the first eight constitutional governments (through Balsemão II) were elaborated by the prime minister. The ministers and the secretary of state (junior minister) gave him a one-page summary of the policies of their respective ministries, normally drawn from the electoral programme. The programme was not discussed with interest groups. In this sense, the prime minister exercised direct control over the programme (Portas and Valente 1990: 334–5).

The 'Central Bloc' Cabinet 1983–1985

Although the coalition agreement of June 1983 between the PS and the PSD is shorter than the previous agreements, it is probably the most interesting of the three. Most of the agreement deals with policies intended to stabilize the economy. Yet, the agreement includes a larger component of rules for coalition governance than its predecessors. The agreement was intended for the duration of the legislative term (four years). The agreement envisaged a consensual approach to the nomination of ministers and public offices, based on the principles of the national interests and professional capacity. For portfolio allocation, this meant that ministers were nominated by their own respective party and confirmed by both coalition partners. This practice was also extended to the nomination of positions in the public economic sector. The parties sought to ensure a smooth running of the government through previous consultations on legislative initiatives in the Assembly of the Republic, regular meetings between the party leaders and the leaders of the parliamentary groups, and inter-party summits between the two leaders of the coalition parties ('Acordo' 1983: 2–3).

Most of the policy commitments in the coalition agreement referred to economic policies. The only other issue area included was social welfare. The austerity programme implied a considerable reduction of public spending. Both governmental parties were affected by intra-party divisions over social and employment policies. The social costs of the austerity programme, which particularly affected disadvantaged social groups, made the coalition quite unpopular inside the respective parties and among the population (Cravinho 1986). Nevertheless, the coalition was able to implement the austerity programme and to establish a system of social concertation around a newly created Permanent Council for Social Concertation (Conselho Permanente para a Concertação Social, CPCS). This regime of social partnership was necessary to gain the support of the social partners for the unpopular measures (Lucena 1989: 552–3). During 1984 and 1985 the coalition came under increasing pressure, as the presidential election drew near. Mário Soares's decision to be a candidate ran counter to the agreement, which defined a common procedure for the nomination of a presidential candidate. The death of PSD leader

Carlos Mota Pinto in May 1985 led to further turbulence. For a short time, Rui Machete became the PSD president, until May 1985 when the XII congress of Figueira da Foz elected Cavaco Silva as the new leader. This charismatic leader terminated the coalition government, forcing Ramalho Eanes to call early elections (Cruz 1995: 142).

Governance Procedures

One of the main features of the agreements is that they are not very detailed with respect to coalition discipline and coalition conflict management mechanisms. There is some commitment to coalition discipline in legislation and other parliamentary behaviour, but de facto any achievement of a majority in the legislature is always accompanied by factionalism and dissent. Coalition governance until 1985 was characterized by a lack of coordination of policies between the prime minister and the other cabinet ministers (Portas and Valente 1990).

In the two-party coalition agreements the general and specific procedures of inter-party cooperation and consultation are well defined in the agreement. In the AD governments the institution of the political cabinet played a role in defining positions in relation to the opposition. All three coalitions include formally or informally rules of discipline in the initiation of legislation in the Assembly of the Republic. Such discipline was also in part enforced at later stages of parliamentary deliberation.

In the two-party coalition governments, the agreements even specify discipline in other parliamentary areas such as the election to parliamentary offices. The largest share of the coalition agreements is dedicated to policies. The short-term nature of the coalitions show that, on the whole, intra- and inter-party conflicts prevented a routinization and stabilization of coalition procedures, although it may lead to the consolidation of democratic procedures in the context of the logics of regime democratization.

There was no election rule until the revision of the constitution in 1982. This was quite evident during the PSD–PS coalition government in 1978. The breakdown of the coalition led to a more active role for the president, who, against the wishes of the political parties, decided to dismiss the prime minister and invest caretaker governments until the end of the legislative term. After 1982, strains on the coalition were usually met with demands for early elections. The breakdown of the coalition in 1985 was conducive to the early elections in October. This chain of events was repeated in 1987, when the PSD minority government lost a motion of censure in parliament. Although the Portuguese constitution does not require early elections when cabinets resign during the legislative term, informally such a practice has evolved. The establishment of this convention has thus removed the need for parties to negotiate election rules in their coalition agreements.

Portfolio Allocation

Office distribution is not a major item in coalition agreements. The prime minister dominates the appointment procedure of both ministers and junior ministers. The coalition partners retain a limited freedom of appointment, however. The choice of ministers was based on the personal trust of the prime minister, or, as in the case of AD governments, the need to give representation to important party factions. The criteria of selection were to a lesser extent related to the rank that a potential minister held within the party or his technical competence. The role of the prime minister was crucial in the selection of cabinet ministers as well as junior ministers (*secretários de estado*) (Portas and Valente 1990: 333–7). The coalition agreement between the PS and the PSD in 1983 mentioned that the allocation of ministers and junior ministers should follow the principle of electoral representativeness (parity). This was also followed in the AD governments between 1979 and 1983. Only the coalition agreement between the PS and the PSD seemed to devote some space to the appointment of non-governmental positions. There one can identify several procedures regulating the appointment of positions in public institutions and in the public sector of the economy.

The Sá Carneiro cabinet included nine members of the PSD and four of the CDS and one of the PPM with one independent. This cabinet structure remained more or less intact throughout all three cabinets. In the ninth Soares III cabinet, an important ministry was allocated to the PPM. The government wanted to stress this element stronger in government policies (Ferreira 1985: 721). While the Balsemão I cabinet was quite unstable due to intra-party factionalism, the Balsemão II cabinet was more successful in keeping the coalition together until late 1982. Afterwards the Ministry of Foreign Affairs changed hands, as did the offices of vice-prime minister and the Ministers for Education and Employment. Moreover, a new Ministry for Parliamentary Affairs was created under the leadership of Marcelo Rebelo Sousa. The government resigned at the end of the year.

In the PS–CDS coalition, it was agreed that eleven ministers should go to the PS and three to the CDS (Foreign Affairs, External Trade, and Administrative Reform), with two independents (Minister of Agriculture Saias and Defence Minister Firmino Miguel). Only five ministers from the previous government retained seats in the new cabinet (Rother 1985: 257–8).

The Soares III cabinet consisted of eleven ministers of the PS and five ministers from the PSD. In spite of some changes during 1984, the government remained very stable between 1983 and 1985. This distribution of offices was agreed in the coalition agreement ('Acordo' 1983: 2).

In sum, coalition governance in Portugal has not been extremely formalized. On the contrary, the prime minister was a dominant figure in the three coalition cabinets. This was further reinforced by the lack of coordination

TABLE 14.6. *Distribution of cabinet and junior ministerships in Portuguese coalitions*

Cabinet number	Cabinet	(1) PM	(2) Deputy PM	(3) Finance	(4) Planning and Coordination	(5) Foreign Affairs	(6) Industry/ Energy	(7) Interior	(8) Defence	(9) Social Affairs
8	Soares II	PS,3i	PS	PS,3i	—	CDS,ps	PS,2cds	PS	I	PS
12	Sá Carneiro I	PSD	CDS	PSD	—	CDS[a]	PSD	PSD	CDS	CDS
13	Sá Carneiro I	PSD	CDS,i	PSD	—	CDS[a]	PSD	PSD	CDS	CDS
14	Balsemão 1	PSD	CDS	CDS, 5psd	—	I,2psd	CDS	PSD	CDS[a]	PSD,2i,3cds
14	Balsemão 2	PSD	CDS	PSD,i,cds	—	I,2psd,cds	CDS,2psd,i	PSD,cds	CDS[a]	CDS,2i
15	Soares III	PS	PSD	I,4psd	—	PSD	PS,2psd	PS,psd	PSD[a]	

Cabinet number	Cabinet	(10) Agriculture/ Fisher	(11) Education	(12) Employment	(13) Justice	(14) Trade/ Tourism	(15) Transport	(16) Housing	(17) Administrative Reform	(18) Environment
8	Soares Ii	I,2ps,cds	PS,28,cds	PS,i	I	CDS,i,ps	PS,i	PS,i,cds	CDS,ps	—
12	Sá Carneiro	PSD	PSD,cds	PSD	PSD	CDS	PPM	PSD	PSD	—
13	Sá Carneiro	PSD	PSD,cds	PSD	PSD	CDS	PPM	PSD	PSD	—
14	Balsemão 1	PSD,2i	PSD,2i,cds	PSD	PSD	PSD,i,cds	PSD,i,cds	CDS	—	PPM,psd,cds
14	Balsemão 2	CDS,2,psd,i	PSD,i,cds	PSD	PSD	PSD	PSD,cds,i	—	—	PPM
15	Soares III	PSD,2ps,4i	PSD,ps,i	PSD,ps	PSD	PSD,2ps	PS,psd	—	—	PSD,i,cds

Cabinet number	Cabinet	(19) Youth	(20) Parliamentary Affairs	(21) European Integration	(22) Sea	(23) Culture	(24) Public Works	(25) Health
14	Balsemão 1	—	—	PSd,i	—	—	—	—
14	Balsemão 2	—	PSD	—	—	CDS	—	—
15	Saores III	—	PS,i	—	PS,psd	PS	—	PS

I/i = non-partisan minister or junior minister

[a] This minister also was deputy prime minister.

Source: Ferreira 1985.

between the Prime Minister's Office and the individual ministers. Policy formulation was carried out by the prime minister. There has been no sophisticated procedure of allocation of cabinet and junior ministerships.

COALITION TERMINATION

In the period between 1976 and 1985, Portuguese cabinets generally did not last more than one year. Since 1985, cabinets have been of longer duration, mainly because of their more cohesive, single-party, nature (see Table 14.3).

A variety of intertwined factors account for the termination of coalition cabinets in Portugal. The single most common reason is intra-coalition conflict. This often leads to a decline of legislative discipline and the loss of a parliamentary majority. The caretaker governments collapsed mainly because of a lack of majority support in the parliament. Single-party governments with only a plurality in the parliament—minority governments formed by the largest party—have mainly been defeated by a motion of censure or no confidence. Although in the first and second legislatures, the termination of a cabinet did not automatically lead to early elections, after 1983 it has been common to opt for this solution when a cabinet breaks down. Terminal events have been minor causes reinforcing technical and behavioural mechanisms of cabinet termination. They played a major role during the unstable period between 1976 and 1985.

The PS–CDS Coalition of 1978

External constraints put severe pressure on the informal PS–CDS coalition. Apart from the growing criticism by the president, pressure groups such as the Confederation of Portuguese Farmers (Confederação de Agricultores Portugueses, CAP), under Manuel Casqueiro, destabilized the coalition in May and June 1978 (Rother 1985: 271). Inside the coalition the CDS called upon the independent Minister of Agriculture, Saias, to speed up the return of land estates to their former owners. Saias's refusal to comply with these demands led to pressure from the junior partner to have him dismissed, which the PS refused. Therefore, the CDS ministers collectively decided to leave the coalition on 24 July 1978. They wanted to give Soares a chance to undertake a cabinet reshuffle. In this situation, Eanes dismissed the government, in spite of the fact that the CR had decided against the dismissal (Rother 1985: 271–2). In response to Eanes, Soares refused to continue to govern in a caretaker capacity. Eanes decided not to call early elections, but instead invested an independent with the task of forming a government. Between 1978 and 1979, three such 'presidential governments' were formed, despite strong opposition from the main parliamentary parties.

TABLE 14.7. *Cabinet termination in Portugal, 1976–1999*

Cabinet number	Cabinet	Mechanism of cabinet termination							Terminal events				Comments
		Technical		Discretionary									
		(1) Regular parliamentary election	(2) Other constitutional reason	(3) Death of prime minister	(4) Early parliamentary election	(6) Cabinet defeated by opposition	(7) Conflict between coalition partners		(9) Elections (non-parliamentary)	(10) Popular opinion shock	(12) Economic	
							Policy	Personnel				
7	Soares I					X						Motion of confidence failed in the Assembly of Republic
8	Soares II						X				X	Inter-party conflict between coalitions partners
9	Nobre da Costa					X						Government was not approved by Assembly of the Republic
10	Mota Pinto		X									Government lacked support in the Assembly of the Republic
11	Pintassilgo				X	X						Caretaker government until interim elections of Dec. 1979
12	Sá Carneiro I	X										Regular parliamentary election
13	Sá Carneiro II			X								Death of prime minister after airplane crash
14	Balsemão				X			X	X			Intra-party conflict (PSD) and inter-party conflict
15	Soares III				X		X	X				Inter-party conflict, withdrawal of PSD ministers
16	Cavaco Silva I				X	X				X		Motion of censure of opposition parties
17	Cavaco Silva II	X										Regular elections
18	Cavaco Silva III	X										Regular elections

The AD Cabinets 1980–1982

The Sá Carneiro cabinet terminated because of the tragic death of its leader in an aviation accident in Camarate on 4 December 1980. The responsibility was taken over by the second vice-prime minister Pinto Balsemão, who became the prime minister afterwards. He was elected president of the PSD on 13 December and designated as new prime minister by Ramalho Eanes on 9 January. The new cabinet was attacked by his own party. These criticisms, coming from Helena Roseta, Cavaco Silva, and Eurico de Melo, against the economic policies of the cabinet, led to the sudden resignation of Balsemão in August 1981 (Gomes 1982: 38–9).

Balsemão called then for solid support from his party for his leadership. In the end, he was able to gain support from the young social democrats, the trade-unionists, the leaders of the autonomous regions of Madeira and Acores, and a large part of the barons from the provinces. This strong support led to a victory over the critical sector inside the party (Gomes 1982: 39).

The second Balsemão cabinet continued to be attacked by its own party. Such intra-factionalism would reappear in late 1982, leading to the fall of the AD government. Although the direct reason was the loss of 4.5 per cent of votes in the local elections of 12 December 1982, he presented as reasons misunderstandings among the coalition partners and tiredness. Vitor Crespo, the vice-president of the National Political Commission, asked Eanes to form a new government (Ferreira 1985: 725). Eanes refused and on 23 February 1983 called early elections. The elections took place on 25 April 1983. The main parties of the coalition, the PSD and the CDS, lost considerably in the elections. The PSD lost 7 seats, the CDS 16, the PPM 5. The new majority party became the PS with 36.1 per cent and 101 seats.

The 'Central Bloc' Cabinet 1983–1985

The Central Bloc government terminated due to growing disagreement between the coalition partners. It began to disintegrate after the death of PSD leader Carlos Mota Pinto in May 1985. But the main cause was the ascension of Anibal Cavaco Silva as the new PSD leader at the XII congress in Figueira da Foz in May 1985. The new leader withdrew the PSD ministers from the coalition. This was reinforced by the announcement by Mário Soares that he wanted to be a candidate for the presidential elections. The electoral results of 6 October 1985 harmed the PS more than the PSD. The PS lost 15.27 per cent of the vote gathered in 1983. Most of the voters defected to the new party PRD, which was created by Ramalho Eanes. The PSD was able to gain 2.67 per cent and formed a minority government under Anibal Cavaco Silva.

In sum, coalition termination has been due to a variety of causes. The PS–CDS coalition ended, because of inter-party conflict, but in the end, it was terminated by the semi-presidential position of President Ramalho Eanes,

TABLE 14.8. *Electoral costs/benefits of government parties in Portugal, 1976–1999* (in % of the vote)

Government	In office at time of election	Election year	PS	PSD	CDS	AD	Government
PS 1976–8	No	1979	−7.54	—	—	—	−7.54
PS–CDS 1978	No	1979	−7.54	—	—[a]	—	—[a]
Presidential cabinets 1978–9	Yes	1979	—	—	—	—	—
AD 1979–80	Yes	1980	—	—	—	2.39	2.39
AD 1980–3	Yes	1983	—	—[b]	—[b]	−4.69	−4.69
PS–PSD 1983–5	Yes	1985	−15.68	2.79	—	—	−12.68
PSD 1985–7	Yes	1987	—	20.35	—	—	20.35
PSD 1987–91	Yes	1991	—	0.58	—	—	0.58
PSD 1991–5	Yes	1995	—	−26.40	—	—	−26.4
MEANS			−11.61	−0.67	—	−1.15	−4

[a] In the elections of 1979 the CDS participated as part of the Democratic Alliance (AD). Therefore it is not possible to identify the electoral costs/gains of the CDS and the PS–CDS government in the 1979 elections.

[b] PSD and CDS had joined forces before the 1979 and 1980 elections. Based on a pre-electoral coalition agreement they run as AD. Therefore it is not possible to give party-specific figures for electoral gains or losses in the 1983 elections. However, some evidence suggests that the CDS lost heavily compared to the PSD.

who decided to dismiss Mário Soares and invest a caretaker government. In the first AD government it was the death of Prime Minister Sá Carneiro, but in the second and third it was due to intra- and inter-party conflict, which led to the calling of early elections by Prime Minister Pinto Balsemão. In the Central Bloc government it started after the death of Vice-Prime Minister Mota Pinto and was caused by intra-party conflict inside the PSD and the jockeying for the presidential elections of late 1985. The withdrawal of the PSD ministers from the government and the call for early elections definitively terminated the coalition.

Government Participation and Electoral Performance

Holding government office has been more of a liability than an asset in Portugal. As Table 14.8 shows, four out of seven governments have suffered in the elections following their term of office. The average electoral performance of a government is a 4 per cent loss, but the variance is unusually large. In 1987, the Cavaco Silva I cabinet actually gained more than 20 percentage points, whereas in 1995 the same prime minister's third cabinet lost a whopping 26.4 per cent. There have been significant systematic differences between coalition governments and single-party governments and between the Socialist Party and the non-socialist parties. While the average electoral performance of coalition governments' has been −5.6 per cent, single-party governments have done much better with a loss of mere 1.8 per cent and whereas the Socialists lost an average of 11.45 per cent, the bourgeois parties have acquitted themselves considerably better, with a mere loss of 1.27 per cent.

CONCLUSIONS

The very fledgling Portuguese democracy has experienced three different coalition government constellations over the past two decades. All of them were minimal winning and were formed in a crucial period of democratic consolidation. Between 1978 and 1985 Portugal had seven governments and three general elections. Cabinet duration was very short. On average, a cabinet lasted 15 months (the shortest period was 6 months and the lengthiest 29 months). The three government constellations were formed at different times in the legislative cycle. In this sense, the Portuguese case offers a wide range of coalition formation constellations, which may be enriching for coalition theory.

The coalition agreements of the two two-party coalition governments were divided into two parts: (1) formal coalition procedures and (2) policies. It is the prime minister who appoints ministers and junior ministers, although limited freedom of appointment could be found in the AD and Central Bloc coalitions. All coalition governments have mechanisms of conflict management and enforcing discipline in legislative behaviour. This extended to other areas of parliamentary behaviour as well. Coalition termination was mainly due to inter-party or intra-party conflict, which may be related to the incipient consolidation of the young party structures. Personalism tended to undermine the work of the coalition government. In one case, the death of the prime minister was a factor in cabinet termination, nevertheless the coalition continued to live on under the leadership of another prime minister. The death of a vice-prime minister was also an indirect cause of the breakdown of the PS–PSD coalition.

In sum, coalition government in Portugal has been very unstable, short-term, and minimal winning. It was formed to achieve short- to medium-term objectives such as economic stabilization and constitutional revision. After or even before fulfilling those tasks, coalitions have tended to collapse. Although coalition government has never been a well institutionalized practice in Portugal, it was an important experiment in managing to deal with the democratic options and rules of game of the new democracy. Since 1985, Portuguese governments have increased in stability and durability. In this sense, coalition government represented an important step towards the establishment of a modern Western European democracy.

REFERENCES

'Acordo Politico PS-CDS' (1978). In Victor Silva Lopes (ed.), *Crise 1977/78: Programa do II Governo*. Lisbon: Centro do Livro Brasileiro.
'Acordo politico, parlamentar e do Governo celebrado entre o PSD e o PS, 1983' (1983). *Povo Livre*, 8 (Jan.): 2–4.
Aguiar, Joaquim (1985). 'The Hidden Fluidity in a Ultra-Stable System', in Eduardo de Sousa Ferreira and Walter C. Opello (eds.), *Conflict and Change in Portugal (1974–1984)*. Lisbon: Teorema.
——(1989). 'Dinâmica do sistema partidário-condições de estabilidade', in Mario Baptista Coelho (ed.), *Portugal: O sistema político e constitucional 1974–1987*. Lisbon: Instituto de Ciências Sociais Universidade de Lisboa.
——(1994). 'Partidos, eleições, dinâmica politica (1975–1991)'. *Análise Social*, 29 (125–6): 171–236.
Alianca Democrática (1979). *Programa Eleitoral do Governo*. Lisbon: PSD.
Assembleia do MFA (1976). 'Criado o Tribunal Revolucionário'. Comunicado, 19 May 1975, in Fernando Ribeiro de Mello (ed.), *Dossier 2 a República*, ii. *25.4.1975–25.11.1975*. Lisbon: Edicões Afrodite.
Browne, Eric (1982). 'Introduction', in Eric C. Browne and John Dreijmanis (eds.), *Government Coalitions in Western Democracies*. New York: Longman.

Bruneau, Thomas, and Macleod, Thomas (1986). *The Politics in Contemporary Portugal: Parties and the Consolidation of Democracy*. Boulder, Colo.: Lynne Rienner.

Corkill, David (1995). 'Party Factionalism and Democratization in Portugal', in Richard Gillespie, Michael Waller, and Lourdes Lopez Nieto (eds.), *Factional Politics and Democratization*. London: Frank Cass.

Costa e Sousa, Vinicio Almeida (1983). 'O Partido Comunista Português (subsídios para o estudo dos seus adeptos)'. *Estudos Politicos e Sociais*, 11 (3–4): 497–543.

Cravinho, Jõao (1986). 'The Portuguese Economy: Constraints and Opportunities', in Kenneth Maxwell (ed.), *Portugal in the 1980s: Dilemmas of Democratic Consolidation*. New York: Greenwood Press.

Cruz, Manuel Braga da (1994). 'O Presidente da República na evolução e genese do sistema do governo português'. *Análise Social*, 29 (1–2): 237–65.

——(1995). *Instituicões Politicas e Processos Sociais*. Lisbon: Bertrand Editora.

Diario da Assembleia da Republica (DAR), governmental programmes (1976–1983).

Di Palma, Giuseppe (1990). 'Parliaments, Consolidation, Institutionalisation: A Minimalist Approach', in Ulrike Liebert and Maurizio Cotta (eds.), *Parliament and Democratic Consolidation in Southern Europe: Greece, Italy, Portugal, Spain and Turkey*. London: Pinter.

Domingos, Emidio Veiga (1980). *Portugal Politico: Análise das Instituições*. Lisbon: Edicoes Rolim.

Duverger, Maurice (1980). 'A New Political System Model: Semi-Presidential Government'. *European Journal of Political Research*, 8: 165–87.

Ferreira, Goncalves F. A. (1985). *Quinze Anos de Historia de Portugal (1970–84)*. Lisbon: no publisher.

Ferreira, José Medeiros (1982). *Ensaio Histórico sobre a Revolução Portuguesa: O Periodo Pre-Constitucional*. Lisbon: Casa da Moeda-Imprensa Nacional.

Gallagher, Tom (1989). 'The Portuguese Socialist Party: The Pitfalls of Being First', in Tom Gallagher et al. (eds.), *Southern European Socialism*. Manchester: Manchester University Press.

Galli, Giorgio (1966). *Il Bipartitismo Imperfetto: Comunisti e Democristiani in Italia*. Bologna: Il Mulino.

Gomes, João Salis (1982). 'Aliança Democrática: Análise de uma coligacao'. *Perspectivas*, Nos. 10–12 (Apr.): 19–40.

Laver, Michael, and Hunt, W. Ben (1992). *Policy and Party Competition*. New York: Routledge.

——and Schofield, Norman (1990). *Multiparty Government: The Politics of Coalition in Europe*. Oxford: Oxford University Press.

Lopes, Pedro Santana, and Barroso, Manuel Durão (1980). *Sistema de Governo e Sistema Partidário*. Lisbon: Bertrand.

Lopes, Victor Silva (1978) (ed.). *Crise 1977–78: Programa do II Governo*. Lisbon: Centro do Livro Brasileiro.

Lucena, Manuel (1989). 'A Herança de duas revoluções: Continuidade e Rupturas no Portugal Pos-Salazarista', in Mário Baptista Coelho (ed.), *Portugal: O sistema político e constitucional 1974–1987*. Lisbon: Instituto de Ciências Sociais Universidade de Lisboa.

Magone, José (1996a). *The Changing Architecture of Iberian Politics: An Investigation* on the Democratic Structuration of Political Systemic Culture in Semiperipheral Southern European Societies. New York: Mellen University Press.

——(1996b). 'Portugal', in Juliet Lodge (ed.), The 1994 Elections to the European Parliament. London: Pinter.

——(1998). 'Party System Change in Portugal', in David Broughton and Mark Donovan (eds.), Party System Change in Western Europe. London: Cassel.

Mendes, Armindo Ribeiro (1989). 'O Conselho da Revolução e a Comissão Constitucional na Fiscalização da Constitucionalidade das Leis', in Mário Baptista Coelho (ed.), Portugal: O sistema político e constitucional 1974–1987. Lisbon: Instituto de Ciências Sociais Universidade de Lisboa.

Morlino, Leonardo (1995). 'Political Parties and Democratic Consolidation in Southern Europe', in Richard Gunther, P. Nikiforos Diamandouros, and Hans-Juergen Puhle (eds.), The Politics of Democratic Consolidation. Baltimore: Johns Hopkins University Press.

Nataf, Daniel (1995). Democratization and Social Settlements: The Politics of Change in Contemporary Portugal. New York: State University of New York Press.

Panebianco, Angelo (1988). Political Parties: Power and Organization. Cambridge: Cambridge University Press.

Pereira, José Pacheco (1987). 'O PCP: Um Partido do Passado Presente—Uma Interpretação'. Revista de Ciência Politica, 5: 5–39.

Pinto, Jaime Nogueira (1989). 'A direita e o 25 de Abril: Ideologia, estratégia e evolucao politica', in Mario Baptista Coelho (ed.), Portugal: O Sistema Político e Constitucional. 1974–97. Lisbon: Instituto de Ciências Sociais.

Portas, Paulo, and Valente, Vasco Pulido (1990). 'O Primeiro Ministro: Estudo sobre o Executivo em Portugal'. Análise Social, 25 (107): 333–49.

Rother, Bernd (1985). Der verhinderte Übergang zum Sozialismus: Die sozialistische Partei Portugals im Zentrum der Macht (1974–1978). Frankfurt a.M.: Materialis.

Stock, Maria José Fernandez (1984). 'Sistema de partidos e governabilidade (Um Estudo Comparado)'. Economia e Sociologia, 37: 43–84.

——(1989a). 'Elites, Facções e Conflito Intra-partidário: O PPD/PSD e o Processo Politico Português de 1974 a 1985', Ph.D. thesis. Universidade de Évora.

——(1989b). 'O centrismo politico e os partidos do poder em Portugal', in Mário Baptista Coelho (ed.), Portugal: O sistema politico e constitucional 1974–1987. Lisbon: Instituto de Ciências Sociais.

Vester, Michael (1984). 'A reforma agrária Portuguesa como Processo Social'. Revista Critica de Ciências Sociais, 18–20: 481–516.

15

Conclusion

Coalition Governance in Western Europe

Wolfgang C. Müller and Kaare Strøm

The European experience with coalition government is complex and evolving. Patterns of coalition membership, formation, governance, and performance vary from country to country and in many cases from era to era. The chapters of this volume have illustrated this diversity with greater specificity and in more intimate detail than any previous study of cabinet coalitions. Such an intensive empirical survey is timely for more than one reason. For one thing, all major existing surveys have become dated, since no comprehensive volume containing studies by country experts has been published since the mid-1980s. More importantly, however, our empirical knowledge of coalition politics has simply failed to grow apace with our theoretical understanding. For many years, the basic features of coalition politics in Europe were better known than understood. Particularly over the past decade or so, however, the theoretical literature on coalition bargaining has rapidly grown much more sophisticated. It has begun to focus on many aspects of coalition governance that have hitherto simply not been empirically explored in any systematic and theoretically guided manner. Thus, our understanding has lept ahead of our knowledge. This volume attempts to redress that shortcoming in our empirical knowledge and, furthermore, to suggest new avenues for theoretical as well as empirical work.

The latter agenda suggests systematic analysis and extensions that go far beyond the confines of this volume. In the remainder of the current volume, we shall attempt something less ambitious and space-consuming, namely to provide an initial overview of the data from the country chapters. This concluding chapter thus summarizes, largely in a country-by-country manner, some of the main features of European coalition politics as presented in the individual chapters. The empirical information summarized here covers the entire post-1945 period, from the first post-war cabinet until 1 January 1999. While in the country chapters both governments and cabinets figure as units of analysis, this chapter will focus on cabinets almost exclusively. Only in the analysis of electoral performance will we depart from this standard. A more exhaustive comparative analysis of the wealth of data provided in this volume is currently being undertaken.

Cabinet Membership

For present purposes, however, let us begin with the most standard information concerning cabinets, their incidence, and basic composition. Table 15.1 provides an overview. Altogether, 343 party-based cabinets have been identified within the parameters of this volume.[1] The countries differ widely in the incidence of cabinets, from a mere eleven in the case of Portugal to forty-eight for Italy. These numbers need to be qualified, however. While for the vast majority of countries, we cover the whole post-war period, beginning in 1945 or even 1944, there are three exceptions. The German case covers the life of the Federal Republic, and the analysis therefore begins in 1949. The French analysis is confined to the Fifth Republic and thus covers the post-1958 period exclusively. Finally, the Portuguese case picks up in 1978 with the consolidation of democracy.

Coalition and Single-Party Cabinets

We begin our survey with two characteristics commonly associated with cabinet strength. Traditionally, it has been thought that in parliamentary democracies strong government requires a single-party cabinet. However, although most countries in our sample have had some experience with single-party cabinets, coalitions account for 69 per cent of the cabinets (238 of 343 cases) analysed here. See also Figure 1.1 in the introductory chapter. Although the figure there presents data on the proportions of time in office, rather than on the relative numbers of cabinets, the results are broadly consistent. Coalitions are the only form of government that post-war Luxembourg and the Netherlands have experienced. They have been by far the most important form of government in Germany, where single-party cabinets make up 15 per cent of the cases (4 of 26) but in reality have been only transitional phenomena. To a lesser extent this is also true for Finland (11% single-party cabinets), Belgium (15%), Austria (23%), France (26%), and Italy (29%). The other countries have a more mixed record: Denmark (45%), Ireland (55%), Norway (61%), Portugal (69%), and Sweden (73%). Thus, three countries have experience more single-party than coalition cabinets, and the top two countries in this regard are both Scandinavian. Our findings thus confirm the Scandinavian tendency towards coalition avoidance (Strøm 1990).

---

[1] There are minor variations in the number of cabinets between the tables because of missing data, in particular for the first post-war cabinets in the Netherlands.

TABLE 15.1. *Parliamentary cabinets*

Country	Number of cabinets[a]	Mean number of cabinet parties	Minority cabinets		Single-party cabinets	
			Number	Percentages[b]	Number	Percentages[b]
Austria	22	1.86	1	5.5	5	22.7
Belgium	33	3.24	3	9.1	5	15.2
Denmark	31	1.97	27	87.1	14	45.2
Finland	44/37[c]	3.49	11	29.7	4	10.8
France	23	2.26	7	30.4	6	26.1
Germany	26	2.08	3	11.5	4	15.4
Ireland	22	1.64	11	50	12	54.5
Italy	49/48[d]	2.88	23	47.9	14	29.2
Luxembourg	16	2.13	0	0	0	0
Netherlands	22	3.23	3	13.6	0	0
Norway	26	1.73	17	65.4	18	69.2
Portugal	14/11[e]	1.91	3	27.3	5	45.5
Sweden	26	1.42	19	73.1	19	73.1
TOTALS	354/343		128		106	
MEANS	27.2/26.4	2.3		37.3		30.9

[a] Excluding the Parri and first De Gasperi cabinets in Italy; the Schermerhorn cabinet in the Netherlands.
[b] Party-based cabinets only.
[c] In all, Finland had 44 cabinets, 37 of which were party-based. The remaining columns take into account only party-based cabinets.
[d] In all, Italy had 49 cabinets, 48 of which were party-based. The remaining columns take into account only party-based cabinets.
[e] In all, Portugal had 14 cabinets, 11 of which were party-based. The remaining columns take into account only party-based cabinets.

Majority and Minority Cabinets

Another salient feature of coalition strength is whether or not the parties in the cabinet also control a legislative majority. In our sample, no fewer than 37 per cent of the 343 administrations are minority cabinets. The rather high frequency of minority cabinets, more than one-third, parallels other recent studies of this phenomenon (Strøm 1990; Laver and Budge 1992). Denmark clearly leads the pack with no less than 87 per cent minority cabinets, followed by Sweden (73%), Norway (65%), Ireland (50%), and Italy (48%). With the single exception of Luxembourg, all the countries covered in this volume have had their experience with this form of government. The countries not yet mentioned fall within the range from 5 per cent (Austria) to 30 per cent (Finland and France) (the actual numbers are: Belgium 10%, Germany 12%, the Netherlands 14%, France 18%, and Portugal 27%). In sum, a large proportion of European cabinets do not fall into the categories that have conventionally been considered 'strong'.

PARTY SYSTEMS

To understand the processes that lead to the formation of cabinets, whether majority or minority, single-party or coalition, we need to examine the context in which bargaining occurs. First and foremost, coalition bargaining takes place within party systems. Whether or not they can be properly regarded as unitary actors (see Laver and Schofield 1990, for the best survey of this issue), parties are surely the key actors in the game of coalition politics. Given the centrality of parties, party system format is a critical contextual factor in coalition bargaining. Consequently, party systems are generally considered *the* major explanatory variable in coalition politics, and debates concerning the motivations of parties, or party leaders, have been central to the development of the field (cf. Dodd 1976; Luebbert 1986; Laver and Schofield 1990; Müller and Strøm 1999).

The main, and typically competing, motivational assumptions have been that the behaviour of parties in coalition bargaining is driven by the pursuits of office (power) or policy, respectively. Pure office-seeking approaches (Riker 1962), which attempt to explain coalition behaviour without regard to the parties' policy preferences, generally have not performed well empirically (Lijphart 1984a; Laver and Schofield 1990: 91-7; Warwick 1994). 'Policy-driven' approaches which take into account the ideological distance between parties have done better (de Swaan 1973; Laver and Budge 1992). Such policy motivations have often been described with the help of models of spatial voting games. In one-dimensional accounts of cabinet formation, the median legislator thesis has proved useful (cf. Laver and Schofield 1990: 113). That is to say, where it is reasonable to portray the preferences driving party behaviour as aligned along a single continuum (often conventionally assumed to be a left–right axis), the party containing the median legislator is in a highly favourable bargaining position. This is because if unified, this party should under majority voting be able to block any move to a position other than its ideal point. We would therefore expect this party to be a frequent, if not constant, cabinet participant, with or without coalition partners (see e.g. Laver and Schofield 1990).

How well does this strong theoretical result hold up in practice? All of our contributors indeed report a left–right ordering of the relevant parties in their respective countries, based on an authoritative cross-national study and relevant country-specific information. Yet, party politics decidedly appears not always to be unidimensional. For ten countries, we have estimates of a second significant policy dimension, and one case (Belgium) even features a third important dimension. We expect the power of the median party to be somewhat attenuated in these cases.

The actual empirical patterns are interesting and somewhat counter-intuitive (Table 15.2). First, holding the median position does seem to give parties important leverage in coalition bargaining, as such parties are clearly over-represented in government. In aggregate, 80 per cent of all party-based parliamentary cabinets that have been formed in our sample have included the median party. Only 20 per cent of the cabinets have not, and the vast majority of these cases (13% of all cabinets, or 64% of the cabinets without the median legislator party) have been minority cabinets. Thus, minority cabinets have been significantly less likely than majority governments to include the median party. This is interesting, since it has been argued that it is precisely because they control the median legislator that many minority cabinets are able to survive (e.g. Laver and Schofield 1990: 111).

There are only four countries in which the median party has been excluded in more than one or two cases. In Italy and the Netherlands, they have been excluded from no cases at all. Proportionally, the exclusion of the median legislator party has been most frequent in Denmark (58% of all cabinets), Belgium (42%), Ireland, and Norway (both 27%). There is probably no single factor that accounts for the anomalies represented by these four countries. The Danish case seems to reflect the frequency with which a smaller party, in particular the Radical Liberals, has controlled the median legislator but failed to participate in the government. This is probably due at least in part to the prevalence of two-bloc politics (socialists vs. non-socialists) and to the informal constraints that this division has imposed on coalition bargaining. In Ireland and Norway, the long-time anti-coalition stances of their respective dominant parties, Fianna Fáil in Ireland and the Labour Party in Norway, must clearly have been of major importance. These two parties have consistently been not only the leading parties in their respective countries, but also centrally placed in policy space. Their refusal to coalesce has ruled out a number of coalition cabinets that would have included the median party.

It is interesting to note, however, that the failure of median parties to participate in government does not seem in any systematic way related to the intrusion of secondary or tertiary policy dimensions. Only in Belgium does the occasional absence of a median party seem attributable to multidimensionality. One of these deviant cases (Denmark) has by our contributor been classified as one-dimensional. In the Norwegian and Irish cases a second policy dimension has been identified, yet at least the Norwegian party system has had a single dominant policy dimension.

Party Systems and Bargaining Complexity

Basic party system features provide a guide to the ease or complexity of coalition bargaining. The more unevenly and the more transparently some parties are favoured by the distribution of power, the more straightforward we would expect the process of forming and maintaining cabinet coalitions to be. Building on previous research along these lines, Warwick (1994) has

TABLE 15.2. *Government participation of parties with median legislator in Western Europe*

Country	Number of party-based cabinets	Median party (1st dimension) in cabinet?		Median party (2nd dimension) in cabinet?		Minority cabinets where median party (1st dimension) is not in cabinet
		yes	%	yes	%	
Austria	22	18	82	8	36	1
Belgium	33	19	56	15	45	2
Denmark	31	13	42	N/A	N/A	18
Finland	37	30	81	24	65	4
France	23	21	91	N/A	N/A	2
Germany	26	24	92	22	85	2
Ireland	22	16	73	15	68	2
Italy	48	48	100	43	90	0
Luxembourg	16	15	94	7	44	0
Netherlands	22	20	91	14	64	0
Norway	26	19	73	17	65	7
Portugal	11	9	82	8	73	2
Sweden	26	22	85	21	81	4
TOTALS	343	274	79.9	194	56.6	44

introduced the notion of 'bargaining complexity'. In his account of cabinet terminations, Warwick contrasts explanations that rest on ideological or policy differences within cabinets (the ideological diversity thesis) with accounts that are premissed on changes in the strength and positions of the coalition parties that in turn provides them with incentives to seek alternative coalitions (the bargaining environment thesis).

There are at least three structural party system features that contribute to the simplicity or complexity of coalition bargaining. The more parties in parliament, all else equal, the more complex we expect the bargaining environment to be. Second, the greater the dispersion of support (e.g. the number of parliamentary representatives), the greater the complexity of the situation. By implication, the complexity of the bargaining environment should correlate positively with indices of party system fragmentation, such as Rae's F (1971) or the effective number of parties (Laakso and Taagepera 1979). Finally, the more policy dimensions, the less simple (more complex) bargaining should be. We expect these various aspects of bargaining complexity to be positively correlated. We also expect to see systematic relationships between these measures and various features of the bargaining process (such as its length and complexity), as well as with properties of the cabinets that eventually form.

Let us first examine the intercorrelations between the different structural correlates of bargaining complexity (Table 15.3). Contrary to what one might expect, there is no very strong relationship between the number of policy dimensions and party system fragmentation. It is true that Belgium, with a three-dimensional (or more) party system also features a large effective number of parliamentary parties. One the other hand, however, one-dimensional Denmark and France have almost as many parties. Overall, the relationship between the number of policy dimensions and party system fragmentation is a weak one, accounted for entirely by Belgium. The mean effective number of parties is 4.40 for systems with only one relevant policy dimension, 3.75 for two-dimensional systems, and 4.96 for the only three-dimensional system, Belgium. Thus, bargaining complexity may be a less straightforward matter than we were first inclined to believe.

TABLE 15.3. *Party system indicators in Western Europe*

Country	Number of relevant policy dimensions	Effective number of parties[a]	Number of parties in parliament[a]
Austria	2	2.68	3.50
Belgium	3	4.96	8.48
Denmark	1	4.48	7.68
Finland	2	5.06	7.73
France	1	4.32	5.04
Germany	2	2.59	4.04
Ireland	2	2.83	4.77
Italy	2	4.01	10.54
Luxembourg	2	3.30	4.81
Netherlands	2	4.68	9.86
Norway	2	3.39	6.42
Portugal	2	5.62	5.36
Sweden	2	3.29	5.35

[a] Mean values per country.

CONSTRAINTS ON COALITION FORMATION

Yet, bargaining complexity is hardly the only factor that explains coalition politics. The formation and performance of parliamentary governments is often heavily affected by any number of factors that restrict the effective range of options available to the bargaining parties. We consider as constraints on coalition bargaining any restrictions on the set of feasible cabinet coalitions that is beyond the short-term control of the players, which in this context normally means the leaders of the coalitionable political parties (Strøm, Budge, and Laver 1994). We can distinguish between two major forms of constraint: institutional ones, on the one hand, and party system features, on the other.

TABLE 15.4. *Institutional rules and conventions concerning cabinet formation*

Country	Formal procedure of government formation	Use of *informateurs*	Discretionary power of head of state	Investiture vote required (First Chamber)	Investiture vote decision rule	Investiture vote required (Second Chamber)	Cabinet responsible to Second Chamber	Requirement of special majorities in legislation
Austria	Yes	No	2	No	N/A	No	No	Yes[a]
Belgium	Yes	Yes	0	Until 1995:Yes Since 1995: No	Until 1995: 50 % + 1 of the votes cast Since 1995: N/A	Yes	Until 1995:Yes Since 1995: No	Yes[b]
Denmark	No	Yes	0	No	N/A	N/A	N/A	No
Finland	Yes	No	4	No	N/A	N/A	N/A	Yes[c]
France	Yes	No	4	No	N/A	No	No	No
Germany	No	No	1	Yes	50% + 1 of all MPs for the proposed Chancellor (quorum 50% + 1)	No	No	Yes[d]
Ireland	No	No	1	Yes	50% + 1 for the proposed PM (quorum 20 MPs)	No	No	No
Italy	Yes	No	2	Yes	50% + 1 for the proposed PM (quorum 50%)	Yes	Yes	No[e]
Luxembourg	Yes	Yes	0	Yes	50% + 1	N/A	N/A	Yes[f]
Netherlands	Yes	Yes	0	No	N/A	No	(Yes)	No
Norway	No	Yes	0	No	N/A	N/A	N/A	No
Portugal	Yes	No	2	Yes	50% + 1 for government programme (quorum 50%)	N/A	N/A	No
Sweden	Until 1975: No Since 1975: Yes	(Yes)[g]	0	Until 1975: No Since 1975: Yes	Since 1975: No majority of all MPs against proposed PM	Until 1970: No Since 1970: N/A	Until 1970: Yes Since 1970: N/A	No[h]

566 Wolfgang C. Müller and Kaare Strøm

TABLE 15.4. cont.

Discretionary power of head of state
 0 No influence
 1 Selection of prime minister only, special situations
 2 Selection of prime minister and parties, special situations
 3 Selection of prime minister only, all situations
 4 Selection of prime minister and parties, all situations

[a] Two-thirds majority in first chamber for constitutional amendments and several other laws.
[b] Two-thirds majority in both chambers for constitutional amendments and several other laws.
[c] Two-thirds majorities for tax laws. Until 1992 a minority of one-third of the MPs had a suspensive veto power which could delay legislation for two to four years. This, in turn, means that the veto could be avoided by rallying more than two-thirds of the MPs behind a specific law.
[d] Two-thirds majority in both chambers for constitutional amendments and majority also in the second chamber (the Bundesrat) for a majority of laws.
[e] A majority is required in the second chamber also.
[f] Two-thirds majority in parliament for constitutional amendments.
[g] President of Parliament (since 1975).
[h] Until 1970 a majority was required in the second chamber also.

Institutional Constraints

Institutional constraints comprise the various and sundry formal rules, constitutional and otherwise, that define the options available to party leaders during coalition bargaining and, just as importantly, in office. Our contributors have paid particular attention to the rules under which cabinet formation takes place, since these have a direct and undeniable impact on coalition membership and policy (Table 15.4). Moreover, it is generally possible to formulate specific hypotheses concerning their effects, ceteris paribus, on coalition politics.

For one thing, parliamentary democracies vary substantially in the extent to which their constitutions, or other statutes or conventions, specify a formal procedure for coalition bargaining and formation. Where such procedures exist, they often privilege the largest parliamentary party, whose bargaining power is then presumably enhanced. As the preceding chapters have shown, European systems exhibit a surprising range of such institutional rules. Whereas the formation processes in Italy and Sweden are heavily regulated (thanks, no doubt, to their modern constitutions), those of Denmark and Norway are surrounded by very few formal rules. In these specific cases it is not clear, however, whether the denser institutional environments of the former states are any more conducive to large-party domination than the latter.

Table 15.5 provides information about the inclusion of the largest parliamentary party in the cabinet. In many political systems there is a strong convention that the largest parliamentary party moves first in cabinet formation. That is, the *formateur* in the first formation attempt comes from this party. As

Baron (1991) has shown, such a first-mover advantage can significantly enhance the benefits flowing to the party so privileged. According to Table 15.5 the largest party indeed seems to have an advantage, being represented in no less than 81 per cent of the cabinets formed. In Austria, for example, the largest party has made it into every post-war cabinet. Party size seems to be least important in the Netherlands and Norway. In both cases the Social Democrats have frequently been excluded from government even when they have been the strongest parliamentary party.

Parliamentary democracies also vary with respect to the role played by the head of state (president or monarch) in the bargaining process. Typically, presidents have more extensive real powers than kings, although formal constitutional rules might not always be of much help in describing these powers. Where the head of state plays a relevant and discretionary part in coalition bargaining, the result may be a potential distortion of that partisan game, in the sense that the weights and spatial positions of the relevant parties may not permit us to make any specific prediction. The Finnish president, for example, has occasionally contributed to coalitional solutions that would not otherwise have been predictable. As Magone and Verzichelli and Cotta show, the presidents of Portugal and Italy, respectively, have at times exercised similar powers.

Investiture vote requirements, such as are featured in the constitutions of Italy and Germany, make majority cabinets, as opposed to minority cabinets, more likely. The expectation that cabinets have to be formally invested by a parliamentary majority may deter some parties from attempting to form minority cabinets. Similarly, positive parliamentarism, in which voting rules require cabinets to have positive majority support rather than mere toleration, makes majority cabinets more likely, whereas negative parliamentarism tends to induce minority cabinets (Bergman 1993).

TABLE 15.5. *Cabinet representation of the largest parliamentary party*

Country	Largest party in cabinet?	Number of cabinets	Percentage
Austria	22	22	100
Belgium	26	33	79
Denmark	21	31	68
Finland	29	37	78
France	21	23	91
Germany	22	26	85
Ireland	16	22	73
Italy	47	48	98
Luxembourg	15	16	94
Netherlands	13	22	59
Norway	17	26	65
Portugal	11	11	100
Sweden	21	26	81

Note: This table excludes non-partisan cabinets.

Moreover, where the cabinet is responsible to a second chamber, broadly based coalitions (more presisely: coalitions which command a majority in both houses) have been more likely. As the contributors have shown, there are a number of countries in which cabinets are formally accountable to a second (upper) chamber, but few where this responsibility is enforced and thus effectively constrains coalition bargaining. Italy, however, is one prominent example. Finally, broadly based coalitions may be favoured by the existence of legislative rules requiring supermajorities for various types of legislation, such as budgets (Finland) or constitutional amendments (Belgium).

Party System Constraints

But constraints on coalition bargaining need not take the form of systemic institutional rules. Various features of the party system may have similar effects on bargaining. Examples are parties that because of their policy positions or histories are precluded from bargaining, parties that voluntarily exclude themselves through anti-coalition pledges, and temporary restrictions that follow from some particular political agenda.

1. *Anti-system or pariah parties.* Such parties may be excluded from coalition politics, which, in turn, reduces the number of feasible coalitions. Parties that have fallen into this category include (*a*) communist parties during the Cold War (e.g. Austria, Belgium, Luxembourg, and Italy); (*b*) populist protest parties (the FPÖ in Austria, the Progress Parties in Norway, Denmark, and temporarily also New Democracy in Sweden, and the ADR in Luxembourg); and (*c*) parties of the extreme right (the Front National in France, the MSI in Italy, and the Vlaams Blok in Belgium).

2. *'No coalition' pledges by major parties.* Ireland (Fianna Fáil) and Norway (Labour) are the classic examples of major (indeed, plurality) parties that have adopted a long-term policy of not entering into coalitions with any other party. Moreover, both Fianna Fáil and the Norwegian Labour Party have frequently made a campaign issue out of their very anti-coalition stance, stressing their coherence and stability in comparison with the unstable compromises of coalition politics.

3. *Constraints imposed by the political agenda.* The examples of situations in which the political agenda has restricted coalitional options include early post-war Austria (where the salient issues gave priority to economic reconstruction and getting the occupational troops out of the country) and Germany, in the case of the formation of CDU/CSU–SPD grand coalition in 1966. In the latter case, the political agenda was dominated by the economic situation and by proposed constitutional amendments.

COALITION FORMATION

Whereas studies of coalition politics normally have confined themselves to the coalitions that actually have been formed, this book is the first to address the government formation process itself in a comprehensive form and for a large set of countries. Our assumptions are that the process of negotiations may matter as much as the final results, and that inconclusive bargaining rounds are interesting in their own right. In previous sections, we have summarized cabinet membership data. The country chapters provide an unusually extensive and up-to-date analysis of these phenomena, but a more original contribution lies in the rich information we have acquired on the process and characteristics of cabinet bargaining and formation.

TABLE 15.6. *Cabinet formation*

Country	Number of parties in parliament		Number of inconclusive bargaining rounds		Number of days required in cabinet formation	
	Range	Mean	Range	Mean	Range	Mean
Austria	3–5	3.5	0–2	0.2	0–129	37.0
Belgium	4–14	8.5	0–7	1.3	0–148	37.8
Denmark	5–11	7.7	0–3	0.5	0–35	8.3
Finland	6–10	7.7	0–6	1.3	0–80	26.9
France	4–6	5.0	0–1	0.1	0–11	2.2
Germany	3–9	4.0	0–2	0.1	0–73	20.2
Ireland	3–7	4.8	0–1	0.1	0–48	15.7
Italy	8–16	10.5	0–3	0.5	1–126	29.5[a]
Luxembourg	4–7	4.8	0–3	0.4	0–52	24.1
Netherlands	7–14	9.9	0–6	2.0	10–208	70.6
Norway	5–8	6.4	0–1	0.1	0–16	4.2
Portugal	4–6	5.4	0–1	0.1	0–45	22.5
Sweden	5–7	5.3	0–2	0.2	0–25	5.4

[a] No data on five Italian cabinets regarding the number of days required in cabinet formation, and they were excluded in this calculation.

Formation Attempts

Coalition bargaining need not be complicated even when they involve a large number of players and strategies. If no uncertainty exists, party leaders should be able to correctly anticipate the behaviour of one another and thus to avoid abortive formation attempts. If the parties to the bargaining also have similar and non-trivial discount rates, cabinet formation should be concluded swiftly and predictably. One very interesting and hitherto inadequately addressed question is the extent to which inconclusive formation attempts actually happen. If inconclusive bargaining attempts are a stubborn empirical regularity, it is a good indication that coalition politics in fact features significant private information. Moreover, under incomplete information, inconclusive bargaining rounds are not necessarily mistakes, but may serve important informational purposes for the parties involved. The chapters in this volume have shown that 'mistakes' and inconclusive bargaining do happen. Yet, they do not occur with anything like the same frequency from country to country. Empirically, we can distinguish three groups of countries:

1. The first group consists of countries in which elections largely decide cabinet composition, and where inconclusive bargaining attempts are rare. These include Portugal, Germany, Sweden, Ireland, Norway, France, and Austria. The average number of failed formation attempts per cabinet formed in these countries ranges from 0.1 to 0.2. In these countries, either elections often result in absolute or 'working' majorities (i.e. pluralities large enough to allow for the survival of relatively stable minority cabinets), or elections are contested on the basis of pre-electoral coalitions, electoral pacts, or other party precommitments. In the former case, the low number of inconclusive bargaining attempts probably reflects a high level of information certainty among the parties. In the latter case, the precommitments made may instead reflect deliberate attempts to deal with a high degree of uncertainty on the part of party leaders and/or voters about coalitional options and/or party preferences.

2. The second category includes countries in which coalition decisions are made after elections, but with clear patterns of what would constitute a feasible government. These systems include Italy, Luxembourg, and Denmark, where the average number of inconclusive bargaining attempts hovers around 0.5. These polities feature established coalition patterns ('formulas' or 'cycles' in Italy), and they tend to be dominated by pivotal parties. Commonly, the pivotal party remains in government regardless of its electoral fortunes (unless it voluntarily decides to seek refuge in opposition as the Luxembourg Christian Democrats did in 1974). This party then seeks a coalition party that represents the recent swing among the voters. Luxembourg is probably the clearest example. Among these countries is also one in which minority governments are the rule, namely Denmark.

3. In the third group, we find countries where post-electoral coalition negotiations are indeed decisive for coalition formation and where parties have a larger menu of choices: Belgium, Finland, the Netherlands. The average number of inconclusive formation attempts in these countries ranges from 1.3 to 2.0. These are systems in which bargaining is often truly complex, and in which uncertainty presumably is high.

Number of Days Required for Cabinet Formation

The number of aborted bargaining attempts sheds important light on the often poorly understood process by which cabinet coalitions, as well as other types of cabinets, come into being. Yet, such data can still conceal substantively important aspects of the formation process. For example, some bargaining rounds may be brief and pro forma. Others may go on for months and directly or indirectly involve scores of negotiators. The duration of the bargaining process, the number of days spent in transition from one cabinet to the next, is therefore an equally interesting and complementary piece of information. Empirically, the coalitional parliamentary democracies of Western Europe sort themselves into four categories: (1) countries where cabinet formation routinely is swift and takes less than 10 days (France, Norway, Sweden, and Denmark); (2) an intermediate category, consisting solely of Ireland, in which cabinet formation on average takes between 10 and 20 days; (3) a set of countries in which cabinet formation is more protracted, taking between 20 and 30 days (Germany, Finland, Portugal, and Luxembourg); and (4) finally the four most complicated countries, in which cabinet formation more often than not takes more than a month (Italy, Belgium, Austria, and the Netherlands).

There is obviously a positive correlation between inconclusive bargaining attempts and the duration of formation. The more common failed negotiations are, the longer cabinet formation tends to take. For example, the Netherlands has experienced the highest average number of inconclusive bargaining rounds. At the same time, the average Dutch formation process has lasted almost twice as long as that in any other country. However, coalition formation may take a relatively long time not only because party systems are complex and therefore offer many possibilities. This is clearly demonstrated by Austria, which has a quite simple party system that does not allow for many alternative coalitions, but where cabinet transitions none the less tend to be lengthy. We will return to this question when we discuss 'tight' and 'loose' coalitions below.

COALITION GOVERNANCE

As we noted in the introductory chapter, the recent theoretical literature reflects a greatly enhanced interest in how governance occurs once a cabinet coalition has been formed. For example, in their influential work Laver and Shepsle (1990 and 1996) argue that coalition members have no effective mechanism to compel cabinet ministers to implement any policy position other than their own ideal points. Therefore, all parties to coalition bargaining resign themselves to the idea that the only feasible policy positions are the ideal points of whatever party holds the respective cabinet portfolios in the various policy dimensions. Cabinet portfolios, in this view, imply a powerful form of agenda control. Yet, it is not obvious that such abdication to ministerial government would be stable. Often, decisive coalitions of parties will prefer other policy positions to the solution implied by the set of ideal points of the cabinet parties in their respective jurisdictions. Under such condtions, it stands to reason that coalition parties would cooperate to limit the power of individual ministers to impose undesirable policy outcomes. Laver and Shepsle argue that there is no way in which the coalition partners could commit themselves to such solutions, but it is not self-evident that such mutually beneficial arrangements can be ruled out. One solution may lie in formal or informal coalition agreements that parties conclude before going into executive branch collaboration. This study has scrutinized such agreements in novel ways. Where coalition agreements have become available, the contributors have analysed their contents and examined the balance between policy commitments, portfolio and other office agreements, and rules by which coalition disputes are settled.

Coalition Agreements

As Table 15.7 demonstrates, of the 238 coalition cabinets analysed in this volume, 150 (63%) have been based on an identifiable coalition agreement. There are none the less great cross-national differences in the incidence of such accords. In Finland, Luxembourg, Norway, Portugal, and Sweden, all coalition cabinets have featured coalition agreements. This has also been the case in Austria ever since 1949. In contrast, coalition agreements are the exception rather than the rule in Italy, where only a single cabinet (or a mere 3%) has relied on such an agreement. The other countries cover the range from 80 per cent (Ireland) to 45 per cent (Germany).

While we refer to the country chapters for details, note that if there is a trend over time, it is towards the use of coalition agreements. Typically, formal coalition agreements have been introduced after some years of experience with coalition politics. Relevant cases are Austria (where this happened as early as 1949, after a mere four years of coalition politics), Belgium (where the first coalition agreement dates from 1958), the Netherlands (where the first coalition agreement was drafted in 1963), Germany (where the first experience with coalition agreements dates from the early 1960s, but where they have become a permanent feature of coalition politics only since 1980), and France (where coalition agreements were introduced as recently as the early 1980s).

Of the 150 coalition agreements (note that our actual observations here are cabinets and not agreements as such, since the latter may remain the same under successive cabinets), 123 (82%) were, when they were drafted, intended for publication. Coalition agreements have invariably been public documents in Finland, France, Ireland, Norway, Portugal, and Sweden. Recall, however, that some of these documents have been pre-electoral coalition

TABLE 15.7. Coalition governance

Country	(1) Coalition agreement	(2) Agreement public	(3) Election rule	(4) Conflict management mechanism	(5) Coalition discipline in legislation	(6) Coalition discipline in other parliamentary behaviour	(7) Freedom of appointment	(8) Policy agreement	(9) Junior ministers	(10) Non-cabinet positions
Austria	14	12	14	CoC, CaC, IC	1, 2	1, 2	17	0, 1, 2, 3	Y	9Y, 8N
Belgium	20	18	0	CaC, PS, IC	1, 2	4	28	0, 1, 2, 3	22Y, 6N	Y
Denmark	8	6	0	IC, CaC, PCa, O	1	1	17	3	N/A	Y
Finland	33	33	0	IC, CaC, PCa	2, 3	2, 3	28	1, 2, 3	N/A	Y
France	8	8	17	CaC, O, PS, CoC	2, 4	2, 4	2	0, 2	N	N
Germany	10	7	0	PCa, Parl, PS, IC, CoC, CaC	1, 2	1, 2	0	1, 2, 3	Y	Y
Ireland	8	8	0	Parl, PS	1, 2	1	10	0, 1, 2	Y	Y
Italy	34	1	0	CoC, PS	2	3	34	1, 2	33Y, 1N	33Y, 1N
Luxembourg	16	16	0	O, CoC, PS	2	4	16	3	9Y, 7N	Y
Netherlands	23	11	12	Parl, IC, CoC	2	4	23	0, 1, 2, 3	20Y, 3N	N
Norway	8	8	0	IC, CaC, PCa	1	2	5	1, 2, 3	5Y, 2N	4Y, 3N
Portugal	6	6	0	CoC, CaC, PS	2, 3	3	6	3	1Y, 5N	N
Sweden	7	7	0	IC, CaC	2	2	7	2, 3	Y	Y

Note: See Table 1.5 of the Introduction to this book for an explanation of the codes used in this table.

manifestos (France, Portugal) or parliamentary bills spelling out alternatives to the government's budget (Norway). It should come as no surprise that these have been public documents. In the Netherlands (91%), Belgium (90%), Austria (86%), Denmark (75%), and Germany (70%), most coalition agreements have been in the public domain. In contrast, the coalition parties in Luxembourg and in the singular Italian case have kept their coalition agreements private.

Our contributors have collected and analysed coalition agreements from 12 of our 13 countries pertaining to 119 cabinets (occasionally, more than one cabinet has been based on the same coalition agreement) The summary data are presented in Table 15.8. Only in Luxembourg are coalition agreements generally not publicly available. In examining these documents, which have never before been subject to a systematic scholarly investigation of this scope, our collaborators have focused on the size, contents, and implications of these documents.

Size

The simplest measure by which coalition agreements differentiate themselves is size. As Table 15.8 demonstrates, the shortest coalition agreement identified and analysed in this volume is just over 200 words long (Finland), while the longest one contains more than 43,000 words (Belgium). The average size of coalition agreements is below 3,000 words in three countries: France, Finland, and Sweden. It is between 3,000 and 10,000 words in Denmark, Germany, Austria, Ireland, and Italy (the last-mentioned observation is based on a single agreement, however), whereas in the following countries it includes more than 10,000 words: Norway, Portugal, Belgium, and the Netherlands. Yet, there is substantial within-country variation. In Austria, for example, the longest coalition agreement on record is more than 30 times the size of the shortest one.

Size, we believe, reflects the bargaining situation and the nature of the inter-party agreement that is reached. Specifically, size is a rough indicator of the extent to which the negotiating parties try to anticipate the cabinet's policy agenda, and the extent to which they feel compelled to seek binding agreements *ex ante*. The more uncertainty the parties face, and the more critical this uncertainty is, the more extensive we expect their formal agreements to be. Also, parties that fear that their coalition partners would renege or drag their feet on any policy commitment not explicitly spelled out may wish to craft a very extensive policy document. Conversely, when the parties have a high degree of trust that potential policy disputes can successfully be sorted out as they emerge, they may content themselves with a very short agreement. A long agreement may thus reflect an attempt to anticipate policy issues in detail, and/or a lack of faith that informal inter-party coordination can be engineered in a more ad hoc manner. Yet, the correlation between uncertainty

TABLE 15.8. Size and content of coalition agreements

Country[a]	Size (in words)		General procedural rules (in %)		Specific procedural rules (in %)		Distribution of offices (in %)		Distribution of competence (in %)		Policies (in %)	
	Range	Mean	Range	Mean	Range	Mean	Range	Mean	Range	Mean	Range	Mean
Austria (14)	700–23,300	6,593	1–50	18.6	0–44	14.1	1–30	10.8	0–24	8.1	0–98	48.2
Belgium (16)	3,150–43,550	14,166	0–5	1.3	0–14	5.0	0–3	0.5	0–3	0.6	83–99	92.8
Denmark (5)	910–5,613	3,619	0	0	6–30	12.4	0	0	0	0	70–94	87.4
Finland (33)	204–4,541	1,163	0–1	0.0	0	0	0	0	0	0	99–100	100.0
France (5)	870–3,390	1,976	0–5	1.0	0	0	0	0	0	0	95–100	99.0
Germany (10)	513–16,536	5,934	0–28	7.4	0–4	1.2	0–1	0.1	0	0	68–100	91.4
Ireland (6)	1,248–18,593	9,348	0	0	0	0	0	0	0	0	100	100.0
Italy (1)	—	3,680	—	38.1	—	23	—	0	—	7.5	—	31.3
Netherlands (11)	3,100–36,000	14,223	0–16	2.9	0–29	4.1	0–3	0.3	0–9	2.4	52–98	90.3
Norway (8)	2,919–31,138	12,435	0	0	0–4	0.5	0	0	0	0	97–100	99.5
Portugal (3)	2,461–34,300	13,746	0–39	16.5	0–14	4.9	0–5	1.5	0	0	60–100	77.1
Sweden (7)	1,100–5,200	2,443	0	0	0–8	2.6	0	0	0	0	92–100	97.4

[a] Numbers in parentheses indicate the number of cabinets on which this table is based. No data on Luxembourg.

and agreement size may not be quite that simple. Alternatively, a very short agreement may, for example, signal a high degree of uncertainty about the future policy agenda of the government. Size also reflects the contents of coalition agreements, as it generally takes more space and words to spell out policy agreements than it does to identify procedural rules.

Note that there is no immediately apparent relationship between the number of participating parties and the length of the coalition agreement. There may be a weak tendency for long agreements to emerge in complex bargaining situations, of which Belgium is a prime example. The length of Dutch and Portuguese agreements, however, suggests that bargaining complexity cannot be a necessary condition for lengthy agreements. These countries have tended to have very lengthy agreements, although the number of parties involved in negotiations has typically been limited. Conversely, the Danish case illustrates that even complex bargaining environments may give birth to short agreements. What these apparently deviant cases may reflect is the impact of the level of trust in the feasibility of informal coordination. Such confidence may be built over time, through iterated interactions, or it may decay for similar experiential reasons.

Contents

Exception for most Austrian agreements and the singular Italian case, the average coalition agreement has been concerned mainly with the policies the new government intends to pursue. As already indicated, however, there are significant cross-national differences in the attention given to policy versus procedural concerns. At one extreme, in Finland, Norway, Sweden, France, Belgium, the Netherlands, and Germany, 90 per cent or more of the contents of coalition agreements have been concerned with policy. At the other extreme, the corresponding figures are 31 per cent for Italy and 48 per cent for Austria, which means that about two-thirds of the single Italian and about half the average Austrian coalition agreement have been devoted to non-policy matters. In between these extremes, the policy content is 87 per cent in Denmark and more than 70 per cent in Portugal.

The second most frequent purpose of coalition agreements in Western Europe has been to lay down the procedural rules of the coalition. There is only one country—Ireland—in which general and/or specific rules of the game have not made their way into coalition agreements. (However, Finland comes very close to Ireland.) On the Western European average, 6.4 per cent of the space in coalition agreements has been devoted to this purpose. As the tables in the country chapters show, though, the countries differ substantially, from 61 per cent of the single Italian agreement, to about one-third of the words in the average Austrian agreement, to less than 0.5 per cent in Norway.

In contrast, there are only few countries in which coalition agreements have dealt with the distribution of offices and competences between the coalition

TABLE 15.9. *The proportion of procedural rules in coalition agreements*

Country	Average share of procedural rules (%)
Austria	33
Belgium	6
Denmark	12
Finland	0
France	1
Germany	9
Ireland	0
Italy	61
Luxembourg	—
Netherlands	7
Norway	0.5
Portugal	21
Sweden	3
MEAN	11.8

partners. Austria has been in the lead, devoting on average almost one-fifth of the references in the coalition agreements' to these purposes. The general paucity of portfolio commitments in coalition agreements should not, however, be taken as an indication that these are minor concerns to bargaining parties. Such an inference would certainly fly in the face of the historical evidence and the interpretations presented by the various contributors. More likely, the coalition parties see formalized and publicized deals of this nature as unnecessary and perhaps embarrassing. As the country chapters and Table 15.7 show, a consensus concerning the distribution of sub-cabinet spoils between the coalition partners is much more frequent than the coalition agreements suggest. Apparently, coalition parties prefer to keep such agreements informal and, it would seem, as private as possible.

Tight and Loose Coalitions

One of the hitherto little-known aspects of coalition politics is the extent and nature of the commitments that exist between coalition parties. Quite obviously, coalition parties, like partners in other human relationships, differ substantially in the degree and ways in which they are tied to one another. We can place coalitions on a continuum ranging from 'tight' to 'loose' commitments. Think of a tight coalition as analogous to a classic Catholic marriage, while a loose coalition has more in common with an 'open relationship'. More specifically, parties which enter tight coalitions commit themselves to unconditional loyalty for the lifetime of their alliance. On the other hand, the looser a coalition is, the more relaxed the attitudes towards coalition loyalty.

The information summarized in Table 15.7 and in the respective country tables allows us to map our 13 countries by employing four variables, namely the degree of coalition discipline exhibited in election rules, legislation, other parliamentary behaviour, and policy agreements. An election rule reflects a very strong tie between coalition partners. Such rules imply that the coalition parties commit themselves to calling an election if they dissolve the coalition. The parties thus agree to subject themselves to immediate popular sanctions in the event that they decide to go their separate ways. Given the fact that voters are generally considered to be hostile to squabbling parties, such a rule may be a powerful deterrent against premature dissolution of the coalition. Of course, election rules can only be enforced under constitutions that allow the cabinet or prime minister (or, in most cases, a parliamentary majority) to dissolve parliament before the end of its regular term. For this reason, election rules are of questionable utility in some countries, e.g. Germany and Sweden, in which the opportunities or incentives for parliamentary dissolution are severely circumscribed. In Norway, such a rule is simply not feasible, since the Norwegian parliament cannot be dissolved before the end of its four-year term. None the less, election rules are in principle enforceable in most of the countries examined here. With respect to actual incidence, France clearly leads the pack, as all coalition cabinets have been based on an election rule. France is followed by Austria, where the vast majority of cabinets (82%) have featured an election rule. The Netherlands comes third with 58 per cent. In no other country have coalition parties ever made the commitments implied by an election rule.

Coalition Discipline

Likewise, coalitions in which the parties commit themselves to coalition discipline in law-making, which in our definition includes the budgetary process, must be considered tighter than coalitions that permit various exceptions, or that do not commit their constituent units to any legislative discipline at all. The same logic applies to discipline in other parliamentary behaviour (e.g. behaviour in committess of investigation, when questioning ministers, etc.). Our operational indicators of coalition discipline have been presented in the introductory chapter. We characterize discipline through the use of a four-category ordinal coding scheme, in which the code 1 means 'always discipline', the code 2 'discipline on all policies except those explicitly exempted', 3 'no discipline, except on those policies explicitly specified', and 4 'no discipline'. Tables 15.10 and 15.11 report cross-national differences in the average frequency of these various forms of coalition commitments.

The countries that exhibit particularly high levels of coalition discipline in legislation are Denmark, Norway, Austria, and Germany. The pertinent coalitions vary, of course, from mainly non-socialist ones in the two Scandinavian countries, to the centrist German ones, to the grand coalitions

TABLE 15.10. *Coalition discipline in legislation*

Country	(1) (Always discipline)	(2) (Exceptions from discipline)	(3) (Discipline as exception)	(4) (No discipline)	N
Austria	15	2	0	0	17
Belgium	2	26	0	0	28
Denmark	17	0	0	0	17
Finland	0	16	17	0	33
France	0	15	0	2	17
Germany	21	1	0	0	22
Ireland	8	2	0	0	10
Italy	0	34	0	0	34
Luxembourg	0	16	0	0	16
Netherlands	0	23	0	0	23
Norway	8	0	0	0	8
Portugal	0	5	1	0	6
Sweden	0	7	0	0	7

of Austria. At the other extreme, Finland and France show particularly low commitments to legislative discipline. Interestingly, both are also countries with strong presidents, as well as countries in which communist parties have occasionally been brought into the orbit of governance. However, whether these commonalities are necessary or sufficient to explain the lack of legislative discipline is beyond the scope of this study.

With respect to other parliamentary behaviour, just as for legislation, we find particularly high levels of coalition discipline in Austria, Denmark, and

TABLE 15.11. *Coalition discipline in other parliamentary behaviour*

Country	(1) (Always discipline)	(2) (Exceptions from discipline)	(3) (Discipline as exception)	(4) (No discipline)	N
Austria	14	3	0	0	17
Belgium	0	0	0	28	28
Denmark	17	0	0	0	17
Finland	0	16	17	0	33
France	0	15	0	2	17
Germany	21	1	0	0	22
Ireland	10	0	0	0	10
Italy	0	0	34	0	34
Luxembourg	0	0	0	16	16
Netherlands	0	0	0	23	23
Norway	0	8	0	0	8
Portugal	0	0	6	0	6
Sweden	0	7	0	0	7

Germany. Ireland is another system in which tight coalition discipline is expected, whereas all the Benelux countries fall at the opposite end of the spectrum. Although coalitions at either end of this scale tend to be similar in their partisan make-up, these commonalities apparently do not extend to the forms that parliamentary cooperation takes within the coalition.

Policy Programmes

As we have seen, most coalition agreements have a large policy component. Yet, coalitions vary substantially with respect to the comprehensiveness of their policy agreements (Table 15.12). As the reader will recall from Chapter 1, coalition policy programmes have been analysed with the help of a four-category ordinal coding scheme, in which the 'highest' category, code 3, means a comprehensive programme, 2 a policy programme with certain exceptions, 1 a progamme in which commitment exists only on a few selected issues, and 0 no common policy agreement. In three countries, Denmark, Luxembourg, and Portugal, all coalition agreements have conformed to the highest level of commitment. In France, at the other extreme, two-thirds of all coalition cabinets have had no commonly agreed policy programme at all. Austria, Belgium, Ireland, and the Netherlands also feature at least one coalition cabinet a piece which fall into the latter category. Austria and the Netherlands exhibit the greatest variance in policy commitment. In both cases coalition agreements have become more policy comprehensive over time and in both cases this has paralleled a decline of traditional party loyalties and an increase in party competition. Coalitions that are based on a comprehensive policy programme should generally be considered tighter than coalitions in which this is not the case. Yet, there may be functional alternatives to comprehensive policy programmes. If the other three conditions of commitment are truly fulfilled, there may be no need for an explicit policy programme in order to 'tighten' a coalition. Austria is a case in point. The grand coalitions from the late 1940s to the early 1960s were certainly tight, even though they were based almost exclusively on procedural rules rather than on a comprehensive policy programme. High levels of commitment to legislative unity, coupled with a strong election rule, sufficed to produce a series of 'tight' coalitions.

Appointment Powers

Although formal coalition agreements tend to be silent on ministerial and other appointment powers, there can be no doubt that such matters weigh heavily on the minds of party leaders. Consequently, rules and norms certainly tend to evolve, and our contributors have used the best available evidence to characterize them. Some coalitions allow their parties full discretion in their choice of cabinet ministers ('freedom of appointment'), whereas others subject such appointments to mutual veto. Freedom of appointment has

TABLE 15.12. Policy agreement

Country	(3) (Comprehensive)	(2) (Variety of issues)	(1) (Only few issues)	(0) (No policy agreement)	N
Austria	5	2	9	1	17
Belgium	15	5	7	1	28
Denmark	17	0	0	0	17
Finland	13	6	14	0	33
France	0	5	0	12	17
Germany	5	8	9	0	22
Ireland	0	7	1	2	10
Italy	0	12	22	0	34
Luxembourg	16	0	0	0	16
Netherlands	8	3	8	1	20
Norway	5	1	2	0	8
Portugal	6	0	0	0	6
Sweden	4	3	0	0	7

been the rule in most of the 13 countries covered in this volume. Finland and Norway have been partial exceptions to this rule, whereas German and French coalition parties have often had little or no freedom of appointment.

Similarly, the coalition partners may include in their deals the appointment of junior ministers (second-level political appointees in various ministerial departments without cabinet rank and voting rights) and other political appointees (e.g. in various agencies in the public sector, or in EU institutions). Junior ministers exist in most of our 13 countries, as only Denmark and Finland do without them. As Table 15.7 shows, most coalitions indeed make the appointment of junior ministers a part of the deal between the coalition partners. Many of the country chapters highlight the role of junior ministers in coalition politics. From a coalitional point of view, junior ministers are particular interesting in those cases where they come from a party different from that of their respective superiors, the cabinet ministers. (Consequently, the portfolio allocation tables in the country chapters have confined themselves to such cases.) Potentially, such junior ministers can foster either coalition stability or instability. If they manage to keep their party informed about potentially unacceptable policy developments in their respective departments, such appointments may allow coalition parties more effective agenda control in ministries that they do not hold, thereby avoiding conflicts in the cabinet or in parliament that could lead to cabinet termination. Yet, this is not the only role that a junior minister may play. Such an appointee may act more as a *'postillon d'amour'* of his or her department, or more as a 'watchdog' of his or her party. However, as long as the prime concern of junior ministers is to prevent major coalition conflicts, we would expect them to ease coalition governance and enhance coalition stability. However, if junior ministers—for career, electoral, or other reasons—are mainly interested in creating conflict, they can certainly be a thorn in the side of their respective ministers. Such relationships can exacerbate conflicts within the coalition and may well shorten its life.

Conflict Management Mechanisms

Table 15.7 also shows whether the coaliton agreements have set up a specific conflict management mechanism, such as a coalition committee. Where such mechanisms do not exist, disputes and uncertainties presumably have to be resolved through existing constitutional mechanisms (such as cabinet deliberations) or through negotiations between coalition party leaders. Again, we have previously had little or no systematic knowledge of how such processes work.

The contributions in this volume have documented a great variety of mechanisms of conflict management. For example, coalition committees of some kind have existed in Austria, France, Germany, Italy, Luxembourg, the Netherlands, and Portugal. Yet, while many of the parliamentary systems of central Europe have experience with this institution, there is no record of its use in any of the Nordic countries. Inner cabinets are an alternative institutional mechanism. The contributors have documented their use in Austria, Belgium, Denmark, Finland, Germany, the Netherlands, Norway, and Sweden. That is to say, this less formal mechanism of coordination has found use in many of the same countries that have also experienced coalition committees. Note, however, that inner cabinets have found somewhat greater favour in Northern Europe, including the Netherlands. At a lower level perhaps, but still within the cabinet, coalition conflicts typically have been managed through cabinet committees in Ireland, Italy, Luxembourg, and the Netherlands. In several countries, coalition parties have sought to contain conflict by drawing on parliamentarians, either exclusively (Ireland, the Netherlands), or in joint fora of MPs or parliamentary leaders and cabinet members (Denmark, Finland, Germany, Norway).

Finally, yet another forum for conflict management is party summits, i.e. meetings of the leaders of the coalition parties, whether or not these hold portfolios in the cabinet. This mechanism has been used in Belgium, France, Germany, Ireland, Italy, Luxembourg, and Portugal. Again, there is no clear separation of the systems in which this institutional vehicle has been in use. Thus, a more definitive account of the choice and effects of different conflict management mechanisms must await further research. There can be no question, however, that conflicts or coordination problems often arise between different cabinet members, and that coalition parties have devised a multitude of institutions to resolve such conflicts and coordinate policy across ministerial jurisdictions. Thus, the real world of coalition politics is a good deal more complex than the Laver and Shepsle model of ministerial government.

CABINET STABILITY AND TERMINATION

Recently, a rapidly growing literature has been devoted to the explanation of cabinet stability, as well as to the circumstances and causes of coalition termination (Warwick 1994; Lupia and Strøm 1995). Once again, the contributors to this volume have added substantially to our knowledge of these phenomena. In our brief summary of these findings, we shall focus first on stability, and then on the specifics of terminations.

Cabinet Stability

As the informed student of parliamentary democracies will know, the countries represented in this volume differ widely in cabinet stability. To be sure, the degree of cabinet stability or instability depends to some extent on the definition of 'government' or 'cabinet' (cf. Lijphart 1984b; Strøm 1988; Damgaard 1994). To reiterate, we define a 'cabinet' as an administration under the same prime minster, representing the same parties and uninterrupted by general elections. For the sake of simplicity, we also ignore differences in the maximum constitutional term of parliament (which ranges from 3 to 5 years in our study). Given these conventions and simplifications, we find clear cross-national patterns in cabinet stability (Table 15.13). Overall, we can distinguish between three rough categories of states: one exhibiting a high degree of goverment stability (with a mean cabinet duration of more than 800 days, including Luxembourg (with a mean of 1,171 days), Ireland (891), Austria (854), and the Netherlands (808)); a second containing countries with a medium degree of goverment stability (with a mean cabinet duration of between 500 and 800 days: Sweden (771), Norway (755), Germany (700), Denmark (626), France (625), Portugal (597), and Belgium (520)); and finally a set of countries with low cabinet stability (a mean cabinet duration below 500 days), namely Finland (453) and Italy (355). The overall cross-national patterns are certainly consistent with previous research and should be familiar to students of coalition politics.

Cabinet Termination

Coalition studies have recently come to the realization that coalition terminations may be as interesting and consequential as coalition formations and that one phenomenon cannot be properly understood except in the context of

TABLE 15.13. *Cabinet duration*

Country	Number of cabinets	Mean duration	Minimum duration	Maximum duration	Standard deviation
Austria	21	854.3	160	1,431	447.2
Belgium	32	520.2	7	1,502	489.2
Denmark	30	626.4	40	1,337	323.9
Finland	36	452.6	36	1,409	365.0
France	22	625.1	31	1,191	376.5
Germany	25	699.5	14	1,452	504.9
Ireland	21	891.1	228	1,532	382.1
Italy	47	355.1	11	1,628	309.9
Luxembourg	15	1,170.5	153	1,936	694.8
Netherlands	22	808.1	80	1,638	539.8
Norway	25	755.3	24	1,435	404.6
Portugal	10	596.8	96	1,506	503.8
Sweden	25	771.0	167	1,468	403.2
MEANS	25.5	702	80.5	1,497	441.9

Note: This table excludes non-partisan cabinets.

the other. Yet, our factual knowledge of the histories of coalition termination has until now been rudimentary. The contributors have therefore made a major contribution to coalition studies by identifying what we have termed the mechanisms and causes of all cabinet terminations.

We distinguish technical from discretionary terminations. Technical terminations are those beyond the control of the relevant parties, namely constitutional mandated elections, the death or personally motivated retirement of the prime minister, and other constitutional provisions that require the cabinet's resignation (e.g. the accession of a new head of state). These causes are mutually exclusive, or at least individually sufficient. Discretionary terminations include early parliamentary dissolutions, voluntary enlargements of coalitions, parliamentary defeats at the hands of the opposition, conflicts between coalition parties over policy or personal matters, and conflict within any coalition party. These discretionary mechanisms need not, of course, be mutually exclusive.

Table 15.14 examines the mechanisms of cabinet termination. Collectively, our contributors have provided termination information on 331 party-based cabinets. While 128 (39%) have been terminated for technical reasons, various discretionary mechanisms account for the vast majority of terminations. Yet, the analysis reveals substantial cross-national differences. Discretionary mechanisms account for more than 80 per cent of all terminations in Ireland, Italy, and Belgium, and more than 75 per cent in Denmark. Clearly, in these cases, our record of cabinet changes is not unduly inflated by the rules by which we have counted cabinets. In other words, the vast majorities of such

TABLE 15.14. Mechanisms of cabinet termination

Country	Number of cabinets	Technical			Discretionary				Conflict between coalition parties		(8) Intra-party conflict in coalition parties
		(1) Regular parliamentary election	(2) Other constitutional reason	(3) Death of prime minister	(4) Early parl. election	(5) Voluntary enlargement of coalition	(6) Cabinet defeated by opposition in parl.		(7)		
								Policy conflict	Personnel conflict		
Austria	21	7	2	0	9	0	0	6	1	3	
Belgium	32	5	1	0	8	2	1	17	2	3	
Denmark	30	1	3	3	18	1	10	2	0	1	
Finland	36	9	7	0	1	4	2	14	0	1	
France	22	4	5	0	4	0	1	2	0	6	
Germany	25	11	0	0	2	3	2	5	2	8	
Ireland	21	0	2	0	16	0	3	3	3	7	
Italy	47	4	0	1	6	5	12	15	12	17	
Luxembourg	15	9	1	0	2	0	0	3	1	1	
Netherlands	22	10	1	0	4	0	1	6	0	2	
Norway	25	13	5	0	0	1	3	2	0	2	
Portugal	10	3	0	1	3	0	2	2	3	0	
Sweden	25	16	2	2	1	1	0	3	0	0	
TOTAL	331	92	29	7	74	17	37	80	24	51	
MEANS/%	25.5	27.8	8.8	2.1	22.4	5.1	11.2	24.2	7.3	15.4	

Note: This table excludes non-partisan cabinets.

changes that have been recorded here, have been due to the actions of the parties themselves, and not artefacts of our definitions.

On the other hand, only one in five cabinet terminations in Sweden reflects an actual discretionary change, and even in Norway and Luxembourg, the majority of resignations have been technical rather than discretionary. Specifically, most of these technical resignations have been due to general elections. In Sweden, this count is inflated by the fact that the parliamentary term for much of the recent decades has been limited to three years. In the remaining systems, the proportion of discretionary terminations ranges from 50 to 60 per cent.

Terminal Events

Our record of 'terminal events' represents the first systematic attempt to catalog the circumstances that have toppled specific cabinets (Table 15.15). These may in many cases be viewed as the initial developments that generate the conflicts discussed above. Critical events have featured prominently in the recent theoretical literature on coalition duration, but they have so far proven resistant to operationalization and empirical analysis. Our five types of events are: non-parliamentary elections, popular opinion developments, national security events, economic events, and personal events. Our contributors have identified terminal events for 91 of 331 cabinet terminations (27%). Personal events (29 cases/32% of terminal events) and economic events (24 cases/26%) have been the most numerous. International and security events account for only 14 (15%) cabinets. However, some of them (in particular, the beginning of the Cold War) have been of lasting importance, excluding some parties from the executive branch for decades. Finally, non-parliamentary elections (presidential and local elections) (13 cases/14%) and popular opinion shocks (11 cases/12%) have accounted for more than one-tenth of cabinet terminations each.

ELECTORAL CONSEQUENCES OF GOVERNMENT PARTICIPATION

What do parties get out of governing? To a large extent, and to most voters, the primary answer has to be found in the policies that these parties have an opportunity to effect. Yet, it is obvious that parties keenly eye their pay-offs in future elections as well. Our contributors have examined the performance of incumbent parties and governments in such electoral terms. In many circumstances, the electoral performance of the government as a whole matters. If a government loses its majority, it is unlikely to remain in office (though occasionally this happens). Likewise, a government that has lost heavily in

TABLE 15.15. *Terminal events*

	Number of cabinets	(9) Elections (non-parliamentary)	(10) Popular opinion shock	(11) International or national security event	(12) Economic event	(13) Personal event
Austria	21	1	1	1	1	0
Belgium	32	0	1	0	0	0
Denmark	30	0	0	1	7	6
Finland	36	6	0	0	2	1
France	22	0	1	6	2	3
Germany	25	0	0	0	2	2
Ireland	21	0	6	0	2	4
Italy	47	4	1	1	0	2
Luxembourg	15	0	0	0	0	1
Netherlands	22	0	0	1	0	0
Norway	25	1	0	4	5	6
Portugal	10	1	1	0	3	0
Sweden	25	0	0	0	0	4
TOTAL	331	13	11	14	24	29
MEANS/%	25.5	3.9	3.3	4.2	7.3	8.8

popular vote may not be returned even if it manages to maintain a parliamentary majority, because political leaders feel the need to respond to signals from the electorate, or because they do not wish to burden an incoming government with the image of decline or defeat. In the final event, however, elections are contested by individual parties. What in most cases matters to the key actors in coalition politics is how their own party performs, not what happens to coalition partners. We therefore also explore the performance of governing parties in the elections that have immediately followed their government participation (Table 15.16).

Governments

When viewed in the aggregate, most governments do not maintain their strength in the elections that follow their term in executive office. Altogether, our contributors have collected data on the electoral performance of 277 governments. Of those, only 92 (33%) have been able to improve their electoral strength (in proportions of votes) in the election following their term in office, while 179 (65%) have suffered losses. Six governments have been returned with precisely the same combined electoral strength as previously. In 11 out of our 13 countries (with France and Germany as the exceptions), the size of the largest recorded loss has been larger, and often considerably larger, than the maximum gains that any governments has made in any election.

Our 13 countries differ widely in the extent to which incumbency has been a liability or an asset. Only in Austria, however, have more than half of all governments improved their strength in subsequent elections. German and French governments have done so in almost half of the cases, whereas Danish and Italian governments have also done comparatively well. In all other countries the vast majority of governments have suffered electoral losses. Seventy per cent or more of the governments in Belgium, Ireland, the

TABLE 15.16. *Electoral gains and losses of government parties* (in % of total popular vote)

Country (N/N[a])	Party			Government		
	Numbers of winning/ losing cases (gains/ losses)	Range of gains/ losses in %	Losses in % of cases	Numbers of winning/ losing cases	Range of winning/ losing cases in %	Losses in % of cases
Austria (26/16)	12/14	4.8/–9.2	54	9/6	5.7/–12.3	38
Belgium (58/27)	20/35	6.4/–8.4	60	6/20	3.5/–15.4	74
Denmark (49/26)	19/30	11.0/–11.7	61	12/14	11.0/–11.7	54
Finland (61/36)	16/44	2.9/–5.0	72	8/27	3.5/–13.9	75
France (24/15)	9/15	27.0/–16.2	63	7/8	26.7/–22.4	53
Germany (30/23)	12/18	14.2/–6.4	60	11/12	11.1/–8.3	52
Ireland (28/17)	7/20	6.0/–12.1	71	2/13	3.9/–15.1	76
Italy (47/37)[b]	22/22	13.3/–18.6	47	16/20	14.3/–35.6	54
Luxembourg (24/12)	6/18	13.1/–8.1	75	2/10	5.8/–11.3	83
Netherlands (50/20)	19/31	6.5/–13.1	62	5/15	4.8/–21.0	75
Norway (32/20)	14/18	10.3/–11.2	56	7/13	7.0/–11.2	65
Portugal (8/7)[c]	4/4	20.4/–26.4	50	3/4	20.4/–26.4	57
Sweden (27/21)	7/19	4.7/–8.9	70	4/16	4.9/–8.9	76
TOTALS	167/288			92/179		
MEANS		10.8/–11.9	61.6		9.4/–16.4	64

[a] Because some elections return the government and/or individual government parties with ±0 gains/losses, the number of winning/losing cases can be smaller than the Ns. The first N is the number of government parties (each counted once per election), the second N is the number of governments.

[b] We have excluded those parties for specific elections which run a joint list (PCI and PSI in 1948, PSI and PSDI in 1968 and 1972).

[c] Though the second Soares government in Portugal included the Socialist Party (PS) and the Centre Social Democrats (CDS), it is not possible to calculate electoral gains/losses for the CDS in the following election because the party joined the Democratic Alliance (AD) in that election with two other parties; for the same reason, it is also not possible to calculate electoral gains/losses for that government. In the four Portuguese governments in which the AD participated, the AD is treated as a single party (though elsewhere it is treated as three separate parties), since it is not possible to break down the AD's electoral performance into the electoral performance of its three component parties.

Netherlands, Luxembourg, Sweden, and Finland have had to face electoral punishment. Portuguese and Norwegian governments on the average have done slightly better (though they have still lost ground in about 60% of the cases).

Government Parties

As our country studies demonstrate, parties serving in the same government often experience different fortunes at the ballot box. Some gain while others lose. Nevertheless, on the average, individual parties have performed exactly as poorly as governments overall. Of the 464 cases (i.e. parties contesting an election after having served in government for a whole or partial term), 288 (62%) have suffered losses, 167 (36%) have made gains, and a mere 9 (2%) have just maintained their electoral strength. Moreover, in 10 out of our 13 countries the largest recorded loss has been greater, and often considerably greater, than the largest gain on record (again with France and Germany, plus Luxembourg, as the exceptions).

It is worth taking a more disaggregated view of our 13 countries. Only in Portugal have as many as 50 per cent of the government parties improved their electoral position in elections following their incumbency (with the other half losing ground). For individual parties, government participation has on average been most likely to result in electoral losses in Finland, Ireland, Luxembourg, and Sweden, where 70 per cent or more of incumbent parties have lost vote shares. The proportion of losers has been above 60 per cent even in Belgium, Denmark, France, Germany, and the Netherlands.

Our brief investigation of the electoral fortunes of government parties is not directly comparable to the classic study by Rose and Mackie (1983), who use different measures and examine a larger set of countries (in particular, by including countries that typically have single-party governments). Nevertheless, our results are quite consistent with theirs. Indeed, our data suggest that government incumbency has been even less of an electoral asset in the 1980s and 1990s than in the 24 post-war years which form the basis of their study.

CONCLUSION

In the introductory chapter to this volume, we discussed the many lacunae that still remain in our knowledge of cabinet coalitions in parliamentary democracies. The literature, we noted, has long suffered from one of the traditional Hollywood biases: much more attention has been given to identifying the right match, and to the process of courtship, than to the actual process of sharing a life (political or otherwise) and working out the concomitant issues. The most important ambition shared by the contributors to this volume has been to go some distance towards redressing that imbalance, by in various ways enhancing our understanding of coalition governance.

The chapters here have been designed to convey detailed insight into the process of coalition governance in all of the 13 main parliamentary coalition systems in Western Europe. In this sample, we have included France, in the belief that its constitutional mechanisms of legislative delegation and accountability are not critically different from other parliamentary systems. We have focused on three general aspects of coalition politics: formation, governance in office, and termination. These, of course, are all identifiable concerns in the existing literature on cabinet coalitions. Our emphasis, however, has shaded much more in the directions of governance, first, and termination, second, than what has hitherto been common. Furthermore, we are convinced that these phases of coalition politics cannot fruitfully be studied in mutual isolation, since the game of coalition politics is so much one of strategy and anticipation. We have aimed to produce data that will facilitate the study of the interactions between different phases of coalition politics. Consequently, this is a much more complete survey of coalition politics than any study previously published, and it is one whose focus is more consistent with recent developments in the theoretical literature.

The bulk of the insight we have gained is contained in the series of country chapters. In this concluding chapter, we have sought to provide a first survey of these results. It has not been possible to analyse these data in detail or to explore the various ways in which formation, govenance, electoral performance, and termination are interrelated. The research team that has produced this volume will pursue these questions in forthcoming publications. The answers, we hope, will interest students of parliamentary democracy, its practitioners, and, not least, those whom such governments are meant to serve.

REFERENCES

Baron, David P. (1991). 'A Spacial Bargaining Theory of Government Formation in a Parliamentary System'. *American Political Science Review*, 83: 1181–1206.

Bergman, Torbjörn (1993). 'Formation Rules and Minority Governments'. *European Journal of Political Research*, 23: 55–66.

Damgaard, Erik (1994). 'Termination of Danish Government Coalitions: Theoretical and Empirical Aspects'. *Scandinavian Political Studies*, 17: 193–211.

de Swaan, Abram (1973). *Coalition Theories and Cabinet Formation*. Amsterdam: Elsevier.

Dood, Lawrence C. (1976). *Coalitions in Parliamentary Government*. Princeton:

Princeton University Press.

Laakso, Markuu, and Taagepera, Rein (1979). '"Effective" Number of Political Parties. A Measure with Applications to Western Europe'. *Comparative Political Studies*, 12: 3–27.

Laver, Michael, and Budge, Ian (1992) (eds.). *Party Policy and Coalition Government.* London: Macmillan.

——and Schofield, Norman (1990). *Multiparty Government.* Oxford: Oxford University Press.

——and Shepsle, Kenneth (1990). 'Coalitions and Cabinet Government'. *American Political Science Review*, 84: 873–90.

————(1996). *Making and Breaking Governments: Cabinets and Legislatures in Parliamentary Democracies.* Cambridge: Cambridge University Press.

Lijphart, Arend (1984a). *Democracies.* New Haven: Yale University Press.

——(1984b). 'Measures of Cabinet Durability'. *Comparative Political Studies*, 17: 265–79.

Luebbert, Gregory M. (1986). *Comparative Democracy: Policymaking and Governing Coalitions in Europe and Israel.* New York: Columbia University Press.

Lupia, Arthur, and Strøm, Kaare (1995). 'Coalition Termination and the Strategic Timing of Parliamentary Elections'. *American Political Science Review*, 89: 648–65.

Müller, Wolfgang C., and Strøm, Kaare (1999) (eds.). *Policy, Office, or Votes? How Political Parties in Western Europe Make Hard Decisions.* Cambridge: Cambridge University Press.

Rae, Douglas W. (1971). *The Political Consequences of Electoral Laws.* New Haven: Yale University Press.

Riker, William T. (1962). *The Theory of Political Coalitions.* New Haven: Yale University Press.

Rose, Richard, and Mackie, Thomas (1983). 'Incumbency in Government: Asset or Liability', in Hans Daalder and Peter Mair (eds.), *West European Party Systems: Continuity and Change.* London: Sage.

Strøm, Kaare (1988). 'Contending Models of Cabinet Stability'. *American Political Science Review*, 82: 923–30.

——(1990). *Minority Government and Majority Rule.* Cambridge: Cambridge University Press.

——Budge, Ian, and Laver, Michael J. (1994). 'Constraints on Cabinet Formation in Parliamentary Democracies'. *American Journal of Political Science*, 38: 303–35.

Warwick, Paul V. (1994). *Government Survival in Parliamentary Democracies.* Cambridge: Cambridge University Press.

Index

Aardal, Bernt 161, 164, 188
accountability 425, 501, 506, 510, 521, 591
Ackaert, Johan 329
Action Committee for Democracy and Pension Justice, ADR (Luxembourg) 401, 406, 569
Action Party, PdA (Italy) 433
Aliança Democática, *see* Democratic Alliance, AD (Portugal)
Adenaur, Konrad 43–5, 50, 53, 58, 61–3, 71, 75–8, 81
agency relations 6, 18, 51
agenda control (setting) 18, 108, 113, 178, 211–12, 288, 366, 376, 382, 388, 461, 572, 582
Agrarian (Centre) Party, CE (Finland) 264–5, 268, 270, 272–3, 281–3, 288
Aguiar, Joaquim 530, 533
Ahern, Bertie 144
Aho, Esko 282, 292
Ahtisaari, Martti 292
Albæk Jensen, Jørgen 236–7, 248
Alen, André 325
Alleanze Nazionale, AN (Italy) 435, 443, 462
All-German Bloc, GB/BHE (Germany) 44, 76–7
Alliance '90, B'90 (Germany) 60
Alt, James 13
Amaral, Freitas do 531
Amato, Giuliano 443, 453, 462
Andenæs, Johs. 166
Anders Lange's Party (Norway) 160
Andeweg, Rudy 149, 381–3
Andrén, Nils 194, 201, 206, 217
Andreotti, Giulio 449, 457, 460–2, 488–9
Arkins, Audrey 131
Arndt, Claus 57
Arrow, Kenneth 6
Arter, David 201
Austen-Smith, David 3, 13
Austrian People's Party, ÖVP (Austria) 86–7, 90–3, 95–7, 99, 101–2, 104–113, 116–17, 120–2
Axelrod, Robert 92

Bäck, Mats 198
Back, Pär-Erik 197
Bakema, Wilma 382, 396
Balladur, Éduoard 502, 505, 511, 525
Balsemão, Francisco Pinto 547, 549, 553, 536, 539, 541, 546, 553, 555
Bangemann, Martin 63
Banks, Jeffrey 3, 13
Barfuß, Walter 104
bargaining:
  complexity 194, 344, 368, 390, 563–5, 576
  power 7–8, 19, 22, 71, 130, 133, 265, 498, 567
  rounds 13–15, 48–9, 96, 272, 312–13, 333, 368, 390, 394, 410–12, 570–2
Baron, David 3, 11, 13, 568
Barre, Raymond 509, 522, 525
Barroso, Manuel Durão 533
Bartolini, Stefano 433, 495
Barzel, Rainer 62, 77
Battegazzorre, Francesco 448, 461, 478
Baum, Gerhart-Rudolf 58
Baunsgaard, Hilmar 250
Bavarian Party, BP (Germany) 34, 39, 45
Bech, Joseph 401, 406, 415, 419, 427, 429
Beel, Louis 387
Belgian Socialist Party, BSP 334, 345
Beller, Dennis 6
Belloni, Frank 6
Bennulf, Martin 198
Bérégovoy, Pierre 525
Berggrav, Dag 178–9
Berglund, Sten 159, 197
Bergman, Torbjörn 7, 11, 29, 90, 167, 192–3, 195, 197, 202, 205, 231, 307, 568
Bergström, Hans 209, 211–12, 214
Berlusconi, Silvio 435, 444, 456, 489
Bermbach, Udo 65
Biesheuvel, Barend 387
Bildt, Carl 212
Bille, Lars 232
Bilstad, Karl-Anders 164
Birgersson, Bengt Owe 193
Bjørklund, Tor 160–1

Björnberg, Arne 172
Blondel, Jean 383
Bogdanor, Vernon 3
Bohman, Gösta 204, 211, 217
Bohnsack, Klaus 47, 57
Bondevik, Kjell 172–3, 181
Bondevik, Kjell Magne 169–70, 174, 183
Bondevik, Odd 180
Borten, Per 173, 179, 181, 185
Bossi, Umberto 443
Bracher, Karl Dietrich 35–6, 48, 50, 65, 75
Brandt, Willy 35, 46, 48, 55, 62, 71, 75
Bratteli, Trygve 169, 173, 186
Browne, Eric 3, 22, 143, 150, 292
Bruneau, Thomas 530, 536
Brundtland, Gro Harlem 167
Bruton, John 144
Budge, Ian 3, 8, 11, 15, 22, 92, 112, 131, 238, 240–1, 269–70, 307, 309, 311, 317–18, 363, 377, 424, 430, 561–2, 565
Busse, Volker 60–1

cabinets:
  caretaker 204, 237, 271, 273, 289, 343, 363, 370, 387, 390, 489, 535–6, 548, 551, 555
  inner 18, 63, 105, 179, 212–13, 246, 352, 381, 396, 415, 417, 583
  investiture 11, 48, 90, 131, 167, 231, 307–8, 311, 317, 322, 324, 343, 352, 363, 372, 399, 404, 409–10, 418, 420, 445, 493, 495, 504–4, 521, 536, 568
  recognition rules 11, 13, 131, 133
  majority 170, 561, 568
  minority 75, 167, 169–70, 174, 189, 192, 202, 225–7, 231, 243, 258, 260–1, 317, 344–5, 452, 561, 571
Calise, Mauro 464
Campbell, David 87
Carducci, Michele 470
Carlsson, Ingvar 203
Carneiro, Soares 535–6
Casqueiro, Manuel 551
Castles, Francis 8, 195
Catholic People's Party, KVP (Netherlands) 358, 364–5, 367
Cavaco Silva, Anibal 529, 531, 536, 546, 548, 553, 555
Centre Democratic Party, CD (Denmark) 233, 236, 239, 245
Centre Party (Finland), see Agrarian (Centre) Party, CE (Finland)
Centre Party, Ce (Sweden) 192–8, 201, 203–7, 209, 211–19, 222–6

Centre Party, SP (Norway) 159–61, 163–6, 169–70, 172–3, 177, 180–1, 186, 188
Centre Party, Z (Germany) 34
Centre Right Parties, CDP/CDS/UC (France) 508, 525, 530–1, 534–45, 551, 553
Chaban-Delmas, Jacques 522
Chagnollaud, Dominique 508
Chiaramonte, Alessandro 446
Chirac, Jacques 501–2, 505, 508–9, 511, 521–2, 525
Christensen, Jørgen Grønnegaard 246
Christian Democratic Appeal, CDA (Netherlands) 362, 364, 367, 377, 393, 395–6
Christian Democratic Party, CD (Sweden) 192, 194, 195, 205, 217
Christian Democratic Party, CSV (Luxembourg) 401, 405, 407–12, 415, 418, 420, 424–8, 430–1, 571
Christian Democratic Union, CDU/CSU (Germany) 33, 35, 38–40, 43–6, 49–50, 53, 57–9, 61–4, 66, 70–1, 75–8, 80, 569
Christian Democrats, CVP/PSC (Belgium) 300–1, 304, 306–7, 312–13, 316–19, 327, 333–5, 341–2, 345, 349, 351–2
Christian Democrats, DC (Italy) 6, 433, 435, 438, 442–5, 446, 449, 451–3, 457, 461–4, 478, 488–90, 493–4
Christian League, CHR (Finland) 265
Christian People's Party, CPP (Denmark) 233, 237, 239, 245
Christian People's Party, KRF (Norway) 159–60, 163–5, 166, 169, 170, 172, 177, 181, 186, 188
Christian Socialist Union, see Christian Democratic Party, CDU/CSU (Germany)
Christoffersson, Ulf 211
Ciampi, Carlo Azelio 443, 456
civil service 60, 112–16, 144, 149, 179, 248, 273, 283, 335, 341, 375, 418, 424, 427
Claeys, Paul Henri 304
Clann na Poblachta, CnP (Ireland) 129
Clann na Talmhan, CnT (Ireland) 129
Cluskey, Frank 140
Coakley, John 193
Coalition Party, see Conservative Party, CON (Finland)
coalitions:
  committee 18, 38, 58–63, 81, 104–5, 110, 140, 383, 396, 583
  coordination 226, 246

discipline 19, 57–9, 105–7, 110–11, 140–1, 178, 180, 209, 246, 278, 281–2, 384, 418, 460, 514, 548, 579–81
  legislative 105, 168, 189, 219, 225
  grand 37, 39, 45, 50, 57, 62, 71, 80, 86–7, 90, 92–3, 95–7, 99, 101–13, 120–2, 135, 138, 433, 461, 569, 579, 581
  renegotiation 132, 406, 447, 452
  theory 4–7, 11, 16, 137, 227, 261, 358, 555
Common Course, CC (Denmark) 233
Communist Party, PCP (Portugal) 530–1, 533–4, 538–9, 541
Communist Party, Com (Denmark) 233, 236
Communist Party, Com (Sweden) 192–3, 197–9, 201, 21–19, 225
Communist Party, FPDU (Finland) 264, 282–3
Communist Party, KPD (Germany) 39
Communist Party, KPL (Luxembourg) 400–1, 406, 424
Communist Party, KPÖ (Austria) 86, 90, 92–3, 120
Communist Party, NKP (Norway) 159–60, 165
Communist Party, PC (France) 501–2, 504, 508–12
Communist Party, PCB/KPB (Belgium) 301, 304, 307, 312, 335, 341
Communist Party, PCI (Italy) 433, 435, 438, 442, 444, 446–7, 449, 452–3, 457, 490, 494
confidence motions 35–7, 75–6, 80, 90–1, 108, 132, 167, 202, 225, 231, 237, 260, 268, 307, 324, 342, 345, 363, 384, 404, 410, 425, 427, 444–6, 448, 457, 460, 470, 478, 490, 495, 505, 514, 521–2
conflict management mechanisms 18, 55, 58–63, 81, 104–5, 140, 178–9, 189, 246, 278, 281, 297, 391, 396, 417, 431, 460–1, 548, 556, 583
Conradt, David 40
Conservative Party, Co (Sweden) 193, 198, 203, 205, 211, 215, 217, 222–4
Conservative Party, CON (Finland) 264–5, 268–70, 282–3
Conservative Party, H (Norway) 158, 161, 165–6, 168–9, 172–4, 177, 179, 181, 183, 186, 188
Conservative People's Party, Con (Denmark) 233, 236, 239–40, 244–6, 253

consociational democracy 80, 94, 390, 396
Corkill, David 531
Cosgrave, Liam 150–1
Cossiga, Francesco 444, 448, 478, 488
Costa e Sousa, Vinicio Almeida 533
Costa, Amaro da 531
Cotta, Maurizio 433, 438, 443, 451, 453, 456, 462, 468
Council of the Revolution, CR (Portugal) 530
Couve de Murville, Maurice 525
Cravinho, João 547
Craxi, Bettino 446, 449, 453, 462, 488–9, 494
Cresson, Édith 522
Criscitiello, Annarita 461, 489
critical events 26, 32, 292, 298, 349, 353, 587
Cruz, Manuel Braga da 531, 536, 539, 548

D'Alema, Massimo 444, 446
D'Alimonte, Roberto 433, 446, 495
D'Hondt, Paula 341
Daalder, Hans 367
Damgaard, Erik 231–2, 236, 238, 248, 253, 255, 584
Danish People's Party, DPP (Denmark) 233
Daudt, Hans 367
De Gasperi, Alcide 449
De Gaulle, Charles 498, 508, 522
De Jong, Jan 367
De Melo, Eurico 541, 546, 553
De Mita, Ciriaco 462, 488, 494
De Quay, Jan Eduard 380
De Ridder, Martine 309
De Swaan, Abram 562
De Valera, Eamon 150
De Winter, Lieven 300–1, 304, 307–8, 310, 316, 324–7, 341–2, 425, 457
Debré, Michel 522
Dehaene, Jean-Luc 326, 345
Della Porta, Donnatella 300
Delors, Jacques 522
Demarez, Pierre 304
Democratic Alliance, AD (Portugal) 531, 535–9, 541–2, 546, 548–9, 553, 555
Democratic Convergence (Portugal) 538
Democratic Left, DL (Ireland) 131, 133, 135, 137, 143
Democratic Left, DS/PDS (Italy) 444, 494
Democratic Renewal Party, PRD (Portugal) 533, 553
Democratic Social Union, DSU (Germany) 50, 75

Den Uyl, Joop 380
Deschouwer, Kris 300, 349
Desmond, Barry 145
Dewachter, Wilfried 312, 322
Dexheimer, Wolfgang 47
Di Palma, Giuseppe 460
Diermeier, Daniel 14
Dini, Lamberto 444, 456, 478, 489–90
Dittrich, Karl 358, 368
Dobler, Helmut 116
Dodd, Lawrence 27, 400, 562
Dogan, Mattei 464
Domingos, Emidio Veiga 535, 546
Dooney, Sean 149
Dorff, Robert 381
Drees, Willem 380
Dreijmanis, John 3, 116
Duhamel, Olivier 505, 508
Dujardin, Jean 325
Dumont, Patrick 301, 307
Dupong, Pierre 406, 415, 427, 429
Duverger, Maurice 501, 530
Duvieusart, Jean Pierre 325
Duynstee, F. J. F. M. 372

Eanes, Ramalho 529, 530, 533, 535–9, 542, 548, 551, 553
Economic Reconstruction League, WAV (Germany) 34
ED Centre Left Parties, (France) 525
Eeckhaut, Laurence 344

Egardt, Peter 212–15, 227
Einaudi, Luigi 445
elections:
  election rule 19, 57, 103, 178, 204, 246, 364, 548, 579, 581
  electoral system 1, 39, 76–7, 90–1, 132, 199, 233, 261, 271, 296, 403–4, 442–3, 446, 456, 494–5, 501, 527
  government performance 4–5, 27–8, 120–1, 151, 155, 186, 188, 193, 223, 226, 258, 293, 349, 391, 428, 431, 490, 493–4, 525, 555, 559–60, 565, 587–8, 591
  campaign 39, 91–2, 160, 169, 173, 197, 222, 272, 508–10, 527, 541, 569
Elklit, Jørgen 233, 253
Engelmann, Frederick 107
Environmental Party, Green (Sweden) 194–5, 198, 218, 219
Erhard, Ludwig 43, 50, 62, 71, 75, 77
Erlander, Tage 204–5, 207, 209, 211–12, 214, 217, 224, 226

Ersson, Svante 269
Eschenburg, Theodor 65
European Union:
  European Commission 333, 408, 415–16, 425, 427
  European Community 95, 160, 169, 172–3, 178, 185, 546
  European Monetary Union 444
  European Parliament 405
  general EU 101, 165, 169, 173, 178, 186, 201, 236, 444, 531, 531
Eyskens, Gaston 317, 329, 334, 345, 349
Eyskens, Mark 317, 325, 344, 349

Fabbrini, Sergio 456
Fabius, Laurent 509–10, 525
Fälldin, Thorbjörn 212, 219, 222
Fanfani, Amintore 448, 478, 488
Farmers' Party, see Centre Party, SP (Norway)
Farrell, Brian 137–8, 149
Feldt, Kjell-Olof 212
Fennell, Nuala 144
Ferreira, Goncalves F.A. 535, 544, 549
Ferreira, José Medeiros 533
Fianna Fáil, FF (Ireland) 126, 129–35, 137–8, 144, 149, 151, 155, 169, 193, 563, 569
Figl, Leopold 90, 97, 116
Fine Gael, FG (Ireland) 129–30, 133–5 137–8, 140–2, 144–5,
Finnish Rural Party, FRP (Finland) 265, 296
Fischbach 416, 428
Fischer, Heinz 97
FitzGerald, Garret 144
Fonsmark, Henning 241, 245
formateur 7, 36, 131, 135, 203, 205–6, 241, 271–3, 282, 297, 308–9, 312, 333, 351, 357, 362–6, 383, 399, 406–8, 411, 431 447, 449, 503, 529, 537, 567
Forza Italia, FI (Italy) 435, 443–4, 462
Franklin, Mark 22, 92
Free Democratic Party, FDP (Germany) 35, 38–40, 43–7, 49–50, 53, 55, 58–9, 61–3, 65, 70–1, 75–8, 80
Free Peoples Party, DA/FVP (Germany) 43, 77
Freedom Party, FPÖ (Austria) 86–7, 90–3, 97, 99, 101–2, 105, 108–9, 111, 117, 120–2, 569
French Speakers' Front, FDF (Belgium) 301, 304, 312, 335, 345
Frendreis, John 292

Frieden, Pierre 401, 420, 427
Frognier, André-Paul 310, 324, 326
Front National, FN (Belgium) 301, 569

Gallagher, Michael 129, 131–3, 138,
    141–2, 145
Gallagher, Tom 541
Galli, Giorgio 533
Gaullist Parties, UNR/UDR/RPR
    (France) 498, 500–2, 508, 509–12, 521,
    525
Gerhardsen, Einar 186
Gerlich, Peter 104, 107
German Party, DP (Germany) 34, 39,
    44–5, 50, 53, 61, 77
German Social Union, DSU (Germany)
    50, 75
Germer, Peter 237
Gibowski, Wolfgang 39
Gilljam, Mikael 194–5, 197–8, 204
Giolitti, Giovanni 464
Giscard d'Estaing, V. 500, 502, 508, 522,
    525
Gleditsch, Nils Petter 160
Gleiber, Dennis 292
Gomes, João Salis 539, 546, 553
Gorbach, Alfons 109
Goria, Giovanni 488
Grausgruber, Alfred 120
Green Alternative, GA (Austria) 86–7, 89,
    91, 95, 122
Green League, GWR (Finland) 265,
    269–70
Green Party (Germany) 34–5, 38–9, 46–8,
    59–60, 71, 80
Green Party (Ireland) 131, 135, 138
Greens (France) 501, 511–12
Greens (Luxembourg) 401, 406
Greens, AGALEV and ECOLO, Belgium
    301, 304
Greens, PEV (Portugal) 533
Groennings, Sven 161
Grofman, Bernard 26
Grønmo, Sigmund 164
Guagnano, Giuseppina 457

Haakon VII, King 172
Hadenius, Stig 192, 199, 205, 222
Hagtvet, Bernt 161
Haider, Jörg 109, 117, 120
Halvarson, Arne 201
Hammerich, Kai 204, 211
Hansen, H. C. 243
Harmel, Pierre 317

Haughey, Charles 150–1
head of state 26, 202–3, 238, 268, 292, 343,
    444–9, 463, 470, 478, 505, 510–11,
    535, 568, 585
Hearl, Derek 8, 232, 236, 304, 318–19,
    400, 404, 407
Hedlund, Gunnar 205
Heidar, Knut 161
Heinemann, Gustav 35
Hellevik, Ottar 160
Heosun, Josef 91
Higgins, Michael 126, 132, 138
Hildebrand, Klaus 46, 50, 77
Hine, David 461
Hobbes, Thomas 394
Hogwood, Brian 51
Holkeri, Harri 268, 282, 292
Holmberg, Erik 194–5, 197–8, 202, 204,
    211
Holmstedt, Margareta 198, 236
Hölzl, Norbert 91
Hondeghem, Annie 341–42
Horner, Franz 87
Horta, Basilio 531
Huber, John 8, 501, 506
Hunt, W. Ben 8–9, 22, 40, 66, 87, 164–5,
    194–5, 198, 233, 236–37, 250, 358,
    362, 400, 530

Ieraci, Giuseppe 489
Independent Party (Denmark) 233, 236
informateur 30, 131, 172, 189, 203, 205,
    238, 241, 271, 308–9, 312, 351, 362–5,
    370, 406–7, 503, 529, 537
Inglehart, Ronald 8, 400
interest groups 35, 95, 193–4, 375, 545,
    547
International Monetary Fund (IMF) 538,
    542, 544
Irwin, Galen 391, 393
Isaksson, Christer 207
Isernia, Pierangelo 433, 438, 443, 451, 462

Jäger, Wolfgang 35–6, 48, 50, 65, 75, 78
Jagland, Thorbjørn 170, 173
Janda, Kenneth 9
Jenny, Marcelo 87
Jensen, Henrik 248
Jensen, Torben 236
Jenssen, Anders Todal 164
Jesse, Eckhard 39–40
Johansson, Olof 223
Jonasson, Gustaf 206, 222
Jonnergård, Gustaf 209, 214

Jospin, Lionel 502–3, 505, 509–10, 512
Juppé, Alain 502, 511, 522, 525
Justice Party, JP (Denmark) 233, 236, 245

Kaarsted, Tage 238, 241, 245
Kaltefleiter, Werner 38, 58, 80
Katz, Richard 446
Kauffeldt, Carl 244
Keane, Fergal 140
Kekkonen, Urho 273, 278, 283
Keman, Hans 22, 112, 311, 377
Kenny, Shane 140
Kiesinger, Kurt Georg 62
king 167, 170, 172, 178, 203, 203–7, 214, 237, 309, 334, 363
King, Gary 3, 12–13
Klestil, Thomas 90
Klingemann, Hans-Dieter 9, 46–7, 192, 319, 400
Kohl, Helmut 38–9, 44, 46–7, 50, 60, 63, 70, 71, 75
Koiranen, Hannu 293
Koivisto, Mauno 268, 271, 282, 292
Kok, Wim 380, 383, 396
Kollman, Eric 90
Körner, Theodor 90
Korte, Karl-Rudolph 60–1, 71
Korvald, Lars 169, 173–4, 177, 179
Koskiaho, Britta 288
Kraft, Waldemar 76
Krag, Jens-Otto 243
Krehbiel, Keith 66
Kreisky, Bruno 97, 99, 117
Krier, Pierre 427
Kristensson, Astrid 211
Kropp, Sabine 38, 47, 55, 57, 59, 65–6
Kuhnle, Stein 161
Küpper, Jost 53, 57, 61

L'Ulivo 462
La Malfa, Ugo 447, 464
Laakso, Markku 33, 194, 232, 358, 564
Laakso, Seppo 273
Labour Party, A/DNA (Norway) 159–61, 164–5, 167–70, 173–4, 177, 186, 563, 569
Labour Party, Lab (Ireland) 130–1, 133, 135, 137–8, 140–5, 148–9, 151
Labour Party, PvdA (Netherlands) 356, 362, 364–8, 370, 374–7, 395
Lambsdorff, Count Otto 63, 78
Lane, Jan-Erik 269
Larsen, Dan 241, 245
Larsson, Sven-Erik 212, 222

Larsson, Torbjörn 217
Laver, Michael 3, 6, 7–9, 11, 13, 15–17, 22, 27, 40, 44, 46, 66, 87, 93, 110, 113, 126, 131–2, 135, 138, 145, 160, 164–5, 193–4, 195, 198, 233, 236–8, 240–1, 250, 269–70, 307, 309, 311, 317–18, 358, 362–3, 370, 372, 387, 400, 416, 424, 430, 530–1, 561–5, 572
League of Independents, VdU (Austria) 86, 90, 93, 96
Leburton, Edmond 316, 324, 326, 345
Leclaire, Alfred 107
Lees, Charles 65
Lefèvre, Théodore 317, 324
Left Party, see Communist Party, Com (Sweden)
Left Socialist Party, LS (Denmark) 233
left–right dimension (scale) 8–9, 40, 87–9, 163–5, 197–8, 222, 225, 227, 233, 236–7, 239–40, 260, 264, 307, 311, 317–18, 362, 367, 400, 439, 506
Leijonhuvud, Sigfrid 222
Leipart, Jørn 164
Leiserson, Michael 16
Lemass, Sean 150
Leone, Giovanni 448
Lewin, Leif 194
Liberal Centre Party, LC (Denmark) 233, 236
Liberal Democratic Party, LDP (Japan) 6
Liberal Democrats, D66 (Netherlands) 356, 358, 367–8, 370, 374–5, 394–6
Liberal Forum, LF (Austria) 86–7, 95, 122
Liberal Party, DP (Luxembourg) 400–1, 407–12, 415, 418, 424–5, 427, 430
Liberal Party, Li (Sweden) 192–3, 195, 203, 205, 207, 211, 215, 217, 223
Liberal Party, Lib (Denmark) 233, 236–7, 244–5, 253–4
Liberal Party, PLI (Italy) 433, 435, 438, 442, 445, 451, 457, 478
Liberal Party, PVV/PLP (Belgium) 300–1, 304, 306, 311–12, 322, 327, 334–5, 341–2, 345, 351–2
Liberal Party, V (Norway) 159–60, 164, 168–9, 181, 188
Liberal People's Party, LKP (Finland) 264
Liberals, VVD (Netherlands) 356, 362, 366–8, 370, 374–5, 377, 380, 391, 393, 395
Lijphart, Arend 8, 27, 94, 307, 390, 396, 584
Lindström, Ulf 159
Link, Werner 35–6, 48, 50, 65, 75, 78

Lipponen, Paavo 269, 282, 289
Lipset, Seymour Martin 9
Listhaug, Ola 188
LO 193
Lopes, Pedro Santana 533
Lösche, Peter 35, 45
Löwenberg, Gerhard 59
Lubbers, Ruud 380, 382, 384–7, 390
Lucena, Manuel 547
Luebbert, Gregory 113, 288, 358, 368, 376, 562
Lupia, Arthur 3, 26, 32, 151, 584
Luther, Kurt Richard 87, 109
Lynch, John 150
Lyng, John 173, 177, 181, 186

Mackie, Thomas 27, 51, 92, 253, 584
Macleod, Thomas 530, 536
Mader, Erik 241
Magone, José 531, 568
Mair, Peter 8, 129–30, 142, 195
Mannheimer, Renato 464
Marchais, Georges 510
Marcic, René 110
Marradi, Alberto 452
Marsh, Michael 131, 133, 142, 149
Martens, Wilfried 316–17, 324–6, 344–5, 349, 351
mass media 103, 122, 147, 172, 218, 297, 375, 381, 390, 393, 407, 409, 503, 533, 539, 545
Mastropaolo, Alfio 456–7
Mattson, Ingvar 180, 192
Mauroy, Pierre 509–10, 522, 525
Mendes, Armindo Ribeiro 535
Mershon, Carol 44, 448, 461
Messmer, Pierre 508, 522, 525
Meth-Cohn, Delia 101, 116
Miguel, Firmina 549
Mikkelsen, Hans 232
Mintzel, Alf 35, 39, 63–4
Mitchell, Paul 47, 131, 133, 135, 137, 141–2, 148
Mitterrand, François 502, 509–11, 522, 525
Moderate Conservative Parties, CNI/RI/UDF (France) 500, 502, 508–12, 525
Moderate Liberals (Norway) 158
Molin, Björn 192, 199, 205, 222
Möller, Alex 62
Möller, Tommy 198, 204
Monarchic People's Party, PPM (Portugal) 539, 546, 549, 553

Monarchist Party, PNM (Italy) 435, 442
Monteiro, Manuel 531
Morgan, Mary-Jane 400
Morlino, Leonardo 443, 456, 534
Moro, Aldo 446, 449, 461, 470, 478
Mota Pinto, Carlos 541, 548, 553, 555
Mouvement Réformateur, Réf (France) 525
Movement of the Armed Forces, MFA (Portugal) 530
Movimento Sociale Italiano, MSI (Italy) 435, 438, 442, 569
Müller, Wolfgang 7, 11, 29, 86–7, 90–2, 95, 97, 99, 101, 103–4, 107–8, 113, 116, 143, 562
Müller-Rommel, Ferdinand 51, 65, 383
Murto, Eero 272, 282
Mussolini, Benito 435

Nannestad, Peter 236
Narud, Hanne Marthe 164, 166, 185, 188, 391, 393
Naßmacher, Karl-Heinz 99
National Democratic Party, NPD (Germany) 34, 77
Nazi Party, Germany 120
Neels, Leo 329
Neisser, Heinrich 104
New Democracy Party, (Sweden) 194–5, 569
no-confidence motions, see confidence motions
Nordby, Trond 158
Nordli, Odvar 186
Norpoth, Helmut 35
North Atlantic Treaty Organization, NATO 427–8
Northern League, LN (Italy) 443–4, 462
Nousiainen, Jaakko 283, 292–3

O'Halpin, Eunan 150
O'Leary, Michael 140
Oberländer, Theodor 76
Oberreuter, Heinrich 35
office-seeking behaviour 46, 148, 297, 424, 462, 562
Olah, Franz 111
Olsen, Søren-Ole 236, 246

Padgett, Stephen 35
Palme, Olof 219
Paloheimo, Heikki 293
Panebianco, Angelo 532

parliamentarism 1, 90, 167, 202, 231, 237, 269, 278, 282, 293, 568
parliamentary government 1, 166–7, 231, 238, 264, 272–3, 278, 293, 296, 565
Parti Radical, PR (France) 508
Party of Democratic Socialism/Left List, PDS/LL (Germany) 34, 80
party system:
　constraints on coalitions 121, 569
　five-party 131, 159, 194
　four-party 400–1, 530, 534
　multiparty 1, 33, 129, 199, 243, 260, 357–8, 498
　parliamentary 7, 26, 192, 194, 232–3, 300, 498, 501, 530
　three-party 34, 264, 272
　two-and-a-half party 301, 313
　two-party 1, 33, 301
Pasquino, Gianfranco 435, 456, 462
Pedersen, Mogens 232–3, 236
Pelinka, Anton 87, 99
Pereira, José Pacheco 533
Pertini, Alessandro 445
Pesonen, Pertti 205
Peterson, Robert 309, 366
Petersson, Olof 195, 207
Pettersson, Åke 212–15, 218, 227
Pfeifer, Helmut 104
Philipp, Wilfried 87, 103, 116
Pholien, Joseph 325
Pijnenburg, Bert 367
Pinto, Jaime Nogueira 532
Plasser, Fritz 87, 120
Pompidou, Georges 508, 522, 525
Portas, Paulo 547–9
Portugese Democratic Movement, MDP/CDE (Portugal) 533
Powell, G. Bingham 27, 188
Prader, Georg 111
premier 170, 420, 429, 462, 539
Presthus, Rolf 179
Pridham, Geoffrey 3
Prodi, Romano 444, 456, 490
Progress Party, FRP (Norway) 160–1, 163, 165, 169, 174, 186, 569
Progress Party, PP (Denmark) 233, 236, 569
Progressive Democrats, PD (Ireland) 130–1, 133, 135, 137–8, 143–4, 150
proportional representation 1, 86, 91, 233, 357–8, 446, 508; *see also* elections
public opinion 75, 188, 226, 393, 494, 522

Quermonne, Jean-Louis 508

Raab, Julius 112
Radical Liberal Party, RL (Denmark) 233, 236, 239, 245–6, 563
Radical Party, PPR (Netherlands) 367
Rae, Douglas 232, 564
Rasch, Bjørn Erik 167, 179
Rasmussen, Erik 238
Rassemblement Walon, RW (Belgium) 301, 304, 312, 335, 345
Rauchensteiner, Manfred 99, 109
Renzsch, Wolfgang 44
Republican Party, PRI (Italy) 438, 442, 449, 451, 457, 462, 478, 490
Reynolds, Albert 144, 150–1
Rihoux, Benoît 310, 324, 326
Riker, William 15, 45–6, 92, 562
Robertson, David 8
Robinson, Mary 132
Rocard, Michel 504, 511, 522, 525
Rodrigues, Nascimento 541
Rokkan, Stein 9, 159
Rommetvedt, Hilmar 161, 162, 166–7, 169, 180
Rose, Richard 27, 253, 584
Roseta, Helena 546, 553
Rother, Berndt 538, 544–5, 549, 551
Rudzio, Wolfgang 61–2, 81, 99
Ruggeri, Andrea 470
Rui, Machete 548
Ruin, Olof 192, 205–6, 209, 214
Rumor, Mariano 448–9
Rusk, Jerrold 236

Sá Carneiro, Francisco 531, 535–6, 538–9, 546, 549, 553, 555
Saalfeld, Thomas 32–3, 45, 80
Saias 545–6, 549, 551
Sainsbury, Dianne 161
Sani, Giancomo 8
Sänkiaho, Risto 273
Santer, Jacques 401, 418, 420, 425, 427
Saragat, Giuseppe 445
Särlvik, Bo 199
Sartori, Giovanni 6, 8, 37, 57, 160, 232, 307, 401, 433
Scalfaro, Oscar Luigi 447
Scelba, Mario 451
Schärf, Adolf 90, 101
Scheel, Walter 35, 48, 76
Schieren, Stefan 44
Schindler, Peter 39, 48
Schlüter, Poul 243
Schmidt, Helmut 43, 46, 50, 58, 62, 71, 75, 77, 78

Schmidt, Manfred 33, 37, 80
Schmitt, Ute 45
Schneider, Kurt 101
Schofield, Norman 3, 6–9, 16, 22, 27, 44, 46, 131, 160, 193, 236, 238, 240, 269, 319, 358, 370, 387, 531, 562–3
Schou, Tove-Lise 198, 232, 236
Schreckenberger, Waldemar 63, 81
Schröder, Gerhard 35, 60, 63, 71
Schüle, Adolf 58, 59
Schwarz, Hans-Peter 50, 59, 77
Secher, Herbert 99, 116
Secker, W. P. 364
Seeber, Gilg 87
Sejersted, Francis 181, 185
Shaffer, William 164, 180
Shepsle, Kenneth 3, 13, 16–17, 22, 110, 111, 113, 132, 135, 372, 416, 572
Sinnott, Richard 131, 133, 149
Sinowatz, Fred 111, 117
Sjölin, Mats 193
Slater, Martin 456–7
Smith, Gordon 53
Soares, Mário 530–1, 533, 535–9, 541–2, 544, 547, 549, 553, 555
Social Democratic Party, PSD (Portugal) 529–30, 533–6, 538–9, 541–2, 547–9, 553, 555–6
Social Democratic Party, PSDI (Italy) 438, 442, 445, 451, 453, 457, 478, 490
Social Democratic Party, PvdA (Luxembourg), see Labour Party, PvdA (Luxembourg)
Social Democratic Party, SD (Denmark) 233, 236–7, 239, 241, 245–6, 250
Social Democratic Party, SD (Sweden) 192–9, 201, 204–9, 212, 217–9, 222, 224–6
Social Democratic Party, SDP (Finland) 264, 268, 270, 278, 281–3, 288, 292
Social Democratic Party, SDP (Luxembourg) 401
Social Democratic Party, SPD (Germany) 35, 38–9, 43–8, 50, 55, 57, 59–60, 62, 64–6, 70–1, 75–8, 80, 569
Social Democratic Party, SPÖ (Austria) 86–7, 90–3, 95–7, 99, 101–2, 104–13, 116–17, 120–2
Socialist Left Party, SV (Norway) 160, 165
Socialist Party, BSP/PSB (Belgium) 300–1, 304, 311–12, 316–17, 327, 333, 335, 341–2, 345, 351–2
Socialist Party, LSAP (Luxembourg)
400–1, 405, 407–10, 412, 415, 418, 420, 424–5, 427–31
Socialist Party, PS (Portugal) 530–1, 533–9, 541–2, 544–9, 551, 553, 555–6
Socialist Party, PSI (Italy) 433, 435, 438, 442, 445–6, 449, 451, 453, 457, 462–4, 478, 488, 490, 494
Socialist Party, SPÖ (Austria), see Social Democratic Party
Socialist People's Party, SF (Norway) 160–1, 233, 236, 241
Socialists, PS/FGDS (France) 501–2, 504, 508–12, 527
Sorsa, Kalevi 281–2, 292
Sousa, Marcelo Rebelo 549
Spaak, Paul-Henri 311, 317, 324, 344–5
Spadolini, Giovanni 446, 449, 462, 488
Spring, Dick 135, 146, 149
Spruyt, Marc 304
Stavang, Per 167
Steffani, Winfried 44
Steger, Norbert 117
Steiner, Jürg 381
Steiner, Kurt 116
Steininger, Barbara 103, 116
Stengers, Jean 308
Stjernquist, Nils 202, 211
Stock, Maria José Fernandez 531, 541–2
Stöss, Richard 35, 76
Strauß, Franz Josef 63, 77
Strøm, Kaare 1, 3, 7, 11, 15, 26–7, 29, 32, 44, 93, 131, 143, 151, 161, 164, 166–7, 179–80, 202, 231, 238, 240–1, 253, 269–70, 273, 297–8, 307, 363, 560–2, 565, 584
Stücklen, Richard 62
Sturm, Roland 38, 47, 55, 57, 59, 65, 66
Svåsand, Lars 161, 179
Svensson, Palle 232, 255
Swedish People's Party, SW (Finland) 264
Swyngedouw, Mark 304
Syse, Jan P. 161, 169, 172, 177–9, 181, 183, 185

Taagepera, Rein 33, 194, 232, 358, 564
Tambroni, Fernando 451
Taylor, Michael 15
Tegenbos, Guy 342
terminal events 186, 258, 349, 551, 587
Thomas, Alastair 205, 231
Thorn, Gaston 418, 420
Timmermans, Arco 202, 319, 325, 329, 367–8, 370, 375–6, 382, 384, 386–7, 396

Tindemans, Léo 310, 316, 317, 325, 328, 345, 351
Tops, Pieter 358, 368
Torp, Olaf 186
Tsebelis, George 47
Tuomioja, Sakari Severi 273

Ulram, Peter 87, 120
unanimity 80, 104, 110, 281–2, 298
Union Démocratique pour le Repect du Travail, UDRT (Belgium) 301
unitary actors 6, 140–1, 110, 281–2, 298
Unity List, UL (Denmark) 233, 236
Uomo Qualunque (Italy) 435
Urwin, Derek 163

Valen, Henry 159–61, 163–4
Valente, Vasco Pulido 547–9
Van Acker, Achille 325, 345
Van Agt, Andreas 375, 380, 386–7
Van Roozendaal, Peter 14, 26
Van Tijn, Joop 384
Van Weezel, Max 384
Vanden Boeynants, Paul 316, 349
Vassallo, Salvatore 456
Vedung, Evert 222
Verzichelli, Luca 453, 456, 463–4, 568
Vester, Michael 538
Virolainen, Johannes 281

Vlaams Blok, VB (Belgium) 301, 307, 569
Völk, Josef Anton 47, 65, 77
Volkens, Andrea 39, 46–7
Volksunie, VU (Belgium) 304, 312, 335
Von Beyme, Klaus 94
Von Heland, Erik 211
Von Merkatz, Heinrich 53
Von Sydow, Björk 206, 222
Vranitzky, Franz 111, 116–17

Waldheim, Kurt 90
Waleffe, Bernard 334
Warwick, Paul 3, 11, 26, 37, 297, 562–3, 584
Wehner, Herbert 45
Welan, Manfried 90, 101, 104
Werner, Pierre 405–6, 415, 420, 428
Westerståhl, Jörgen 193
Westholm, Anders 192
Wewer, Göttrik 62
Whitten, Guy 188
Wiberg, Matti 289, 293
Wieslander, Hans 192, 199, 205
Willoch, Kaare 169–70, 172, 174, 177–9, 181, 183, 186
Withalm, Hermann 109

Zoli, Adone 478